What they're saying about *Pea in a Pod*

"Up-to-date information and ideas"

"With health care in turmoil in the US and many of our pregnancy outcome markers headed in the wrong direction, people are searching for a GPS map to help them arrive at a normal birth. This book offers a great guide to that wonderful journey with up-to-date information and ideas in an easy-to-read and use format."

Charles Mahan, MD, FACOG
Dean and Professor Emeritus, University of South Florida—
College of Public Health and College of Medicine

"An invaluable resource"

To say *Pea in a Pod* is "a comprehensive 'one-stop-shopping' guide that provides solid, accurate information for expectant parents" is an understatement! As a first-time expectant mom, I cannot think of a single question unanswered after reading this book. It is an invaluable resource!

Rosemary Banks, MPH, CHES
Lecturer, Department of Public Health Sciences
University of North Carolina at Charlotte

"A must for your pregnancy library"

Pea in a Pod offers couples sound, up-to-date information that focuses not only on physician/hospital care and deliveries, but also on the midwifery model of care throughout the pregnancy cycle with options of hospital, birth center, and home births. This book is a must for your pregnancy library.

Sandy Williamson, CNM, MSN
Founder, Special Beginnings Birth & Gynecology Center
Former President, Florida Alliance of Birth Centers

"Well-balanced, comprehensive"

Pea in a Pod is a well-balanced, comprehensive guide that every mother-to-be will want to keep close at hand throughout pregnancy, during breastfeeding, and into early parenthood.

Rae Davies, BSH, CHE, CD (DONA), LCCE, IBCLC
Board member, International MotherBaby Childbirth Organization
Coordinator, World Alliance for Breastfeeding Action Health Care Practices Task Force

"[A] wealth of information"

The author's experience in birth centers and hospitals contributes to the uniqueness and wealth of information contained within the pages of this book. The easy-to-read text, helpful tips for moms and dads, and eloquent photos and illustrations make this a must-have book for expectant and new parents.

Laura J. Hart, BSN, RN, IBCLC
Parent educator, lecturer, founding member of Breastfeeding Education Network

"A wonderful guide"

This is a wonderful guide to the experience of early parenthood. The proper balance of science and professional wisdom provide the new parent with knowledge that otherwise would have taken years to attain.

Miles M. Landis, MD, FAAP
Pediatrician

"An amazing book"

Linda Goldberg has written an amazing book for expectant families. It is thorough, well-researched, packed with facts and suggestions for couples that want to be well informed about their journey through pregnancy, labor, birth and the newborn period.

Karen Kesler, BSN, RN, FLCCE
Manager, Parent Education & Lactation Center
Florida Hospital Women's Services

Pea in a Pod

YOUR COMPLETE GUIDE TO PREGNANCY, CHILDBIRTH & BEYOND

Linda Goldberg

RN, CCE, IBCLC

SQUAREONE

The health, medical, and nutritional information in this book is based on the training, personal experience, and research of the author. Every effort has been made to provide the most complete, current, and accurate information as possible. Because each person and situation are unique, the author and publisher urge the reader to check with a qualified healthcare professional before using any procedure whose appropriateness may be of concern. It is a sign of wisdom, not cowardice, to seek a second or third opinion. As there is always some risk involved, the author and publisher are not responsible for any adverse effects or consequences resulting from the use of any of the suggestions or procedures described in this book.

Cover Designer: Jeannie Tudor
Cover Illustrator: Rob Bolster
Back Cover Photographer: Lisa DeVore
In-House Editor: Marie Caratozzolo
Typesetter: Gary A. Rosenberg

Square One Publishers
115 Herricks Road
Garden City Park, NY 11040
(516) 535-2010
(877) 900-BOOK
www.squareonepublishers.com

Library of Congress Cataloging-in-Publication Data

Goldberg, Linda.
    Pea in a pod : your complete guide to pregnancy, childbirth & beyond / Linda Goldberg.
        p. cm.
    Includes bibliographical references and index.
    ISBN 978-0-7570-0181-9 — ISBN 0-7570-0181-5
  1. Childbirth—Popular works. I. Title.

RG525.G513785 2008
618.2—dc22

                        2007050718

Printed in Singapore

10   9   8   7   6   5   4   3   2   1

Contents

Credits, vi

A Word About Gender, viii

Acknowledgments, ix

Introduction, 1

1. Birth, Your Way, 3

2. Pregnancy, 17

3. Questions and Concerns, 33

4. Prenatal Care and Testing, 47

5. Nutrition, 83

6. Prenatal Exercise, 113

7. Tools for Labor, 137

8. Labor and Birth, 177

9. Labor Variations, 217

10. Medications and Anesthesia, 229

11. Interventions During Labor
    and Birth, 245

12. Cesarean Birth, 263

13. The Newborn, 283

14. Baby Care and Concerns, 301

15. Breastfeeding, 343

16. Alternative Feeding Methods, 389

17. The New Parent, 403

Glossary, 437

Trimester Checklists, 447

Resources, 449

Notes, 457

Bibliography, 465

About the Author, 471

Index, 472

Credits

The figures appearing on pages 28, 29, and 30, illustrating the woman's body at the end of each trimester, are from *Pregnancy in Anatomical Illustrations.* They are used courtesy of Carnation Nutritional Products.

The illustrations on pages 189 and 218 depicting various categories of fetal presentation, and the illustration on page 266 of the prolapsed cord are from "Obstetrical Presentation and Position," Clinical Education Aid No. 18 by Abbott Laboratories. They are used with permission.

The pudendal block illustration on page 232 is from "Regional Anesthesia in Obstetrics," Clinical Education Aid No 17 by Abbott Laboratories. It is used with permission.

The skin incision illustrations on page 275 and the uterine incision illustrations on page 276 are adapted from an illustration copyrighted © 1980 by Childbirth Graphics Ltd. Used with permission.

The illustrations for the Reverse Pressure Softening technique on page 377 were drawn by Kyle Cotterman and used with permission by K. Jean Cotterman.

The table "Methods of Contraception Used in the United States" on pages 428 through 435 is adapted from "Family Planning Methods of Contraception." It is used courtesy of DHEW Publication No. (HAS) 80-5646, Department of Health and Human Services, Public Health Service, Health Services Administration.

Dedication

To my first son, Jeff, whose birth inspired me to this calling of teaching and working with pregnant and nursing women. To my daughter, Becky, whose challenging birth showed me my strength. And to my youngest son, Jon, whose birth with a nurse-midwife in a birth center showed me how natural birth can be. This book is also dedicated to my wonderful parents, Bertha and John Pitcavage. And most of all, to my husband, Bill, who has supported me with his love, kindness, cooking (or picking up dinner) each step of this long journey.

I would also like to dedicate this book to the thousands of couples I have taught as a childbirth educator or have worked with as a lactation consultant. You have all touched my life. I have learned as much from you as you have learned from me.

A Word About Gender

In an effort to avoid awkward phrasing within sentences, it is our publishing style to alternate the use of generic male and female pronouns according to chapter. This means that when referring to a "third-person" caregiver or a baby, odd-numbered chapters will use female pronouns, while even-numbered chapters will use male.

Acknowledgments

Just as an optimum birth experience requires the support of caring individuals, the birth of *Pea in a Pod* was accomplished thanks to the efforts of a great many people.

Special thanks to my previous co-authors, Jan Kukar and especially Ginny Brinkley, whose hard work in former books helped establish the framework for this publication. For sharing their professional expertise, I would also like to thank Harvey Karp MD and Jean Cotterman RNC, IBCLC, who reviewed the information related to their topics and offered helpful suggestions.

For their artistic contributions, I would like to acknowledge Melissa Brenner and Penny Banks, as well as my son, Jeff (my "in-house" artist), who spent many hours creating artwork to my detailed specifications. I would also like to acknowledge the photographic artistry of Susan Torregrosa, Terry Cuffel, Gary W. Fox, Lisa DeVore, and my husband, Bill, whose contributions have added visual interest and clarity to the book.

For graciously agreeing to either appear in the book's photos or share their personal photographs, a great number of people deserve special recognition. Heartfelt thanks go to Helen, Peter, and Andrew Alberse; Debbie and Logan Baker; Traci, Jon, and Samantha Balao; Tracy, Zach, Jeff, and Skylar Baumann; Brenda Bradshaw-Csonka; Jennette and Renee Bremer; Rocket Brinkely; Zachary and Nathan Burns; Camie Carson; Natalie, Kevin, and Elizabeth Casey; Becky and Nathan Collins; Yaara Dagan Colmenero and Elena Colmenero; Kelli Conley; Jill and Levi Corns; Carolyn Daily; Rita and Kolohe Del Carmen; Jeannie, Lynn, and Jared Denbrook; Sariah, Darren, and Kerra Ellsmore; Nancy Fishalow; Colleen and Tyler Goehrig; Bill, Jeff, and Jon Goldberg; Aubrey and John Harman; Maryanne Hewitt; Nancy and Allison Hillis; Maritza, Jerry, and Katarina Jenarine; Adriene Johnson and Dawn White; Ashlen Johnson; Paula Jones-Marek; Leslie and David Jordan; Diana Konz; Heather and Matt Kubis; Mari Beth and Cade Langston; Jenny, Alex, and Kaela Maer; Roberta Mattix; Casey and Jesse Mizzone; Lisa and Sam Nasrallah; Chiaki and Wendy Nishikawa; Josephine and John Oetjen; Suzanne Paszkowski; Jackie, Joseph, and Addison Perri; Bethany, Bob, and Lily Pisani; Susan Robinson; Clare Rogers; Takako Saito and Mark Pohlhammer; Leslie, Joe, and Armando Santiago; Amanda and Henry Schalich; Karen and Nathaniel Scheer; Brette Petway Sears; Pamela and Thomas Shipley; Kendra Shortle; Gina and Brian Stalvey; Julianne Stowell; Nicole, Vincent, and Tiana Tristram; Christina Varnell; Kimberly and Kayla Vincent; Ericka Waters, Kenneth Redd, and Christopher; Christine, Damon, Evan, and Ava Watts; Veronica and Derrick Watts; and Karen and Savannah vonRabenau.

I would also like to thank Brian Leatherwood, Fenna Roberts, Joanna Rivera, Amy and Owen Busch, and Keva Ambre, whose memorable quotes (uttered during class) appear throughout the book. I owe a debt of gratitude to Laura Hart who was my mentor on my path to becoming a lactation consultant, and to the certified nurse-midwives who gave me the opportunity to observe and teach normal birth in a nurturing environment. They are Robbie Mattix, Camie Carson, Suzanne Paszkowski, Terri Nesbitt, Cathy Rudolph, and especially Sandy Williamson, who had the vision to open Special Beginnings Birth and Gynecology Center.

This book would not have been possible without the help of two important people: My publisher, Rudy Shur, who was instrumental not only in this project, but also in guiding me through my evolution as a writer over the past three decades. And also Marie Caratozzolo, my editor, whose knowledge, diligence, and attention to detail has made this book reader friendly and complete. It has been a joy to work with both of them.

And finally, I must extend an extra special thanks to my family for both their contributions to the book as well as their unending support. To my son Jeff for his outstanding drawings; to my daughter, Becky, and her husband, Nathan, who became my "models;" to my son Jon for his helpful suggestions; to my mom, who gave up mother/daughter time so I could work on the book; and especially to my husband, Bill, who is always there for me.

Introduction

"Honey, I'm pregnant!" For most couples, this phrase elicits a wide range of feelings—from joy and anticipation to anxiety and concern. Most of all, it results in lots of questions. Being pregnant for the first time throws most women into an exciting world of unknowns and new experiences. It is often the first time they start thinking about the food they are eating or what they should or should not do to help ensure a healthy baby. Being well-informed during this time is key.

Today, many women learn about childbirth from television shows or movies, which often paint unrealistic or inaccurate pictures of the experience. The Internet, another popular source of information for expectant mothers, may (or may not) be accurate, depending on the reliability of the specific site. While it is, of course, possible to obtain good information from any of these venues, prenatal classes with certified instructors, which provide personal interaction, are usually the best sources. This book —whether used alone or in conjunction with classes—can be considered another.

Up-to-date and complete, *Pea in a Pod* is a comprehensive "one-stop-shopping" guide that provides solid, accurate information for expectant parents. With topics that begin with preconception and continue through pregnancy, childbirth, and baby's first year, this book could easily be called *Absolutely Everything You Could Possibly Want or Need to Know About Pregnancy, Birth, Breastfeeding, and the Newborn*. In addition to a wealth of practical information, it includes the latest developments in the field of obstetrics, pediatrics, and breastfeeding, as well as the most current policies issued by organizations such as the American Academy of Pediatrics, the American College of Obstetricians and Gynecologists, the American Heart Association, the Academy of Breastfeeding Medicine, the World Health Organization, and the United States Department of Agriculture.

The book opens with a general discussion of the many birthing options and caregiver choices that are currently available for expectant mothers. Today's woman can opt for an unmedicated birth in a home, hospital, or birth center; she can decide to have a high-tech delivery that employs gadgets, machines, and plenty of medication. She can even have a prescheduled induced labor or a planned cesarean for the sake of convenience. To assist her in giving birth, she can be aided by a doctor or midwife, have the support of one or more labor partners, and employ the services of a doula, who is specially trained to help women in labor. Because so many options are now available, it is even more important for expectant couples to educate themselves before making decisions. Only by becoming familiar with the benefits and risks of all the available options can a couple make wise choices.

To help guide you through pregnancy, *Pea in a Pod* provides a wealth of pertinent information, starting with a detailed description of conception and fetal development, and continuing with informative discussions on the physical and emotional changes that occur during each trimester. It offers important nutritional guidelines, explanations of required and optional prenatal tests and procedures, and answers to the most commonly asked questions (the do's and the don'ts) of expectant couples. It also provides a variety of easy-to-follow prenatal exercises—both for relieving the minor discomforts of pregnancy and for preparing your body to give birth.

Subsequent chapters are designed to prepare you (and your partner) for the upcoming labor and the birth of your baby. They offer a wide variety of relaxation techniques and breathing methods that you can practice at home in preparation for the event. Detailed discussions offer a clear understanding of what to expect during this time and how to best cope. And since every labor is different and may not necessarily go "by the book," labor variations are also discussed. You will become aware of common labor interventions and medications, along with their benefits and risks. An entire chapter is devoted to cesarean birth.

Once your precious baby has made an entrance into the world, you can expect to have a fresh supply of questions—especially if this is your firstborn. The final chapters of this book are devoted entirely to this time, during which most new parents find themselves concerned over their newborn's actions or appearance —"Is her head supposed to have that shape?" "How do I care for the umbilical cord?" "Why is he crying so often?" "If I hold her a lot, will I spoil her?" These and other common concerns are addressed. Also presented are helpful tips for best managing your time (to avoid exhaustion), for baby proofing your home, and for knowing when a call to the pediatrician is in order. Clear, step-by-step instructions for handling emergencies, such as choking, are included, as well as directions for performing infant CPR. And as breastfeeding is the gold standard for infant feeding, helpful suggestions are offered to make this choice a successful one. A section on pumping and bottle-feeding (especially helpful for working moms) is also included, as is information regarding the use and preparation of breastmilk substitutes. Completing the book is a chapter on parenting, which incorporates helpful tips on preparing your other children (and even pets) for the new arrival. It also discusses the importance of remaining close to your partner, and offers suggestions for maintaining a strong, loving relationship.

The purpose of this book is twofold. First, it provides the tools to be utilized by you, the expectant couple, throughout the pregnancy and birth. It can be used in conjunction with early pregnancy, childbirth preparation, and breastfeeding classes, as well as classes for new mothers. The chapter on cesarean birth also makes it an appropriate manual for cesarean preparation. Second, the book conveys an attitude, one of awareness and responsibility. It is through this attitude that couples come to understand the impact and importance of their decisions.

The birth of a baby is one of the most significant events in a person's life—one that will be remembered in great detail even decades later. Making well-thought-out decisions can help ensure an optimum birth experience and positive memories. Whether this is your first birth or your first "prepared" birth, the information in this book will enable you to make the journey from pregnancy to parenthood a truly rewarding and memorable experience.

Birth, Your Way

or Decisions, Decisions

Pregnancy is a time of heightened awareness. You become aware of changes in your body, in your way of thinking, and in your priorities. You must also become aware of the available choices that can help determine how you feel about your birth experience, your baby, and yourself as a parent. You have the right as a consumer to know the different options from which you can choose. You have the responsibility to learn as much as possible—through classes, your doctor or midwife, and independent research—to make informed, considered choices from among those options.

After presenting a brief history of childbirth in the United States, this chapter offers an overview of current trends and options that all expectant parents should consider. Topics range from choosing a caregiver to determining where to have your baby to deciding on the childbirth method that best suits your needs. Subsequent chapters offer more detailed information on these and other topics to help you make the most of this important, life-changing experience.

HISTORY OF CHILDBIRTH IN THE UNITED STATES

Over the last century, the experience of childbirth has undergone numerous changes. In the early 1900s, most births took place in the home, attended by women who were skilled in delivering babies, by midwives, and/or by family physicians. By the middle of the century, the act of giving birth had largely moved from the home to the hospital, and it was male physicians who began delivering the majority of babies. Giving birth changed from a normal, healthy, at-home occurrence to a medical event within the hospital environment. Normal, healthy childbirth was determined only after a woman had given birth without complications.

Pregnancy and birth during the 1940s and the 1950s were managed largely by physicians. Women in general were not informed about their bodies and they knew very little about the process of giving birth. They simply followed the advice of their doctors without question. In the hospital, the use of narcotics and an amnesiac drug called *scopolamine* was common during labor. During birth, women were given a general or spinal anesthesia, and babies were often delivered with forceps. Women no longer trusted their bodies alone to give birth, nor did they feed babies from their breasts. Formula feeding became the norm, as women placed their trust in medical experts and the scientific approach to infant feeding.

In the late 1960s, as a result of the woman's movement and several natural child-birth pioneers, women became more informed about their bodies and the process of birth. Suddenly, they began investigating the benefits and risks of the common procedures that had turned the normal event of giving birth into a technological experience. This heightened awareness resulted in the natural childbirth movement, which gave women more control over their labor and birth. For the first time, husbands were allowed in the labor and delivery rooms. Expectant mothers began questioning child-birth methods and procedures that their own mothers—just a few decades earlier—had blindly followed upon the advice of their doctors. Needless to say, many physicians saw this consumer movement as a loss of control.

Some women began choosing to have their babies at home to avoid common medical interventions. And out-of-hospital birth centers started to spring up, giving women the option to control their childbirth experience with expert midwifery care. During the 1980s, hospitals began responding to these actions with birthing suites—rooms that were designed to give the hospital a home-like appearance. Much of this was just interior decorating as the use of technology continued to increase. Fathers were routine in birthing rooms, and the choice of midwives as caregivers for labor and birth became more popular. Consumer-based childbirth classes were slowly replaced by hospital-based programs. These programs typically provided information that was specific to a particular hospital or group of physicians.

During the 1990s, a number of standard hospital procedures became less common. Routine episiotomies, for example, were on the decline, as were repeat cesarean sections. More and more women attempted vaginal births after having cesareans. Women became aware of the beneficial services provided by doulas—trained labor support persons—who assisted them in achieving the birth experience that they desired. On the other hand, epidurals became the norm. Fewer couples attended child-birth classes or they preferred shortened classes that fit into their busy schedules. Television and the Internet became primary sources for information on pregnancy and childbirth, and couples, once again, began relying on their physicians to make decisions for them without question.

Today, at the start of the twenty-first century, the approach to childbirth has become one of convenience. With everyone's busy schedules, preparation for this event has taken a back seat. Many first-time pregnant women give birth to their babies without attending either childbirth or breastfeeding classes. The number of labors that are being induced without medical indications are skyrocketing. Women are choosing to deliver their babies when it is most convenient, or when their favorite obstetrician is on call. Maternal exhaustion (a term that simply means "tired of being pregnant") is another growing reason for inducing labor at thirty-eight or thirty-nine weeks.

The Lamaze method of childbirth preparation, which first gained popularity in the 1970s, was referred to as "painless childbirth." Today's "painless childbirth" means that the woman gets an epidural as soon as medication (Pitocin) is started to induce her labor. This prevents her from experiencing any painful contractions. Cesarean deliveries are again skyrocketing, as scheduled cesarean births are becoming more frequent. Women who have had a cesarean delivery but desire giving birth vaginally with subsequent pregnancies are generally discouraged from doing so. Doctors inform them, as well as women who have already experienced a vaginal birth after cesarean (VBAC), that they no longer allow women to labor and must have another cesarean.

Women who desire a VBAC often have to go to great lengths to find a caregiver who will support them in their decision. Another alarming trend involves the number of planned cesarean births for first-time mothers who are supposedly carrying "large" babies—a determination based on a sonogram report, which may be off by over a pound. Even more disturbing, just because they are preferred, cesareans are being performed upon request with no medical indications.

On the positive side, in-hospital lactation services, which assist women in the early days of breastfeeding, are becoming more common. But even so, it is not unusual for women to stop nursing within the first weeks if breastfeeding doesn't come easily. Many hospitals continue to offer formula supplementation without a medical reason.

The journey of pregnancy and childbirth is one of the most significant events in a woman's life—one in which taking an active role is vital. Healthy, normal birth should be considered the standard for care. If there is interference in the normal birth process, the flow of labor may be interrupted and result in an altered outcome. It is imperative for expectant mothers (and fathers) to become aware of all aspects of pregnancy and childbirth, and to take an active role in the many decisions involving this experience.

MAKING DECISIONS

When you announce your pregnancy, you may be surprised at the number of people who will begin to share their birth stories with you. Even after many years have passed since giving birth, most women are able to recount their personal experiences in vivid detail. Some of the stories will be positive and heartwarming; others may instill you with fear. Just keep in mind that the events surrounding your child's birth are unique memories that will last a lifetime. That is why it is so important to be aware of and involved with all of the decisions that need to be made during this special time.

Early in your pregnancy, take the time to examine your feelings about labor and birth. Talk to family and friends about their pregnancies and birth experiences. Discover what choices they've made that were positive and negative, and find out what they would change if they had to do it over again. Understand that there are certain factors over which you have no control, but the choices that you *do* make, including your choice of doctor or midwife and your place of delivery, will have an impact on the birth experience. Your health insurance may cover specific facilities, and they may provide a list of caregivers from which to choose. If you desire to use a caregiver or facility that is not on the list, be prepared to pay the difference to ensure the type of birth that you desire.

In addition to becoming knowledgeable about pregnancy, labor, and childbirth, you can enhance the experience by eating well, exercising, and practicing relaxation and breathing techniques. All of these factors, which are discussed in later chapters, can influence this very important event in your life.

CHOOSING YOUR CAREGIVER

Your caregiver is the person you select to provide your prenatal care and to attend your birth. It is the doctor or midwife that you hire to be your healthcare provider. This very important person can have a significant influence on the course of your labor and birth and the type of experience you have. It is important to decide which "model of care" best suits your particular needs. Taking the time to interview different caregivers will help you decide on the one that is best for you. Remember, these models of care, which are discussed beginning on page 7, are general guidelines that describe how a particular healthcare service is usually delivered. Some midwives may practice more like physicians and some physicians may have incorporated midwifery practices into their care.

Early in your pregnancy, there is sufficient time for interviewing and exploring the options. However, even in late pregnancy, women have successfully changed caregivers. If possible, include your support person (husband, father of the baby, significant other, family member, friend, or whoever plans to be with you during labor and birth) in the interviews with potential caregivers. He or she may want to be an integral part of the entire experience, including the prenatal visits. Interestingly, many women have reported that caregivers seem to spend more time with them during the initial interview and subsequent visits when their partner attends. The amount of information you receive during office visits, especially the first one, can be overwhelming. Having a second set of ears will help you remember all the instructions and details that are discussed. A partner can also assist you in remembering any questions that you need answered by your caregiver.

Communication is key. It is up to you to express your desires to potential doctors or midwives, and discover if they are willing to accommodate you. If any of their policies are unclear, be sure to have them explained. An open exchange of views establishes a good rapport and a feeling of mutual trust and security.

A conscientious, caring doctor or midwife will take the time to discuss your feelings. He or she will also promote good nutrition, and encourage you to educate yourself on pregnancy and childbirth through reading and by attending classes. During interviews, you may want to ask caregivers what percentage of their deliveries are cesarean sections, as well as the percentage of cesareans performed in the hospitals where they deliver. And find out the reasons they consider non-negotiable for performing this procedure. For example, some caregivers automatically perform cesareans for twins, a breech baby, or if a woman has had a previous cesarean. You may also want to verify the credentials of the doctors and midwives you are considering.

Many women in the United States prefer to have obstetricians (OBs) as their caregivers because of an OB's training in handling any problems that may arise, especially during labor and delivery. Midwives care for the majority of normal healthy women in most other countries; and even in the United States, the number of births attended by midwives has steadily increased over the years. In 1975—the year that certified nurse-midwives (CNMs) were noted on birth certificates for the first time—they attended the births of 19,686 infants, or 0.6 percent of all births that year. In 2002, CNM-attended births had risen to 307,527, which accounted for 7.6 percent of all births that year, or over 10 percent of all spontaneous vaginal births that year.[1]

According to Charles Mahan, MD, OBG, dean of the University of South Florida College of Public Health and former State Health Officer for the State of Florida, "Midwives are willing to start in early labor and sit with a woman fourteen hours. I'm not willing to do that. Most of my colleagues aren't either. For low-risk women, they are better off with a midwife."[2]

Physician Model of Care

Physicians—obstetricians, perinatologists, and family practice physicians—deliver the majority of the babies born in the United States, and most deliveries take place in a hospital setting. *Obstetricians* care for the majority of pregnant women. Their training focuses on diagnosing and treating high-risk pregnancies. A *perinatologist* is an obstetrician who has additional training and certification in the treatment of high-risk pregnancies. Most perinatologists only take care of women with high-risk pregnancies; they may care for these women during part of the pregnancy in consult with their obstetricians or family practice physicians. Both obstetricians and perinatologists diagnose and treat complications and manage diseases that affect pregnant women and their fetuses. *Family practice physicians* also deliver babies, although this is not a common practice. These physicians, who practice mainly in rural areas, may need to consult an obstetrician or perinatologist if the woman develops complications.

In the United States, most pregnant women choose obstetricians as their healthcare providers, even though midwifery care is an excellent alternative for healthy women, and at a lower cost. The care of most obstetricians is two-fold: focusing on the woman's physical changes and testing to rule out possible complications. They focus on the "pathologic potential of pregnancy and birth."[3] Obstetricians perform many interventions "just in case." Women with chronic medical problems such as diabetes or high blood pressure, or who become high-risk during pregnancy greatly benefit from the expertise of an obstetrician or perinatologist. But women with normal, healthy pregnancies who choose these physicians as their providers are often managed in the same manner as women who are high-risk. This means they are likely to undergo frequent and unnecessary testing during pregnancy. Furthermore, during labor, they will probably to be confined to a bed while hooked up to a continuous electronic fetal monitor, and they may not be permitted to eat or drink. Although there is no medical reason for it, their labor may be induced and they will probably request an epidural.

Choose a caregiver with whom you feel comfortable and can agree with on a birth plan.

Although some physicians wait for labor to start on its own, many women with no medical reason to be induced are being offered the option, even before their due date in some cases. Today, it is unusual for a pregnancy to go beyond forty-one weeks, even though this time period is still normal. At forty-two weeks, women are considered overdue and induction is recommended if they have not spontaneously gone into labor.

In hospitals, it is the nursing staff that tends to women during labor. Doctors rely on nurses to provide information on the laboring women's progress. Patients may receive occasional visits from the OB, but just for a quick check of the cervix. In many cases, the first time a woman in labor sees the doctor is during the pushing stage. And most nurses—who have multiple duties and who are assigned to more than one patient—rarely stay with a woman during her labor for any length of time. Most women who deliver in a hospital have continuous electronic fetal monitoring that can be viewed at a central nurse's station. Intravenous fluids, the use of oxytocin to induce or augment labors, and epidurals are commonplace. As a result, women are less inclined to get out of bed and move around during labor. They are limited to sucking on ice chips or ice pops and sipping clear liquids.

In most hospitals, when the doctor arrives to deliver the baby, the labor bed is transformed into a delivery table. The bottom third of the bed is dropped down or removed and the woman's feet are placed into foot rests. Her bottom half is then is draped with a sterile sheet during the delivery. The newborn is placed on her abdomen, which is usually covered with a blanket. After a short time, the baby is removed, so the nursery staff can perform the admission procedures.

Some obstetricians and hospital nursing staffs discourage women from attempting an unmedicated birth. They view the pain of labor as unnecessary and may offer medication or epidurals throughout labor instead of other pain-relief methods, such as breathing techniques, relaxation exercises, and laboring in water. If you desire an unmedicated, non-intervention type of birth experience, it is very important to seek out a doctor who agrees with your philosophy and who will support your desires when you enter the hospital. Upon arrival at the hospital, request a nurse who has experience in supporting women who choose to deliver naturally. A doula or trained labor companion can be another important addition to your support system.

Midwifery Model of Care

Midwives are experts in assisting women who are experiencing a normal pregnancy and childbirth. In addition to being a registered nurse, a certified nurse-midwife (CNM) has completed training and passed an exam in midwifery. She may even have a master's degree. Certified nurse-midwives can have hospital privileges, as well as attend births in out-of-hospital birthing centers or homes.

A few states recognize licensed midwives (LMs), who have completed training according to the requirements of their states. LMs may or may not be nurses. Certified professional midwives (CPM) must pass a test, but their training is informal and can include self-study and an apprenticeship. Lay midwives may or may not be registered in their states and their training and qualifications vary. Births by midwives other than CNMs usually take place in a birthing center or home.

Midwives view pregnancy as a transition into motherhood that has physical implications, as well as cultural, spiritual, and emotional ones. They consider the entire woman—whom they refer to as a client, not a patient. During prenatal visits, along with monitoring physical changes, a midwife will spend time exploring her client's emotional needs. Time is typically spent discussing such topics as nutrition, exercise, and the avoidance of harmful substances. In an effort to get a complete picture of her client, a midwife may ask about her home environment and perhaps question her sexual history. Because pregnancy changes the family dynamics, whether it is a first baby or a later pregnancy, family participation during these meetings is welcomed.

Midwives, who view birth as an important passage into motherhood, are experts at enhancing the process of labor, delivery, and breastfeeding. They have an innate trust in the ability of a woman's body to give birth. During labor, the midwife stays with the woman to support and monitor her progress. She is less likely to intervene in a normal labor, but allows the woman to decide which coping techniques work best for her. Unless the woman is post-term (forty-two weeks) or develops a medical condition that warrants induction, labor is allowed to begin on its own. During labor, women are encouraged to eat, drink, walk, and assume any position that is comfortable. They can even sit in a

Choose your options wisely.

Looking for a Midwife?

To find a certified nurse-midwife (CNM) in your area, call The American College of Nurse-Midwives toll-free at 888-MIDWIFE (643-9433), or logon to its website at www.midwife.org.

warm bath. And intravenous (IV) fluids are not used routinely. Babies are monitored at regular intervals by a *fetoscope* or a hand-held fetal monitor, not by continuous fetal monitors. Family members are welcome to share in the entire labor and birth experience.

During birth, the woman may assume whatever position feels most comfortable—lying on her side, semi-reclining, kneeling, squatting, or even standing. She can push while sitting on a birthing chair or stool, or while lying in a warm bath or on a regular bed. If the birth takes place on a bed, sterile drapes are not placed over the woman's legs and abdomen. (If the birth occurs in a hospital, the labor bed will remain intact; it is not transformed into the standard delivery position with the bottom third removed.) The woman and her partner are encouraged to touch the newborn immediately. They are able to reach down and bring the baby up and onto the mother's bare abdomen. The baby is dried off, but stays skin to skin on the mother's chest for the next hour to facilitate bonding and breastfeeding.

Interventions are not routine; they are used only when the pregnancy or labor changes from normal to high-risk. When a normal pregnancy develops complications, the midwife either consults with her physician backup or transfers the care of the woman to the physician's practice.

PLACE OF BIRTH

When deciding where to have your baby, ask yourself a few important questions. Do I feel safest in a hospital environment? Do I want to give birth in a hospital where the latest technology is available for high-risk women and babies? Do I prefer a smaller community hospital, even though it may require transferring to another hospital if my baby or I need special care? Do I feel more comfortable in an out-of-hospital birthing center that is close to a hospital if a transfer is necessary? Do I want to deliver my baby in a hospital setting that has a home environment? Or do I prefer to give birth at home in my own familiar, comfortable surroundings?

Along with interviewing caregivers, try to visit the various facilities and ask questions. A hospital may appear very home-like, but may, in fact, treat all women as if they are high-risk, discouraging them from walking the halls or laboring in water. Speak to labor nurses. Share your desires with them, and ask if the hospital will support your choices. Does the doctor or midwife you have chosen deliver at the hospital you prefer?

Despite claims that the hospital is the safest place to have a baby, studies show that women having a normal healthy pregnancy can safely deliver in alternative settings.[4] A midwife can attend your baby's birth unless a cesarean or instrument delivery is necessary. So if you choose a midwife, be sure to find out if she has hospital privileges in case a transfer is necessary. If she does not, determine who will care for you in case of complications. Some women want a midwife to attend the birth of their baby, but prefer the hospital environment. In certain instances, the midwife must deliver the baby in the hospital if the mother has had a previous cesarean section or has certain medical conditions, such as gestational diabetes or anemia. Certain potential problems with the newborn that were discovered during pregnancy may also prevent the woman from giving birth out of the hospital.

Hospitals

Hospital facilities range from small community-based sites to large, high-risk units with level-3 intensive care nurseries that can provide care for critically ill newborns. A woman who is at risk for delivering a very preterm baby or who is having serious

Hints for the Mother-to-Be

✓ Make a list of the things that you wish to discuss with your caregiver.

✓ Start asking questions early in your pregnancy.

✓ Ask a few questions at each obstetric visit, rather than a long list of questions at one visit.

✓ Take your partner with you to the visits during which you want to discuss important issues. Your caregiver may be more willing to discuss these issues with both of you present.

✓ Ask labor and delivery nurses for recommendations of supportive doctors and midwives.

**Looking for a
Birth Center?**

To find a birth center in your
area, logon to the American
Association of Birth Centers
at www.birthcenters.org.
Centers that have met
national standards will be
recognized as accredited
by the Commission for the
Accreditation of Birth Centers.

pregnancy complications will benefit from the advanced technological equipment found at a high-risk facility. Keep in mind, however, that a woman who is experiencing a normal, healthy pregnancy may also be treated as if she is high-risk, which means she may be subjected to many of the same interventions. Also, be aware that small community hospitals may not have twenty-four hour anesthesia coverage or an obstetrician in house. These criteria may be important if your pregnancy is high-risk.

Free-Standing Birth Centers

Most out-of-hospital birth centers are independently owned and managed by midwives or physicians; others are financed by hospitals, but located outside the main building. Birth centers offer normal, healthy women the opportunity to birth their babies using few medical interventions. They usually cost less than hospitals, while still providing a high quality of care. Many insurance companies cover the cost of these centers for maternity care. Several states actually require insurance companies to offer the option of birth centers to their clients.

Many midwives who manage birth centers, also have physicians in the practice. These centers deliver comprehensive prenatal, labor, birth, and postpartum care. Discharge from a birth center usually occurs within four to six hours after birth. Cesarean rates for women in labor who require transfer to a hospital are low—4.4 percent according to the National Birth Center Study.[5] Nurse-midwives have protocols in place in case there is need for such a transfer.

The New England Journal of Medicine published the National Birth Center Study, which showed that normal, healthy women could be safely cared for in a birth center environment. Even more important, the satisfaction rate for women delivering there is very high. In a study of women who were transferred from a birth center to a hospital, 97 percent said they would recommend the birth center; 83 percent said they would have their next baby in the birth center.[6]

Home Birth

Women who choose to have their babies at home usually do so to avoid unnecessary intervention or to be in a comfortable, familiar environment. A woman who is experiencing a normal, healthy pregnancy and who has had excellent prenatal preparation is a good candidate for a home birth. Lay or licensed midwives assist in delivering babies in homes. It is important, however, to be within thirty minutes of a hospital in case of an emergency. It is also imperative for the midwife to recognize when a transfer is needed and to have a plan in place if an emergency occurs.

The majority of those in the medical community do not support home births However, a study of over 5,000 home births of low-risk women who used certified professional midwives, showed outcomes that were similar to women who had given birth in a hospital. Giving birth at home did not result in a greater number of infant deaths.[7]

BIRTH PLANS

Over the years, *birth plans*—the desires and wishes of expectant parents during labor and delivery—have evolved from long detailed requirements to a few simple requests. Keep in mind that a long list of demands is likely to be met with resistance and negativity by physicians and hospital staffs. Instead of fostering an environment of cooperation and trust, it may create an adversarial response. Doctors and nurses may feel that lengthy requests show a lack of trust by the expectant parents.

During your pregnancy, discuss your desires with your physician or midwife and then write out a simple plan expressing your wishes. This "wish list" will then be placed on your chart so that the hospital staff will be aware of your choices. If an option is important to you, but your caregiver does not seem willing to accommodate it, encourage him to explain his reasoning. Following the discussion, if you are still not comfortable with his response, consider seeking care elsewhere. If you make this decision, be sure to let your original caregiver know why you are leaving his practice.

Assessing Your Options for Labor and Birth

Only you can determine your particular needs for ensuring a positive birth experience. The following lists are intended to help you design your desired birth plan. Some subjects may not be of any interest you, while others may be very important. Once you've researched the topics (detailed information is found within the chapters of this book) and have decided on their importance, discuss them with your doctor or midwife. If you aren't prepared and don't express your desires prior to giving birth, then your choices will be limited once labor has begun.

Possible Labor and Birth Options

During the time of labor and birth, I would like to:

- Have one or more support persons present, including children, if desired.

- Have a doula or other professional support person present.

- Move about and assume a variety of comfortable positions.

- Labor and/or give birth in water.

- Have liquid nourishment and high-carbohydrate, low-fat snacks as desired.

- Have personal items (nightgown, music, photographs, flowers, etc.).

- Have intravenous fluids or a saline lock *only* if medically necessary.

- Have the baby's fetal heart rate monitored with a fetoscope or a hand-held ultrasound device. Use of an electronic fetal monitor (either intermittently or continuously) is to occur *only* if it is medically necessary.

- Allow the membranes of the amniotic sac to rupture spontaneously.

- Have an episiotomy *only* if needed.

- Have a gentle birth.

- Have medication administered only when I have requested it, and only after I have been given full information regarding the possible effects it will have on me, my baby, and my labor.

- Avoid any inducing or augmentation of labor unless there is a medical indication for it.

- Maintain a comfortable and efficient pushing and delivery position. I do not want to be in a supine position or use stirrups.

- Have regional anesthesia *only* if medical or surgical intervention becomes necessary.

- Have the newborn placed immediately on my bare abdomen or in my arms.

- Delay the cutting of the umbilical cord until the pulsating stops.

- Have the father cut the umbilical cord.

- Have the blood from the umbilical cord collected for banking.

- Have the baby breastfeed within the first hour after birth (or as soon as possible).

- Delay giving the baby antibiotic ointment or a vitamin K injection until after bonding.

■ Avoid separating me and my baby during the recovery period unless it is medically necessary. The baby is to remain with me and go with me to my post-partum room instead of spending time in the nursery.

■ Allow the placenta to spontaneously detach from the uterine wall.

■ Allow the taking of photos or videos.

Possible Postpartum Options
After giving birth, I would like the following:

■ The baby to be breastfed on demand.

■ No supplements (water or formula) or pacifiers given to the baby.

■ To be discharged from the hospital or birth facility as early as possible.

■ Full twenty-four hour rooming in.

■ The father to stay in the room.

■ Delaying of the circumcision (if male and if planning to circumcise) until the baby is feeding well and has recovered from birth.

After carefully considering the various options you desire during labor and delivery, as well as those that are important to you after you've given birth, it's time to discuss them with your caregiver and then write out your birth plan. Have your caregiver sign a copy, which you will have placed on your chart for the hospital staff to see. The Sample Birth Plan for Uncomplicated Labor and Birth on page 14 serves as a guide.

Assessing Your Options for a Planned Cesarean Birth

In addition to considering the various options for a normal labor and birth, if you are having a planned cesarean, it is important to think about the following preferences as well. Once you have determined your desires, write out your birth plan. See the Sample Birth Plan for Planned Cesarean Birth on page 15 to serve as a guide. (See Chapter 12 for a detailed discussion of cesarean birth options.)

Cesarean Birth Options
Before, during, and after the cesarean procedure, I would like to:

■ Allow labor to begin naturally to ensure that my baby is ready to be born.

■ Avoid any preoperative sedation.

■ Have my support person present for the surgery.

■ Have a spinal or epidural anesthesia for the surgery.

■ Have the drape lowered or mirrors provided during the delivery so I can see the birth.

■ Begin breastfeeding the baby as soon as possible after birth (in the recovery room).

■ Allow the taking of photos/video of the birth.

■ Have my support person remain with the baby after the surgery, and bring the baby to me in the recovery room.

■ Be able to hold the baby in the operating room if possible, or have her remain in the operating room with me rather than being admitted to the nursery.

■ Allow rooming in for my support person, so he/she can assist with the baby.

CHILDBIRTH CLASSES

Childbirth preparation is more than breathing techniques. It prepares you mentally for the emotional demands and the work involved with labor. Today's trend in childbirth involves the administration of epidural anesthesia—which causes a loss of sensation from the abdomen to the toes—as early as possible during labor. Women who plan to have epidurals often do not feel the need to take childbirth classes or to prepare for dealing with labor pain. But keep in mind that the administration of an epidural may be delayed due to a woman's stage in labor, her medical condition, or the unavailability of the anesthesiologist. Furthermore, epidurals do not always work, which means that if you have not learned other pain-coping techniques, you are likely to have a very difficult time dealing with labor.

As mentioned earlier, preparing for childbirth helps prepare you for the work involved with labor, and labor helps prepare you for the job of parenthood. Women are often surprised at the overwhelming feeling of satisfaction and empowerment that a natural birth provides. To plan for the work involved with this event, it is important to be aware of the process, as well as the coping mechanisms that can help assist you in having a good childbirth experience. In addition to providing information on labor and birth, childbirth classes also share helpful guidelines on such subjects as breastfeeding, normal appearance and characteristics of newborns, baby care, and coping with the job of parenthood.

While the Internet can provide a wealth of information, a class environment allows you to ask questions and interact with other couples. Furthermore, it can be a social experience. Many long-lasting friendships have developed in childbirth class.

There are many types of childbirth preparation options. Most hospitals offer Lamaze classes with emphasis on what is standard practice at that particular facility. Consumer-based classes may offer a more nonbiased approach to labor and birth, and teach a variety of techniques, such as the Lamaze and Bradley methods, as well as

A childbirth instructor assists an expectant couple with relaxation techniques during class.

HypnoBirthing. You can also find classes that focus on early pregnancy, as well as specific aspects of parenting, such as breastfeeding, infant care, babysitting, grandparenting, and managing siblings. Happiest Baby on the Block classes, which are offered in some areas, teach parents coping techniques for crying babies. Classes that train parents in administering cardiopulmonary resuscitation (CPR) and other emergency procedures are also available. After your baby is born, you may want to take advantage of a mother's support group, breastfeeding support group, and infant massage classes. There are a number of community resources that you may find helpful during this exciting time in your life.

Sample Birth Plan for Uncomplicated Labor and Birth

To Dr. Smith and the labor and delivery staff of Memorial Hospital:

I am a normal, healthy pregnant woman who is expecting an uncomplicated labor and birth. My desire is to have a natural, unmedicated childbirth experience. My partner and I have prepared for this by taking childbirth classes, and by practicing relaxation and breathing techniques. I would like to have the freedom to change positions, drink fluids, and relax in water during labor.

Please assign a nurse to me who is experienced in assisting natural deliveries and who will help me accomplish these goals. I request that the anesthesiologist/ nurse anesthetist or any other staff member refrain from asking me if I want medication or an epidural. If I feel that I need medication, I will ask for it. To facilitate walking during labor, my physician has agreed that I do not need intravenous fluids. I can also be monitored intermittently with an electronic fetal monitor.

After the birth, as long as my baby is healthy, please place her on my abdomen and let her stay with me for the first hour after she is born. I would appreciate any admission procedures and examinations to be performed while the baby is in my arms or within my sight. I also want to initiate breastfeeding as soon as my baby is interested, so please do not offer her any bottles or pacifiers, as they may interfere with the breastfeeding process.

During labor or birth, if a situation arises regarding my baby's care that requires intervention, I wish to be part of the decision-making process. If I need to have a cesarean delivery, I would like to be given a spinal or epidural and have my partner remain with me during the operation. I also wish to be reunited with my baby in the recovery room if her condition is stable. That way, I can start breastfeeding as soon as possible.

I am looking forward to delivering my baby in your facility. Thank you for your assistance in making this experience special.

Sincerely,
Leah Jacobs

INFORMED CONSENT

During the course of pregnancy, labor, birth, and/or breastfeeding, you may need to take certain medications or undergo specific tests or procedures. Giving your informed consent for such medical interventions means that you have discussed them with your healthcare provider and are fully aware of what is involved, including benefits and risks. Informed consent is your authorization to undergo the test or procedure based upon that information. Along with explaining the potential value and risks of the medications and/or procedures, your healthcare provider should discuss possible alternative treatments and their benefits and possible side effects. Finally, the ramifications of avoiding the medical interventions altogether should be presented as well.

To Dr. Jones and the labor and delivery staff of University Hospital:

I have been scheduled for a cesarean section in your facility on May 10th of this year. My husband, who will be my support person during the surgery, and I are looking forward to experiencing a family-centered birth. After the surgery, if the baby is stable, I would like her to remain in the operating room with us. If, however, she needs to go to the nursery for observation, please let my husband go with her. Please allow me to touch and hold my baby prior to her admission to the newborn nursery.

As long as the baby is in stable condition, I would like her brought to me in the recovery room so I can begin breastfeeding. Please do not offer her a bottle or pacifier in my absence, as this may interfere with the breastfeeding process. Please inform my husband and me of any necessary interventions that you feel are necessary for my baby.

My husband is planning to stay with me in the hospital to assist in caring for our newborn. We would like her to room in with us.

Once again, I am looking forward to delivering my baby in your facility. Thank you for your assistance in making this experience special.

Sincerely,

Jessica James

Sample Birth Plan for Planned Cesarean Birth

If you face an emergency situation, there may not be time to discuss alternatives and you will have to trust your caregiver's decisions. But if it is not an emergency, be sure to ask questions that will help determine if the intervention is most acceptable to you. Here are some sample questions to discuss with the caregiver:

- What is the benefit or benefits of this medical intervention?
- What information will the test or procedure give you?
- What are the possible risks for both me and my baby?
- If I undergo this test or procedure, will additional tests be necessary?

- Can this medical intervention be delayed? If so, for how long?
- What will happen if I refuse this medical intervention?
- Are there any alternative treatments I can try instead?

As always, knowledge is empowering. No one should blindly follow a doctor's advice without discovering all there is to know about the subject. Remember, educated choices can be made only when you have all of the facts.

DECISIONS, DECISIONS, DECISIONS

If you were going to buy a new car, you wouldn't plunk your money down without first learning about the car. You would do Internet searches, read auto magazines, and visit auto showrooms. You would learn about the car's various safety features, the kind of gas mileage it gets, and the colors it comes in. There is a lot to consider; after all, buying a car is important.

When it comes to having your baby, nothing is more important. The decisions you make during pregnancy and childbirth can impact your life and the health of your baby. Your perception of the birth experience will last a lifetime, so make it positive—one that will enhance your parenting abilities and give your baby the best possible start.

While no physician or midwife intentionally prescribes treatments that are harmful, every medical procedure, surgery, and medication has risks and side effects. That's why it is so important to have trust in your doctor or midwife, and allow her to make decisions for you in the event of an emergency.

There are many choices open to today's expectant parents. Some want to allow nature to take its course; they do not want to interfere with the body's ability to give birth naturally without medications or other interventions. Others plan to use breathing and relaxation techniques to deal with labor pain, but only until they can get an epidural. Still others want to schedule their baby's birth, induce labor, and avoid any pain by receiving an epidural during early labor. Women who have already had a cesarean delivery can elect to have a vaginal birth after cesarean (VBAC); but the number of women who choose this option is decreasing, and so is the number of doctors who will care for them. Of greater concern are the increasing number of women who are requesting and having planned cesarean deliveries for their first child, even when there are no medical indications for doing so. A cesarean section is major surgery. The risks of a surgical delivery are greater than a vaginal birth and should not be taken lightly.

It is imperative to be knowledgeable before making any decisions regarding your baby's birth. The choices you make can have a profound impact on the birth experience, your baby, and on any future births. For a listing of organizations that can help you make informed decisions on such subjects as childbirth methods, birthing centers, and breastfeeding, see the Resources beginning on page 449.

CONCLUSION

This chapter presented general guidelines to help you make some basic, yet very important decisions on the childbirth experience—choosing a caregiver, a delivery method, and where to give birth. The chapters that follow offer more detailed discussions on these and other topics regarding pregnancy, childbirth, and life with your newborn.

Hints for the Father-to-Be

✓ Join your partner for interviews of prospective caregivers.

✓ Tour local hospitals and birth centers with her.

✓ Help her write her birth plan. Discuss the plan with her caregiver and have it signed. Make sure that it is placed on her chart when she enters the hospital or birth center.

✓ Bring an extra copy of the signed birth plan with you to the hospital or birth center.

Pregnancy
or Conception and Myth-Conceptions

Pregnancy begins with conception and continues until the moment of birth. It is that special time in life when your body envelops the growth of a new being. Everything you do, everything you eat, and even your emotions can have an effect on the development of that new life. It is, therefore, very important to be aware of both the actions you can take and those you should avoid to best benefit the development of your baby. Understanding the normal course of pregnancy, which is one of the topics presented in this chapter, will aid you in gaining this awareness.

Every pregnancy is unique. Each woman's experience differs in some ways from every other woman's. In fact, different pregnancies in the same woman usually vary. However, some aspects of pregnancy—certain physical and emotional changes that result in similar physical and emotional needs—are common to all women. This chapter takes a look at some of those common factors.

FERTILIZATION

A baby is created from the union of an *ovum* (egg cell) from a woman's body and a *sperm cell* from a man's. This union is called *fertilization* or *conception* and marks the beginning of pregnancy. Each egg and sperm cell contains half of the genetic material, or *chromosomes,* necessary to begin human life. These chromosomes contain thousands of *genes,* which determine various characteristics of the child. The male and female each contribute twenty-three chromosomes for a total of forty-six. Because of the billions of possible combinations that can be produced by these chromosomes and their thousands of genes, every child is unique.

The woman's biological contribution begins in one of her two *ovaries.* Every month, a pituitary hormone causes an egg *follicle* in one of the ovaries to ripen and swell. The walls of the follicle that surround the ripening ovum produce *estrogen,* which causes the lining of the *uterus,* or *womb,* to thicken. (The top of the uterus is called the *fundus;* the bottom section is the *cervix.*) Estrogen also causes an increase in cervical mucus, making it more receptive to sperm. When the egg is mature, it bursts from the follicle and is released near the *fimbria*—the fringed end of the *fallopian tube.* This release, called *ovulation,* usually occurs fourteen days before the next menstrual period, or about midway through the cycle.

The *fallopian tubes* are muscular canals lined with fine hairs called *cilia.* As seen in Figure 2.1 on page 18, the cilia, which move with a wavelike action, draw the egg

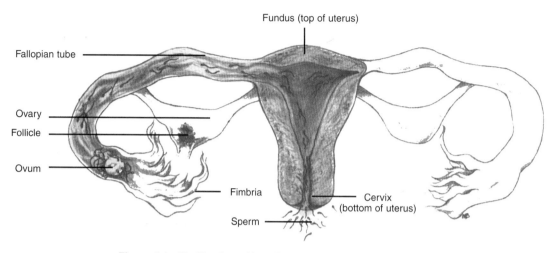

Figure 2.1. Fertilization taking place in the female reproductive organs.

into the tube and then move it toward the uterus. At the same time the egg is traveling through the fallopian tube, the follicle, stimulated by a pituitary hormone, begins producing another hormone called *progesterone,* which causes the uterine lining to thicken further. The progesterone also slows down contractions in the uterus, which facilitates implantation of the fertilized egg. If fertilization does not occur, the lining of the uterus is shed during the woman's monthly period.

The man's biological contribution to the baby begins with the production of sperm cells in his *testes,* the two organs that hang outside his body in a sac of skin called the *scrotum.* (See Figure 2.2.) Sperm cells, or *spermatozoa,* are produced in the *seminiferous tubules* within the testes and are propelled into the *epididymis* for storage until ejaculation. As the sperm pass from the epididymis through the *vas deferens* to the *urethra,* secretions are added from the *seminal vesicles,* the *prostate gland,* and the *Cowper's gland.* The purpose of these secretions is to provide a nourishing fluid that helps the sperm move through the vagina, where they are deposited during intercourse.

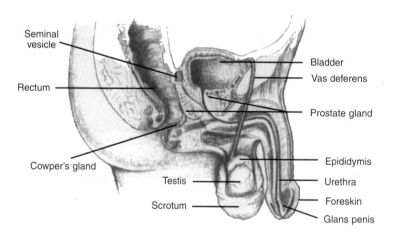

Figure 2.2.
Male reproductive organs.

During sexual excitement, the penis becomes erect as blood rushes to its spongy layers, and the veins leaving the penis begin to constrict. Upon further stimulation, the muscles around the seminal vesicles, the vas deferens, and the prostate gland contract, driving the semen into the urethra. During ejaculation, the muscles in the penis contract and push the semen through the urethral opening. Although 300 to 500 million sperm are ejaculated, only about 20,000 are still viable in the uterus; by the time they reach the egg, there are usually fewer than 1,000.

For fertilization to occur, sperm—which can remain viable within the woman for up to five days—must reach the egg within twenty-four hours of ovulation. It takes sperm from thirty minutes to two hours to swim from the upper vagina, where they are usually deposited, to the outer third of the fallopian tube, where fertilization takes place. Only one sperm out of the hundreds that may complete the journey actually fertilizes the egg. As soon as this sperm penetrates the egg wall, an enzyme is released that toughens the egg's outer membrane and prevents penetration by any other sperm.

Many people mistakenly believe that if penetration has not taken place, or if the penis is removed from the vagina prior to ejaculation, pregnancy cannot occur. The truth is that sperm can reach an egg even if they are deposited externally on the vulva. The vaginal area is moist, so sperm that have been ejaculated close to the vaginal opening are capable of making their way into the vagina. And remember, it takes only one sperm to produce a pregnancy.

"May the best sperm win!"

Assisted Reproduction

Women who are unable to become pregnant due to infertility or lack of a male partner can utilize other methods to conceive. Artificial insemination, which involves a low level of technology, is the most common. In vitro fertilization and intracytoplasmic sperm injections are other effective methods. Unlike artificial insemination, they involve significantly more cost, time, and personal commitment.

Artificial insemination is a procedure in which previously collected semen—either from a partner or other donor—is deposited deep into the vagina or uterus with a catheter. Usually performed in a doctor's office, this procedure can also be attempted at home by the woman herself. Over a million babies have been conceived through artificial insemination, which has been performed since the 1970s.

During *in vitro fertilization (IVF),* which takes place outside the uterus, the woman first takes hormones to stimulate her ovaries to produce multiple eggs (rather than just one) during the monthly cycle. Through a special procedure, as many eggs as possible are removed and then fertilized with the sperm of her partner or a donor. After three to six days of in vitro development, typically two to four of these fertilized eggs are placed in the woman's uterus, where implantation will hopefully occur. Adding multiple eggs increases the chance that at least one will implant and result in a successful pregnancy. This also increases the chance of a multiple pregnancy. Waiting five to six days until the fertilized egg becomes a blastocyst (the stage just prior to implantation) results in higher implantation rates than for eggs that are transferred after only three days of in vitro development.

For cases in which very low sperm counts or other sperm abnormalities are the cause of fertilization difficulties, *intracytoplasmic sperm injections (ICSIs)* can significantly improve chances. In an ICSI procedure, a single sperm is injected into a mature egg.

Using any of these alternative fertilization methods may take more than one attempt to achieve a pregnancy, just as it does when trying to conceive through sexual intercourse. If you are having trouble getting pregnant, speak to your doctor, who should be able to refer you to a fertility specialist. Fertility specialists counsel women on the best methods of conception for their particular situation. Alternative methods can also be expensive and involve risks—additional reasons it is important to be informed.

IMPLANTATION

Upon fertilization, the egg cell, now called a *zygote,* divides into two cells, then into four, and so on. By the fourth day, it is a cluster of sixteen cells called a *morula.* By the time it travels through the fallopian tube and reaches the uterus, a journey that takes three to four days, it has become a *blastocyst*—a hollow ball resembling a tiny blackberry. About eight days after fertilization, the blastocyst implants itself in the uterus, usually on the upper back wall. Tiny hairlike projections on the outside of the blastocyst, called *chorionic villi,* help it attach to the thick inner lining of the uterine muscle. The blastocyst can then tap into the woman's blood supply for nourishment. The villi eventually develop into the placenta.

FETAL DEVELOPMENT

The terms used to date a pregnancy can be confusing. Once the pregnancy is confirmed, your caregiver will estimate your *due date* (also referred to as the *estimated date of confinement* or EDC) by counting from the first day of your last menstrual period. In a normal twenty-eight day menstrual cycle, fertilization usually takes place approximately two weeks after your period, so you are considered two weeks pregnant at the time of fertilization. Throughout your pregnancy, your progress will be measured in weeks of gestation (pregnancy) and the baby will be given a gestational age as measured from the first day of your last menstrual period. For example, when you are twelve weeks pregnant, the fetus is actually only ten weeks old; but it is referred to as a twelve-week-old fetus, or as being twelve weeks gestational age.

Pregnancy is also divided into three trimesters, each consisting of three calendar months. In addition, lunar months are used to describe events that occur during the pregnancy. A lunar month equals twenty-eight days, and a pregnancy lasts ten lunar months.

Most of the fetal organ development takes place during the first trimester. At the beginning of this phase, the ovum is a single cell, but by the end of the twelfth week, or third lunar month, the fetus is recognizable as a human. The placenta is fully functioning, exchanging nutrients and waste products. The second trimester is a time of continued development. Most of the fetal growth and organ maturation takes place during the third trimester.

First and Second Weeks

During the two weeks prior to fertilization, the woman's body is actually preparing for pregnancy. Her eggs are ripening, her uterine wall is becoming thick, and there is an increase in cervical mucus. Fertilization typically occurs at the end of the second week when the woman ovulates and a single sperm penetrates the egg.

Third Week

During the third week of gestation or the first week following fertilization, the single cell (zygote) divides again and again, forming a hollow ball of three cell layers (blastocyst). Hairlike chorionic villi appear on the outside and help the blastocyst burrow into the uterus, usually on the upper back wall.

Fourth Week

By the end of the fourth week of gestation or two weeks following fertilization, the hollow space in the blastocyst has developed an *amniotic sac,* which is filled with fluid, and a *yolk sac,* which will produce small blood vessels and cells. As the developing being begins producing its own blood cells, the yolk sac will degenerate. The amniotic sac serves three functions—to protect the developing baby from shocks, to keep the temperature constant, and to serve as a barrier against infection from the outside. It is composed of two membranes that will eventually fuse together. The *amnion,* or inner layer, produces the amniotic fluid, and the *chorion* forms the outer layer.

At this point, the woman will have missed her period and may suspect that she is pregnant. Most pregnancy tests show positive results at this time; some tests show results even earlier.

Fifth Week

During the fifth week of gestation or three weeks after fertilization, the developing being becomes an embryo. During the embryonic stage, which lasts five weeks, the cells differentiate and develop into specific organs. The embryo is made up of three layers, which contain the foundations of specific organ systems. The top layer develops into the brain, nerves, skin, nails, and hair. The middle layer becomes the heart, kidneys, muscles, blood vessels, and reproductive organs. The bottom layer forms the stomach, liver, intestines, lungs, and urinary tract. (At the end of the embryonic phase, all of the organs are functioning and the embryo becomes a fetus.)

The chorionic villi, which are imbedded into the wall of the uterus, provide nutrients and remove waste from the embryo. These villi multiply and will eventually become the placenta.

Sixth Week

At six weeks, the embryo is about $^3/_{16}$ inch long (the size of a lentil). As seen in Figure 2.3, the nervous system and brain are beginning to grow, and the face is forming a mouth, a lower jaw, and dark circles where the eyes will be. The heart is beating and pumping blood through the developing blood vessels. Little buds that will become the arms and legs are also beginning to appear.

Seventh Week

By the end of the seventh week, the embryo is about $^1/_2$ inch long (the size of a blueberry). The brain, spinal cord, and nervous system are more developed. As shown in Figure 2.4, the head has increased in size, and the nostrils, lips, and tongue are visible. The limb buds have grown into arms and legs.

Eighth Week

By the end of the eighth week, the embryo is about $^5/_8$ inch long (the size of a kidney bean). Figure 2.5 shows that the head is quite large compared to the trunk. External ears form elevations on either side of the head. A skeleton made of cartilage, not real bone, has appeared; and a tail is apparent at the end of the spinal cord. Fingers and toes have also formed.

Ninth Week

The embryo is almost an inch in length (the size of a grape) by the end of the ninth week. The brain is visible through the fine skin that covers the head. The eyes can be seen through the closed lids. As small muscle fibers begin to grow, the body may start to move. Bone has begun to replace the cartilage, and the tail has almost disappeared. The embryo is now uniquely human, with most of its internal organs present.

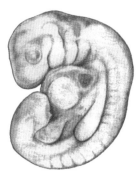

Figure 2.3.
The embryo at six weeks.
It is about $^3/_{16}$ inch.

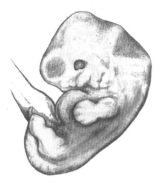

Figure 2.4.
The embryo at seven weeks.
It is about $^1/_2$ inch.

Figure 2.5.
The embryo at eight weeks.
It is about $^5/_8$ inch.

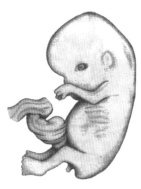

Figure 2.6.
The fetus at eleven weeks.
It is about 1$^1/_2$ inches.

Tenth Week

From the tenth week until birth, the developing baby is called a fetus. By the end of the tenth week, the fetus is approximately 1$^1/_4$ inches long (the size of a blackberry) and weighs about 2 grams ($^1/_{15}$ ounce). The jaws and other facial features are more clearly developed, and teeth are forming. The arms begin to bend at the elbow and are long enough to touch the face. If the fetus is male, its penis is apparent. If it is female, a clitoris has developed.

Eleventh Week

By the end of the eleventh week, the fetus is starting to look more human, as seen in Figure 2.6. It measures about 1$^1/_2$ inches in length (the size of a peanut shell) and weighs about 4 grams ($^1/_6$ ounce). Most of the major structures and organs are formed—development now consists of the growth and maturing of the existing structures. At this stage, the fetus has fingernails, toenails, and hair follicles; in males, a scrotum is apparent.

Third Lunar Month

By the end of the third lunar month, or twelve weeks, the fetus is over 2 inches in length (the size of a kiwi) and weighs about 7 grams ($^1/_3$ ounce). As seen in Figure 2.7, its face is well developed with eyelids that are present although fused. The fetus can move its facial muscles; it can also squint, purse its lips, and open its mouth. Its arms, hands, fingers, legs, feet, and toes are fully developed and, although the woman cannot feel it, the developing baby can make a fist and kick with its feet. The external genitalia show definite signs of a male or female sex, and a hand-held ultrasound monitor called a Doppler, can detect the fetal heartbeat. The woman's uterus can be felt just above her pubic bone.

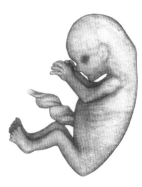

Figure 2.7.
The fetus at three lunar months. It is over 2 inches.

Fourth Lunar Month

Figure 2.8 shows the fetus at the end of the fourth lunar month, or sixteen weeks. It is almost 5 inches long (the size of a baking potato) and weighs about 100 grams (3 ounces). All of its essential body systems are now present, and most of the remaining changes will be in size. To facilitate growth, the placenta is growing rapidly. The fetus has eyebrows and eyelashes, and it is also developing several layers of thicker, less transparent skin. It may suck its thumb, as well as swallow amniotic fluid, which is passed out as urine. (Fetal urine now makes up 99 percent of the amniotic fluid for the remainder of the pregnancy.) Waste products, called *meconium,* are beginning to collect in the intestinal tract. Between the sixteenth and eighteenth weeks, some women feel the first faint fluttering movements of the fetus called *quickening.* Initially, this is commonly felt between the pubic bone and navel, and is often confused with gas.

Fifth Lunar Month

By the end of the fifth lunar month, or twenty weeks, the fetus is about 8 inches long (the length of a carrot) and weighs around 240 grams (8 ounces). This is the midpoint of a pregnancy. Although some fat has been deposited under its skin, the fetus is still quite thin. Its skin is becoming less transparent and hair is appearing on its head. The body is covered with downy hair called *lanugo.*

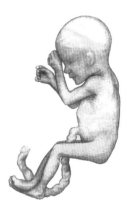

Figure 2.8.
The fetus at four lunar months is almost 5 inches.

Sixth Lunar Month

By the end of the sixth lunar month, or twenty-four weeks, the fetus is almost 11 inches long and weighs about 500 grams (1 pound 2 ounces). *Vernix caseosa,* a creamy coating that protects the skin from its watery environment, has developed. The fetus can hear; its eyes are open; and it has fingerprints and footprints. Between 40 and 60 percent of the babies born at this time survive.

Seventh Lunar Month

By the end of the seventh lunar month, or twenty-eight weeks, the fetus is close to 13 inches long and weighs about 900 grams (2 pounds). Its eyes can perceive light; it can hear, smell, taste, and respond to touch; and it has definite awake and sleep periods. If the fetus is male, testicles have descended into the scrotum. Over 90 percent of the babies born at this point survive.

Eighth Lunar Month

By the end of the eighth lunar month, or thirty-two weeks, the average fetus is about 15 inches long and weighs 1,500 grams (3 pounds 5 ounces) or more. Its skin is red but becoming less wrinkled, and its fingernails are long. If born at this point, the baby's chance of survival is better than 95 percent.

Ninth Lunar Month

By the end of the ninth lunar month, or thirty-six weeks, the baby is almost 17 inches long and weighs between 2,160 grams (4 pounds 12 ounces) and 2,500 grams (5 pounds 9 ounces). During the last two months of gestation, the fetus gains about an ounce a day. This weight gain is important because it provides the fetus with a layer of fat under the skin that will help keep the body temperature constant when outside the uterus. The once-red skin has faded to pink and has become smoother. Most of the lanugo has been shed and remains only on the arms and shoulders. The lungs are maturing and producing *lecithin,* a nutrient that is necessary for respiration.

Tenth Lunar Month

Figure 2.9 shows the fetus at the end of the tenth lunar month, or forty weeks. During this last lunar month, a typical fetus gains about 8 ounces per week. By the fortieth week, it averages 20 inches in length and 7 to $7^{1}/_{2}$ pounds in weight. The number of brain cells has greatly increased—a growth that will continue for the first five to six months after birth. During these last few weeks of gestation, 96 percent of all fetuses are positioned head down. During the final two to four weeks, the head or other presenting part settles into the top of the woman's pelvis. The baby is ready to be born!

LIFE WITHIN THE WOMB

We now know that even while all of this physical development is taking place, the unborn child is becoming an aware, reacting human being. At as early as eight weeks, he can express his likes and dislikes with well-placed kicks and jerks. At twenty-eight to thirty-two weeks, his emerging sense of awareness transforms his physical responses into feelings. His mother's emotional state can and does have an effect on the way he perceives his world—warm and friendly or cold and hostile. When a woman is under chronic stress, her fetus has a fast heart rate and is very active. This is not to say

Figure 2.9.
The fetus at ten lunar months.

that fleeting anxiety will negatively affect your unborn child. It does, however, mean that chronic anxiety or stress, especially of a personal nature, or deep ambivalence about motherhood can affect your baby.

Ultrasound images have observed fetuses rooting, sucking, swallowing, breathing, grasping, stretching, yawning, and smiling. Unborn babies alternate between being awake and active to quiet and sleeping. Many mothers describe their babies as mellow, active, or quite energetic. Fetuses that are active during the night usually continue to follow the same pattern after they are born. As you become aware of your baby's pattern, use the alert and active times to communicate with him. Touch or pat your abdomen and notice his response.

Studies have shown that the unborn child hears well from the twenty-fourth week on. By weeks twenty-five and twenty-six, he will become startled at the sound of a loud noise. According to a recent discovery, the noise level inside the uterus is much higher than previously thought. The mother's constant heartbeat and intestinal rumblings are magnified by the amniotic fluid, providing a continuous rhythmical background for the fetus. The kinds of sounds he hears will have an emotional effect. Soft, soothing sounds and gentle music are calming, while loud noise and blaring music can cause the fetus to punch and kick aggressively. Some women who played soft music while resting during the last months of pregnancy found that their babies associated music with rest time after they were born.

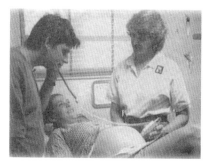

A father-to-be listens to the fetal heartbeat with the help of a certified nurse-midwife and a handheld ultrasound device.

Both parents and siblings are encouraged to read stories and sing to the baby. Studies have shown that the newborn remembers patterns or rhythms of speech when heard repeatedly during the last six weeks of pregnancy.[1] The fetus memorizes its mother's voice while in utero and can differentiate it from other women's voices after birth. Within the first week of life, the newborn can also recognize the father's voice.

While in utero, the fetus swallows amniotic fluid and tastes different flavors from the foods eaten by the mother. Its taste receptors are developed between twenty-eight and thirty-six weeks.[2] Consuming large amounts of sugar or caffeine can have an effect on the activity level of the fetus.

Most fetuses blink their eyes at twenty-eight weeks, but blinking has been observed as early as twenty-six weeks. External clicking sounds have produced an immediate blinking response of the eyes.[3] (Some researchers, however, have questioned if this reaction is a response to the sounds or to the vibrations felt in the fluid.) Fetuses can also respond to visual stimulation—they have been found to follow the beam of a flashlight that is being moved over their mothers' abdomens.

A Myth Disproved

At one time, the placenta was considered a "barrier" that blocked harmful substances from reaching the fetus. It is now known, however, that almost everything that enters the woman's body passes to the fetus.

The exciting aspect of this knowledge about fetal emotions is that you can begin shaping a positive relationship with your child before he is born. While you are pregnant, talk soothingly to your baby and send him loving thoughts. Encourage your partner and other children you might have to do the same. It's a good way to get your family involved in the pregnancy. Try to spend a portion of each day in a relaxed, anxiety-free state of mind. Both you and your unborn child will benefit.

THE PLACENTA

The function of the *placenta,* or *afterbirth,* is to supply the growing fetus with the oxygen and nutrients it needs from its mother's blood system, and take away the waste products, such as carbon dioxide, that it does not need. Two weeks after fertilization, the placenta has already started to develop. This formation begins with the villi that are embedded in the lining of the uterus. They start forming primitive blood vessels that tap into the woman's blood supply.

Fetal blood is always separate from maternal blood. Substances are passed back and forth through a semi-permeable membrane. At one time, the placenta was believed to act as a barrier to materials that might hurt the fetus. However, it is now known that almost everything that enters the woman's body—including viruses, drugs, nicotine, and alcohol—is passed to the fetus.

The placenta continues to grow until about two months before delivery, when it reaches its maximum size. At that time, it weighs from one to two pounds and is usually the size and shape of an eight- to nine-inch dinner plate. As seen in Figure 2.10, the side that is attached to the uterine wall is dark red and has lobular sections called *cotyledons,* which resemble circular puzzle pieces. This tissue may also have small white areas. These are areas that have degenerated and calcified. Women who smoke during pregnancy have more of these calcified areas than women who do not smoke. Figure 2.11 shows the side of the placenta that is next to the fetus. White and smooth, it is covered by the amniotic sac.

Nutrients from the mother pass into the blood vessels of the placenta. From the placenta, they move through the umbilical cord into the blood that is circulating within the fetus. There are three blood vessels inside the umbilical cord—one large vein and two smaller arteries—as illustrated in Figure 2.12. Nutrients travel from the placenta to the fetus through the vein. Waste products return to the placenta through the arteries and are then passed back to the mother. A gelatinous substance called *Wharton's jelly* surrounds the blood vessels and helps protect them.

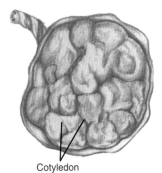

Cotyledon

Figure 2.10.
The maternal side of the placenta. This side is attached to the wall of the uterus.

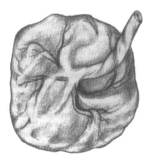

Figure 2.11.
The fetal side of the placenta. The amniotic sac originates on this side.

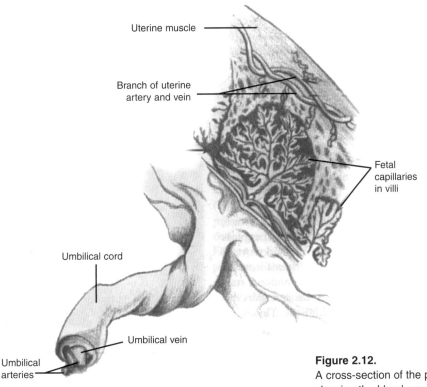

Uterine muscle

Branch of uterine artery and vein

Fetal capillaries in villi

Umbilical cord

Umbilical vein

Umbilical arteries

Figure 2.12.
A cross-section of the placenta showing the blood supply and circulation.

Hints for the Father-to-Be

✓ If your partner is experiencing morning sickness, bring her a snack such as crackers or dry toast before she gets out of bed.

✓ Accompany your partner on her prenatal visits.

✓ Take photos of your partner during each month of her pregnancy and put them in a "pregnancy scrapbook." Also record any important national, international, local, or personal events that occur during this time.

✓ Remind your partner how beautiful her changing body has become.

✓ If you feel uncertain or ambivalent about the pregnancy, give yourself time to adjust. It's not uncommon to initially feel this way.

The umbilical cord begins to develop during the second week after conception and usually grows to about eighteen inches in length, although it is possible to grow to anywhere from twelve to forty inches. After the baby is born, the cord is clamped and cut. A stump remains, but within seven to fourteen days, it dries up and falls off.

LENGTH OF PREGNANCY

The average length of pregnancy is 280 days. This is about nine calendar months or ten lunar months. A lunar month, which was discussed earlier in this chapter in the section on fetal development, is twenty-eight days—the time it takes to go from one full moon to the next.

Your doctor calculated your estimated due date by adding seven days to the first day of your last normal menstrual period and then counting back three months. For example, if the first day of your last menstrual period was February 15, your doctor would add seven days, bringing the date to February 22. Then he would subtract three months for an expected due date of November 22. This date is about 280 days after February 15. The baby would be only about 266 days old on November 22, but the date of the last menstrual period is used because the actual date of conception is usually unknown and could be as early as day five or six of the menstrual cycle. Only about 4 percent of women carry their babies for exactly 280 days, but 66 percent deliver within the ten days before or after their due dates. The due date is only an estimate, based on an average of all pregnancies. Your baby may take more or less time to develop, the same way that some babies take more or less time to get their first tooth.

PHYSICAL AND EMOTIONAL CHANGES

Pregnancy is divided into three trimesters—three periods of three months each. Most women experience the same general changes during each trimester. Throughout the pregnancy, physical changes occur in both the expectant mother and the fetus at the same time. Along with physical changes, the mother will also experience emotional changes. You and your partner can use these changes as opportunities to grow, to expand your awareness of yourselves and of each other, to deepen your sense of responsibility, and to become aware of what millions of other parents-to-be have experienced.

First Trimester

The first trimester includes the first three calendar months of the pregnancy, or the period from the first through the fourteenth week of gestation. You will experience many physical and emotional changes during this time, although most of the physical changes will be more noticeable to you than to anyone else. For an illustration of the woman's body at the end of the first trimester, see Figure 2.13 on page 28.

Physical Changes

A number of major physical changes occur during the first trimester of a pregnancy. These changes include the following:

■ **Uterus.** A missed menstrual period is the first sign of pregnancy for many women. Some women may continue to have very light periods for the first two or three months. Lack of a regular period is due to the high levels of estrogen and progesterone that the body produces to maintain the uterine lining, which nourishes the developing embryo. Many women spot slightly on the day the ovum attaches itself to the uterine wall. This is called *implantation bleeding,* not menstrual bleeding. By the time the fetus is twelve weeks old, the placenta has formed. The uterus will grow to the size of a grapefruit (with its top reaching just above the pubic bone) and the cervix will begin to soften.

■ **Vagina.** Due to the increase in pregnancy hormones, the vagina will begin to thicken and soften. An increased blood supply to the area may cause it to become bluish or violet in color. Vaginal secretions will become more noticeable and increase as the pregnancy progresses.

■ **Breasts.** A tingling or prickling sensation is often felt in the breasts during the early weeks of pregnancy. This is because the blood supply is increasing and the milk-secreting glands are beginning to grow. After a few weeks or months, this sensation will disappear, but typically, the breasts will continue to grow until the third trimester. Around the eighth week, veins may start to become visible under the skin, and small round elevated areas may appear on the *areola*—the dark area surrounding the nipples. These elevated areas are the *Montgomery glands,* which secrete a substance that lubricates and protects the nipples during pregnancy and breastfeeding.

■ **Urination.** Many women experience an increased need to urinate during the first trimester because the uterus is growing and pressing on the bladder. This need usually eases during the second trimester as the uterus rises out of the pelvic area. Even though it means more trips to the bathroom, you should drink plenty of fluids to maintain good kidney function and to provide the water necessary to metabolize the protein you eat.

■ **Digestion.** Up to 85 percent of pregnant women experience regular bouts of nausea (often to the point of vomiting) during early pregnancy. Some feel nauseous during the entire pregnancy. Although this condition is called *morning sickness,* it can occur at any time of the day. Morning sickness is caused by an increase in hormone levels, low blood sugar, and/or a lack of vitamin B_6. According to the American College of Obstetricians and Gynecologists (ACOG), the best way to fight morning sickness is by taking supplements of B_6 or ginger.[4] Eating foods that are high in B vitamins and consuming small high-protein meals throughout the day may also help. (For a further discussion on morning sickness, see "First Trimester" on page 91.)

In addition to nausea, some women experience indigestion and heartburn. The hormones *relaxin* and *progesterone* relax the smooth muscles in the body, including the sphincter located at the top of the stomach. This muscle helps keep food from rising out of the stomach and backing into the esophagus. Progesterone is also responsible for relaxing the intestines somewhat. This slows digestion, making constipation more likely. Eating a diet that is high in fiber (fresh fruits and vegetables, and whole grains), drinking plenty of fluids, and exercising regularly help to minimize constipation. (For additional heartburn remedies and preventives, see "Heartburn Fighters" on page 31.)

■ **Skin.** The hormones that are released during pregnancy can have an effect on your skin. Many women find that their skin radiates with the "glow" of pregnancy. Others are not as fortunate and may develop acne. Continue to eat a good diet and drink plenty of water. Wash your face two or three times a day with a gentle cleanser and apply moisturizer to dry areas. Avoid the temptation to pick at or squeeze the blemishes—it will only increase the likelihood of infection and scarring. Choose makeup that does not clog the pores, or at least try to limit the amount of time you wear it. Keep applicators clean

Dad Has Cravings Too!

"Soon after she announced the pregnancy, I started to crave tacos from Taco Bell. For two weeks straight, I made late-night runs there between 11 PM and 12:30 AM. Once the craving stopped, I couldn't look at another taco."

Brian
Expectant father

or purchase new cosmetic brushes or powder "puffs." If the acne is severe, you may need to see a dermatologist. Just make sure that he knows you are pregnant. Two common acne medications, Accutane and Retin A, should *not* be used during pregnancy.

■ **Stamina.** Expect to feel more tired than usual during the first trimester. Pregnancy brings change to every system in the body, and these changes require a great deal of physical and emotional energy. Proper rest is extremely important for an expectant mother, so don't feel guilty about napping during the day or going to bed early. Your body needs the rest.

Emotional Changes

Many expectant mothers spend the first trimester accepting the fact that they are pregnant and coming to terms with the implications. (This is true for other family members as well.) You may find yourself drawing inward and focusing on the changes in your body, as well as your fears and dreams. You may worry about miscarriage or feel increasingly vulnerable to danger.

Even when the pregnancy is wanted, most expectant parents will worry: Can we afford a child? How will our lifestyle change? Will we have jealousy problems with our other children? The woman may wonder: Will I have to quit work? Both parents-to-be may feel a sense of panic at the additional responsibilities. Such ambivalent feelings toward the pregnancy are very common in the early months. They are neither bad nor wrong. Acknowledging any concerns and discussing them with your partner may help you cope with them—and accept the pregnancy. Facing your doubts and fears will aid in emotional growth.

Many couples find themselves enjoying increased sexual activity during this time of adjustment, while other couples desire less. It is important for you and your partner to talk to each other openly about any feelings or fears you may have regarding this change. Keeping such concerns pent-up can damage your relationship. (For a further discussion of sexual intimacy during the first trimester, see "Sexual Relations During Pregnancy" on page 36.)

By the end of this first trimester, you may find that you have begun to examine your feelings toward your own parents. You may think about how, as a parent, you expect to be different from or similar to them. During this time, you may also experience feelings of excitement, increased creativity, and increased sensuality. You may simply feel "special." You can also expect possible mood swings, which may become extreme during pregnancy—increased hormone levels can have you laughing or crying over the most insignificant matters. While the hormones do not actually cause moodiness, they tend to intensify your feelings.

Women experiencing a second or subsequent pregnancy often find that they are less preoccupied with all of these changes than they were with their first. The major adjustment to parenthood seems to come with a first pregnancy. With later pregnancies, most women have less time available and feel less of a need to ponder the meaning of each physical change they experience.

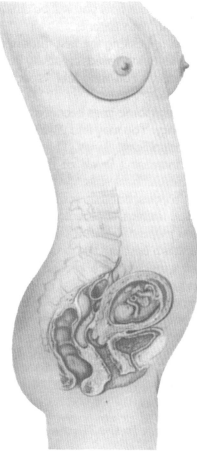

Figure 2.13.
The woman's body at the end of the first trimester.

Second Trimester

The second trimester of pregnancy includes the middle three months, or the period from the fifteenth through the twenty-eighth week of gestation. For many women, this trimester is the most enjoyable of the three. The initial adjustment period has passed, and fatigue and nausea are usually less of a problem. It is also during this time that your pregnancy becomes obvious to other people, and you may frequently be the center of attention. Your body, though larger, is not cumbersome, and it is still fairly easy to move around. The woman's body at the end of the second trimester appears in Figure 2.14 below.

Physical Changes

Women experience a growing number of significant physical changes during the second trimester, most of which are visibly apparent. These changes typically include the following:

■ **Uterus.** By the fourteenth week, the uterus begins to expand out of the pelvic area and into the abdominal cavity. By week twenty, which is midway through the second trimester, the uterus is usually at the level of the navel. Women who are pregnant for the first time usually begin to feel the movements of the fetus at about sixteen to eighteen weeks. Those who have already given birth often feel these movements earlier. When the movements are first perceived, the fetus is usually about 7 inches long and weighs around eight ounces. During this time, some women experience mild uterine contractions known as *Braxton-Hicks* contractions.

■ **Vagina.** Throughout this trimester, the tissues of the vagina continue to soften and become more elastic in preparation for the baby's passage at birth.

■ **Pelvis.** Hormones cause the cartilage in the pelvic joints to soften and widen, providing additional mobility and relaxation. This will allow the baby to pass through the pelvis more easily.

■ **Breasts.** *Colostrum,* a clear yellow fluid that precedes mature breastmilk, is often present in the breasts by the sixteenth week.

■ **Circulation.** By the end of the second trimester, the blood volume has increased by 40 to 60 percent and the heart has begun pumping more blood with each beat. Because of this increased blood volume, as well as pressure from the enlarging uterus and an increase in estrogen, *edema* (swelling) may occur, usually in the feet or ankles, and sometimes in the hands. Standing for long periods may result in edema. Putting your feet up or lying on your side will improve circulation and help decrease the swelling. Increasing your protein intake will also help. Be aware that some amount of swelling is normal during pregnancy, but it should decrease with rest. If, however, the swelling occurs in the face, comes on suddenly, and/or is significant, notify your doctor immediately. This could be a sign of preeclampsia, a serious condition that must be addressed immediately. (For more information on preeclampsia, see "Hypertension" on page 71.)

■ **Linea nigra.** Another physical change that is attributed to the hormonal activity of pregnancy is the appearance of the *linea nigra,* a dark line that

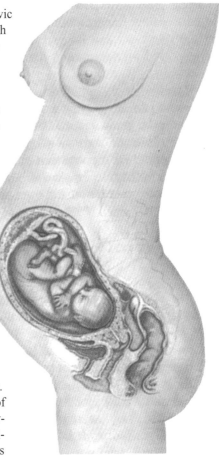

Figure 2.14.
The woman's body at the end of the second trimester.

Hints for the Father-to-Be

✓ Be understanding of your mate's mood swings.

✓ Massage oil or lotion into her abdomen to help reduce the number and severity of stretch marks.

✓ Attend her ultrasound examinations. Ask the doctor or technician for a copy of the procedure.

✓ Encourage her to rest and take naps.

extends from the navel to the pubic bone. This line, which occurs in women of all skin colors, fades after delivery, although it may continue to be visible for a number of months.

■ **Stretch marks.** Many women develop at least some stretch marks, or *striae gravidarum,* during pregnancy. These red or pink lines appear when the skin's connective tissue is stretched to the point of rupturing. Stretch marks may appear on the abdomen, thighs, and/or breasts. After delivery, they fade to white. Many women find that massaging oil or lotion into the vulnerable areas prevents stretch marks, although heredity seems to be more of a factor.

■ **Mask of pregnancy.** Some women develop dark facial blotches known as the *mask of pregnancy* during this time. This pigmentation is believed to result from increased levels of melanocyte stimulating hormone (MSH). The mask usually disappears after pregnancy when the production of MSH drops. Deficiency of folic acid, a B vitamin, is another possible cause of this skin discoloration. Your prenatal vitamins should include folic acid to meet your increased requirement.

Emotional Changes

Most women find the second trimester to be a more positive experience than the first, as they are now beginning to feel the movements of the life within them. Most husbands (or partners), who initially may have experienced ambivalent feelings toward the pregnancy, have accepted it and are often just as excited about the baby's movements. During this trimester, as the pregnancy progresses, many women begin to feel more vulnerable and need more attention from their partners. They may also expect their partners to become more involved with the pregnancy and the baby. Some women find themselves becoming overly concerned for their partners' safety.

Fathers-to-be react differently to their expectant partners' growing needs and dependence. Some are very interested and involved, offering unwavering support throughout the pregnancy, while others may suddenly seem to be more interested in work or a hobby. A number of expectant fathers experience a phenomenon called *Couvade syndrome* in which they go through symptoms of pregnancy—weight gain, cravings, nausea—right along with their partners!

Expectant mothers and fathers deal differently with the changes and stresses brought on by pregnancy. It is important for both partners to be aware of and to talk about their feelings, concerns, and fears, especially those that may be a source of friction between them. During this trimester, a woman's dreams may suddenly become very real and sometimes disturbing, often involving misfortune to her or her baby. Dreams are a way of bringing fears to consciousness, where they can be dealt with more easily. Refusing to acknowledge them can result in increasing anxiety.

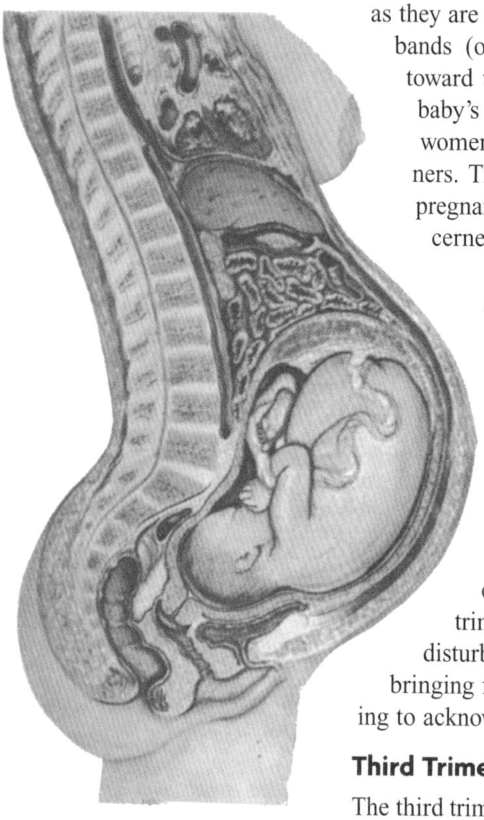

Figure 2.15. The woman's body at the end of the third trimester.

Third Trimester

The third trimester of pregnancy includes the last three months, or the period from the twenty-ninth through the fortieth week of gestation. It is a time of preparing for the birth—physically, mentally, and emotionally. The woman's body at the end of the third trimester appears in Figure 2.15 at left.

Physical Changes

As the fetus continues to grow during the third and final trimester of life inside the womb, the woman experiences continued physical changes as well. These changes include the following:

■ **Uterus.** Toward the end of pregnancy, the uterus measures about 11 by 14 inches and reaches the breastbone. *Lightening*—the settling of the baby's head downward into the pelvis, and possibly engaging in the pelvic inlet—occurs from one to six weeks before delivery. Braxton-Hicks contractions become stronger and more apparent as the time for delivery approaches. (For a further discussion of Braxton-Hicks contractions and false labor, see "Warm-Up Signs of Labor" on page 185.) Moving suddenly can cause sharp pains in the groin. This pain is caused by a spasm in or the stretching of the round ligaments, which are the main support of the uterus and extend into both sides of the groin area. During the last few weeks, the cervix becomes softer and may begin to thin out and open up a little in preparation for labor.

■ **Vagina.** As the pregnancy nears its end, the vagina produces increased amounts of mucus in preparation for the baby's passage. Vaginal swelling also increases at this time and may result in discomfort during sexual intercourse. (For a discussion of sexual intimacy during the third trimester, see "Sexual Relations During Pregnancy" on page 36.)

■ **Digestion.** After eating, many women experience bouts of indigestion during this trimester. This usually happens because of the growing uterus, which puts increased pressure on the stomach and intestines. Heartburn may also occur because pregnancy hormones cause certain muscles, including the sphincter located at the top of the stomach, to relax. When this muscle is relaxed, the gastric contents of the stomach can escape into the esophagus and cause heartburn. Problems with constipation are likely to continue at this time as well. (For heartburn remedies and preventives, see the "Heartburn Fighters" at right.)

■ **Breathing.** Shortness of breath is common during this trimester because the uterus is pushing up on the diaphragm. Breathing will improve, however, after lightening—when the baby moves downward into the pelvis. Many women also experience nasal congestion and even nosebleeds during this time.

■ **Vision.** Some women experience a change in their vision—even to the point where they may require new glasses or find themselves unable to wear their contact lenses. Changes in vision can also be the result of gestational diabetes, preeclampsia, or another serious problem. Be sure to report any vision changes to your caregiver.

■ **Circulation.** Increased pelvic pressure caused by the growing fetus, as well as the decrease in blood return from the lower body can cause *varicose veins,* which may develop in the legs, vulva, and/or rectum (hemorrhoids). Varicose veins usually diminish after giving birth.

■ **Urination.** The need to urinate usually increases, especially after lightening occurs. This is caused by the pressure of the baby on the bladder.

■ **Stamina.** Carrying around the extra weight usually causes fatigue to return during the last trimester.

Heartburn Fighters

Many women have found the following suggestions helpful in preventing or alleviating heartburn. Your caregiver may offer other recommendations as well.

✓ Eat frequent small meals.

✓ Avoid fried and spicy foods.

✓ Do not drink a lot of liquid with meals.

✓ Eat a small amount of yogurt before meals.

✓ Drink milk or eat ice cream when heartburn occurs.

✓ Chew gum.

✓ Never overfill your stomach with food or liquid.

✓ Take an antacid as recommended by your caregiver.

✓ Take a papaya enzyme supplement with meals.

✓ Do not lie down after eating.

✓ Sleep with your head elevated.

✓ Avoid bending at the waist after eating.

✓ Avoid clothing that is tight around your abdomen or waist.

Expectant Dads Can Feel Pregnant Too!

A number of fathers-to-be experience symptoms of pregnancy right along with their partners—a phenomenon known as *Couvade syndrome*. It is not unusual for expectant dads to experience weight gain, food cravings, abdominal cramping, and an increase in heartburn, backaches, and toothaches. Some men have reported suffering from symptoms of morning sickness even though their pregnant partners did not.

Emotional Changes

During the third trimester, most women focus more and more on the baby, labor, and birth. For many parents-to-be, the search for the perfect name has become an important pastime, along with preparing the house for the baby. At this point, most women view their babies as real people, separate from themselves.

Time during the third trimester may seem endless. Many women count on their due date to bring an end to their growing physical discomfort, and they may become very discouraged if they go a week or more beyond it. (If you find yourself in this situation, don't be tempted to ask your doctor to induce labor, unless there is a medical reason for it.) Because of their large size, some women experience a drop in self-esteem during this trimester. They need the people around them, especially their husbands or partners, to reassure them that they are still attractive.

You can use your preoccupation with labor and birth to your advantage at this time. Gather as much information about the birth experience as possible. Read books, take classes, and talk to new mothers. However, avoid people who attempt to discourage you from taking prepared childbirth classes or who dwell on negative birth experiences. You need to keep a confident, relaxed attitude toward the upcoming event. Do not avoid your fears, but at the same time, do not allow negative thinking to dominate your thoughts. To a great extent, your chances for a positive birth experience are determined by your attitude. Fear and anxiety can create a negative one.

CONCLUSION

This chapter has presented many of the common physical and emotional aspects of a normal pregnancy—from the moment of conception to the end of the third trimester. It was designed to offer a good idea of what you, your partner, and the baby you are carrying will experience during this very special time. Keep in mind that pregnancy is a natural condition—one of wellness, not illness. With few exceptions, you should be able to continue the same daily activities and experience the same good health and lifestyle that you enjoyed prior to becoming pregnant.

Common Questions and Concerns

or the Do's and Don'ts

When a woman becomes pregnant, she has many questions regarding her health and the health of her unborn child. Which activities can I continue to participate in and which do I need to modify? Can I perform the same job at work or do I need to make some adjustments? Is it safe to travel? Do I need to stop or refrain from taking any medication? How do alcohol, cigarettes, and recreational drugs affect my unborn baby? What about caffeine and artificial sweeteners? Can my partner and I continue to have sexual relations? This chapter addresses these and other common concerns of pregnant women.

PREGNANCY AND ACTIVITIES OF DAILY LIVING

Many normal everyday activities can continue without interruption when a woman discovers she is pregnant. As long as she maintains a healthy lifestyle and remains low risk, she does not have to greatly alter her normal activities. The following topics cover some of these areas.

Working

More than 1 million working women become pregnant each year. For most, continuing to work until right before their due dates is not a problem. As long as you and your fetus are healthy and your job presents no greater risks than those encountered in everyday life, working should not cause any added concerns.

Certain conditions, however, do require that you take precautions. If, for example, your job includes a lot of lifting, standing, or walking, your caregiver may suggest that you cut back on your hours. If your job exposes you to potentially toxic materials, including x-rays, lead, and chemotherapy medications, you should be reassigned to another area. If reassignment is not possible, your caregiver may advise you to quit your job. If you work with any substances that you feel may be harmful, be sure to discuss this with your caregiver.

Everyone encounters some stress in life, but if your job is unusually demanding, it could lead to possible problems in your pregnancy. You will need to modify your work environment to provide less stress, or learn some stress-relieving techniques to help you deal with the situation. Additionally, certain medical conditions—diabetes, kidney disease, heart disease, back pain, and high blood pressure—may prevent you from working or require you to restrict your activities. If you have had a previous mis-

carriage or preterm birth, or if you are experiencing a multiple pregnancy, your caregiver may advise you to stop or cut back on your work.

In rare cases, a condition related to your pregnancy may qualify you as disabled and prevent you from working. Even such symptoms as nausea, dizziness, and swollen ankles may cause a temporary disability. More serious complications such as infection, bleeding, premature labor, premature rupture of the membranes, heart disease, uncontrolled diabetes, or high blood pressure are other possible causes. If your caregiver determines that your pregnancy is disabling, she can sign a statement verifying this. Your employer will be required to give you the same preferences and benefits that are provided to any other disabled employee. If your employer does not routinely provide disability benefits, you may be eligible for benefits from the state.

There may be times during your pregnancy when you find it difficult to cope with your job. If you have morning sickness or are extremely tired or sleepy, making it through another day at work can be a challenge. Make maximum use of your breaks to rest and elevate your feet. Keep nutritious snacks handy to provide energy and relieve nausea. If you sit all day, remember to maintain good posture. Get up and walk around often to improve your circulation and prevent or reduce swelling. Above all, listen to your body's signals. You may find it best to cut back on your hours or just take a day or two of vacation. With common sense on your part and cooperation from your employer, you should be able to make it over the rough spots.

Place the belt under your abdomen and the shoulder strap between your breasts.

Car Safety

Most pregnant women wonder if it is advisable to wear a seat belt while riding in a car. The answer is a resounding *yes.* By protecting yourself from injury, you are also protecting your baby. Pregnant drivers who do not wear seat belts and are involved in a car crash are twice as likely to experience excessive maternal bleeding and three times more likely to have a fetal death than drivers who use seat belts.[1]

Some women are concerned that the seat belt will squeeze the baby and cause a miscarriage. There is no evidence that wearing a seat belt results in fetal injury, no matter how serious the collision. Your baby is well cushioned inside your body, surrounded by amniotic fluid and your organs. A properly worn seat belt is your unborn child's best protection. As shown in the photo at left, place the lap portion of the belt underneath your abdominal bulge, as low on your hips as possible. Never put it above your abdomen. Position the shoulder portion of the belt between your breasts. Do not slip the belt off your shoulder. Adjust both parts as snugly as possible.

Traveling

If you are like most women, traveling during pregnancy is not a problem. You should, however, adhere to the following guidelines:

■ Check with your caregiver to make sure there are no specific healthcare concerns that prevent you from traveling.

■ Try to plan trips during your second trimester, when comfort is the greatest.

■ While traveling, walk often to improve circulation and prevent or reduce swelling.

■ Wear comfortable shoes and clothing.

■ Take along light snacks and juice to prevent hunger and avoid nausea.

■ Do not take motion sickness pills or any other medications before first checking with your caregiver.

■ Take time to eat regular, nutritious meals.

■ Eat plenty of high-fiber foods to prevent constipation.

■ Get your usual amount of sleep and rest often, elevating your feet when possible.

■ When traveling far from home, take a copy of your medical record and get the name of an area doctor or facility where you could go for treatment if necessary.

■ If traveling overseas, drink only bottled beverages and do not use ice in your drinks. Avoid eating raw, unpeeled fruits or vegetables, as well as raw or undercooked meat. Make sure that any milk you drink has been pasteurized.

■ If traveling by car, avoid riding for more than six hours a day. Stop every one to two hours to walk around—and always wear a seat belt.

■ If traveling by air, sit in an aisle seat for the greatest comfort. Wear layers of clothing so that you can make adjustments as the cabin temperature changes. Drink plenty of fluids to prevent dehydration.

■ Avoid flying in small aircrafts that do not have pressurized cabins. When flying over 7,000 feet, oxygen levels for the baby may be affected.

Many airlines have policies for pregnant travelers. Although they do not have any restrictions during the first and second trimesters, some airlines require both a letter from the doctor (signed within seventy-two hours of travel) and clearance from the airline for passengers who are traveling close to their due date. Check for specific details with your airline before making travel plans.

The best guideline you can follow when traveling is to keep your plans flexible and change them according to your body's signals. If you use common sense, traveling during pregnancy can be a pleasure, not an inconvenience.

Dental Care

Many pregnant women experience gum tenderness or bleeding due to an increase in hormone levels. It is important to continue daily brushing using a soft-bristled toothbrush and fluoride toothpaste. Brushing after every meal or at least twice a day and flossing can reduce the chance of developing the gum infection *gingivitis* during pregnancy. The bacteria that cause gingivitis and cavities have been associated with preterm labor. If left untreated, gingivitis can lead to periodontitis in which the infection erodes the bones and surrounding tissues. Maternal periodontal disease is associated with an increased risk for preeclampsia according to a study in 2003.[2]

Continue to keep your regular dental checkups. The American Dental Association recommends that pregnant women avoid x-rays until after delivery, but if they are necessary, a special apron must be applied to prevent fetal exposure. In addition, a protective thyroid collar should also be used. One study concluded that even low doses of radiation around the head and neck increase the woman's risk of delivering a low birth weight baby.[3]

Hints for the Father-to-Be

✓ Place your head close to your partner's abdomen and talk or sing to your baby.

✓ Continue the romance.

✓ Be aware that your desire for sexual relations with your partner may increase or decrease after you learn of the pregnancy. This is normal.

✓ Sexual relations will not harm the fetus in a normal pregnancy.

✓ If you are having trouble with your regular love-making positions, try alternate ones.

If you need dental work, a local anesthetic can be administered and most antibiotics can be taken. Always inform your dentist that you are pregnant and check with your obstetrician or midwife if you have a question about the prescribed medications.

Sexual Relations During Pregnancy

The way in which you and your partner react to your changing body, coupled with how comfortable you are discussing these feelings will play a role in your attitude toward lovemaking. Your partner may find you even more desirable now because your body is carrying his child. Or he may worry that sexual intercourse might cause the growing baby harm or cause you to have a miscarriage. Unless you have a history of miscarriage or other medical problems, this concern is unnecessary. Check with your caregiver for reassurance.

At the beginning of your pregnancy, together, you and your partner should decide to remain physically close, even if you go through times of lessened sexual activity. Touching, snuggling, caressing, or massaging—not necessarily leading to sex—can keep both of you feeling open, warm, and loving toward one another. Accepting both positive and negative feelings is a necessary part of dealing with and coming to terms with the pregnancy. Openly communicating with one another and, of course, with your caregiver will help ensure that your pregnancy gets off to good start.

Early pregnancy classes are good places to talk about sexuality and your changing body in relation to lovemaking. Prepared childbirth classes are also good for discussing this subject; however, by the time you take them, much of your pregnancy will be behind you.

The first trimester can be an exciting time for both you and your partner. It is common to feel very good about yourself and your pregnant body. You may feel unusually close to your mate and very beautiful, exhilarated at the thought of a new life growing within you. You might also find yourself easily fatigued, nauseated, anxious, and very emotional. Your partner may be proud and excited about the new life he has helped to create. At the same time, he may feel anxious or rejected because you are now concentrating your love and attention on your developing child.

The first three months are certainly a time of adjustment for both you and your mate. Wide mood swings will be normal for both of you. You will also experience changes in your body and in your relationship. While you continue to love each other as much as or even more than before the pregnancy, your physical expression of that love is likely to be altered—sometimes to a surprising degree! Please be assured that this is not unique to you. Whatever your feelings, desires, needs, or concerns, they have been experienced by countless other couples. Be aware that pregnancy encompasses a wide range of emotions, needs, and concerns. Some women experience increased sexual desires during the first trimester; others, especially if they are feeling nauseated or fatigued, have less of a desire. Even if you are nauseated, you will still appreciate soothing touches and caresses (as well as good back rubs) from your partner. Both of you will enjoy warm hugs and kisses.

During the second trimester, your growing uterus will begin to bulge, although not to the extent that it is in the way or makes sex uncomfortable. Some women experience a decline in sexual enjoyment as the pregnancy advances, while others feel increased pleasure. Again, if you are open with each other and responsive to each other's sexual needs, you can eliminate most problems before they begin.

Some of your initial physical complaints will probably disappear by the third or fourth month. Usually, the nausea and fatigue have passed, and you will feel more relaxed now that the chance of miscarriage has diminished.

As you move into the third trimester, however, you may find that simple movements, such as getting in and out of bed, bending forward, and even standing, walking, or sitting, can be very awkward and difficult. This physical clumsiness may keep you from enjoying sexual intercourse. On the other hand, increased pelvic congestion may arouse sexual desires that are relieved by orgasm. Your partner may also feel some restraints in enjoyment. He may be uncomfortable feeling the baby move during lovemaking sessions. He may also initiate sex less frequently as he assumes a more protective role. Do not misinterpret this as rejection.

As your waistline expands and your body enlarges, you may start to view yourself differently and find it difficult to feel sexy. This feeling may be reinforced by other people's attempts at humor when they comment on your changing shape. Just remember, you are pregnant, not fat, and this growth is essential for a healthy baby. You can be assured that your former figure will return after you have given birth.

You may have already tried a variety of positions to increase your comfort during intercourse. If your pregnancy has advanced to the point where it is almost "in the way," you may find that having your partner on top but slightly to the side will avoid the discomfort that was caused by his weight pressing on your abdomen. This position also gives you more mobility and lessens penetration of the penis. You may discover that being on top is more comfortable, as you can better control the degree of penetration. Some couples, however, find that this position results in deeper penetration and causes more discomfort.

Side-lying positions can be comfortable and satisfying, as can entry from behind while you are lying on your side or as you kneel or stand while using the bed for support. In these positions, you can control the degree of penetration and relieve abdominal pressure. You can also lie close to the edge of the bed and have your partner support your legs with his arms or shoulders. Needless to say, experimenting to find the position that affords the most comfort and satisfaction is important, as is a sense of humor!

Many couples find alternatives to intercourse at this point in the pregnancy. Remember that massaging, touching, and caressing provide close physical contact, which is just as important as intercourse for both of you. Some couples find that genital manipulation and mutual masturbation provide sexual gratification. Even self-masturbation can be relieving. Some couples enjoy oral sex. However, a word of caution here is necessary. Air should *not* be forced into the vagina at any time during pregnancy. Because of increased vascularity during pregnancy, air that passes into the uterus can enter the woman's bloodstream and cause an *air embolism*—a rare phenomenon that can result in death. If you enjoy oral sex, it is fine to continue the practice as long as you are aware of this one restriction.

Unless you are spotting or have a history of miscarriage, consider your pregnancy a sign of physical health. This means you should continue your life as normally as possible, keeping in mind that intercourse will not harm your baby and can be continued throughout pregnancy. If you experience pain in your pelvic region or observe blood or fluid, contact your caregiver immediately.

When to Avoid Sex During Pregnancy

✓ If you are at risk for preterm labor.

✓ If you have a placenta previa (low-lying placenta).

✓ If you have an incompetent cervix.

✓ If you experience vaginal bleeding.

✓ If your membranes have ruptured or you are leaking fluid.

✓ If you have an active herpes lesion.

✓ If you experience pain with intercourse.

✓ If you have a vaginal infection or an undiagnosed vaginal discharge.

Be aware that orgasms will cause the uterus to contract. However, the uterus contracts the same way with Braxton-Hicks contractions, which are perfectly natural during pregnancy. But, if are at risk for preterm labor and your caregiver advises against orgasms, you must understand that this means via masturbation as well. You may also need to adjust two other practices. First, avoid touching your nipples as this releases *oxytocin,* a hormone that causes uterine contractions. Second, if you are permitted to continue having intercourse, your partner may need to wear a condom. This is because semen contains prostaglandins, which can also stimulate contractions. In addition, your caregiver should let you know if you have a medical problem that requires you to alter your position or frequency of intercourse, or to stop altogether. Otherwise, most professionals believe that couples can continue to enjoy intercourse until labor begins. Therefore, experiment and enjoy!

FOOD PRODUCTS

A number of food items contain certain substances—caffeine, artificial sweeteners, food additives, and particular herbs—that may have an effect on the developing baby. Over the years, new research and information has caused the Food and Drug Administration (FDA) to review and alter its recommendations regarding the use of these items by pregnant women. The most current guidelines for these products are presented in the following discussion.

Caffeine

Caffeine is a stimulant that is present in coffee, tea, cola drinks, chocolate, and some over-the-counter medications. Researchers have looked at the effects of heavy caffeine consumption (over 300 milligrams per day) on pregnancy and the developing fetus.

While some studies have linked caffeine with miscarriage, other studies have disagreed. One report reviewed fifteen epidemiologic studies and decided that due to limitations in the methods used to collect the data, the link between caffeine and miscarriage was inconclusive.[4] Some studies have linked high caffeine intake to low birth weight and preterm delivery.[5] But other factors such as maternal smoking may have also contributed to these problems. These effects, however, were not observed with moderate caffeine consumption.[6]

Upon ingestion, caffeine quickly crosses the placenta to the fetus. The amount of caffeine in the fetal blood remains higher for a longer period of time due to the developing baby's immature metabolism.[7] In the last months of pregnancy, the woman metabolizes caffeine at a slower rate, so the effects on the fetus may be increased. Moderate caffeine can affect fetal heart rate, causing an irregular heartbeat; it can also affect the baby's movement.[8] Once the woman removes caffeine from her diet, these effects are reversed. According to the authors of *Drugs in Pregnancy and Lactation,* moderate caffeine consumption does not pose a "measurable risk to the fetus." When used in moderation, there is no proven association with congenital malformations, spontaneous abortions, preterm birth, and low birth weight.

Caffeine is found in many common food and nonfood items. It is also present in a number of products that may surprise you. Table 5.1 on page 103 lists a number of these foods, along with their caffeine content. Fortunately, many delicious decaffeinated coffees and teas are now available. Do keep in mind, however, that coffee, tea, and soft drinks have no nutritional value. Milk, water, and fruit juices should make up the bulk of your fluid intake for maximum nutrition.

Artificial Sweeteners

Artificial sweeteners are added to many foods, drinks, and medications. They can also be purchased in individual serving sizes and/or in bulk for use in cooking. Although the question of their safety has been a matter of controversy, the FDA has deemed the following artificial sweeteners safe—even for pregnant women:

- Aspartame (NutraSweet, Equal, NatraTaste)
- Neotame
- Sucralose (Splenda)
- Acesulfame potassium (Sunett)
- D-Tagatose (Naturlose)
- Saccharin (Sweet'n Low)

Aspartame, which has been on the market since the 1980s, is added to many food products and beverages. Sold as NutraSweet, Equal, and NatraTaste, this artificial sweetener is available in blue individual serving packets. Because it does not retain its sweetness when exposed to heat, aspartame is not used in cooking or baking. The most studied food additive, aspartame does not pose a risk to the fetuses of normal mothers.[9] However, women with the genetic condition known as phenylketonuria (PKU) must avoid aspartame because it contains phenylalanine. Neotame, a derivative of aspartame, was approved by the FDA in 2002. Unlike aspartame, neotame does not break down during cooking.

Sucralose, known by the trade name Splenda, is derived from table sugar (sucrose). When ingested, sucralose is not metabolized, so it is almost calorie free. Sold in individual yellow packets as well as bulk form for cooking, Splenda is used in a variety of products including baked goods, baking mixes, beverages, puddings, salad dressings, coffee and tea products, jellies, syrups, and chewing gum.

Acesulfame potassium, sold under the brand name Sunett, has been approved since 1988 as a tabletop sweetener, and more than ninety studies verify its safety.[10] It is often combined with other sweeteners and has a long shelf life. D-Tagatose is another artificial sweetener that is generally considered safe by the FDA. It is found in many food products including candy, light ice cream, cereals, chewing gum, and diet sodas.

Saccharin is the original artificial sweetener and is widely available in the form of Sweet'n Low (in the pink packets). Early studies identified saccharine as a carcinogen, and packets of Sweet'n Low contained a warning label stating that its use caused cancer in laboratory animals. But in 1997, the US National Toxicology Program removed it from the list of established human carcinogens.[11] The Program claimed that "extensive data obtained during the past twenty years on saccharin clearly demonstrate that the bladder tumor findings in rats are not relevant to humans." Over thirty human studies indicate saccharin safety at human levels of consumption.[12]

Artificial sweeteners used in moderation should not pose a health risk to you or your baby. Since many products that contain artificial sweeteners have no nutritional value or are considered junk food, it is wise during the pregnancy to limit your intake of these products. Avoid soft drinks altogether and opt for water, milk, or juice instead.

Herbs

A variety of herbal remedies are readily available in the form of pills or tinctures. Although a number of herbs can be useful during pregnancy, over-the-counter products are unregulated, making it difficult to determine the amount of active ingredients in the different brands. Because of this, the FDA does not recommend the use of medicinal herbal products during pregnancy. Some practitioners, however, are specialists in their use; they can provide advice if you choose to use herbs while pregnant.

If you enjoy herbal teas, choose those with familiar ingredients such as mint, orange extract, strawberry leaf, fennel seed, lemon verbena, rosehips, alfalfa, or lemon grass leaf. Many women have found ginger root and peppermint leaf teas to be helpful when coping with morning sickness. Be aware that while some herbs may be fine in small doses, larger quantities may be a concern. For example, the use of rosemary in cooking should not pose a problem, but large quantities taken medicinally might stimulate contractions. Women with a history of miscarriage or preterm labor should also avoid large quantities of red raspberry leaf tea as it may cause uterine contractions. It's best to refrain from drinking this tea or at least waiting until the second trimester.

Many herbs stimulate the uterus or hormonal activity and are unsafe for all pregnant women. Do not use blue or black cohosh, pennyroyal, mugwort, ephedra (ma huang), dong quai, St. John's wort, feverfew, saw palmetto, goldenseal, or yohimbe.

Food Additives

Many of the processed foods we eat contain food additives. Preservatives increase shelf life and reduce spoilage; flavor enhancers make food taste better; and color additives make them look better. Although most additives are considered safe to consume during pregnancy, there are a few that you should avoid:

■ **Nitrates.** Nitrates prevent rancidity and bacterial growth in meats and meat products. They are commonly found in cured meats, such as bacon, hot dogs, and luncheon meats. Nitrates have been linked to cancer-causing substances in animals, so they should be avoided not only by pregnant women, but by everyone. It's best to eat only fresh meats, poultry, and fish; but when choosing cured meats, look for brands that do not contain nitrates.

If your water comes from an underground source, have it tested for nitrates and nitrites. Nitrates, which convert to nitrites when consumed, are often used in fertilizer and can enter the water system through the soil. Excessive levels in drinking water can cause serious health risks. In children, it can interfere with blood's ability to carry oxygen, which can be fatal. Excessive long-term exposure can also affect the spleen.

■ **Olestra.** An artificial fat substitute, olestra is used in a growing number of snack foods, such as potato chips, crackers, corn chips, and tortilla chips. Olestra is not absorbed by the body, but it has been linked to abdominal cramping and diarrhea in some individuals. Because olestra hasn't been tested thoroughly enough, it is wise to avoid it during pregnancy. In addition to snacks containing olestra, you should limit your intake of all processed snack foods, which are typically high in fat, sugar, and/or salt. Choose fresh fruit, raw vegetables, or other healthy snack choices instead.

■ **Monosodium glutamate (MSG).** A flavor enhancer commonly added to soups, bouillon, canned vegetables, processed meats, and Asian food, MSG has been classified by the FDA as a food ingredient that is "generally recognized as safe." It has, however, been linked to a number of adverse short-term reactions, such as headaches, facial tingling or tightness, sweating, mouth numbness, and heart palpitations. The symptoms are mild in most people, although some experience more severe reactions.

Minimize or avoid consumption of foods and beverages that contain these additives. Be sure to always read food labels carefully.

MEDICATIONS

As Americans we are a drug-oriented society. We routinely take—and encourage our children to take—medicine, often without considering that even those sold over-the-counter are drugs. Virtually all drugs and medications that are taken during pregnancy cross the placenta and reach the baby, who often gets an equal amount of the drug dosage. Fetal growth and development are so rapid that a drug can have a profound effect on the baby, even though it is considered mild. Many drugs are harmful when taken at particular stages of the pregnancy or if they are used in conjunction with other drugs or agents. The exact connections between some drugs and birth defects are difficult to trace, since humans are not used as experimental subjects. Therefore, be careful about taking or using *any* drug during pregnancy. No drug is *known* to be safe, even though it may not be considered harmful. Always weigh the potential risks against the possible benefits before taking any medication.

Often, a drug-free treatment can provide relief. For example, a headache may be caused from tension or by going for a long period without eating. Lie down, put on some relaxing music, and apply an ice bag to your head. Try eating, if you haven't done so in awhile. Some people have found headache relief by applying firm fingertip pressure to acupressure points—the temples, the area midway between the eyebrows, and the back of the neck along the hairline. You may find circular massage to be more effective than direct pressure for this. The pressure points will be tender to the touch, which will help you locate the correct spots. (For more information on acupressure and pain relief, see page 162.)

Backaches are often caused by poor posture. Using good body mechanics and the Pelvic Rock (see page 125) can be more beneficial for relieving backache than taking a pill. Constipation can be avoided by consuming a high-fiber diet, drinking plenty of fluids, and getting enough exercise.

If you do develop a medical problem, such as a urinary tract infection, or you have a pre-existing condition, such as diabetes, asthma, or heart disease, you may have to take medication. Not treating these conditions properly can be more dangerous to the fetus than the medication. If you have a chronic health problem, be sure to discuss it with your doctor so she can review the medications and determine which can be used safely during pregnancy. Most caregivers try to avoid prescribing any medications during the first trimester unless it is absolutely necessary.

If you have pain or fever, your doctor may recommend acetaminophen (Tylenol). Take only the recommended dose as taking more can affect the liver. Do not use aspirin or ibuprofen (Advil, Motrin), as these products can cause bleeding. Occasionally, your caregiver will prescribe aspirin for women who are at risk for complications from preeclampsia. Do not take aspirin without specific orders from your doctor.

If you get a cold or flu during pregnancy, remember that most medications for these illnesses will only relieve symptoms. Taking them will not cure you any faster and may actually harm your baby. Try treating your symptoms with nondrug methods instead. Drink plenty of fluids and rest. Saline nasal spray or a vaporizer may relieve a stuffy nose. If, however, your symptoms are severe, your caregiver may recommend a decongestant such as Sudafed. If you have sinus pressure, placing warm compresses over the sinus area may provide relief. If you have a cough, sucking on a cough drop or using a product such as Robitussin DM, which contains *guaifenesin* (an expectorant) and *dextromethorphan* (a cough suppressant), may help. Do not take zinc lozenges without the approval of your doctor.

Since asthma attacks can be life threatening, asthma symptoms should always be treated. Treating mild to moderate asthma symptoms can inhibit intrauterine growth restriction (IUGR), low birth weight, and preterm birth.[13] These conditions are possibly the result of a decrease in oxygen to the fetus. Asthma medications that are inhaled are preferred.

Heartburn is a common complaint during pregnancy. For relief, it is safe to take an antacid such as TUMS, Maalox, Mylanta, Gas-X, and Di-Gel. (See page 31 for a list of heartburn remedies.)

Retinoid drugs, which are used to treat acne, are extremely hazardous to the developing fetus. Taking them can result in miscarriage, preterm delivery, or infant death. Even small doses can cause birth defects, such as hydrocephaly (excess fluid in the brain), microcephaly (small head), mental retardation, eye and ear abnormalities, cleft lip and palate and other facial abnormalities, and heart defects.[14] Women who take Accutane (isotretinoin), Amnesteem, or Claravis, should stop taking the drug and wait over a month before trying to conceive. Also avoid topical treatment for acne and sun damaged skin that contains Retin-A, Renova (tretinoin), or Differen (adapalene), as their safety is still being studied.

Soriatane (acetretin), another retinoid drug used to treat severe psoriasis, has been implicated in a number of serious birth defects, including craniofacial and heart deformities, spina bifida, and limb defects. Do not get pregnant for at least three years after using this drug.[15] If you have consumed alcohol either while taking Soriatane or during the two months after taking the medication, the alcohol will convert the medication to Tegison (etretinate), another psoriasis medication that should never be used by women who plan to have children. This drug stays in the system indefinitely.[16] Vesanoid (tretinoin) is a drug used to treat a certain form of leukemia. It should not be taken during pregnancy as it can cause birth defects. Women should not get pregnant for one month following treatment with this medication.[17]

Unless it is absolutely necessary and taken under the approval of your caregiver, avoid using any medication during pregnancy, particularly during the first trimester. Even over-the-counter drugs can affect the developing baby.

CIGARETTE SMOKING

Smoking during pregnancy is considered one of the leading preventable causes of low birth weight, one of the leading causes of infant illness, disability, and death. Cigarette smoke contains nicotine, carbon monoxide, and many other chemicals that constrict blood flow to the fetus. This reduces the amount of oxygen and nutrients that the infant receives. Consuming high amounts of caffeine in addition to smoking increases the risk of delivering a baby with lower birth weight than smoking alone.[18] A recent study showed that smoking during pregnancy also increases the risk of having a baby born with defects such as fused, extra, or missing fingers or toes.[19] If a woman stops smoking by the end of her first trimester of pregnancy, she is no more likely to have a low birth weight baby than a woman who has never smoked.

Pregnant smokers typically give birth to babies who weigh about eight ounces less than those of nonsmokers. They also have a greater chance of miscarriage, ectopic pregnancies, placental malformations, preterm births, placental abruptions, and stillbirths. Their babies also have a higher incidence of sudden infant death

"Those cigarettes are killing me!"

syndrome (SIDS) and are more likely to have developmental difficulties, such as a short attention spans and hyperactivity. Expectant mothers who smoked more than twenty cigarettes a day were more likely to have infants with cleft lip and palate.[20] After delivery, babies of smokers may also experience withdrawal symptoms—they may be jittery and difficult to soothe.

If you smoke, try to stop or cut down as much as possible. A direct relationship exists between the number of cigarettes a woman smokes per day and the degree to which her baby is affected. And if you are a nonsmoker, try to avoid being around heavy smokers. Nonsmoking pregnant women who are regularly exposed to second-hand smoke are more likely to have babies with a lower birth weight.

Even if their mothers did not smoke during pregnancy, infants who are living in households where people smoke are more than twice as likely to die of SIDS than those living in smoke-free environments.[21] They suffer from more lower-respiratory illnesses like bronchitis and pneumonia, as well as ear infections. They are also at greater risk of developing asthma. Research indicates that women who smoke are less likely to breastfeed, thus depriving their infants of this important immunity booster.

If you are a smoker, pregnancy is the best time to stop. The immediate and future benefits for you and your unborn baby are immeasurable.

ALCOHOL

Beer, wine, wine coolers, and liquor all contain alcohol, which depresses bodily functions such as breathing and heart rate. If you drink alcohol during your pregnancy, it will quickly cross the placenta and saturate the fetal blood supply in the same concentration that is present in your blood. This can have a toxic effect on the developing fetus. Drinking during pregnancy increases the risk of miscarriage, low birth weight, and stillbirth. A study published in the *Journal of the National Cancer Institute* in 1996 links consumption of alcohol during the last six months of pregnancy with infant leukemia, a rare disease.[22]

Babies born to women who are heavy drinkers have a 50-percent chance of having fetal alcohol syndrome (FAS). Common characteristics of this serious condition include mental retardation, slowed body growth before and after birth, learning disabilities, behavioral problems, vision and hearing problems, and damage to the central nervous system. Abnormal facial features, unusually small heads and brains, and heart defects are other FAS characteristics. In the United States, fetal alcohol syndrome is the leading preventable birth defect associated with impairment of mental and behavioral abilities.

A study in the March 2004 issue of *The Journal of Pediatrics* reported that newborns whose mothers drank alcohol heavily during pregnancy had damage to the nerves in the arms and legs. The nerve damage was still present when the children were re-examined at one year of age.[23]

There is no known safe level of alcohol consumption for a pregnant woman. In 2005, the US Surgeon General released a statement urging women who are pregnant or who may become pregnant to abstain from alcohol.[24] Even two drinks a day may cause a lowered birth weight in babies. Be sure to avoid any type of heavy drinking during pregnancy or even if you suspect that you are pregnant. Binging even once is not worth the risk to your baby. Obviously, the wisest course is to give up alcoholic beverages completely during this time.

Hints for the Father-to-Be

Encourage your partner to:

✓ Use nondrug therapies for her headaches, backaches, and colds.

✓ Avoid alcohol and recreational drugs.

✓ Stop smoking (if she does). And if you smoke, stop as well.

"I wish I could tell her what those drinks do to me."

RECREATIONAL DRUGS

Recreational drugs, including marijuana, cocaine, heroin, amphetamines, and LSD, can all have a negative effect on the developing fetus. Furthermore, any addictive drug that is used throughout pregnancy can cause the newborn to suffer withdrawal symptoms. Women who use recreational drugs are also more likely to smoke cigarettes or consume alcohol. What follows is an overview of these drugs and their possible effects.

■ **Marijuana.** Studies have indicated that women who smoke marijuana (grass, pot) during pregnancy are at risk for giving birth to a baby with low birth weight. In addition to possibly affecting fetal growth, smoking pot can cause newborns to experience tremors and other withdrawal symptoms. Scientific research also indicates that children who are exposed to marijuana in the womb are at greater risk for developing problems with concentration, memory, and behavior.

■ **Cocaine.** Cocaine (coke, crack) is another commonly abused drug. It can be injected into a vein, snorted through the nose, or smoked (freebasing). The effects of cocaine on a fetus are alarming. This drug has been implicated in miscarriage, low birth weight, physical malformations, and stillbirth. Babies who are exposed to cocaine in the womb experience severe withdrawal symptoms. Cocaine constricts the blood vessels and can cause a sharp rise in the mother's blood pressure. A stroke or heart attack, preterm labor, or an abruption of the placenta can result. Follow-up studies on children whose mothers used cocaine during pregnancy concluded that this exposure "has a significant effect on three-year cognitive abilities as measured on the Stanford-Binet scale."[25]

■ **Heroin.** During pregnancy, using heroin, which is either smoked or injected into a vein, can cause preterm birth, stillbirth, and low birth weight. Heroin and methadone, which is given to replace heroin at drug treatment centers, are believed to affect the baby's developing brain and may cause behavioral problems later in childhood. The newborn will be addicted to these drugs and suffer severe withdrawal symptoms. She may have to be gradually weaned off them.

■ **Hallucinogens.** Popular hallucinogenic drugs such as PCP (angel dust), ketamine (Special K) and LSD (acid) alter the user's mental state, often to the point where reality is distorted. Because these drugs cause uterine contractions, miscarriage is a risk among pregnant users.

■ **Stimulants.** Ecstasy, amphetamines (speed, uppers), and methamphetamine are stimulants that can cause insomnia, agitation, and loss of appetite. Pregnant women who take these drugs often do not eat well and may become malnourished. Their babies may have low birth weight, and experience rapid heart rate.

Inhaling the fumes of certain solvents such as airplane glue and paint thinners is another method for a temporary high. During pregnancy, this has been known to cause miscarriage, preterm birth, and birth defects. Another method of getting high—injecting a mixture of the prescription painkiller pentazocine and the antihistamine tripelennamine (T's and Blues)—may cause the fetus to experience slowed growth and suffer withdrawal at birth. Abusing oral prescription painkillers can also cause the newborn to experience withdrawal symptoms.

By taking recreational drugs, you run the risk of compromising your child's health and development. The dangers to your unborn child are not worth the temporary high you may experience.

ENVIRONMENTAL CONCERNS

Using hair dye, lying in the sun, sitting in a hot tub, and a number of other activities may be of special concern to you during pregnancy. What follows are some of the most common ones.

Tanning

During pregnancy, be cautious about tanning either in a tanning bed or in the sun. The elevated hormones in pregnancy can cause patches of darker pigmentation, also known as the *mask of pregnancy.* Tanning will exacerbate this condition. Instead, use self-tanning sprays containing dihydroxy-acetone, which is not absorbed by the skin.

Hot Tubs and Saunas

Prolonged exposure to high heat can increase a pregnant woman's body temperature, which can have a negative effect on the baby. When the body is immersed in hot water or subjected to an enclosed heated area for a prolonged period, it cannot release the heat that has built up and, in some cases, can cause fever. During the first trimester, the use of hot tubs and saunas has been associated with neural tube defects (spina bifida). And fetal death may result if there are multiple prolonged exposures to this type of high heat.

If you enjoy using a hot tub, make sure that the water temperature does not go above 99°F, as this will elevate your body temperature. (You can monitor the temperature with a thermometer.) Also minimize your exposure to the heat by limiting your time in a hot tub to less than ten minutes. And don't submerge yourself up to your neck. Keep your upper body out of the water so that it can release some of the heat. Unlike sitting in a hot tub, taking a warm bath is completely safe.

Hair Dyes

There is no evidence that hair dyes are harmful during pregnancy. However, to be on the safe side, it is always best to delay their use until after the first trimester. Also be aware that the hormonal changes that occur during pregnancy may cause hair colorants to be less effective or produce a different result than you are accustomed to.

Plastic Containers and the Microwave

Many of the plastic wraps and containers used for food are "microwave safe." These products have been specially designed to withstand the heat of a microwave without warping or melting—and they have been tested by the manufacturer. If the item is safe for microwave use, it will be labeled as such.

The FDA has set stringent safety standards for *all* plastic items that are intended for food use, whether they are designed for the microwave or not. This means that microwaving food in a plastic container that is not labeled as microwave safe is not necessarily unsafe. What it does mean is that the item has not undergone testing to evaluate its suitability in the microwave. And according to the FDA, it is not likely that microwaving food in non-microwave safe containers will cause any health risk. There is, however, a possibility that these containers will melt or warp and cause accidental burns. For this reason, it is best to avoid using plastic items such as butter or margarine tubs, whipped topping bowls, and takeout containers in the microwave.

Paint, Solvents, and Other Hazardous Material

Exposure to lead, carbon monoxide, mercury, solvents, cleaning solutions, paint, paint thinners, benzene, and formaldehyde during pregnancy can result in higher incidence of miscarriage and birth defects. Try to avoid or greatly minimize your exposure to all of these products, especially during the first trimester.

After the first trimester, if you plan to paint a room in your home, make sure the area is well ventilated. Minimize exposure even further by wearing protective gear such as gloves and a face mask. If you are planning to remove old paint, first have it checked for lead content. Homes built before 1960 (and even some built after) have a good chance of containing lead-based paint. The Consumer Product Safety Commission warns that there is "no completely safe method for 'do-it-yourself' removal of lead-based paint."[26] Hire a professional for this job.

Art paints can also contain various toxic elements such as lead, chromium, cadmium, cobalt, mercury, nickel, and manganese. Flake white (white lead) and Naples yellow (antimony yellow) are the two lead-containing pigments used in oil paints that should be avoided. If you are using these colors, don't use techniques like spraying or airbrushing, which can cause you to inhale the mist. Using a brush is recommended.

Pesticides

Exposure to pesticides and herbicides during pregnancy has been associated with an increase in cancer, miscarriage, and birth defects. Many of these products have been determined as hazardous to humans and have been removed from the marketplace. But the soil in which fruits and vegetables are grown can still be contaminated. To be on the safe side, always peel or wash fresh fruits and vegetables before eating.

If you have your home sprayed for insects, do not be present while the spraying is being done. Allow several hours for the product to dry and avoid direct contact with the insecticide.

Electromagnetic Radiation

Some concern exists about the possible correlation between exposure to electromagnetic radiation and miscarriage. Sources of this radiation include computer monitors and video display terminals, electric blankets, waterbed heaters, and power lines and substations. There is no conclusive evidence to support this concern; however, to be on the safe side, try limiting your exposure to these sources.

CONCLUSION

Once you know what to expect, as well as what to avoid during the next few months, you can feel positive and confident about your pregnancy—a normal, natural condition of wellness. This chapter has shown that you can continue most of the same daily activities and experience the same good health and lifestyle that you enjoyed before becoming pregnant.

Prenatal Care and Testing

or Information Overload

You should begin receiving prenatal care the moment you suspect you are pregnant. All of your baby's vital organs will have already begun forming. The person you choose as your caregiver will be the one providing your prenatal care. He will chart your progress during your pregnancy and watch for any signs that indicate a potential problem. Most practitioners will not schedule your first visit until you are approximately eight weeks pregnant unless you are having problems or have previous medical conditions that need to be addressed.

PHYSICAL EXAMINATIONS

When you visit your caregiver's office for your first prenatal appointment, you will give your complete medical history. If you smoke, you will be advised to stop. You will also be told to avoid the use of alcohol and drugs, and to modify your nutritional habits. You may be advised of the benefits of exercise and counseled on sex, hygiene, and any other relevant topics. You will also be given a physical examination, which will probably take about an hour. This first exam will include the following:

■ A breast examination.

■ A pelvic (vaginal) examination to: confirm the pregnancy; take a pap smear; take a vaginal culture for gonorrhea and chlamydia; and estimate the size and shape of your pelvis. Typically, a pelvic exam will not be done again until the last month of pregnancy.

■ Blood tests for: blood type, Rh factor, and antibody screen; a complete blood count; rubella titer (to determine if you are immune to German measles); syphilis and hepatitis B; immunity to chicken pox (if you haven't had chicken pox or weren't vaccinated).

Some clinics and offices also provide other blood chemistry checks for a more complete analysis of the woman's health. Additional blood tests that may be offered after counseling include those for human immunodeficiency virus, toxoplasmosis, and alpha-fetoprotein. If your racial or genetic background dictates, you may be tested for sickle cell disease, Tay-Sachs, thalassemia, or cystic fibrosis. (All of these conditions are discussed in this chapter.)

■ Urine tests for a complete urinalysis and to check for infection, if indicated.

After this first examination, you will probably be given checkups on a monthly basis. Starting in the seventh calendar month, the checkups will become biweekly. In the ninth calendar month, they will become weekly. All of these checkups will typically include:

- Checking your weight.

- Checking your blood pressure.

- Testing your urine for: protein—high levels may indicate preeclampsia (see "Hypertension" on page 71); sugar—high levels may indicate diabetes (see "Gestational Diabetes" on page 70); and infection.

- Checking your abdomen for: growth of the uterus to estimate the progress of the pregnancy; size and position of the fetus; the fetal heart rate, which is checked with a hand-held ultrasound device.

A mother-to-be takes an active part in her prenatal care by checking her own weight during regular monthly office visits.

Beginning at thirty-six weeks, vaginal exams will be done to check the status of the cervix and the position of the baby. A culture of the vaginal and rectal areas will be taken to check for the presence of group B streptococcal infection. (See "Group B Strep" on page 67.) In some practices, this test may also be done when the woman is in labor. If the doctor or midwife has concerns about preterm labor, these exams may be done earlier than thirty-six weeks.

TESTS PERFORMED DURING PREGNANCY

Various tests and procedures are performed to monitor the pregnancy and evaluate maternal and fetal well-being. They can identify certain risk factors and help maintain a healthy pregnancy. Certain tests can provide important diagnostic information for the high-risk woman. Ask your caregiver about the risks and benefits of the different procedures. Make sure you understand the purpose of the tests and how the results can impact your care. While some of the tests are noninvasive and carry little risk to the fetus, others are considered invasive and can cause miscarriage or other complications.

These tests are commonly performed during a specific trimester, which is how they are presented in the following discussion.

FIRST TRIMESTER

Blood Type and Rh Factor

Early in your pregnancy, your blood will be tested to determine your blood type and Rh factor. Blood type is identified by two major components—a letter (A, B, AB, or O) and the Rh factor. If your blood contains the Rh factor, you are considered Rh positive; if it lacks this factor, you are Rh negative. Therefore, if your blood type is AB and you are Rh negative, you are said to have AB-negative blood.

During pregnancy, it is important to be aware if you are Rh negative. If an invasive procedure is performed, such as chorionic villus sampling or amniocentesis, you will need a shot of Rho(D) Immune Globulin, commonly known as RhoGAM. This shot will prevent you from developing antibodies that will attack the fetal blood cells if the fetus is Rh positive. (See "Rh Incompatability" on page 77.)

Women who have type O blood may give birth to babies who are more susceptible to developing jaundice. (See "Blood-Type Incompatibility" on page 291.)

Chorionic Villus Sampling

Chorionic villus sampling (*CVS*) is a test that can detect genetic abnormalities earlier than amniocentesis can. It is usually done between ten to twelve weeks of gestation. However, it is not available in all locations.

A *chorionic villus* is one of the fingerlike projections covering the developing embryo. It contains cells that have the same genetic composition as the embryo. In CVS, a sample of chorionic tissue (about the size of a grain of cooked rice) is removed and tested. In one removal method, which is done vaginally, a suction catheter is inserted into the uterus through the cervix under the visual guidance of ultrasound. In another method, a needle is inserted into the uterus through the abdominal wall. Both methods take about thirty minutes to complete. This procedure should not be performed through the vaginal route if the woman has genital herpes or an active vaginal infection.

There are a number of advantages to CVS. It can be performed early in pregnancy and the results can be obtained in one to two weeks (amniocentesis results usually take three or four weeks). In some cases, particularly for the woman who is considering termination of the pregnancy, the earlier this information is available, the better. The possible risks of CVS include infection, Rh sensitization (women with Rh negative blood should receive RhoGAM after the procedure), bleeding, miscarriage, and perforation of the fetal membrane. In addition, studies in England have indicated that fetal limb deformities may result from CVS, especially if performed early in the pregnancy (before sixty-six days).[1]

Nuchal Translucency Screening

Nuchal translucency screening, also called the *nuchal fold scan,* is performed precisely between eleven and fourteen weeks gestation. It helps to determine the baby's risk of Down syndrome or other chromosomal abnormality.

There is a clear or "translucent" space in the tissue at the back of the fetus's neck that can be measured under ultrasound. Babies with certain chromosomal abnormalities have a tendency to accumulate extra fluid in this area during the first trimester. This measurement, along with the baby's exact age and the mother's age can indicate the risk of a possible abnormality. The woman can then decide whether or not to have additional, more invasive diagnostic testing, such as chorionic villus sampling or amniocentesis, which will give a definitive result.

The accuracy rate of detecting Down syndrome through this screening can be increased by combining the nuchal fold measurement with a blood test that measures two proteins in the blood. This is called the *first trimester combined screening test.* One advantage of nuchal translucency screening is that it is a noninvasive procedure; another advantage is that it can be done in the first trimester. The disadvantages are that it is not widely available, it does not detect neural tube defects, and the results are not definitive. Because of this, the test results may cause increased anxiety or false reassurance.

Carrier Screening for Genetic Diseases

A *carrier screening* is a blood or saliva test that detects carriers of a genetic mutation that can result in a number of disorders. These genetic disorders are recessive, which means both parents must be carriers of the gene in order to pass it on to the fetus. Carriers have no symptoms and are unaware that they carry the gene.

If both parents carry the defective gene, genetic counseling is recommended. If only one parent is a carrier, the baby will not inherit the disease; however, he may be

A Hint for the Mother-to-Be

Some tests performed during pregnancy involve risks. Make sure that you understand the potential benefits and risks of any procedure before you agree to it.

a carrier. Your caregiver will take a detailed history to determine your risk of having any of these disorders. Risk factors include having a certain ethnic background or having a family member who either has the disease or is a known carrier. Carrier screening tests are available for the following:

■ **Cystic Fibrosis.** An incurable genetic disease, cystic fibrosis (CF) impairs breathing and increases the risk of respiratory infections due to the production of thick mucus in the lungs. It also produces thick secretions in the pancreas that interfere with food absorption. CF is most common in Caucasians but can affect other races.

■ **Sickle Cell Disease.** The sickle-shaped red blood cells in this inherited blood disorder can block small vessels and cause damage to various organs. Anemia, jaundice, and gallstones are common complications. One in twelve African Americans carries the gene for this disease. Descendants from the Caribbean, Central and South America, and the Mediterranean are others who are at risk.

■ **Tay-Sachs Disease.** Tay-Sachs is a progressive neurological genetic disorder. Children born with Tay-Sachs appear to be normal for the first few months of life, but then a rapid deterioration of mental and physical abilities starts to occur. Most do not live past four years old. The incidence of Tay-Sachs is high among people of Eastern European ancestry and Askhenazi Jewish descent.

■ **Thalassemia.** Thalassemia is a diverse group of genetic blood diseases resulting in varying degrees of anemia. While some types are mild, others, such as Cooley's anemia, which is the most severe form of beta thalassemia, is life threatening. Beta thalassemias affect those of Mediterranean (Greek, Italian, Middle Eastern), Asian, and African descent. Alpha thalassemias affect people of Southeast Asian, Indian, Chinese, and Filipino ancestry.

SECOND TRIMESTER

Multiple Marker Screening

Multiple marker screening, also known as *triple screen, quad screen,* or *maternal serum alpha-fetoprotein (AFP) screening,* is a blood test done between fifteen and twenty weeks of pregnancy (sixteen to eighteen weeks is the ideal time) to screen for fetal abnormalities. This is done by measuring the presence of AFP—a protein produced by the baby's liver—in the mother's blood. A high level of AFP indicates a possible open neural tube defect, such as spina bifida or anencephaly. It may also be caused by a multiple pregnancy or a miscalculation of gestational age. A low level may indicate Down syndrome (Trisomy 21) or another rare chromosomal anomaly called Edwards syndrome (Trisomy 18). Insulin-dependent diabetics can also have lower AFP levels. This test may also be a predictor for preeclampsia, premature birth, or miscarriage.[2]

In addition to measuring AFP levels during this test, most labs measure two or three additional substances—human chorionic gonadotropin (hCG), a hormone produced by the placenta; unconjugated estriol (uE3), a byproduct of estrogen; and inhibin A, a substance produced by the ovaries. Testing for more than just AFP increases the accuracy of the test for Down syndrome.

Unfortunately, AFP testing has a high rate of false positive readings, so further testing should be done if the results indicate an abnormality. The additional tests could include another AFP blood test, ultrasound for accurate determination of gestational age, or amniocentesis for a more accurate diagnosis.

Glucose Screening

One hour after drinking a liquid that is high in sugar or eating a specific high-carbohydrate snack, blood is drawn to check the mother's glucose level. A high level is an indication of gestational diabetes. This test is done between twenty-four and twenty-eight weeks gestation, but if there is a family history of diabetes, or if the woman has given birth to large babies in the past or she has a history of gestational diabetes, it may be performed earlier, at around sixteen weeks. If the glucose level is above the normal limit on the glucose screening, then a three-hour glucose tolerance test is given to confirm the diagnosis.

Glucose Tolerance Test

During the *glucose tolerance test (GTT)*, which determines if the woman has gestational diabetes, a blood sample is taken after the woman has fasted at least eight hours. She then consumes a sugary drink (glucose) and her blood is drawn and tested after one hour, two hours, and three hours. The GTT evaluates how she metabolizes a large amount of sugar. Women who are unable to drink the liquid can eat specific foods instead. For more information on gestational diabetes, see page 70.

Antibody Screening

In an Rh-negative woman, at the same time that blood is drawn for the glucose screening, an additional sample of blood is sent to check for antibodies. At her next visit, usually at twenty-eight weeks, she will be given an intramuscular shot of the Rh-immune globulin RhoGAM.

Ultrasound (Sonogram)

Ultrasound was developed during World War I when high-frequency sound waves were used to detect enemy submarines. The *sonogram*, which uses intermittent sound waves, is the form of ultrasound used in pregnancy testing. The ultrasound transducer—the device that emits the sound waves—is either placed on the abdomen (transabdominal) or inserted into the vagina (transvaginal). Transvaginal scans are used in the first trimester to detect problems that would be difficult to see through the abdomen. The sound waves are directed into the woman's abdomen or pelvic area, and an outline of the baby, placenta, and other structures involved in the pregnancy are transmitted to a video screen. A fetal heartbeat can be observed as early as six weeks.

A sonogram is often used to determine fetal position, to estimate the maturity of the baby, or to confirm a multiple pregnancy. In addition, the location of the placenta can be pinpointed when placenta previa (low-implanted placenta) is suspected. Ultrasound is also used to visualize the baby and placenta when amniocentesis or CVS is being performed. During nuchal translucency screening, practitioners use sonography to look for abnormalities in the fetal neck fold.

Many doctors use ultrasound routinely to determine the due date. When the test is performed between the fourteenth and twentieth week, it is accurate to within one week before or after the estimated date. Later in pregnancy, and especially after the thirty-second week, it is not as accurate because of variations in fetal growth. In a high-risk pregnancy, an accurate due date is important for making sure that the infant is delivered at the best time. Routine ultrasound is usually done between the sixteenth and nineteenth weeks of pregnancy. In addition to determining the due date, it also shows the baby's basic anatomy, including the heart, spine, stomach, kidneys, bladder, and umbilical cord, which are examined for abnormalities. If the doctor has concerns, a more detailed level II ultrasound can be done to detect structural defects or to provide additional information.

Some physicians may recommend an ultrasound as early as seven weeks if the woman experiences vaginal bleeding or if she has had infertility treatments (to check for multiple fetuses). Ultrasound may also be recommended between seven and thirteen weeks if the woman is unsure of her last period—measuring the distance from the crown of the baby's head to his rump during this time can determine age within three or four days. In late pregnancy, ultrasound can be used to measure the length of the cervix if the woman has signs of preterm labor. If the baby is positioned correctly, its sex can also be determined through ultrasound, sometimes as early as sixteen weeks.

Three-dimensional (3D) ultrasound is a new technology that provides more lifelike images of the fetus than traditional sonograms, which produce images that are grainy and unclear. The still photos taken from 3-D ultrasound are also very lifelike. There is also four-dimensional (4D) imaging—the continuous three-dimensional scanning of the baby, which allows couples to see the baby moving. Your facility should provide a CD, video, or DVD with the images for you to keep. Avoid "baby boutiques" that take ultrasounds to provide expectant parents with "keepsake videos" for entertainment purposes only. These are not diagnostic ultrasounds. They are not covered by insurance and the sonographers may not be certified to perform this service. In 2002, the FDA stated that ultrasound should not be administered without a prescription. In an official statement, the American Institute of Ultrasound in Medicine strongly discouraged the "non-medical use of ultrasound for psychosocial or entertainment purposes."[3]

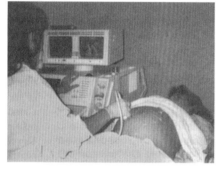

During a sonogram, a technician moves a transducer over a woman's bare abdomen to check the condition of the developing fetus. The gel on the woman's abdomen helps improve the quality of the sound waves.

Sonograms can also be used to measure the biophysical profile of a fetus, usually in the third trimester. This type of profile assesses fetal movements, muscle tone, amount of amniotic fluid, and fetal breathing movements. The test is usually done in higher-risk pregnancies to assure fetal well-being and to determine the best time for delivery.

During routine examinations, ultrasound can also be used to listen for a fetal heart rate using a hand-held ultrasound device called a Doppler. During labor, the heartbeat is usually checked with an electronic fetal monitor. (See page 246 for a discussion of these monitors.).

Diagnostically, ultrasound is preferred over x-rays. However, many doctors now use ultrasound routinely during labor, as well as recommending one or more sonograms during pregnancy. As with other procedures, ultrasound should not be used indiscriminately—you have the legal right to refuse it. A six-year study by the National Institute of Child Health & Human Development, a division of the National Institutes of Health (NIH), concluded that no benefit is derived from the routine use of ultrasound in low-risk pregnancies. This study, the largest ever conducted, found that perinatal outcome was not improved by routine screening when compared with the selective use of ultrasonography based on the caregiver's judgment. The investigators estimated that $1 billion a year could be saved if sonograms are limited to high-risk pregnancies and other cases in which they are medically indicated.[4]

If your caregiver requests a sonogram and you do not have insurance to cover the cost, ask if the procedure is medically necessary. Find out what information your caregiver hopes to receive from it, and if that information will mean a change in your prenatal care. In addition, if you are going to have a sonogram, you may want to ask about the credentials of the person performing and interpreting the test results. Does that person have training or certification in ultrasonography? Be aware that the FDA has guidelines regarding the intensity of the machines and the amount of time a fetus should be exposed.

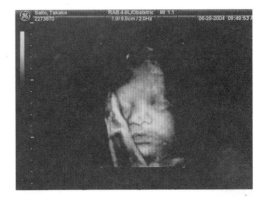

Ultrasound often provides expectant parents with the first "photograph" of their child.

The results of an ultrasound can depend on several factors. A normal sonogram should never be considered 100 percent accurate. Some abnormalities are difficult to visualize or may not be obvious with early sonograms. The skill of the sonographer and the quality of the equipment may also be a factor. If the woman is obese or there is little amniotic fluid the images may be fuzzy. Or the baby may not be in an ideal position to aptly visualize all of the parts (occasionally couples are informed they are having one sex and it turns out to be the other). Estimates of fetal weight can also be off by as much as a pound. Some women have opted for a planned cesarean section because they thought they were having a large baby, only to discover at the birth that the baby was within normal weight.

Because so much information can be gained about the fetus through diagnostic ultrasound, and because studies have not shown any long-term effects on babies, many doctors feel strongly that the benefits of routine ultrasounds in pregnancy outweigh any potential risks. Others, however, limit its use to those with a medical indication.

Amniocentesis

Amniocentesis is a diagnostic procedure for detecting a number of chromosomal and structural abnormalities and genetic disorders in the developing fetus. It may also be performed late in the pregnancy to assess fetal lung maturity if an induced labor or cesarean delivery is indicated.

During amniocentesis, after a local anesthetic is administered, a thin hollow needle is inserted through the abdominal and uterine walls, and a sample of amniotic fluid is withdrawn. This procedure is usually done in conjunction with ultrasound, which shows the location of the fetus, the placenta, and the umbilical cord. The amniotic fluid is sent to a lab for culturing and testing. Certain tests—such as those for Tay-Sachs disease, Hunter's syndrome, neural tube defects, and fetal lung maturity—can be performed immediately.

Most tests for chromosomal abnormalities such as Down syndrome and Edward's syndrome, and genetic disorders like cystic fibrosis and sickle cell anemia, require that the fetal cells be isolated and given sufficient time to multiply, usually one to two weeks. Then a complete chromosomal analysis is performed to detect for these types of abnormalities. Amniocentesis can also verify the sex of the baby, so if the expectant couple does not want to know this information, it is important that they inform the doctor of this.

When amniocentesis is used for detecting abnormalities, it is generally performed between fifteen and eighteen weeks gestation. There is usually an insufficient amount of amniotic fluid before fourteen weeks. When testing for gestational maturity, the procedure is done in the last trimester. Amniocentesis does not detect every birth defect. It will not, for example, identify a cleft lip or palate.

Amniocentesis is a very valuable diagnostic procedure, but it does come with possible risks. There is a slight chance that it can cause a miscarriage or possible injury to the fetus, placenta, or umbilical cord. The procedure may result in an infection or uterine bleeding. And women who are Rh negative should receive a shot of RhoGAM after this procedure.

Amniocentesis should never be done just to satisfy curiosity about the baby's sex. And unless you plan to terminate your pregnancy if an abnormality is found, or unless your doctor plans to alter your care, having this test done purely for genetic information is a personal decision that you will need to consider.

THIRD TRIMESTER

Fetal Movement Evaluation

Around week twenty-eight, your caregiver may suggest that you keep track of your baby's movements—a healthy baby moves about the same amount each day. This *fetal movement evaluation,* sometimes called a *fetal kick count,* is a noninvasive "test" that can provide valuable information about your baby's health and well-being. To perform this evaluation, set aside a certain time each day and record how long it takes your baby to move ten different times. The chart below serves as an example. Sometimes the movements will be quick kicks, other times they will be long, slow stretches. It's best to choose a time when your baby is normally active, such as after a meal. Remem-

FETAL MOVEMENT TRACKING CHART

The following chart, which has been partially filled out, is helpful for keeping track of your baby's movements during the third trimester. It is best to set aside a certain time each day—during the baby's normal active period—and record how long it takes your baby to kick or move ten times. Contact your caregiver if you discover a noticeable decrease in these movements.

Date	Start Time	End Time	Total Time	Kick/Movement Counts
May 2	1:15 pm	1:30 pm	15 minutes	THL THL
May 3	1:00 pm	1:40 pm	40 minutes	THL THL
May 4	1:10 pm	2:15 pm	1 hour, 5 minutes	THL THL
May 5	12:35 pm	12:45 pm	10 minutes	THL THL
May 6	1:30 pm	1:58 pm	28 minutes	THL THL
May 7	12:45 pm	1:30 pm	45 minutes	THL THL
May 8	12:50 pm	1:22 pm	32 minutes	THL THL
May 9				
May 10				

ber, your baby has awake and sleep cycles, so you will want to choose a time when he is awake and active.

If you notice a dramatic decrease in the baby's movements, or if you haven't felt any movement for an extended period of time (several hours) and you cannot stimulate it by gently touching your abdomen or making a loud noise, contact your caregiver immediately. This could be the sign of a problem and should be addressed right away.

Group B Strep Culture

At thirty-five to thirty-seven weeks gestation, a routine culture of the vaginal and rectal areas will be taken to check for the presence of group B streptococcus (GBS). Many healthy pregnant women harbor these bacteria, although most display no symptoms. If the culture comes back positive, the woman will receive antibiotics during labor so the baby doesn't become infected during a vaginal birth. A detailed discussion of group B strep is found on page 67.

Fetal Fibronectin Test

Fetal fibronectin (fFN) is an adhesive protein that serves as "natural glue" on the placenta. It changes into a lubricant just before labor begins. fFN's presence in the cervical/vaginal secretions after the twenty-second week of pregnancy indicates a high risk of delivering within the next two weeks.[5] If a woman is experiencing signs of early labor, an fFN test will determine the presence of this protein. The absence of fFN is a fairly reliable predictor that the pregnancy will continue for at least two weeks from the date of the test. This information can reduce the need for medical interventions. A positive fFN reading, while less reliable, allows for preventive measures to delay labor. It could also indicate giving the mother corticosteroids to hasten fetal lung maturity if the baby is delivered prematurely. The test results are usually available within one or two days.

Non-Stress Test

Once you pass your due date, or if you are high risk and in the last month of pregnancy, a *non-stress test* can be a reliable, noninvasive way to determine fetal well-being. During this test, the fetal heart rate is measured in response to fetal activity.

The woman is placed on an electronic fetal monitor and a baseline heart rate is noted. Then she is given a controller, which she pushes each time she feels the baby move spontaneously. When pushed, the controller places a mark on the readout. If the baby is sleepy or not active, the woman may be asked to eat or drink something or the technician may gently nudge her abdomen to encourage movement. The technician may also stimulate the baby by placing a small transducer over his head that makes a buzzing sound. When this is done, the test is called a *vibroacoustic stimulation test (VST)*. An increase in the fetal heart rate after fetal movement indicates fetal well-being. If the result is negative, additional testing, such as a biophysical profile or an oxytocin challenge test (described on page 56) is usually performed.

Non-stress test results can be affected if the fetus is in a sleepy state. Eating prior to the test can help stimulate the fetus to move and decrease the time it takes to complete the test.

Biophysical Profile

A *biophysical profile (BPP)* is a comprehensive noninvasive test that combines the non-stress test with an ultrasound evaluation. It is often performed during the third trimester of high-risk pregnancies, usually for women with diabetes or high blood pressure. If you are past your due date, or if your caregiver is concerned that the baby is not growing as expected, a BPP may be recommended. This test is also performed to determine the level of amniotic fluid.

The BPP measures the following five components, rating each with 0 (abnormal), 1, or 2 (normal) points:

- The baby's heart rate (in response to movement during a non-stress test).

- Movement and activity (assessed through ultrasound).

- Muscle tone—flexing of the arms and legs (assessed through ultrasound).

- Breathing movements—ability to move the chest muscles (assessed through ultrasound).

- Amniotic fluid volume (assessed through ultrasound).

A total score of 6 to 10 is considered normal. A low score of 0 to 2 means the baby needs to be delivered immediately. If the score is in the intermediate range, 3 to 5, repeated testing and close follow-up is necessary. If the amniotic fluid volume (AFV) is 0, immediate delivery is usually recommended. The biophysical profile is an alternative to the oxytocin challenge test.

Oxytocin Challenge Test

Performed in the hospital, the *oxytocin challenge test (OCT)*, also known as a *contraction stress test (CST)* helps determine how well the baby will undergo the stress of labor. While reclining at a 45-degree angle, the woman is given oxytocin (Pitocin), which causes uterine contractions. She is given this drug intravenously until she has three, forty-five-second contractions within a ten-minute span. At the same time, the baby's heart rate is electronically monitored to check the effect of the contractions. If the results are positive or *nonreassuring*—that is, the fetal heart rate appears abnormal during the stress of the contractions—the baby may not be able to tolerate the stress of labor and the doctor may recommend a cesarean birth. If the results are negative or *reassuring*—that is, the heart rate remains normal during the contractions—the baby is likely to do well during labor

This OCT may take several hours. It has to both stimulate and maintain regular contractions, as well as allow the contractions to cease after the medication is stopped. This test should be avoided by women who are at risk for preterm labor or placental abruption; those with placenta previa; or those who have a "classical" (vertical) uterine incision from a previous cesarean delivery. Many caregivers now prefer the noninvasive biophysical profile instead of this test.

The OCT test is very reliable for determining if the baby will be able to tolerate the stress of labor. It may, however, give false-positive results, which indicate that the baby *cannot* tolerate labor when he actually can. These false readings, which could lead to unnecessary interventions, can be caused by a variety of factors. If, for instance, the uterus is hyperstimulated by oxytocin, it can experience long, strong contractions. These contractions may decrease the blood flow to the baby and make it appear as if he is in distress. If the woman takes the test while lying on her back, a drop in blood pressure can result. This, in turn, will decrease oxygen to the fetus—and possibly cause the appearance of fetal distress.

Cordocentesis

Cordocentesis, also called *percutaneous umbilical blood sampling (PUBS),* can be performed any time after eighteen weeks gestation. Using ultrasound for guidance, the doctor inserts a needle through the woman's abdomen and uterus and into the umbilical cord to withdraw a fetal blood sample, to give a blood transfusion, or to administer medication. This test can also diagnose Rh incompatibility, sickle cell anemia, infections such as rubella or toxoplasmosis, hemophilia, and other abnormalities with faster results than amniocentesis, usually within seventy-two hours. This test is commonly performed if the amniocentesis or CVS results were unable to be performed or inconclusive. PUBS cannot detect neural tube defects.

The risks for cordocentesis are higher than for amniocentesis and require a high skill level to perform. Possible complications include miscarriage, bleeding from the umbilical cord, blood clot formation in the cord, infection, preterm labor, premature rupture of the membranes, placental abruption, and irregular fetal heart rate. This procedure is available only at large high-risk diagnostic facilities.

Doppler Blood Flow Study

The *Doppler blood flow study* uses a Doppler ultrasound device to gather information about the blood flow in the umbilical artery, the fetal blood vessels, and the mother's uterine artery. This provides important data about the fetal circulation as well as the blood flow between the uterus and placenta. The information may be helpful in the treatment of certain conditions, such as intrauterine growth retardation (IUGR) or hypertension in pregnancy, in which the blood flow to the uterus is compromised. This test is not widely used and available only at large high-risk diagnostic centers.

Magnetic Resonance Imaging

Magnetic resonance imaging (MRI) uses a super-conductive magnet to provide a multi-layered view of the organs. This allows a noninvasive examination of the fetal organs and blood vessels, and the maternal structures. This test is not commonly performed for fetal examinations as it is expensive and other tests can provide similar information. Also, since the fetus moves, it is more difficult to obtain good images with an MRI. This type of test may, however, be helpful for diagnosing maternal problems such as deep vein thrombosis. Its use is not recommended during the first trimester.

WARNING SIGNS IN PREGNANCY

Your caregiver will discuss a number of symptoms or warning signs during pregnancy that may (or may not) indicate a serious complication. If you experience any of the following signs, notify your caregiver immediately:

❑ Vaginal bleeding. It is never normal to bleed during pregnancy.

❑ Persistent nausea or vomiting.

❑ Frequent dizzy spells or fainting.

❑ Sudden and excessive swelling of the face, hands, or feet.

❑ Severe and persistent headaches.

❑ Visual disturbances, such as dimness, blurring, flashes of light, or dots in front of the eyes.

❑ Marked decrease in the frequency of urination.

❑ Pain or burning upon urination.

❑ Any persistent dull or sharp pains.

❑ Fever higher than 100°F.

❑ Vaginal discharge that is irritating or has a foul odor.

❑ Genital sores.

❑ Redness or pain in the legs, particularly the calves.

❑ Sharp abdominal pain or severe cramping.

❑ Loss of fluid from the vagina.

❑ Any signs of labor before thirty-seven weeks of pregnancy.

❑ Noticeable decrease in fetal movement.

❑ Any other sign that you think is unusual.

These warning signs during pregnancy can be indications of possible illness, infections, miscarriage, or impending labor. It is important to recognize these signals and act on them; however, it is just as important to remain calm, since there may be nothing wrong. Just be sure to contact your caregiver as soon as possible to address the issue. Often, just speaking to him can be calming and reassuring.

ILLNESSES DURING PREGNANCY

During your prenatal testing, you will be screened for several diseases, including syphilis, hepatitis B, group B strep, and possibly HIV. Whether or not you have immunity to rubella or chicken pox will also be determined. Developing a fever or other symptoms during pregnancy may indicate the presence of a bacterial or viral infection, or other condition that may have a negative effect on you and/or your growing child. During this time, it is especially important to be aware of (and try to avoid) these illnesses, which include common childhood sicknesses, sexually transmitted diseases, food-borne infections, and infections transmitted by animals.

Childhood Illnesses

Most children have been immunized against measles, mumps, rubella, and chicken pox before they enter kindergarten. The incidence of these diseases has decreased dramatically since the widespread use of vaccinations, but some areas of the population remain unvaccinated. Even if you were vaccinated as a child, you will be screened for immunity to rubella at your first prenatal visit since it may have faded as you got older—this increases your susceptibility to contracting rubella. You may also be screened for immunity to chicken pox if you have not had the disease or have not been vaccinated.

Pregnant women who do not have immunity to rubella or chicken pox must be careful not to come in contact with children who have these illnesses. Children with cytomegalovirus, coxsackie, fifth disease, and pinworms should also be avoided.

Chicken Pox

Chicken pox (varicella) is a viral infection caused by the herpes zoster virus, also known as the varicella-zoster virus. Symptoms include fever, headache, body aches, and fatigue followed by the appearance of lesions. The lesions start as red spots that become fluid-filled blisters that progress to pustules and then scabs. Chicken pox commonly occurs in childhood. It is spread by breathing in droplets from the sneeze or cough of an infected person or through direct contact with his lesions. A person is considered infectious from two days before the rash appears until about seven days later, or until all the lesions have formed scabs. Most cases are mild and provide life-long immunity. The older a person is when contracting chicken pox, the more serious the complications can be. Today, most children are vaccinated against chicken pox, but lifelong immunity after vaccination is unknown.

If a woman develops chicken pox during pregnancy, she and her developing fetus are both at risk. When contracted during the first twenty weeks, chicken pox can result in miscarriage or birth defects. If she contracts the disease in the second half of pregnancy but more than five days before giving birth, the infant will be fine. This is because the mother will develop antibodies and pass them on to the fetus. If she develops chicken pox twenty-one days before giving birth, her newborn may develop the illness, but it is usually not serious as he has received his mother's antibodies. If the disease is contracted during the third trimester, the woman is at risk for encephalitis or varicella pneumonia, which can be fatal. Pregnant women who are exposed to chicken pox can be treated with varicella-zoster immune globulin and antiviral medications, which may prevent or lessen the illness and its side effects.

The newborn is at the greatest risk of becoming seriously ill if he is born within five days of the mother contracting the disease, or during his first two days of life. These infants should be treated with varicella-zoster immune globulin immediately after birth. If they develop chicken pox within the first two weeks, they should receive the antiviral medication acyclovir.

Reactivation of the virus, which can remain dormant in the body for decades, is most likely to result in shingles—a crop of painful blisters that appears on one area of the body, usually the torso. Those with active blisters can spread chicken pox to others who have never had it or who have not been vaccinated against it. Shingles pose little risk to the pregnant woman or fetus.

Coxsackie

Also known as *hand, foot, and mouth syndrome, coxsackie* is a viral infection. Symptoms include tiny blister-like sores in the mouth, on the palms of the hands, and on the soles of the feet that are accompanied by a mild fever, a sore throat, and painful swallowing. Coxsackie lasts approximately seven to ten days and is contagious from one day before the blisters appear until one day after. There is no cure, but symptoms can be treated. Diagnosis can be confirmed with a blood test.

Pregnant women should avoid contact with children who have coxsackie. Although there is currently no clear evidence that this type of virus causes adverse reactions during pregnancy, some studies have linked it to miscarriage and neurologic developmental delays in the child.

Cytomegalovirus

Cytomegalovirus (CMV) is the most common virus to be transmitted in utero. It is spread through close contact of infected persons via blood, saliva, urine, breastfeeding, or sexual contact. Symptoms include fever, fatigue, and flu-like symptoms. CMV infection is determined through blood tests or culturing of amniotic fluid. Newborns can be diagnosed through blood tests or a blood or urine culture. Good hand washing in daycare centers, hospitals, schools, or other institutions is one key to prevention.

If a woman has a primary infection during pregnancy, her infant is at greater risk than if it is a recurring infection. Most fetuses are unaffected, but a primary CMV infection during the first trimester can cause possible serious conditions, including intrauterine growth retardation, deafness, delayed psychomotor development, and eye problems. A small percent of asymptomatic newborns develop hearing loss or developmental delays during the first two years of life and should have frequent hearing evaluations and developmental checkups. There is no treatment for CMV infection of the fetus during pregnancy.

Fifth Disease

Fifth disease or *erythema infectiosum* is a contagious but mild viral illness that is caused by the parvovirus B19. Much more common in children than adults, the illness begins with a low-grade fever followed by a facial rash that appears as if the child has been slapped on the cheeks. A generalized rash on the body comes next. Fifth disease is transmitted through close, usually respiratory, contact. The name comes from a numerical system of identifying rashes that was used in the early 1900s. Fifth disease usually occurs in outbreaks among elementary or junior high students during the winter or spring.

Adults with fifth disease, which can be confirmed by a blood test, rarely have the facial rash, but they may develop a rash on the body. More commonly, they experience pain in the joints or flu-like symptoms. A blood test can look for antibodies to parvovirus B19 to confirm the diagnosis.

While the risk is low, if a woman contracts the disease while pregnant, the fetus can experience severe anemia, heart failure, edema, and even death. A small number of babies have been treated in utero with blood transfusions. No vaccination for fifth disease is available at this time. Pregnant women who work with school-age children should use extreme caution during outbreaks.

Measles

Measles (rubeola) is a viral infection commonly associated with childhood. It is spread through direct or indirect contact with the respiratory secretions of an infected person. Symptoms typically include fever, cough, runny nose, conjunctivitis, and spots on the lining of the mouth before the eruption of a rash appears on the body. Adults with the disease can develop severe complications, including pneumonia and encephalitis. Although most children are immunized against the measles, immunity can fade with age. A blood test confirms the diagnosis.

Pregnant women with measles are at risk for miscarriage or premature labor. They can receive immune globulin within six days of exposure to prevent or decrease the risk of contracting the disease. There is no syndrome associated with infants born to mothers who contracted measles during pregnancy. If the mother has measles near the time of delivery, the infant can become infected within twelve days of birth. The baby can receive immune globulin to prevent or lessen the severity of the disease.

German measles (Rubella)

Rubella or *German measles* is a viral infection that is transmitted through respiratory contact with an infected person. Symptoms of the illness include fever, swollen lymph glands, and a rash that appears on the face and spreads to the lower body. It lasts three days. Rubella has decreased dramatically since the widespread introduction of vaccinations, although there has been a moderate resurgence of the disease in those who have not been vaccinated.

If a pregnant woman contracts rubella, her developing baby can be affected. The greatest risk occurs during the first trimester, although the risk continues during the second trimester. If infected during this time, the baby may develop *congenital rubella syndrome.* Symptoms include intrauterine growth retardation, cardiac defects, deafness, vision problems, and mental retardation. Congenital rubella syndrome can be confirmed with chorionic villus sampling or amniocentesis.

During the first prenatal visit, all women are given a blood test and screened for immunity to rubella. Vaccination during pregnancy is not recommended for those women who are not immune. A vaccination is, however, suggested after giving birth, with the warning not to get pregnant for at least three months. Avoidance of the disease is the best prevention.

Mumps

Mumps is an acute viral illness caused by the mumps virus. It is spread through direct contact with the saliva or respiratory secretions of an infected person. Symptoms include fever, body aches, and loss of appetite followed by swelling of the salivary and parotid glands, which are located in the neck/cheek area. The infectious period is from three days before the symptoms appear until nine days after. Severe complications from the mumps are rare; however, if acquired during the first trimester, it can increase the risk of miscarriage. There is no evidence of a link between the mumps and birth defects.

Pinworms

Pinworms are caused by a small white intestinal parasite called *Enterobius vermicularis.* During sleep, the female pinworms leave the intestines and deposit eggs on the anus. This causes intense anal and perineal itching. Pinworms are transmitted by the ingestion of eggs after contact with contaminated surfaces. Women should not be treated for pinworms during pregnancy, but the rest of the family should receive treatment. The eggs can survive up to two weeks on bedding, clothing, and other objects. These items should be washed in hot water with chlorine bleach to avoid reinfection. There is no risk to the fetus if the mother contracts pinworms.

Sexually Transmitted Diseases

Genital sores, unusual vaginal discharge, and other types of genital discomfort are often warning signs of *venereal* or *sexually transmitted diseases (STDs)*. Contracting a venereal disease while pregnant puts the developing fetus at serious risk. Inform your caregiver if you suspect you have an STD or if have had one in the past. That way, you can be treated, if necessary, during your pregnancy. Your partner may also need to receive treatment for certain infections.

Chlamydia

Chlamydia is caused by the bacterium *Chlamydia trachomatis.* Symptoms in females include a vaginal discharge and pelvic pain or pain during urination. Chlamydia can be passed to the newborn during a vaginal delivery. Neonatal chlamydia can cause eye or lung infections that appear five to twelve days after birth. If the woman has a history of chlamydia infections, she should be cultured late in the pregnancy and treated with oral antibiotics prior to delivery. Her partner may also need to be treated to prevent reinfection.

Genital Herpes

Genital herpes is a common sexually transmitted disease caused by the herpes simplex virus (HSV). Although it may not display visible symptoms, this virus can produce outbreaks of painful fever blisters and sores in the genital area. If the disease is acquired for the first time during pregnancy, especially during the third trimester, there is a high rate of viral shedding and complications for both the mother and baby. The mother may develop encephalitis, pneumonitis, or hepatitis.[6] The baby is at a high risk for premature birth, intrauterine growth retardation, or even death. If the outbreak is not a primary infection, risks to the mother and fetus are low.

Ninety percent of neonatal herpes infections are transmitted during birth through contact with an active lesion in the genital area. If herpes is contracted during birth, complications to the newborn include skin lesions, encephalitis, and neurologic disability.[7] Newborns with HSV infection that was acquired during birth have a 65-percent mortality rate if untreated and a 25-percent mortality rate if treated.[8] Antiviral medication may be used for both mother and baby to treat or reduce the symptoms.

If the woman does not have active genital lesions at the time of delivery, she may deliver vaginally. If she has a history of herpes and develops lesions close to term, the lesions should be cultured at three-to-five-day intervals to determine if a vaginal delivery is safe. Lesions that are not in the genital area can be covered to prevent contact. Women with active genital lesions should deliver by cesarean section to prevent neonatal infection. The surgery should be performed within four to six hours after the membranes rupture.

Genital Warts

Genital warts, or *condylomas,* are caused by the *human papillomavirus (HPV)* and can appear on the vulva, cervix, vagina, and anus. The warts are difficult to treat and often recur. Genital warts usually increase in size during pregnancy as a result of high progesterone levels. They decrease after delivery.[9] If lesions are present in the genital area, a cesarean section may be preferable to reduce bleeding and possible transmission of the infection to the infant. Because HPV can be present but not active, it is possible for warts that were transmitted during delivery to appear up to three years after the baby is born.

Treatment during pregnancy may be recommended to prevent complications. A number of treatment options, including laser therapy, cryotherapy, and trichloracetic acid, are safe for pregnant women.

In June 2006, the US Food and Drug Administration approved a new vaccine that protects women against four strains of HPV. Called *Gardasil,* this vaccine is given in three doses over six months and should not be used during pregnancy. Two of the most common strains that the vaccine protects against account for about 70 percent of cervical cancers. The other two strains cause about 90 percent of genital warts. The vaccine does not protect against all strains of the virus.

Gonorrhea

Gonorrhea—caused by the *Neisseria gonorrhoeae* bacterium—is a common, highly contagious sexually transmitted disease. Spread most often through sexual contact with an infected person, gonorrhea can also be spread through contact with infected bodily fluids. This means a mother could pass this disease on to her newborn during childbirth.

Although many women with gonorrhea have no symptoms, others may experience vaginal discharge, pain with urination, and pelvic pain. Routine testing for gonorrhea is standard during the first prenatal visit. Women who test positive often have chlamydia as well. Pregnant women who need to have chorionic villus sampling, should first have a negative culture for gonorrhea. This is to prevent spreading the infection to the uterus.

Pregnant women with gonorrhea have an increased risk of miscarriage or premature delivery. An infected mother can also pass the infection to her baby during delivery. This can result in joint infection or an eye infection, which can lead to blindness. Treating gonorrhea as soon as it is detected will lessen the risk of these complications. Antibiotic ointment is routinely administered onto the eyes of newborns within the first hour after birth to prevent eye infections from gonorrhea.

Hepatitis B

Caused by the *hepatitis B virus (HBV), hepatitis B*, which affects the liver, can be spread through sexual activity or contact with infected blood. Symptoms can be mild or severe and may include fatigue, fever, headache, nausea and vomiting, and jaundice. If a pregnant woman has an acute hepatitis B infection during the third trimester or is a chronic carrier of the virus, she can transmit it to her newborn during delivery. If she is exposed during pregnancy, she can receive hepatitis B immune globulin and hepatitis B vaccine within two weeks of exposure to prevent the infection. If the mother is a carrier, the newborn can be treated in the same manner within the first hours after birth. Left untreated, hepatitis B can develop into chronic liver disease.

Hepatitis C

Hepatitis C is a liver disease caused by the *hepatitis C virus (HCV)*. It is spread through contact with infected blood. Most people have no symptoms or mild symptoms of the disease, such as fatigue, nausea, fever, and headaches. Pregnant women are at no greater risk of being infected with HCV than other women. Only those who have high risk factors for the disease should be tested. A small number of infants born to women with the disease become infected during delivery—and there is no treatment or vaccine to prevent it.

Human Immunodeficiency Virus

Human immunodeficiency virus (HIV) is a sexually transmitted disease that can also be acquired through contact with infected blood. It can progress to *acquired immune deficiency syndrome (AIDS)*. Pregnant women with HIV are more susceptible to infections. They are also capable of passing on the virus to their unborn children. It is important to be tested for HIV early in the pregnancy because early treatment can dramatically decrease the risk of transmission to the fetus. Antiviral medications can be given to the mother during pregnancy and labor, as well as to the newborn. Since this protocol was initiated in the United States, the transmission rate of HIV from mother to baby has dropped from 28 percent to 0 to 2 percent.[10] Breastfeeding is usually discouraged as the virus can be transmitted in breastmilk. There are no birth defects associated with HIV.

Syphilis

Caused by the *Treponema pallidum* bacterium, *syphilis* is a sexually transmitted disease that can affect the entire body. Initially this disease produces an open sore, usually in the genital area, mouth, or wherever the bacteria entered the body. Left untreated, the sore can progress to a highly contagious rash that is accompanied by fever and painful swollen glands. Eventually, the late stage of syphilis may result in damage to the heart, eyes, and central nervous system. Antibiotics effectively treat this disease during any stage; however, treatment cannot reverse the damage caused during the late stage.

Pregnant women are routinely checked for syphilis, which can result in miscarriage, premature birth, and stillbirth. They can pass the disease—*congenital syphilis*—to their babies through the placenta. Possible complications can include blindness, deafness, mental deficiencies, and bone deformities. Congenital syphilis can be prevented if the mother is treated with antibiotics before twenty weeks gestation.[11] Treatment and follow-up during the pregnancy are important to prevent reinfection.

Trichomoniasis

Spread primarily through sexual intercourse, *trichomoniasis* is an infection caused by a protozoan parasite called *Trichomonas vaginalis*. Symptoms in women include a greenish-yellow vaginal discharge with a foul odor, vaginal itching, and pain during urination or intercourse. Although there are no birth defects associated with this infection, it can increase the risk of preterm delivery. Certain medications can be taken during pregnancy to treat this sexually transmitted disease.

Food-Borne Infections

Food poisoning is a common, sometimes life-threatening problem. A number of food-borne infections pose serious risks to the unborn child. As a pregnant woman, you should be aware of these risks, so you can choose the safest foods to nourish yourself and your baby. For a complete list of guidelines that can decrease your risk of contracting a food-borne illness, see "Foods to Avoid During Pregnancy" on page 100.

In addition to avoiding foods that have a high risk of contamination, be sure to follow proper handling and food preparation methods. According to recommended guidelines of the Food and Drug Administration, wash your hands with hot soapy water before and after handling food. Be sure to wash utensils, cutting boards, and other work surfaces that have come in contact with raw meat, poultry, or fish. Wash fresh fruits and raw vegetables before eating, and remove surface dirt with a scrub brush. Remove and discard the outer leaves of cabbage, lettuce, and other leafy greens. Promptly refrigerate leftovers. Avoid eating any cooked food that has been out of the refrigerator more that two hours.

Listeriosis

Listeriosis is an infection caused by the bacterium *Listeria monocytogenes,* which is found primarily in soil and water. Listeria has been found in many types of uncooked or undercooked meats, poultry, and seafood, as well as raw vegetables and unpasteurized milk (and foods made from it). Other possible sources include cold cuts, hot dogs, and other processed meats, and soft cheeses like feta, Brie, Camembert, and blue-veined varieties. Although this bacterium is killed through pasteurization and proper processing methods, it can still be present if the equipment is contaminated or appropriate preparation guidelines are not followed.

Symptoms of listeriosis include fever, chills, and other flu-like complaints, plus headache, nausea and vomiting, and diarrhea. They can occur two to thirty days after ingestion of the contaminated food.

Listeria does not pose serious harm to healthy adults, but it is very dangerous to pregnant women and their fetuses. Pregnant women are at an increased risk of miscarriage, stillbirth, or premature delivery. The infant can also be born with the infection. There is no routine screening test to determine if you have listeriosis during pregnancy. If you display symptoms of this infection, consult your doctor immediately. A blood test will confirm the diagnosis.

According to Dr. Boris Petrikovsky, chief of maternal-fetal medicine at North Shore University Hospital on Long Island, New York, listeria is "the number-one food-borne infection that kills fetuses."[12] During pregnancy, it is recommended to cook meats and vegetables well, and to avoid any products, such as processed meats and soft cheeses, which might be contaminated with listeria.

E. Coli

E. coli is an abbreviation for *escherichia coli*—a broad group of bacteria that live in the intestinal tract of healthy humans and animals. They play an important role in the absorption of certain vitamins, but a few strains can cause serious food-borne illness. While most cases of E. coli are linked to undercooked ground meat, the bacteria can also contaminate raw fruits and vegetables, such as melons, lettuce, sprouts, tomatoes, spinach, and green onions. It has also been discovered in raw seafood, unpasteurized dairy products, and contaminated water.

Most people who become ill will experience abdominal cramping and diarrhea for a few days. A more virulent strain of E. coli produces a toxin that damages the lining of the small intestine, leading to intense abdominal cramps and severe, bloody diarrhea. In rare cases, kidney failure can occur. Because it is important for the bacteria to be excreted from the intestines, antidiarrheal medications are not recommended. Antibiotics are also not indicated.

Since E. coli inhabits the intestines of animals, the meat can be contaminated during slaughter and processing. Grinding meat for ground beef can cause the bacteria to become mixed with the meat. Milk can become contaminated when the bacteria is present on the cow's udders. Pasteurization kills these bacteria. Water from feedlots can pollute water that is used to irrigate crops, or manure that is used for fertilizer can be contaminated. Persons with wells should have their water checked for the presence of E. coli. Petting zoos have also been a source of this infection.

To reduce your chance of contracting E. coli, always cook meat, especially hamburger, until there is no pink and the thermometer registers 170°F. Never place cooked hamburgers back on the plate that held the raw patties. Wash your hands, utensils, plates, and counters with hot soapy water after touching raw meat. Wash fresh fruits and vegetables, and remove the outer leaves from heads of lettuce. Drink only pasteurized milk, fruit juices, and cider. Pregnant women should avoid alfalfa sprouts. When swimming, avoid swallowing lake water or pool water in which children who may not be potty trained swim.

Salmonella

Salmonella enterica is the strain of bacteria that can be found in the intestinal tract of infected animals and people. This bacterium causes fever, intestinal cramping, and diarrhea, twelve to seventy-two hours after ingestion, and can last up to seven days. Most people will recover without treatment, but for those with depressed immune systems, the infections can be fatal if they are not treated with antibiotics. Salmonella can be present in dairy, poultry, and meat products, as well as fruits and vegetables. Chickens and eggs are particularly high-risk foods. The unwashed hands of an infected food handler can contaminate food. Cooking foods thoroughly will kill this bacteria.

The best way to prevent contamination is to wash your hands and surfaces before preparing foods. After handling high-risk foods, wash your hands, cutting boards, dishes, and utensils with hot soapy water. Separate raw meat, poultry, and seafood from other foods in your refrigerator. Refrigerate leftovers promptly.

Poultry should be cooked to an internal temperature of 185°F. Pregnant women should be especially careful not to eat sushi that contains raw fish; they should also avoid eating raw oysters, which have been known to harbor salmonella bacteria. Keep eggs refrigerated and do not consume raw or runny eggs, or unpasteurized milk.

Those who have reptiles (turtles, iguanas, lizards, snakes) or birds as pets need to pay extra attention to hand washing as these animals are also known to carry salmonella. Do not handle these pets when pregnant, and be careful not to touch the feces. Make someone else responsible for cleaning their tanks or cages. If you must do the cleaning, be sure to wear rubber gloves.

Giardiasis

Consuming water or food that is contaminated with the *Giardia intestinalis* parasite, also known as *Giardia lamblia,* can cause *giardiasis*—an infection characterized by gas, bloating, and watery diarrhea. Symptoms of giardiasis normally begin one to two weeks after becoming infected and can last two to six weeks.

Treatment includes the consumption of additional fluids to prevent dehydration and the return to a normal diet as soon as possible to prevent weight loss. There are no reports of transmission to the fetus, but severe dehydration and weight loss can result in complications during pregnancy. Medications for treating giardiasis are not advised.

Giardia is easily spread in day care centers through its accidental ingestion from surfaces (bathroom fixtures, changing tables, diaper pails, toys, etc.) that are contaminated with feces from an infected person. Swimming pools, hot tubs, fountains, lakes, rivers, ponds, and streams can be contaminated through sewage or feces from humans or animals. When traveling in countries where the water supply might be unsafe, do not drink tap water or use ice to cool your beverages. Always drink bottled beverages without ice. Food that has been washed in contaminated water, exposed to manure, or prepared by an infected person's unwashed hands can contain giardia as well.

Animal-Transmitted Infections

Toxoplasmosis and lymphocytic choriomeningitis are two animal-transmitted viral diseases that can be harmful during pregnancy. Both infections are spread primarily through waste products.

Toxoplasmosis

Toxoplasmosis is caused by the *Toxoplasma gondii* parasite, which multiplies in the intestines of cats. The parasite is shed in their feces and found mainly in litter boxes and garden soil. In addition to getting toxoplasmosis by handling cat litter or soil in which there is cat feces, you can also get it from eating unwashed fruits and vegetables, and the undercooked meat of animals that are infected with the parasite.

When first infected, mild flu-like symptoms occur and then the person develops immunity to the infection. Pregnant women who develop toxoplasmosis during pregnancy can pass the infection to the unborn child. Infected babies can develop brain damage, vision loss, and hearing loss; they can also experience seizures and even death. When toxoplasmosis is diagnosed during pregnancy, antibiotics can help reduce the severity of symptoms in the newborn.

To minimize the chance of developing toxoplasmosis while pregnant, avoid changing litter boxes or wear rubber gloves while doing so. Also wear gloves while working in the garden, where contaminated soil can be present. Be aware that cats like to use children's sandboxes as litter boxes, so be sure to cover them when not in use. Try to control the presence of flies and roaches as they can spread contaminated soil or cat feces onto food. Avoid eating undercooked meat or poultry and unwashed fruits and vegetables. And be sure to wash your hands with hot soapy water after petting cats, touching soil, or handling raw meat.

Lymphocytic Choriomeningitis

Lymphocytic choriomeningitis (LCMV) is a rodent-borne infectious viral disease that causes meningitis and/or encephalitis. Field mice are the most common carriers, although wild mice from breeders and those sold in pet stores can also carry the virus and infect hamsters, guinea pigs, and other rodents. Infection with LCMV occurs after exposure to the fresh urine, droppings, saliva, or nesting materials from an infected rodent, as well as a bite from one.

If contracted during pregnancy, birth defects such as hydrocephalus, cerebral palsy, mental retardation, seizures and blindness or impaired vision can result. Pregnant women should avoid handling pet rodents or cleaning the cage to avoid breathing in the virus contained in the waste.[13] If you do handle a pet rodent, wash your hands with soap and hot water or a waterless alcohol-based hand cleaner, even if your hands are not visibly soiled. When cleaning a rodent's waste materials from the floor, avoid using a vacuum or broom, which will stir up dust that may contain the virus.

Other Infections

Several other infections can affect pregnancy and the unborn child. Be sure to notify your caregiver if you develop any symptoms of these infections.

Group B Strep

The *group B streptococcus (GBS)* bacterium is commonly found in the gastrointestinal tract; it can also colonize in the vaginal area. Up to 30 percent of healthy pregnant women harbor this bacteria. Most show no signs of the illness, but it puts them at an increased risk for kidney infections, premature rupture of the amniotic membranes, preterm labor, and stillbirth. The biggest danger is to infants, who can become infected during birth. While not all infants contract the infection, those who do can suffer serious complications. Factors that increase the risk of complications include prematurity, fever during labor, high levels of bacteria, and prolonged rupture of the membranes prior to delivery.

According to the 2002 revised guidelines from the Centers for Disease Control (CDC), a culture of the vaginal and rectal area to check for group B strep should be performed on all pregnant women at thirty-five to thirty-seven weeks of pregnancy. If no test results are available, a culture can be taken upon admission to a facility during labor. Women who have tested positive during pregnancy with either the genital culture or urine culture, or who have previously had an infant with a GBS infection, should be treated during labor with antibiotics. Women who did not have a culture done or whose culture results are not known should be given antibiotics if they are less than thirty-seven weeks pregnant, have had ruptured membranes for longer than eighteen hours, or have a temperature of over 100.4°F.

Treatment with antibiotics during labor has been shown to be highly effective in preventing complications in newborns if the antibiotic is administered four or more hours prior to delivery. The incidence of infants with group B streptococcal disease has declined over 70 percent since the increased use of intrapartum antibiotic prophylaxis (the use of antibiotics in labor to prevent GBS in newborns).[14] If the infant is born less than four hours following the administration of antibiotics or shows signs of infection, a partial or full septic workup may be required. This may include blood tests, a spinal tap, chest x-rays, and/or intravenous administration of antibiotics.

According to the CDC guidelines, women who are having planned cesarean deliveries and have not begun labor or do not have ruptured membranes do not need intrapartum antibiotic prophylaxis even if the GBS culture is positive.[15] In addition, if a woman has had a negative vaginal and rectal culture within five weeks of delivery, she does not require antibiotics in labor even if she develops the risk factors (delivery before thirty-seven weeks gestation, ruptured membranes over eighteen hours, or a temperature over 100.4°F.)[16]

In 1997, the American Academy of Pediatrics recommended that if treatment is necessary, two doses of antibiotics should be administered prior to delivery. But many women deliver prior to receiving a second dose. Treated infants should be observed in the hospital for forty-eight hours or until they meet the criteria for discharge. If a healthy-appearing baby is over thirty-eight weeks gestation at delivery and the mother received antibiotics over four hours before delivery, the baby may be discharged as early as twenty-four hours after birth, if the parents are able to observe for signs of infection and transport the infant to an appropriate healthcare facility if clinical signs of sepsis develop.[17]

Testing GBS positive during a previous pregnancy is not an indication for antibiotics in subsequent deliveries. Screening to detect this bacteria in each pregnancy should determine the need for antibiotics during labor in that pregnancy. However, women who have previously given birth to an infant with an invasive GBS infection should always receive antibiotics during labor. For these women, it is not necessary to do prenatal cultures. Vaccines are currently under development that may reduce the number of women who require antibiotics in labor.

Bacterial Vaginosis

Bacterial vaginosis (BV) is a common infection caused by an imbalance of the normal bacterial flora found in the vagina. Symptoms include a nonirritating milky discharge with a fishy odor that is most noticeable after sexual intercourse. Pregnant women with BV are at risk for preterm labor, premature rupture of the membranes, or chorioamnionitis—an infection of the membranes. Following both vaginal and cesarean births, women with BV have developed serious infections of the uterus and recurring urinary tract infections. The infant is at risk for preterm birth.

Antibiotics are the usual treatment for bacterial vaginosis. Women with a history of preterm birth will be screened for BV during pregnancy.

Lyme Disease

Lyme disease is a bacterial illness caused by a spirochete bacterium called *Borrelia burgdorferi*. Transmitted through the bite of a deer tick, Lyme disease occurs most commonly in rural and suburban areas in the northeastern United States. Typically, within days of the tick bite, the surrounding skin develops into an expanding red ring. The outer part of the ring may be brighter than the center, giving it a "bulls-eye" appearance. One to four weeks after the bite, flu-like symptoms occur. If untreated, cardiac and neurologic symptoms, or pain in the muscles and joints can develop. These problems can become chronic.

There are no negative effects on the fetus if the pregnant woman receives appropriate antibiotic treatment for Lyme disease.[18] Pregnant women with untreated Lyme disease have an increased risk of miscarriage, premature delivery, and stillbirth.[19]

To avoid getting Lyme disease, keep away from tick-infested areas, especially long grass. If walking in these areas is unavoidable, be sure to dress appropriately. Keep your legs, ankles, and arms covered. Wear a long-sleeved shirt and long, light-colored pants that are tucked into socks. Inspect for ticks as soon as possible—noticing them early will decrease the risk of developing Lyme disease. Caution should be used with the tick repellent DEET, which is considered toxic in high doses. If DEET is used, the spray should be applied to clothing, not directly on the skin. Citronella oil may be a safer alternative that can also be applied to clothing.

Viral Influenza

Influenza, more commonly known as the *flu,* is caused by a variety of viruses. Major symptoms of the flu, which is spread through close contact with an infected person, include fever, headache, chills, muscle aches, cough, congestion, runny nose, and sore throat. There is no specific treatment other than bed rest and drinking fluids. The CDC recommends the flu vaccine for all pregnant women. They should be vaccinated prior to flu season but preferably after the first trimester. The inactive version of the vaccine should be used rather than the live vaccine. Pregnant women who are at greatest risk for flu complications include those with chronic cardiac or pulmonary diseases, chronic metabolic diseases such as diabetes, or those with suppressed immune systems.

Yeast infections

Yeast infections are caused by an overgrowth of a normal fungus that is present in the vaginal tract. During pregnancy, women are more susceptible to these infections, which are characterized by an itchy, painful vaginal discharge that resembles cottage cheese.

Yeast infections can also cause an itchy rash on the nipples or other moist areas of the body. Although they are uncomfortable, yeast infections are not harmful to pregnant women or their babies. Topical antifungal creams or natural remedies are recommended. Avoid the use of antibiotics, which can increase the occurrence of yeast infections.

HIGH-RISK PREGNANCY

Certain conditions cause some women to be classified as high-risk during pregnancy. Women who have diabetes, heart disease, or high blood pressure, or those who develop these conditions during pregnancy or labor fall into this category. Also considered high risk are women who are carrying their fifth (or later) child; those carrying more than one baby; those under seventeen or over thirty-five; those who are over thirty and carrying their first child; and those who develop signs of preterm labor. The degree of risk varies with each of these conditions and should be explained by your doctor.

If you are in the high-risk category, the management of your pregnancy, labor, and birth may need to vary from that of a woman who is experiencing a normal pregnancy. Consequently, not all options discussed in this book may be available to you. What follows are some of the more common conditions that place women in the high-risk category.

Gestational Diabetes

Diabetes is a condition characterized by a high level of sugar (glucose) in the blood. When it occurs in pregnancy, it is called *gestational diabetes.* During pregnancy, the *human placental lactogen (HPL) hormone* causes the body's insulin to be less effective at metabolizing glucose. While this allows more available glucose for fetal growth, the resulting high blood sugar can lead to complications for both the woman and baby.

Women who have diabetes in pregnancy are more likely to develop preeclampsia—a condition resulting from uncontrolled hypertension (see page 71). To determine fetal well-being, practitioners may order some of the tests discussed earlier in this chapter, such as ultrasounds, the non-stress test, or a biophysical profile. They may also encourage a fetal movement evaluation to keep track of the baby's activity level. To prevent stillbirths, doctors may induce labor before or on the due date. If the induction is not successful, a cesarean section will be performed. Infection and postpartum hemorrhaging are also more common in diabetic women.

Babies of untreated diabetic women tend to be very large, making delivery more difficult. Other complications can include respiratory difficulties, jaundice, a high level of red blood cells, a low level of calcium in the blood, and stillbirth. If the diabetes is not controlled, the baby may develop hypoglycemia (low blood sugar) after birth. This occurs because the baby, while in utero, produces high levels of insulin to absorb the mother's high blood sugar. When the umbilical cord is cut at birth, the baby stops receiving glucose. What results is a high level of insulin in the baby that may cause his own blood sugar level to drop very low. Babies of diabetic mothers will have their blood sugars checked regularly until they are stable. Breastfeeding soon after birth helps to prevent hypoglycemia in the newborn.

The diabetic condition disappears after pregnancy for the vast majority of women, although about a third become gestational diabetics with subsequent pregnancies. In later life, they are also more likely to develop noninsulin-dependent diabetes. Most women whose blood sugars are well controlled during pregnancy have good pregnancies and healthy babies.

A family history of diabetes is one of the risk factors for developing gestational diabetes. Giving birth to large babies in the past, or having already had gestational diabetes are others. The condition is also more common in women over age twenty-five who are obese, or whose urine samples test positive for sugar during prenatal checkups. Women with any of these factors are likely to be screened for gestational diabetes early in the pregnancy. Most practices screen all women for this condition at twenty-eight weeks. Once a positive diagnosis is confirmed, the woman is placed on a diabetic diet. Home monitoring of blood sugar is performed several times a day. If diet alone does not control the blood sugar, insulin may have to be given. The woman may be referred to a diabetic clinic or dietician who will provide the necessary education about this condition. Along with a good balanced diet, exercise can help to keep blood sugar within normal limits.

After pregnancy, women who were gestational diabetics should not use the progestin-only pill for contraception. This has been associated with an increase risk of developing type 2 diabetes.[20]

Hypertension

Hypertension (high blood pressure) is characterized by a blood pressure reading of 140/90 or above for two separate readings. For accuracy, both readings should be taken by the same person and by using the same device. Pregnant women who develop high blood pressure after the twentieth week have *pregnancy-induced hypertension (PIH),* formerly known as *toxemia.* Most women who develop PIH did not have hypertension before they became pregnant and won't have it after. Women with high blood pressure prior to pregnancy have *chronic hypertension.* Those taking blood pressure medication should notify their caregivers to ensure that it is safe for use during pregnancy. Both types of high blood pressure pose serious risks to the mother and baby during pregnancy. For this reason, they are treated aggressively.

While the cause of PIH is unknown, the risk factors for developing this condition include first pregnancies and multiple pregnancies (those with more than one fetus). Other factors include stress, poor diet, age (under twenty or over thirty-five), and being overweight. A history of preeclampsia (discussed below), chronic hypertension, kidney disease, lupus, and diabetes are additional factors for developing hypertension in pregnancy.

At each prenatal visit, the blood pressure is taken, weight is monitored, and a urine sample is checked for protein, which can detect kidney damage from high blood pressure. Mild PIH, which may be treated with bed rest, poses little effect on the mother and baby as long as the blood pressure is kept under good control.

Persistent hypertension affects both the mother and fetus. High blood pressure constricts the blood flow to the uterus. This means the baby receives less oxygen and nutrients, which can affect his growth (intrauterine growth retardation). Additional ultrasounds may be indicated to monitor the baby's progress. A more serious complication is *placental abruption* in which the placenta separates from the uterine wall prematurely and can result in severe bleeding and shock.

If hypertension is untreated or uncontrolled, the woman can develop *preeclampsia,* which can damage her kidneys, liver, and brain. The only treatment for this condition is the birth of the baby, although the woman can develop symptoms up to forty-eight hours after delivery.

Call your doctor immediately if you have any of the following danger signs for preeclampsia:

✓ Sudden and excessive swelling of the face, hands, or feet.

✓ Severe and persistent headache.

✓ Pain in the upper abdomen.

✓ Visual disturbances such as dimness, blurring, flashes of light, or dots in front of the eyes.

✓ Marked decrease in the frequency of urination.

Preeclampsia may require hospitalization. It may be also necessary to induce labor or perform a cesarean section if the blood pressure is not controlled. The need for early delivery will be determined by lab work, blood pressure readings, and if the baby is at greater risk remaining in the uterus or being delivered prematurely. During labor, magnesium sulfate is administered intravenously to prevent the woman from having convulsions. This medication is usually continued for twenty-four hours after birth.

If preeclampsia is not controlled, it can progress to *eclampsia*—which is marked by convulsions, coma, and possible death of the woman and/or baby. A critically ill woman may also develop *HELLP syndrome*, which indicates complications involving the liver and blood. HELLP stands for **H**emolysis (breakdown of red blood cells), **E**levated **L**iver enzymes, **L**ow **P**latelets. Women who have progressed to this level of illness are cared for in the intensive care unit.

The effects of the uncontrolled hypertension can be serious. Early detection and treatment is key to a healthy mother and baby.

Multiple Pregnancy

If you are pregnant with more than one baby—twins, triplets, or more—it is considered a multiple pregnancy. Twins occur in 1 of every 33 pregnancies. Triplets, quadruplets, or higher multiples occur 1 in 555 pregnancies. Fraternal twins (the result of two sperms fertilizing two eggs) are more common than identical twins (the result of one sperm fertilizing one egg, which then separates). Fraternal multiples may run in families, as multiples are more likely to occur in women who hyper-ovulate (release more than one egg during ovulation). If the father's side has multiples, his generation will not be affected, but his daughter may carry the tendency to hyper-ovulate. Identical multiples are more likely a random event. Fraternal twins, triplets, etc. may or may not be the same sex and they may be unlike in physical appearance. Since identical siblings carry the same genetic material, they are always the same sex, always look alike, and always have the same blood type. They may be mirror images of each other.

Your doctor or midwife may suspect more than one baby if your uterus measures larger than normal, if two or more heartbeats are detected, or if your weight gain is more rapid than expected. You are more likely to be carrying more than one baby if you became pregnant while undergoing fertility treatments, if you have already had a set of multiples, or if multiples run in your family. Other factors that may increase your chance of having multiples are age (older women tend to be likely candidates), many previous pregnancies, and being of African descent. Multiples are less common in Hispanic and Asian women.

An increased demand is placed on the bodies of women who are carrying more than one baby. The discomforts of pregnancy are accentuated, since there is an increased demand on the circulatory system and the uterus is larger in size. The chances of miscarriage, preeclampsia, placental abruption, and preterm labor are also greater. Half of the multiple pregnancies deliver before thirty-seven weeks. Frequent ultrasounds are indicated to ensure that all the babies are growing at a proper rate.

One complication for twin pregnancies is a rare condition called *vanishing twin syndrome* in which two fetuses are diagnosed early in the pregnancy but only one survives. It is believed that the lost twin was reabsorbed or miscarried, sometimes with no symptoms. Another rare complication in identical twins is called *twin-to-twin transfusion syndrome* in which one twin receives the other twin's blood supply through their shared placenta. Early detection can save the lives of both babies.

Women experiencing a multiple pregnancy have higher protein and caloric requirements for the adequate growth of their babies and to ensure good muscle tone of their overly distended uteruses. They also have increased vitamin needs, requiring 600 micrograms of folic acid a day and between 30 and 60 milligrams of daily iron to prevent anemia. An increase of fluid intake is also vital to prevent dehydration, which can increase the chances of premature contractions. Weight gain with twins should be between thirty-five and forty-five pounds. Your caregiver will give you specific guidelines if you are carrying more than two babies. Gaining too much weight increases the risk of complications, including the need for cesarean section. (Detailed information on dietary and nutritional requirements during pregnancy, including multiple pregnancies, is presented in Chapter 5.)

Twins can be carried in the uterus in many different positions. If the first baby is positioned head down (the vertex position), the possibility of having a vaginal delivery increases. If the second baby presents feet first (breech), many physicians will deliver the baby vaginally while still in this presentation. They may also attempt to turn him to a head-down position during the delivery. Some doctors are not comfortable delivering breech babies vaginally and will perform a cesarean section for the second baby. If the first baby is breech or if the babies are positioned sideways (a transverse lie) in the uterus, most physicians will schedule a cesarean section. Many hospitals prefer to deliver multiples in the operating room rather than a birthing room in case an immediate cesarean section is necessary. If you are carrying more than two babies, you will most likely have a cesarean section.

Women who eat well during pregnancy decrease their chances for complications and increase their chances for delivering healthy babies at term. Although many physicians place women who are carrying twins or multiples on bed rest at twenty-eight weeks, there is no evidence that bed rest prevents preterm labor.

Local and national groups, including The National Organization of Mothers of Twins Clubs (NOMOTC) and The Triplet Connection provide mothers of multiples with helpful information and support. Contact information for these and other organizations is provided in the Resources beginning on page 449.

Preterm Labor

If a baby is born before the thirty-seventh week of pregnancy—more than three weeks early—the birth is called *preterm* and the baby is considered *premature*. Preterm births represent the greatest health risk to newborns. Babies born prematurely have an increased risk of neonatal problems. Their lungs and other organs may not be ready to function. Respiratory distress is the greatest concern. Premature babies often have difficulty maintaining their body temperature, their sucking ability may be weak, and they tend to be more susceptible to infections, including a serious inflammatory intestinal condition called *necrotizing enterocolitis.*

Preterm labor occurs in 8 to 10 percent of all births. Certain women are at a higher risk for this occurrence than others. They include those who:

■ have had a previous miscarriage or preterm birth.

■ have experienced bleeding during pregnancy.

- have an overly distended uterus from a multiple pregnancy or from an excess of amniotic fluid.

- smoke, abuse alcohol, or take drugs (especially cocaine).

- were malnourished before or during the pregnancy.

- are under the age of eighteen or over thirty-five.

- are African American.

- gave birth less than eighteen months earlier.

- have a urinary tract or vaginal infection (particularly bacterial vaginosis or trichomoniasis).

- have an infection of the amniotic sac membranes.

- experience a high degree of emotional distress.

- have jobs that involve standing for long periods.

- work under stressful conditions.

Women who have structural abnormalities of the uterus such as fibroids or an atypical shape are also at greater risk for preterm labor, as are those with cervical abnormalities or insufficiencies. Women whose mothers took the drug diethylstilbestrol (DES) while pregnant with them may experience preterm delivery. DES was once prescribed during pregnancy to prevent miscarriages and premature deliveries; it was eventually linked to a rare form of cancer. Other women who are at risk for early delivery include those who have experienced abdominal trauma or have undergone abdominal surgery during the pregnancy, as well as those with hypertension, diabetes, sickle cell anemia, lupus, periodontitis, or problems related to the placenta, such as placenta previa or abruption.

It is imperative to contact your doctor, midwife, or other caregiver if you experience symptoms of preterm labor. The following signs are possible indications:

- More than four uterine contractions, which may be painless, in a one-hour period.

- Menstrual-like cramps that are constant or intermittent.

- Abdominal cramps, with or without diarrhea.

- Persistent diarrhea.

- Backache that is constant or intermittent.

- Pelvic pressure or the feeling that the baby is pushing down.

- Sudden increase in vaginal discharge that is watery, bloody, or mucous-like.

- A feeling that something is wrong.

Your caregiver may perform several tests to determine if your symptoms are normal Braxton-Hicks contractions or other typical changes in pregnancy, or if you are actually in preterm labor. You may be given a vaginal exam to check the cervix for possible changes and to assess whether or not the membranes have ruptured. An ultrasound evaluation of the cervix may also provide a more accurate measurement. If you are having contractions, you may be placed on a fetal monitor for evaluation.

You may also be given a test to detect the presence of fetal fibronectin in the cervical/vaginal secretions. As explained earlier in this chapter, the absence of this protein is a reliable indication that the pregnancy will continue for at least two more weeks. If the test is positive and fibronectin is present, or in cases of impending preterm birth between twenty-four and thirty-four weeks gestation, you will be given corticosteroids to improve the baby's outcome. This medication reduces the incidence of respiratory distress syndrome and brain hemorrhage in newborns and dramatically reduces the death rate. Most deaths of premature infants occur among those who are born before the thirty-second week of pregnancy.

You may be instructed to reduce or stop physical activity; to stop having sex or to use a condom; and to stop smoking if you haven't already. The most common method for trying to stop preterm labor is bed rest, antibiotics for infection (if indicated), and medications that relax the uterus to stop the contractions. The American College of Obstetricians and Gynecologists (ACOG) reported, however, that while bed rest, home uterine activity monitoring, hydration, and sedation are among the common treatments to help prevent or stop preterm labor in the United States, there is little evidence that any of them work.[21] Despite advances in technology, there has been no decrease in the incidence of preterm labor/delivery in the past four decades and, in fact, the rate has increased slightly.[22]

Until effective strategies to stop preterm labor are discovered, the report recommends that efforts should be aimed at preventing newborn complications by administering antibiotics for infections, using corticosteroids, and avoiding traumatic deliveries of very premature infants.[23] Women who are at risk for delivering very premature babies should be cared for in a high-risk center that is experienced in treating these infants. Doctors may try to delay the labor of women who are very preterm and whose amniotic membranes have ruptured but there is no labor. This will allow the baby to mature. Antibiotics will be given to prevent infection, and blood work and temperatures will be monitored. The physician must determine if it is safer for the baby to remain inside the woman or be delivered prematurely and cared for in the nursery.

Pregnant women who have previously lost several babies in mid-pregnancy—the result of cervical insufficiency or an unknown reason—may undergo a procedure called *cerclage* around thirteen to sixteen weeks. During this surgery, the cervix is stitched closed; late in the pregnancy, the stitches are removed. Infection is the biggest risk with this procedure. Cerclage is rarely done later than twenty-four weeks in pregnancy as an emergency method to prevent dilation. Bed rest to help prevent pressure on an already dilated cervix is the recommended alternative.

Bed Rest During Pregnancy

Up to 25 percent of pregnant women are placed on bed rest for a variety of reasons. The most common are incompetent cervix, placenta previa, vaginal bleeding, premature rupture of membranes, preterm labor, edema, hypertension in pregnancy, pre-eclampsia, multiple pregnancy, and intrauterine growth retardation.[24] Bed rest helps to decrease pressure on the cervix and to reduce uterine contractions, although there is no evidence that it can stop preterm labor. It can also lower your blood pressure. Lying on your left side can increase oxygenation of the placenta.

Bed rest can be recommended for a few days or many weeks. If your caregiver has recommended bed rest for you, he may also ask you to stop working or reduce your work hours; avoid lifting anything heavy, including your other children; and/or avoid any strenuous housework. More extensive restrictions may mean spending weeks in bed, getting up only to use the bathroom. Some women may even be hospitalized. Pelvic rest means avoiding sexual stimulation—this includes intercourse as well as nipple stimulation, which can bring on contractions. If sex is permitted, your partner may need to wear a condom because semen contains prostaglandins, which may stimulate contractions. You may also be told to stop performing Kegels, exercises of the pelvic floor muscles (see page 130).

The side effects of long-term bed rest can include decreased muscle tone, a loss of calcium and bone, dizziness upon walking, constipation, an increased risk of blood clots, depression, and a longer postpartum recovery. If you are instructed to be on bed rest for a prolonged period of time, the following suggestions can help you cope:

■ Have a bedside table set up with activities to keep you busy. Start a craft project such as knitting, embroidering, or crocheting (booties, blankets, and bibs are great possible projects).

■ Watch movies; read books and magazines.

■ Have a computer set up next to your bed or use a laptop.

■ Shop online for nursery items.

■ Eat healthy foods and drink plenty of fluids. Choose high-fiber meals to avoid constipation.

■ Plan the meals for the week and make a grocery list for your partner.

■ Before your partner leaves for work, have him prepare your lunch, snacks, and drinks, and place them in a bedside cooler.

■ Look for massage therapists or hair stylists that will come to your house.

■ If you have a job, perhaps you will be able to do some work from home.

■ Follow your baby's development week by week, as he gets closer to maturity.

■ Begin writing a journal for your baby.

■ Start a baby book for your soon-to-be-born child.

If you are unable to attend childbirth classes, inquire about alternatives. Some facilities prepare a "bed rest packet" of information for those who are unable to attend. You may even be able to borrow videos from the facility or the library. You can also use this book to learn the techniques that will help you cope with labor.

Do not refuse offers from friends and family who want to bring you food, run errands for you, or just want to pay you a visit. If you are permitted to be up for a short time during the day, move to a different room—preferable one with a sunny window—for a change of scenery. And although you may not be able to do housework or other strenuous activities, you can still fold the laundry or pay bills.

If bed rest has been prescribed for you, be sure to ask your caregiver the following questions:

- How many hours a day must I lie down? How much walking/standing can I do?
- Can I get up to go to the bathroom or to take a shower?
- Can I drive a car?
- Do I need to quit work or reduce my hours?
- Can I lift anything?
- Can I perform any exercises while I am in bed?
- Can I continue to have sex?
- Can I do any household chores?

It is important to be clear on what you can and cannot do during this period. Knowing the answers to these questions will ensure this awareness.

Rh Incompatibility

During your first prenatal visit, you will have blood drawn to determine your blood type and Rh (D) factor. As explained earlier in this chapter, you are Rh-positive if your blood contains the Rh (D) factor and Rh-negative if it does not. If you are Rh-negative, additional blood tests will be performed during the pregnancy to check for antibodies. If people who are Rh-negative receive Rh-positive blood, they will become sensitized and their bodies will produce antibodies that attack the foreign red blood cells. This is a significant consideration for a pregnant woman who is Rh-negative because if her mate is Rh positive, their child can also be Rh positive. During amniocentesis or during the delivery of the placenta, it is possible for the baby's blood to come in contact with the mother's. If this happens, the mother's body will produce antibodies that attack the Rh-positive cells and cause them to die, resulting in *hemolytic disease of the newborn.* If many blood cells are destroyed, the baby will be born with anemia. In severe cases, he can experience heart failure. Fortunately, this is rare since the use of RhoGAM (see below).

Since the sensitization usually does not occur until after the birth, a woman's first baby will not be affected—unless the woman was previously sensitized and not treated. If a woman is not treated and becomes pregnant again with an Rh-positive baby, the antibodies will cross the placenta and kill the fetus's red blood cells.

To prevent hemolytic disease of the newborn, Rho(D) immune globulin, commonly known as RhoGAM, is administered intramuscularly after the birth of an Rh-positive infant, as well as after a miscarriage, abortion, or amniocentesis. It is also given at twenty-eight weeks of pregnancy as a preventive. RhoGAM acts by suppressing the specific immune response of Rh-negative individuals to Rh-positive red blood cells. Since the woman does not produce antibodies, subsequent pregnancies will not be affected, and the woman can give birth to healthy newborns in the future. In the rare instance in which the woman has become sensitized and the fetus is compromised, an intrauterine blood transfusion can be performed or the baby may be delivered early to receive treatment.

Chronic Health Problems

It is extremely important for women with chronic health problems to discuss pregnancy plans with their physicians and to take whatever special precautions are necessary to ensure a healthy baby. In some areas, perinatologists, who are experts in high-risk pregnancy, may be available for consultation or management.

Prior to becoming pregnant, insulin-dependent diabetics should have their weight and blood sugars under control. Diabetics who do not normally take insulin may need to take it during pregnancy. Tight controls and close medical supervision can help to reduce possible complications.

Women with chronic hypertension or heart disease will also need close supervision. If taking medication, they must make their physicians aware of this. Angiotensive converting enzyme (ACE) inhibitors, commonly used to lower blood pressure, should be avoided during pregnancy. Other types of blood pressure medication will be prescribed.

Women with phenylketonuria (PKU) will have to follow a special diet to prevent mental retardation and/or birth defects in their offspring. Blood levels of the amino acid phenylalanine (a protein) must be carefully monitored to ensure that they are within a safe range. Other chronic health problems, such as digestive disorders, autoimmune diseases like lupus, epilepsy, kidney problems, or lung disease, may also be of concern and require special needs during pregnancy. It is important that caregivers are aware of any chronic problems. Specialists may be needed to help ensure the health of both mother and baby.

SPECIAL SITUATIONS AND CONCERNS

In addition to the high-risk pregnancy conditions just discussed, the following topics may be of special importance to you.

Teen Pregnancy

Most teen pregnancies are unplanned. It is not unusual for some girls to initially hide their condition for any number of reasons—denial, embarrassment, fear. This causes a delay in initiating prenatal care, which should begin as early in the pregnancy as possible. Many teens do not seek healthcare during the first four months of their pregnancy (or until they start to look pregnant), which puts them and their babies at risk.

Because a teenager's body is still growing, it is especially important for an expectant teen mother to be diligent about following guidelines of good nutrition, exercise, and proper healthcare. This will help ensure adequate growth for her body as well as that of the developing baby. Like all pregnant women, she should begin taking prenatal vitamins at the onset of the pregnancy. Expectant teens also have greater calcium needs than pregnant women who are over age eighteen.

Proper eating habits are particularly important for expectant teens, who, compared to adult women, are less likely to eat properly and gain adequate weight during pregnancy. This can lead to babies with low birth weight, which is associated with infant illness, disability, and even death. Pregnant teens are also at higher risk for hypertension, anemia, preterm labor, and long labors. Good nutritional counseling is essential, as is regular prenatal care.

Pregnancy Over Age Thirty-Five

Many women delay starting a family until they are in their mid-thirties. Those who are in good physical condition can have healthy pregnancies with few complications. With age, however, certain problems, such as diabetes and chronic hypertension, tend to be more common. During pregnancy, those over age thirty-five are more likely to miscarry, develop gestational diabetes, and have an infant with low birth weight. Cesarean section rates are higher for women in this age group as well.

The risk of having a child with birth defects also increases as a woman ages. Most doctors will offer women over thirty-five the option of genetic counseling to assess the risk of having a child with a birth defect. They may offer the option of amniocentesis or chorionic villus sampling to test for genetic problems.

Most women of this age group enjoy healthy pregnancies and give birth to healthy babies. As with expectant women of all ages, the major contributors of a positive pregnancy include good prenatal care, proper diet, and exercise.

Ectopic Pregnancy

During a normal pregnancy, the fertilized ovum implants itself on the interior wall of the uterus. In an *ectopic pregnancy* (ectopic means "out of place"), the fertilized ovum attaches itself outside the uterus, usually in one of the fallopian tubes, although it can also implant itself on the ovary, within the cervix, or in the abdominal cavity. Unlike the uterine wall, these areas have neither the space nor the type of tissue needed to nurture the developing embryo. As the embryo grows, the woman is likely to experience pelvic or abdominal pain, vaginal spotting or bleeding, and/or lower back pain. As it is impossible to transplant an ectopic pregnancy in the uterus, termination—usually through surgery—is the only option.

If an ectopic pregnancy is left untreated, the embryo will continue to grow until it ruptures and damages the fallopian tube (or other organ to which it is attached). This will cause heavy internal bleeding that can result in death. Even if a fallopian tube has been damaged, future pregnancies can occur as long as the other tube remains intact and functioning.

Early detection of an ectopic pregnancy is key to avoiding serious complications. Contact your caregiver immediately if you experience any signs of this condition.

Miscarriage

A *miscarriage*, also called a *spontaneous abortion,* is the loss of the baby before the twentieth week of pregnancy—most often, this happens during the first twelve weeks. It is often difficult to determine the cause of a miscarriage, especially if it occurs during the first trimester. Miscarriages that take place early in the pregnancy are often due to chromosomal abnormalities, a blighted ovum (a pregnancy sac that develops but contains no embryo), and ectopic pregnancies. Other causes can include infections, abnormalities of the uterus, chronic health conditions, and even medical procedures.

Signs of miscarriage typically include cramping, vaginal spotting or bleeding, backache, or sudden loss of pregnancy symptoms. Contact your caregiver immediately if you experience these signs. He will be able to determine if a miscarriage has occurred. Be aware that there is no treatment to stop an impending miscarriage. Bed rest, however, may be recommended to possibly stop the bleeding and prevent the miscarriage from occurring.

It is normal to experience grief, depression, and even guilt following a miscarriage. It's also important to allow yourself time to mourn your loss. A miscarriage may make you fearful or anxious about becoming pregnant again. It's important to acknowledge your feelings and work through your emotions and pain. Allow yourself time to complete the grieving process for the lost baby. Support groups are available to help you and your partner cope.

Understanding why miscarriages occur can help you to come to terms with your own loss. Most important, realize that having a miscarriage does not mean that you can't have a normal, healthy pregnancy in the future.

Obesity and Pregnancy

The term "obese" refers to anyone who weighs more than 30 percent over their ideal body weight. Those who are obese (and even marginally overweight) are at risk for a number of serious illnesses, such as diabetes, cardiovascular disease, and arthritis. Pregnant women who are obese may face several serious health complications, including preeclampsia and gestational diabetes. They also experience higher rates of miscarriage, preterm delivery, and prolonged and difficult labor that may result in the need for a cesarean section.

Babies of obese women are also affected. They are at risk for *macrosomia*—a condition in which they gain too much weight during development, making labor and vaginal delivery difficult. Because of their size, some of these babies injure their shoulders (shoulder *dystocia*) when exiting the birth canal. Offspring of obese women are at a greater risk of developing neural tube defects such as spina bifida. They are also more likely to become obese themselves by age four.

If you are obese and have become pregnant, *do not* try to lose weight. Dieting at this point can prevent your developing baby from getting the nutrients necessary for proper growth. Instead, focus on gaining weight in moderation. Most women who are obese need to gain between fifteen and twenty-five pounds during pregnancy—most of that weight should be added during the last trimester. You can also exercise to reduce your risk of possible complications. Speak with your doctor about an exercise program that would fit you best.

Hyperemesis Gravidarum

Many women experience some degree of *morning sickness* during pregnancy. Characterized by nausea that is often accompanied by vomiting, this condition usually occurs during the first trimester. Rapidly rising levels of estrogen and other hormones are believed to be the cause of this discomfort. Eating small, frequent meals, snacking on dry foods like crackers and bread, eating ginger or foods that contain ginger, and sipping seltzer or sparkling water may provide relief.

Although some degree of nausea and vomiting in pregnancy is considered normal, if it becomes excessive and persistent—a rare condition called *hyperemesis gravidarum*—it can interfere with the weight gain needed to sustain the pregnancy. Most seriously, it can result in dehydration, which can be harmful to both the mother and child.

Under the watchful eye of a physician, women with this condition may be given medication to alleviate the nausea. Severe cases may require hospitalization, in which intravenous fluids are given to restore hydration and provide nutrition.

DES Daughters

From the 1940s until the early 1970s, *diethylstilbesterol (DES)*—a synthetic estrogen—was sometimes prescribed to pregnant women who were at a heightened risk for miscarriages and premature deliveries. This practice was eliminated when a high incidence of reproductive organ abnormalities and a rare type of vaginal cancer called *clear cell adenocarcinoma* were discovered in the daughters born to these women. Regular gynecological checkups and pap smears are especially important for the daughters of women who took DES.

DES daughters also experience a higher incidence of infertility. Those that do become pregnant are at a higher risk for miscarriage, ectopic pregnancy, and premature labor and delivery. All DES daughters need careful monitoring during pregnancy.

Victims of Domestic Violence

Domestic violence can involve physical and/or emotional abuse. A woman who lives in fear of a partner who exerts extreme control over her through intimidation or coercion can also be in an abusive situation. Approximately 8 percent of pregnant women are physically hurt by their partners or by another man. Homicide is now the leading cause of injury deaths in pregnant women and in women within one year after giving birth.[25]

Physical abuse during pregnancy, especially trauma to the abdomen, can result in miscarriage, hemorrhaging, uterine rupture, preterm labor, or premature rupture of the membranes. If you are in an abusive relationship, discuss this situation with your caregiver or contact the National Domestic Violence Hotline for assistance. For contact information, see the Resources beginning on page 449.

History of Sexual Abuse

Women with a history of sexual abuse may have more difficulties in labor and birth than the average woman. The frequent vaginal exams and a loss of privacy at this time can contribute to increased feelings of discomfort and lack of control. Certain phrases or words may be used by the doctor or staff that the abuser may have uttered during the attack. These "trigger" phrases or situations may affect the woman's ability to relax or to push during labor. Her tension and anxiety may impede the normal labor process and result in the need for interventions.

If you have a history of sexual abuse, share this information with your caregiver. Discuss any concerns or fears you may have as a result, so they can be carefully dealt with throughout your pregnancy and during childbirth.

CONCLUSION

For most women, pregnancy is a time of health and happiness. Many of the routine tests and examinations help to ensure that the pregnancy is just that. But if your pregnancy falls out of the "normal" range, your doctor will discuss some of the additional tests reviewed in this chapter.

The next chapter discusses an aspect of your pregnancy that you *can* control—nutrition. The food choices you make at this time can help you feel good and ensure a well-nourished baby.

Nutrition

or Food for Thought

Because Americans are among the wealthiest people in the world, they are often thought to be the most well nourished. Unfortunately, this is not true. The average American diet includes a good deal of fat, sugar, and highly processed food. This "junk food" provides only empty calories—that is, it has a high caloric content with little or no nutritional value.

A junk food diet is not healthy for anyone, but for a developing fetus, it is disastrous! Your baby's entire body—including her liver, heart, bones, and brain—is formed completely from the nutrients you provide. She is not a parasite drawing from your body's reserves. Only the nutrients you consume are available for her formation and growth. For your baby to develop to her full potential, both physically and mentally, you must eat right throughout your pregnancy. Even her intelligence quotient (IQ) in later life can be affected by your diet, since her tiny brain cells need adequate protein for proper development. Remember this as you plan your meals every day.

If you are already nutrition conscious and eating a healthy diet, your main concern will be to simply increase your protein intake. If, however, you are a "junk food junkie," now is the time to change. By eliminating empty calories from your diet, as well as increasing your consumption of protein, you can feel confident that you are providing your baby with the optimum building blocks. And as a bonus, you will feel better, too!

Fortunately, many women begin to pay closer attention to their diets during pregnancy. Some are motivated by a desire to do everything possible to ensure a healthy child. Others want to avoid problems such as constipation, heartburn, morning sickness, and fatigue. An expanding abdomen and weight gain are factors that concern still other women, who fear that they will never lose the added pounds. It is important for you to realize that gaining weight is necessary during pregnancy and that you *will* lose the added weight afterwards.

A poor diet can cause a multitude of problems for the woman, including anemia, infection, placental malfunction, difficult labor, cesarean delivery, and poor postpartum healing. It can result in a baby that is preterm, has a low birth weight, or even has birth defects. This chapter discusses the nutritional needs of mothers-to-be. It explains why they require certain foods, and recommends the best dietary approaches for getting them.

NUTRITIONAL FOCUS DURING PREGNANCY

During pregnancy, many changes occur in a woman's body to ensure that her baby receives adequate nutrition. The following discussion presents these important changes and explains how they are influenced by proper diet and good nutrition.

The Placenta

When a woman is pregnant, she is growing not only a baby, but also a placenta. The placenta carries out all of the essential life functions for the developing baby. It absorbs nutrients, oxygen, and other vital substances from the mother's blood, and passes it to the fetus through the umbilical cord. Like the baby, the placenta needs to be adequately nourished to ensure proper implantation and development for efficient functioning. It is an important part of the baby's life-support system.

The placenta, in providing nourishment for the baby, works very much like a fuel pump. If the fuel is of poor quality or the wrong octane, the pump will not work effectively (it may even stop completely). If the pressure or volume of the fuel is affected, the pump's efficiency will be altered as well. Think of the nutrients in your bloodstream as fuel. An unhealthy diet results in nutritionally poor fuel that moves through the "placental pump." And if the volume of fluid in the bloodstream is inadequate, the pressure of the fuel coming through the pump will be weak. Nutrients will not be able to get through in sufficient quantity to adequately nourish the fetus.

Bodily Fluids

During the last half of pregnancy, the body's blood volume needs to increase by more than 50 percent to enable the placenta to be an efficient pump. This increase requires an adequate intake of sodium (salt), along with a sufficient intake of fluids. Many women experience an increased desire for salt during pregnancy. This is the body's way of ensuring that it receives the necessary salt supply. Restricting salt intake may hinder the body's performance of this vital function.

Sufficient fluid intake is also needed for the production of amniotic fluid. By the last weeks of pregnancy, the amniotic sac contains about one quart of fluid to cushion and protect the baby. This fluid, which is constantly circulated by the fetus (who swallows and excretes it through urination), is replaced every three hours. In addition, the fluid in the woman's tissues increases by an estimated two to three quarts during pregnancy. Every day, you need to drink at least two quarts of liquid—water, milk, and fruit juices are recommended— to maintain these levels and to ensure a healthy pregnancy. Stay away from alcohol and drinks that contain caffeine.

During pregnancy, some degree of swelling is normal. The enlarging uterus presses on the veins of the legs and can cause edema (swelling) in the lower extremities, especially in women who stand or sit for long periods. In addition, estrogen, which is manufactured by the placenta during pregnancy, causes the tissues to retain extra fluid. Before you became pregnant, you may have experienced signs of water retention (bloating, swelling) just before your menstrual period. This was caused by an increased level of estrogen in your body. Women taking birth control pills may also experience swelling for the same reason.

In the past, doctors often treated normal swelling with diuretics (water pills) and encouraged a salt-restricted diet. Because of potential side effects, this practice is no longer followed. If the swelling is a result of *hypovolemia* (low blood volume), diuretics may drive salt and water from the blood, lowering the volume even further. This

Hints for the Mother-to-Be

✓ *Do not* restrict your salt intake unless your doctor gives you documented proof that it is necessary in your particular case.

✓ *Do not* take a diuretic for normal swelling.

✓ *Do not* restrict your calories to "hold down" your weight gain.

✓ *Do not* go for even twenty-four hours without nutritious food.

could actually cause or increase high blood pressure, which the diuretic may have been prescribed to prevent. At times, however, diuretics may be indicated in pregnancy—if, for example, abnormal swelling occurs due to heart or kidney disease.

Rather than resort to diuretics or salt restriction, the normal pregnant woman should make certain that her protein consumption is ample and that her salt intake is adequate. Salt is contained naturally in many foods. During pregnancy, "salt to taste" is a good rule to follow.

Pregnant women with high blood pressure who experience a sudden, abnormal swelling of the hands, feet, and/or face, should contact their caregiver immediately. These symptoms are a possible indication of preeclampsia.

The Liver

Your liver performs about 500 functions. It helps to maintain the increased blood volume during pregnancy by providing *albumin,* a protein that keeps water in the bloodstream. Inadequate protein intake prevents the liver from producing enough albumin to maintain the water, which leaks into the tissues and creates abnormal puffiness.

The liver also filters the pregnancy-induced hormones that are manufactured by the body, and it rids the body of toxins normally produced in the lower bowel. The liver is under increased stress as the baby grows. To counteract this stress, you must increase your intake of calories, protein, vitamins, and sodium during the last half of your pregnancy.

Fetal Brain Development

The baby's brain grows the most during the last two months of pregnancy. An adequate intake of protein is essential at this time for building brain cells. Even if your diet has been unstructured up to your seventh month, an increase in your protein intake during the last two months can still greatly benefit your baby. Conversely, if your diet has been adequate up to your seventh month, but you begin restricting calories in an effort to control weight gain, your baby may suffer.

Fetal Iron Stores

During the last weeks of pregnancy, the baby will store vital minerals and body fat that are essential for survival. She stores iron because her diet will be low in this mineral for the first six months of life. Therefore, during the last months of pregnancy, you must eat foods that will provide you and your baby with a sufficient amount of iron. After birth, breastfeeding will help maintain this supply. Although it contains only a small amount of iron, breastmilk is efficiently absorbed and utilized by babies. Infant formula also contains an iron supplement, but it is poorly absorbed by babies.

Weight Gain

Weight gain, which is often the focus of too much concern during pregnancy, is expected and necessary for the well-being of the mother-to-be and the baby. The amount of weight gained during pregnancy varies from woman to woman, as does the pattern of gain. Total weight gain is determined by prepregnant weight, eating habits, daily activities, and metabolism. Since every woman is unique, there is no specific weight gain that is correct for all pregnant women. It is, however, recommended that the average woman eat between 2,100 and 2,500 calories per day and gain twenty-five to thirty-five pounds during the pregnancy.

Women who were underweight before becoming pregnant will need to gain more weight than what is expected of the average woman—approximately twenty-eight to forty pounds. Overweight women who become pregnant must *never* try to diet during pregnancy. Dieting for any woman can prevent developing babies from getting the nutrients they need for proper growth. Replacing high-calorie junk foods with nutrient-rich choices will adequately nourish babies. A daily calorie intake of less than 2,100 will not provide the proper amount of nutrients for the baby, nor will it allow the woman to gain an adequate amount of weight.

The nutritional needs of women who are experiencing a multiple pregnancy, are greater than for those carrying a single baby. Each day, they need to consume an extra 20 to 25 grams of protein and 300 extra calories for each additional baby. Expectant mothers of twins, for example, should gain between thirty-five and forty-five pounds. Women who are pregnant with multiples also have higher vitamin requirements. They need 600 micrograms of folic acid a day and between 30 and 60 milligrams of iron, which prevents them from developing anemia. They also require an increase in fluid intake to prevent dehydration, which can increase the chance of premature contractions and possible premature birth.

Physiologic swelling is even more exaggerated for women carrying multiples, as they may have additional placentas or one very large placenta that produces a greater quantity of estrogen. A larger, heavier uterus also restricts the blood flow in the leg veins more than normal, increasing edema in the lower extremities. Women carrying multiples need to be especially conscious of a high-quality nutritious diet to help ensure their babies are of normal weight and that they deliver at term.

Women with special dietary needs must speak with a nutrition counselor if they are unable to meet the increased needs of pregnancy. Vegetarians, women who are have food allergies, and those who are lactose intolerant, for example, will have to alter their diets to ensure proper nutrition. See "Special Dietary Concerns" on page 102 for more information.

NUTRITION BASICS

Food is made up of a number of basic elements. These food components, some of which are discussed below, are an important part of good nutrition and a healthy diet.

Protein

Proteins are the building blocks of all cells. They are composed of amino acids and are necessary for the growth and repair of tissues, for building blood and amniotic fluid, and for forming antibodies in both the pregnant woman and her developing baby. There are two kinds of protein—complete and incomplete. A complete protein, which comes from animal sources, supplies all eight essential amino acids. Vegetable proteins are incomplete, supplying some but not all of these amino acids. If you are a vegetarian and do not eat meat, you will need to plan a diet that provides all eight essential amino acids through a combination of vegetables, legumes, and grains. Good protein sources include red meat, fish, poultry, eggs, milk, cheese, dried beans and peas, peanut butter, and nuts.

Carbohydrates

Foods that are derived from plants contain *carbohydrates*, which the liver breaks down into simple sugars—the major source of energy. Carbohydrates fall into two main categories—simple and complex. The big difference between the two is how quickly they are digested and enter the blodstream. *Simple carbohydrates* are quickly broken down by the body to release energy. They are found in fruits, milk products, and table sugar. *Complex carbohydrates* are broken down by the body more slowly, providing a slow, steady release of energy. Foods such as unprocessed vegetables, whole grains, beans, and nuts are examples of complex carbs.

Carbohydrates are especially important during pregnancy because they supply the woman with energy, allowing protein to be spared for the important work of building tissues. Be aware that many processed snack foods—such as potato chips, cookies, and candy—are largely simple carbohydrates that supply empty calories and little else. Vegetables and fruit supply not only energy, but vitamins and minerals that benefit both the woman and the developing baby. Some carbohydrates also provide fiber, which helps minimize the possible problem of constipation.

Fat

Like carbohydrates and protein, dietary fat is an important source of energy. Although a low-fat diet is generally healthier than one that is higher in fat, our bodies need a certain amount of fat for the body's normal growth and development; for processing fat-soluble vitamins (A, D, E, and K); and for maintaining healthy hair, skin, and nails. Fats also help the body maintain its temperature in cold weather, and they are necessary for healthy nerve function and proper wound healing.

There are several types of fats. *Saturated fats,* which can raise cholesterol levels, are considered unhealthy. They come primarily from animal foods such as beef, pork, lamb, and other fatty meats, as well as butter, whole milk, and whole-milk products. Saturated fat is also found in certain plant foods such as peanuts and coconut, palm, and palm kernel oils. Less than 10 percent of daily calories from should come from saturated fats.

Unsaturated fats, which come primarily from vegetable sources, consist of polyunsaturated and monounsaturated fats, which are both considered "good." They are healthiest type and help to protect your heart and lower blood cholesterol. *Polyunsaturated fats* are found in corn, soybean, and safflower oils, and certain fish, including sardines, anchovies, herring, salmon (choose wild rather than farm raised) and mackerel (avoid king mackerel, however, which is high in mercury). *Monounsaturated fats* are optimal and contained in olive oil and canola oil.

Two important polyunsaturated fats are omega-3 and omega-6. They are considered essential fatty acids (EFAs) because they cannot be manufactured by the body and must be provided through diet or supplements. *Omega-3 fatty acids,* which are present in dark green leafy vegetables, canola oil, flaxseeds, hemp seeds, soybeans, walnuts, and fish, such as tuna, salmon, herring, and sardines, can help lower LDL (bad) cholesterol and reduce the risk of coronary heart disease. They also aid in brain development, blood clotting, and controlling inflammation. Many caregivers are now recommending an omega-3 supplement during the third trimester of pregnancy to enhance fetal brain and eye development. Adequate amounts of omega-3 may also decrease the risk of preterm labor, preeclampsia, and depression. If taking fish oil supplements for omega-3 fats, avoid those derived from fish livers (such as cod liver oil). They contain high levels of retinal vitamin A, which can cause birth defects.

Omega-6 fatty acids also help lower LDL cholesterol and are essential for normal development and function of the brain, adrenal glands, and eyes. They are found in whole grains, eggs, poultry, and most vegetable oils. It is important to consume omega-6 and omega-3 fats in the proper ratio. A diet that is too high in omega-6 and too low in omega-3 can lead to chronic inflammation and a number of other health problems.

It is important to avoid consuming *trans fats*—manufactured fats that increase the shelf life of oils and many foods. They increase cholesterol levels as well as the risk of heart disease. Sources include hydrogenated and partially hydrogenated vegetable oils that are used to make shortening and commercially prepared baked goods, snack foods, fried foods, and margarine.

Reducing the intake of "bad" fats, while increasing consumption of "good" fats is a wise decision for anyone. During pregnancy, however, it is especially important for the health and development of your unborn child.

A Hint for the Mother-to-Be

Make sure your daily diet includes 400 micrograms of folic acid.

Calcium

Calcium is one of the body's most important minerals. It helps build and maintain bones and teeth, aids in blood clotting, regulates the body's use of other minerals, and functions in muscle tone and relaxation. Milk, yogurt, cheese and other dairy products are the best calcium sources. Foods such as broccoli; dark green leafy vegetables, like collard and mustard greens; and some seafood, including sardines, clams, oysters, and shrimp, are other good sources. Because vitamin D helps the body absorb calcium, be sure to get enough of this vitamin, which is found in egg yolks, fortified milk, and dark-meat fish like salmon. Most multivitamins contain the recommended daily amount of vitamin D. Your body also naturally produces vitamin D from sunlight.

The body's calcium absorption increases during pregnancy, especially during the second and third trimesters when babies need this extra calcium for the proper development of teeth and bones. If they don't get the calcium they need from their mother's diet, they will take it from her bones.

Women who have a low dietary intake of calcium during pregnancy need to take supplements to have adequate stores for their babies as well as themselves. Decreased amounts are associated with decreased strength in infant bones. Calcium may also be helpful in moderately decreasing the risk of normal women developing high blood pressure during pregnancy. Taking a calcium supplement is even more important for women who already have high blood pressure. One study stated that pregnant women should have a daily calcium intake of 1,500 to 2,000 milligrams a day.[1] This has been shown to have a substantial benefit to reduce high blood pressure in women who are at risk for developing preeclampsia.[2] Avoid carbonated soft drinks, refined snack foods, and processed meats. They contain phosphorus, which can have a negative effect on the availability of calcium to the body's cells. Continue to eat good sources of calcium.

Iron

Iron is essential for the formation of hemoglobin, which carries oxygen to the tissues and cells. Because of an increase in the body's total blood volume during pregnancy, the ratio of hemoglobin to blood volume decreases in the last trimester. This is normal, although it is sometimes confused with true anemia. During pregnancy, iron intake must be increased to build up the baby's supply while preventing the mother from developing anemia. If necessary, an iron supplement may be recommended along with the prenatal vitamins. Iron supplements, however, can cause constipation and nausea. If you experience these uncomfortable side effects, tell your caregiver. She may recommend another iron supplement that agrees with your digestive system.

Good sources of dietary iron include red meat, egg yolks, shellfish, blackstrap molasses, dried fruit, dried beans and peas, enriched whole grain breads, and fortified ready-to-eat or cooked cereals. Animal liver is another rich source of both iron and protein; however, it is not recommended during pregnancy. Because it functions as one of the body's filtration systems, liver may contain toxins and is best avoided during this time.

Folic Acid, Zinc, and Other Vitamins and Minerals

Vitamins and minerals are essential for good health. Their functions are many, ranging from maintaining the body's energy level and immune system to repairing damaged cells and tissues.

The optimum way to obtain vitamins and minerals is through a diet that includes the water-soluble B-complex and C vitamins, the fat-soluble A, D, E, and K vitamins, and minerals such as calcium and iron. Diet alone, however, may not supply enough of these vital nutrients during pregnancy, so supplements are also recommended. It is important not to rely solely on supplements, which are essentially just that—supplements. They are not adequate substitutes for a healthy diet.

During pregnancy, taking supplemental folic acid—one of the B vitamins—is strongly recommended. Folic acid plays an important role in the production of blood cells. It supports the growth of the placenta as well as the baby, and is vital in the production of DNA as the cells multiply. Low levels can lead to prematurity, low birth weight, and hypertension in pregnancy.[3] The daily consumption of 400 micrograms (but not more than 1,000 micrograms) of folic acid, beginning before pregnancy and continuing through the first trimester, can prevent up to 70 percent of neural tube defects like spina bifida. It is important to begin taking this vitamin prior to pregnancy since neural tube defects occur in the first month, often before the pregnancy is confirmed. There is also evidence that folic acid may prevent cleft lip and palate, and certain heart and limb defects.[4]

Good dietary sources of *folate,* the natural form of folic acid, include oranges, orange juice, strawberries, green leafy vegetables, beets, broccoli, cauliflower, peanuts, and dried beans and legumes. Since 1998, the FDA has required manufacturers to fortify grain products, including breads, flours, cornmeal, pasta, and rice, with folic acid to ensure that women receive this important vitamin. In 2002, the National Center on Birth Defects and Developmental Disabilities reported a 31 percent decrease in the number of babies born with spinal bifida.[5]

Certain women may have an even higher daily requirement of folic acid. This includes those who have already had a baby with a neural tube defect, and women with diabetes, epilepsy, or obesity, as they are already at a higher risk for this type of birth defect. Women with epilepsy who take the anticonvulsant drug valproic acid also need larger doses of folic acid because this drug decreases the body's absorption of folate.

Zinc is an essential mineral that is a basic building block of cells, enhances the immune system, is a component of insulin, and plays an important role in forming healthy sperm and eggs. Low zinc levels are associated with poor fetal growth and development, a long labor, and a prolonged pushing stage before giving birth. Good dietary sources of zinc include red meat, eggs, seafood, fortified cereals, and, to a lesser degree, legumes, nuts, and whole grains. The amount of zinc contained in prenatal vitamins is sufficient. Additional supplements are not necessary.

Some women who experience morning sickness or periods of nausea and vomiting have found relief by taking supplemental vitamin B$_6$ (pyridoxine) and eating foods that are rich in this vitamin. Chicken, pork, salmon, tuna, and eggs are among the best vitamin B$_6$ sources. Others include carrots, cabbage, cantaloupe, bananas, soybeans, brown rice, oat bran, fortified cereals, and soy-based meat substitutes. Speak to your caregiver before taking B$_6$ supplements to treat morning sickness and check to see how much is included in your prenatal vitamins. The typical dosage for treating morning sickness is 10 to 25 milligrams three times a day.[6]

Not all vitamins are safe when taken in higher amounts than the recommended dosage. Extra vitamin A, for example, may cause birth defects if taken in early pregnancy. A study published in *The New England Journal of Medicine* in 1995 cautions that more than 10,000 international units (IUs) of vitamin A each day may be dangerous to the fetus. The problems involve malformations of the face, head, heart, or nervous system.[7] Most prenatal vitamins contain 4,000 IUs of vitamin A. Some multivitamins, especially those sold in health food stores, contain higher levels; and vitamin A capsules may have as much as 25,000 IUs. It is also recommended that women be careful not to combine vitamin supplements with large servings of liver, which is high in vitamin A, or with vitamin-enriched cereals, which may contain 5,000 units of vitamin A per bowl. Fish oil derived from livers, such as cod liver oil, also contains very high levels of vitamin A and should not be taken during pregnancy.

High protein supplements should also be avoided. Although they may have a small benefit by increasing weight in small babies born full term, they do not reduce the rate of preterm births.[8] In multiple trials, although it was found that balanced high protein/energy supplements may increase a mother's energy level, isocaloric protein (high protein without energy supplements) for healthy or overweight women (to limit calories) have shown no benefit to mothers or babies and may potentially be harmful.[9]

Taking Prenatal Vitamins and Supplements

Prenatal vitamins do not contain all of the necessary ingredients for a developing baby, but they can ensure that you get the required amounts of vitamins and minerals if they are lacking in your diet. If your doctor or midwife is concerned about your diet, she may encourage you to take additional supplements, such as calcium or iron.

Some women have difficulty taking prenatal vitamins because they cause nausea or constipation. If you are experiencing this discomfort, try taking the vitamins with meals. If this doesn't seem to help, tell your caregiver, who can recommend an alternative that you may be able to tolerate better.

If you are anemic, iron supplements may be prescribed. Take them on an empty stomach or with orange juice, as vitamin C increases the absorption of iron. Do not take them with milk, tea, coffee, or a calcium supplement, which can interfere with iron absorption.

NUTRITIONAL CHANGES DURING PREGNANCY

As your pregnancy progresses, the nutritional demands made on your body increase. A look at these growing needs by trimester provides further insight.

First Trimester

During the early weeks of pregnancy, there is a good chance that you are not aware of the baby growing within you. For this reason, you should begin following a healthy diet and taking folic acid even before you become pregnant. Once your pregnancy is confirmed, be sure to continue eating nutritious foods and taking supplemental folic acid. If you experience morning sickness, you may not have much of a desire to eat; however, you must try your best to eat properly. It's important. With the exception of added folic acid, your dietary nutritional requirements at this time are the same as those for nonpregnant women.

A number of natural remedies have been helpful in treating morning sickness, which most commonly occurs during the first trimester. A vitamin B_6 deficiency is believed to be one possible cause of this condition. As mentioned in the previous section, increasing your vitamin B_6 intake (through both foods and supplements) can be effective. Low blood sugar is believed to be another cause of morning sickness. It commonly occurs in the morning after not eating all night. Eating a few crackers or some dry toast before getting out of bed has been known to help. To avoid nausea during the day, try not to go for long periods without eating. Other natural remedies for treating morning sickness are found in the margin at right.

If natural remedies do not seem to help, and nausea and vomiting are becoming excessive and persistent, contact your doctor. Extreme morning sickness can cause dehydration, which can be harmful to both you and the baby. In such severe cases, medication can be prescribed. Gratefully, morning sickness usually disappears by the fourth month.

Second Trimester

Nutritional needs increase during the second trimester, when you should begin consuming additional calories, vitamins, and minerals as instructed by your doctor. Although the baby will put on very little weight during this time, your body will start to undergo some noticeable changes. You will begin to lay down a store of fat that your body will utilize during lactation, and your uterus and breasts will begin to enlarge. During this trimester, the volume of amniotic fluid will increase, the placenta will grow in size, and your blood volume will begin to expand. Therefore, increased protein and fluid intakes are essential.

Third Trimester

During the last trimester, the baby will gain weight rapidly. It is important to continue taking in a sufficient amount of calories and protein to ensure optimum development of the baby's brain and body, which grows the most during the last two months. It is also the time that the baby's liver builds up iron stores. Continue following the pregnancy diet recommendations during this time (and beyond, if you breastfeed). Do not try to minimize your weight gain by dieting during the last trimester or fasting before office-visit weigh-ins.

Natural Remedies for Morning Sickness

If you suffer from morning sickness, consider the following suggestions:

✓ Increase your intake of vitamin B_6 through supplements or foods.

✓ Eat foods that contain ginger, such as candy and cookies. Drink real ginger ale (be sure ginger is included on the ingredient label).

✓ Sip seltzer or sparkling water throughout the day.

✓ Eat dry toast or crackers before rising in the morning.

✓ Eat frequent high-protein snacks during the day and at bedtime.

✓ Take prenatal vitamins with meals, not on an empty stomach.

✓ Ask your doctor to prescribe different prenatal vitamins.

✓ Avoid greasy, fried, or highly spiced foods.

✓ Cut a slice of lemon and inhale the fragrance.

✓ Wear "acupressure" wristbands that are designed to prevent motion sickness by applying pressure to certain areas of the wrist. (They are sold in dive shops and sporting goods stores.)

✓ Try acupuncture.

Your caregiver may recommend other natural remedies.

If you experience increased swelling as your due date approaches, try adding more protein to your diet. In rare cases, swelling may put pressure on the nerves in the wrist, resulting in carpal tunnel syndrome. Tingling, numbness, and/or pain in the hands and fingers are symptoms of this condition. Additional vitamin B_6 may also help relieve this problem or prevent its further development. A hand splint may be necessary to provide relief. The symptoms of carpal tunnel syndrome will gradually subside following delivery.

DIETARY GUIDELINES

In 2005, in an effort to provide a science-based program that promotes health and reduces the risk for major chronic illnesses, the United States Department of Agriculture (USDA) established new dietary guidelines. These guidelines support a well-rounded diet that encompasses a variety of foods from different food groups, as well as a daily exercise regimen. (See Chapter 6 for information on exercise during pregnancy.) These dietary guidelines have been adapted for average pregnant women to help them meet their increasing nutritional needs, as well as those of their developing babies. Daily recommendations are as follows:

My Personal Dietary Pyramid

For more specific dietary guidelines during pregnancy and breastfeeding—based upon your particular age, height, weight, and other factors—visit the following USDA website: *www.MyPyramid.gov/ MyPyramidmoms/index.html*

Food Category	Daily Servings
Fats and sweets	2 servings (maximum)
Fruit	4 servings
Grain products (breads, cereals, pasta, rice)	7 to 8 servings
Milk and other dairy products	3 servings
Protein (meat, fish, poultry, eggs, beans/legumes, nuts, seeds)	6 to $6\frac{1}{2}$ servings
Vegetables	6 servings

To accurately follow these guidelines, it is important to understand serving sizes. Often what constitutes a typical helping is actually more or less than one serving. See "Know Your Servings" on page 93.

When choosing foods and beverages, it is important to consume nutrient-dense foods and limit the intake of saturated and trans fats, cholesterol, added sugars, salt, and alcohol.[10] Pregnant women should choose foods that are high in or fortified with iron. Foods that are fortified with B vitamins are also important. Eating iron-rich foods along with foods or beverages that are high in vitamin C (oranges, orange juice, tomato juice) will help with the absorption of iron.

Select foods and beverages that provide the most nutrition for the fewest calories. For example, opt for reduced-fat milk rather than whole, which has the same amount of calcium but a significantly higher calorie count. (See Table 5.2 on page 106.) Preparation methods can also alter calorie content, but not the nutritional value. Baking or grilling, for instance, is a healthy alternative to frying.

Be aware that many foods, such as ground beef, whole milk, and tender steaks, contain hidden fat; the skin of chicken and turkey have a high fat content as well. Added sugar is found in many sweetened beverages, desserts, syrups, and canned fruits. Keep added fats, oils, and sugar to a minimum, especially if you are putting on more weight than is recommended.

Know Your Servings

The following information presents serving information for various types of food. It will help you make proper dietary choices every day.

Fats and Sweets

- Butter, margarine, oil = 1 tablespoon
- Limit sweeteners like sugar and honey, and sweets such as candy and pastries. They offer no nutritional benefit, only calories.

Use additional fats sparingly. Consider them discretionary calories (see page 94).

Fruit

- Whole piece (apples, pears, etc.) = 1 medium
- Melon = 1 wedge (4-x-8-inches)
- Fresh berries = 1 cup
- Canned fruit = $1/2$ cup
- Dried fruit = $1/4$ cup
- Juice = $3/4$ cup

Opt for fresh fruits over canned and dried varieties, which often contain added sugar and extra calories.

Grain Products (bread, cereal, rice, pasta)

- Bread = 1 average slice
- Cooked cereal = $1/2$ cup
- Ready-to-eat cereal = 1 ounce
- Cooked rice = $1/2$ cup
- Cooked pasta = $1/2$ cup

Choose whole grains (whole wheat, rye, whole grain oatmeal, brown rice) rather than refined (white bread, enriched pasta, white rice) for better nutrition. At least half of the grains eaten every day should be whole grain varieties; the rest can come from enriched products.

Milk and Other Dairy Products

- Milk = 1 cup
- Yogurt = 1 cup
- Cheese = $1 1/2$ to 2 ounces

Try to choose fat-free or low-fat products. (Calcium-fortified soymilk is included in this category.) High-fat ice cream and dairy desserts should be eaten sparingly due to their fat and sugar content.

Protein (meat, fish, poultry, eggs, beans/legumes, nuts, seeds)

- Cooked lean meat, poultry, and fish = 1 ounce (a "typical" portion of these foods is 3 ounces, which is equivalent to three 1-ounce servings)
- Nuts = $1/3$ cup or $1 1/2$ ounces
- Seeds = 2 tablespoons or $1/2$ ounce

The following portions are equal to 1 ounce of meat:

- Cooked dry beans/legumes = $1/2$ cup
- Eggs = 1 large
- Nut butters = 2 tablespoons

When choosing meats, always opt for lean cuts.

Vegetables

- Raw = $1/2$ cup
- Cooked = $1/2$ cup
- Leafy greens = 1 cup (raw or cooked)

Include a variety of vegetables—dark green (broccoli, spinach, collards, romaine), deep yellow (carrots, sweet potatoes, pumpkin, squash), and starches (white potatoes, corn, green peas).

DAILY NUTRITIONAL NEEDS

The chart below will help you keep track of your daily dietary intake to ensure that you are meeting the recommended nutritional requirements.

Each week, make a copy of this chart, keep it in a convenient location, and check off the boxes as you fill each requirement.

	Dairy Products 3 servings	Protein/Meats 6 to 6½ servings	Fruits 4 servings	Vegetables 6 servings	Grain Products 7 to 8 servings	Fats/Sweets Sparingly
Sunday	☐☐☐	☐☐☐☐☐☐	☐☐☐☐	☐☐☐☐☐☐	☐☐☐☐☐☐☐	☐☐
Monday	☐☐☐	☐☐☐☐☐☐	☐☐☐☐	☐☐☐☐☐☐	☐☐☐☐☐☐☐	☐☐
Tuesday	☐☐☐	☐☐☐☐☐☐	☐☐☐☐	☐☐☐☐☐☐	☐☐☐☐☐☐☐	☐☐
Wednesday	☐☐☐	☐☐☐☐☐☐	☐☐☐☐	☐☐☐☐☐☐	☐☐☐☐☐☐☐	☐☐
Thursday	☐☐☐	☐☐☐☐☐☐	☐☐☐☐	☐☐☐☐☐☐	☐☐☐☐☐☐☐	☐☐
Friday	☐☐☐	☐☐☐☐☐☐	☐☐☐☐	☐☐☐☐☐☐	☐☐☐☐☐☐☐	☐☐
Saturday	☐☐☐	☐☐☐☐☐☐	☐☐☐☐	☐☐☐☐☐☐	☐☐☐☐☐☐☐	☐☐

Discretionary Calories

The food servings presented in the previous section are in their nutrient-dense, lean, or low-fat forms without any added sugars. Within the 2,100 to 2,500 calorie allowance for pregnant women, approximately 300 calories are considered discretionary. *Discretionary calories* are those added calories that do not provide any nutritional value to the food. Food preparation methods and food choices will determine how you use your discretionary calories.

For example, when the USDA gives allowances for a 2,100-calorie diet, they are counting the calories in nonfat milk. If you choose whole milk, those extra calories need to be counted. Cheese and even low-fat milk and milk products contain fat, which is counted as part of the discretionary calories. The servings of meat are for very lean cuts with no added fat for cooking. A piece of meat that has a higher fat content, such as ground beef or a tender steak with marbling, adds additional calories without nutritional value. These calories are considered discretionary as well.

Servings of grain products should be whole grain. Avoid sweetened cereals, muffins, or other refined grain products, which typically contain added sugars and/or added fat, and, therefore, added calories. Vegetables should be either raw or cooked without fat. They do not include foods such as French fries. The fruit choices do not include canned varieties or juices that contain added sugars. The fats included in the serving guidelines are amounts that meet essential fatty acid needs and also contribute toward vitamin E needs.

Keeping Track

Keeping track of what you eat every day and making sure that you are consuming the right number of servings can be difficult. The Daily Nutritional Needs chart above is designed to help you keep track of your daily food intake. Make a copy of the chart and check off the boxes as you fulfill each requirement.

NUTRITIONAL HINTS

There are a number of helpful guidelines you can follow to make the best dietary choices during pregnancy. For instance, try to choose fresh foods over canned or frozen varieties, and prepare your meals from scratch rather than eating over-processed prepared or ready-to-eat foods. Many of these "meals of convenience" are also high in fat, sugar, and sodium. When possible, eat foods, such as fruits, in their natural state. This means, for example, it is better to eat an apple rather than drink a glass of apple juice. Making homemade meals instead of ordering take-out or eating in restaurants gives you control over how the food is prepared as well as portion size. Portions served in restaurants are often oversized and high in fat and salt. When dining out, if you are presented with a large plate of food, eat only part of the meal and take the remainder home. Take-out food can be divided into correct portions and enjoyed for more than one meal.

When preparing meals, avoid frying foods or using large amounts of fat, which increases calories. When using fats, choose polyunsaturated vegetable oils or monoun-saturated varieties, such as olive or canola oil. They are healthier choices than butter, margarine, or other hydrogenated products.

All packaged foods have a "Nutrition Facts" label that lists serving size, calories, and the amount of fat, cholesterol, sodium, carbohydrates, and protein the product contains. It also provides the product's percentage of daily vitamin requirements. These values are based on a 2,000-calorie diet. Pregnant women need additional iron and calcium. Many processed foods are now enriched and can provide additional calcium, iron, folic acid, and other important vitamins and minerals. Be sure to read labels.

Get in the habit of fortifying almost everything you cook. You can do this by adding products like wheat germ or brewer's yeast to many foods. Wheat germ—the finely milled center of the wheat kernel—contains high concentrations of protein, vitamin B_1 (thiamine), vitamin E, and iron. Versatile and nutritious, it can be added to almost any dish. To fortify cakes, muffins, and pancakes, add about a half cup of wheat germ to a regular-size box of mix or an average recipe. To bolster the nutritional content of burgers, meat loaf, or most other ground meat recipes, include a half cup of wheat germ for every pound of meat. Wheat germ, which can be enjoyed plain or toasted, also makes a great topping for casseroles. Try mixing some with peanut butter for a nutritious sandwich spread. Top it with milk for a crunchy, nut-like cereal, or add it to cooked or cold cereal. Wheat germ can be used in almost any cookie recipe in addition to or in place of nuts. Let your imagination create new uses for this nutritional powerhouse.

You can also boost the nutritional value of many foods by adding brewer's yeast—a rich source of protein and B-complex vitamins. Because of its somewhat strong flavor, brewer's yeast is commonly added to recipes that require cooking, which seems to make its taste milder. When baking cookies, add about one tablespoon to an average-sized batch. You can also add brewer's yeast to bread dough, and cake and pancake batters. And for instant energy, stir one to two tablespoons into twelve ounces of vegetable or fruit juice. Readily available in health food stores, brewer's yeast comes in different forms. The powdered variety is the strongest-tasting and most nutritious, while the instant flakes dissolve better and are milder in taste. Tablets are also available, but this is a weak form, and requires huge quantities to be of value. Unflavored varieties are also available.

Infants Cultivate Their Taste Preferences

A study found that six-month-old infants preferred cereal prepared with carrot juice as compared to water when their mother's drank carrot juice either during pregnancy or during breastfeeding. Infants in a third group whose mother's drank only water showed no preference.

24-HOUR DIETARY RECALL CHART

During pregnancy, it can be difficult to know if you are getting the right amount of calories, protein, calcium, and iron from your daily diet—recommended amounts are found at the top of each column. To help you keep track, make copies of this chart and use one each day to write down the foods and beverages you consume. Use Table 5.2, beginning on page 106, to determine each food's protein, calcium, iron, and calorie counts.

Food / Drink	Protein Count (71 gms)	Calcium Count (1,000–1,300 mgs)	Iron Count (27 mgs)	Calorie Count (2,100–2,500)

Keep in mind that sweeteners—granulated sugar, honey, brown sugar—should have a limited place in your diet. Honey is a natural sweetener that contains vitamins, minerals, and antioxidants, making it a more nutritious choice than processed white table sugar. However, the best way to obtain sugar is by consuming fruits, vegetables, and milk. A word of warning: *Do not* give raw honey to a baby under one year of age (never dip a pacifier in honey to encourage the baby to accept it). Spores may be present in the honey that can cause the baby to develop infantile botulism.

Cooking nutritionally is a challenge, but it can also be fun. There are plenty of cookbooks and Internet sites that offer nutritionally superior recipes that are delicious and easy-to-prepare. Get in the habit of bolstering the nutritional value of almost everything you cook. For example, doctor up a pizza with a sprinkling of wheat germ, fresh tomato slices, freshly cooked ground beef, and some extra cheese.

If your family has well-established but poor eating habits, make dietary changes slowly. You will neither reach your nutritional goals nor have a happy family if you try to change a lifetime of eating habits in one week. Make only one change at a time—and do not mention it! For instance, replace half of the ground beef in your favorite meat loaf recipe with leaner ground turkey. Instead of using full-fat cheese in your casseroles, use reduced-fat varieties. Unless you tell them, your family won't notice the change. Gradually, as the weeks turn into months, you will all be eating—and enjoying—truly nutritious meals. The highly refined and valueless foods will have fallen by the wayside, forgotten and not missed.

24-HOUR DIET RECALL

One way to determine if you are eating well is through a 24-hour diet recall. In addition to helping you keep track of your calorie count, this will help you focus on your intake of specific important nutrients. The average pregnant woman needs to eat a daily diet that contains 2,100 to 2,500 calories. She also needs to eat foods that are high in protein, calcium, and iron. According to the USDA's Dietary Reference Intakes (DRIs)[11] —an updated version of the Recommended Dietary Allowances (RDAs)—pregnant women require daily amounts of the following:

- **Calcium**: 1,000 to 1,300 milligrams (fourteen to eighteen year olds need 1,300)
- **Protein**: 71 grams   ■ **Iron**: 27 milligrams   ■ **Calories**: 2,100 to 2,500

To make sure you are eating properly and getting sufficient dietary nutrients, make a copy of the chart at left and use it to write down everything you eat and drink during the day (a 24-hour period). Refer to the food listing in Table 5.2, beginning on page 106, to find the protein, calcium, iron, and calorie counts for each food you list, and add up the totals at the end of the day. (For packaged food items that are not listed in the table, check the "Nutrition Facts" panel on packages.) The totals should come close to the daily recommended amounts. Keep in mind that it is very difficult to obtain sufficient iron through dietary methods alone. Your prenatal vitamins contain supplemental iron and a small amount of calcium. They do not, however, contain protein, which comes primarily from diet. It is, therefore, important to eat a sufficient amount of protein every day. If you discover that you are deficient in your consumption of a protein or a certain nutrient, refer back to Table 5.2 to find foods that contain high amounts.

Let's say that . .

One night after dinner, you tally up your food counts and notice that you need additional protein and calcium. Having a cup of yogurt or some nuts would be a better snack choice than a piece of fruit.

VEGETARIAN DIET

The term *vegetarian* loosely refers to people who avoid eating red meat, poultry, and products containing these foods. Their dietary nutrition comes primarily from fruits, vegetables, legumes, and grains. Although all vegetarians eliminate red meat from their diets, they also follow different dietary guidelines. Depending on their eating practices, vegetarians fall into various categories—lacto, ovo, lacto-ovo, nouveau, and vegan. *Lacto vegetarians* eat dairy products but not eggs; conversely, *ovo vegetarians* eat eggs but avoid dairy products. *Lacto-ovo vegetarians* eat both eggs and dairy products, while *vegans* follow a strict plant-based diet. *Nouveau vegetarians* avoid red meat and poultry, but consume fish, eggs, and dairy products. Vegetarians who follow a macrobiotic diet eat the same plant-based foods as vegans, although they also include an occasional small amount of fish.

Eating enough protein each day is critical during pregnancy. Most expectant mothers get the bulk of their protein from meat, milk, cheese, and eggs. Because these foods contain all of the essential amino acids (the building blocks of protein) they are considered "complete" proteins. Pregnant women who follow a vegetarian diet and avoid these foods must turn to other protein sources, such as whole grains, rice, corn, beans, legumes, oatmeal, peas, peanut butter, and soy foods. These "incomplete" protein foods contain some but not all of the essential amino acids. This means, in order to get complete proteins, vegetarians must eat a variety of foods from the following categories—legumes, nuts and seeds, and grain products—every day. At one time, it was believed that these foods had to be eaten in a certain combination during each meal, but research has shown that they can be eaten any time throughout the day.[12] (See "Creating Complete Proteins" on page 99.)

Because vegetarians may be deficient in vitamin B_{12}, vitamin D, and zinc, it is important for them to get these nutrients through supplements during pregnancy. Lacto-ovo vegetarians can get adequate vitamin B_{12} if they consume dairy foods and eggs on a regular basis. Vitamin D can be obtained from exposure to the sun (your body naturally produces this vitamin from sunlight) and from eating foods that are fortified with vitamin D. Women who live in sunless climates or who receive little sun exposure due to clothing or use of sunscreen are more susceptible to vitamin D deficiency. Women with dark skin are also less likely to absorb vitamin D.

Before discussing the iron and calcium needs of vegetarians during pregnancy, it's important to understand the term *bioavailability*. This refers to the capacity of a substance (vitamin, mineral, chemical, drug, etc) for absorption and utilization by the body. In other words, it is the amount of the substance that the body can use.

The iron in plants is less bioavailable than the iron in animal products, so vegetarians have a higher need for iron. In addition to taking supplements, pregnant women should increase their consumption of iron-rich foods. Good sources include soybeans and soy products; legumes; nuts, such as cashews and almonds; pumpkin, squash, and sunflower seeds; fortified bread; oatmeal; cream of wheat; dried fruit; and blackstrap molasses. Be aware that calcium, certain teas, coffee, and cocoa can inhibit iron absorption, while vitamin C can enhance it.

Calcium in the vegetarian diet can be obtained from many plant foods, soy foods, and foods that are calcium-fortified, such as soymilk, Almond Breeze, Rice Dream, fruit juices, tomato juice, and breakfast cereals. Foods such as broccoli, Napa cabbage, bok choy, collards, kale, okra, and turnip greens have a higher calcium bioavailability (49 to 61 percent) than calcium-set tofu, and calcium-fortified cow's milk and fruit juices (31 to 32 percent). Fortified soymilk, sesame seeds, almonds, and red and white beans have the least calcium bioavailability (21 to 24 percent).[13] Even though spinach, beet greens, and Swiss chard have a high calcium content, the calcium is not a good bioavailable source. Other factors that enhance calcium absorption are protein and an adequate intake of vitamin D.

Daily Food Guide for Vegetarians

If you follow a vegetarian diet, base your meals on the Daily Nutritional Needs chart on page 94. You will, of course, have to make some adaptations according to your personal food choices. Substitute nondairy calcium products for milk and other dairy products, and choose meat substitutes, dry beans, nuts, and seeds for protein. And be sure to check the information on serving sizes found on page 93. To determine if you are getting adequate intakes of protein, calcium and iron, keep track of what you eat through 24-hour recalls (see page 97).

Creating Complete Proteins

If you follow a vegetarian diet, combine foods from each of the following categories every day. This will ensure that you are consuming complete proteins, which are necessary for good nutrition. For additional food suggestions (and serving sizes), see Table 5.2 beginning on page 106.

LEGUMES AND SOY PRODUCTS

Cooked varieties (¹/₂ cup)

Black beans	Kidney beans	Soybeans
Chickpeas/garbanzo beans	Lentils (1 ounce)	Split peas
Great Northern, navy, and other white bean varieties	Lima beans	Tofu/soybean curd
	Pinto beans	

NUTS AND SEEDS

Nuts (¹/₄ cup), Seeds (¹/₄ cup), Butters (2 tablespoons)

Almonds	Peanuts	Sesame tahini
Cashews	Pumpkin seeds	Sunflower seeds
Peanut butter	Squash seeds	

GRAINS AND GRAIN PRODUCTS

Breads (1 slice), Ready-to-Eat Cereals (¹/₂ cup), Grains (¹/₂ cup cooked)

Barley	Oatmeal	Wheat germ (2 tablespoons)
Bulgur	Pasta, soy or whole wheat	Whole wheat or white enriched bread
Cereal, ready to eat	Rice, brown or wild	
Cream of wheat		

FOODS TO AVOID DURING PREGNANCY

It is very important to stay away from a number of foods and beverages that you may have enjoyed before becoming pregnant. These foods may contain harmful bacteria such as listeria, salmonella, and E. coli; parasites like Toxoplasma gondii; or dangerous levels of environmental pollutants like mercury. Serious health risks for both mother and baby can result. (Details of these harmful food elements are presented in Chapter 4.)

Many of the following foods should be avoided altogether, while others may be consumed in limited amounts only.

Unpasteurized Foods and Beverages

To rid raw milk of bacteria, especially listeria, it goes through a pasteurization process. Consuming unpasteurized milk can cause *listeriosis*, a serious infection that can result in miscarriage. A number of foods, particularly soft cheeses, are made with unpasteurized milk and may contain listeria. For this reason, it is important to avoid the following varieties: feta, goat, Brie, Camembert, blue and other blue-veined varieties, and the Mexican cheeses queso freso and queso blanco.

Soft cheeses made with pasteurized milk are safe to eat. Also safe are firm varieties like cheddar, semi-soft types such as mozzarella, pasteurized processed cheese slices and spreads, cream cheese, and cottage cheese.

Undercooked Meats and Seafood

Raw or undercooked meats and fish (particularly sushi and shellfish), can result in food-borne illnesses caused by salmonella or E.coli bacteria. Toxoplasmosis, caused by the *Toxoplasma gondii* parasite, is another danger. In addition to causing nausea and diarrhea, these illnesses are associated with preterm birth and miscarriage.

Always take precautions when preparing meat. Make sure steak and other red meats reach an internal temperature of 170°F. This includes pork, as well as hamburgers, meat loaves, and other ground beef dishes, which should be cooked until no pink remains. The internal temperature of poultry must reach 185°F.

Processed Meats and Spreads

Hot dogs and deli meats may be contaminated with listeria. They, however, are safe to eat during pregnancy as long as they are cooked until steaming. Because listeria has also been found in refrigerated pâtés and other meat spreads, as well as refrigerated smoked fish, choose only canned or shelf-safe varieties of these foods.

Raw Eggs

Any dish that contains raw eggs can contain salmonella bacteria and result in food poisoning. Severe cases can stress the baby and even cause preterm delivery. Some types of mayonnaise, homemade ice cream, custard, Caesar salad dressing, and Hollandaise sauce may contain raw eggs. When dining out, be sure to ask before ordering these items. When commercially prepared, these products are made with cooked eggs and are safe to eat. When buying eggnog, be sure it is pasteurized, and don't be tempted to sample even just a little of your uncooked cookie dough.

Certain Fish

Fish is a good source of omega-3 fatty acids, which are important for the vision and brain development of the baby. Certain varieties, however, should be avoided because they are characteristically high in methyl mercury, which can result in neurological damage. In 2004, the FDA and the EPA issued a joint consumer advisory about mercury levels in fish and shellfish. In order to minimize mercury exposure, women who may become pregnant, women who are pregnant, nursing mothers, and young children should adhere to the following advice:

■ Do not eat shark, swordfish, king mackerel, or tilefish, which are especially high in mercury.

■ Eat up to 12 ounces (two average portions) a week of fish and/or shellfish, such as shrimp, canned light tuna, salmon, pollock, and catfish. These varieties are characteristically lower in mercury. Albacore (white) tuna has more mercury than canned light tuna—one serving a week is recommended.

■ Check local advisories about the safety of fish caught in local waters, which may be contaminated with bacteria, mercury, or harmful PCBs. If no advisory is given, eat only one portion per week, and do not eat any other fish.

Mercury ingestion in children can impair motor function, learning capacity, vision, and memory, and cause a variety of other symptoms related to neurological damage. According to Kathryn Mahaffey, division director in the EPA's Office of Prevention, Pesticides, and Toxic Substances, umbilical cord blood has higher concentrations of mercury than the mother's blood. During pregnancy, choose fish with lower mercury levels but higher levels of omega-3 fatty acids. Good choices include Sockeye salmon and herring. Also choose wild salmon rather than farm-raised varieties. A report from the Environmental Working Group, a Washington DC environmental research organization, stated that farm-raised salmon had significantly higher levels of PCBs and dioxins than salmon caught in the wild. They also had less omega-3 fatty acids. Limiting intake of farm-raised salmon and eating a variety of fish is the safest option.[14]

Liver

Although liver is a good source of protein and iron, most experts advise against eating it during pregnancy. There is concern because one function of this organ is to detoxify the blood, which means it may contain toxins or pesticides that may be harmful to the fetus. Liver also contains high amounts of the retinol form of vitamin A, which can be toxic.

Unwashed Vegetables

The parasite that causes toxoplasmosis may be present in soil. Soil may also be contaminated with E. coli bacteria. For these reasons it is very important to wash raw fruits and vegetables—which may have been grown in contaminated soil—before eating them. It is also recommended to peel away and discard the outer leaves of cabbage and lettuce varieties before eating.

Alcohol

When an expectant mother drinks a glass of wine or any other alcoholic beverage, her baby does also. The alcohol passes through the placenta and robs the baby of oxygen and important nutrients for proper development. No amount is safe during pregnancy. Depending on the amount and timing, alcohol consumption during pregnancy can lead to fetal alcohol spectrum disorders. The most serious of these disorders is *fetal alcohol syndrome,* characterized by abnormal facial features, problems of the central nervous system, and learning disabilities. Alcohol should also be limited during breastfeeding.

Artificial Sweeteners

The FDA has approved the use of artificial sweeteners, including aspartame (Equal, NutraSweet) and sucralose (Splenda) for use during pregnancy. According to extensive studies, these sweeteners have not shown any detrimental effects to the developing baby. However, since most products that contain artificial sweeteners are low in food value, their intake should be limited. Women with phenylketonuria (PKU), a rare metabolic disorder in which the person is unable to metabolize phenylalanine (an ingredient in aspartame), should not consume aspartame because it will place her fetus at risk if he inherits this disorder. (See "Phenylketonuria" on page 104.)

The FDA also considers saccharin (Sweet'n Low) to be safe for the general public. Earlier studies had indicated that there was a link between saccharin and bladder cancer, but the National Toxicology program later dismissed this claim.

Caffeine

Caffeine is a stimulant that is present in coffee, tea, soft drinks, chocolate, and some over-the-counter medications. While a moderate intake of caffeine does not seem to be harmful to the developing fetus, it *can* affect the baby's heart rate and movement. Caffeine is, however, a diuretic, which eliminates fluids from the body resulting in water/calcium loss. Water, juice, and milk are preferred beverages.

Although limiting caffeine is recommended, as a general rule, do not exceed more than 300 milligrams per day. Table 5.1 on page 103 lists the amount of caffeine contained in a number of common food and beverage sources. This information will help you keep track of your caffeine consumption. As you can see, a number of items contain a "range" of caffeine. This is due to a number of factors, including the variety of coffee or tea, how finely the product is ground, and the preparation methods used.

SPECIAL DIETARY CONCERNS

Many pregnant women have medical conditions or other problems that may affect their diet during this time. As proper nutritional intake is critical, be sure to make the necessary adjustments if you have any of the following conditions.

Milk Allergies and Lactose Intolerance

People with a milk allergy react to one or more of the proteins found in milk. This is different from those who are lactose intolerant. Lactose intolerance is characterized by

TABLE 5.1. CAFFEINE LEVELS IN COMMON FOODS AND BEVERAGES

Source	Serving Size	Caffeine (mgs)
Coffee		
Coffee, decaffeinated, brewed	5 ounces	3
Coffee, drip method	8 ounces	96–288
Coffee, percolator method	8 ounces	64–272
Coffee, instant prepared	8 ounces	48–92
Cappuccino, instant	8 ounces	25–102
Espresso	1 ounce	90
Tea		
Brewed, major US brands	8 ounces	33–144
Brewed, imported brands	8 ounces	40–176
Instant prepared	8 ounces	40–80
Iced, bottled	16 ounces	15–100
Green	8 ounces	40
Other Beverages		
Caffeinated soft drinks, carbonated	12 ounces	30–60
Caffeinated water	16 ounces	20–125
Cocoa, prepared	8 ounces	6–42
Chocolate milk	8 ounces	2–7
Energy drink (Red Bull)	8 ounces	80
Ice Cream		
Cappuccino flavored	1 cup	8–15
Coffee flavored	1 cup	40–85
Chocolate flavored	1 cup	4–10
Chocolate		
Milk chocolate	1 ounce	1–15
Dark chocolate, semi sweet	1 ounce	5–35
Baker's chocolate	1 ounce	26
Chocolate flavored syrup	1 ounce	4
Drugs		
Excedrin Migraine	1 tablet	65
No Doze, Vivarin	1 tablet	200

Make Your Own Peanut Butter

Naturally cholesterol-free, peanuts are packed with protein and vitamins, and are a good source folate. When buying peanut butter, avoid commercial brands, which often contain too much salt, sugar, extra (often unhealthy) fat, and other additives. Instead, purchase freshly ground or natural peanut butter, which is available in health food stores and some supermarkets. Better yet, try your hand at making your own. It's fun and easy! The following recipe yields about 1½ cups.

2 cups roasted peanuts

½ teaspoon sea salt*

2 tablespoons peanut, canola, or other vegetable oil

*Omit if using salted peanuts.

1. Place the peanuts and salt in a food processor, blender, or nut grinder. Process until the nuts are finely ground.

2. Add the oil and continue processing until the mixture reaches the desired degree of smoothness. Add more oil if necessary.

3. For chunky-style peanut butter, stir in ½ cup chopped roasted peanuts.

4. Use immediately, or cover tightly and store in the refrigerator.

the inability to digest milk products properly. It is caused by the inactivity or absence of the lactase enzyme. Pregnant women with either of these conditions must rely on nondairy sources to obtain calcium. Foods such as broccoli; dark green leafy vegetables like collard and mustard greens; and some seafood, including sardines, clams, oysters, and shrimp, are good calcium sources, as are calcium-fortified beverages.

Phenylketonuria

Phenylketonuria (PKU) is a genetic metabolic disorder. Those with this condition are unable to metabolize phenylalanine, an amino acid. A buildup of phenylalanine in the brain causes mental retardation. All babies are screened for PKU when they are infants. If they have it, a special diet is necessary, especially during infancy and childhood, to prevent mental deficiency. A diet low in phenylalanine is recommended throughout life, but many people do not follow it as they mature. High-protein foods, such as meat, fish, poultry, eggs, cheese, milk, dried beans, and peas should be avoided. Pregnant women with this condition must adhere to a strict low phenylalanine diet to prevent damage to the fetus if the disorder is inherited.

Peanut Allergies

Peanut allergies affect about 1 percent of the country's population. One out of every four affected people experiences severe reactions, including respiratory distress. It has been suggested that some children with this reaction to peanuts were sensitized in utero. Although research on fetal sensitization is limited, it is believed that a fetus can, in fact, be exposed to peanut and other food allergens. And if the mother has a food allergy or a family history of allergies, there is an increased chance that the fetus will develop an allergy as well.

Because of this, expectant mothers who fit this profile should avoid eating peanuts. And be aware that peanuts are found in trace amounts in a wide variety of packaged products. Read food labels carefully. Also, when dining out, consider how the food is prepared. Some restaurants, particularly Thai and Asian, are known for using peanuts and peanut oil in their dishes.

Eating Disorders

Pregnant women who have an eating disorder such as anorexia or bulimia may have an especially difficult time dealing with the weight they need to gain. They may limit their food intake, which will deprive the baby of much-needed nutrition. Research indicates that eating disorders are associated with premature birth and newborns with low birth weight. Nutritional counseling, as well as professional psychological guidance, is very important for expectant mothers with eating disorders.

Crohn's Disease

Women with Crohn's disease or irritable bowel syndrome may have difficulty absorbing nutrients. They are at risk for low weight gain and, in severe cases, zinc deficiency, which is characterized by hair loss, diarrhea, and loss of appetite. Increased zinc supplements are often recommended. It is important for women who are taking the drug sulfasalazine for Crohn's disease to increase their folic acid intake as this drug reduces folic acid absorption. Most women with Crohn's disease have normal pregnancies and healthy babies.

Pica

Pregnant women often have unusual food cravings. Those who experience pica, however, crave and ingest bizarre often nonfood items, such as laundry starch, detergent, clay, dirt, flour, baking powder, baking soda, and frost that accumulates in the freezer. Other nonfood items that expectant women have reported craving include burnt matches, charcoal, mothballs, coffee grounds, toothpaste, and soap. Some of these cravings indicate mineral deficiencies, and some may be harmful. Eating large amounts of ice or frost during the last two trimesters may indicate low iron levels, while the consumption of soap may indicate a zinc deficiency. Clay from specific geographic areas, such as Georgia and Mississippi, has been found to impair the absorption of iron, although the clay from Texas does not. Mothballs contain naphthalene, which is toxic. Pregnant women who sniff or ingest mothballs can have infants born with hemolytic anemia.

In certain geographic areas of the country, pica is culturally accepted. Women believe that eating certain nonfood items is good for the developing baby or that it makes the baby beautiful. The hazard of this practice is that the craved items are often eaten in place of nutritious food. It may also cause profuse salivation, bowel impactions, or intestinal parasitic infections. If you experience pica, be sure to inform your caregiver.

CONCLUSION

Every day, you make dietary decisions that affect your health. You choose which foods and beverages to consume and which ones to avoid. These decisions are particularly important when they also affect the health and development of another person—that tiny being growing inside you who is totally dependent on your choices. Providing your developing baby with the best possible building blocks is the most important thing you can do while you are pregnant. Typically, women who are well nourished have better pregnancies, shorter labors, and healthier babies.

TABLE 5.2. PROTEIN, CALCIUM, IRON, AND CALORIE COUNTS

	Amount	Protein (gms)	Calcium (mgs)	Iron (mgs)	Calories
Daily Pregnancy Requirement		71	1,000–1,300	27	2,100–2,500
Fats and Oils					
Butter	1 tablespoon	trace	3	trace	102
Margarine	1 tablespoon	trace	4	trace	101
Mayonnaise	1 tablespoon	trace	2	0.1	99
Oil, olive	1 tablespoon	0	trace	0.1	119
Milk and Dairy Products					
Cheese					
American, processed	1 ounce	6	163	0.2	93
Cheddar	1 ounce	7	204	0.2	114
Cream	1 tablespoon	1	12	0.2	51
Feta	1 ounce	4	140	0.2	75
Parmesan, grated	1 tablespoon	2	69	trace	23
Swiss	1 ounce	8	272	trace	107
Cottage cheese, 1%, creamed	1/2 cup	14	69	0.2	82
Frozen yogurt, vanilla	1/2 cup	3	103	0.2	114
Ice cream, vanilla	1/2 cup	2	84	0.1	133
Milk					
Whole	1 cup	8	291	0.1	150
2%	1 cup	8	297	0.1	121
Skim	1 cup	8	302	0.1	86
Yogurt, plain, made from nonfat milk	1 cup	13	295	0.1	120
Meat, Poultry, Fish, and Eggs					
Bacon, crisp	3 slices	6	2	0.3	109
Beef, lean					
Ground, 83% (broiled)	3 ounces	22	6	2.0	218
Sirloin (broiled)	3 ounces	26	9	2.9	166
Chicken					
Breast (fried)	1/2 average	35	28	1.8	364
Breast (roasted)	1/2 average	27	13	0.9	142
Drumstick (fried)	1 average	16	12	1.0	193

	Amount	Protein (gms)	Calcium (mgs)	Iron (mgs)	Calories
Daily Pregnancy Requirement		71	1,000–1,300	27	2,100–2,500
Chile con carne with beans, canned	1 cup	20	67	3.3	255
Eggs					
Whole	1 large	6	25	0.7	75
Whites	from 1 large	4	2	trace	17
Substitute	$1/4$ cup	8	33	1.3	53
Fish, flounder (baked)	3 ounces	21	15	0.3	99
Fish sticks, breaded (baked)	1 average	4	6	0.2	76
Ham					
Baked	3 ounces	25	6	1.0	179
Deli-style	2-ounce slices	11	4	0.4	75
Hot dog (broiled) $1\frac{1}{2}$ ounces	1 hot dog	5	5	0.5	144
Oysters (fried)	3 ounces	7	53	5.9	167
Pork chop, boneless (broiled)	3 ounces	26	26	0.7	172
Salmon (broiled)	3 ounces	23	6	0.5	184
Sausage, pork	2 links or 1 patty	5	8	0.3	100
Shrimp, meat only, canned	3 ounces	20	98	2.6	102
Tuna, light, canned in water	3 ounces	22	9	1.3	99
Turkey					
Dark meat	3 ounces	24	27	2.0	159
Light meat	3 ounces	25	16	1.1	133
Dry Beans and Legumes (cooked)					
Black beans	1 cup	15	46	3.6	227
Black-eyed peas	1 cup	13	41	4.3	200
Chickpeas	1 cup	12	77	3.2	286
Great Northern beans	1 cup	15	120	3.8	209
Kidney, red	1 cup	13	61	3.2	218
Lentils	1 cup	18	38	6.6	230
Lima beans	1 cup	15	32	4.5	216
Navy beans	1 cup	16	127	4.5	258
Pork and beans	1 cup	13	142	8.3	248
Refried beans	1 cup	14	88	4.2	237

	Amount	Protein (gms)	Calcium (mgs)	Iron (mgs)	Calories
Daily Pregnancy Requirement		**71**	**1,000–1,300**	**27**	**2,100–2,500**
Nuts and Seeds					
Almonds (roasted)	1 ounce	6	70	1.2	164
Cashews (roasted)	1 ounce	4	13	1.7	163
Peanuts (roasted)	1 ounce	7	15	0.6	166
Peanut butter	1 tablespoon	4	6	0.3	95
Pine nuts	1 ounce	7	7	2.6	160
Pumpkin/squash seeds	1 ounce	9	12	4.2	148
Sunflower seeds	1/4 cup	6	22	1.2	186
Tahini, sesame	1 tablespoon	3	64	1.3	89
Soybeans and Soy Products					
Boca burger	1 patty	13	100	1.8	90
"Chik" patty	1 patty	9	0	1.8	150
Soybeans, cooked	1 cup	29	175	8.8	298
Soymilk, calcium-enriched	1 cup	7	300	1.0	90
Soy nuts	1 ounce	12	60	1.0	120
Tofu, calcium-set	2.5 ounces	7	100	1.0	70
Tofu crumbles	2.5 ounces	7	60	1.6	55
Veggie protein foods					
"Cheese"	1 1/2 slices	6	300	1.0	60
"Hot dog"	1 hot dog	9	20	0.4	45
"Turkey"	3 slices	15	20	1.0	80
Fruits					
Apple	1 medium	trace	10	0.2	81
Apricot					
Fresh	1 medium	trace	5	0.2	17
Dried	10 halves	1	16	1.6	83
Avocado, Florida	1 ounce	trace	3	0.2	32
Banana	1 medium	1	7	0.4	109
Blackberries	1 cup	1	46	0.8	75
Blueberries	1 cup	1	9	0.2	81
Cantaloupe	1 cup cubes	1	18	0.3	56
Fig, dried	2 figs	1	55	0.8	97
Grapefruit	1/2 medium	1	14	0.1	39

	Amount	Protein (gms)	Calcium (mgs)	Iron (mgs)	Calories
Daily Pregnancy Requirement		71	1,000–1,300	27	2,100–2,500
Grapes, seedless	1 cup	1	18	0.4	114
Orange	1 medium	1	52	0.1	62
Peach					
Fresh	1 medium	1	5	0.1	42
Canned, in juice	1 cup	2	15	0.7	109
Pear	1 medium	1	18	0.4	98
Pineapple, fresh	1 cup	1	11	0.6	76
Prune					
Uncooked	5 medium	1	21	1.0	100
Stewed	1 cup	3	57	2.8	265
Raisins, dark	1/2 cup	2	35	1.5	220
Strawberries, fresh	1 cup	1	23	0.6	50
Watermelon	1 cup cubes	1	12	0.3	49
Vegetables					
Asparagus (cooked)	4 medium spears	2	12	0.4	14
Broccoli, fresh (cooked)	1 cup	5	72	1.3	44
Brussels sprouts (cooked)	1 cup	6	37	1.1	65
Cabbage (cooked)	1 cup	2	47	0.3	33
Carrot, raw	1 medium	1	19	0.4	31
Cauliflower (cooked)	1 cup	2	20	0.4	29
Chinese cabbage (cooked)	1 cup	3	158	1.8	20
Coleslaw (with mayo)	1 cup	2	54	0.7	83
Collards (cooked)	1 cup	4	226	0.9	49
Corn					
Fresh, on the cob	1 average ear	3	2	0.5	83
Canned	1 cup	5	11	0.9	166
Cucumber	1 cup slices	1	17	0.2	14
Green beans (cooked)	1 cup	2	58	1.6	44
Kale (cooked)	1 cup	2.	94	1.2	36
Lettuce					
Iceberg	1 cup	1	10	0.3	7
Romaine	1 cup	1	20	0.6	8

	Amount	Protein (gms)	Calcium (mgs)	Iron (mgs)	Calories
Daily Pregnancy Requirement		**71**	**1,000–1,300**	**27**	**2,100–2,500**
Mushrooms (cooked)	1 cup	3	9	2.7	42
Okra, frozen (cooked)	1 cup	4	177	1.2	52
Peas, canned	1 cup	8	34	1.6	117
Peppers, bell	1 medium	1	11	0.5	32
Plantains (cooked)	1 cup	1	3	0.9	179
Potatoes, sweet	1 average	3	41	0.7	150
Potatoes, white					
Baked	1 average	5	20	2.7	220
French fries, frozen (oven heated)	10 fries (2 inches)	2	4	0.6	100
Mashed	1 cup	4	55	0.5	223
Spinach					
Fresh	1 cup	1	30	0.8	7
Frozen (cooked)	1 cup	6	277	2.9	53
Tomato, fresh	1 medium	1	6	0.6	26
Turnip greens (cooked)	1 cup	2	197	1.2	29
Grain Products					
Bagel	3½ inch	7	53	2.5	195
Biscuit	1 average	2	5	0.7	93
Bread					
Italian	1 slice	2	16	0.6	54
Rye	1 slice	3	23	0.9	83
White	1 slice	2	27	0.8	67
Whole wheat	1 slice	3	20	0.9	69
Cereal, cooked					
Cream of wheat	1 cup	4	50	10.3	133
Oatmeal	1 cup	6	19	1.6	145
Cereals, ready-to-eat					
Cheerios	1 cup	3	55	8.1	110
Corn Flakes	1 cup	2	1	8.7	102
Raisin Bran	1 cup	6	35	5.0	186
Rice Krispies	1 ¼ cups	2	3	2.0	124
Shredded Wheat	2 biscuits	5	20	1.4	156

	Amount	Protein (gms)	Calcium (mgs)	Iron (mgs)	Calories
Daily Pregnancy Requirement		**71**	**1,000–1,300**	**27**	**2,100–2,500**
Special K	1 cup	6	5	8.7	115
Total	3/4 cup	3	258	18.0	105
Wheaties	1 cup	3	55	8.1	110
Cracker, saltine	4 crackers	1	14	0.6	52
English muffin	1 muffin	4	99	1.4	134
Granola bar					
Hard variety, plain	1 bar	3	17	0.8	134
Soft, chocolate-coated peanut butter	1 bar	3	31	0.4	144
Matzo	6-inch square	3	4	0.9	112
Muffin, from mix					
Blueberry	1 average	3	13	0.6	150
Corn	1 average	4	38	1.0	161
Oatbran	1 average	4	36	2.4	154
Pancake	4 inch	2	28	0.6	74
Pasta (cooked)					
Enriched	1 cup	7	10	2.0	197
Whole wheat	1 cup	7	21	1.5	174
Pita	6 1/2 inch	5	52	1.6	165
Popcorn	1 cup	1	1	0.3	55
Rice (cooked)					
White, long-grain, enriched	1 cup	4	16	1.9	205
Brown, long-grain	1 cup	5	20	0.8	216
Rice cake, plain	1 cake	1	1	0.1	35
Tortilla					
Corn	6 inch	1	46	0.4	58
Flour	6 inch	3	40	1.1	104
Tortilla chips	1 ounce	2	44	0.4	142
Waffle, frozen, toasted	4 inch	2	77	1.5	87
Wheat germ	1 tablespoon	2	3	0.6	27
Beverages					
Almond Breeze	8 ounces	1	200	0.4	90
Apple juice	8 ounces	trace	15	1.5	117
Orange juice	8 ounces	2	25	0.4	110

	Amount	Protein (gms)	Calcium (mgs)	Iron (mgs)	Calories
Daily Pregnancy Requirement		71	1,000–1,300	27	2,100–2,500
Orange juice w/calcium	8 ounces	2	350	0	110
Prune juice	8 ounces	2	31	3.0	182
Rice Dream					
Enriched	8 ounces	1	300	0.2	120
Original	8 ounces	1	20	0.2	120
Soft drinks, carbonated					
Cola	12 ounces	0	14	0.1	152
Ginger ale	12 ounces	0	11	0.7	124
Root beer	12 ounces	0	19	0.2	152
Soymilk, calcium-enriched	8 ounces	7	300	1.0	90
Tomato juice	8 ounces	2	22	1.4	41
Vegetable juice cocktail	8 ounces	2	27	1.0	46
Miscellaneous					
Brownies, from mix	1 average	1	3	0.3	84
Cheesecake (17 ounces)	$1/6$ slice	4	41	0.5	257
Cookies					
Chocolate chip	1 average	1	3	0.3	48
Oatmeal	1 average	1	14	0.4	61
Sandwich, chocolate	1 average	trace	3	0.4	47
Doughnuts, cake type	1 average	2	21	0.9	198
Pickle, dill	$3\frac{3}{4}$ inch	trace	6	0.3	12
Pie (8 inch)					
Apple	$1/6$ slice	2	13	0.5	277
Cherry	$1/6$ slice	2	14	0.6	304
Pumpkin	$1/6$ slice	4	65	0.9	229
Pizza, cheese (12 inch)	$1/8$ slice	8	117	0.6	140
Potato chips	1 ounce	2	7	0.5	152
Pretzels	10 twists	5	22	2.6	229
Soup, ready-to-serve					
Chicken noodle	1 cup	13	24	1.4	175
Clam chowder, New England	1 cup	5	17	0.9	117
Vegetable	1 cup	4	55	1.6	122
Spaghetti sauce, jarred	1 cup	4	55	1.8	143
Trail mix, w/raisins, chocolate chips, nuts, seeds	1 cup	21	159	4.9	707

Adapted from *Nutritive Value of Foods, Home and Garden Bulletin #72* by Susan E.Gebhardt & Robin G. Thomas. Beltsville, MD:U.S. Department of Agriculture, 2002.

Prenatal Exercise
or Moving Through Pregnancy

Most experts agree that women who exercise during pregnancy feel better, look better, and get back into shape faster after their babies are born than women who do not exercise. Regular exercise helps strengthen muscles, promotes energy, improves mood, reduces swelling and bloating, and even aids digestion. Good body mechanics can also improve posture, reduce backaches, and help you sleep better. If you exercised regularly or participated in a sport or other physical activity before becoming pregnant, for the most part, you can continue. This depends, of course, on the specific activity (discussed later in this chapter) and on the approval of your doctor. As your pregnancy progresses, however, you may need to shorten or limit some of your activities. Even women who exercised regularly found that their performance declined as the pregnancy progressed.

If you are not in the habit of exercising, now is a good time to start. The purpose of exercise during pregnancy is to remain healthy and feel good—not to lose weight. Exercising regularly or participating in some other physical activity throughout pregnancy causes an increased secretion of *endorphins,* natural painkillers that are produced by the body. These natural opiates give a feeling of well-being during and after exercise. In addition, they cross the placenta and may provide pleasant sensations to the baby. Researchers have found that women who exercise regularly have higher levels of endorphins while exercising than women who exercise only occasionally.

There are three types of exercise—aerobic/cardiovascular, strength training, and stretching/flexibility. *Aerobic exercise* strengthens the cardiovascular system (heart, lungs, and circulation) through brisk physical activity. Its major goal is to increase heart and breathing rates by promoting the circulation of oxygen through the blood. Running, brisk walking, swimming, and bicycling are popular aerobic exercises. *Strength training,* which commonly includes working with weights or some other form of resistance, helps build and maintain muscle tone and increase endurance. If you regularly worked with weights before becoming pregnant, you can continue your current regimen—unless your doctor recommends differently. He may suggest, for instance, that you decrease the amount of weight used or the number of repetitions performed. *Stretching* exercises, which include yoga, gentle stretching, and Pilates, promote flexibility. They will help you avoid injury while performing other forms of exercise and improve muscle tone so you will experience fewer common discomforts of pregnancy.

This chapter presents specific exercises to prepare the body for labor and delivery. Proper body mechanics are also discussed, as are measures to relieve some of pregnancy's minor discomforts. Rounding out this chapter is a section on helpful massage techniques.

GUIDELINES AND PRECAUTIONS

Women with certain chronic health conditions, such as high blood pressure, cardiac disease, or a respiratory condition, should avoid strenuous activity during pregnancy. Their physicians should offer specific exercise limitations and guidelines. Doctors will also limit the activity of women who experience bleeding or placenta previa, or who develop signs of preterm labor. Women with a history of miscarriage, incompetent cervix, or preterm labor may also be cautioned about strenuous exercise.

When exercising, your pregnancy is going to force you to make certain concessions. For example, your circulatory and respiratory systems have more work to do when you are pregnant, so you may not be able to exercise as long as you did before. You may also find that you require more time to rest and recover after exercising. Never exercise to the point of breathlessness. If you are out of breath, your baby is likely to be low on oxygen as well. You should always be able to talk as you exercise. If you cannot, slow down and catch your breath.

Overdoing an exercise session can have negative effects on the fetus, including elevated fetal temperature, changes in the blood flow through the placenta, reduced levels of maternal glucose, and increased uterine contractions.[1] Regular twenty- to thirty-minute sessions several times per week are safer than one long weekly session.

If you choose to exercise during your pregnancy, be sure to observe the following guidelines:

- Check with your caregiver before participating in any exercise program or physical activity.
- Wear loose, comfortable clothing and a support bra.
- Always include warm-up and cool-down periods.
- Start slowly, gradually increasing the length and intensity of your sessions.
- Stop and rest if you feel out of breath.
- Choose activities with smooth, continuous movements rather than jerky, bouncy ones.
- Avoid straining and overstretching.
- Stop if you feel pain or experience any other warning signs.
- After twenty weeks of gestation, do not lie on your back when exercising.
- Do not hold your breath while exercising.
- Drink plenty of fluids during exercise sessions or other physical activities.
- As you get larger, avoid exercises that require balance.
- Make sure your pulse rate does not exceed 140 beats per minute.
- Avoid exercising in hot, humid weather.
- Avoid hot tubs, steam rooms, and saunas.

After your fourth month of pregnancy, avoid doing exercises on a firm surface while lying on your back. The weight of the uterus can press on your vena cava (the large vein that returns blood to the heart) and reduce your blood pressure. As a result, the amount of oxygen the baby receives is also reduced.

Stop exercising and consult your caregiver if you feel pain. At the very least, you may have performed an exercise incorrectly, or you may have overdone it a bit. Discontinue if you begin bleeding or cramping, and get an okay from your caregiver before beginning again. Be careful not to overstretch while exercising or even when doing such everyday activities as getting out of bed. During pregnancy, the body secretes a hormone called *relaxin,* which loosens joints and ligaments slightly in preparation for giving birth. This hormone makes it easier to strain ligaments and muscles during physical activities. In addition, as the baby grows and your uterus enlarges, your center of gravity changes. This increases the risk of sprains, stress fractures, and falls. Because of all these physical changes, it is best to avoid certain exercises while pregnant. Weight-bearing activities, such as running and racquetball increase pressure on the bones and joints of your legs and feet to bear the brunt of your body's weight. Non weight-bearing activities, such as swimming and water aerobics, are preferred.

As your abdomen expands, use caution when performing abdominal exercises, which can cause a separation of the *rectus abdominis* muscles. These two muscles, which are separated by a band of connective tissue, run parallel up the abdomen from the pubic bone to the sternum. Because the growing uterus stretches these muscles, doing sit-ups or crunches may cause them to separate.

The American College of Obstetricians and Gynecologists supports exercise for women who have been performing it regularly and do not overdo it. In a recent study,

EXERCISE/ACTIVITY RECOMMENDATIONS

Before beginning or continuing any activities during pregnancy, always speak with your caregiver. Depending on your specific needs and physical profile, he may have you adhere to certain exercise guidelines and limitations. For the most part, expectant mothers can follow the recommendations listed in the chart below.

Can be *started* by anyone during pregnancy	Can be *continued* if regularly performed prior to pregnancy	Should be *avoided* by everyone during pregnancy
Bowling	Basketball (non-competitive)	Competitive sports
Bicycling (preferably stationary)	Hiking	Contact sports
Golf	Jogging	Hang-gliding
Low-impact aerobics	Racquetball (non-competitive)	Horseback riding
Pilates	Running	Scuba diving
Spinning	Skiing (cross-country)	Skiing (downhill)
Stairmaster	Softball (non-competitive)	Sky diving
Swimming	Tennis (preferably doubles)	Snowmobiling
Walking	Volleyball (non-competitive)	Surfing
Water aerobics	Weight training	Water skiing
Yoga		

brisk walking was the exercise preferred by pregnant women. The researchers found that the exercise group in the study experienced less maternal weight gain, but greater infant birth weight and gestational age. They also experienced shorter labors. The women in the sedentary group complained of more discomforts such as swelling, leg cramps, fatigue, and shortness of breath.[2]

Among the exercises and activities that are considered safe to begin during pregnancy are swimming, walking, and low-impact aerobics. On the other hand, activities such as scuba diving, horseback riding, and surfing, pose a high risk to both pregnant women and their babies. This is true even for those women who had been regular participants in these activities before becoming pregnant. The chart on page 115 presents a more extensive list of exercises and other physical activities that are recommended during pregnancy and those that should be avoided. No matter what kind of exercise you choose, begin it as early in your pregnancy as possible. Start slowly and gradually increase your workout regimen as your stamina improves.

PROPER BODY MECHANICS

The term "body mechanics" refers to the way you use the different parts of your body to move. Moving your body properly is especially important during pregnancy to help minimize discomfort as your body gets larger and changes shape. As you will see in the following discussion, there is a correct way to sit, climb stairs, lift objects, lie down, and get up from a lying position.

Standing

Good posture is essential throughout pregnancy because your center of gravity changes. As your abdomen grows, you will be tempted to compensate for this change by slumping when you stand. Try to maintain the same good posture you had before becoming pregnant. Standing erect helps prevent or alleviate back discomfort, improve digestion, and enhance body image.

While standing, the way you hold your head influences the position of the rest of your body. If you let your head hang forward, your body will droop like a wilted flower. Think tall! Hold your head up with your chin tucked in and your neck straight. Lift your shoulders up and pull them back. This position will keep you from cramping your rib cage, which can make breathing difficult and possibly cause indigestion.

Pay special attention to your pelvic area, which contains the weight of the growing baby. Think of your pelvis as a bowl filled with liquid. To prevent the liquid from spilling out, tilt the "bowl" back by tightening your abdominal muscles and tucking your buttocks under. This position prevents excess tension in the lower back muscles. To help maintain proper pelvic alignment, bend your knees slightly and keep your body weight over your feet—and balance yourself on the center of each foot, never on the inside. When standing for long periods, place one foot on a small stool to flex the hip. This reduces strain on the ligaments in the groin.

Good Posture
Standing erect lessens back discomfort, improves digestion, and enhances body image.

Poor Posture
Slumping forward can cramp the rib cage, making it difficult to breathe and causing indigestion.

When walking, maintain all of the aspects of good posture just discussed. When taking steps, bring your legs straight forward from the hip. Do not swing them sideways in a "waddle."

Sitting

While sitting in a chair, try not to slump forward. Use the back of the chair as a guide to sit up straight. For this reason, straight-back chairs are preferred over cushioned ones during pregnancy. Place a pillow behind your neck and/or the small of your back for increased comfort. The full length of your thighs should rest on the seat, which should be high enough to keep your knees even with your hips.

Sitting in a cross-legged position on the floor, called *tailor sitting,* is excellent during pregnancy. In addition to being comfortable, it improves the circulation in the legs, while stretching and increasing the flexibility of the inner-thigh muscles. Sit this way whenever possible—when watching television, reading the newspaper, or folding the laundry. If your legs become tired, stretch them out in front of you.

Lying Down

Lying flat on your back—the supine position—for extended periods of time is not recommended after the fourth month of pregnancy. This is because the increasing weight of the baby and the uterus will compress your vena cava, the major blood vessel that returns blood to the heart. This can lower your blood pressure, which, in turn, will reduce the amount of blood traveling to the placenta and the baby. If you must lie on your back (during an examination, for example), modify the position by bending your knees and placing a pillow under the small of your back for support. Refrain from doing any exercises that require you to lie on your back.

While sleeping, lying on your back is not as critical due to the softness of the mattress. There is more concern when lying on a firm surface. However, if sleeping on your back concerns you, place a small pillow behind your back. This will prevent you from rolling onto your back as you sleep.

Lying on your side takes the weight of the baby off your back and groin, and allows the joints in these areas to relax. Placing a pillow lengthwise between your legs adds comfort and makes it easier for you to rest. Positioning another pillow under your abdomen takes the strain off your lower back. You may feel even more comfortable lying further over on your abdomen in a three-quarter position. Place your lower arm behind your back and bring your upper arm and leg forward, supported by pillows.

To get up from a lying position, first roll onto your side and then push yourself to a sitting position with your arms. If you are in bed, swing your legs over the side. Be careful not to twist your body as you get up. This technique will help you to avoid straining both your back and abdominal muscles.

Climbing Stairs

Be careful when climbing stairs. Lift your body up by using your legs, rather than holding onto a railing and pulling yourself up with your arms. Lean forward slightly and place your entire foot on each step as you climb—and climb slowly. After you have given birth, during the postpartum period, continue to climb steps slowly while tightening your abdominal and pelvic floor muscles.

Use the back of the chair as a guide to sit up straight.

Tailor sitting is comfortable; it also improves circulation in the legs and increases flexibility of the inner thigh muscles.

To get up from a lying position, roll onto your side and then push yourself to a sitting position with your arms.

Lifting incorrectly using the back muscles can cause back strain. Instead . . .

lower yourself to one knee, grasp the object, then return to a standing position by pushing yourself up with your rear foot.

Lifting

Because improper lifting can put excessive strain on the back and the muscles of the pelvic floor, it is important to avoid picking up anything heavy while pregnant. The general rule is to pick up only what you can easily lift with one arm. Many women, however, especially those with small children or toddlers, find that sometimes moderately heavy lifting is necessary during pregnancy. If you find yourself in such a situation, it's important to lift the object properly. Get close to the object and lower yourself into a squat, bending at the knees, not at the waist. Keep your feet parallel and your back straight, and as you lift the object, straighten your legs without twisting your body. An alternate method is to place one foot in front of the other and slowly lower yourself to one knee. Lift the object by pushing yourself up with your rear foot while keeping your back straight. If you are lifting a small child, first have him climb onto a stool or chair. This will allow you to lift him without straining your back.

SHOES AND CLOTHING

The kind of shoes you wear affects your posture. During pregnancy, it is best to wear flat shoes with good support. High-heeled shoes thrust your body weight forward, putting strain on your lower back and the ligaments of your hips and knees. They can also make it difficult to maintain your balance. Habitually wearing high heels causes the calf muscles to tighten and actually become shorter. If you regularly wore high heels before becoming pregnant, suddenly changing to flats can result in strained calf muscles. To prevent this from happening, gradually wear progressively lower heels; this will allow the leg muscles to stretch slowly. You may also find that support hose, which helps prevent varicose veins, relieve your tired leg muscles.

A good support bra is another important wardrobe "must" during pregnancy. As your breasts become larger and heavier, proper support will help minimize upper backache and improve your posture. Select a maternity/nursing bra with wide straps that can be used both during pregnancy and later while breastfeeding. For tips on purchasing a good bra, see page 367.

Many women have found that a maternity support or support band, which provides extra reinforcement to the growing abdomen, is useful for relieving back or lower abdominal pain. Other women find the extra support helpful during physical activities like walking, jogging, or low-impact aerobics. This type of support is especially helpful for women carrying more than one baby. Generally made of a washable spandex-type material, a maternity support—either a one-piece body suit with or without shoulder straps, or a band that passes under the abdomen and across the lower back—also helps lift the uterus and may relieve pelvic and bladder pressure. A maternity support is not a girdle.

The kind of panties you wear is another important consideration. Those made of cotton are preferable over nylon because the fabric breathes and absorbs moisture. This helps prevent irritation and infection. (Actually, this is a good recommendation for *all* women, pregnant or not.) Maternity clothing in general should be made of absorbent fabric that does not trap body heat. During pregnancy, women often feel warmer than usual, so it is especially important to avoid clothes made from nonabsorbent fabrics like nylon and polyester. Cotton clothes are more comfortable. Maternity clothing should also be loose fitting and allow for growth.

AEROBIC EXERCISES

Aerobic exercise strengthens the cardiovascular system through brisk physical activity. Running, brisk walking, swimming, and bicycling are popular aerobic choices. For obvious reasons, during pregnancy it is best to avoid high-impact aerobics—such as jumping, high kicking, leaping, and fast running. Low- or no-impact options are best.

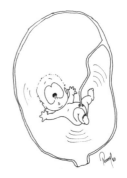

I know she needs to exercise . . . but on a TRAMPOLINE?!

If you have not exercised regularly before becoming pregnant, it's a good idea to begin with a low-impact activity such as walking. A brisk walk of fifteen to twenty minutes each day helps develop cardiovascular strength and uses almost every muscle in the body. Even women with little extra time can usually find time to walk. Bicycling (ideally on a stationary bicycle for safety reasons) is another excellent sustained aerobic exercise. In addition to improving cardiovascular strength, it develops the abdominal muscles that support the baby.

Swimming and other types of water exercise are excellent physical activities during pregnancy. Because the buoyancy of the water helps support the baby, you can use your leg, arm, and back muscles more freely. Swimming for fifteen to twenty minutes several times a week builds muscle tone and strength. When exercising in water, be sure to use the steps or ladder to enter the pool. Avoid jumping in because pool water could be forced into the vagina. And do not dive into the pool as this may exert too much force on your expanding abdomen. When exercising your lower torso, hang onto a kick board or other flotation device. If you develop a sore back, you may be arching your back too much.

Check out your local fitness center. Many offer water aerobics classes specifically for expectant mothers, or they have classes for seniors, which also provide good workouts. If you are unable to join a water-exercise class, you can perform the following recommended exercises on your own.

Arm Circles in Water

Benefits: Strengthens muscles of the chest, upper back, and upper arms.

Directions: Stand in chest-deep water with your feet comfortably apart and your arms outstretched to the sides. Bend your knees until the water covers your arms. Make small circles to the count of 10. Reverse the position and repeat.

Frequency: 1 to 2 repetitions

Freestyle Swimming in Place

Benefits: Strengthens muscles of the chest, upper back, and upper arms. Increases flexibility of the shoulders.

Directions: Stand in chest-deep water with your feet comfortably apart and your arms

Arm Circles.

extended forward at chest level. Bend your knees until the water covers your arms. Extend your hands and arms one at a time as if you are swimming.

Frequency: 10 to 20 repetitions

Caution: Keep your back straight while doing this exercise.

Freestyle
Swimming in Place.

Starting position.   With arm extended.

Breaststroke Swimming in Place

Benefits: Strengthens muscles of the chest, upper back, and upper arms.

Directions: Stand in chest-deep water with your feet comfortably apart and your palms together against your chest. Bend your knees until the water covers your arms, then extend your arms in front of you. When your arms are fully extended, separate your hands and bring them around toward your back.

Frequency: 10 to 20 repetitions

Caution: Keep your back straight while doing this exercise.

Breaststroke
Swimming in Place.

Starting position.   With arms extended.

Jogging in Water

Benefits: Increases flexibility of the lower extremities and improves circulation.

Directions: Stand in waist-deep water and jog in place, raising your knees as high as is comfortable.

Frequency: 1 to 3 minutes, increasing length of time as your stamina improves.

Bicycling in Water

Benefits: Strengthens leg muscles and improves circulation.

Directions: In deep water, while holding onto a kick board or flotation device, move your legs as if riding a bicycle.

Variation: Perform this exercise while holding onto the side of the pool with one hand and facing sideways.

Frequency: 1 to 2 minutes

Caution: Do not point your toes as this may cause a leg cramp.

Leg Kicks in Water

Benefits: Strengthens leg muscles and improves circulation.

Directions: Holding onto the top step or side of the pool, or to a flotation device, lie in the water belly-down and let your legs float to the surface behind you. Kick your legs as if you are freestyle swimming.

Frequency: 1 to 2 minutes

Caution: Do not point your toes as this may cause a leg cramp.

Jogging.

Bicycling.

Leg Kicks.

Leg Kicks in Water While Sitting

Benefits: Strengthens leg muscles and improves circulation.

Directions: Sit on the top step of the pool. Place your hands on the step to support yourself. Allow your legs to float to the surface. Kick your legs as if you are doing the backstroke.

Frequency: 1 to 2 minutes

Caution: Do not point your toes as this may cause a leg cramp.

Leg Kicks While Sitting.

STRENGTH-TRAINING EXERCISES

Strength training tones and builds muscles to help you adjust to your body's physical changes and to prepare you for the work of labor and birth. If you had previously used weights while exercising, your doctor is likely to approve of your continuing to use them during pregnancy. Lifting two- to five-pound hand or ankle weights will build muscle tone without straining. Using resistance bands is another good option.

When working with weights, don't hold your breath. Exhale as you lift and inhale as you lower the weights to the starting position. Always exhale when expending the greatest work. When taking a walk, carry weights for a better cardiovascular workout. If you don't have weights, you can use soup cans or bottles of water instead. Generally, arm exercises can be performed while standing; however, if you feel lightheaded or unstable, you can do them while sitting. After the first trimester, do not lie on your back to lift weights or perform any type of exercise. Do not use machines or equipment that involve bars or weights that can accidentally slip onto your chest or abdomen. And always have someone working with you. The safest way to perform weight-training exercises is under the watchful eye of a qualified instructor. Be sure to inform him of your pregnancy, so he can set up a safe and personalized workout regimen for you.

Some suggested strength-training exercises follow. Use two- to five-pound weights for the Bicep Curls, Arm Raises, and Overhead Press. Weights are not necessary when Rowing or performing Wall Squats.

Bicep Curl.

Bicep Curls

Benefits: Strengthens muscles of the upper arms.

Directions: Stand with your feet comfortably apart and knees slightly bent. While holding a weight in each hand, keep your arms at your sides with palms facing inward. Keeping your arms close to your body, bend your elbows and raise your hands to your chest while rotating your palms toward your shoulders. Hold for 1 second, then slowly lower your arms back to the starting position.

Variation: If you feel lightheaded or off-balance, perform this exercise while sitting in a chair.

Frequency: 8 to 12 repetitions.

Note: Tighten your abdominal muscles as you perform this exercise. Be sure to exhale as you lift the weights and inhale as you lower them.

Arm Raises

Benefits: Strengthens muscles of the upper back and arms.

Directions: Stand with your back straight, knees slightly apart, and feet flat on the floor. While holding a weight in each hand, keep your arms at your sides with palms facing inward. Keeping your arms straight, raise them above your head, then slowly lower them back to the starting position.

Variation: If you feel lightheaded or off-balance, perform this exercise while sitting in a chair.

Frequency: 5 to 10 repetitions.

Note: Tighten your abdominal muscles as you perform this exercise. Be sure to exhale as you lift the weights and inhale as you lower them.

Arm Raises.

Overhead Press

Benefits: Strengthens shoulder muscles.

Directions: Sit with your back against the back of a straight-back chair. Hold a weight in each hand just above the shoulders with your elbows out to the side and your palms facing forward. Raise your hands above your head until your elbows are almost straight. Slowly lower to starting position.

Frequency: 5 to 10 repetitions.

Caution: Do not arch your back. Do not lock your elbows.

Overhead Press.

Wall Squats

Benefits: Strengthens muscles of the abdomen and thighs.

Directions: With your back to the wall, stand about 10 to 12 inches away from it with your feet about hip-width apart. Place your hands on your thighs and press your back and hips against the wall. Slide your torso down the wall until your thighs are parallel to the floor (sitting position). Hold for 2 seconds. Slide back up the wall to a standing position.

Frequency: 8 to 12 repetitions.

Caution: To prevent strain on the knees, do not bend them past the sitting position— they should not extend over your toes.

Note: Tighten your abdominal muscles as you perform this exercise. Be sure to exhale as you bend your legs and inhale as you straighten up.

Rowing

Benefits: Strengthens muscles of shoulders and upper back

Directions: Sit on the floor with your legs out in front of you. (For comfort, sit on a pillow and/or place a small rolled-up towel under your knees.) Wrap a resistance band around the balls of your feet and hold the ends with your hands. Keeping your legs extended and your arms at shoulder height, draw your hands in toward your chest as if rowing a boat. Slowly extend your hands back to the starting position.

Frequency: 5 to 10 repetitions.

Variation: This exercise can be done while sitting in a chair and using weights.

Wall Squat.

Rowing.

STRETCHING/FLEXIBILITY EXERCISES

Stretching exercises improve muscle tone and flexibility, and help relieve tension and a number of minor discomforts. Be sure to perform all of the following stretches slowly and smoothly; quick jerky movements can overstretch tendons and ligaments, and possibly dislocate joints. At first, perform each exercise only two to three times per session, then gradually increase the number until you reach the recommended amount. For maximum benefit, stretch twice a day. Make sure you continue to breathe normally as you stretch—don't hold your breath. For ease of practice, perform the following exercises in the order they appear.

Rib Cage Stretch

Benefits: Relieves tension in the shoulders. Strengthens muscles of the upper back. Helps relieve indigestion.

Directions: Inhale slowly while raising both arms over your head to the count of 5. Then exhale while slowly lowering both your arms to the count of 5, first straight out in front, then down by your sides, and finally behind your back.

Frequency: 5 repetitions. Also perform this exercise whenever you feel tension in your upper body or have indigestion.

Caution: Do not arch your back while doing this exercise.

Note: Raising your arms above your head will *not* harm the baby, as an old wives' tale suggests.

Arm Circles

Benefits: Strengthens muscles and relieves tension in the upper back and upper arms.

Directions: With palms facing up, extend your arms out to your sides. Make small clockwise circles to the count of 10, gradually increasing the size of the circles. Then reverse direction, starting with large circles and gradually decreasing their size to another count of 10.

Frequency: 2 repetitions.

Shoulder Rotations

Benefit: Helps prevent upper backache.

Directions: Place your fingertips on your shoulders and make large backward circles with your elbows to the count of 10. Then reverse direction and make forward circles.

Frequency: 10 repetitions. Also perform this exercise whenever you have an upper backache.

Rib Cage Stretch.

Raise your arms above your head . . .   then lower them behind your back.

Arm Circles.   Shoulder Rotation.

Calf Stretch

Benefits: Helps prevent leg cramps and improve circulation in the legs.

Directions: Stand facing a wall or your partner with one leg well in front of the other, and the foot flat on the floor (lunge position). Stretch the back leg behind you with the knee straight and the foot flat on the floor. Press your hands flat against the wall or your partner's hands. Lunge forward, bending the front leg at the knee and stretching the other calf. Stretch gradually for 15 to 20 seconds. Switch the position of the legs and repeat.

Frequency: 3 to 5 repetitions per leg. Also perform this exercise whenever you have a leg cramp.

Pelvic Rock

Benefits: Improves posture. Relieves back discomfort and pelvic congestion. Increases abdominal muscle tone.

Directions: Kneel on the floor on your hands and knees (do not let your spine sag). Align your head with your spine (you should be facing the floor). Tuck in your buttocks, pull up your abdominal muscles, and press your spine up toward the lower back just enough to erase the spinal curve. Do *not* hump your back. Hold this position for a few seconds, then return to the starting position. Repeat this exercise using a constant rhythm and a rocking motion.

Variation: Stand erect. Place one hand on your pubic bone and the other on the small of your back (to help you get the motion), and rotate your pelvis forward while tucking in your buttocks and abdomen. Release and repeat, using a constant rhythm and a rocking motion. (To make sure you are standing erect, perform this exercise in front of a mirror and check your posture from the side.)

Frequency: 10 repetitions. Also perform this exercise during labor if you are experiencing back pain.

Note: This exercise can be performed in several positions. The ones presented here are the most popular.

Calf Stretch.

Pelvic Rock
while standing.

Pelvic Rock
while kneeling.

Kneel on your hands and knees . . .   then press your spine up toward the lower back.

Tailor Press.

Tailor Press

Benefits: Stretches the ligaments and muscles of the inner thighs and increases their elasticity.

Directions: Sit on the floor with the soles of your feet pressed together and pulled toward your body. Using only the muscles of your legs, press your knees downward and hold for a count of 5. You will feel your inner thigh muscles pull slightly.

Variation: Sit on the floor with soles of your feet pressed together and pulled toward your body. Cup your hands around the outsides of your knees, then pull your knees up with your hands while pushing them down with your leg muscles. (There should be no movement, just counter pressure.) Hold for a count of 5. Next, place your hands on top of your knees and press them down with your hands while pulling them up with your leg muscles. Hold for another count of 5.

Frequency: 10 repetitions.

Caution: Do not bounce your knees. Discontinue the exercise if you feel pain around your pubic bone, which may indicate some separation at the joints. Do not do this exercise after giving birth until the perineum has healed.

Note: Practicing this exercise helps prepare the ligaments and muscles of the inner thighs for the birth process. It also promotes comfort and helps you relax and feel at ease in this position while giving birth.

Tailor Press variation.

Pull your knees up while pushing them down with your leg muscles.

Push your knees down while pulling them up with your leg muscles.

Tailor Stretch

Benefits: Stretches the ligaments and muscles of the inner thighs and increases their elasticity. Also stretches the muscles of the lower back and calves.

Directions: Sit on the floor with your legs stretched out in front of you and as far apart as comfortably possible. Lean forward and either reach each hand to its corresponding ankle (right hand to right ankle and left hand to left ankle), or slide both hands down the same leg until you reach the toes. Repeat with the other leg.

Frequency: 10 repetitions.

Caution: Discontinue this exercise if you feel pain around your pubic bone, which may indicate some separation at the joints.

Tailor Stretch.

Relieving Common Pregnancy Pains

Painful leg cramps are not uncommon during pregnancy. Simply pointing your toes can bring them on. And pain caused by pressure on the sciatic nerve, which runs down the buttocks and along the backs of the legs, is also a common complaint of pregnant women. If you experience either of these painful, sometimes agonizing conditions, the following stretches may help.

LEG CRAMPS

1. Sit on the floor with your legs straight out in front of you.

2. Have your partner place his hand on the knee of your affected leg and press down.

3. With his other hand, have him grasp your foot and, using steady pressure, push your toes toward your head.

4. He should continue applying pressure until the cramp is relieved.

You can also relieve a leg cramp by performing the Calf Stretch on page 125.

Relieving a leg cramp.

SCIATIC PAIN

1. Stand about two feet from the wall with your palms flat against the wall.

2. Start walking your hands down the wall until your back is parallel to the floor and your legs are straight.

3. Point your toes inward and hold this position for about a minute or as long as comfortable.

4. Perform this stretch twice a day if experiencing sciatic pain.

You can also ease hip or sciatic pain by alternately applying heat and cold (twenty minutes of each) to the upper outer quadrant of the affected buttock.

Relieving sciatic pain.

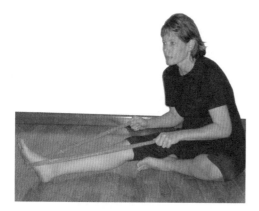

Hamstring Stretch.

Hamstring Stretch

Benefits: Stretches the hamstring muscles (located on the back of the thighs) and relieves tension in the lower back.

Directions: Sit on the floor with your right leg straight out in front of you. Bend your left leg and place the sole of your left foot against the inside of your right thigh. Loop a towel or resistance band around your right foot and hold both ends, applying tension. Lean forward from your hips until you feel a slight stretch in the hamstring muscles. Hold for the count of 10. Repeat with the other leg.

Frequency: 3 to 5 repetitions per leg. Also perform this stretch at the end of an exercise session or after sitting in a chair for a long period of time.

Note: This is a good stretch to perform while watching television.

Foot Stretch

Benefits: Improves circulation. May help prevent varicosities, swollen ankles, and leg cramps.

Directions: Sit or lie down and elevate your legs. Flex your ankles, drawing your toes toward you. Rotate your feet first in one direction, then in the opposite direction.

Frequency: 10 repetitions. Whenever you sit for long periods, perform 1 repetition three to four times an hour.

Caution: Do not point your toes, as this could cause leg cramps.

Neck Stretch

Benefit: Relieves tension in the neck and shoulder area.

Directions: Face forward in a sitting or standing position (you can even do this in the shower). Slowly tilt your head to the right, so that your right ear is parallel to the shoulder, then slowly tilt your head to the left side. Repeat 5 times. Next, slowly lower your chin toward your chest, then return to facing forward position. Repeat 5 times.

Frequency: 1 to 2 repetitions. Also perform this exercise whenever you feel tension in your neck or shoulders.

Caution: If you have ever had a neck injury, move your head very slowly and carefully when performing this stretch.

Prenatal Yoga

Prenatal yoga, which improves muscle flexibility, strength, and tone, has been increasing in popularity over the years. It is an excellent way to prepare your body for the work of labor and birth. In addition to targeting muscles, yoga promotes good posture and aids digestion. Many women who regularly perform yoga have reported a decrease in low back pain and other common discomforts of pregnancy. Another component of yoga is relaxation through controlled breathing, an essential skill during labor and childbirth. Yoga also encourages a sense of emotional well-being and self awareness.

A growing number of yoga or fitness centers, gyms, and even hospitals offer prenatal yoga classes. Attending these classes is not only physically and mentally empowering, it also gives you an opportunity to meet and share experiences and concerns with other pregnant women.

PREPARING PELVIC FLOOR MUSCLES

The muscles of the pelvic floor play an important role in the birth process. These are the muscles that are stretched as the baby passes down the birth canal. The muscles of the pelvic floor are like a hammock—attached to the pubic bone in the front and the coccyx in the back. Because of its position, this muscle group is also known as the *pubococcygeus muscle.* Figure 6.1 below shows a well-toned pelvic floor, while Figure 6.2 shows one that is poorly toned. As seen in Figure 6.3, part of this group, the *sphincter muscles,* forms a figure eight around the urethra and vagina in the front and the anus in the back.

Kegel exercises, which are explained on the following page, are designed to keep the pelvic floor muscles toned in preparation for giving birth. In addition to Kegels, there are also instructions for performing prenatal perineal massage, which will mentally and physically prepare you for the sensations of giving birth.

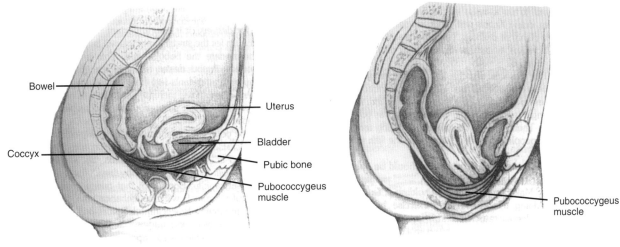

Figure 6.1. A well-toned pelvic floor.   **Figure 6.2.** A poorly toned pelvic floor.

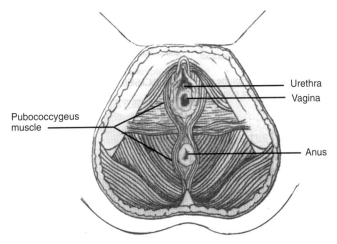

Figure 6.3. Cross-section of the pelvic floor muscles.

Kegel Exercises

Kegel (pronounced *KEE gull*) exercises are named after Dr. Arnold Kegel, a gynecologist who developed them back in the 1940s to help women with weak bladder control—a direct result of giving birth. They are designed to strengthen the pelvic floor muscles, which support the bladder, as well as the uterus, urethra, and rectum.

By performing Kegels regularly during pregnancy, you can achieve voluntary control of the pelvic floor. This will enable you to relax the area consciously during birth. Relaxed pelvic floor muscles will allow your baby an easier passage and perhaps eliminate the need for an episiotomy. During birth, these muscles are stretched, which can result in a prolapsed (sagging) uterus, a prolapsed bladder, and/or urinary stress incontinence (uncontrolled urine leakage caused by coughing, sneezing, or other sudden movement). Performing Kegel exercises during and after pregnancy can help prevent such problems. And when done shortly after birth, Kegels help restore the muscle fibers that were stretched during delivery. After an episiotomy, they increase blood flow to the area, which helps reduce swelling and encourage healing.

The benefits of Kegels are not limited to the period of giving birth. They extend into the immediate postpartum period and can continue throughout life. Performing Kegels helps improve the muscle tone of the vagina, causing it to become tighter, snugger. (Your partner will also appreciate this extra snugness!) It also enhances nerve ending response, resulting in heightened vaginal sensitivity during intercourse.

Performing Kegels

Before performing Kegels, you must first locate the pelvic floor muscles. Do this by contracting the muscles around the urethra as if you were trying to hold back urine. Next, at a time when your bladder is not full, start to urinate and then stop the flow. Do this a few times. Stopping the flow tightens the pelvic floor; releasing the flow relaxes it. Another way to check for pelvic floor tension is to tighten your vaginal muscles around your partner's penis during intercourse. If he feels you "hugging" his penis, you'll know that you are tightening your pelvic floor muscles effectively. Once you are aware these muscles, you can begin doing Kegels. Do not, however, perform them while urinating—initially, you did this only to identify the proper muscles. Instead, practice them when your bladder is empty.

Women have traditionally been taught to perform Kegels by rhythmically contracting and releasing the pelvic floor muscles—approximately fifty to one hundred a day. Well-known childbirth educator and author Penny Simkin developed an improved version of this exercise called the *Super Kegel.* To do a Super Kegel, contract the pelvic floor by lifting and tightening the muscles and holding for a count of twenty seconds. (Make sure you are doing this without tightening your buttocks or squeezing your legs together—use only your pelvic floor muscles.) Try to maintain the contraction. If you feel the muscles relaxing, tighten them again. Perform one repetition of this exercise ten times a day. Super Kegels are more effective than regular Kegels in increasing the awareness and strength of the pelvic floor muscles.

Along with Super Kegels, another variation of this exercise, sometimes called *Elevator Kegels,* will help you achieve deeper muscle control in preparation for pushing during childbirth. To perform this exercise, envision your pelvic floor as an elevator. Contract the muscles upward, from the first floor to the fifth floor, stopping at each floor and increasingly tightening the muscles as you go higher. Then, gradually relax the muscles as you move downward from the fifth floor to the first, releasing a little tension at each floor. Continue moving downward to the basement level where you relax the muscles completely by giving them a slight push. This is the degree of relaxation you will need to achieve while pushing the baby down the birth canal. Always return to the second level to maintain a constant degree of tension in the pelvic floor—the same way that a hammock returns to its normal, higher position when you get up.

With continued practice, you should develop enough control to lift the elevator ten floors. Make sure that you breathe normally as your pelvic elevator moves upward and down—do not hold your breath. Practice this exercise at least twice a day.

Practicing Tips

Start performing a few Super Kegels a day, gradually increasing both the number you perform and the length of each contraction until you are doing ten a day for twenty seconds. Make them part of your daily routine—while washing dishes, watching television, or when stopped at red lights. Do one as you are making breakfast in the morning, or as soon as you get into bed at night. Since it is best to perform Kegels on an empty bladder, get into the habit of doing one while washing your hands after urinating. After the baby comes, doing a Super Kegel with every diaper change will ensure plenty of practice.

Keep in mind that you should practice Kegels for the rest of your life, not just while you are pregnant. They will help you maintain optimum muscular condition of the pelvic floor. According to Penny Simkin, this is the most important exercise a woman of any age can do.

Perineal Massage

Just as you prepare your muscles for delivery by toning them through exercise, you should also prepare your perineum—the area between the vaginal opening and the anus—for the stretching required to accommodate the baby's head. Perineal preparation is especially important if you want to avoid an episiotomy. Many caregivers feel that preparing the perineum increases the chance of keeping it intact during delivery.

Prenatal preparation of the perineal area begins with good nutrition. Eating properly will contribute to healthy tissues that stretch and heal rapidly. Practicing Kegels and pushing techniques (presented in the next chapter) will help you gain additional control over the perineal area, which is very important during labor. And perineal massage will prepare you for the stretching sensations that you will feel during your baby's birth. It also increases the elasticity of the perineal tissues.

Begin performing perineal massage around the thirty-fourth week. You can either do this yourself or have your partner do it for you. It's important that whoever performs the massage has clean hands and short fingernails. For lubrication, you can use a little K-Y jelly, some vitamin E or vegetable oil, or your body's own secretions. Some women find that taking a warm bath prior to the massage is helpful. You may want to use a mirror when massaging the area—especially the first few times—for optimum vision.

To perform the massage yourself, insert your thumbs into your vagina about one inch and press them toward your rectum. With your thumbs, slowly stretch your perineal tissues outward toward your thighs. (Keep the knuckles of your thumbs together to prevent overstretching.) You should feel a stinging or burning sensation. Continue to maintain this pressure for two minutes, until the perineum becomes somewhat numb and the tingling is less distinct. Then gently slide the tips of the thumbs back and forth as you continue to stretch the tissues outward. Continue this action for another couple minutes. If your partner performs the massage, he should insert his index fingers into

Hints for the Father-to-Be

To help the mother-to-be stay in good physical condition:

✓ Exercise with her.

✓ Do not let her lift heavy items.

✓ Discourage her from performing strenuous exercise on hot, humid days.

✓ Compliment her on her good posture.

✓ Remind her to do her Kegels.

✓ Take walks with her.

✓ Discourage her from using hot tubs, saunas, or steam rooms.

✓ Offer to give her massages (including perineal massage after the thirty-fourth week of pregnancy).

your vagina and keep his thumbs on the outside. The knuckles of his index fingers should remain together. If you have a scar from a previous episiotomy, spend additional time massaging vitamin E oil into the scar tissue.

Do not practice perineal massage if you have active herpes lesions or another vaginal infection. Also, to prevent a bladder infection when performing perineal massage, avoid the urethral area.

BODY MASSAGE DURING PREGNANCY

Massage has been a vital part of prenatal and postpartum care in many cultures for centuries. In this country, women have only recently begun to experience the pleasures and benefits of this practice. Much of the stress and discomfort that the body undergoes during pregnancy can be alleviated through proper massage, including:

- Relief from muscle spasms and cramps, especially in the back and neck.

- Increased blood circulation, which brings more blood to the tissues and placenta. This means greater nutrition for tissues and enhanced waste product removal.

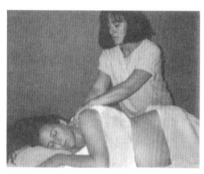

- Increased circulation of the lymphatic system, which results in less swelling and more energy.

- Improved muscle tone.

- Stress reduction.

- Increased relaxation brought about by the sedating effect of the massage on the nervous system, as well as by the release of endorphins.

- Development of sensory awareness.

- Alleviation of pressure on weight-bearing joints.

- Emotional support and physical nurturance.

An expectant mother enjoys a massage administered by a licensed massage therapist trained in working with pregnant women.

If you are interested in experiencing a professional massage, be sure to use a licensed therapist, preferably one who is trained in working with pregnant women. This type of therapist will be aware of any massage restrictions, such as the avoidance of deep tissue work.

Instead of going to a professional, you may prefer to have your partner give you a massage. This can be a pleasurable experience for you both, as long as he uses a gentle touch. You can receive the massage while sitting up or straddling a chair backwards. Or you can lie on your side with pillows under your neck and abdomen and between your legs. If you are lying on the edge of a bed, your partner can kneel on the floor or sit in a chair while massaging one side of your body. Then you can roll to the other side of the bed so he can massage the other side. Choose whatever position you find most comfortable. To create a soothing, relaxing atmosphere, select a warm, quiet place, and perhaps light scented candles and play soft music. Using oil or lotion during the massage will make stroking easier and avoid causing friction. Following the massage, it is important to take a few minutes to rest and have assistance when getting up. Afterward, make sure you drink plenty of water to flush out the toxins that are released during the massage.

The following massage routines are recommended for your partner to perform on you. He can vary the techniques according to your preferences and as he feels comfortable. Be sure to let him know if his stroking, squeezing, or rubbing causes pain or discomfort. And have him use oil or lotion for a smooth, comfortable experience.

Head, Back, and Shoulder Massage

The following routine is excellent for relieving tension in the head, neck, back, and shoulder areas.

1. Have the woman sit backwards on a chair and lean over a pillow. Stand, kneel, or sit on another chair directly behind her.

2. Place your fingertips on her scalp and move your fingers as if you are gently shampooing her hair. Do this for several minutes.

3. Pour a little oil or lotion in the palm of your hand, then rub your hands together until they are warm. Place your palms on her lower back on either side of her spine. Slowly and gently move your hands up her back, across her shoulders, and then down along the sides of her back. Repeat several times, covering her whole back with oil.

4. Place your palms on her lower back and position your thumbs in the grooves on either side of the spine. Using moderate pressure, make small circular movements with your thumbs while slowly moving up the spine. When you reach the top, open your hands with your palms against her back, and gently slide your hands down her back. Repeat three times.

5. Cup one hand on the back of her neck at the base of the skull. Gently squeeze, then gradually move your hand down her neck, continuing to squeeze and release. Repeat three times.

6. Cup both hands on her shoulders close to her neck. Using full hands, squeeze her shoulders and release. Repeat while gradually moving your hands to the ends of her shoulders. (When squeezing, be careful not to pinch.). Repeat three times.

7. Finish with a light full-hand massage, beginning at the top of her neck and slowly moving down her back to her buttocks. Repeat three times.

8. Allow her to rest a few minutes before getting up. Or have her remain seated while you give her the following hand and arm massage.

Gently move your hands up her back, across her shoulders, and then down along the sides of her back.

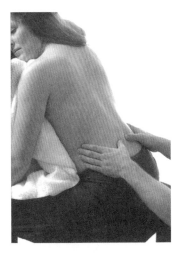

Make small circular movements with your thumbs.

Cup your hand on her neck and gently squeeze, gradually moving down.

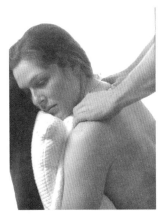

Squeeze her shoulders using your full hands.

Hand and Arm Massage

The following routine is helpful for relaxing the hand and arm muscles.

1. Have the woman sit backwards on a chair and lean over a pillow. Stand in front of her and slightly to her side.

2. Pour a little oil in the palm of your hand, then rub your hands together until they are warm. Gently lift one of her arms at the wrist with both hands. Apply gentle traction and use an easy jiggle motion to relax her arm.

3. Turn her hand palm up. Use your thumbs to make small circles over the entire palm.

4. Turn her hand over (palm down) and, starting at the pinky fingernail, apply light pressure as you move up the entire length of the finger. When you reach the base, gently pull the finger toward you. Repeat with the remaining fingers and thumb.

5. Hold her wrist with one hand, and begin massaging her outer arm. Start at her wrist and slowly move up the entire length of her arm. You can use long strokes or a gentle cupping and squeezing motion. Repeat three times.

6. Switch hands to hold her same wrist, and stroke the inner length of her arm. Repeat three times.

7. Massage the muscle at the top of her shoulder using your full palm and a circular motion.

8. Finish by massaging her entire arm, using long strokes or a cupping and squeezing motion, beginning at the shoulder and moving down to her fingertips.

9. Repeat the entire sequence with her other hand and arm.

Apply gentle traction and use an easy jiggle motion to relax the arm.

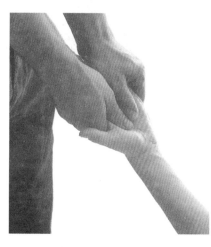

Use your thumbs to make small circles over the entire palm.

Lightly compress the entire length of each finger.

Hold her wrist with one hand as you massage her outer arm.

Foot Massage

The following massage soothes not only the feet, but also the entire body.

1. Have the woman sit in a chair, while you sit in another chair facing her. Place a pillow on your lap and rest one of her feet on top.

2. Pour a little oil in the palm of your hand, then rub your hands together until they are warm. Place one of your hands on the bottom of her foot and the other hand on top. Pull your hands down and off her foot as if you were "pulling" out her tension. Repeat three times.

3. Cup your hand around her heel and gently squeeze the back of her foot several times.

4. Cup your hand under her heel and place your thumb just below her inner ankle bone. Using firm pressure, gently circle this area with your thumb. *It is very important that you do not massage any higher than the ankle bone. An acupressure point is located just above the ankle; stimulating it could initiate labor.*

5. Gently work the arch of her foot with both thumbs, using circular motions over the entire area.

6. Lightly stroke each toe, working from the big toe to the little one.

7. Finish by placing one of your hands on the bottom of her foot and the other hand on top, and then pulling your hands down and off her foot (as in Step 2). Repeat three times.

8. Repeat the entire sequence with her other foot.

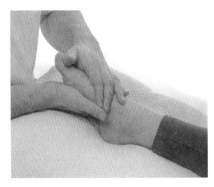

Pull your hands down and off her foot, as if you were "pulling" out her tension.

Cup your hand around her heel and gently squeeze.

Place your thumb just below her ankle bone and gently circle.

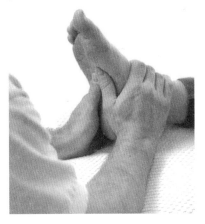

Gently work the arch with your thumbs, using circular motions.

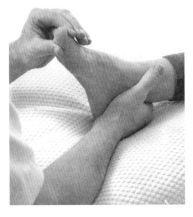

Lightly stroke each toe.

CONCLUSION

If you did not exercise on a regular basis before becoming pregnant, now is a good time to start. Exercising can increase your energy, relieve aches and pains that are common to pregnancy, stimulate the baby, and condition your muscles for the birth experience. It will also help you feel better mentally, knowing that you are doing something positive for yourself and your baby.

Choose the type of exercise that suits you best and that fits into your particular lifestyle. Some women prefer to exercise alone while others find it easier to stay motivated if they join a pregnancy exercise or yoga class. Toward the end of your pregnancy, you will need to taper your workout regimen. You can, however, always include walking as part of your daily routine, even during the last month before giving birth.

Always speak with your healthcare provider before participating in any type of exercise or physical activity during pregnancy. Depending on your physical condition and specific needs, you may need to follow certain restrictions and guidelines.

Tools for Labor

or This Is Not Your Mother's Lamaze

Childbirth training prepares you for birth on three levels—mentally, emotionally, and physically. You prepare mentally by learning all that you can about the natural process of labor and birth, as well as the possible complications that can arise. You also become aware of various comfort measures that can reduce pain perception and provide relief. Emotionally, you are encouraged to think positively about your birth experience and openly face your anxieties and fears. Physically, you practice exercises that promote comfort during pregnancy and birth, as well as techniques that encourage relaxation, offer distraction, and help focus attention during labor.

Chapter 6 presented physical exercises to enhance comfort during pregnancy and to prepare your body for giving birth. Chapter 8 will discuss the physical process of labor and birth, as well as normal hospital and birthing center procedures. This chapter focuses on the relaxation techniques, breathing patterns, and other comfort measures—for both you and your partner—that will become your responses to uterine contractions during labor.

COPING WITH LABOR PAIN

Descriptions of the labor experience will vary from woman to woman; they are also likely to differ for the same woman's various pregnancies. Labor has been described as easy, empowering, hard physical work, controllable, awesome, difficult, unmanageable, or intensely painful. Pain during labor can be caused by a number of factors, including fear, tension, stretching of the cervix, pressure of the baby's head on the nerves in the vaginal and cervical areas, the stretching of the pelvic floor muscles and the vagina, and pressure on the bladder and rectum.[1] The position and size of the baby, whether or not the woman was induced, and the length of labor can also affect pain, as can a woman's physical and mental conditions. Confident women who are well nourished and well rested, and who have good emotional support are more likely to have a positive experience than those with unresolved emotional issues or who are unprepared, stressed, or overly tired from lack of sleep.

Pain during labor is a signal to your body. It is telling you to respond by changing your position or using additional comfort measures. It is also a sign that it's time to get to the hospital, birthing center, or wherever you plan to give birth. It is important to remember that labor pain is different from pain you experience during an illness. It is not continuous. During a normal labor, the process starts slowly with mild

The Empowerment of Natural Birth

After giving birth without medication in an out-of-hospital birth center with a certified nurse midwife, Fenna told a childbirth class, "My body is awesome! I'm never going to be concerned again with negative traits about my body. I trusted my body to do what it needed to do, when I needed to do it."

contractions that gradually build in intensity and frequency. This allows you to gradually adapt. Each contraction is like a wave that builds in strength until it peaks and then gradually decreases. A pain-free break between contractions allows you to rest and prepare for the next wave. Keep in mind that even if your labor lasts twelve hours, approximately nine of those hours will be spent resting. Most important, remember that labor will end!

This chapter provides a variety of effective tools and techniques to use during labor. Most are designed to help distract you from and lessen the pain sensations brought on by contractions (see "The Gate Control Theory of Pain" below). Familiarize yourself with these various methods and individualize them to suit your needs. Every woman deals with pain in her own way. Think back to the last time you were ill with the flu or had a bad headache. Did you want your partner right next to you, hugging you, talking to you, and spoon-feeding you chicken soup? If so, you will probably want touch and close contact with your partner during contractions. Or did you tell him to leave the soup, close the door, and let you rest? While many women find touch soothing and relaxing, others find it irritating. Some women find comfort in their partner's voice; others find that it interrupts their ability to remain focused.

It is only through an awareness of the various labor tools and techniques that you can determine which ones will work best for you.

CHILDBIRTH PREPARATION METHODS

A number of popular labor and childbirth methods are designed to help you prepare for this very unique, very special experience. Although the Lamaze method is the most popular (and the one whose philosophy and practices are supported in this book), the Bradley method and certain hypnosis techniques—also briefly discussed in this chapter—can be effective as well.

These childbirth preparation methods stem from the work and principles of Dr. Grantly Dick-Read. A British physician, Dr. Dick-Read was instrumental in promot-

---

The Gate Control Theory of Pain

Pain sensations travel to the brain through a limited number of pathways. According to the *Gate Control Theory of Pain*, the "gate" through which pain sensations make their way to the brain can be manipulated through certain distraction techniques. Closing this passage allows fewer sensations to get through. Athletes, for example, have been known to concentrate so intensely on the game that, although injured, they are able to play through the pain. They don't perceive the intensity of the pain until the game is over and they begin to focus on it. Similarly, have you ever had a headache, but temporarily "forgot" about it while engrossed in an exciting movie, only to have it return when the movie ended?

While going through painful contractions, a woman in labor is able to distract herself from perceiving the full intensity of the pain by keeping her mind busy. She can do this by concentrating on a specific breathing pattern or focal point, and/or through visualization. Such distractions will help her adjust the pain gate mechanism and allow fewer pain sensations to get through to the brain. Other effective methods of distraction involve the physical stimulation of specific points on the body. Included among these methods are massage, acupressure, and the application of hot and cold compresses.

Some of the most popular childbirth preparation methods, including Lamaze, the Bradley method, and self-hypnosis, all incorporate distraction techniques to reduce pain perceptions during labor.

ing natural childbirth beginning in the 1920s. He believed that giving birth is a normal healthy function of women and, as with all normal bodily functions, it should not cause pain. His 1944 book, *Childbirth without Fear: The Principles and Practice of Natural Childbirth,* was considered controversial for its time.

Dr. Dick-Read first identified the fear-tension-pain cycle as a major contributor to the pain of childbirth. This cycle accurately describes the labor experience of an unprepared woman who enters labor full of fear—fear of the unknown; fear of what she was taught to expect from television, books, and the people around her; as well as the fear of being alone. In response to this fear, she tenses her muscles . . . which intensifies the pain of the contraction . . . which makes her even more fearful of the next contraction . . . which is even *more* painful due to the increased muscular tension. Not only does the fear-tension-pain cycle continue, it increases in intensity as the labor progresses.

Adequate preparation, however, breaks the cycle. Gaining information on what to expect during labor and birth helps eliminate fear and promote a positive attitude. Breathing and other relaxation techniques relieve tension, thereby reducing the painful sensations of labor. Being prepared helps break the fear-tension-pain cycle before it can even begin. Now, let's take a look at some of these effective childbirth preparation methods.

The Lamaze Method

While working in Russia during the 1940s, French obstetrician Fernand Lamaze first realized the importance of preparing for childbirth. There, he observed women in labor and delivery using *psychoprophylaxis* (mind prevention) techniques—breathing and relaxation methods—to reduce their awareness of pain. Upon returning to France in the early 1950s, Dr. Lamaze modified the techniques (which have since become synonymous with his name) and began practicing them in his clinic. After delivering a baby under Dr. Lamaze's guidance, Marjorie Karmel introduced his method to the United States through her 1959 book, *Thank You, Dr. Lamaze.*

The Lamaze method is based primarily on the principles of conditioned response, discovered by Russian physiologist Ivan Pavlov during his experiments with dogs. Each time Dr. Pavlov fed the dogs, he would ring a bell. When the dogs saw the food, they would naturally salivate. After a period of time, whenever the dogs heard the bell—even without seeing food—they would salivate. In other words, their response became a conditioned one.

When preparing for childbirth, you will learn new, positive responses to the contractions of labor. When you feel a contraction begin, you will learn to consciously relax and breathe rather than hold your breath and tense your muscles the way an unprepared woman would. Your preparation will also break the fear-tension-pain cycle as you learn effective tension-relieving techniques. Through the use of breathing, relaxing, and other distraction methods, your perception of pain during labor will be altered.

In France, during the early days of Lamaze, the laboring woman was accompanied and aided by her *monitrice,* the woman who taught her the relaxation techniques. In the United States, this position is filled by the labor companion—generally someone who is emotionally close to the woman, such as her husband, boyfriend, mother, sister, or close friend, who is also trained in the techniques. In addition, some women choose to hire a *doula,* a professional labor support person. The love and support of the labor companion or companions are important factors in creating a confident, positive attitude toward the childbirth experience.

Since Lamaze was first practiced, its preparation has dramatically changed over the years. The organization that promotes Lamaze techniques, originally called The American Society for Psychoprophylaxis in Obstetrics (ASPO), is now known as Lamaze International to honor the memory of Fernand Lamaze. Strict patterned breathing and pushing techniques, which were the focus of early Lamaze, are no longer the hallmarks of this method. The heart of today's Lamaze is based on a philosophy that provides the foundation and direction for women as they prepare to give birth and become mothers. Birth is viewed as a normal, healthy event. Women are encouraged to trust their inner strength and wisdom and to make educated, informed decisions regarding the birth experience.

In 2003, Lamaze International published a position paper that states its mission—"to promote, support, and protect normal birth through education and advocacy." The paper, which was updated in 2007, outlined six evidence-based normal birth practices, adopted from the World Health Organization (WHO), as a guide for creating a "birth environment that lets you tap into your innate birth wisdom and give birth simply and easily. Regardless of your baby's size, your labor's length and complexity, or your confidence level, these care practices will help you keep your labor and birth as normal as possible." They are:

1. *Labor begins on its own.* When the woman's body is allowed to go into labor spontaneously, it is ready to give birth and the baby is physically ready to be born. Unless there is a medical reason for inducing labor, it is best to wait for labor to start on its own.

2. *Freedom of movement throughout labor.* Walking, squatting, and rocking help you cope with painful contractions and encourage the baby to rotate through the pelvic bones and move into the birth canal.

3. *Continuous labor support.* Surround yourself with people you trust who will encourage and support you through labor.

4. *No routine interventions.* Continuous electronic fetal monitoring, restrictions on eating and drinking, episiotomies, IV fluids, and other common interventions are not necessary in most cases, and could even be harmful.

5. *Spontaneous pushing in upright or gravity-neutral positions.* When it is time to push the baby out, get into whatever position is most comfortable and push in response to how you feel.

6. *No separation of mother and baby after birth with unlimited opportunities for breastfeeding.* Your healthy newborn should be placed skin to skin on your abdomen or chest. Any immediate care can be performed while the baby is there.

The information in this book supports the philosophy and practices of Lamaze childbirth preparation. For additional information, or to find a Lamaze certified instructor in your area, either call your local hospital or contact Lamaze International. (For contact information, see the Resources beginning on page 449.)

Most hospitals offer childbirth classes that teach Lamaze techniques. Be aware, however, that some hospitals with high epidural rates may call their childbirth classes "Lamaze," although the focus is more on routine interventions than nondrug methods of pain relief. Prior to signing up for classes, whether in a hospital, birthing center, or private home, ask to speak with the instructor or coordinator to decide if the material being presented corresponds with your desires for labor and birth. In some communities, an independent instructor or a consumer-based group will provide a nonbiased approach.

The Bradley Method

A strong advocate of unmedicated birth and instinctual behavior during labor, obstetrician Robert A. Bradley, MD, developed a method of natural childbirth in 1947. He pioneered the practice of bringing fathers into the labor and delivery rooms. In 1965, Marjie and Jay Hathaway sought out Dr. Bradley for the birth of their fourth child. Together, they developed a formal class series with Dr. Bradley and founded the American Academy of Husband-Coached Childbirth (AAHCC).

Bradley method classes usually last twelve weeks, which is longer than most childbirth preparation classes. This is believed to be the time needed to mentally, physically, and emotionally prepare the body for the upcoming labor and birth. The Bradley method places a strong emphasis on nutrition and the avoidance of drugs during pregnancy, labor, birth, and breastfeeding. Women and their partners are taught exercises to prepare their bodies for the childbirth experience, as well as relaxation and natural breathing techniques. Bradley also encourages talking with the caregiver to verify that she will accommodate the desired birth wishes. To give personalized attention to students, Bradley class size is small, averaging three to six couples per class. According to AAHCC, "of over 200,000 Bradley-trained couples nationwide, over 86 percent have had spontaneous, unmedicated vaginal births."[2]

If you are interested in learning more about the Bradley method, or in finding a class near you, contact the American Academy of Husband-Coached Childbirth. (For contact information, see the Resources beginning on page 449.)

Hypnosis Methods

The use of hypnosis during childbirth has grown in popularity over the past several years. Based on the principles of Dr. Grantly Dick-Read, hypnosis methods have proven effective in breaking the fear-tension-pain cycle of labor, resulting in painless childbirth without the use of medications. During labor, the woman enters a deep hypnotic state through self-hypnosis techniques, visualization, guided imagery, and breathing methods, yet she is still able to move around and achieve a gentle birth. She tends to be relaxed and experience a relatively short labor without the need for medication or other interventions. Women who use hypnosis also tend to experience fewer complications.

Parents (or the expectant mother and her labor partner) can take classes to learn hypnosis techniques, or they can do so through home-study courses, which utilize books, CDs, or audiotapes. It's important for both people to learn and practice the techniques consistently so they are both prepared. The partner must be able to help the laboring woman maintain control. If you are interested in learning more about the use of hypnosis in labor, or in finding a class near you, contact HypnoBirthing or Hypnobabies. (For contact information, see the Resources, beginning on page 449.)

RELAXATION

Learning to relax is not just a tool for labor; it is also a skill for life. It will benefit both you and your partner, who should also learn these techniques.

Before discussing the topic of relaxation, it's important to understand stress and the negative effects it can have on the body. Stress refers to anything that disrupts or upsets your mental or emotional balance. It causes an increased production of the hormones adrenaline and cortisol, which speed up heart rate and increase blood pressure, among other physical changes. These changes are part of what is known as the body's *fight-or-flight response.* During prehistoric times, this inherent mechanism protected man against danger. When he was faced with a stressful challenge, such as a wild animal, the resulting rush of adrenaline that shot through his body gave him the burst of energy needed to either pick up a spear and "fight" or turn on his heel and take "flight." Once the crisis was over and the adrenaline was used up, his body returned to normal.

Most of the stress people face today is mental or psychological, often caused by the pressures of everyday life. It still, however, triggers the fight-or-flight reaction, causing the release of stress hormones. When stress occurs too often or persists for too long, it can wear the body down. Medical research has recognized that people who suffer from constant high stress levels are more likely to develop heart conditions, gastrointestinal distress, irritability, skin conditions, and sleeping problems than those whose lives are more relaxed.

Women with many stress-producing factors in their lives tend to develop a greater number of complications during pregnancy, labor, and birth. During pregnancy, stress has been cited as a cause of fatigue, insomnia, headaches, nausea and vomiting, high blood pressure, and preterm labor. Long-term stress may be linked to a low birth weight baby. This is because of the stress hormones, which constrict the mother's blood vessels and, thereby, reduce the amount of nutrients and oxygen that reach the fetus. In addition, these hormones cross the placenta and enter the baby's circulatory system, possibly predisposing her to increased irritability, restlessness, crying, and digestive upsets.

During labor, stress hormones can contribute to fatigue, a longer and more painful labor, and an increased need for interventions. They can also reduce blood flow to the uterus and placenta, which can put the baby in distress. Both fetal distress and a labor that fails to progress can increase the need for a cesarean section. Relaxation techniques help minimize stress and relax tense muscles during labor. Pain is intensified when muscles are tense. Learning how to relax your body is the single most important skill to develop as you prepare yourself for labor.

A Skill for Life

Relaxation is not just a tool for labor, but also a skill for life.

Labor is hard work. During labor, the uterine muscle will contract intermittently over a period of hours to open the cervix and move the baby down the birth canal. This takes a great deal of energy. It has been estimated that the same amount of energy is expended during labor as during a nonstop twelve- to eighteen-mile hike. Relaxing all of your muscles except the uterus (the one that *needs* to contract) will help reduce pain intensity and preserve energy and oxygen. This will make you less likely to become fatigued and to require medical intervention.

When you hear the word "relaxed," certain images—a rag doll, a drooping flower, a floppy hat—may come to mind. These are all images of extreme passiveness. A sleeping child is the ideal picture of passive relaxation. What you will learn in the following pages is a more active, conscious form of relaxation in which the mind is alert while the body is relaxed. Active relaxation involves the awareness and intentional release of tension. To understand this concept, slowly contract the muscles of your right arm. Now let the arm flop. This is an example of passive relaxation. Again, slowly contract the muscles of your right arm. Now, with concentration, slowly relax the different parts that arm. Begin with your biceps, then move down to relax your lower arm, then your hand, and finally your fingers. This is an example of active relaxation. Through it, you will learn to consciously relax your body—a process called *neuromuscular control* (mind control of the muscles)—during labor.

This section presents a number of exercises that are designed to help you become skilled at relaxation. First, however, it is helpful to take a moment and consider some relaxation basics.

Relaxation Basics

When practicing relaxation exercises, the following simple suggestions will help you make the most of your efforts. Begin by choosing a physical environment that is conducive to relaxing—a warm, comfortable room is best. Wear loose clothing and no shoes. While practicing, play soft, soothing music that you can take with you to the hospital or birth center. Make sure the supporting surface on which you practice—bed, reclining chair, mat—is firm. If it sags or bends, support will be lost, resulting in strain and muscle tension.

Assume a comfortable position in which all parts of your body are completely supported. Otherwise, the force of gravity will cause the unsupported muscles to tighten. Try to keep all of your joints bent, which also helps reduce muscle tension. The following positions are comfortable for practicing relaxation exercises:

■ **Semi-reclined position.** To assume this position, lie back at a 45-degree angle with pillows under your head, back, knees, and arms. While in this position, your partner can easily check your muscle tension. This makes it the best position to begin practicing your relaxation techniques.

A Hint for the Mother-to-Be

Relaxation will become automatic in labor if practiced frequently during pregnancy.

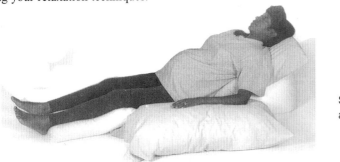

Semi-reclined position at a 45-degree angle.

■ **Side-lying position.** For this position, lie on your side with pillows under your head and abdomen, and between your legs and feet. During labor, many women find that this is the most comfortable position while lying in bed.

■ **The Sims' position.** In this position, named for gynecological pioneer Dr. James Marion Sims, lie on your side but position your body further over your abdomen. Place your lower arm behind your back and bring your upper arm and leg forward. Lie with pillows under your head, front shoulder and arm, abdomen, and upper leg. When in the Sims' position, the weight of the uterus is off the back, making it an excellent position for resting during pregnancy. It is also a good posture for alleviating back pain during labor.

The Sims' position.

As you develop skill in relaxing, you can also assume different positions while practicing your techniques. Try performing them while sitting up or kneeling.

Notes for the Labor Partner

Your role as labor partner is one that involves a number of important responsibilities. Helping your partner stay relaxed during labor is one of them. This means you must recognize any sign of tension she displays, and then help her release it. When in labor, she may be so involved with what her body is doing that she may become tense without even realizing it.

During your practice sessions, you will be checking her both visually and physically for signs of tension. However, to avoid disturbing her during actual labor, you will be checking her only visually. In early labor, you will be observing her for tension during contractions; but as labor progresses, you will also be checking her between contractions to ascertain that she is resting completely. If you observe signs of tension, you can use one or more of the techniques presented in this chapter to help her relax. Because each woman is different and will respond differently to the various comfort measures, it will be up to you to determine which ones are the most effective. Additionally, certain techniques may be more effective at different times during her labor.

While practicing, it's important to learn how to check your partner for both visual and physical signs of tension. As mentioned earlier, during these sessions, it is best for her to get into the semi-reclined position described on page 143. Begin by checking her visually. Is she frowning? Is her jaw clenched? Do her shoulders and neck look rigid? Are her toes flexed or curled? Are her fingers clenched? Are her eyes closed tightly? These are all signs of tension.

Next, check your partner physically by doing the following:

■ Check her neck for tension by gently turning her head from side to side. If her head moves easily, her neck is relaxed.

■ Place your hands on her shoulders and gently move them from side to side. Tense shoulders stay put, while relaxed ones move easily.

■ Gently pick up one of her arms, firmly supporting it under the elbow and wrist. Her upper arm, lower arm, and wrist should each move separately and feel heavy in your hands. If your partner helps lift her arm for you, or if any part of her arm is rigid and stiff, it is a sign of tension. Gently lower her arm back to the supporting surface; never drop it! If you move her arm too abruptly, she won't trust you. She will become tense—rather than relax—at the feel of your touch. Repeat with the other arm.

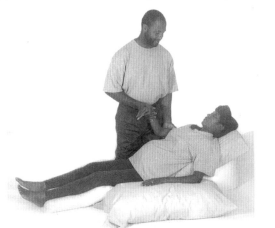

Checking the arm for relaxation.

■ Place your hands on the outside of each hip and gently move her pelvis from side to side. Relaxed hips move easily.

■ Lift one of her legs, supporting it under the knee and ankle. Her upper leg, lower leg, and foot should each move separately and feel heavy in your hands. If your partner helps lift her leg for you, or if any part of her leg is rigid and stiff, it is a sign of tension. Gently lower her leg back to the supporting surface. Her knee should flop to one side. Repeat with the other leg.

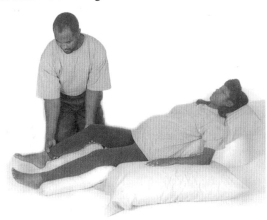

Checking the leg for relaxation.

While checking your partner for muscle tension, you may find certain areas of her body that are not completely relaxed. When this happens, try one of the following techniques:

■ Gently, quietly say to your partner, "Let your [name the specific body part] relax." Repeat as necessary.

■ Tell your partner to tense the body part as tightly as possible, and then slowly release it to the count of ten.

■ Firmly stroke the tense body part or lightly massage the area using a circular motion.

You may find that one of these tension relievers works better than another, or that a combination of techniques is most effective. Do whatever works best.

Relaxation Techniques

Several steps are involved in learning to achieve total relaxation. Begin with the Body Tension Awareness Guide (page 147). Once you and your labor partner have mastered this basic application, you can move on to more advanced techniques for achieving a relaxed state, including one for Total Body Relaxation, another for Touch Relaxation, and others involving visualization techniques.

Body Tension Awareness

The first step in learning relaxation involves developing a sense of body awareness and learning to recognize muscle tension. The goal of this first technique is to make you aware of what your different body parts feel like when they are tense and when they are relaxed. Practice with your labor partner.

The guide beginning on the next page presents easy-to-follow steps. It begins with a verbal cue or instruction, which ideally is given to you by your labor partner. This cue instructs you to tense a specific body part. What follows next are your instructions for responding to that cue—this involves tensing and then relaxing the specified body part. Also included in this guide are instructions for your labor partner to both visually and physically check that body part and verify that it is relaxed.

When you are given a verbal cue, breathe in slowly through your nose while tensing the specified body part. Feel the tightening of the muscles that are used to perform the action. Then breathe out slowly through your mouth and relax the body part. Feel the release as you relax the muscles. Your partner's job is to observe the physical appearance of the tensed muscles, and then check the body part for the degree of relaxation. For ease of checking, it is best to practice this exercise in the semi-reclined position.

Go through this exercise in the order it appears in the guide. When you have finished tensing and relaxing the final body part, take a few moments to mentally go back over your body. For areas that are still tense, repeat the tensing and releasing of that muscle group. Before getting up, take several deep breaths, then slowly rise to an upright position.

BODY TENSION AWARENESS GUIDE

The following technique is designed to help you recognize the way different parts of your body feel when they are tense as well as when they are relaxed. Performed with the help of a labor partner, the following steps should be practiced in the order given below. For best results, practice while lying in a comfortable semi-reclined position as seen on page 143).

Partner's Verbal Cue	Woman's Response	Partner's Evaluation
1 *"Pull up your toes."*	Inhale slowly through nose and tense toes. Exhale slowly through mouth and relax toes.	Visually observe tensed toes, then visually and physically check for relaxation.
2 *"Turn out your ankles."*	Inhale slowly through nose and tense ankles outward. Exhale slowly through mouth and relax ankles inward.	Visually observe tensed ankles, then visually and physically check for relaxation.
3 *"Bend your knees."*	Inhale slowly through nose and flex knees with feet on floor. Exhale slowly through mouth and straighten legs, letting knees flop outward.	Visually observe tensed knees, then visually and physically check for relaxation.
4 *"Squeeze your thighs together."*	Inhale slowly through nose and press thighs inward. Exhale slowly through mouth and let thighs relax outward.	Visually observe tensed thighs, then visually and physically check for relaxation.
5 *"Press your thighs toward the floor."*	Inhale slowly through nose and press thighs downward. Exhale slowly through mouth and relax thighs.	Visually observe tensed thighs, then visually and physically check for relaxation.
6 *"Tighten your buttocks."*	Inhale slowly through nose and tense buttocks. Exhale slowly through mouth and relax buttocks.	Visually observe tensed buttocks, then visually and physically check for relaxation.
7 *"Arch your back."*	Inhale slowly through nose and tense upper and lower back. Exhale slowly through mouth and relax upper and lower back.	Visually observe tensed back, then visually and physically check for relaxation.
8 *"Pull in your abdomen."*	Inhale slowly though nose and tense abdomen. Exhale slowly through mouth and relax abdomen.	Visually observe tensed abdomen, then visually and physically check for relaxation.
9 *"Expand your chest."*	Inhale slowly through nose and fill lungs with air, tensing chest. Exhale slowly through mouth and relax chest.	Visually observe tensed chest, then visually and physically check for relaxation.

Partner's Verbal Cue	Woman's Response	Partner's Evaluation
10 *"Press your shoulder blades back."*	Inhale slowly through nose and tense shoulders, pressing them back as far as possible. Exhale slowly through mouth and relax shoulders.	Visually observe tensed shoulders, then visually and physically check for relaxation.
11 *"Shrug your shoulders."*	Inhale slowly through nose and lift up shoulders. Exhale slowly through mouth and relax shoulders.	Visually observe tensed shoulders, then visually and physically check for relaxation.
12 *"Clench your hands and make fists."*	Inhale slowly through nose and make tight fists. Exhale slowly through mouth and relax hands.	Visually observe tensed hands, then visually and physically check for relaxation.
13 *"Extend your head backwards."*	Inhale slowly through nose and tense neck muscles. Exhale slowly through mouth and relax neck muscles.	Visually observe tensed neck muscles, then visually and physically check for relaxation.
14 *"Grimace."*	Inhale slowly through nose and tense lips. Exhale slowly through mouth and relax lips.	Visually observe tensed lips, then visually and physically check for relaxation.
15 *"Frown."*	Inhale slowly through nose and tense mouth area. Exhale slowly through mouth and relax mouth area.	Visually observe tensed mouth area, then visually and physically check for relaxation.
16 *"Clench your teeth."*	Inhale slowly through nose and tense jaw. Exhale slowly through mouth and relax jaw.	Visually observe tensed jaw, then visually and physically check for relaxation.
17 *"Wrinkle your nose."*	Inhale slowly through nose and tense area above nose. Exhale slowly through mouth and relax area above nose.	Visually observe tensed nose area, then visually and physically check for relaxation.
18 *"Close your eyes tightly."*	Inhale slowly through nose and close eyes tightly. Exhale slowly through mouth and relax eyes.	Visually observe tensed eyes, then visually and physically check for relaxation.
19 *"Lift up your eyebrows."*	Inhale slowly through nose and raise eyebrows as high as possible. Exhale slowly through mouth and relax eyebrows.	Visually observe tensed eyebrows, then visually and physically check for relaxation.

Total Body Relaxation

Once you have become proficient at recognizing tension in your body, it's time to begin refining your relaxation skills with Total Body Relaxation. This technique will help you become conditioned to relaxing your entire body, not just individual body parts. Like the last technique, Total Body Relaxation is done by responding to verbal instructions that ideally are given by your labor partner. The guide beginning on page 150 presents the steps. The verbal cues or instructions should be given in the order in which they appear.

When you have completed the entire sequence, your partner can physically check your body for relaxation. Then take a moment to come back to the present. Take a few deep breaths, open your eyes, and slowly get up with your partner's assistance. After performing these steps several times, you may be able to mentally take yourself through the routine without the verbal cues.

Touch Relaxation

Another technique that can aid dramatically in developing your skill at relaxation is one that involves touch. During touch relaxation, your partner places his hand on your tensed muscles. In response, you relax your tensed muscles toward his hand. Practicing this form of nonverbal communication will help you learn to respond with complete relaxation to your partner's touching, stroking, and massaging during labor. Verbal cues won't be necessary at that time—your muscles will be conditioned to relax automatically in response to your partner's touch.

When practicing the touch relaxation technique, your partner will give you a verbal cue, instructing you to tense a specific set of muscles. Then he will lay his hand upon the contracted muscles. As soon as you feel your partner's touch, begin to release the contracted muscles toward his hand. The guide beginning on page 152 presents the steps, which should be done in the order they appear. Touch relaxation is one of the best techniques to use during labor.

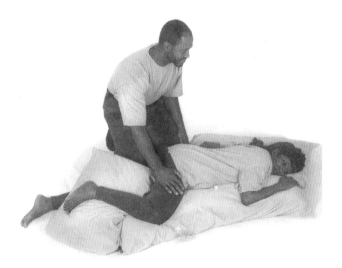

Touch relaxation is an effective technique to use during labor.

TOTAL BODY RELAXATION GUIDE

Following the steps of this guide will help your entire body reach a state of complete relaxation. Although this technique is meant to be done with the aid of a partner, after performing it several times, many women find they can take themselves through the routine through mental images alone. Relax in any comfortable position while performing this technique.

Note for the labor partner: All of the verbal cues are to be given slowly.

Partner's Verbal Cue	Woman's Response	Partner's Evaluation
1 *"Close your eyes, take several deep breaths, and begin to let the tension flow from your body. (PAUSE) Release any tightness in your head starting at the top of your scalp, then moving down the sides and back of your head."*	Relax scalp area.	Observe relaxation of the forehead.
2 *"Lower your eyebrows."*	Let eyebrows drop.	Observe relaxation of eyebrows.
3 *"Close your eyes. Feel your eyelids becoming heavy, your eyes sinking back into your head."*	Relax eyes, eyelids, temples, and forehead.	Observe relaxation of eye area.
4 *"Let your jaw drop. Part your lips slightly."*	Relax jaw and slightly open mouth.	Observe relaxation of jaw.
5 *"Allow your head to rest against the pillow."* (If her head is not supported, say: *"Slightly lower your chin."*)	Relax head against support (or lower chin).	Observe relaxation of head.
6 *"Feel your shoulder blades open outward like a dress falling off a hanger."*	Relax neck, shoulders, and upper arms.	Observe relaxation of upper body.
7 *"Starting at your right shoulder, move any tightness down your upper arm (PAUSE) past your elbow (PAUSE) down your lower arm (PAUSE) past your wrist (PAUSE) through your hand (PAUSE) and out your fingers."*	Slowly relax right arm from shoulder down to fingers.	Observe relaxation of right arm.
8 *"Starting at your left shoulder, move any tightness down your upper arm (PAUSE) past your elbow (PAUSE) down your lower arm (PAUSE) past your wrist (PAUSE) through your hand (PAUSE) and out your fingers."*	Slowly relax left arm from shoulder down to fingers.	Observe relaxation of left arm.
9 *"Concentrate on your breathing. Slowly breathe in oxygen through your nose and send it to your baby; slowly exhale through your mouth, releasing carbon dioxide and tension. With each out-breath, sigh out a little more tension."*	Exhale and relax body further. Be aware of tension release.	Observe relaxation of chest and shoulders.

Partner's Verbal Cue	Woman's Response	Partner's Evaluation
10 *"Breathe in through your nose and out through your mouth, making each breath a little longer, until you feel very relaxed. Try to feel as if you are breathing right down your back, starting at the base of your neck and slowly moving down your upper back* (PAUSE) *past your ribs* (PAUSE) *down into your waist* (PAUSE) *and into your hips."*	Focus on breathing and relax back muscles.	Observe relaxation of back.
11 *"Starting at your right hip, move any tightness down your thigh* (PAUSE) *past your knee* (PAUSE) *down your calf* (PAUSE) *past your ankle* (PAUSE) *through your foot* (PAUSE) *and out your toes."*	Relax right leg from hip down to toes.	Observe relaxation of right leg.
12 *"Starting at your left hip, move any tightness down your thigh* (PAUSE) *past your knee* (PAUSE) *down your calf* (PAUSE) *past your ankle* (PAUSE) *through your foot* (PAUSE) *and out your toes."*	Relax left leg from hip down to toes.	Observe relaxation of left leg.
13 *"Feel every limb become heavy—your feet* (PAUSE) *lower legs* (PAUSE) *thighs* (PAUSE) *hips* (PAUSE) *hands* (PAUSE) *arms* (PAUSE) *shoulders."*	Experience feeling of heaviness from feet to shoulders.	Observe relaxation of arms and legs.
14 *"Feel the force of gravity pulling you down and into the earth."*	Experience feeling of sinking.	Observe relaxation of body.
15 *"Your knees feel very heavy. Let them flop apart to the sides."*	Feel legs become limp.	Observe relaxation of legs.
16 *"Feel your whole body melting and spreading across the floor."*	Feel sensation of tension flowing outward.	Observe relaxation of body.
17 *"Now take a minute to go over your body. is there any area still holding tension? If so, think about bringing some heat to that area."*	Feel the warmth of the sun on any tense area.	Observe relaxation of entire body, then physically check for total relaxation.
18 *"Take a few deep breaths and release them slowly."*	Inhale deeply and exhale slowly.	Observe relaxation of entire body.
19 *"Open your eyes* (PAUSE) *sit up* (PAUSE) *slowly get up."*	Sit up, then slowly rise.	Assist her in getting up.

TOUCH RELAXATION GUIDE

Practicing the following techniques will help condition your tense muscles to relax upon feeling the simple touch of your partner's hand. During practice, tense the specified muscles according to your partner's verbal cues. Then relax those muscles when he places his hand on them. All of these steps can be done while semi-reclined or in a comfortable side-lying position.

Note to the labor partner: Touch the contracted muscles with a relaxed but firm hand. Slowly mold your hand to the shape of the body part. If touching does not bring about complete relaxation, stroke or massage the body part until relaxed.

Partner's Verbal Cue	Woman's Response	Partner's Response
1 "Tense your forehead."	Raise eyebrows.	Place hands on sides of head near temples.
	Lower eyebrows.	Feel the forehead relax.
2 "Tense your jaw."	Grit teeth and clench jaw.	Place hands on sides of jaw.
	Relax jaw.	Feel jaw drop.
3 "Tense your neck."	Raise chin in air and contract back of neck.	Rest hand on back of neck.
	Relax neck.	Feel chin fall forward and muscles relax.
4 "Tense your shoulders."	Press shoulders back against supporting surface or partner's hands.	Rest hands on front of shoulders.
	Relax shoulders.	Feel shoulders move forward.
5 "Tense your right arm."	Clench right fist, and extend and clench entire arm.	Rest hands on fist, stroke palm with thumbs, then slowly move hands up sides of arm to shoulder and press shoulder firmly.
	Relax right arm.	Feel muscles gradually relax from hand up to shoulder.
6 "Tense your left arm.	Clench left fist, and extend and clench entire arm.	Rest hands on fist, stroke palm with thumbs, then slowly move hands up sides of arm to shoulder and press shoulder firmly.
	Relax left arm.	Feel muscles gradually relax from hand up to shoulder.
7 "Tense your abdomen."	Pull in abdomen.	Rest hand on curve of upper abdomen.
	Relax abdomen.	Feel abdomen expand outward.
8 "Tense your back."	Arch small of back.	Rest hands on sides of sacrum.
	Relax back.	Feel back drop toward floor.

Partner's Verbal Cue	Woman's Response	Partner's Response
9 *"Tense your thighs together."*	Press thighs together.	Touch outside of thighs.
	Relax thighs.	Feel legs fall outward.
10 *"Tense your thighs downward."*	Press thighs and knees against floor.	Rest hands on top of thighs.
	Relax thighs.	Feel legs rise and fall outward.
11 *"Tense your right leg."*	Straighten and stiffen right leg, pointing toes upward.	Firmly touch instep of foot, then stroke instep with fingers. Slowly move hands up to knee and then up to top of leg.
	Relax right leg.	Feel muscles gradually relax from foot to top of leg, with thigh falling outward.
12 *"Tense your left leg."*	Straighten and stiffen left leg, pointing toes upward.	Firmly touch instep of foot, then stroke instep with fingers. Slowly move hands up to knee and then up to top of leg.
	Relax left leg.	Feel muscles gradually relax from foot to top of leg, with thigh falling outward.

At the completion of this technique, your labor partner may continue instructing you to add tension to any muscle group that is not already included in the steps above.

Visualization

Visualization is another effective relaxation technique that helps prepare women for labor and birth. Also known as *imagery,* visualization involves picturing an image in your mind. This technique is commonly used among athletes, who use it to prepare for competition. Prior to competing in an event, a gymnast will visualize her routine, a downhill skier will visualize the gates on the run, and an ice skater will mentally run through the jumps she will be attempting during an upcoming performance. As an expectant mother, practicing visualization can help you relax throughout the pregnancy; it can also help you develop and maintain a positive mental attitude toward the birth experience. During labor, it can keep you relaxed and focused on your body.

The two sample visualizations that follow—"A Special Place" and "Birth"—will help prepare you for labor and delivery. With the help of a partner, preferably your labor partner, practice them during your pregnancy. From these sample visualizations, choose the phrases and images that work best for you.

To practice, sit or lie in a comfortable, supported position. To help set a calming mood, play soft, soothing music in the background. (If possible, use this same music during labor.) Your sessions will be most effective if, while reading the visualizations, your partner uses a soft, soothing tone of voice and speaks slowly, pausing frequently to allow the images to develop. While reading, he should pause for a count of one whenever he sees a dot. (This means three dots in a row should prompt a pause of 1-2-3.) Pauses should be slightly longer at the end of a paragraph.

"A SPECIAL PLACE"
VISUALIZATION

For many women, entering the unfamiliar environment of a labor unit can be an unsettling experience. During labor, using this visualization during contractions will help mentally transport you from the labor room to a more familiar, secure place.

During practice sessions, close your eyes while your labor partner slowly reads the following:

Take in a deep breath . . . . exhale . . . . and relax your body . . . . starting at your head . . . . and moving down to your toes . . . . Take in another deep breath . . . . exhale slowly . . . . and once more, slowly breathe in . . . . and out . . . . You will not fall asleep, but you will be calm and fully aware . . . . As you relax, picture in your mind a place that makes you feel very comfortable . . . . a place where you feel safe and secure . . . . a place where you are so protected that nothing can harm you or interfere with your thoughts . . . . a place where you can leave all your worries and surrender yourself to being at peace.

This special place may be a room in your home . . . . or in the home where you spent your childhood . . . . or a favorite vacation or honeymoon spot . . . . or a place you have dreamed about visiting . . . . . It may be from a scene in a book . . . or a movie . . . . or even from a fantasy, a place that does not exist . . . . Enter this place and look around . . . What colors do you see? . . . . . Do you hear any sounds? . . . . Is the temperature warm or cool? . . . . . What are you wearing? . . . . Are you aware of any familiar fragrances? . . . . . . Take a few moments to familiarize yourself with your special place.

As you gaze at your surroundings, focus on an object . . . . Stare at this object and allow it to become your focal point . . . . As you continue to stare at the object . . . concentrate . . . breathe slowly . . . and allow yourself to enter a level of deeper relaxation. (Take a longer pause before continuing.)

Now, take several deep breaths . . . . mentally travel back to your present environment . . . . and slowly open your eyes . . . . Think about the serenity and peace you just expserienced . . . and know that you can go back to that place whenever you choose.

Become familiar with this visualization by practicing it during pregnancy. When you are in labor, you can then close your eyes and return to that special place during every contraction. Or you can keep your eyes open and stare at a focal point—preferably the same focal point you used in your visualizations. Use either the object itself or a picture of it. If your special place was a secluded beach, a house on a lake, or some other place near water, you may find that laboring in a tub or shower will enhance your relaxation. Bring any fragrance from your visualizations (in the form of potpourri, a scented candle, or scented oil) with you. Finally, during labor, play any recorded sounds from your visualizations, including music or sounds of nature, such as the rain, ocean waves, or chirping birds.

"BIRTH"
VISUALIZATION

This visualization, adapted from *Birthing Normally* by Gayle Peterson, will help you prepare emotionally for viewing birth as a normal, healthy event. It encourages you to use your imagination to picture the process of labor and delivery. To be most effective, it is best to practice this visualization when you are relaxed, such as after performing the "Special Place" Visualization or completing one of the relaxation exercises in this chapter. You will be more receptive to suggestion when in a calm, relaxed state. During practice sessions, your partner should maintain a soothing tone of voice when he reads. When describing contractions, though, his soothing voice should increase in volume and speed as the contractions accelerate, and become softer and slower as the contractions recede. Close your eyes while your labor partner slowly reads the following:

Hints for the Labor Partner

While reading visualization instructions to your mate:

✓ Play soothing music.

✓ Speak slowly and pause frequently. This will allow the images to develop in your partner's mind.

Concentrate on your breathing . . . . breathe deeply and peacefully . . . With each breath, allow yourself to let go more and more . . . . You will not fall asleep, but you will be calm and fully aware . . . . . . As you relax, picture in your mind a special place where you would like to have your baby . . . . . . Take yourself there and make yourself comfortable . . . . . Notice the surroundings . . . . What do you see? . . . . Are you aware of any fragrances? . . . . . What textures do you feel? . . . . . Do you hear any sounds?

As you continue to breathe slowly and deeply, picture your uterus in your mind . . . large and pear shaped . . . round and full at the top . . . tapered and narrow at the bottom . . . a strong, muscular organ, capable of much hard work. See the round, healthy, red placenta on the back of the uterine wall . . . See the umbilical cord sending oxygen and food to your baby . . . . Watch your baby floating freely and peacefully in the warm, clear amniotic fluid . . . . Her head is down in the pelvic cradle, just waiting for the day she will be born . . . . Hear your baby's heartbeat, strong and sure . . . . See the downy lanugo hair . . . . Look at the vernix covering her body like a protective coat . . . . Count her fingers and toes . . . Look at how long her nails have grown . . . Your baby is continuing to grow and waiting for the day to be born.

From your baby's point of view, look down at the cervix . . . See it puffy and soft with the mucous plug sealing its opening . . . much like a cork in the neck of a bottle . . . protecting your baby from infection until it is time to be born.

Now take yourself forward in time to the day labor begins . . . . . Picture the cervix . . . . the mucous plug is gone . . . As your uterus begins to contract, the cervix is getting shorter and shorter. . . . Feel your baby's head pressing firmly against the cervix . . . helping it stretch . . . and become thinner . . . and thinner . . . and slowly open up.

You feel a contraction starting, like a train approaching on a distant track . . . getting closer and closer, and the contraction is getting stronger and stronger. Your baby's head is pressing harder and harder on the cervix. The cervix is stretching more and more, and the baby's head is coming down and

Allow Yourself Options

Some women find relaxation techniques sufficient for dealing with the sensations of labor. Others need additional coping strategies. Learning effective breathing techniques, or allowing yourself to assume various positions during labor are other helpful ways to achieve comfort during labor. To be properly prepared, it is best to learn all of these techniques. Then you can use whichever ones you need during your unique labor situation, modifying them as you desire.

down, and you open and open more, and the contraction begins to fade and fade, just as the train moves off into the distance . . . . Feel your body relax . . . Let all the tension go . . . Gather strength from within for the next contraction. . . you rest, and your baby rests. (Repeat this paragraph two more times.)

As the next contraction comes, feel it growing in intensity, much like a large wave, rising higher and higher. Feel your cervix stretching and stretching as the baby's head moves down, down, down into the cervix. Now feel the contraction subsiding . . . just as the wave comes to shore, as you know it always will . . . you rest, and your baby rests. (Repeat this paragraph one more time.)

Quickly, another contraction begins to build, getting stronger and stronger, and stretching the cervix further and further as the uterine muscles pull it up and back, over the baby's head. Feel your baby straining to get through as the amniotic sac bulges into your vagina. Feel relief and warmth as the sac ruptures and the amniotic fluid gushes onto the bed and the contraction subsides as the baby slips back.

Now you feel another contraction. It is very hard and builds rapidly. See your vagina unfold to receive the baby's rapidly advancing head, just as the petals on a flower open up. Feel the head moving through the pelvis and under the pubic bone. Then the contraction begins to fade . . . you rest, and your baby rests.

And still another contraction comes, massaging your baby's skin, preparing her to breathe on her own very soon, very soon. Feel the pressure of your baby's head on your perineum . . . . As your perineum stretches more and more, you feel burning and stinging, and you are panting, panting, relaxing your pelvic floor muscles so that your baby can ease her way out. Slowly, very slowly, here comes the baby's head . . . which she turns to the side . . . Next, the top shoulder is out . . . then the bottom shoulder . . . Hear your baby breathe . . . . Now reach down and slowly lift your baby onto your chest . . . . Feel her warm wetness against your skin . . . . Watch her chest rise and fall as she begins to breathe and her color turns from blue to pink . . . . She looks intently at your face . . . then begins rooting for your breast until she finds it and begins nursing . . . . Such peace and joy . . Your baby has been born!

And now, as you are enjoying the sensations of touching, seeing, hearing, and smelling your new baby, you are aware of another contraction, a milder contraction as your placenta is delivered . . . Your uterus continues to contract very firmly to prevent bleeding, just as it should.

Now bring yourself back to the present and know that your baby is growing and getting ready for that day when she will be born . . . It is still a few weeks off, but getting closer with each passing day . . . Continue to breathe deeply and relax. In a moment, you can open your eyes, feeling renewed and refreshed, knowing that your body will perform just as it should when the baby's birth day arrives.

Continue to sit or lie quietly for as long as you wish. When you are ready to get up, do so slowly. The positive feelings that you are experiencing can remain with you throughout the day.

BREATHING TECHNIQUES FOR LABOR

Along with using strategies that help relax the body during labor, many women find breathing techniques to be effective coping tools as well. Popular breathing methods that were once at the heart of the Lamaze method have changed from specific patterns to breathing normally in a slow, steady rhythm. Rapid panting, for example, which had been one of those coping techniques performed during active labor or transition, is now discouraged. This is because breathing too fast is not only exhausting, it could cause you to hyperventilate. Slow breathing, on the other hand, is effective and the only breathing method you need to practice.

Slow Breathing

Breathing in a slow rhythmical pattern maintains a constant, balanced exchange of oxygen and carbon dioxide to ward off hyperventilation and to ensure a good oxygen supply to the working uterus, the placenta, and the baby. In addition, as explained by the Gate Control Theory of Pain earlier in this chapter, the focusing that is required to maintain breathing at a slow controlled rate can reduce your perception of pain.

As you practice slow breathing, keep in mind that every woman's breathing rate is different and should be customized for her personal comfort. Before you begin, determine your normal breathing rate by having your partner count your breaths for one full minute. When you practice slow breathing, breathe slower than normal—about half your normal rate. And try to maintain a slow, steady rhythm in a relaxed and comfortable manner. Some women mentally count as they breathe to maintain focus. (*Breathe in 2, 3, 4 and out 2, 3, 4.*) Inhale and exhale any way you prefer—in through your nose and out through your mouth, in and out through your nose, or in and out through your mouth. (If your nose is congested, mouth breathing may be easiest.)

During practice and actual labor, begin and end each contraction with a *relaxing breath*—a smooth, deep, faster breath that is inhaled through your nose, and then exhaled like a sigh through your mouth. This breath produces a good boost of oxygen for the baby and your uterus at the start of the contraction. It is followed by your slow breathing pattern, which extends throughout the contraction. A relaxing breath is also a signal to your labor partner that the contraction has begun or ended. While slow breathing through a contraction, many women prefer to close their eyes, which allows them to block out their surroundings and tune into their bodies. Other women prefer choosing a focal point to focus on during the contraction.

When practicing slow breathing, have your partner give you the verbal cue "Contraction begins." Take a relaxing breath, and then begin slow breathing. Have your partner call out the passing time in fifteen-second intervals using sixty seconds as the average length of a

Using a Focal Point

During contractions, some women choose to concentrate on a focal point—a special photograph, a religious symbol, a painting, etc. This enables them to focus on something outside themselves, lessening their awareness of the strength of the contractions.

Steps for Practicing Slow Breathing

1. Labor partner says, "Contraction begins."
2. You take a deep relaxing breath and release the tension from your body.
3. Close your eyes or concentrate on a focal point and begin slow breathing.
4. Labor partner clocks the timing of the contraction, calling out the passing seconds in fifteen-second intervals for a total of sixty seconds.
5. At sixty seconds, the labor partner says, "Contraction ends."
6. You take another deep relaxing breath and totally relax your body.

During practice, rest for a few moments, then repeat these steps.

contraction. At the end of each contraction, have your partner say, "Contraction ends." Finish the contraction with a second relaxing breath. Remember, during labor, your partner will no longer need to give verbal cues as you will automatically begin and end the breathing technique using the actual labor contractions as your guide.

When you are in labor, be aware that your breathing will accelerate naturally in response to your contractions. At first, your breaths will be slow and steady, but expect them to gradually increase in number as the contraction builds. As the contraction subsides, they will slowly decrease. Some women have found that humming or moaning in low tones while exhaling is helpful for getting through contractions. Others like to vocalize during contractions by reciting a phrase, such as "I can do this," or "I am strong."

Breathing During the Premature Urge to Push

Pushing before your cervix is sufficiently dilated for your baby's head to pass through is a waste of energy. Your caregiver will instruct you whether or not it is time to push when you feel this urge, which may be felt during transition.

If, during a contraction, you feel a strong urge to push and your cervix is not completely dilated, pant (say "hee, hee") or take a quick breath and then forcefully blow out the air from your mouth. Do this repeatedly. It is difficult to bear down or push effectively when you are blowing out air this way. Remember to breathe in air before you blow out. When the urge to push is gone, return to slow breathing.

POSITIONS FOR LABOR

Moving around and changing positions during labor can help decrease pain perception, shorten labor, and reduce the need for medication and interventions. Unfortunately, many women assume they must remain in bed once admitted to the hospital, where they are often routinely hooked up to an electronic fetal monitor and/or given intravenous fluids. Obviously, such interventions make it more difficult to move about freely. Be aware that you can request intermittent monitoring or ask to be monitored while out of bed. And the use of IVs may not be necessary, or you may request a saline lock (see "Intravenous Fluids" on page 245).

During labor, trust your body and get into whatever position makes you most comfortable. Try several positions and change them frequently. As you will see, certain postures can encourage proper rotation of the baby as she moves down through the pelvis.

Upright Positions

Upright positions are most beneficial for moving the baby through the pelvis. Standing takes advantage of gravity, which helps the baby descend. Adding movement aids this even further. Standing upright also decreases the perception of pain while producing more effective contractions, which may help to shorten labor. This position also encourages the proper rotation and descent of the baby through the pelvis. If a shower is available, using it will give you the added benefit of warm water on your body. Some facilities even provide a hand-held showerhead, which allows you or your partner to direct the spray over your lower back or abdomen.

Avoiding Hyperventilation

One significant reason for breathing slowly during labor is to avoid hyperventilation, which results from exhaling too much carbon dioxide. Symptoms of hyperventilation typically include dizziness, and/or numbness or tingling in the fingertips, nose, or tongue. If you experience these symptoms, breathe into your cupped hands or a small paper bag and slow down your breathing rate. This will allow you to rebreathe the same air and alleviate the symptoms.

Walking between contractions, standing next to the bed or against a wall, and lunging are all effective upright positions. When standing by a bed, you can lean over and use the side rail or the bed itself for support during contractions. When in this position, a fetal monitor can be used, and your partner can easily massage your lower back. If you experience back pain during labor, press your fists into your lower back while standing with your back against a wall.

If you walk between contractions, your partner can support you by holding onto your arm. When a contraction begins, you can face him, bend your knees, place your arms around his neck with your head on his shoulder, and allow him to support your weight. If your partner is much taller than you, lean your head against his chest and allow your arms to drop to your sides as he places his hands around your waist for support. Or you can press your back against your partner and have him wrap his arms beneath your abdomen, supporting it with his hands. While in these positions, some women have found that swaying their hips, as if dancing, can be soothing.

Getting into the lunge position can help to widen your pelvis, especially if the baby is in a posterior position. To get into this position, stand beside the bed or a chair. With one foot firmly planted on the floor, place your other foot on the mattress or seat of the chair. During a contraction, repeatedly lunge sideways and hold the position for five to ten seconds, using your partner for support. If you know which side of the pelvis the back of the baby's head is facing, lunge with that leg. If you do not know, lunge in the direction that is most comfortable. During lunges, you should feel a stretch in the inner thigh.

Lunge position.

When in an upright position, you can also make use of an elastic exercise rope or a long cloth sling that is securely suspended from above. While holding onto the rope, you can bend your knees to stretch, sway, lunge, or squat. Or you can secure the sling around your back for support to accomplish the same positions. For obvious safety reasons, securing these devices firmly is extremely important.

Sitting

Sitting—whether on a chair, the labor bed, or a birth ball—is another position many women find comfortable during labor. It also provides the benefit of gravity (although not as much as standing does), which encourages the baby to move through the pelvis. A fetal monitor can be used when in this position. Rocking back and forth can offer additional comfort while sitting (sitting in a rocking chair or on a birth ball can be especially soothing). If you are experiencing back pain, sit on the edge of the bed or straddle the chair and lean forward so that your partner can rub your lower back. (For more information on birth balls, see page 164.)

Side-Lying

Side-lying is another comfortable position during labor for most women. It is especially beneficial during long labors in which the woman needs to rest. For maximum comfort, place pillows under your head and abdomen and between your legs. Side-lying does not restrict the use of a fetal monitor or other interventions. It also helps to lower blood pressure, and is a good option for women who are medicated.

Kneeling

Kneeling on the hands and knees is one of the most comfortable positions when experiencing back labor. It takes the weight of the baby off the spine and may also encourage proper rotation. While in this position, doing the Pelvic Rock (page 125) can add further relief; your partner can also apply firm counter pressure to the painful areas. If kneeling on the bed, you can raise the head of the bed and lean your upper body against the elevated section, using pillows for support. If kneeling on the floor, you can do so in front of a chair with your upper body resting on the chair seat. Or you can lean against a birth ball. The photos at left show various kneeling positions during labor.

Kneeling on the hands and knees.

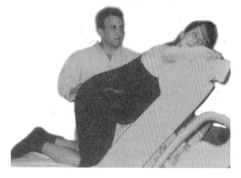

Kneeling against the elevated section of a bed.

Kneeling with the aid of a birth ball.

OTHER TOOLS AND TECHNIQUES FOR LABOR

As you have seen, relaxation, slow breathing, and comfortable labor positions are very effective for reducing pain perception during labor. They are not, however, the only means. Massage, acupressure, and laboring in water are among the many other comfort measures that women can experience either alone or with the help of their partner. Techniques such as acupuncture and transcutaneous electrical nerve stimulation (which require professional assistance) are other effective measures.

It's a good idea to become familiar with all of these nondrug choices—doing so will give you a wider range of options to use during labor. They may also reduce the need for medications and other interventions.

Labor Massage

Massage can be an effective tool during labor to promote relaxation, relieve stress, conserve energy, facilitate breathing, and assist in relieving muscle cramping and pain. While some women prefer not to be touched at all during labor, others appreciate the relief massage can bring, as well as the loving care and support it represents.

The previous chapter presented a number of body massage techniques beginning on page 132 that are designed to relax and comfort you during your pregnancy. Your labor partner can use any of these methods to soothe you during labor.

Another form of massage that is commonly used during contractions is called *effleurage*—a light fingertip massage that can be performed either by you or your labor partner. Lightly place the fingertips of both hands on your abdomen just above your pubic bone. Using light pressure, slowly bring your fingertips upward near the top of your abdomen. Then gently draw them outward, down, and back to the starting point in a circular motion. Continue drawing these circles on your abdomen for the duration of the contraction. You can also draw them in sync with the rhythm of your breathing.

What follows are some additional massage techniques that can help you relax during labor. Your partner can:

■ Gently stroke your arms with his full hand, moving upward from your wrists to your shoulders.

■ Gently stroke your legs with his full hand, moving upward from your ankles to your thighs.

■ Gently massage your face, lightly stroking your jaw area to help relax it during active labor.

■ Apply fingertip pressure along the base of your skull between contractions.

■ Grasp and lightly hold together the first three toes (the big toe and the two next to it) on each foot during contractions. Rhythmically grasping and releasing these toes helps relax the pelvic floor.

■ Gently rub your neck and shoulders.

Effleurage is a light fingertip massage that encourages relaxation during contractions.

Along with using their hands, many labor partners have discovered that hand-held massage tools—which come in a wide variety of styles—can also be effective. Any non-electrical device is acceptable. You can find these massagers at department stores, specialty gift shops, and sporting goods stores, as well as through Internet searches. Along with the devices made specifically for massage, other items can prove to be effective as well. For instance, your partner can use a tennis ball to roll over the tense muscles of your back or use them to apply counter pressure for relief. Water "noodles"—those long, flexible flotation devices made of foam and used in swimming pools—can be cut into foot-long sections and used for back massage. Octagonal-shaped water noodles are the most effective.

Finally, you may want to hire a professional massage therapist to attend your labor. Because of her knowledge and expertise, she would be able to incorporate such relaxation techniques into her massage as reflexology (the release of tension through pressure points on the feet) and acupressure (the release of tension through pressure points on the body).

Counter Pressure

The application of counter pressure is another technique that can help relieve lower back pain during labor. If you are experiencing such pain, you will have to show your labor partner its exact location on both sides of your back. Using his fists or the heel of his hands, he can apply firm pressure to the area during contractions. (You will also have to let him know the amount of pressure you desire.) Be aware that the pressure points will become lower as your labor progresses and the baby's head descends through the pelvis.

Performing the Double-Hip Squeeze is another counter pressure method that can help relieve back pain. For this technique, you can either stand while bending over at the waist and supporting your upper body against a chair or a bed, or you can kneel on all fours. Your partner, who stands or kneels behind you, places his hands high on your

Double-Hip Squeeze.

Knee Press.

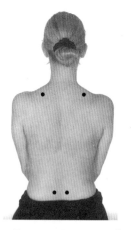

Pressure to upper points
can relieve neck/upper arm
pain and headaches.
Pressure to low points
relieves lower back pain.

Applying pressure to this point
on the bottom of the foot
promotes relaxation and a
general sense of calmness.

buttocks (on the meatiest areas). Using his full hands, he then presses your hips together during contractions, which helps open the outlet at the pubic joint.

Another counter pressure method is the Knee Press. For this technique, sit in a straight-back chair with a small pillow or towel supporting your lower back. Your labor partner kneels in front of you and places his hands on your knees. The heels of his hands should be resting at the lower margin of your knee, where the tibia ends. During a contraction, your partner leans forward and presses your upper legs toward the back of the chair.

Acupressure

The Russian theorists who originated the idea of reducing pain awareness during childbirth through certain mind-prevention techniques included acupressure in their approach. They identified certain "pain prevention points" in the body and recommended applying pressure to them to aid in pain relief. Acupressure interferes with and alters pain impulses as they travel to the brain, as described in the Gate Control Theory of Pain (page 138). It may also encourage the body's release of "feel good" endorphins. This technique was omitted as a component of prepared childbirth when the Lamaze method became westernized.

Also known as *pressure point massage,* acupressure involves the application of physical pressure—often by the thumbs or fingertips—to certain points on the body. When stimulated, these points, which exist in pairs, relieve pain in specific areas of the body. When applying pressure, the fingertips either remain stationary or they move in very small circles over the pressure points. No lubricants are used. When the point has been accurately located and pressure is applied, the person being treated will feel a tenderness or tingling sensation at that spot. If this feeling is *very* painful, it may be necessary to begin with light pressure, and then gradually increase. Pressure should be applied for five or ten seconds, and may be repeated. Since acupressure points exist in pairs, one on each side of the body, remember to treat both sides. And keep in mind that using acupressure along with slow breathing can enhance the effects of both.

Although you can perform acupressure on yourself, most women find it more effective when performed by their partner. The positive support and reinforcement of another person's touch tends to have a more soothing effect that promotes relaxation.

The following acupressure techniques are for dealing with some of the more common discomforts of pregnancy, labor, and the postpartum period:

■ To relieve headache or pain in the neck or upper back, place your fingers or thumbs on the muscles at the tops of the shoulders, slightly toward the back and in a vertical line with the nipples. Press firmly and apply circular pressure.

■ For low-back discomfort, pelvic pain, or pelvic pressure, place fingertips in an inward direction on either side of the spine just below the waist. During contractions, use firm circular pressure. Between contractions, use circular or intermittent pressure.

■ To assist in relaxation and to produce a general calming effect, apply firm fingertip pressure just below the ball of the foot. This may be helpful during the transition period of labor, when the woman may tend to panic.

The following acupressure techniques are also effective during labor. *They must not be used before the thirty-eighth week of pregnancy because they can cause labor to begin:*

■ To relax the vagina and cervix, and speed up the progress of a difficult labor, apply firm pressure to the point at the end of the crease between the thumb and forefinger.

■ To aid a difficult labor, apply strong, steady pressure to the point located about three finger widths above the inner ankle. To find the correct point, press around this entire area until you locate the tenderest spot.

■ For pain relief during contractions, pinch or apply strong pressure to the outside corners of both little toes and hold for seven to ten seconds.

Applying pressure between the thumb and forefinger may help speed up a difficult labor.

Acupressure is an effective, noninvasive technique that is easy to learn and simple to perform. Add it to your repertoire of pain-relief methods to be called upon and utilized as needed.

Aromatherapy

The use of fragrances in labor can evoke a sense of calm and well-being. Bring your favorite scent or the one you used as you were practicing your "Special Place" visualization. Lavender, jasmine, and lemon verbena are popular fragrances used by expectant mothers during labor. Bring the scent in the form of potpourri, scented oil, scented candles, or as an added fragrance to a homemade rice sock.

Music

More and more expectant mothers are making music a part of their birth experience. Music helps create a mood, which is a great relaxation aid during labor. It can also be a great distraction technique. The choice of music will be different for everyone. For some women, it will be classical or easy listening, while others will choose songs with familiar lyrics that they can focus on or sing along to. Others will select inspirational songs with meaningful messages to help encourage their progress during labor. Bring along the same music you listened to during your relaxation practice sessions at home. When practicing to the same music week after week, you will become conditioned to automatically relax when you hear the familiar tunes.

Applying pressure to this point above the inner ankle can stimulate labor.

Many women find that listening to different types of music during the various stages of labor is most effective. Generally, slower, more relaxing music is helpful during early stages of labor, while more spirited music with a faster tempo is better when the contractions become more intense.

Use of Heat

During labor, muscles of the shoulders, lower back, and lower abdomen can become particularly tense, resulting in soreness and possible spasms. The use of heat during labor can be soothing and provide pain relief to these areas. When warmth and heat penetrate tense or sore muscles, blood flow increases. This relaxes the muscles and helps reduce or prevent painful spasms.

Applying heat can be accomplished through various methods, such as hot water

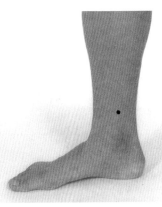

Pinching or applying pressure to this spot on the little toes can provide pain relief during contractions

The Birth Ball

A large, inflatable ball that is sturdy yet very flexible, the birth ball is a useful tool specifically designed for expectant mothers. It provides a firm, yet soft and wonderfully comfortable place to sit, forcing good posture while decreasing muscle strain. Available in a variety of sizes, most birth balls inflate to a diameter of 65 centimeters (about 26 inches) to accommodate the average-sized woman.

Simply place the ball against a wall, bed, or sturdy piece of furniture to prevent it from rolling, and then lower yourself onto it, keeping your legs out to the sides for balance and support. This comfortable sitting position allows your legs to rest while allowing your pelvis to rock or gently sway from side to side. During labor, this movement helps the baby get into position to travel down the birth canal. Many women find that a birth ball is the only comfortable place to sit during the last weeks of pregnancy. Sitting on one regularly can help encourage the pelvis to open in preparation for childbirth. Furthermore, it can be used during prenatal and postpartum exercise.

While many hospitals and birth centers have birth balls available to use, you may prefer to buy your own and use it during your pregnancy. Look for one that is resistant to puncturing and has a safety feature that allows it to deflate slowly in case of a hole. Birth balls are available at sporting goods stores, toy stores, maternity shops, medical supply stores, and through a variety of Internet sites.

Homemade Heat Pack

Make your own heat pack by filling a long cotton sock with rice or deer corn. Place the sock in the microwave for two minutes. It will remain warm for fifteen to twenty minutes. *Caution:* To avoid burns, do not overheat the pack or lie directly on top of it.

bottles, heat packs, prewarmed blankets, and hot compresses (both wet and dry). Over-the-counter heat wraps, which can maintain heat for up to eight hours, are also effective. Do not use electric heating pads or blankets. Letting the hot water of a shower target sore areas is another good option, as is sitting in a hot bath. Laboring in water is especially helpful if you are experiencing back labor. Also, be aware that during the pushing stage, as the perineum stretches, the area will burn. Applying hot compresses to this area will help increase the elasticity of the skin and alleviate the burning sensation.

Use of Cold

When cold is applied to the body, it provides a numbing effect. For this reason, the application of cold packs or compresses—especially during back labor—can offer substantial pain relief. You can use an ice bag, frozen gel packs, a rubber glove filled with crushed ice, a washcloth or small towel that has been soaked in ice water, a cold can of soda, or even a bag of frozen vegetables (a bag of peas molds nicely). To avoid burning your skin, place a layer of cloth between your skin and the ice pack, and limit the application to twenty minutes at a time. If you are standing, ask the nurse to place the ice pack under the elastic strap used to secure the fetal monitor.

Using a Birth Ball

During labor, many women have found that using a birth ball—either to sit on or to support the upper body while kneeling—helps ease some of the discomforts of labor.

Sitting or squatting on this very large, soft ball causes a natural forward tilting of the pelvis, which encourages the baby to move down into the birth canal. It is also easy to rock one's hips while sitting on the ball, further facilitating the baby's positioning and descent. A portable accessory, the birth ball can also be used as a support in the bathtub, in bed, or on the floor. For more information, see "The Birth Ball" on page 164.

Laboring in Water

More and more birthing facilities are providing tubs or showers for laboring women. Many women find that being in warm water aids relaxation. Submersion in a tub reduces external stimuli and provides buoyancy to eliminate pressure on the joints. Pain medication is required less often, as the body is able to produce endorphins, which reduce the perception of pain. Studies have shown that women who have high blood pressure experience lowered pressure within ten to fifteen minutes after entering a tub.[3]

Laboring in water has not been associated with any increase in complications, such as infection, even if the membranes have ruptured. The temperature of the water should not exceed 100°F to prevent elevation of the body temperature. Since your contractions may slow down if you are in early labor, it is best to wait to get into the tub until you are in active labor. A portable hand-held electronic fetal monitor can be used to check the baby's heart rate while you are in the tub. If a traditional electronic fetal monitor—one that uses wires to attach the transducer to the machine—is used, you will have to use the tub between monitorings.

If a shower is available, have the nurse place a chair in the stall so that you can rest. If the shower has a hand-held showerhead, you or your partner can direct the spray onto your abdomen or lower back, if desired. You can also use a water mister to spray your face while in the water. It will help keep you cool.

Repetition/Rituals

Many women find that repeating the same behavior with each contraction helps them focus. What follows are some suggestions:

■ Recite a favorite poem, biblical verse, or other passage in your head.

■ Sing a song in your head.

■ While breathing, make a low sound as you exhale, such as "oh" or "hmmm."

■ Recite a mantra, such as "I can do this" or "I am strong."

■ Picture the sky with clouds. As you breathe out, visualize blowing a cloud away.

■ Receive a hand massage from your partner during contractions. Have him start by massaging your palm for about thirty seconds, then have him move to each finger, timing it so that by the time he reaches the last digit, the contraction is over. When he switches from your palm to your fingers, you will know that the contraction is about half over.

■ Have your partner call out the fifteen-second intervals during contractions. When he says "Thirty seconds," you will know that the contraction is winding down.

Don't Forget . . .

Along with your other labor supplies, be sure to bring along several frozen sixteen-ounce water bottles. If necessary, use them as cold packs during labor. As they melt, you can sip the cold water to quench your thirst.

"Okay, honey, I'm ready to help now!"

Once you have found the ritual that works for you, stay with it. Partners should not suggest trying something else. It is up to you—the laboring woman—to decide if you need a different technique.

Distraction and Attention-Focusing Techniques

Combining techniques during contractions can enhance your ability to cope. Stimulating some or all of your senses can help decrease pain sensations from reaching the brain.

- **Sight.** Open your eyes and stare at a focal point. Close your eyes and visualize your "Special Place," or picture your cervix opening up around the baby's head.

- **Hearing.** Listen to music or your partner's voice. Or listen to the sound of your own voice by chanting or moaning during contractions.

- **Smell.** Sniff a specific fragrance or a variety of fragrances.

- **Touch.** Have your partner give you a massage. While hugging your partner, move your body (rock, sway, slow dance) in rhythm with his. Tap out a rhythm with your fingertips.

- **Taste.** Between contractions, suck on a lollipop or an ice pop. The taste will linger during the contractions.

You can also mentally recite a poetry verse or lyrics to a song. Some women have found that actually singing a song can be an effective distraction during contractions. It is also recommended that you move around and get your body into different positions. If you're standing, move your hips as if you are slow dancing. Use any of the other tools presented in this chapter as needed.

Transcutaneous Electrical Nerve Stimulation

Transcutaneous electrical nerve stimulation (TENS) units are most commonly used to treat chronic pain, but have been helpful for some women in labor. The unit is a small hand-held device that is connected to the skin by electrodes. Controlled by the person wearing it, a TENS unit provides a stimulating, tingling sensation to the area that can help alleviate pain. The unit's intensity can be increased during contractions. Obviously, it cannot be used by women who labor in water.

Intradermal Water Blocks

It is believed that intradermal water blocks—injections of sterile water directly under the skin in specific locations—cause the release of "feel good" endorphins, which decrease the perception of pain sensations. During labor, this technique is sometimes used to relieve lower back pain. Usually four injections, which form small blister-like bumps, are given over the lower back bone, or *sacrum.* (See Figure 7.1 at left.) Initially, the injections cause an intense stinging sensation that lasts no more than thirty seconds. This is followed by about sixty to ninety minutes of back pain relief. Intradermal water blocks must be given by a professional who is trained in this technique.

A Hint for the Mother-to-Be

If you intend to utilize certain comfort measures, such as intradermal water blocks, acupuncture, or professional therapeutic massage; or if you plan to use a TENS unit during labor, you may need to make arrangements beforehand.

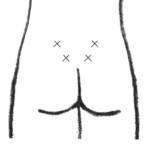

Figure 7.1.
Site of sterile water injections for intradermal water blocks.

Acupuncture

Acupuncture is one of the main treatment methods used in traditional Chinese medicine. It involves the insertion of very fine needles into specific points on the body where the flow of energy is blocked. Stimulation of these points is believed to open up the blockage, which, in turn, provides pain relief to specific areas (depending on the location of the needles). During labor, acupuncture can be used to help reduce labor pain and increase the strength of contractions. It can also be used to induce labor if the woman is overdue. Inform your caregiver if you would like to use this technique, which must be performed by a professional who is trained in its administration.

PUSHING DURING THE SECOND STAGE OF LABOR

When your cervix is completely effaced and dilated, you can actively help the uterus move the baby down the birth canal by bearing down or pushing along with the contractions. Most women feel a strong desire to push at this time, but a few do not. If you do not immediately feel this urge, just continue to breathe through the contractions until your body is ready to bear down. This waiting period is called *laboring down.* The baby's head may not be deep enough into the pelvis to press on the sensors that trigger the bearing-down reflex. To help her descend, assume an upright position.

It has been found that typically, if a woman delays bearing down, she will eventually feel the urge to push, but if she starts pushing without having the urge, she may never feel it. Absence of this urge makes the pushing stage more difficult and less satisfying. If you do not feel the desire to push as the result of an epidural, request that the medication be turned down and delay pushing until you feel the urge.

You should also assume the position for pushing that you prefer, not necessarily the one that you practiced in childbirth class or observed in films. You may find side-lying, squatting, standing, kneeling with your upper body elevated, or kneeling on all fours to be the most comfortable for you and the one most advantageous to your baby's descent. For any pushing position, tuck your chin down into your chest as if you are looking for the baby to come out. This will get your body into a "C" position, which curves your lower back and aids the baby's descent under the pubic bone. Avoid the temptation to throw your head back, which causes an unnatural arch in your back. Your partner can remind you to "look for the baby.".

Spontaneous Pushing

It is best to respond to your body's natural signals and bear down or push only as your uterus commands. This is called *spontaneous pushing* or *woman-directed pushing.*

When the contraction begins, take relaxing breaths until the urge to bear down is so powerful that you cannot resist it. You may, for example, desire to bear down for short bursts or you may feel a need to push with all of your strength. You may hold your breath as you push (no longer than six seconds) or slowly release air as you bear down with the urge. Unless they are directed otherwise, most women use a combination of short-breath holding and exhaling during contractions. Making noise while bearing down, which surprises many women, is also common. Try to use low moans or deep guttural sounds, rather than high-pitched screams or squeals. Low tones encourage a relaxed pelvic floor.

Hints for the Labor Partner

✓ Learn about alternative methods of pain relief for labor and discuss them with your partner.

✓ Learn the acupressure points for pain relief.

✓ Recite visualizations for your partner.

✓ Encourage daily practice sessions during the last month of pregnancy.

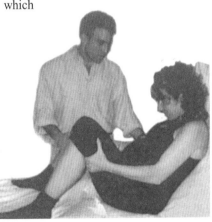

"Look for the baby."

Spontaneous pushing may not produce results as quickly as forceful directed pushing does, but there is no evidence that a longer pushing stage may be harmful to the baby (the exception is for babies who are in fetal distress). In fact, babies may actually benefit from the experience of a slower, gentler birth, rather than a forceful surge down the birth canal.

Directed Pushing

As just discussed, most women will experience a strong urge to bear down and can use their own natural sensations to push the baby down the birth canal. But, if you do not feel the urge to push, perhaps as a result of an epidural, or if you do not develop one within twenty to thirty minutes after changing positions (as described earlier), you may need to use *directed pushing*. With directed pushing, the hospital staff provides the cues for when and how long you should push. Your partner may also watch the fetal monitor to see when the contraction is starting and ending. Directed pushing should not be encouraged if the woman is experiencing a natural urge to push—the staff's instructions of when and how long to push may not correspond with her natural sensations. Directed pushing may, however, be indicated if the caregiver needs the baby to be born at a faster rate.

During directed pushing, you will take two or three relaxing breaths, and then hold your breath and bear down to the count of six. You must be careful not to hold your breath for too long (ten seconds or longer) while pushing with force. Called the *Valsalva maneuver*—this type of sustained forceful pushing can cause a drop in blood pressure, which will decrease the amount of oxygen to the baby. Prolonged pushing can also damage the vagina, as the rapid descent of the baby does not allow for a slow stretching of the tissues. This increases the risk of tearing. Unless the baby is showing signs of distress and the caregiver needs to deliver the baby quickly, prolonged breath holding and forceful pushing should be avoided.

Breathing Patterns

As stated previously, the ideal way to push is to just allow your body to instinctively direct your breathing and bearing-down efforts. During your practice breathing sessions for labor, you may also want to practice the breathing patterns that are effective for the various types of pushing.

During Spontaneous Pushing

Spontaneous pushing is the preferred method for helping the baby down the birth canal. As the contraction begins, take relaxing breaths until you feel the urge to push. Then inhale deeply to expand your lungs, tuck your chin down into your chest, and bear down using your diaphragm. You can either hold your breath for six seconds or let the air out slowly. Picture your baby moving through the pelvis as you relax your pelvic floor muscles. When you need to take another breath, lift your head, take a couple quick breaths, and repeat. Continue this breathing pattern until the contraction ends. Then take several relaxing breaths and try to completely relax your body until the next contraction begins.

During Directed Pushing

Pushing while holding your breath for short periods, also known as the *modified Val-*

salva maneuver, is used by women who do not feel the urge to push or who need to apply more force when helping their babies down the birth canal. As the contraction begins, take relaxing breaths until you feel the urge to push or until directed by your caregiver. Then inhale deeply, let a little air out, tuck your chin down into your chest, hold your breath, and bear down using your diaphragm. Direct the air downward, rather than hold it in your cheeks—this reduces neck and facial tension, and lessens the chance of breaking small blood vessels in your face or the whites of your eyes. Picture your baby moving through the pelvis as you relax your pelvic floor muscles.

To pace your effort while holding your breath and pushing, have your partner slowly count to six. When he reaches six, release your breath, then take a couple quick breaths and repeat this pattern as many times as needed during the contraction. When the contraction ends, gradually stop pushing as you exhale slowly. Take one or two relaxing breaths and relax completely.

To Prevent Pushing

As your baby's head begins to stretch the perineal tissues, your doctor or midwife will instruct you to stop pushing—even though the urge to do so will be *very* strong. Pushing the head out too quickly can cause these tissues to tear. A slow, controlled descent of the head is necessary to allow the perineum to stretch out gradually. To prevent yourself from pushing at this time, repeatedly blow out forcefully or pant. Continue until your caregiver instructs you to begin pushing again.

Pushing Positions

The positions that you use during your pushing effort should be determined by your comfort and desires. Frequently your caregiver's preferences will dictate your position for delivery. Upright positions, which include sitting, squatting, standing, and kneeling, are the most advantageous and result in a shorter pushing stage and less abnormal fetal heart patterns. Women also report fewer episodes of severe pain when in an upright position.[4] Side-lying positions are also comfortable for some women.

Most nurses and doctors encourage the sitting or a semi-reclined position. When in these positions, make sure your back is elevated in the birthing bed. Birthing rooms in hospitals contain beds that can be adjusted to your comfort. They can also be transformed into delivery tables, complete with stirrups. Most birth centers are equipped with regular beds that the labor partner can get into while offering support and helping the woman maintain a proper position with pillows or a birth ball.

Discuss all of the possible pushing positions with your caregiver to learn what she prefers and to let her know what you would like. Then practice pushing in all of them, so that you can use whatever feels best while in labor.

Sitting

Sitting in a semi-reclined position is the most common one used in the birthing room. It is comfortable for most women and provides a good visual field for the caregiver. If you have back labor, however, this position is not recommended, as it places the weight of the baby on your back and increases discomfort. The head of the birthing bed can be elevated 70 degrees, and you can place your feet on the bed or in the footrests (if available). The bottom third of the birthing bed can also be lowered six to twelve inches and used as a footrest.

Semi-reclined position.

To practice pushing in the semi-reclined position, have your partner sit behind you as your back support. Place pillows between his legs and your back. Lie against him at a 70-degree angle, making sure to sit on the small of your back, not on your rectum. Bend your knees, spread your legs, and place your feet flat on the floor or bed. Rest your hands on his knees or your inner thighs to keep your legs and perineum relaxed. If you need to hold something while pushing, grasp your inner thighs and draw them toward you. Then begin your selected breathing pattern, tuck your chin onto your chest, and *push.* When the contraction is over, lie back and relax.

A birthing stool or birthing chair can also help you push while in the sitting position; however, this may also contribute to an increase in second-degree tears and postpartum hemorrhage. One study noted that women who sat in birthing chairs for an extended period of time also had more perineal swelling and hemorrhoids.[5] Many midwives encourage women to change their position when birth is imminent.

Women delivering in birth centers are often encouraged to sit on the toilet for pushing. This encourages the pelvic floor to relax, which results in effective pushing.

Squatting

Squatting is physiologically the best position to use while pushing. You can support yourself in a squat by keeping your feet flat on the floor and holding onto a bed rail or your partner. Many birthing beds come equipped with a squat bar to hold onto for support. Squat only during the contraction, and either stand up or kneel during the rest period. During a long labor, it may be necessary for your partner to assist you out of the squat. As with other pushing positions, tuck your chin into your chest while bearing down.

There are a number of squat variations for which your partner can offer support. A comfortable *supported squat* can be accomplished by having your partner sit on a chair while you squat between his legs with your arms draped over his thighs. In

Supported squat.

Lap squat.

Double squat.

a *lap squat,* which reduces stress on your knees, your partner sits on a chair while you face him and straddle his knees during contractions. In a *double squat,* you lock hands with your partner, who squats with you to provide leverage. As another variation, you can place a long, sturdy shawl, such as a Mexican *rebozo,* around your back and under your arms. As you squat, your partner can hold up the ends of the scarf to support you.

The *standing squat,* which places less strain on the knees and hips, can be achieved in several ways. For instance, you can have your partner stand with his back against a wall while you place your back against his chest and abdomen. As you begin to bear down, your partner will slide down the wall so that his knees are bent. Then you can squat while supporting yourself against his thighs. The *dangle* is another form of the standing squat position. To do this, have your partner sit on the edge of the birthing bed with his feet on the footrests. Stand with your back to him and your arms draped across his thighs. As you begin to push, bend your knees and squat, while "dangling" from your partner's legs for support.

You can also place a bar overhead in a doorway and hold onto it while squatting. Or you can securely hang a cloth sling or an exercise rope with handles from the ceiling or a door and hold onto it while squatting or lunging.

Squatting is an ideal pushing position because it allows gravity to assist the uterus, which makes the contractions more efficient, longer, and more frequent. The pelvic outlet is at its widest, the birth canal is shortened, and episiotomies are needed less frequently. Delivery time is shortened because pushing is more effective. Do not, however, get into this position before the baby's presenting part is engaged, because the descent and engagement could be hampered. In case of complications, squatting may present some manual and visual inconveniences for the caregiver, and it may become necessary to assume a different position.

Using a Rebozo

A rebozo is a traditional Mexican shawl, approximately four to five feet in length. During pregnancy it can be worn around the abdomen to lift and support the uterus and lower back. It can also be used during labor. As the woman kneels, her partner can place the rebozo under her abdomen and hold up the ends while standing above her. He can then use it as a "cradle" to gently "rock the baby" between contractions. If the woman squats during contractions, the rebozo can be placed around her back and hips and used to support her like a giant sling as her partner holds up the ends.

Squat with rebozo.   Standing squat.   Dangle squat.

Kneeling

Some women prefer the kneeling position during pushing. Physiologically, it is effective because it takes advantage of the force of gravity. It may be especially helpful if your baby is slow in coming down the birth canal or if you are having back labor. As you push, be sure to tuck your chin into your chest to improve the angle of your pelvis.

For the basic kneeling position, kneel on the bed while facing your partner. Put your arms around his shoulders for support, and don't forget to tuck your chin while you push. When the contraction is over, relax.

There are a number of variations for this position. For example, while kneeling, you can lean forward against the raised head of the birthing bed or pillows. Or you may want to try placing one knee and the sole of the other foot on the bed, and then lunge with each contraction. You can also kneel on the floor and support your upper body on pillows that are placed on the seat of a chair. Kneeling on all fours is another option. In this position, you can do the Pelvic Rock if you are experiencing back pain. Many women whose babies are in a posterior position find that this position eases discomfort.

Kneeling with the aid of a chair.   Lunging while on one knee.

Side-Lying

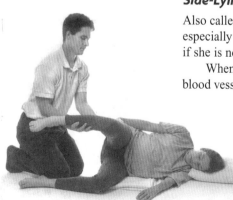

Side-lying position.

Also called the *lateral Sims' position,* side-lying is very comfortable for most women, especially those having back labor or leg cramps. It can aid rotation of the baby's head if she is not yet in a facedown position, and it can help in a breech delivery as well.

When lying on your side, your uterus will not press on the vena cava—the large blood vessel next to your spine that returns blood to the heart from your lower extremities. This reduces your chances of developing *supine hypotension* (low blood pressure when lying on your back). In this position, your perineum is relaxed, which means it is less likely to tear or require an episiotomy. Side-lying, however, does not utilize the force of gravity as well as squatting does, and your view of the baby's birth will not be as good. If a difficult forceps delivery or repair of lacerations is necessary, this position is not recommended.

To get into the side-lying position, lie on your side with pillows supporting your head. Try to lie on your left side because this improves blood flow to the uterus. When you are ready to push, curve your upper body into a "C" shape by tucking your chin onto your chest. Have your partner support your upper leg with his arms or hands, or place the leg on the lowest bed rail, which you can pad with pillows. When the contraction is over, lower your leg onto the bed, where it is supported by pillows, and relax.

Supine Position

Lying flat on your back with your feet in the stirrups, called the *supine* or *lithotomy* position, should be avoided. While this position is advantageous for the doctor—it allows him to easily observe your abdomen and perineum, check the fetal heart rate, apply forceps or the vacuum extractor, if necessary, and manage postpartum hemorrhage—it has definite disadvantages for you.

Pushing in the lithotomy position reduces your pelvic outlet to its smallest diameter. Because of the narrowed vaginal opening (and tautly stretched perineum), there is a greater chance that you will need an episiotomy. In addition, lying on your back may cause your contractions to become more irregular and less frequent. With your legs in stirrups, the strength of your contractions might actually lift your hips off the table, which means you will be pushing your baby uphill, against gravity. The weight of the uterus will be on your vena cava, which may lower your blood pressure and, thereby, decrease the amount of oxygen reaching your baby.

Studies have found that women who lie flat on their back have longer pushing stages, fewer spontaneous births, and an increase in abnormal fetal heart patterns and fetal distress. This position is strongly discouraged.

Practice Sessions for Pushing

Once you feel comfortable with the breathing patterns used for pushing, practice them in various sitting, squatting, and side-lying positions. While practicing, do not push forcefully—push only enough to get the proper feeling. You may find it helpful to push as if you are forcefully emptying your bladder. Also visualize your baby coming down lower and lower as you push, and consciously relax your legs and perineal area.

Begin each practice push with two or three relaxing breaths followed by a deep breath to expand your lungs. Using your diaphragm, start bearing down while either slowly exhaling or holding your breath for the count of six. Try to push three or four times during each practice contraction. While bearing down, also do the following:

- Tuck your chin into your chest and "look for the baby."

- Bulge your lower abdominal muscles down and forward.

- Totally relax your pelvic floor by doing Elevator Kegels. Your perineum should feel as if it is bulging out.

- Take a couple of breaths between pushes.

During your actual second stage of labor, the early pushes will gradually move the baby down the birth canal. Your partner may even see a little of the baby's hair showing as you push. But the hair will disappear as the baby moves back up at the end of the contraction. Slowly lessen your pushing effort as the contraction comes to an end. This will help maintain the baby's position in the birth canal and prevent her from moving back up.

When the top of the baby's head stays in view between contractions, it is called *crowning*. At this point, your caregiver may ask you to stop pushing, which means it is time to pant or blow out forcefully. As explained earlier, it is important to allow the baby's head to gradually stretch the perineum.

PRACTICE FOR LABOR

Try to practice your conditioning exercises, relaxation exercises, and slow breathing every day during the last trimester, especially during the last few weeks. If possible, get in two sessions per day—one alone and one with your labor partner. You can perform the relaxation exercises and breathing patterns at the same time as the conditioning exercises or in separate sessions. It is best to practice when you are rested and can fully concentrate on your efforts.

Mentally rehearse the labor and birth of your baby. Start with early labor and continue through transition, pushing, and birth. Learn your role so completely that you automatically start slow breathing and relaxing your body when a contraction begins.

The following is a suggested sequence for practicing the exercises, breathing patterns, and pushing techniques presented in this chapter. It will prepare you well for the actual labor and birth of your baby. Add to it as you learn new techniques. Each day:

1. Perform your choice of aerobic, stretching, and strength-training exercises.

2. Practice a relaxation exercise (vary the choices).

3. Practice slow breathing with contractions that last sixty seconds each. Perform a series of five contractions with one-minute rest periods between each. Practice each contraction in a different position—standing, sitting, side-lying, etc.

4. Practice a massage technique or other method of distraction as a comfort measure. Perform one technique or a combination of two or more. (For example, listen to music while practicing effleurage.)

5. Practice two or three labor (transition) contractions lasting ninety seconds each with thirty-second rest periods between them. During one or more of these contractions, have your partner call out a premature urge to push lasting fifteen seconds. Pant or blow out forcefully and continuously until your partner signals that the urge to push has passed. Return to slow breathing to finish the contraction.

6. Practice spontaneous pushing three times. Have each contraction last sixty seconds, with one to two minutes of rest between them. Try exhaling during pushing or use short-breath holding (six seconds) to see which technique you prefer. Practice in the different pushing positions.

7. Practice directed pushing for one or two contractions that last sixty seconds each, with one to two minutes of rest between them. Have your partner count to six as you hold your breath.

For the Labor Partner

Your job as labor partner cannot be underestimated. The ways in which you can help out during pregnancy, labor, and birth are innumerable. This book has already shown you many ways in which you can lend support. Here are a few more:

Before Labor:

■ During practice sessions, have her try out different distraction techniques while she is holding an ice cube or frozen water bottle in her hand. This will help her determine which techniques are likely to work best to distract her from the pain of eventual contractions (which are simulated by the icy pain she is experiencing in her hand).

■ Encourage her to take advantage of any Braxton-Hicks contractions she may experience for practicing relaxation and breathing patterns.

During Labor:

■ Observe your partner for tension, both during and between contractions. The longer the labor continues, the greater the chance of the tension slowly spreading. Use both touch and verbal cues as needed to encourage relaxation.

■ Help your partner maintain her breathing rhythm during contractions by counting or breathing with her. Tapping on a hard surface or moving your hand in front of her face may also keep her on track.

■ During contractions, be sure to call out the passing time in fifteen-second intervals. Pacing the contraction this way will help her keep her perspective.

"Gee, honey, can't you loosen up just a little?"

Helping the expectant mother throughout her pregnancy and during the actual labor and birth is an important key to her success. With a little common sense, imagination, and teamwork, pregnancy and childbirth can be one of the more fulfilling times in a relationship.

CONCLUSION

By practicing the exercises in this chapter and Chapter 6, you and your labor partner will learn a number of specific skills while developing into a strong team. The ability to work together—to communicate clearly and to trust each other—is as important to the labor experience as the skills you are learning. Teamwork takes time to develop, however, so be sure to encourage each other and offer positive feedback, especially in the beginning. As you become more and more comfortable working with each other, begin to discuss ways in which you can improve your efforts. *Take time each day to practice together.* The quality of your labor experience will depend greatly upon the amount of time you prepare together and the quality of those sessions.

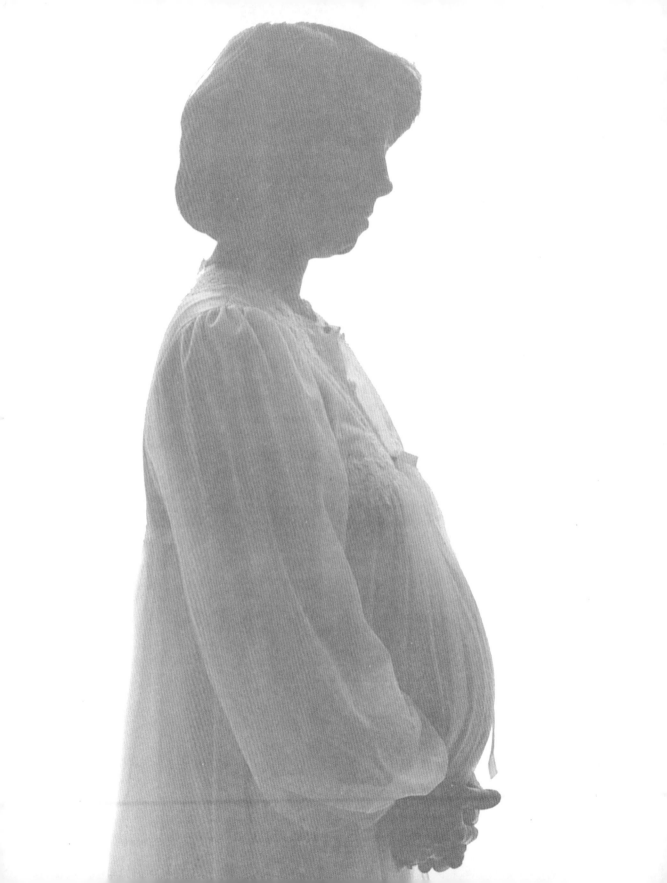

Labor and Birth
or I Gotta Get Outta This Place

For nine months, your body has been working to nurture your growing baby. During the last weeks of pregnancy, your body will undergo a number of changes in preparation for the baby's entrance into the world. It is during this time that he will start to descend into the pelvis. The occasional mild contractions you may have felt earlier in your pregnancy, will begin to increase in frequency and begin the job of thinning and opening your cervix. These "warm up" contractions will become stronger and more frequent during labor and eventually push your baby out.

Labor is the natural process at the end of pregnancy that begins with regular uterine contractions and culminates in the birth of the baby. Each labor is unique. Some of the factors that will affect the course of your labor are your physical health, emotional makeup, nutritional profile, the size and shape of your pelvis, how prepared you are for the experience, and how well you have practiced relaxation and breathing techniques. The size and presentation of the baby are also important factors. Additionally, the emotional support you receive, and the use of any medical interventions may also affect the course of your labor.

Even though each labor is different, certain aspects of all labors are similar. For ease of explanation, labor is divided into four stages. The first stage begins with the onset of labor and ends with the complete effacement and dilation of the cervix. The second stage, expulsion, begins with the complete dilation of the cervix and ends with the birth of the baby. The third stage is the delivery of the placenta. The fourth stage, which occurs during the first hours after birth, is the recovery period.

Before discussing the four stages of labor, this chapter presents some practical tips to help you get ready for your approaching due date.

THINGS TO DO BEFORE YOUR DUE DATE

As your due date approaches, you will want to make sure that you have completed your preparations for labor and for the arrival of your baby. Confirming your labor partner choice, taking a tour of the hospital or birthing center, and preregistering for your admission are just a few ways in which you can become prepared for the upcoming experience.

Confirm Your Choice of Labor Partner

Your labor partner is the person who will be with you during labor and birth to provide you with emotional support, as well as assist you with the comfort measures and techniques that you learned in childbirth class. He or she will also serve as your go-between with the medical staff. Many women choose their husband, boyfriend, or father of the baby as their labor partner. Others choose a close friend or relative. Some choose more than one person.

Your labor partner should prepare for the birth by attending childbirth classes with you, by helping you practice relaxation and breathing techniques, and by learning as much as possible about the childbirth experience. *The Birth Partner* by Penny Simkin is an excellent book on the subject that is aimed at the labor partner.

In addition to a labor partner, some women hire their childbirth instructor or a nurse or midwife who is not associated with the facility in which they plan to deliver. Other women hire a doula, who is specifically trained to assist women and their partners during labor. Doulas go through special training to become skillful in providing a reassuring, nurturing, and constant presence during labor. Studies have shown that the presence of a doula significantly reduces the chance of complications. Women tend to have shorter labors, require less Pitocin (to induce or augment labor) and pain medication, and have fewer epidurals and forceps deliveries. In addition, the risk of having a cesarean is reduced by 50 percent.[1] Doulas can also provide postpartum support and breastfeeding advice. You can hire a doula through DONA International or the International Childbirth Education Association. (For contact information, see the Resources beginning on page 449.)

Take a Tour of the Hospital or Birth Center

Taking a tour of the hospital or birth center where you plan to have your baby will allow you to become familiar with your labor setting before checking in. It also gives you an opportunity to discuss your desires with the staff and learn about the various policies of the facility. If you are planning to have your baby at a birth center, you may also want to tour the affiliated hospital. It's a good idea to be familiar with the hospital just in case you have to be transferred there during labor.

Among the many questions you may ask when taking your tour, be sure to inquire about security. Find out what measures they will take to protect your baby from abduction. (See "A Word About Hospital Security" on page 285.) Some facilities restrict the use of cameras or video equipment during the birth. If you and your partner plan to take photos at this time, be sure it is permitted. Whatever questions or concerns you have about the facility—

"If only giving birth were as easy as getting pregnant!"

whether it involves the availability of tubs or showers, or their visitation rules during labor or after your baby is born—try to discover the answers before it's time for you to check in.

Preregister

To shorten the admission procedure when you arrive in labor at the facility, you can preregister. Try to do this during your last trimester, but don't wait until the last minute. If you are planning to deliver at a birth center, you may also want to register at the affiliated hospital.

To complete the required forms, you will need your insurance information and a photo identification card, such as a driver's license. Before signing any consent forms regarding possible surgery, epidural anesthesia, circumcision, etc., read the forms carefully and modify them according to your desires. You may also be asked to sign a paper indicating whether or not you have a living will. During preregistration, many facilities require a monetary deposit. Call ahead to find out what the policy is, so you can be prepared.

Arrange for Cord Blood Banking

It is now possible to collect and store the blood from your baby's umbilical cord and save it for future use. Cryobanks throughout the country freeze this blood and store it. Many couples are donating this otherwise discarded blood, which can be used in place of bone marrow transplants. There is usually no charge for this service. Some families—usually those with a history of leukemia or other cancers, blood or immune disorders, sickle cell anemia, hemophilia, or another disease that may require a bone marrow transplant—prefer to bank the cord blood for their own possible future use. Minority and mixed-race families often use this option since tissue matches for them are much more difficult to obtain. Families who bank blood for their own use are charged a collection and yearly storage fee.

Umbilical cord blood contains a high level of stem cells. These immature cells produce the oxygen-carrying red blood cells, the white blood cells that make up the immune system, and the platelets that help blood clot. There are many benefits to using cord blood instead of bone marrow. The concentration of stem cells is greater in cord blood, and since the cells have not built up antibodies, they are more compatible when donated. Unlike the traditional bone marrow transplant, the stem cell collection procedure is not invasive and involves no pain to the donor. The collection is usually done after the cord has been cut and before the placenta is delivered.

If you are interested in cord blood banking, contact your nearest cryobank and make arrangements prior to your due date. Also make sure that your caregiver is aware of your desires so that the collection will be performed. (For a listing of these companies and organizations and their contact information, see the Resources beginning on page 449.)

Choose Your Baby's Pediatrician

Unless you have already decided on a pediatrician, it's a good idea to begin your search during the last trimester. For recommendations, you may want to ask friends and family members who have small children. Your obstetrician, midwife, or primary care physician may also offer recommendations.

Before making your decision, there are a number of factors to consider. For instance, is the office in a convenient location? Are the hours suitable? Many practices have several locations, and offer evening and weekend hours. If it is a solo practice, find out who will cover for the physician when he isn't available. If it is a group practice, discover how many doctors are in the group. Are they all board certified? Can you request a certain pediatrician during visits?

Hints for the Father-to-Be

✓ Help decorate the nursery.

✓ Stock up on baby supplies when you shop.

✓ Baby proof the house.

✓ Buy an infant safety seat and install it in the car.

✓ Have the installed infant seat inspected by someone certified (fire department or sheriff's office) to make sure you have done it correctly.

"But you said I could bring more than one person!"

Some practices also have pediatric nurse practitioners and certified lactation consultants on staff. Find out who will answer your questions if you call the office. Will you speak with the doctor, a nurse, or the receptionist? How are emergencies handled that occur after office hours? Does the office have both a "sick" and a "well" waiting room? What is the average wait time? With which hospitals are the doctors affiliated? What are the costs for an office visit? Do they accept your insurance?

To help make your decision, arrange for a prenatal interview with the doctor, either in a group setting or a personal meeting (some pediatricians charge for private consultations). Make sure you are prepared with a list of questions you want answered. In addition to the questions above, you may find it important to discuss the pediatrician's philosophy on such baby care topics as breastfeeding (and at what point he recommends supplementation and/or solid foods), circumcision, and vaccinations. After the interview, you should have a good feeling about him and his practice.

Prepare Your Home for the Baby

Gather all of the baby equipment and furniture you will be needing and have it set up before giving birth. It should be ready to use when the baby comes home. (Once you bring your newborn home, you will want to focus all of your attention on him.) Assemble the baby clothes, wash them, and put them away. During the last months of pregnancy, it is a good idea to reorganize your home, making it safe for a small child. Lock up all medicines, cleaning products, and other poisonous materials. Insert childproof plugs into electrical wall outlets and cover the sharp corners of furniture. Ask friends who have small children to help you spot potential hazards. (For a list of suggestions, see "Baby Proofing Your Home" on page 326.)

Organize Your Household and Plan Ahead

Organize your household for the time you will be gone, and take measures to simplify your work when you return with the new baby. If relatives or friends will be coming by to offer help, be sure they understand that they will be needed (and greatly appreciated) to help with the housework, not to take care of the baby. Organize your grocery shopping and cleaning on a weekly or monthly basis. Whenever possible, stock up on groceries and store as many nonperishable items as you have room for. When preparing casseroles, spaghetti sauce, soups, and stews, make double portions and freeze some for later use. Stock up on disposable items, such as paper plates, cups, and napkins.

Try to locate a 24-hour pharmacy or one that will deliver to your home. (Some deliver only prescriptions, while others may have a minimum purchase policy.) Also stock up on sanitary pads—you will need plenty of them the first two weeks you are home. If you plan to nurse, you may also want to purchase nursing pads. Men's handkerchiefs and squares of old diaper material also serve this purpose well.

You can save yourself a lot of time after the baby arrives if you buy things such as gifts and cards for upcoming birthdays, graduations, and other holidays beforehand. If you have other children, you may want to pick up some special gifts for them, as well as several "busy things," such as coloring books and crayons, marking pens, and perhaps a video game or favorite movie that you can bring out on a rough day. (For more suggestions, see "Helping Your Other Children Adjust" on page 410.)

Celebrate with a "Birth Circle"

Many pregnant women prepare for their new babies with birth rituals. Traditionally, this ritual is a baby shower—a joyous party that, typically, is complete with games, food, cake, and gifts for the new baby. Another type of festivity is the spiritual baby shower known as a *birth circle* or *blessing way.* This practice originated with the Navajo Indians and consisted of chanting, prayers, and the lighting of candles. Its focus is on the mother-to-be and is meant to bring her blessings and love, and to let her know she is not alone.

A birth circle is meant to prepare the woman emotionally for birth. Usually, it is an all-women gathering, although sometimes the father of the baby participates. At this spiritual baby shower, birth stories are shared and reassurances are given that birth is a normal, healthy event that should be celebrated. It is a time when the expectant mother can express her concerns, fears, and desires, while feeling safe and cared for.

The activities at this type of ceremony can be quite

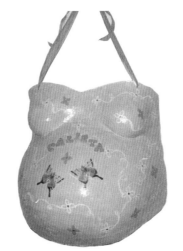

A plaster cast celebrates the pregnant shape.

varied. At some birth circle gatherings, comfort foods are served, poems are recited, and prayers are chanted. A necklace is sometimes made with charms that are symbolic of special people or good wishes for the woman's upcoming labor. The participants often write messages of good wishes for a healthy baby or an easy labor on paper and place them in a cloth bag that the woman can take with her during labor. At some gatherings, symbols are drawn on the pregnant abdomen with henna. Or a plaster cast of the woman's pregnant belly is made, which is then painted with decorations or decorated with dried flowers.

At some of these gatherings, friends pamper the mother-to-be. They clean and decorate her house, prepare and freeze food to feed the family after the birth, and/or give her a massage. The birth circle celebration encourages a sense of community among women. It reminds the expectant mother of the millions of women who have given birth in the past and reassures her of her own ability to do so.

If someone will be helping you care for your other children after you bring home the new baby, have a schedule ready for their meals, naps, bedtimes, school hours, car pools, and after-school activities. Also be sure to specify anything that is an absolute no-no. Leave a list of important numbers (pediatrician, school, car-pool drivers, neighbors, and friends) next to the phone.

Finally, address and stamp the envelopes for your birth announcements before going to the hospital. Then you will only need to fill in the details, which you can do in the hospital.

As your due date approaches, it is a good idea to pack the following bags—a Lamaze bag for items you will need during labor, a "personal" bag for any items you may want during your hospital stay, and a "baby" bag that contains items for your newborn. Having them packed by your thirty-fifth week (especially the Lamaze bag) is not too early. It means one less thing to worry about if your baby decides to make an early entrance.

A Lamaze Bag

The Lamaze bag should contain all of the items that you and your labor partner might need during labor, such as:

- This book for reference.

- A copy of your birth plan, signed by your caregiver. (The original should be attached to your chart.)

- Playing cards, books, magazines, or games to help pass the time during early labor.

- A watch with a second hand to time your contractions.

- A notebook and pencil to record your contractions. You can also use a hand-held computer that has a labor contraction timer program installed.

- A comfortable pair of shoes for walking during labor.

- The item you plan to use as your focal point.

- Extra pillows for support and comfort.

- Your favorite fragrances for aromatherapy.

- A rice sock (to warm up in a microwave) or a thermal wrap for heat therapy.

- Tennis balls that are tied in a sock—for applying counter pressure to a possible aching back.

- A wooden roller-type foot massager (see photo below) to help reduce labor pain through acupressure.

- Cornstarch, oil, or lotion to reduce friction during massage.

- A washcloth for cooling your face.

- Sour lollipops to help prevent your mouth from becoming dry.

- A toothbrush, toothpaste, and mouthwash to help moisten a dry mouth.

- Lip balm or lip gloss to soothe dry lips.

- Heavy socks to keep your feet warm.

- A hand-held fan for your partner to cool you.

- MP3 player or CDs of the music you want played during labor. Also bring a CD player in case one is not available in the labor room.

- Snacks for your labor partner to keep his energy up without having to leave the room to get food.

- A camera, a tape recorder, and/or video camera to record the birth or the first photos of the baby.

- Your newborn's "baby book," in which the staff can immediately record his footprints.

- A list of all the people you or your labor partner need to notify, as well as their phone numbers and, if necessary, a calling card.

While packing your Lamaze bag, remember to also have some beverages chilling in the refrigerator. When it's time to leave for the hospital or birth center, pack the cold drinks in an insulated bag. Your labor partner will appreciate something cold to drink while assisting you during labor. Also, as mentioned in Chapter 7, bring along a few frozen water bottles, which you can use as cold packs during labor. As they melt, you can sip the cold water.

A wooden roller-type foot massager can provide pain relief during labor through the acupressure points on the bottom of the feet. Place the foot massager on the floor in front of a chair, then move your feet over the roller as you sit in the chair and rock.

Your Personal Hospital Bag

Your personal hospital bag or suitcase should contain all of the items you will be needing during your hospital stay. Typically, it includes the following items:

■ Nightgowns. (If you plan to breastfeed, make sure that they button in the front or are special nursing gowns.)

■ A robe and slippers.

■ Two nursing bras. (For help in purchasing this important undergarment, see "How to Select a Nursing Bra" on page 367.)

■ Your usual cosmetics, toiletries, and other grooming aids.

■ Your going-home clothes, preferably a loose-fitting dress or maternity clothes, since it will be some weeks before you regain your prepregnant figure.

■ Birth announcements.

■ A shower cap.

■ Shower shoes.

■ A few pairs of underwear.

■ Sanitary pads (plain pads, not ones with a hi-tech woven barrier, which can "catch" perineal stitches).

■ Peri-care items such as a squeeze bottle, medicated cleansing pads, and anesthetic spray. Please note that these items are usually supplied by the hospital and charged to your bill. If, however, you have inadequate or no insurance, you can save money by purchasing them yourself. Just remember to inform the nursing staff, so you will not be billed, and then *double-check your bill when you receive it.*

■ Non-perishable snacks (chips, granola bars, candy, mints) and drinks.

■ Cell phone charger (if cell phones are allowed at the facility).

■ Breastfeeding pillow (if you plan to breastfeed).

■ Camera.

■ Laptop computer to email baby's first photos to family and friends.

You may also want to add items of personal significance, such as photographs of your other children to keep on your nightstand. However, leave items of value, such as jewelry, at home.

There is no need to bring this bag into the hospital when checking in. Leave it in the car until after you have given birth and have been moved into a room.

Baby's Hospital Bag

Pack a hospital bag for the baby that contains any items you will need to bring your newborn home. Generally, this bag includes:

■ A sweater or warm outer covering (depending on the weather).

■ Diapers.

■ A receiving blanket and, outer blanket (optional).

■ A pair of socks or booties.

■ A going-home outfit and/or an outfit for taking a picture.

■ A hat (optional).

This bag can be left in the car until you are settled in your room. It can even be left at home and brought to you just before you and your baby will be leaving the facility.

Prepare an Emergency Birth Kit

If you have a history of rapid labors, live some distance from the hospital, or just want to be prepared in case your baby arrives unexpectedly, pack an emergency birth kit. The items that you might need for an emergency delivery include the following:

- A flashlight for better vision or at night.

- Clean towels, newspapers, or crib pads to absorb the amniotic fluid.

- Clean handkerchiefs to wipe the newborn's face.

- Blankets, including baby blankets and soft towels, to dry off the infant and a larger one to keep the mother and baby warm.

- A new bulb syringe to suction the newborn's mouth and nose if necessary.

- New shoelaces to tie the umbilical. (You do not need to cut the cord.)

- A large plastic bag to hold the placenta when it is delivered. Take the placenta with you to the hospital for examination.

Keep all of these items tightly wrapped in a clean plastic bag. Store the bag in a convenient place and take it with you when you leave for the hospital. (For additional tips, see "Giving Birth Without Medical Assistance" on page 223.)

Buy and Install a Car Safety Seat

In addition to preparing the Lamaze bag, hospital suitcase, baby's hospital bag, and emergency birth kit, have a car safety seat ready for the ride home. The safest place to install the seat is in the middle of the back seat, facing the rear of the car. If your car has dual air bags, *never* place the safety seat on the front passenger seat. The force of a discharged air bag can propel an infant seat and cause serious brain and neck injuries, or possibly death. In fact, no child under age thirteen should ride in the front seat of a car with dual air bags. The impact of a discharged air bag can seriously or fatally injure a child who is facing forward.

When installing the seat, carefully follow the instructions. In addition, check your car's owner's manual for information on installing car seats. It may be necessary to obtain an additional seat belt or a locking clip to ensure that the seat is securely fastened. The car seat should not slide side-to-side or forward when tugged. If it does not pass the tug test, it may be necessary to exchange your safety seat for another model. It is recommended that a certified Child Passenger Safety (CPS) Technician check your safety seat for correct installation. (Contact information for CPS Technicians is found in the Resources beginning on page 449.)

If you purchase a new seat, send in the warranty card. You will be notified directly of any recalls. If you have a seat that was previously used, it is important to confirm that that particular model has not been recalled. To check, call the manufacturer or the National Highway Traffic Safety Administration (NHTSA), which has an Auto Safety Hotline. (For contact information, see the Resources beginning on page 449.) Never use a car seat after it has been involved in a moderate or severe accident. Such a seat is no longer considered safe. All fifty states have passed laws that require infants and small children to ride in safety seats. (For a further discussion on safety seats, see "Automobile Safety" on page 330.)

Arrange Care for Your Pets

If you have pets, arrange to have them taken care of while you are at the hospital or birth center. Ideally, the person you choose should already be familiar with your pets. Provide your "pet sitter" with clear written instructions and a house key. Call him when you go into labor before heading for the hospital.

Spend Time Together

The last weeks of pregnancy are a time of waiting and expectancy. If this is your first baby, it will be the last time you will be just "a couple." Spend time together enjoying favorite activities, going out to eat, taking a weekend trip, or enjoying quiet evenings at home. Soon your life will change forever. If you already have other children, include them in the preparations so that they also feel important.

WARM-UP SIGNS OF LABOR

Prior to the onset of labor, you will notice several signs that indicate it is approaching. Some will happen several days or even weeks in advance. Others will occur when labor is imminent.

One of the first indications that labor is approaching is the settling of the baby's head into the pelvis. Called *lightening* or *dropping,* this generally occurs from two to four weeks before labor, especially with first babies. With subsequent pregnancies, lightening may occur even earlier or not until labor begins. After lightening, your abdomen may appear lower and protrude more. (See Figures 8.1 and 8.2 below.) You will be able to breathe easier and to eat more at one time. In addition, if you have been experiencing heartburn, you may find that it occurs less frequently. Lightening does, however, increase pressure in the pelvis, which could cause an increased need to urinate. You may experience increased backache because of the lowered position of the fetus as well as its greater size. Your center of gravity will also change with the new angle of the baby and may cause you to become more awkward when walking. In addition, finding a comfortable sleeping position may be difficult. Using relaxation techniques and extra pillows can help.

"We're still 'just a couple,' but I think something is coming between us!"

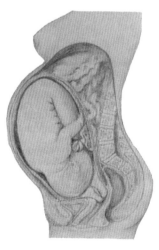

Figure 8.1. The position of the baby before lightening.

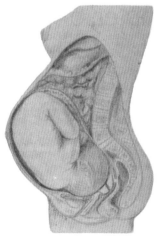

Figure 8.2. The position of the baby after lightening.

Hints for the Labor Partner

To help your partner during the warm-up phase before labor begins:

✓ Spend time with her—take her out to eat, accompany her on long walks, take her out on a "date."

✓ If you have been giving her prenatal perineal massages, continue to do so.

✓ Help her pack her Lamaze bag and place it in the car—and make sure the gas tank is full!

In addition to lightening, you are likely to experience other signs that your body is nearing labor, including the following:

■ An increase in vaginal secretions during the last weeks of pregnancy as your body prepares for the baby's passage.

■ A softening or "ripening" of the cervix as it prepares to start thinning and opening. The cervix may also begin to move from a posterior position to a more anterior one (towards the front). Internal exams to assess cervical changes usually begin around the thirty-sixth week of pregnancy.

■ Effacement (thinning) and dilation (opening) of the cervix, which may start weeks before the onset of labor.

■ Release of the mucous plug.

■ Feelings of anxiety or depression, which are very common as the due date approaches (or if it passes). Try to remain occupied and active.

■ A loss or leveling off of weight in the last few days before labor begins. You could lose as much as two to three pounds due to the excretion of excess tissue fluid.

■ A spurt of energy about twenty-four to forty-eight hours before labor. This may give you the urge to clean the entire house, wash floors or carpets, clean closets, or do some other chore that requires a great deal of physical work. *Do not give in to this "nesting" urge!* Nature gives you this extra energy to help you during labor.

■ Frequent bowel movements, usually within the forty-eight hours before labor. This cleansing of the lower bowel is the body's way to prepare for giving birth.

You many also experience an increase in Braxton-Hicks contractions, which some women feel as early as the fourth month of pregnancy. These "practice" contractions, named after the English physician who first described them in the 1880s, prepare the uterus for labor and may cause some effacement and dilation of the cervix during the warm-up period. They do not ordinarily cause pain, but during the last weeks of pregnancy, they may increase in strength and regularity. These signs of prelabor or false labor are sometimes confused with true labor. Although an internal exam is the only way to determine true labor from prelabor, there are certain signs that can help distinguish the two. See "Contractions—Prelabor or True Labor?" on page 187.

WHAT CAUSES LABOR TO BEGIN?

Although researchers continue to analyze various factors that may cause labor to begin, the exact reason is not known. Evidence does, however, point to hormonal changes in both the baby and the mother. Current research suggests that it begins with the baby's hypothalamus gland, which is located in his brain. The hypothalamus sends a hormone to the baby's pituitary gland that causes his adrenal glands to increase their production of a chemical that the placenta turns into estrogen. This estrogen then causes the placenta to produce hormones called prostaglandins, which cause the uterus to contract.

Contractions—Prelabor or True Labor?

While prelabor contractions can cause changes in the cervix, these changes occur over several weeks. Contractions that occur during true labor effect changes in the cervix within hours, causing it to thin out and open, while encouraging the baby to descend through the pelvis. The only way to distinguish prelabor from true labor with certainty is through an internal examination. Both types of contractions, however, are characterized by certain symptoms that can help you differentiate between the two. For a more detailed discussion, see "Signs of Labor" on page 188.

Prelabor

Contractions are felt more in the abdomen.

Contractions do not increase in intensity or length, even though they may be strong and close together.

Contractions slow down or become less intense with a change in activity or a warm bath or shower.

There is no bloody or pink mucous discharge.

Contractions slow down or stop after eating.

True Labor

Contractions are felt more in the back.

Contractions become increasingly stronger, last longer, and come closer together over time.

Contractions continue or become more intense with a change in activity. A bath may cause them to slow down during early labor.

A bloody or pink mucous discharge is usually present.

Contractions continue after eating.

This same hormone also stimulates the baby's lungs to mature—another reason it is so important to allow your body to go into labor when your baby is ready to be born. Not only does choosing to have an induced labor for non-medical reasons mean a possible difficult labor as your cervix is not ready, it also means your baby's lungs may not be mature.

HOW TO TIME CONTRACTIONS

Contractions are the periodic tightening and relaxing of the uterine muscles. For most women, they start in the back and radiate to the front and the abdomen becomes very hard to the touch. Some women feel them just in the lower back or hip area. Many women describe contractions as exaggerated menstrual cramps or pressure in the groin or upper thighs. Others perceive them as severe gas pains, which they sometimes confuse with flu symptoms or intestinal disorders.

A contraction gradually builds in intensity until it reaches a peak or strongest point, and then it gradually subsides—many women describe it as a wave action. Contractions are intermittent, with a rest period following each one.

The easiest way to time contractions—the amount of time from the beginning of one contraction to the beginning of the next—is by writing down the time (the exact minute) each one starts. Use the "Sample Chart of Timed Contractions" on page 188 as a guide. It shows the time that each contraction began as well as how long they lasted. Using this chart, you would tell your caregiver, "The contractions started at 10:00 and were 10 minutes apart, lasting 45 seconds. Now they are 3 to 4 minutes apart, lasting 60 to 65 seconds."

Contraction Timer

A variety of websites offer a free labor contraction timer that can be downloaded onto handheld computers. To locate these sites, simply do an Internet search using the keywords "free contraction timer."

SAMPLE CHART OF TIMED CONTRACTIONS

Start of Contraction	Duration of Contraction
10:00	45 seconds
10:10	45 seconds
10:15	60 seconds
10:20	55 seconds
10:25	60 seconds
10:29	60 seconds
10:33	65 seconds
10:37	60 seconds
10:40	60 seconds
10:43	65 seconds
10:47	60 seconds
10:51	60 seconds

Signs of Labor

The signs of true labor are:

✓ Progressive contractions.

✓ Rupture of the amniotic membranes.

✓ Release of the mucous plug from the cervix.

Call your caregiver if you are in labor.

SIGNS OF LABOR

When going into labor, a number of signs will be present. If you experience any of these signs before your thirty-seventh week, contact your caregiver immediately—you could be experiencing preterm labor. The signs of labor include the following:

■ **Progressive contractions.** The contractions of labor become longer, stronger, and closer together as labor advances. When timed, they show some regularity or pattern. Persistent contractions that have no rhythm but come less than seven minutes apart should be reported to your caregiver. If you are experiencing frequent backaches or symptoms of intestinal discomfort, place your hand on your abdomen. If your uterus becomes firm, you are having a contraction.

■ **Rupture of the amniotic membranes.** The rupture of the membranes of the amniotic sac may be noticed as a gush or uncontrollable leakage of fluid from the vagina. In a small percentage of women, this occurs as a first sign of labor. More commonly, the membranes remain intact until late in labor. Amniotic fluid can usually be distinguished from urine or heavy vaginal secretions. It is colorless, odorless, and cannot be stopped by doing Kegel exercises. If you are uncertain, your caregiver can perform a test on the fluid to determine its source.

Contact your caregiver as soon as the amniotic membranes rupture because a passageway will now be open for infection. Do not douche, insert a tampon, or have intercourse at this time. Contractions generally start within six to twelve hours following this rupture. If they do not start on their own, your caregiver may want to induce labor with the drug Pitocin. This is especially true for women with a positive culture for group B strep to prevent infection of the baby. Antibiotics will be started upon admission to the hospital or birth center.

Although most doctors insist that babies be delivered within twenty-four hours after the amniotic sac ruptures to prevent infection, some allow women to labor longer with good results. Frequent temperature checks and white blood cell counts can be used to monitor for infection. Of utmost importance is the avoidance of vaginal exams to prevent the introduction of bacteria into the vagina.

Some women may be concerned that once the amniotic membranes have ruptured, they will experience a "dry birth." Such a concern is unwarranted because there is actually no such thing as a dry birth. Approximately one-third of the amniotic fluid is replaced every hour. Also, the pressure from the baby's head acts as a cork against the cervix, preventing complete loss of the fluid. You may even notice intermittent leakage with the contractions as the pressure forces a small amount of amniotic fluid around the baby's head.

■ **Release of the mucous plug from the cervix.** Loss of the mucous plug is indicated by the presence of thick mucus. Pink or brownish in color or tinged with blood from capillaries that break as the cervix begins to dilate, this mucus is also called a *bloody show*. Although this plug is usually passed twenty-four to forty-eight hours before labor begins, it may be released as much as a week in advance. Sometimes it is passed when labor is well established. The loss of the mucous plug without the other signs does not indicate true labor.

Once labor is established, notify your caregiver. Be prepared to tell him how far apart the contractions are, their length, and their intensity; whether your amniotic membranes have ruptured and, if they have, the time of the rupture and the color of the fluid. Also be prepared to tell him if the mucous plug has been released. He will give you instructions on when to leave for the hospital or birth center.

UNDERSTANDING THE PROCESS OF LABOR

The process of labor and birth involves rhythmical contractions of the uterus that shorten and open the cervix and move the baby down through the pelvic bones. Once the cervix is open wide enough for the baby to exit the uterus, he can descend down the birth canal, assisted by the woman's pushing.

Some of these changes can begin during the last weeks of pregnancy as lightening occurs and the cervix starts to efface and dilate. Becoming aware of the various terms that relate to the baby's position and movements during labor will enable you to communicate with your caregiver and better understand your progress.

Fetal Presentation

The term *presentation* refers to the way the baby is situated in the uterus. The part of the baby that is closest to the cervix is considered the *presenting part.* In a normal birth, the head is lowest in the uterus and is, therefore, the presenting part. This type of presentation, called a *cephalic presentation,* is shown in Figure 8.3. More specifically, if the top of the head is felt at the cervix, it is called a *vertex presentation.*

For *breech presentations,* which account for 3 to 4 percent of all deliveries, the buttocks present first. Labor may be longer than with a vertex presentation because the buttocks are not as efficient a dilating wedge as the top of the head. Since most breech babies are born by cesarean delivery, this type of presentation (and other variations) will be discussed further in Chapter 10.

Position

The baby's *position* refers to the relation of his presenting part to the woman's pelvis. In a cephalic or vertex presentation, the baby's *occiput,* or back of the head, is the point of reference. The most common position during labor is the *anterior position,* in which the back of the baby's head is toward the woman's abdomen, as seen in Figure 8.4. A less common position is the *posterior position,* in which the back of the baby's head is against the woman's spine, as shown in Figure 8.5. A posterior position often results in prolonged labor accompanied by a great deal of back discomfort. (For more information on back labor, see page 222.)

Your caregiver may use letters—such as ROA, LOT, ROP, or OP—to identify your baby's position. The first letter—*R* or *L*—designates your right or left hip. The letter *O* refers to the baby's occiput, and the last letter can be either an *A* for anterior position, a *P* for posterior position, or a *T* for transverse position. (In the transverse position, the back of the baby's head is toward your side.) If the baby is breech, an *S* would be used to designate where the baby's sacrum (lower back) is positioned. For example, if your caregiver says that the position of the baby is ROA, it means the back of his head is toward your abdomen, but slightly toward your right side, as illustrated in Figure 8.4. In an OP position, the back of the baby's head is directly against your spine, and your baby is "sunny side up." Figure 8.5 shows the baby in ROP, a posterior position in which the back of his head is toward the mother's spine and slightly towards her right hip. A normal labor begins with the baby entering the pelvis in a transverse position and then rotating to an anterior position.

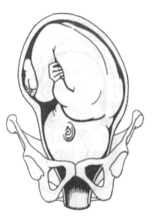
Figure 8.3. Cephalic or vertex presentation.

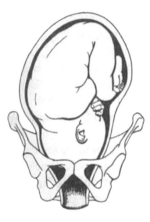
Figure 8.4. Anterior position.

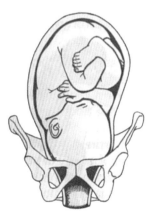
Figure 8.5. Posterior position.

Cardinal Movements

The *cardinal movements* of labor are the rotations of the baby as he moves through the pelvis. During labor, the baby must make specific rotations so that the widest diameters of his head and shoulders will match the widest diameter of the pelvis. The uterine contractions move the baby down the pelvis as he follows the path of least resistance. Ideally, when the baby enters the pelvis, his head faces sideways. As he moves down the pelvis during labor, his head turns so that by the time the woman is ready to push, he is looking at her back. This also places his shoulders in correct alignment to enter the pelvis. After the baby's head is delivered, his head rotates again to look at the woman's thigh with his shoulders lined up to come under the pubic bone.

Effacement

Effacement refers to the shortening and thinning of the cervix. It is expressed in percentages, from 0 percent (long and thick) to 100 percent (completely thinned out). Figure 8.6 shows the cervix in four stages of effacement and dilation.

Figure 8.6.
Effacement and dilation
of the cervix.

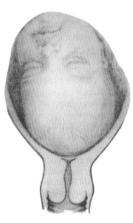

No effacement or
dilation of the cervix.

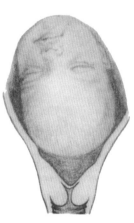

Cervix effaced 60 percent.

Cervix effaced 90 percent
and dilated 2 centimeters

Cervix effaced 100 percent
and dilated 10 centimeters.

Dilation

Dilation refers to the opening of the cervix. It is measured in centimeters, from 0 centimeters (closed) to 10 centimeters (completely opened). This range of dilation is shown in Figure 8.7. Dilation may also be expressed in fingers, with five fingers equal to 10 centimeters (approximately 4 inches). Dilation is complete when the cervix has opened enough for the baby's head to pass through it and into the vagina.

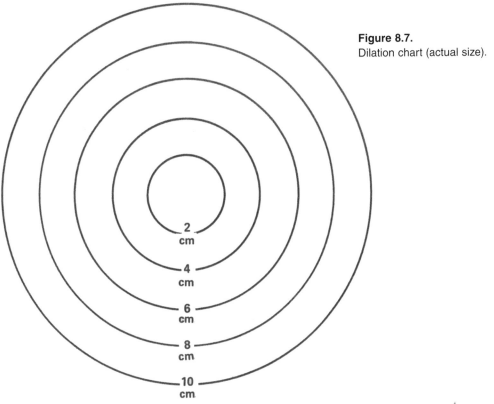

Figure 8.7.
Dilation chart (actual size).

2 cm

4 cm

6 cm

8 cm

10 cm

Station

The word *station* is another term to measure labor progress. It refers to the location of the baby's presenting part, usually the head, in relation to the level of ischial spines (shown in Figure 8.8) of the woman's pelvis. The station of the baby indicates the degree of his descent through the pelvis. It is expressed in centimeters above (minus) or below (plus) the level of the ischial spines (zero station). The head is usually engaged when it reaches zero station.

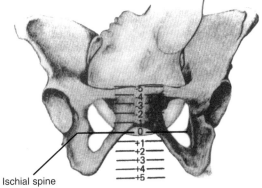

Ischial spine

Figure 8.8. The baby's head at "zero station," which is even with the woman's ischial spines.

Labor Overview

As mentioned earlier, labor is divided into four stages. During the first stage of labor, the contractions of the uterine muscles cause the cervix to efface and dilate. The second stage of labor begins at full dilation and effacement, and ends with the birth of the baby. The third stage of labor is the delivery of the placenta or afterbirth. The fourth stage of labor includes the first hours after delivery or your recovery period.

Your caregiver or a nurse will determine your progress during labor by vaginal examination. He or she will insert two fingers into the birth canal to measure the effacement and dilation of the cervix and determine the station of the baby. Though sometimes uncomfortable, these examinations will help assess your progress.

The average labor for a woman having her first baby is twelve hours. Women having subsequent babies usually experience a shorter labor, about seven hours. These numbers are just averages—the length of labor can vary greatly.

GOING TO THE HOSPITAL OR BIRTH CENTER

At some point during early or active labor, you will have to leave for your place of birth. When you go will depend on a number of factors, such as whether or not this is your first baby, the distance to the facility, your previous labor history, and your caregiver's recommendation. If you had a positive group B strep culture, your caregiver may want to start intravenous antibiotics in early labor. Some physicians recommend that once the amniotic membranes rupture, it is time to get to the hospital. Learning to recognize the signs of the various labor phases will allow you to judge your progress and avoid arriving too early.

"Now let's see . . . did I forget anything?"

Hospital Procedures

When you leave for the hospital, don't forget your Lamaze bag. Also take the bag or suitcase with your personal belongings, but leave it in the car. Be sure to leave your jewelry and any other valuables at home. When arriving at the hospital during the day, you will probably have to check in at the admissions office; when arriving at night, you may have to use the emergency room entrance. In many hospitals, you can go directly to labor and delivery.

Once in the labor and delivery unit, your partner may be directed to a waiting area while you are examined in a triage unit or preadmission room. This allows the nurse to speak privately with you and to determine whether or not to admit you to the labor unit. If you wish to remain together, inform the nurse. And be aware that some hospitals have restrictions on the number of support persons who can remain with you during labor. Confirm this prior to your arrival.

During this initial exam, you will be asked questions about your medical history, your allergies to medications, and your present labor symptoms. You will be placed on a fetal monitor to observe the pattern of contractions. You will also be asked if you plan to breastfeed or bottle feed. If you are planning to labor without medication, inform the nurse and request a labor nurse who will help you reach your goal. Discuss your birth plan, and request that no staff member suggest medication or an epidural. If you change your mind during labor, you can request medication at that time. If a contraction starts during the questioning, stop talking and go into your breathing pattern. The nurse will wait. Finally, you will be given a vaginal exam to determine cervical dilation and effacement, and station of the presenting part.

After your labor has been verified and you have been admitted, you may be asked to undergo certain procedures depending on your caregiver's written orders. If you have previously discussed your birth plan with your caregiver, and, for example, he has agreed that you do not need an IV or continuous monitoring, clarify this with the nurse to ensure it appears on the doctor's orders. Depending on the progress of your labor, certain procedures may or may not be necessary.

You will be placed on an electronic fetal monitor to determine the regularity and duration of the contractions. The nurse will also observe the baby's heart rate to assess fetal well-being in response to the contractions. (For a further discussion, see "Electronic Fetal Monitor" on page 246.) If a nurse-midwife is your caregiver, after evaluating your baby's tolerance of labor for thirty minutes on the electronic monitor, she will periodically assess your baby's heart rate using a hand-held fetal monitor and continue to observe your contractions for strength and frequency. Many midwives who practice in the hospital remain with the women during labor, just as they would in a birth center. Your blood pressure, temperature, pulse, and respiration will be taken. You will provide a urine sample, your blood will be drawn, and a vaginal culture may be taken to detect the presence of group B strep if there is no report on your chart.

If you are still in early labor, you may be instructed to walk around for a while to help increase the strength of the contractions. In years past, physicians ordered an enema, but this practice is no longer common. Many caregivers feel that it is unnecessary, especially if you've had a good bowel movement within the previous twenty-four hours. A woman may request an enema if she has been constipated or if she feels that she will not be able to effectively relax her bottom during the pushing stage for fear of soiling the bed. In this case, a small disposable enema will suffice.

Many facilities provide tubs or showers for laboring women. After the stress of the trip to the hospital and the admission procedures, relaxing in water can be soothing; it can also lower your blood pressure. The warm water provides buoyancy and reduces external stimuli, which allows you to relax both physically and mentally. Your relaxed body is better able to produce endorphins, the body's natural pain relievers. The more comfortable a woman is, the less likely she is to produce stress-related hormones, which can raise her blood pressure or slow the labor. Laboring in water, even after the amniotic sac has ruptured, will not cause infections or other complications. Avoid getting into the tub too early, though, as it can slow down early labor.

At one time, it was a standard procedure for laboring women to have their pubic hair shaved to reduce the risk of infection. Studies have shown, however, that this practice actually increases the risk, so it is no longer done. This also spares the woman the itching and discomfort associated with the hair regrowth. If the hair is long, it may be trimmed with scissors or clippers. And many women routinely wax their bikini area, so fewer arrive in labor with significant pubic hair.

An IV drip may be started if indicated. To allow for increased mobility, some physicians place a saline lock in the vein. The procedure is the same as for starting a standard IV, but the bag of fluid is not connected and the line is occasionally flushed with saline (a salt solution) to keep the vein open. (For a further discussion, see "Intravenous Fluids" on page 245.)

Birth Center Procedures

"Couldn't we just talk first?"

If you are giving birth in an out-of-hospital birth center, you are already familiar with the environment since you have been going there for your prenatal care. Most birth centers are not staffed twenty-four hours a day. If you are in labor during office hours, call the center and speak with the midwife on call. This will alert her to the possibility that she may have a client (midwives refer to women as "clients," not "patients") in labor. She may have you come in for an exam or to start antibiotics if your group B strep culture was positive. It will also allow her to organize her day in case she will have to be up all night. Most birth centers will give you a backup number to call after hours. If you are calling the midwife late at night, she will not have your chart in front of her. It is your responsibility to inform her of any pertinent information, such as your history of short labors, need for antibiotics, long drive to the center, etc.

When arriving at the facility, the midwife will greet you at the door and discuss your symptoms. She will also check your vital signs (blood pressure, temperature, pulse, and respirations). She will have you check your urine with a dipstick and report the results or she will read the results herself. She will also monitor your contractions and listen to your baby's heart rate with a hand-held fetal monitor. If you are in labor, you will remain at the birth center. If you are having strong regular contractions, but are still in early labor, she may request that you eat something and maybe take a walk, and then come back for another assessment.

Once you are admitted in labor, the midwife will remain with you to monitor your contractions and the baby's heart rate at regular intervals. At some point, she may call in a birth attendant, who will assist her during the birth and help care for your infant after he is born.

Interventions are not routine. Most women delivering in a birth center do not have routine IVs, electronic fetal monitoring, or restrictions on positions during labor and birth. Women may eat as they desire and are strongly encouraged to drink to prevent dehydration. Most facilities provide a list of items that the client should bring for comfort during labor.

You will wear your own clothes and may invite additional support persons to help you during labor. After the baby is born, you will remain in the center for four to six hours before leaving for home.

Home Birth

If you are having your baby at home, your caregiver will instruct you on the necessary supplies to have on hand. You will also be instructed on when to call. Once the caregiver arrives, she will remain with you throughout labor and the recovery period.

For the Labor Partner—Your Role as a Support Person

Your primary job as labor partner is to provide comfort, support, and encouragement to the laboring woman, and to remind her of her breathing and relaxation techniques and other comfort measures. Some women have more than one support person. If you and another person are serving as labor partners, at times you can work together, while allowing each other an occasional break. If the other labor partner is a trained professional, she can supply technical expertise while you provide the emotional support.

If you are separated from the mother-to-be during admission, you will probably be reunited within thirty to forty-five minutes. When you see her again, you may find her tense and somewhat lost without your assistance. Immediately start encouraging her to relax and help her with slow breathing. Some couples do not want to be separated at all during labor. If you want to stay together, make this request during the admission procedure. A few physicians still ask the labor partner to leave during exams and other procedures. If you want to be present, discuss this with your caregiver in advance. For a summary of the labor partner's role during the four stages of labor, see Table 8.1 on page 210.

THE FOUR STAGES OF LABOR

Labor is divided into four stages. The first stage begins with the onset of labor and ends when the cervix is completely effaced and dilated. The second stage begins with the completely dilated cervix and ends with the baby's birth. The third stage involves the delivery of the placenta. The fourth stage, considered the recovery period, includes the first few hours after giving birth.

FIRST STAGE OF LABOR

The first stage of labor is the longest of the four stages. It is divided into three phases— early, active, and transition.

Early Labor

Also called the *latent phase,* early labor is the easiest but longest phase, usually lasting from two to nine hours. Along with effacing, the cervix dilates from 0 to 4 centimeters during this time. Contractions, which are commonly from thirty to sixty seconds long, are usually fifteen to twenty minutes apart initially, and get progressively closer until they are about five minutes apart. They start out mild to slightly uncomfortable, and become stronger and longer as labor progresses. You will probably be at home for most of this phase.

During the rest period between contractions, you should feel good. You are likely to be talkative and able to walk around and continue normal activities. Eat, drink, and empty your bladder every one to two hours during this phase. Women who have prepared themselves for labor generally feel very confident during this time and handle it well. Some women, however, may suddenly express anxiety, realizing that once labor has begun, it will not stop.

If labor starts during the day, walk around and keep active to help stimulate the contractions. If labor begins at night, try to get some sleep or rest so that you can better handle the upcoming active phase. Take a warm bath, which will slow down the early labor contractions so you can sleep. Be assured that when your contractions become strong, you will awaken!

During early labor, you can enjoy decaffeinated tea, apple juice, and sports drinks, as well as Jell-O, broth, and ice pops. Avoid diet and caffeinated beverages, milk, and citrus juices. Nutritious snacks that are high in carbohydrates and low in fat, such as crackers, fruit, toast, pasta, cereal, and waffles, are recommended choices. These foods provide the nourishment that is needed for labor. In one study, women who were encouraged to eat and drink during labor required fewer pain relief medications and less Pitocin. They also experienced a shortening of their labor by an average of ninety minutes.[2] Digestion slows during more active labor, and the woman's desire for food diminishes.

The needs of a woman in labor are similar to those of an athlete. Prior to an event, an athlete loads up on carbohydrates in order to have the energy supplies that his body

Trust Your Body

It is most important that you go into labor trusting your body. Women have been giving birth successfully since the beginning of time. Your body was built for carrying and nourishing your baby, and for safely delivering him into the world.

Early labor.

needs during the event. These needs are similar during labor and especially during the hard physical work of pushing. Fasting may lead to a labor that progresses slowly, dystocia (a difficult labor), and a "cascade of interventions culminating in a cesarean delivery."[3] Frequently, IVs are started during labor to prevent dehydration, electrolyte imbalance, and ketosis. Many women who were required to fast during early labor have stated that those feelings of hunger increased their stress during labor. If women were encouraged to simply eat and drink as they desire, these negative side effects would be reduced. Permitting them to do so provides hydration, nutrition, increased comfort, and a feeling of being in control.[4]

Eating during labor remains a controversial issue because of the possibility of vomiting and aspirating the stomach contents into the lungs if general anesthesia is given. General anesthesia, however, is seldom used, so if a woman vomits while she is awake, there shouldn't be a problem. And aspiration of the stomach contents by a person who has fasted is more serious than it is for someone who has just eaten. This is because the contents will be highly acidic from the acid that is produced in the stomach. Current anesthesia guidelines require that all laboring women be treated as if they had eaten and require certain techniques to prevent aspiration of stomach contents.

For the Labor Partner—Your Role in Early Labor

Early labor is a time of preparation. Make sure the Lamaze bag and your partner's suitcase with her personal belongings are packed and ready to go. Check the traffic report and, if necessary, find an alternate route to the facility. Make sure there is gas in the car. If you have children or pets that need to be taken care of, alert the sitters with whom you have made prior arrangements. If a doula and/or other support people will be attending the birth, inform them of the labor status. Since you will probably be spending most of this early labor period at home, help pass the time by playing cards, watching a movie, or taking a walk. Encourage your partner to eat carbohydrates and drink fluids.

This is the time to become familiar with contractions. If you place your hand on your partner's abdomen, you can feel her uterus become very hard. Sometimes you can feel a contraction beginning even before your partner is aware of it, so you can help prepare her. Also help out by timing the contractions and making sure that she is relaxing and breathing slowly with them. If you notice her tensing or expressing discomfort during contractions, encourage her to relax by massaging or stroking the tense area. You can also encourage her to change positions or remind her to urinate (a full bladder often causes discomfort during labor). Suggest that she take a shower but discourage her from lying in a warm bath as it can slow down early labor. If, however, she is not well rested, a warm bath could slow down labor enough for her to take a nap.

Active Labor

During active labor, the cervix dilates from 4 to 8 centimeters. After 5 centimeters, labor may progress very rapidly. In fact, labor is more than half over at this point, with the contractions becoming stronger and peaking faster. The peaks also last longer now. During this phase, the contractions usually last from forty-five to sixty seconds and are two to four minutes apart. If the amniotic membranes rupture at this time, they

Hints for the Labor Partner

To help your partner during early labor:

✓ Time her contractions.

✓ Help her determine if she is experiencing true labor or prelabor.

✓ Encourage her to sleep if labor begins at night.

✓ If you are walking with her, stop and support her during contractions.

✓ Remind her to urinate every one to two hours.

✓ Offer her snacks and liquids.

✓ Offer her massages or back rubs.

✓ Tell her what a great job she's doing.

usually do so with a gush. Many women notice an increase in the intensity of the contractions after the membranes rupture.

Active labor is the time to go to your place of birth or, if you are delivering at home, to call your caregiver. If you are in active labor during office hours, call your doctor or midwife and report your symptoms. If it is at night, and you are giving birth in the hospital, your caregiver may want you to go to the labor and delivery unit for an examination. The staff will inform him if you are in labor.

During the active phase, your mood will become serious and very birth-oriented. You may not want to be distracted and may begin to doubt your ability to cope with the contractions. You will no longer want to play cards or games, you will be less talkative between contractions, and you may need more help in remaining relaxed. You may want to change positions or try laboring in a tub or shower.

Active labor.

For the Labor Partner—Your Role in Active Labor

During this more intense, active phase of labor, continue reassuring and encouraging your partner. It is important to keep her informed of her progress at this time. Help her maintain focus during contractions and assist her with breathing if necessary. If she is moaning, or vocalizing during contractions, encourage her to make low-pitched sounds. She may want to use your eyes as her focal point. Keep your commands to your partner short, since she may not be interested in long conversations. Continue to remind her to empty her bladder every one to two hours.

Offer comfort measures as needed. If her mouth is dry, help her sip juice, suck on ice chips or an ice pop, brush her teeth, or rinse with mouthwash. For dry lips, help her apply lip balm or gloss. Wiping her face with a cool cloth may help her feel refreshed. If you are walking with her, you may need to stop and support her during a contraction. If she is in bed, have her change position often, about every twenty to thirty minutes, and help her adjust the bed for comfort. You can start to utilize some of the other tools for labor, such as massage, counter pressure, acupressure, hot or cold compresses, or whatever is appropriate.

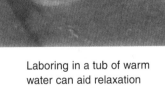

Your partner may need to add additional comfort measures to remain relaxed and focused. If you find a technique or combination of techniques that works, repeat it with every contraction. (See Chapter 7 for suggestions.) Do not change to a different strategy unless she tells you that the current one is not working or asks you to stop.

Many women find the sound of voices irritating during active labor. If other people are in the room, encourage them to keep their voices low while talking or ask them to remain quiet during contractions.

Laboring in a tub of warm water can aid relaxation during active labor.

Transition

The transition from the first stage of labor to the second stage is the shortest phase, but it is also the most intense. During this time, the cervix dilates from 8 to 10 centimeters. The contractions are usually sixty to ninety seconds in duration and peak very suddenly, sometimes more than once. In addition, the contractions may be as close as a minute and a half to three minutes apart. Even though there is a short rest period between contractions, some women have claimed that the contractions felt as though they were right on top of one another with no relief. Transition may last from ten minutes to an hour and a half. Think positive—at this point, labor is almost over!

Certain signs will alert you and your labor partner to the fact that you are in transition. These signs, which you may or may not experience, are:

- Premature urge to push or bear down. You may mistakenly think you need to move your bowels.
- Belching or hiccups.
- Nausea and/or vomiting.
- Shaking or uncontrollable trembling of your legs or body.
- Chills and/or extreme warmth.
- Loss of modesty. You may throw off your covers.
- Cramps in your legs and buttocks.
- Sensitivity to touch. You may not want to be touched.
- Spontaneous rupture of the membranes if it has not yet occurred. At this point, it usually happens with a gush.
- Flushed face.

- Dopey feeling; amnesia or sleeping between contractions. This is probably caused by the release of endorphins.
- Increased bloody mucous discharge.
- Confusion and/or a tendency to give up. You may say, "I can't do it," or "I can't take another contraction."
- Feeling of getting nowhere, that labor will never end.
- Panic, especially if left alone.
- Susceptibility to suggestion, especially if offered medication.
- Inability to comprehend directions and a need for your labor partner to do the breathing patterns with you.
- Irritability and restlessness.
- Feeling out of control and overwhelmed by contractions.

Remember that these are *possible* signs. Be assured that you will not experience all of them.

For the Labor Partner—Your Role in Transition

During transition, your encouragement and presence are vital. *Do not leave your partner during this time for any reason.* She may panic if left alone, even for a short period. At this time, she is likely to accept any medication that is offered, or she may even ask for it (even though her original intention was not to use drugs). Remind her that she is in transition and any medication taken at this time may not take effect until the phase is over. An epidural, for instance, may not begin to provide relief until the pushing stage, at which time she will need to be able to feel the sensations to push effectively. Any drugs taken now might have a strong effect on the baby. Narcotics given intravenously may transfer to the baby and cause him to experience depressed respirations at birth. Many women find that relaxing in water during transition provides sufficient pain relief to avoid the need for medication.

"During my labor, I imagined myself floating in the ocean and each contraction was a wave. I stayed relaxed by floating on top of the wave. I knew if I started to panic I would drown."

Joanna

If she requests medication, ask the doctor or midwife to give her an internal exam, even if one was performed recently. She may be surprised to find that she has made significant progress. Just hearing the change may cause her to decide that medication is unnecessary. On the other hand, if she has remained the same and is having great difficulty, she may decide that medication is now an option.

If she says that she needs to move her bowels or begins to bear down, inform the nurse so that an examination can be performed. If the cervix is not fully dilated but is stretchy, the nurse may instruct the woman to bear down with the contraction to see if the cervix will open completely. But if the cervix is unyielding and tight around the baby's head, pushing will only cause exhaustion. In this case, you will have to instruct your partner to blow out forcefully during the urge to push.

You must make sure during transition that your partner "catches" each contraction. If she sleeps or has amnesia between them, you must make sure that she starts her breathing pattern in time. Let her know when the contraction ends and help her relax in between. *Remain calm.* Even if your partner yells at you, do not argue. Make your commands short and precise. If your partner becomes confused, have her sit up in bed.

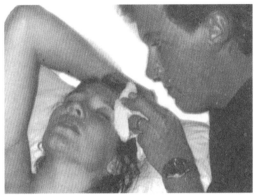

A cool cloth on the forehead can be soothing during transition.

If your partner says that she wants to give up, keep reminding her that this is transition and that labor is almost over. Just hearing the word transition can reassure her. Let her know that the contractions will not get any worse. Encourage her to rest between them.

Occasionally, a woman will want to squeeze something. Be careful what you offer her! If her fingernails are long, they may dig into your skin. Give her a pillow to hold. Offer her two fingers to grasp, rather than your full hand, especially if you wear a ring. Firmly massage her hand and fingers. She may have great difficulty staying completely relaxed. Do not worry. It is just important that you are there to support her and help her get through this difficult period.

Start a rhythmical activity such as tapping, swaying, or rocking. If this is comforting, repeat it with every contraction. You may have to use multiple distraction techniques to get through this part of labor. Your partner may want you to stay close and stroke her arm, or she may want you to sit beside her, but without touching her. Remember, every woman labors differently, and just because she does not want to be touched, it does not mean she doesn't want your presence.

If you notice that your partner is not using a focal point, is rocking her head from side to side, or is gripping the bed sheet, your hand, or a bed rail, she may be starting to panic. She may also stop her breathing pattern and hold her breath, yell, or cry out. She may even thrash around in the bed. To help her regain control, first stand up. This puts you in a position of authority. Grasp her face or wrists with your hands and call her name. Bring your face close to hers and do the breathing pattern with her. If she is vocal, encourage low moaning, but direct high squeals to a lower octave. You may need to be firm with her during this time and take full command of the situation. Generally, when the contractions become unbearable, transition is almost over, with just a few contractions left. Be sure to tell your partner this.

Transition.

Ask your doula, midwife, or supportive nurse for assistance at this time. Often, they can suggest techniques that have worked for other women. This is one of the great benefits of having a professional who remains with you throughout the labor and birth. Midwives and doulas have observed and assisted many women in labor and will stay by your side to help you through the difficult times. If you have a nurse who doesn't have other patients, she may also be able to stay with you and help you cope.

Continue with the other comfort measures as needed. If your partner's back is uncomfortable, perform counter pressure or acupressure, massage the area, or apply a

Hints for the Labor Partner

To help your partner during active labor and transition:

✓ Be positive.

✓ Do not leave her for any reason.

✓ Tell her that she is wonderful.

✓ Wipe her face with a cool cloth.

✓ Offer her ice chips or sips of liquid.

✓ Try acupressure.

✓ Stay calm.

✓ Begin a rhythmical activity and continue with each contraction.

✓ Maintain eye contact if she becomes confused or panicky.

✓ Tell her that labor is almost over.

✓ Encourage her to breathe evenly and slowly.

✓ Get her to focus on you and imitate your rate of breathing.

✓ If she starts hyperventilating and begins to feel "tingly," have her breathe into a paper bag or into her cupped hands.

warm or cool cloth. Put warm socks on her feet if they are cold. If her legs are trembling, firmly massage her inner thighs or grasp her legs. Keep a cool cloth on her forehead or neck if she is nauseated. Tell her she is doing wonderfully and keep her informed of her progress. Above all else, keep a positive attitude!

SECOND STAGE OF LABOR

The second stage of labor, also called the *pushing stage,* begins when the cervix is completely dilated and effaced, and ends with the birth of the baby. The contractions during this stage are more like those experienced during active labor, lasting approximately sixty to seventy-five seconds. They slow in frequency and are usually three to five minutes apart. The pushing stage may last from ten minutes to two or more hours. For women who have given birth before, this stage is generally short.

You might find yourself enjoying a rest period between the first and second stages of labor. The contractions may stop for ten to fifteen minutes. Use this opportunity to rest and to prepare for the hard work of pushing.

During the pushing stage, your mood will greatly improve. You will become sociable, even talkative, and you will feel more positive about your progress. If you have been blowing to combat a premature urge to push, you will feel tremendous relief at being able to work actively with the contractions. Many women feel great satisfaction while pushing the baby down the birth canal, even though it is hard work. Some women even equate the baby's emerging from the vagina with an orgasmic experience.

During the peaks of the contractions, you will feel a strong urge to push. If you do not feel this urge, ask to wait to begin pushing and continue labor breathing, also known as *laboring down.* Get into a more upright position and allow gravity to aid the descent of the baby in the pelvis, so that his head will stimulate the urge to bear down. Avoid pushing until you feel the urge develop. Pushing without your body's direction is difficult and unsatisfying. If you were given an epidural, ask to have the medication reduced so that you can feel the contractions. If you are unable to move your legs or feel the contractions, it may take a while for the epidural's effects to diminish. Your pushing will be more effective if you wait until you can feel the urge to push and are able to move your legs. Once the baby descends deep enough in the vagina, you will begin to feel the urge.

As you begin to push, you may feel a strong urge to have a bowel movement. You may respond to this urge by tightening the pelvic floor so that you will not soil the bed. This feeling is a normal sensation as the baby's head presses against the bowel. In some facilities, women are permitted to sit on the toilet to start pushing. This alleviates the fear of having a bowel movement in the bed. (It is not unusual for a small amount of bowel movement to be passed during pushing, unless the woman has emptied her bowels earlier in labor.) Do not react to this sensation by tensing. Instead, concentrate on relaxing your bottom for maximum comfort and progress. If you relax your jaw, your pelvic floor will also relax. When you practice your Kegel exercises, notice that if you tense your jaw, you will feel a tightening in the pelvic floor. Conversely, if you relax your jaw, your pelvic floor will also relax.

Use spontaneous or non-directed pushing and bear down as your body guides you. Feel the cues and work with your body to push with the urges. (It is similar to vomiting or having diarrhea—when your body is ready to expel its contents, it is almost impossible to hold back.) Push lightly with a mild urge and use more effort if the urge is strong. There is no evidence that a more rapid second stage is beneficial for the mother or the baby. As long as the mother and the baby are stable, there should not be a rigid time limit on the pushing stage.[5] Avoid sustained breath holding while bearing down. If you do hold your breath, do not hold if for more than six seconds. If possible, get into an upright position to allow gravity to help the descent of the baby. Do not lie flat on your back when pushing as this can cause the weight of the uterus to press on your vena cava and cause the baby to receive less oxygen and have distress.

If you are having difficulty with pushing, tell the nurse or midwife, who can help by giving verbal directions or by applying pressure in the vagina to direct your bearing down efforts. You can also use a mirror to see your progress. When you observe the bulging of the perineum, you will know you are pushing correctly.

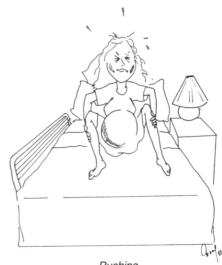

Pushing.

As the baby descends the birth canal, you may experience an increased bloody show, a burning or splitting sensation, or leg cramps. Your face may turn red or begin perspiring, and you may have a look of intense concentration. You may grunt or groan involuntarily as you actively work with the contractions. Your partner may misinterpret these normal responses as expressions of pain. Some women express discomfort or pain with pushing, which is usually associated with an unusual presentation or position of the baby, poor position of the woman, a large baby, or an unrelaxed pelvic floor. If you experience discomfort, change position and focus on relaxing your bottom. Visualize the vagina opening up to allow the passage of the baby.

Some women stop pushing out of fear, concerned about tearing the perineum or damage to the vagina. Other women express anxiety about their partner viewing the vagina stretching to such a degree that he will lose his desire for sex. If the doctor has not arrived, and the birthing bed has been converted to a delivery bed with the bottom third removed, the woman may be afraid that she will push her baby out and onto the floor. Also, women with a history of sexual abuse may have difficulty being placed in such a vulnerable position. It is very important to discuss this issue with the caregiver prior to the birth so that specific words and phrases that may trigger negative emotions are avoided.

If you experience these feelings of fear during your second stage of labor, try to focus on the positive idea that your pushing efforts will result in the birth of your baby. Tell yourself that you will see your baby soon. Many nurses instruct women to push into the pain to move past it. You may want to visualize pushing your way through a tight hallway or passageway as you bear down.

You will feel a large amount of pressure or a burning sensation as the baby nears the perineum. Your caregiver may apply warm compresses or perform perineal massage to stretch the tissues. While pushing during contractions, you may notice the baby's head at the vaginal outlet, along with some bulging of the perineum and separation of the vaginal lips, as seen in Figure

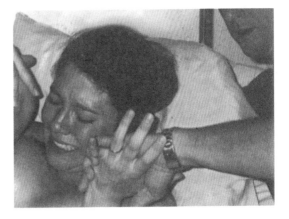

This woman's face reflects the intensity of pushing.

8.9 on page 202. The head may appear wrinkled and covered with wet hair. It will recede between contractions until the top of the head finally remains visible between contractions. This is called *crowning,* which may be accompanied by intense burning known as the *ring of fire.* With the next few contractions, the baby's head will be born. It will then rotate with the face turning toward your thigh. Next, the shoulders will be delivered, and the body will slide out with ease, often accompanied by a gush of amniotic fluid. Many couples help with the birth of the baby. Once the shoulders are free, the woman (and/or labor partner) can reach down and pull the baby onto her abdomen. The labor partner can then cut the umbilical cord after it has stopped pulsating.

At this point, you and your labor partner will probably be so overwhelmed by the sight, sound, and feel of your new infant that you will not notice any of the other activity going on around you.

For the Labor Partner—Your Role During the Second Stage of Labor

During the pushing stage, help your partner get into a comfortable position, preferably upright. Avoid giving her instructions on how and when to push. Encourage her to follow her natural sensations, bearing down only when she feels an urge. If others in the room are "coaching" her to bear down forcefully, discourage this practice. If the baby is moving down the birth canal rapidly, encourage her to reduce her efforts. This will help to avoid tears and a delivery that is too rapid. A baby that is born too quickly is more likely to retain fluid in his lungs and experience rapid breathing after birth.

If your partner holds her breath while pushing, count for her. In addition, make sure that she releases a small amount of air before holding her breath. Check her jaw to make sure that it is relaxed.

Place warm wet compresses or washcloths on her perineum. This will be very comforting and can help ease the burning sensation. It may also help her relax and possibly reduce her chance of needing an episiotomy. As the baby's head is emerging and the caregiver instructs your partner how to push and when not to push, you may need to repeat the instructions to her.

This is the time to have your camera or recording equipment ready (if permitted by the facility). Make sure that the mirror is adjusted correctly and your partner is

"After this experience, I am in awe of the human body."

Amy
After a birth without medication

Figure 8.9.
Birth of the baby's head.

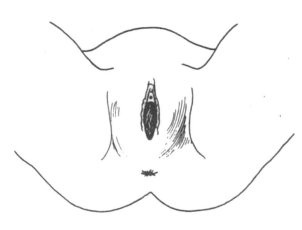

Head visible.   Crowning.

wearing her contacts or glasses if needed to watch the birth. Encourage her to keep her eyes open while pushing so that she can see her progress in the mirror and not miss the actual birth.

Some caregivers encourage the partner to be actively involved in the birth and to be the person to place the baby onto the mother's abdomen. If you are going to "catch" the baby, carefully follow the instructions of the caregiver.

Cutting the Cord

Once the baby is born and breathing on his own, he no longer needs the umbilical cord. After the caregiver clamps the cord, he may ask the labor partner if he wants to cut it. Some caregivers do this immediately after birth. Others wait until the cord has stopped pulsating, which may take up to five minutes. Dr. Frederick Leboyer, a noted French obstetrician, advocated delay in cutting the cord. He believed that this benefits the infant, who will be receiving oxygen from two sources—his lungs and the placenta—until his circulatory system changes from fetal to newborn circulation. While the baby is in utero, blood bypasses his lungs through a blood vessel between his pulmonary artery and aorta called the *ductus arteriosus,* and he receives oxygen via the umbilical cord. Once he begins to breathe, the ductus arteriosus closes and blood goes to the lungs for oxygenation.

Placing the baby on the mother's abdomen after delivery and waiting for the cord to stop pulsating will allow optimal blood volume within the baby. Holding him below the mother will cause gravity to increase the amount of blood that he receives. Once the placenta has detached, usually within minutes, the infant no longer receives oxygen via the umbilical cord. Also, when the cord is exposed to air, the Wharton's jelly that surrounds the vessels in the cord begins to expand and compresses the vessels. If the cord is tight around the baby's neck or the baby needs resuscitation, the cord may need to be cut earlier. If you made arrangements to have the cord blood collected, it will be done at this time.

Hints for the Labor Partner

To help your partner during pushing:

✓ Assist her in finding a comfortable position, preferably upright.

✓ Encourage her to follow her natural "pushing" urges.

✓ Remind her to "look for the baby" as she bears down.

✓ Apply warm washcloths to her perineum.

✓ If she is holding her breath while pushing, make sure she first lets a little air out, then pace her efforts by counting to six.

✓ Provide a mirror so she can see her progress.

✓ Continue telling her that she is doing great.

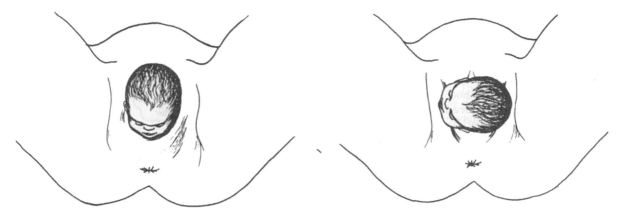

Birth of the head.

External rotation.

Procedures in Out-of-Hospital Birth Centers and Hospital Birthing Rooms

Out-of-hospital birth centers and in-hospital birthing rooms offer a number of options to couples expecting an uncomplicated labor. Most birthing centers are run by certified nurse-midwives, with a backup physician in case a complication arises. They are usually located outside a hospital and accept only normal healthy women as clients. Licensed midwives (LM), certified professional midwives (CPM), and lay midwives also deliver outside the hospital. (For more information on midwives, see page 8.) In-hospital birthing rooms offer many of the same options as birthing centers, but they are located in the labor and delivery area of a hospital and utilize the hospital staff. If your caregiver is a physician, the nursing staff will monitor and care for you during labor. Your physician will arrive for the delivery. Occasionally, if your physician is in the hospital, he may visit several times during your labor. If you have chosen a nurse-midwife as your caregiver, she will often remain with you during labor to monitor your progress, as well as to perform the delivery.

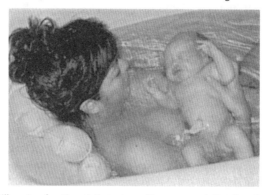

Only a few hospitals still require women to labor in one room, transfer to a delivery room, move to a recovery and bonding room, and finally go to a postpartum room. The majority of hospitals have birthing rooms, also known as LDRs (labor, delivery, recovery), where a woman stays until she is transferred to a postpartum room. The newest form of birthing room is the LDRP (labor, delivery, recovery, postpartum), where a woman remains for her entire hospital stay. This type of birthing room is the closest in concept to the birth center.

In both birth centers and birthing rooms, attractive surroundings make the room homelike, with the necessary medical equipment hidden within the furniture. Restrictions on visitors are often minimal or nonexistent. Some hospitals do restrict the number of visitors, especially at the time of the birth. (In case of a cesarean section, only one support person is usually permitted in the operating room.) Siblings may even be present for the birth. If you are delivering in the hospital, your doctor may have to give permission for this to occur.

During labor, a woman is free to move about the room and halls, and to labor in a comfortable recliner or rocking chair. Many facilities offer showers or tubs in which women can relax during labor. This is more likely to occur if the woman is under the care of a midwife or if she has expressed these desires to her physician. When there is a strong emphasis on inductions and epidurals, fewer women utilize these options during labor.

Care Given to the Baby at Birth

Immediately after the birth, the baby is placed onto the mother's abdomen and quickly dried to prevent him from getting cold. After the cord is cut, he can remain skin to skin on the mother's chest, covered with warm blankets. Request that assessments by the nurse be performed in this position as long as the baby is healthy and stable.

Your baby will be given his first exams in life at one minute after birth and again at five minutes after birth. This two-part evaluation, called the Apgar score, is designed to show how well the baby handled labor and delivery, and how he is adjusting to life outside the uterus. For detailed information, see "The Apgar Score" on page 206.

In out-of-hospital birth centers or during midwifery care, few interventions are used and only if medically necessary. IVs, fetal monitors, and draping, for example, are not routine. Women are encouraged to eat and drink as they desire. Most birth centers have regular beds, which allow the woman to choose whatever position feels most comfortable. She may even deliver standing, sitting on a birthing chair, squatting, or while lying on her side or in water. Bright lights are avoided and the temperature in the birth room is warmed to prevent cold stress in the newborn. At the moment of birth, the mother and labor partner can reach down and lift their baby up and onto the mother's bare abdomen. The baby is dried off and then remains on the mother, skin to skin, covered with warm blankets. Some fathers participate even more by "catching" the baby while under close supervision. The infant is never separated from the parents to go to a nursery; all exams are done in the same room.

Several hours after birth, when the mother is ready to get washed, she may take her baby into the tub with her for his first bath. Birth center philosophy considers not only the mother's physical needs, but also her emotional and spiritual concerns. Families play an integral part in providing a safe birth in a loving, caring atmosphere. The woman and the baby usually go home within four to six hours after the birth. They are followed up closely by the nurse-midwife via telephone conversations and an office or home visit during the first days.

Most women who deliver in the hospital will have IVs and continuous electronic fetal monitoring. They are permitted only ice chips, ice pops, or sips of clear liquids. Since the induction rate and the use of early epidurals has increased, fewer women are observed walking, laboring in water, or attempting to give birth without medication.

Most in-hospital birthing rooms have birthing beds that can be maneuvered into various positions. A common delivery position elevates the woman's back and places her feet in footrests or stirrups. The lithotomy position (lying flat on the back) should be avoided. Many doctors and midwives are willing to try alternate positions that are more comfortable for the woman. At the time of birth, the bottom of the bed is removed, an antiseptic solution is poured over the woman's perineum, and her legs are draped. Not all doctors or midwives require stirrups or leg drapes to be used. Others do not use abdominal drapes, recognizing the importance of the skin-to-skin contact that occurs when the newborn is placed on the mother's bare abdomen following delivery.

Many supportive doctors hand the newborn right to the mother to touch and caress as the family begins the bonding process immediately after birth. In some birthing rooms, a nurse may want to take the baby to a warmer within that room to perform admission procedures. Unless it is medically neccesary, ask to delay removing your baby from you for the first hour. Both of you should be covered with warm blankets to maintain body heat, to help regulate his blood sugar, and to facilitate breastfeeding. Removing him early will cause stress and is unnecessary in a normal healthy baby.

If you choose to deliver in a hospital, discuss these and all options with your caregiver to ensure an optimum birth experience.

After you have had an opportunity to hold and soothe your newborn, the nurse may "borrow" him to perform admission and identification procedures. Since the birthing room will probably be about twenty degrees cooler than body temperature, your baby must be kept warm if he is separated from you. During the procedures, therefore, he will be placed under a warming light. When he is with you and covered with a blanket, he will not need a warming light because mothers are the best baby warmers! If the nursery returns him all bundled up, remove the blanket and resume skin-to-skin contact. Breastfeeding should be initiated within the first hour when the baby is receptive and in an alert state.

The Apgar Score

The first test given to a newborn was designed by anesthesiologist Virginia Apgar to quickly evaluate the baby's physical condition after birth and to determine any immediate need for additional medical care. The test is given twice—once at one minute after birth, and again at five minutes after birth.

Five signs/characteristics of the newborn are evaluated during this test, and easily recalled by the acronym APGAR. They are **A**ctivity (muscle tone), **P**ulse (heart rate), **G**rimace (reflexes), **A**ppearance (color), and **R**espiration (breathing). As shown in the scoring chart below, each characteristic is rated with a score of 0, 1, or 2 (with 2 being the strongest). Then the numbers are totaled.

A baby whose score is 7 or above at one minute after birth is generally considered in good health and needs only routine post-delivery care. A lower score between 4 and 6 does not necessarily mean there is something wrong with the baby. It indicates only that he may need some special immediate care, such as stimulation to bring on crying (this is done by drying him vigorously). And don't expect a perfect score of 10 either—most babies don't have pink hands and feet during the first hours after birth. A score of 3 or lower alerts the staff that the baby is in distress and needs assistance.

When the Apgar score is recalculated at five minutes after birth, if the baby's score is 6 or lower, he may need medical attention and will be closely monitored. Your caregiver will determine what steps need to be taken.

APGAR SCORING CHART

Sign/Characteristic	0 Points	1 Point	2 Points
Activity (muscle tone)	Limp; no movement	Some flexing of the extremities	Active movement
Pulse (heart rate)	Absent	Less than 100 beats per minute	More than 100 beats per minute
Grimace (reflex response)	No response.	Grimaces.	Sneezes, coughs, or pulls away.
Appearance (skin color)	Entire body is bluish-gray or pale.	Body is pink; hands and feet are bluish.	Entire body is pink.
Respiration (breathing)	Absent.	Weak cry. Slow, irregular breathing.	Strong cry. Normal breathing rate and effort.

THIRD STAGE OF LABOR

The third and shortest stage of labor, which involves the delivery of the placenta, generally lasts from five to twenty minutes. After the baby is born, the uterus continues contracting, although with less intensity than during the first two stages. The placenta spontaneously separates from the wall of the uterus and is expelled. You may be asked to push with the contractions to deliver the placenta, or your caregiver may guide the placenta out using firm fundal pressure. The placenta should be allowed to separate without strong traction or pulling on the cord. Otherwise, placental tissue may be left inside the uterus, which can result in postpartum hemorrhaging. Your caregiver will massage the uterus to make sure it is firm. If it isn't, he will vigorously massage the fundus and possibly administer medication. This will cause the uterine muscles to contract and prevent excessive bleeding.

Once the placenta is delivered, your caregiver will determine if it is intact. If necessary, he may do an internal examination of the uterus to make sure that no placental tissue has been retained. This examination is uncomfortable, but you can reduce the discomfort by using your relaxation and breathing techniques.

FOURTH STAGE OF LABOR

The fourth stage of labor is your recovery period and lasts for one to two hours. During this stage, your caregiver will repair the episiotomy, if one was done, as well as any vaginal or perineal lacerations. If the repair work becomes uncomfortable, ask for a local anesthetic. If you had a cesarean birth, this time will be spent in a recovery room.

While you are bonding with your new baby, you will be closely observed. The nurse will monitor your vital signs—blood pressure, pulse, and respiration—as well as check your uterus for firmness and for position in the abdomen. Your uterus should feel like a grapefruit, with the fundus at the level of your belly button. To keep the uterus in a contracted state, a nurse will massage your fundus or instruct you to do so. Massaging this area can be very uncomfortable, especially if the uterus is not firm.

If you were given medication to help contract the uterus or if you have already started breastfeeding, you may feel *afterpains.* These uterine contractions are more painful following the birth of a second or subsequent child. After you have given birth, expect a normal discharge of blood, excess tissue, and fluid from the uterus. The amount and consistency of this discharge, called *lochia,* will be closely monitored by a nurse, who will also apply an ice pack to your perineum and rectal areas to reduce swelling and decrease pain. She will also check for hemorrhoids and unusual bruising or edema in the perineal tissues.

You will be asked to urinate before you are allowed to leave the birthing room because a distended bladder can force the uterus up and out of position and cause it to relax. It's possible that you may not feel the need to urinate, since other sensations after giving birth can mask awareness of a full bladder. If necessary, a nurse will insert a catheter into your bladder to empty it.

During this time, you may feel exhilarated and very excited about the baby. If your labor was long or difficult, you may feel relieved or exhausted. Your legs and/or body may tremble involuntarily. A warm blanket will help stop the trembling. You may also be hungry and thirsty. The nursing staff should give you some well-deserved nourishment. If a meal or snack is not offered, ask for one.

During recovery, try to do Kegels. Contracting the pelvic floor muscles increases blood flow to the area. This also helps reduce swelling and speeds healing of the stitches from an episiotomy or tear. If you do not have stitches, you should still do Kegels to help restore the muscle tone of your pelvic floor.

Both you and your partner will experience an emotional high, feeling proud of your accomplishment. Together, you will probably relive the details of the birth over and over again. Limit your visitors at this time so that you can breastfeed and enjoy some private time with your newborn.

"Labor was amazing. it was intimate, private, and I was able to assist her. I wouldn't do it any other way. It is a powerful experience."

Owen
First-time father

Bonding

Bonding refers to the attachment that a mother and father feel for their child. This process actually begins before birth, when the parents-to-be feel their baby's movements, see the baby on an ultrasound, talk to and name their unborn child, and anticipate his arrival. The feeling is heightened at the first sight of the newborn. The importance of keeping the mother and baby together without interference is well documented. Human touch is vital to the newborn. The feel, smell, sight, taste, and sounds of the mother stabilize the infant and help him adjust to the outside world. As a result of this research, neonatal intensive care nurseries encourage parents to visit, touch, and hold their babies skin to skin for extended periods of time—called *kangaroo care.* They are even encouraged to assist in the care of their premature or sick newborns during hospitalization.

In the 1970s, Drs. Marshall Klaus and John Kennell published *Maternal-Infant Bonding,* a book that was instrumental in changing hospital practices regarding care of the newborn. They believed that after the birth, the father, mother, and infant should be allowed to spend at least one hour together in privacy, and stay together as much as the mother desires while in the hospital. If the baby must go to the nursery, it should be for short periods. During the first one to two hours of life, the baby is in a quiet alert state, awake and responsive to his environment. He looks intently at his mother's face and gazes into her eyes. It is now known that babies can see at birth and that they focus best on objects eight to ten inches away—the distance between an infant's face and his mother's during breastfeeding. It is suggested that a newborn's eyes not be treated with antibiotic ointment or silver nitrate drops (a standard procedure) until after this initial bonding period to avoid interference with his vision.

Most hospitals no longer separate mothers and infants right after birth. Parents begin bonding with their newborns in the birthing room, operating room, or recovery room if the woman had a cesarean delivery. At this time, new parents can explore and marvel at their creation. The mother can hold her naked infant close to her bare breast, and begin the nursing relationship. Both parents can hold, talk to, and caress the baby. Do not be surprised if you find yourselves talking to your newborn in high-pitched voices. This is almost instinctive, and babies respond very positively to these sounds.

When you hold your baby in your arms, you will notice that he is especially attracted to your eyes and facial features. He will respond by gazing, listening, imitating, possibly crying (he can be soothed by you or the father's familiar voice), and following you with his eyes. He is so new, yet so alert!

Bonding.

Ideally, breastfeeding should also be initiated soon after birth. Many studies have shown that if the baby nurses within this first hour, he and his mother will be more successful at breastfeeding. In addition, the *colostrum* that the baby ingests during the first nursing period provides him with protection against infection and acts as a laxative to help cleanse his system of mucus and meconium. The mother also benefits from early nursing. The baby's sucking releases the hormone oxytocin, which enhances maternal feelings. Oxytocin also causes the uterus to contract and reduces blood loss following birth.

A positive childbirth experience usually fosters the bonding process. Similarly, a negative childbirth experience may adversely affect a mother's feelings toward her child for a while and cause a delay in maternal attachment. Some parents simply take a little longer to develop loving emotions toward their newborns. In these cases, bonding usually takes place in the weeks following birth, rather than during the first few minutes. The newborn stage is not the only time in a baby's life that a strong parent-baby bond can be established. The initial bonding period can be compared to a honeymoon: If a couple become ardent, completely satisfied lovers, then so much the better. But a less-than-perfect honeymoon does not doom a marriage. Nor does a less-than-perfect birth-bonding experience doom the parent-child relationship.

Any medications used during labor and delivery may also adversely affect the bonding experience. If a mother is heavily sedated, she will not be able to interact with her baby immediately. In this case, she should bond with her baby as soon as she is able. In addition, the father can arrange to bond with the baby right after birth. Fathers who spend uninterrupted contact with their newborn in the first days will feel more confident and nurturing. A baby who received medication via the placenta may be sleepy and less responsive right after birth. The medication may remain in his system for long periods of time and possibly affect his responses and sucking ability. Bonding is more difficult in this situation.

Active participation in the birth enhances the parents' strong feelings of attachment toward the baby. In addition, when a couple works together to bring about the birth of their baby, they feel a closeness toward one another that is not easily forgotten. The bonding between them can be tremendous. They should work to maintain this close feeling, especially during those difficult first few weeks after birth.

Bonding is very important in family-centered maternity care, enabling parents to love and cuddle their new baby as they welcome him into their lives. Make the most of this opportunity. Find out about your hospital's policies on bonding and twenty-four-hour rooming-in. Discuss your desires for extended contact with both your caregiver and your baby's pediatrician.

ROOMING-IN

Rooming-in is available in all hospitals and should be initiated as soon after birth as possible. It allows the mother to keep the baby in the room with her for all or part of the day. With complete rooming-in, the baby stays with his mother day and night. With partial rooming-in, he stays with her from morning until evening and then goes to the nursery for the night (the mother can have him brought to her for nighttime feedings). With flexible rooming-in, the baby stays with the mother but can be returned to the nursery whenever the mother desires.

Even with complete rooming-in, many hospitals return the baby to the nursery for a short period each morning for a pediatric examination or other testing. During this time, the mother can shower and receive any required nursing care. In some hospitals, the pediatrician examines the baby in the mother's room.

The bond of affection formed immediately after birth can grow and deepen during the hospital stay. The close association and interaction between mother and baby continue as she cares for her infant. Mothers who opt for rooming-in feel more confident and competent at caring for their babies than do mothers who are separated from their babies by traditional hospital routines. Since hospital stays are approximately twenty-four to forty-eight hours after a vaginal birth, and forty-eight to seventy-two

TABLE 8.1. LABOR PARTNER'S SUMMARY		
Stage of Labor	**What Is Going On?**	**How Is She Feeling?**
WARM-UP *Before Labor Begins*	Lightening. Increased frequency of Braxton-Hicks contractions. Early effacement and dilation. Increased vaginal discharge. Leveling off or loss of weight.	Excited; a sense of anticipation. Depressed. Difficulty sleeping; very tired. Spurt of energy.
Beginning of Labor	Contractions. Loss of the mucous plug. Leaking or rupture of the membranes. Frequent bowel movements.	Excited. Apprehensive. Talkative.
Early Labor	Contractions from 5 to 20 minutes apart, lasting from 30 to 60 seconds, becoming longer, stronger, and more frequent. Effacement and dilation from 0 to 4 centimeters.	Confident. Sociable. May doubt this is true labor.
FIRST STAGE *Active Labor*	Contractions from 2 to 4 minutes apart, lasting from 45 to 60 seconds, with greater intensity and longer peaks. Dilation from 4 to 8 centimeters, with more effacement. Labor is more than half over at 5 to 6 centimeters.	Anxious. Apprehensive; doubts her ability to handle labor. Serious mood; birth-oriented. Attention turned inward. Quiet.
Transition	Contractions from $1\frac{1}{2}$ to 3 minutes apart, lasting from 60 to 90 seconds, extremely strong and erratic, possibly with more than one peak. Dilation from 8 to 10 centimeters. Effacement complete.	Panicky; wants to give up. Irritable. Does not want to be touched. Forgetful; disoriented; amnesic. Rectal pressure; premature urge to push. Nausea; vomiting. Alternating between feeling hot and cold. Trembling legs.

What Should She Do?	How Can I Help?
Simplify the housekeeping. Pack suitcases and Lamaze bag. Conserve energy; take naps. Preregister at the hospital; take a tour. Practice exercises, relaxation, and breathing daily.	Assist her with the household chores Encourage her to rest. Provide diversion (take a walk together, take her out to eat). Help her practice relaxation and breathing.
If it is nighttime, try to sleep. If it is daytime, continue normal activities. Take a walk. Take a shower; wash hair; shave legs. Eat carbohydrates; drink juice/fluids.	Time the contractions. Reassure her of her readiness for labor. Call the babysitter and/or pet sitter. If it is nighttime, encourage her to sleep; sleep yourself.
Relax with the contractions. Begin slow breathing if necessary. Stay in an upright position as much as possible. Empty bladder every hour. Call caregiver. Drink sweetened liquids; eat light snacks.	Time and record the contractions. Remind her to relax; use touch relaxation. Encourage and praise her. Help her with the breathing pattern if necessary. Encourage her to walk. Remind her to urinate. Use distractions (play cards or games; watch a movie).
Continue relaxation and breathing. Use a focal point. Do effleurage. Relax in a tub or shower. Change position frequently. Continue to urinate hourly. Drink liquids. Adjust pillows for comfort. Go to the hospital or birth center or call midwife if a home birth.	When walking, stop and support her body during contractions. Administer massages or back rubs. Give her a cool washcloth for her face. Give her ice chips or ice pops to suck on. Offer her cool liquids. Remind her to change position and to urinate. Keep her informed of her progress. Encourage her to relax and help her to do slow breathing. If her breathing seems ineffective, add other distractions. Start a ritual. Watch for signs of transition.
Remember that this phase is intense but short. Take the contractions one at a time. Alter breathing as needed, remember to moan. Eliminate the relaxing breath if the contraction peaks immediately. Blow with a premature urge to push. Slow breathing down between contractions.	*Do not leave her for any reason.* Remind her that the labor is almost over—the baby is coming. Praise her lavishly for her efforts. Communicate with the medical staff. Keep her calm; do not argue with her. Apply counter pressure to her back. Call the nurse if she feels an urge to push. Breathe with her; have her mimic you. Help her catch the contractions at the start. Help her relax between contractions. If she asks for medication, first request a cervical check.

	Stage of Labor	What Is Going On?	How Is She Feeling?
SECOND STAGE	**Birth of the Baby**	Contractions from 3 to 5 minutes apart, lasting from 60 to 75 seconds, with an urge to push at the peak. Effacement and dilation complete. Baby is moving down the birth canal. Head is crowning. Delivery of the head, the shoulders, and then the rest of the body.	Strong urge to push. Relieved to be able to push. Renewed energy level. Great deal of rectal pressure. Burning, splitting sensation. Sociable again between contractions.
THIRD STAGE	**Delivery of the Placenta**	Mild uterine contractions. Separation and expulsion of the placenta.	Exhilarated. Fatigued.
FOURTH STAGE	**Bonding and Recovery**	Perineal repair if necessary. Identification procedures for the baby. Intermittent uterine contractions. Checking of the mother's physical status. Transfer of mother and baby to postpartum unit.	Emotionally high. Proud. Happy. Tired. Motherly. Hungry and thirsty.

hours after a cesarean birth, the more time you can spend with your baby under the guidance of a nurse, the more competent you will feel when you take him home. Many hospitals have lactation consultants on staff that can assist you with breastfeeding.

As a result of extended contact with their babies, rooming-in mothers seem to develop maternal feelings more quickly and are able to resume physical activities earlier than mothers who do not have their babies room-in. Babies who interact with just one caregiver—the mother—appear to be more content. They cry less and organize their sleep-awake rhythms and feeding patterns more quickly than babies who interact with several caregivers and are fed on a rigid schedule. Rooming-in on a twenty-four-hour basis provides the best opportunity for successful breastfeeding.

Rooming-in also gives the father a chance to hold, care for, and enjoy his baby before bringing him home. This strengthens the paternal bond and helps the father feel more confident in caring for the new baby. Most hospitals encourage fathers to be active caregivers and to also stay with in the room with the mother and baby. Rooms usually have a cot or a special chair that can be converted to a bed for the father.

SIBLING VISITATION

A mother's ability to adjust to a home situation that includes other children will be greatly improved if they are allowed to visit her in the hospital. This type of visit will help reduce any separation anxieties the children may be experiencing, plus it allows them to meet their new brother or sister. Many hospitals allow these visits—some also permit children to be present for their sibling's birth. (See "Children at the Birth" on page 214.) Early involvement by all family members enhances family bonding. Children other than siblings of the newborn are usually not permitted in the maternity unit of most hospitals.

What Should She Do?	How Can I Help?
Assume a comfortable position. If you do not have an urge to push, become upright and wait for the urge. Use spontaneous pushing as your body directs. Push only when feeling the urge. Pant or blow as the head is delivered. Relax the perineum. Keep eyes open.	Help her assume a comfortable position for pushing. Allow her to decide when and how to push. If she is holding her breath, count to 6 to pace her pushing. Make sure she lets a little air out before holding her breath. Remind her to relax her bottom; check her face for relaxation. Tell her to pant or blow as the head is delivered. Remind her to keep her eyes open. Be sure she can see the birth in the mirror. Take pictures as the baby is born.
Push with the contractions as instructed. Hold and soothe the new baby. Initiate breastfeeding. Use slow breathing if necessary.	Take pictures of the mother and baby. Hold the baby.
Examine, caress, nurse, and talk to the baby. Make eye contact with the baby. Take pictures of the father and baby. Massage the fundus of the uterus. Eat and drink.	Share in bonding with the baby. Take more pictures. Make telephone calls.

HOSPITAL STAY

The length of the hospital stay will be determined by the health of the mother and baby, the type of health insurance, the needs of other children at home, and monetary concerns. A federal law that went into effect in 1997 mandates insurance companies to pay for no less than a forty-eight-hour stay for women following a vaginal delivery and no less than ninety-six hours following a cesarean. Some mothers choose to be discharged within twenty-four hours after a vaginal birth, while others prefer to stay the full two days. Most birth centers allow mothers to go home four to six hours after delivery, but they provide daily phone consultations and a follow-up visit within three days after birth.

Have all visitors, whether at the hospital or at home, wash their hands well before handling the baby.

The 1997 law grew out of great concern over the decreasing amount of time women stayed in the hospital. A primary worry was that many breastfeeding women did not recognize the signs that an infant was not receiving enough milk. Early discharge from the hospital is appropriate only as part of a comprehensive program of care that includes intensive prenatal education and close postpartum and newborn follow-up. One benefit of early discharge is the avoidance of hospital-induced infections. The problems of early discharge are generally related to lack of education and follow-up, rather than the time of discharge.

During the hospital stay, the nursing staff will provide medical care for both you and your baby. To prevent infection and promote healing of your perineum and vagina, you will be taught *peri-care*. If you had an episiotomy or laceration, or if you have hemorrhoids, you will be offered medicated pads and an anesthetic spray or foam. Ice pack applications to the perineum during the first twenty-four hours will reduce swelling and decrease pain. After twenty-four hours, a warm-water soaking of the area,

Children at the Birth

Many facilities now offer children the opportunity to be present for the birth of their sibling. The decision to include your child at this "event" should be discussed first with your partner. During pregnancy, as you talk about the new baby, you can begin to offer your child the opportunity to learn more about the changes in your body and about the actual birth. If he shows an interest in being present at the birth, you may want to prepare him in greater detail. Make sure that the information is age appropriate.

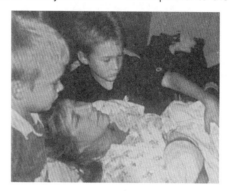

Discuss anatomy and show him pictures of fetal development as it corresponds to your week of gestation. You should become more comfortable with your child seeing your undressed pregnant body. As you get closer to the end of pregnancy, discuss labor and birth. Show photos, slides, and films, and discuss the presence of blood and fluids. Reinforce that these are normal and expected, since most children associate blood with injuries and death.

Some films also show the delivery of the placenta. Do not be surprised if the child describes the placenta as gross or disgusting. You can ask if he would like to help the father cut the umbilical cord. Reassure him that this procedure is not painful to the baby. Ask him to draw pictures of how he envisions different aspects of what he will be seeing. These drawings will offer insight into his level of understanding of the information and also provide clues about his concerns.

Prepare your child for the sights and sounds associated with hard labor and giving birth. Practice your breathing and pushing in front of him, making sure to demonstrate different positions and simulate moans, grunts, and groans.

Have your child attend your prenatal visits. He will become familiar with the staff and comfortable with your examinations. It will also be exciting for him to hear his sibling's heartbeat. Some offices have birthing dolls that can be used for demonstration. If you are

Hints for the New Father

During the hospital stay:

✓ Room-in with the mother and baby.

✓ Bring in a cake with a "0" candle and have a "birth day" party.

✓ Bring your mate her favorite snacks and other foods.

✓ Offer to change the baby's diaper.

✓ Encourage your partner to empty her bladder and do a Super Kegel every two hours.

called a *sitz bath,* can provide relief. In the first twenty-four to forty-eight hours after birth, your body will begin to eliminate the fluid that was retained during pregnancy. The nursing staff may ask you to urinate into a container several times to ensure that you are emptying your bladder adequately.

Your perineum will be sore, you may have hemorrhoids, and your abdominal muscles will be relaxed, so moving your bowels may be difficult. If a proper diet (fresh fruits and vegetables, whole grains, and sufficient water) does not help, ask to have a stool softener prescribed. When cleaning yourself, make sure that you wipe from front to back to avoid fecal contamination and infection.

Along with monitoring your vital signs, the nursing staff will periodically check the height of your fundus and tone of your uterus. They will also observe the consistency and amount of lochia being discharged from your uterus and the condition of your perineum. You can expect a daily visit from your caregiver and the baby's pediatrician. You may also receive a visit from a lactation consultant if your facility has one on staff.

If you are an Rh-negative mother who gave birth to an Rh-positive infant, you will be given an injection of RhoGAM within seventy-two hours after giving birth. This injection will prevent your body from producing antibodies that could endanger sub-

having your baby in a birth center, show your child the birthing rooms and have him assist you in your choice of room for the birth. If you are delivering in a hospital, take a tour of the facility and meet the staff. This will allow him to be comfortable in the hospital environment. Sibling classes can also alleviate concerns and prepare your child.

Choose a support person for the child that he likes and knows well. It is important that the child feels comfortable talking to or expressing his feelings to this person. Occasionally, children need to remove themselves from the birthing room because of boredom or concerns. The support person needs to understand that she must accompany the child, even if this means missing the birth. This person should also attend sibling preparation classes with the child so she knows what information the child is given.

Allow the child to make the final decision about attending the birth. Give him the freedom to be present in the room as much or as little as he chooses, and to even decide if he does not want to attend. Discuss the possibility of changes in the birth plan, such as a transfer from an out-of-hospital birth center to a hospital; interventions, including delivery with forceps or a vacuum extractor; and even a cesarean section. Occasionally, a woman goes into labor while the child is asleep or in school, or the labor progresses much faster than expected. Preparing children for the unpredictability of labor will help prevent disappointments.

During labor, provide diversions for the child such as books, crafts, video games, or DVDs. Young children may want to bring a favorite stuffed animal or doll, or a blanket and pillow for naptime. Pack plenty of drinks and snacks. If the labor is long, make sure the child eats regular meals. Give him several tasks to perform during labor, such as offering you drinks, wiping your face with cool washcloths, or selecting your music. An older child may want to be responsible for taking photographs or videotaping.

Participation in the birth of a sibling can be a rewarding experience for a child. It can start the bonding process and make him feel like a special part of the birth. But, if you have any reservations or your child seems unsure, alter the plans to make this a positive experience. Rather than have your child present for the actual birth, you may want to have him arrive soon after. Celebrate the birth with a "birth day" party and make this a memorable experience for everyone.

sequent babies during pregnancy. If you are no longer immune to rubella (German measles), you will receive a vaccination prior to discharge so that future pregnancies are not at risk. Do not get pregnant for three months following this injection.

Hopefully, you can utilize the first few days of your baby's life to the fullest in establishing a close family bond. Most hospitals have policies that promote mother-father-baby-sibling contact. If your hospital allows family involvement, make sure you take full advantage of it. Interaction and bonding of the family members during the first days after birth will help promote a loving, thriving family. If it does not allow the options that are important to you, request them anyway. You need to make your wishes known. Perhaps the hospital will make allowances to accommodate your desires.

Before leaving the hospital, you will be given instructions to follow once you have been discharged from the facility. This will include guidelines and advice pertaining to your care as well as the baby's once you get home. Among this information will be a list of symptoms that warrant a call to the obstetrician or pediatrician. You will be informed of any follow-up visits for you and your baby, or for any lab work that may be necessary, such as a blood test for jaundice. It is important to follow these instructions and ask any questions you may have.

CONCLUSION

The act of giving birth is something that will remain with you for the rest of your life. It can be a positive, empowering experience, providing an opportunity for you to grow as a woman. Trust your body to do the work of labor and of giving birth to your baby. A woman's body is perfectly designed to perform this miraculous natural function. Allow yourself to view birth as healthy and normal, rather than a medical or surgical procedure. There will be hard work and pain, but the incredible feeling of accomplishment that follows will provide great satisfaction that will positively impact the rest of your life. Experience the joy of actively bringing forth your baby into this world, confident that your body knows exactly what to do.

Labor Variations
or Any Which Way You Can

The last chapter presented the stages of labor for a typical normal birth. The type of labor that you experience may be considered normal and yet not progress exactly "by the book." Remember that each woman's labor is unique. Variations in the way the baby is presenting or positioned may require a modification or adjustment of standard labor techniques. This is why it is so important be prepared for any situation that might arise.

Before presenting the different labor variations, this chapter begins with a discussion of the many ways in which a baby can be positioned in the uterus, as well as differences in presentation. These variations have a direct impact on altering normal labor techniques. Gentle birth variations, such as the Leboyer method and underwater birth, are also discussed. Rounding out this chapter are guidelines for giving birth without medical assistance.

VARIATIONS IN FETAL PRESENTATIONS AND POSITIONS

At term, most babies lie in the uterus upside down and facing the woman's spine. There are, however, a variety of fetal positions that may require the need for interventions, such as a cesarean delivery. What follows is a discussion of the various in utero presentations and positions.

Presentation Variations

As discussed in Chapter 8, presentation refers to the way in which the baby is situated in the uterus. The part of the baby that is closest to the cervix is called the *presenting part*. At term in a normal pregnancy, the head is lowest in the uterus and, therefore, considered the presenting part. This is called a *cephalic presentation* (see Figure 8.3 on page 189). More specifically, if the top of head is felt at the cervix, it is called a *vertex presentation*. The baby's brow or face can also be the presenting part, but this is much less common and can cause difficulty at delivery. If the face is presenting, a cesarean section is usually performed.

A very small percentage of births involve a *transverse lie,* or *shoulder presentation.* For this, the baby lies sideways in the uterus with her shoulder as the presenting part (see Figure 9.1 on page 218). With a transverse lie, a cesarean is mandatory.

In a *breech presentation,* the buttocks present first. Breech presentations account for 3 to 4 percent of all deliveries. The most common types include the *complete*

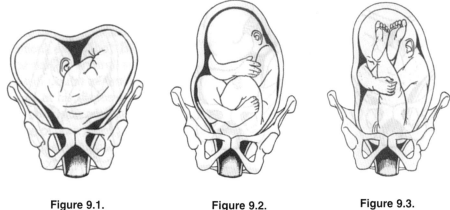

Figure 9.1.
Shoulder presentation,
or transverse lie.

Figure 9.2.
Complete breech
presentation.

Figure 9.3.
Frank breech
presentation.

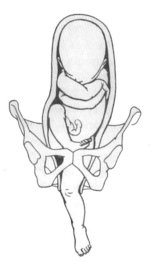

Figure 9.4.
Footling breech
presentation.

breech, in which the fetus sits cross-legged in the bottom of the uterus (see Figure 9.2), and the *frank breech,* in which the fetus's legs are straight up with the feet near the face (see Figure 9.3). Less common is the *footling breech,* which is similar to the complete breech, but in which one or both feet present first (see Figure 9.4). The rarest form of breech presentation is the *knee breech,* in which the knee, instead of the foot, presents at the cervix.

The risk to the baby is increased in a breech delivery, so the possibility of obstetrical intervention is also increased. Most doctors routinely perform cesareans for breech presentations. Labor may be longer than with a vertex presentation because the buttocks are not as efficient a dilating wedge as the top of the head. While the baby's buttocks may pass easily through the pelvis, his larger head may have difficulty and become stuck. There is also greater risk of a prolapsed umbilical cord as the buttocks do not fill the pelvis as tightly as the head. During birth, the cord is also more likely to be compressed by the head at the cervical outlet or in the vagina and cause fetal distress. When determining the method of delivery, the doctor takes into account fetal size, type of breech presentation, the woman's pelvic dimensions and architecture, and progress in labor. He also factors in his own experience in handling vaginal breech deliveries. Many obstetricians (especially newer ones) have no experience in delivering breech babies vaginally.

The doctor or midwife may not realize before labor begins that the fetus is in a breech presentation. An ultrasound will be done if a breech is suspected. If confirmed, your doctor may attempt external version (see page 219) to rotate the baby or, more likely, a cesarean will be performed immediately.

Turning a Breech Baby

Prior to thirty weeks, a baby has plenty of room to turn around in the uterus and his position is insignificant. If your caregiver discovers that your baby is breech after thirty weeks, you may be able to rotate him into a vertex presentation by performing the *breech tilt position.* As seen in the photo on page 219, lie on your back with your knees bent and feet flat on the floor. Lift your pelvis into the tilt position by placing several pillows beneath your lower back and buttocks to elevate your pelvic area nine to twelve inches. Stay in this position for ten to fifteen minutes, three times a day, preferably before meals for the greatest comfort. While in this position, you may want to visualize the baby turning in the uterus. And be sure to relax your body to decrease abdominal muscle tension. Continue getting into this position until the baby rotates, at which point you should stop—or he may return to breech. Walk a lot to help the baby settle further down in the pelvis. Your caregiver will confirm the baby's change in presentation.

If your baby is in a breech presentation, this breech tilt position will encourage him to rotate.

This position is also effective in rotating a baby who is lying transverse in the uterus. Always check with your caregiver before getting into the breech tilt position to make sure there is no medical reason why you should not do it.

Some women have reported success in turning a breech baby by placing headphones on the lower abdomen and playing music. Babies are able to hear and may turn to get closer to the music. This can be done in combination with or separate from the breech tilt position. When your partner talks to the baby, he should place his head low on your abdomen. Some women have used flashlights, pointing the beam at the top of the uterus and then slowly moving it down the abdomen. Since your baby can see at this time, he may try to follow the beam of light. While these methods are anecdotal, they involve minimal risk and may increase the chance of success.

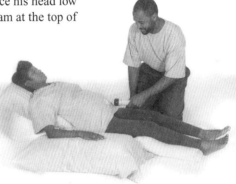

This couple hopes their breech baby will follow the flashlight beam and turn before labor begins.

Other women have sought out Chinese medicine techniques to stimulate fetal activity and correct a breech presentation. *Moxibustion* involves the burning of the herb artemisia (mugwort) to stimulate the acupuncture point beside the outer corner of the fifth toenail (Zhiyin). According to a study reported in the *Journal of the American Medical Association (JAMA),* this technique was effective in 75 percent of the women treated.[1] Women have also sought out specialists to try hypnosis, acupuncture, or chiropractic manipulation in an attempt to turn a breech baby.

It is also possible to turn a baby from a breech or transverse lie through *external version.* Using the visual guidance of ultrasound, the doctor manipulates the baby into a head-down position by applying firm yet gentle pressure to the woman's abdomen while pressing on the baby's head and hip. External version is usually performed in a hospital. Prior to this procedure, the woman may be given medication to relax her uterine muscle, making it easier for the doctor to manipulate the baby.

External version is usually performed at thirty-seven weeks of pregnancy. Prior to that, the baby's lungs may not be mature enough if the woman suddenly goes into labor, or if the baby cannot tolerate the procedure and an emergency cesarean is necessary. After thirty-seven weeks, external version may be more difficult (although not impossible) to perform. The doctor is less likely to be able to rotate the baby because of reduced amniotic fluid. In addition, the baby is larger and may have settled into the pelvis. This procedure can, however, be attempted even if the breech is not diagnosed until labor.

The risks associated with external version include initiation of labor, soreness to the woman's abdomen, and, on rare occasions, shearing of the placenta from the uterine wall, which would necessitate an emergency cesarean. Only a doctor who is experienced in performing external version should attempt the technique.

Hints for the Labor Partner

During pregnancy, if you discover the baby is breech:

✓ Place your head near your partner's pubic bone when you talk to the baby.

✓ Use a flashlight to encourage the baby to "move to the light."

✓ Encourage your partner to assume the breech tilt position.

Position Variations

As discussed in the last chapter, during a normal labor, the baby's head rotates through the pelvis. He enters the pelvis with the back of the head, called the *occiput,* facing the side of the pelvis and rotating towards the front of the woman in an *anterior position* (occiput anterior). If the baby does not rotate through the pelvis correctly, the woman can experience a difficult labor.

The most common malposition is a *posterior position* (occiput posterior) in which the back of the baby's head faces the woman's back. A woman whose baby is in the posterior position is most likely to experience a back labor. (See "Back Labor" on page 222.) A baby whose head is tilted, called the *asynclitic position,* does not fit through the pelvis as easily and can result in a difficult labor. Also, since the head is not well centered, the cervix may not dilate evenly. You may be told that the cervix has a "lip." This means that although most of the cervix is completely thinned out, a portion that did not receive as much pressure from the head is still a bit thicker. Try different positions, such as standing while swaying your hips, kneeling and doing Pelvic Rocks, or sitting and bouncing on a birth ball to encourage the baby to move through the pelvis.

During the last six weeks of pregnancy (or the last three weeks if you have given birth before), focus on the following suggestions daily.[2] They will encourage your baby to assume an anterior position prior to labor.

■ Perform the Pelvic Rock (page 125).

■ Do a lot of walking.

■ Sit with your knees lower than your hips, using a birth ball or by straddling a chair.

■ Sleep in the Sims' position (page 144), using pillows for comfort.

These recommendations encourage the heavier part of the baby (the spine) to turn toward your abdomen, and may inhibit him from getting into a posterior position.

LABOR VARIATIONS

Although each labor is different, the majority follow somewhat of a pattern. Five types of labor that vary significantly from the "norm" include preterm labor, precipitate labor, prolonged prelabor or early labor, prolonged labor, and back labor.

Preterm Labor

A *preterm labor* is one that begins before thirty-seven weeks gestation. This is a concern because babies born prior to thirty-seven weeks may not be mature enough and may require intensive nursing care to survive or to prevent long-term health problems. Your physician will attempt to stop preterm labor with bed rest, home monitoring, medication, or hospitalization. On a positive note, an increasing number of preterm babies are surviving due to advances in medical technology. For a complete discussion on preterm labor and suggestions for coping with extended bed rest, see page 75. Information about medications that are used to help stop preterm labor is presented in the following chapter.

Precipitate Labor

A *precipitate labor* is one that lasts three hours or less. This short duration may sound appealing, but it presents its own special problems. The contractions in a precipitate labor are usually quite intense and may be misinterpreted as a very difficult early labor. Because the contractions may be hard to control, the labor partner should remain with the woman at all times and use all the comfort measures at his disposal. If left alone, the woman may experience confusion and fear because of lack of knowledge about her labor's progress. These feelings can be complicated by the rushing around of the hospital or birth center staff upon discovery of the labor's advanced state.

If you suspect you are having a precipitate labor, you must trust your own feelings about your body. Be sure to request a vaginal examination as soon as you arrive at your place of birth to determine your progress. Your own control and the directions of a good labor partner are crucial. You will need to concentrate on relaxing, even though it may be difficult. In addition, before requesting medication, try using comfort measures and other distraction techniques along with your breathing. Also try changing your position. Your labor is almost over!

In some cases, the labor progresses so rapidly that there isn't enough time to get to the hospital or birth center. Instructions on what to do in such a situation is found in "Giving Birth Without Medical Assistance" on page 223.

Prolonged Prelabor/Early Labor

Occasionally, women have regular contractions that do not make significant changes in the cervix. These episodes may last for hours and intermittently start and stop, or they may persist for over twenty-four hours. This *prolonged prelabor,* also called *prodromal labor,* is mentally and physically exhausting. It is important to eat, drink, and sleep during this type of labor so that when active labor begins, you will have the energy to cope with the stronger contractions. If you are unable to sleep, try relaxing in a tub of warm water. It may slow down the contractions enough so that you can fall asleep.

Your caregiver may suggest taking a medication such as a tranquilizer or sedative, or drinking a glass of wine to relax and help you rest. It is important to remember, however, that the baby will also receive the effects of these products. Your doctor or midwife may also suggest stimulating labor by stripping the membranes or by inserting prostaglandin gel or pills. Both methods can stimulate contractions that may initiate labor. Or he may recommend inducing labor by rupturing the membranes or starting a Pitocin drip. Usually, once the woman enters the active phase of labor, it will progress normally.

Prolonged Labor

A *prolonged labor* is one that lasts twenty-four hours or more. Ineffective contractions, breech presentation, posterior position, a large baby, a small pelvis, extreme anxiety or tension, too much medication, early administration of an epidural, fasting during labor, and malnutrition during pregnancy are some of the causes.

Considerable patience is required during a long labor, along with creativity in the use of breathing techniques, comfort measures, and relaxation. Fatigue is difficult to combat, and dozing between contractions may make it even harder to be ready for the next one. If you experience a prolonged labor, you and your partner must work together, using all the techniques and comfort measures you can to avoid discouragement, tension, and fatigue. Encouragement from your labor partner is essential. You need to relax as much as possible to conserve your energy. Labor in a tub of warm water if you become fatigued or are tense. If you have been confined to bed, ask to be allowed to walk around, as walking often helps to speed up the labor process. Also, try stimulating your nipples to release oxytocin, which may help strengthen the contractions.

Hints for the Labor Partner

If your partner is having a precipitate labor:

✓ Remain calm and drive carefully to the birth facility.

✓ Encourage her to perform relaxation and slow breathing techniques.

✓ Remind her that the labor is almost over.

✓ If she says "the baby is coming," get ready to assist her in the birth.

If your partner is having a prolonged labor:

✓ Encourage her to walk.

✓ Provide snacks and drinks.

✓ Have her change position.

✓ Massage her back.

✓ Help her into the tub or shower.

✓ Try stimulating her nipples to release oxytocin.

✓ Stay positive.

Prolonged labor.

During a prolonged labor, a nurse or a fetal heart monitor must keep a watchful eye on the condition of the fetus. If the woman has not been allowed to eat or drink, she will probably receive IV fluids to prevent dehydration. Pitocin is usually administered to increase the strength of the contractions.

If your labor is prolonged or extremely difficult, make sure that you understand your situation—know what is happening to you, as well as any suggested procedures. If you have questions, ask your caregiver. And remember, labor is not an endurance contest. If you become too fatigued and can no longer cope with the more powerful Pitocin-augmented contractions, consider medication or an epidural.

Back Labor

Back labor is felt primarily in the back or hips, and produces extreme discomfort during and often between contractions. About one out of four women experiences back labor to some degree. Back labor is usually caused by a posterior position of the baby, but it can also be brought on by a breech presentation, variations in the woman's anatomy, tension, or laboring while lying on the back.

"Dancing" through a contraction can help ease the pain of back labor.

Because discomfort is also felt between contractions, rest and relaxation are more difficult to achieve with back labor. In addition, the labor may last longer. If you experience back labor, take the contractions one at a time and experiment with the following suggested comfort methods.

Get the baby off your back. Do not lie or sit in any position that places the weight of the baby on your spine. Get into a position that encourages the baby to rotate. The most effective positions are those in which you are upright because they give you the advantage of gravity. You can also walk between contractions, and when one begins, use your partner or the back of a chair for support and sway your hips as if dancing. Perform the Lunge or have your partner do the Double-Hip Squeeze. Get into the shower and have your partner direct the spray at your lower back.

You may want to try sitting backwards while straddling a chair and using pillows for support. Or try sitting forward on the edge of the chair while leaning against your partner (who is kneeling in front of you) for support. If you are in bed, sit on the side of the bed, put your feet on a chair, and lean on the over-bed tray table or a pillow that is positioned on your lap. Keep your legs apart and your knees lower than your hips.

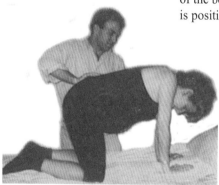

If you experience back labor, kneel on all fours and do the Pelvic Rock.

Several kneeling positions are also very comfortable. Try the Pelvic Rock on all fours. You can also try kneeling on the floor, using the seat of a chair as your upper-body support. If you are in bed, kneel on all fours against the raised head of the bed, or kneel with your upper body elevated on pillows. While you are kneeling on all fours, have your partner gently sway your abdomen back and forth. He can use his hands or a long cloth to gently rock the baby.

Side-lying while in bed or a tub may be a comfortable position during back labor. If you are in bed, make sure that you are well supported by pillows under your head, uterus, and upper legs. Lie with your body three quarters over, hugging a pillow. You may want to try changing position from side-lying to kneeling on all fours to side-lying on the opposite side. Repeat this sequence, remaining in each position for fifteen minutes.

Another position that may be uncomfortable for the baby and encourage his rotation is one in which you lie on your back with a rolled-up blanket tucked beneath the small of your back to increase the angle of your spine. Alternate this position with side-lying every fifteen minutes. If your baby does not rotate, however, and is still posterior when you begin pushing, you can also push in this position to encourage rotation. Your partner can hold up your legs, or you can bend your knees slightly and rest your heels on the bed. Once the baby has rotated, you can continue pushing in a more comfortable position.

The best position for pushing if your baby is in the posterior position is the squat. Squatting increases your pelvic capacity by as much as 30 percent.[3] To do the dangle squat (see page 171), have the nurse remove the bottom third of the birthing bed and insert the foot rests. Have your partner sit on the edge of the bed with his feet on the foot rests, while you stand between his legs with your back toward him. During the contraction, rest your forearms on his thighs, bend your knees, and perform a partial squat. Other pushing positions you may want to try if your baby continues to be posterior are side-lying and kneeling. One recommended variation of the kneeling position has you place one knee and the sole of the other foot on the bed. During the contraction, lunge in this position to expand the pelvis.

This labor partner uses a rebozo (a Mexican shawl) to "rock the baby."

In addition to changing position frequently, many women want their partners to perform counter pressure or acupressure. Several of these methods have been used with success. For instance, have your partner press the heel of his hand or his fist against the area of your back that is causing the greatest discomfort. Have him use as much force as is comforting to you. He can also kneel on the bed with one knee pressed against your lower back as you lie on your side. Or you can lie on your own fists, a roll of toilet tissue, or several tennis balls that are tied up in a sock. These last counter pressure suggestions can be especially helpful during vaginal exams, when you may need to be on your back. Having your partner massage your lower back with lotion or oil may also be effective.

You may find it comforting to have your partner apply warm or cold compresses to your back. You can use heat packs, commercial heat wraps, or washcloths that have been soaked in hot water. Also try laboring in a warm tub or shower. For cold compresses, use washcloths that have been soaked in ice water. You can also use ice packs, "blue ice," frozen juice cans, or frozen water bottles that are wrapped in towels. You can also wrap a towel around a hollow plastic rolling pin that is filled with cold water or crushed ice.

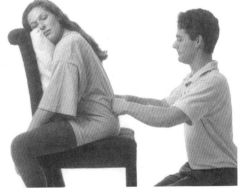

Counter pressure can ease the pain of back labor.

Other measures that may help reduce the pain of back labor include touch relaxation and slow, deep breathing between contractions, which promotes relaxation Additional distraction techniques may be necessary as well. Finally, an encouraging and supportive labor partner is the best tool for handling this kind of labor.

GIVING BIRTH WITHOUT MEDICAL ASSISTANCE

If your labor progresses very rapidly or you fail to recognize that you are in the final phase of labor, you may end up giving birth at home or on the way to the facility. In most cases, such a birth is uncomplicated, and the baby is born healthy and vigorous. Since anesthesia and medications are not used, the baby usually breathes immediately and is very alert.

Hints for the Labor Partner

If your partner is at home and birth is imminent:

✓ Remain calm.

✓ Call 911.

✓ Make her comfortable.

✓ Get out the emergency birth kit.

✓ Place a pad under her.

✓ Have her pant or blow as the head is born.

✓ When the baby's head is out, if the cord is around her neck, lift the cord over her head.

✓ Support the baby's head as the shoulders and body emerge.

"Okay, honey, I'm ready to deliver now!"

Nevertheless, both you and your labor partner may feel some uneasiness and fear about handling such a situation. This section is, therefore, directed toward the labor partner, to give him support and confidence should he find himself in the position of being your caregiver.

A woman almost always knows if birth is imminent. Take her word for it. She may feel the baby's head coming down the birth canal, feel a strong urge to push, or feel a burning pressure. If you are in the car when this happens, resist the temptation to drive fast or take chances to reach the hospital or birth center. Instead, when it is safe to do so, pull off the road, put on the emergency flashers, turn on the heat in the car, get out the emergency birth kit (see page 184), and assess the situation.

If this is the woman's first baby and the baby's head is not yet visible at the vaginal opening, you probably have time to get to the birth facility if you are within fifteen to twenty minutes driving time. If this is not the first baby or if the baby's head is visible, you are better off staying where you are. If you have a cell phone, call 911 and be prepared to tell them your location. Help your partner get comfortable in the back seat and then let the baby be born. Make sure the baby is breathing well before you continue on to the birth facility.

If you are home, call 911. Emergency medical personnel are trained to handle this kind of situation. Wash your hands and arms. Help your partner get into a comfortable position on the bed. Place a crib pad, blankets, or towels under her buttocks to protect the mattress. Turn off the air conditioner and fans to allow the room to warm up. Do not leave her alone. She will need your calm support to keep from panicking.

Whether you are at home or in a car, let her uterus do all the work. Once the baby's head is visible at the vaginal opening, coach your partner to pant until the head is born. A slow, controlled birth will reduce the chance of tearing the perineal tissue. As the baby's head begins to emerge, support your partner's perineum with your hand wrapped in a clean handkerchief. If the amniotic membranes are still covering the head, break them with your fingernail, then pull them away from the baby's face to allow him to breathe. You can wipe off any mucus and fluid with a cloth. Check to see if the cord is around the baby's neck. If it is, gently lift it over the head before the rest of her body is born.

When the baby's head rotates to face her mother's thigh, the shoulders are ready to emerge. Support the baby's head with your hands as your partner bears down lightly with the next contraction. *Do not pull on the baby's head*—this could permanently injure her spinal cord. Once the shoulders are born, the rest of the body will slide out easily. When birth is complete, place the baby face down on her mother's abdomen, dry her body, then cover them both with a blanket. The face-down position will help the baby cough up or drain out any mucus that is in her nose or throat. You can further help the baby by gently wiping out her mouth with a clean handkerchief or, if needed, suctioning it with a soft rubber bulb syringe. If using a syringe, compress the bulb before inserting it into the mouth or nose, and release the pressure gently.

If the baby does not breathe right away, vigorously rub her back or the soles of her feet. *Do not panic.* If the placenta is still attached, the baby is continuing to receive oxygen via the umbilical cord. However, if she does not begin breathing within one and a half minutes, you will need to give her artificial respiration. To do this:

1. Place the baby on her back and position her with her head tilted back slightly.

2. Cover both her nose and mouth with your mouth, and place your fingers on her chest.

3. Gently breathe out with only the air in your mouth. You will feel the baby's chest rise slightly. Do not blow hard because forcing too much air into her small lungs could cause them to rupture. Give two breaths.

4. Check for a pulse. You can feel this in the cord, close to its insertion at the abdomen. If you are unable to feel a pulse, start chest compressions (see "Cardiopulmonary Resuscitation" on page 324).

Do not worry about cutting the cord. This can be done when you reach the birth facility or when the paramedics arrive. If the cord is long enough, help the mother put the baby to her breast as soon as she is breathing well. The baby's sucking will stimulate her uterus to continue contracting and expel the placenta. It will also prevent hemorrhaging. In addition, the colostrum the baby receives from the breast will help remove the mucus from her digestive tract. When the cord stops pulsating, tie it with a shoestring.

Do not pull on the cord in an attempt to deliver the placenta. When the placenta is ready to be expelled, you will notice the cord lengthening. The woman may also feel pressure and the need to push. If the placenta is expelled before help arrives, place it next to the baby in a bag or wrap it up with her for extra warmth. It should be taken to your birth facility so your caregiver can examine it.

Some bleeding is normal while the placenta is being delivered and right afterwards. Nursing the baby immediately after giving birth is usually sufficient stimulation to keep the uterus firmly contracted. The uterus should feel as firm as a grapefruit and it should be at the level of the woman's navel. If the bleeding seems excessive—that is, more than two cups worth—massage her abdomen at the navel using a deep circular motion to encourage contractions. If the baby refuses to nurse, you can stimulate the release of oxytocin, which encourages uterine contractions, by gently massaging the woman's nipples.

If the baby is born in the car, you can now resume driving to the hospital or birth center. If the baby is born at home, wait for assistance to arrive or call your caregiver and follow his instructions.

When arriving at the hospital, you may want to request immediate rooming-in to prevent isolating the baby, which some hospitals do routinely with babies born outside the facility. If all is well, the woman may feel like returning home within a few hours. She also has the option of staying one or two days for observation.

GENTLE BIRTH

The concept of *gentle birth* takes into consideration what birth is like from the baby's point of view. It attempts to minimize the stress and trauma experienced by the infant as she passes through the birth canal to make her entry into the world more pleasant. Types of gentle birth include Leboyer delivery, underwater birth, and birth without interventions.

Hints for the Labor Partner

If your partner has given birth at home:

✓ Place the baby face down on the mother's bare abdomen and dry her off, which will help stimulate her to breathe.

✓ Wipe or gently suction the mucus from the baby's mouth.

✓ To keep them warm, cover mother and baby with dry blankets. (Make sure to turn off fans or the air conditioner.)

✓ Watch the baby move to her mother's breast as soon as she is interested.

✓ Tell your partner how proud you are of her.

✓ Congratulate yourself on a good job.

Leboyer Delivery

French obstetrician Frederick Leboyer originated the concept of gentle birth in the 1970s. He believed that birth is a traumatic experience for the newborn and that certain routine delivery procedures increase the trauma. Otherwise, why do babies cry and look so unhappy at birth? In his view, the infant moves from a peaceful womb through the "assault" of labor into a world of bright lights and loud voices. She is held upside down, her cord is cut, and she is immediately removed from her mother. Dr. Leboyer stated that a newborn's senses are very acute and that she perceives the intense sensations of birth, often very vividly.

Dr. Leboyer's method for bringing a newborn into the world was popularized in his 1975 book *Birth Without Violence*. A Leboyer delivery incorporates several techniques that make birth a more soothing experience for the infant. What follows is a description of gentle birth:

The room is dimly lit, allowing the baby to adjust slowly to the light. The bright lights that are normally used in delivery rooms are blinding to the eyes of a baby who has been in semidarkness for nine months. Think about what it is like to be in a dark room for a while and then to suddenly have bright lights directed at your face. It's no wonder that newborn babies shut their eyes tightly.

To keep the baby from becoming chilled, the temperature of the birthing room is adjusted for the baby's needs, rather than for the hospital staff's comfort. Talking is kept to a minimum or a whisper. Loud voices and exclamations may seem deafening to the new baby's ears.

As the baby emerges from the birth canal, she is gently lifted up and placed onto her mother's bare abdomen for skin-to-skin contact. She is not held upside down by her feet, which would straighten her spine—a position exactly opposite of the one she had in utero. She is not stimulated to cry, but allowed to begin breathing spontaneously. Her mother can gently soothe her through massage or stroking. Her nose and mouth are not suctioned unless they need to be.

The cord is not clamped and cut immediately after birth, but delayed until it stops pulsating. This allows the baby to continue receiving oxygen-carrying red blood cells. Delayed cord cutting also means that the baby does not have to be rushed into breathing, since she is still receiving oxygen from her mother via the cord. This makes the transition from intrauterine life to breathing on her own much easier.

The baby is given to her father, who can place her in a warm bath to simulate a return to the security of the womb. Many babies completely relax and stop crying while they gently float in the water. The baby is then dried, wrapped, and given to her mother.

Opponents of delayed cord cutting argue that the baby receives extra red blood cells, which increases the risk of jaundice. However, unless the newborn is held below the level of the placenta or the cord is "milked" (compressed and stroked toward the baby), equal amounts of blood enter and leave the baby while the cord is pulsating.

Caregivers who specialize in Leboyer deliveries have found no increase whatsoever in infection, heat loss, undetected distress, or other complications attributed to gentle-birth procedures. Since the parents are intimately involved during this type of birth, bonding may be encouraged more than in a non-Leboyer birth, and the parents' competence at caring for their new baby may be enhanced.

Interestingly, many of Leboyer's techniques are being incorporated into regular birthing room routines. For example, caregivers no longer hold babies upside down by their feet, but instead, deliver the infants up and then onto the mother's abdomen where they can remain for extended contact. Women are also taking less IV medication, so babies are being born more alert and do not need to be stimulated or "spanked" after delivery. Most babies today are being welcomed into the world more gently, with their comfort in mind.

Even if your caregiver does not practice Leboyer techniques, he may agree to incorporate some of the aspects of this type of delivery that appeal to you.

Underwater Birth

Some women have taken the concept of gentle birth one step further by choosing to deliver their babies underwater. Just as laboring in warm water has been found to promote relaxation, making contractions less painful and more efficient, delivering while in water can reduce the stress of birth on the baby.

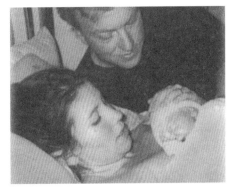

This new mother, father, and baby take a well-earned rest after birth.

For this type of birth, the woman rests in a tub of water that is heated to around 98°F. After the baby is born, she is gently lifted from the water and handed to her mother, or the mother reaches down and lifts her out of the water. According to proponents of this method, the physiological mechanism that causes the baby to breathe is not stimulated until her face is exposed to changes in temperature and air pressure. In other words, the baby does not take her first breath until after she is removed from the water. While in the water, she continues to receive oxygen from the placenta through the umbilical cord.

The concept of giving birth underwater originated in France at the Pithiviers Hospital Maternity Unit under the direction of Dr. Michel Odent, who developed and headed the unit. After learning of Dr. Leboyer's delivery techniques, Dr. Odent created an atmosphere in his own hospital for gentle births. Women were able to labor and give birth however they felt most comfortable. He began by gradually removing the traditional obstetrical technologies, which he felt created barriers between the parents and child. He incorporated the use of dimmed lights and reduced noise, and had the staff remain out of the way unless needed. In finding their most comfortable labor and birthing positions, women began opting to get into the tub of water provided for them. Underwater birth became a natural outgrowth of these efforts. Dr. Odent saw that delivering in this manner reduced the trauma of birth to its minimum, and he began actively promoting underwater birth. Over the years, his name has become almost synonymous with this type of birth.

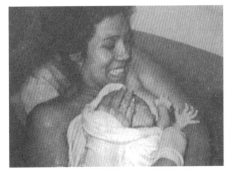

Waterbirth allows the infant a very gentle entry into the world.

According to Barbara Harper, RN, an author and expert on waterbirth, being in water helps some laboring women relax so much that fear and resistance are almost totally eliminated, allowing for the easiest delivery possible.[4] Sometimes, women get into the tub just to labor and the birth happens before they can get out. Another benefit of waterbirth is that it causes the perineum to be more elastic, reducing the chance of tearing and the need for an episiotomy. Dr. Odent reported that in one hundred waterbirths he attended, there were no episiotomies and only twenty-nine cases of superficial tearing.[5]

Many women who have given birth underwater felt that it allowed them to be more in tune with their bodies and work with the labor process more effectively. They felt that birthing in this manner gave them the opportunity to really "give birth," rather than "being delivered."

A number of doctors, however, feel that the risks of waterbirth are too great. They believe that the chance of a baby drowning, no matter how slight, prevents this from being an acceptable procedure.

Have It Your Way

If you want to have a gentle birth, begin your search for an accommodating caregiver and birth facility early in your pregnancy.

Waterbirth is available in certain areas in the United States. If you are interested in this type of experience, begin by checking with the nearest birth center. You can also contact Waterbirth International, which is part of Global Maternal/Child Health Association—a group that provides practitioner referrals and information on the subject. Contact information for Waterbirth International is provided in the Resources beginning on page 449.

Birth Without Interventions

A birth without interventions, one in which the woman is allowed to do whatever feels best during labor and delivery, is a truly natural birth. In other words, the woman acts instinctively to birth her baby. She may, for example, instinctively choose to kneel on all fours during parts of her labor and to squat while pushing out the baby. Because there are no interventions (other than listening to the baby's heart rate with a fetoscope or hand-held electronic fetal monitor), her positions and movements are not restricted by any tubes, wires, or medications. She feels free to make whatever noise is comforting to her, and she is not rushed by anyone's schedule to "get the baby out."

Because doctors are trained in a medical setting, the majority of physicians and nurses have never witnessed a natural birth, one without any interventions. They are trained to see birth as a medical event, something that requires managing and regulating. Women who experience a birth without interventions usually do so with a midwife, either in a birth center or at home. Most advocates of natural or "instinctive" birthing do not teach a method of childbirth, such as patterned breathing techniques. Instead, they encourage a woman to look within herself for the resources to cope with labor. Dr. Michel Odent has stated that when laboring women follow their instincts, there is "almost nothing to teach."[6] In his words, "One simply cannot help an involuntary process; one can only disturb it."

CONCLUSION

While the majority of women have a normal progress of labor, others may hit some "bumps" along the way that may alter their birth plan. Be flexible in your desires so that if your labor varies from the normal course, you can make adjustments and still have a wonderful birth experience.

Medications and Anesthesia
or How Do You Spell Relief?

Whenever possible, it is always best to avoid the use of medications during pregnancy, labor, birth, and the postpartum period. The importance of their avoidance during pregnancy was covered in Chapter 3. This chapter focuses on the various types of drugs and anesthesia that may be used during labor and delivery, as well as their possible risks and benefits. Also discussed are the special situations for which certain medications are needed.

USING DRUGS DURING CHILDBIRTH

In a normal, uncomplicated labor and birth, the use of medication is often unnecessary. Relaxation, slow breathing, and other comfort measures can be very effective in combating the sensations of pain. The presence of a loving support person is probably the best tranquilizer available. In addition, the encouragement given by the hospital staff and your caregiver may affect your need for medication. If you are given positive reinforcement ("You're doing great!" "It's almost over!"), if you are permitted to move about freely, and if you receive a minimum of medical interventions, you will probably experience very little need for medication. On the other hand, if you are frequently asked if you need something for pain, if you are made to lie in one position, or if medical interventions are used, you may have an increased desire for some type of medication.

Nature has provided its own painkiller for laboring women. Labor prompts the pituitary gland to release *endorphins,* morphine-like natural pain relievers that are said to be several times more potent than morphine. Endorphins produce a sensation of enormous pleasure after a tremendous exertion, such as that experienced during labor. Scientists have found that if a woman is given any kind of drug during labor, production of this natural painkiller is disturbed.[1]

Knowledge of the labor and birth process can also enhance a woman's ability to cope. During labor, before you decide to take a medication, request a cervical exam to verify your dilation. Even if it has been only a short time since you were examined, get checked once again, just to be sure of your progress. If you are in transition, it means your labor is almost over and you may have just a few more contractions left before completing the first stage. By the time the nurse goes out, prepares the medication, and returns with it, you may have dilated to 10 centimeters and no longer need it. Medication taken at this time may make you sleepy, interfering with your ability to push during the second stage and to bond with the baby immediately after birth. Plus, it may have a strong effect on the baby. If you request an epidural, it may take as long as thirty minutes to be administered and take effect—and you do not want to be numb for the pushing stage.

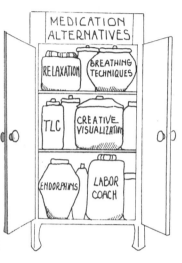

Before going into labor, discuss with your caregiver which medications and types of anesthesia you will be offered if the need arises. Also make sure that your labor partner is aware of your desires long before your due date arrives. Labor is stressful and not the time to decide which medication or anesthesia is best for you. If you wait until you are in active labor or transition, you may agree to something that is really not acceptable to you.

Know your alternatives and understand how they will affect both your participation and your partner's during the labor and birth. When you discuss medications with your caregiver prior to labor, or when you are deciding whether to accept a medication or any prescribed treatment during labor, ask the following questions:

"Look! All benefit and no risk!!"

- How will this medication (or treatment) affect my labor, my baby, and me?
- What are the benefits and the risks?
- If I decide not to accept this medication (or treatment), what will happen?
- Is there an alternative form of treatment?

Even though relaxation and breathing work extremely well for many women, some find that these tools do not provide enough pain relief or promote adequate relaxation. You may want to try some of the additional techniques suggested in Chapter 7. If you are still experiencing unbearable pain, medication or anesthesia is available. In a prolonged or difficult labor, some women feel they need medication to help them cope with their contractions. During a complicated delivery, such as one in which forceps or a vacuum extractor is necessary, anesthesia may be beneficial. For a cesarean section, anesthesia is a necessity.

No one perfect medication exists for all circumstances. Since you cannot foresee what your labor will be like, except in the case of a planned cesarean, you must remain flexible in your attitude. Every medication and anesthetic has benefits and risks, and you need to be aware of them to make an informed decision. Only when the benefits outweigh the risks should you consider using a particular medication.

The Benefits

In a difficult labor, a small amount of medication can decrease some of the pain sensations and may aid relaxation, especially between contractions. Analgesics (pain relievers) such as Stadol or Nubain are common choices. It is important to realize that an analgesic will not take away all of your pain. It may, however, lessen it enough to help you cope better. In a prolonged labor, a narcotic may relax the cervix, helping to speed up labor. It may also provide some needed rest if the woman has been in early labor for many hours without sleep.

An epidural, which offers the most effective pain relief during labor (and will be detailed later in this chapter), is the most popular choice. If a woman previously had a cesarean after a long, hard labor and is afraid to attempt a vaginal birth, an epidural may give her the reassurance to go through labor again.

When an intervention such as the use of forceps or a cesarean section becomes necessary, a regional anesthetic, such as epidural anesthesia, can relieve pain, while allowing you to be awake for your baby's birth. Epidural anesthesia, which partially or completely numbs the abdominal area and below, also presents fewer risks to the woman and baby than general anesthesia for a cesarean birth. In addition, after the surgery, injecting a narcotic through the epidural catheter can provide further pain relief for twelve to eighteen hours. And it does so without the disadvantages of repeated intravenous (IV) or intramuscular (IM) narcotic injections, which can cause drowsiness, itching, nausea, vomiting, intermittent pain relief, and pain at the injection site.

For a list of the medications commonly used during labor and delivery, see Table 10.1 on page 234. This table offers a complete summary of when and how the drugs are given, their uses and benefits, and their possible side effects for both the mother and baby.

The Risks

When weighing the risks of accepting a medication or anesthesia, you must take many factors into consideration. While the dosage of a medication is geared to the woman, two individuals are involved, and one is a much smaller individual. All medications affect the fetus in one way or another. The American Academy of Pediatrics' Committee on Drugs has warned that there is no medication that has yet been proven safe for the unborn child.

The fetus may be affected either directly or indirectly by medication used during labor or delivery. Both effects are highly influenced by the dosage and the time it is given before the baby is born. With an epidural, there is a continuous infusion of medication. When given over a period of many hours, the baby has an increased risk of side effects. When a single IM or IV injection of medication is given to the woman, her liver will start to break it down. If enough time passes between the administration of the medication and the baby's birth, much of the medication will be metabolized by the woman. This means a decreased risk of infant side effects. If, however, the baby is born while a large amount of the medication is in his system, his immature liver will have to excrete the medication on its own. Liver enzyme activity is immature in the fetus and newborn, taking four to eight weeks after birth to reach adult capacity. In a premature infant, the effects of medication are even greater.

The direct effects of medication on the baby may include toxicity or alteration of his central nervous system, respiratory system, and/or temperature-regulating centers, as well as change in his muscle tone. The use of the narcotic meperidine (Demerol) during labor and the postpartum period should be avoided as it remains in the system a long time. It can cause central nervous system depression in the newborn and adversely affect his ability to suck.

The indirect effects of medication on the baby are caused by the drug's influence on the woman's physiology. If the medication depresses the woman's respirations or blood pressure, the infant will receive reduced amounts of oxygen.

The use of medications or anesthesia may increase the need for additional interventions. For example, oxytocin intensifies contractions, which, in turn, may increase the woman's need for pain medication. Stronger contractions may also decrease the amount of oxygen the fetus receives. Conversely, some pain medications can slow down or prolong labor, thus increasing the need for oxytocin. Certain anesthetics dull the urge to push, which can increase the need for an assisted delivery with forceps or a vacuum extractor.

The decision to accept or refuse medication is not an easy one. You must learn what is available, and then, if the need arises, you can choose the medication with which you are most comfortable. If you have an allergy to a medication, make sure to tell your caregiver, who should note it on your chart. And before accepting any medication, ask, "What are you giving me?" Also, if you are very sensitive to medication, ask your caregiver to prescribe a reduced dose. If the smaller dose is not sufficient, you can always ask for more. If the dose is too strong, however, you may not be able to handle the contractions effectively. Remember, once a medication has been given, it cannot be taken back.

REGIONAL ANESTHETICS AND ANALGESICS

During childbirth, regional analgesics and anesthetics target specific areas of the body. A regional *analgesic* provides adequate pain relief to the area without affecting motor abilities or level of consciousness. A regional *anesthetic* provides excellent pain relief and, depending on the dosage, causes a complete or partial loss of motor ability. The epidural is the most frequently used method of regional anesthesia. Other common methods include local infiltration, the pudendal block, the spinal, and the combined spinal/epidural.

Regional anesthetics numb a large area of the body, while local anesthetics target smaller areas. To numb a specific area, a local anesthetic—a "caine" drug, such as procaine, bupivacaine, lidocaine, and ropivacaine—is injected into the tissues or nerves. During childbirth, lidocaine is the most common local anesthetic given to numb the perineal area when repairing tissues after an episiotomy or a laceration. This is called a *local infiltration.* A caine drug is also given prior to the insertion of the epidural or spinal needle to numb the tissues in the back. In addition, a local anesthetic is used for a *pudendal block,* in which the injection is given through the vaginal walls and into the pudendal nerves to numb the vagina (see Figure 10.1 at left). For a *paracervical block,* which is rarely done, the medication is injected directly into the cervix.

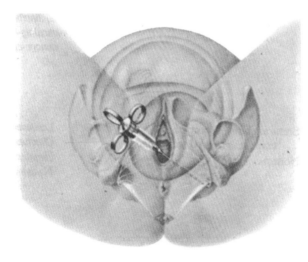

Figure 10.1.
A pudendal block numbs the vagina and perineum.

While most people think that the medication administered during a local infiltration does not reach the baby, research has shown that lidocaine, the local anesthetic injected into the perineum prior to an episiotomy, quickly enters the mother's circulation, crosses the placenta, and can remain in the baby's system for up to forty-eight hours.[2]

The Epidural

The use of epidural anesthesia (sometimes called the "Cadillac of anesthesia") for pain relief during labor has increased dramatically over the years. In many hospitals, more than 70 percent of women use epidurals during labor. While they are an excellent anesthesia for cesarean delivery, epidurals have their downside. It is important to be aware of these shortcomings before choosing one for an uncomplicated birth.

As mentioned earlier, it can take more than thirty minutes for an epidural to be administered and take effect. This means, if you are well into transition, an epidural may not kick in until you are ready to push. Also, you will have to deal with the intense contractions of transition in an uncomfortable position. During the second stage of labor when it's time to push, you will find it very difficult to bear down without feeling the natural urge. If you do receive an epidural during labor, you could request that the dosage be reduced. Then you can delay pushing until you feel pressure or an urge to bear down. Waiting for this urge will enable you to push more effectively.

On the positive side, an epidural can help a woman who is experiencing a prolonged labor or a difficult back labor to relax and cope better. It can also provide relief to women who experience increasingly intense contractions after being given Pitocin.

Epidural medication consists of two types: local anesthetics (lidocaine and other "caine" drugs), which cause the complete loss of sensation and motor control, and narcotics (fentanyl, sufentanyl), which provide analgesia or pain relief. The single or combined use of these two drugs can be adjusted for different results. Low-dose and ultra-light epidurals administer narcotics with little or no caine drugs. They allow women to retain motor function while providing adequate pain relief.

In some facilities, a low dose of medication is administered continuously through the epidural catheter. If the woman needs additional relief, she can bolus herself with a PCA (patient-controlled analgesia) device. When she presses the button, a mini dose of medication is administered. The unit monitors the dosage and timing of the medication to prevent an overdose.

If you decide to accept an epidural, you will need to undergo several procedures. An IV will be started and you will be given one to two liters of fluid to reduce the chance of your blood pressure dropping. You will be asked to sit on the edge of the bed or lie on your side with your back curved while an anesthesiologist or certified registered nurse anesthetist (CRNA) administers the epidural. First, the injection site is numbed through a local anesthetic. Then, as shown in Figure 10.2, the epidural needle is inserted into the epidural space and the epidural catheter is threaded through the needle into place. The needle is withdrawn and the catheter is taped into place. A test dose is usually given to insure correct placement.

In addition to an IV, you will be attached to a fetal monitor and an automatic blood pressure cuff. Since your mobility and your ability to feel sensations will be greatly diminished, you will be restricted to the bed and may need to have a urinary catheter inserted. This is to prevent a full bladder, which could impede the baby's progress through your pelvis.

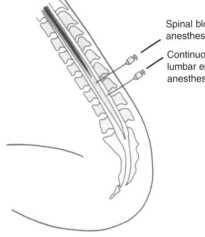

Spinal block anesthesia

Continuous lumbar epidural anesthesia

Figure 10.2.
The spinal needle (for a spinal block) is placed into the spinal fluid. For epidural anesthesia, the needle and catheter are positioned in the epidural space, just outside the membrane that encases the spinal fluid.

TABLE 10.1. MEDICATIONS AND ANESTHETICS COMMONLY USED IN CHILDBIRTH			
Type	**How Given**	**When Given**	**Uses and Benefits**
Sedatives **Hypnotics** *Seconal* *Nembutal* *Restoril* *Phenobarbital*	Orally	Prelabor. Early labor. (Rarely used due to side effects).	Help differentiate prelabor from true labor. Effects depend on dose. Sedatives allay anxiety/excitement and induce rest, but do not relieve pain. Hypnotics may induce sleep.
Tranquilizers **Antiemetics** *Vistaril (Atarax)* *Compazine* *Phenergan* *Valium* *Versed*	Orally IM IV	Early labor. Active labor or transition, alone or combined with analgesic. After a cesarean during repair.	Relieve tension and anxiety. Promote relaxation. Prevent nausea and vomiting when used with analgesic; also enhance effects of analgesics. Reduce anxiety during surgical repair.
Analgesics *Fentanyl* *Morphine* *Stadol* *Nubain* *Demerol*	IM IV	Active labor.	Reduce or alter pain perception. May speed labor that is slowed due to stress.
Narcotic **antagonist** *Narcan*	IM or IV to woman. IM or in umbilical vein to baby.	Second stage of labor. After birth.	Reverses respiratory depression caused by narcotics.
Oxytocics (synthetic hormones to contract uterus) *Pitocin* *Syntocinon* *Oxytocin* *Ergotrate* *Methergine*	IV (dosage best controlled when diluted in IV fluid). IM (postpartum only).	Prior to labor. During labor. Postpartum.	Induce or stimulate contractions. Control postpartum bleeding.

IV = intravenously, IM = intramuscularly.

* Dependent on maternal dosage and timing in relation to birth.

† The cord level indicates the amount of medication that is in the baby's bloodstream as compared to that in the woman's.

Possible Risks and Side Effects for Woman	Possible Risks and Side Effects for Baby*
Slow down labor if given too soon. Disorientation. Drowsiness. Lowered blood pressure.	Accumulation in tissues. Respiratory depression. Decreased sucking ability. Cord level: 70%†
Drowsiness. Confusion. Blood pressure changes. Heart rate changes. Versed causes amnesia; may not remember birth or bonding time.	Heart rate change. Decreased sucking ability. Decreased muscle tone. Lowered body temperature. Decreased attention, increased restlessness. Increased jaundice. Cord level: 95%–100%†

Dizziness.
Dry mouth.
Euphoria, hallucinations.
Nausea.
Respiratory depression.
Lowered blood pressure.
Drowsiness and possible difficulty concentrating
  on breathing or pushing if dose too large.
Sleepiness during delivery.
	Depressed respiration.
	Decreased sucking ability.
	May affect fetal heart rate.
	Altered behavioral responses for many days or weeks.
	Cord level: Demerol, 80%–130%†
	FDA requires Demerol to carry warning label
	  of possible adverse effects on infant.
	Nubain may cause fetal bradycardia, respiratory
	  depression, apnea, low muscle tone, and cyanosis.

Rapid heart rate. Elevated blood pressure. Nausea and vomiting. Sweating. Trembling. Return of pain. Withdrawal symptoms if woman is addicted to narcotics.	Same as for mother. Severe seizures if mother is addicted to narcotics. Little is known about long-term effects. Effects of antagonists are shorter than those of narcotics, and depression may recur.

Lowered blood pressure; anxiety; increased heart rate;
  edema; water intoxication.
Tetanic (very strong) contractions or rupture of uterus.
Increased desire for pain medication.
Increased need for coaching and support.
Ergotrate or methergine given postpartum can
  increase blood pressure or cause severe "afterpains."
FDA warns that oxytocin should not be used for elective
  induction for convenience of doctor or woman.
Oxytocin is released naturally during breastfeeding.
	Heart rate changes.
	Fetal asphyxia due to tetanic contractions.
	Increased jaundice.

Type	How Given	When Given	Uses and Benefits
Regional anesthesia (uses local anesthetics or "caine" drugs such as procaine, bupivacaine, lidocaine, or ropivacaine).	See below.	See below.	Does not affect alertness. Does not affect cough reflex— less danger of aspiration if vomiting occurs. Does not affect labor partner's participation in labor and birth.
Local infiltration	Injection into perineum.	Second stage of labor. Prior to perineal repair.	Numbs perineum for repair of episiotomy or lacerations. Response time: 3 to 4 minutes. Duration: 1 to 2 hours.
Pudendal block	Injection into pudendal nerves via vagina.	Second stage of labor.	Numbs birth canal and perineum for forceps delivery, episiotomy, or tissue repair. Response time: 2 to 3 minutes. Duration: 1 hour.
Epidural (uses either "caine" drug; narcotic such as morphine, Demerol, fentanyl, or sufentanil; or combination of the two).	Continuously through catheter inserted into epidural space (low spinal area).	Active labor. Second stage of labor. Prior to cesarean birth.	Completely or partially relieves pain from uterine contractions, birth, and repair, depending on dose. Avoids spinal headache if done correctly. Response time: 10 to 15 minutes. Duration: continuous.
Spinal (intrathecal) Saddle block (low spinal) *Note: If used during labor, only a narcotic is given.*	Single injection into spinal fluid.	Active labor. Second stage of labor. Prior to cesarean birth.	Pain relief during labor. Woman can walk. Numbs from pubic area to toes for forceps delivery. Numbs area from above navel to toes for cesarean delivery. Requires small dose. Response time: 1 to 2 minutes Duration: 3 to 10 hours for labor (narcotic); 1 to 3 hours for delivery ("caine" drug).

Possible Risks and Side Effects for Woman	Possible Risks and Side Effects for Baby*
See below.	See below.
Burning and stinging upon administration.	Decreased muscle tone. Absorbed by fetus and can remain in system up to forty-eight hours after birth.
Blocked urge to push—coaching needed during birth. Possible toxicity caused by required large dose. (Rarely performed.)	Fetal depression caused by required large dose.
Possible ineffectiveness—technical difficulty may cause it not to work or to take only on one side. Prolonged labor. Lowered blood pressure. Increased maternal temperature (fever), resulting in treatment for nonexistent infection. Increased need for medical supervision and interventions (IV, fetal monitor, urinary catheter, Pitocin). Relaxation of pelvic floor muscles along with diminished urge to push, prolonging second stage of labor, and increasing need for forceps or cesarean delivery. Backache, either short or long term. Increased chance of cesarean delivery. Difficulty urinating. Shivering. Spinal headache if dura is punctured.	Decreased oxygen and lowered heart rate if mother's blood pressure drops. If mother has fever, may cause rapid fetal heart rate; lower one-minute Apgar score; increased need for resuscitation, oxygen; increased risk for seizures in neonatal period. Testing needed to rule out infection if mother or baby has fever. Subtle behavior alterations. Reduced muscle tone. Nursing difficulties. Increased risk of jaundice.
Nausea, vomiting, itching, prolonged labor, and respiratory depression if narcotic is used during labor. Lowered blood pressure. "Caine" drugs cause loss of the urge to push. Spinal headache. Difficulty urinating.	Decreased oxygen and heart rate if mother's blood pressure drops.

Type	How Given	When Given	Uses and Benefits
General anesthesia (unconscious) *Sodium pentathol (IV). Nitrous oxide (gas). Isoflurane (gas).*	IV Via tube inserted into windpipe.	Prior to cesarean birth.	For emergency cesarean when time is too short to administer regional anesthetic.
Postpartum analgesics *Acetaminophen (Tylenol). Ibuprofen (Advil, Motrin). Darvocet. Tylenol with Codeine. Percocet, Tylox.*	Orally	Postpartum.	Oral medication reduces pain from episiotomy, afterpains, hemorrhoids, and cesarean. Compatible with breastfeeding.
Demerol Morphine Duramorph Fentanyl	IM IV by patient-controlled analgesia (PCA)—woman pushes button to release small dose into IV. Epidural catheter.	First 12 to 24 hours after cesarean.	Epidural narcotics give good pain relief up to 18 hours after cesarean without additional medication. Does not affect mobility.

Studies have also shown that if the blood pressure drops as the result of an epidural, the amount of blood flow to the uterus and placenta is reduced. This means the baby's heart rate may drop to a level that can lead to interventions and even a cesarean delivery due to fetal distress.[3]

Multiple studies have shown that epidurals prolong both the first and second stages of labor. Women are more likely to require Pitocin to improve contractions. Epidurals also relax the pelvic floor muscles, which affects the rotation of the baby through the pelvis. This increases the chance that assistance with forceps or a vacuum extractor will be necessary. It also increases the chance of needing a cesarean for an abnormal fetal head position.[4] Women having their first babies are two to three times more likely to have a cesarean for an abnormal or prolonged labor if they accept an epidural before 6 centimeters dilation. If given before 2 centimeters, an epidural causes prolonged labor.[5]

Although most caregivers state that the epidural medication does not reach the fetus, studies have indicated that the drugs do, in fact, enter the baby's circulation.

Possible Risks and Side Effects for Woman	Possible Risks and Side Effects for Baby*

Nausea and vomiting; aspiration of vomit if intubated incorrectly.
Deep anesthesia produces:
  Skeletal muscle weakness.
  Depression of central nervous system—requires constant monitoring.
  Cardiac and respiratory depression; irregular heart pattern; lowered blood pressure.
  Depression of liver, kidney, and gastro-intestinal tract function.
Incompatible with prepared childbirth.
Labor partner often not allowed to be present.
	Crosses placenta rapidly.
	Effects of deep anesthesia are same as for mother.
	Cord level: up to 85%[†]

Drowsiness. Codeine and Percocet can decrease motility of bowels (increase gas pains).	Percocet has been found in moderate amounts in breastmilk—has insignificant effect on full-term infant, but very preterm or ill newborn should be observed for sedation and lowered respirations. Rarely, a woman carries a gene that causes her to rapidly metabolize codeine into morphine, which could result in an overdose in the baby. Observe for extreme sedation.
Repeated IM injections are painful. IM and IV medications cause drowsiness and give intermittent relief. Narcotics via epidural can cause itching. All narcotics can cause nausea, vomiting, and depressed respirations.	Insignificant in normal infants. At high maternal IV or IM doses, infant should be monitored for sedation, poor feeding, and respiratory depression. Avoid Demerol as it remains in the system longer.

This occurs as the medication diffuses from the epidural space into the woman's veins and then crosses the placenta. The concentration increases with the length of the epidural. The baby's level is approximately one-third of the amount found in maternal blood.[6]

Many women have been extremely satisfied with their choice of epidural anesthesia. Others, especially those who experienced side effects, have not been quite as enthusiastic. Occasionally, an epidural does not provide adequate pain relief or its numbing effect "takes" only on one side. It is also responsible for a number of possible side effects, including itching, nausea, vomiting, a drop in blood pressure, uncontrollable shivering, and difficulty in urinating postpartum, which may require catheterization. Epidural anesthesia also increases the risk of postpartum hemorrhage. Residual backache, sometimes lasting for months after giving birth, is another common complaint. It is uncertain if this is from the procedure or, more likely, the stressful position that the woman is placed in during the second stage of labor—because she is numb, she cannot tell if her position is actually harmful to her back.

Less frequently, a severe headache results from the epidural needle inadvertently puncturing the *dura,* the membrane that separates the epidural space from the spinal fluid. While the risk of a spinal headache is low, the needle used for an epidural is larger than for a spinal, as it must be big enough for a catheter to be threaded through it. This results in a larger hole if the dura is punctured. These spinal headaches, which can include neck aches and migraines, may start within days of the birth and last up to eight years.[7] The first method of treatment for spinal headaches is caffeine that is given intravenously or consumed orally. The most effective treatment for a dural puncture is a blood patch to seal the hole and eliminate the headache. For this invasive procedure, a small amount of the woman's blood is injected over the puncture site. This may require an additional epidural injection if the epidural catheter has been removed.

When an epidural is given for longer than five hours, the body's ability to regulate temperature becomes altered, and one-third of women and newborns develop fevers. This may lead to admission into the intensive care nursery for diagnostic procedures to determine if the infant's fever is caused by an infection. The procedures may include a complete blood count (CBC) and blood cultures. If a septic workup is ordered, the newborn will also have to undergo a spinal tap. This also means prolonged hospitalization of both the mother and baby for treatment with antibiotics for a possible nonexistent infection.

According to a recent study, researchers found that if the woman develops a fever of 101°F or above, her infant is four times more likely to have a one-minute Apgar score of under 7. These infants are also more likely to need resuscitation with a bag and mask at delivery, need oxygen in the nursery, and have a seizure in the neonatal period.[8] Babies born to mothers with fever are often hypotonic (low muscle tone), which can impact breastfeeding.

Epidurals can also affect the fetal heart rate. If the mother develops a fever, the fetal heart rate may accelerate to over 160 beats per minute (tachycardia). A slow heart rate of less than 100 beats per minute (bradycardia) can occur after the initial injection or bolus injections of medication into the epidural. During the end of the first stage of labor or during the second stage, late or variable decelerations of the fetal heart rate are more common, which can indicate distress and may lead to interventions.[9]

Epidural anesthesia during labor can also increase the rate of jaundice in the infant.[10] More severe (but extremely rare) complications due to epidurals include an allergic reaction to the medication, convulsions from an overdose, and numbness in the chest that makes breathing difficult. On very rare occasions, a woman must be placed on a respirator until the effects wear off.

The cost of an epidural is another consideration. For families who are paying out of pocket, the cost of the procedure and its possible impact on the method of delivery may be significant. For instance, if a cesarean delivery is also required, the additional cost will be considerable.

Before deciding on an epidural, also consider how it might affect your perception of your role in giving birth. Some women report that rather than being active participants in the birth, they were only observers because of the epidural. While many people assume that labor is always painful and requires relief, others view it as a normal function in which pain can be minimized or relieved through other measures. In many cases, the discomfort of labor causes a woman to find a more comfortable position, and this new position can actually facilitate labor. As one anesthesiologist stated, "The practice of obstetric anesthesia is unique in medicine in that we use an invasive and potentially hazardous procedure to provide a humanitarian service to healthy women undergoing a physiological process."[11] Even though the incidence of severe side effects is low, every woman should carefully weigh the benefits and risks before deciding on an epidural or any other medication during childbirth.

Spinal Analgesia and Anesthesia

Spinal analgesia, in which a narcotic (only) is administered into the spinal fluid, is available in some facilities during labor. It provides a rapid onset of pain relief with no loss of motor control for three to ten hours, depending on the medication used.

A traditional spinal (intrathecal) anesthesia uses lidocaine or another "caine" drug, which is injected into the spinal fluid, as shown in Figure 10.2 on page 233. This provides complete loss of sensation and movement from the injection site to the lower part of the body. A low spinal, known as a *saddle block,* usually numbs just the perineum, buttocks, and inner thighs (the area that touches a saddle). It can be used for a vaginal delivery. A higher spinal provides complete anesthesia and loss of motor control from below the ribs to the toes. It can be administered prior to a cesarean.

Unlike an epidural, spinal anesthesia takes effect quickly and does not give one-sided or patchy relief. Also, the medication dose is very small to reduce the risk of toxicity. Possible side effects of narcotics include nausea, vomiting, urinary retention, itching, prolonged labor, respiratory depression, and spinal headache.

Combined Spinal/Epidural Analgesia

During the administration of a combined spinal/epidural, the anesthesiologist first inserts an epidural needle. Through this needle, he guides a thinner, but longer spinal needle past the epidural space and dural membrane, and into the spinal fluid. A small dose of narcotic is given, and the spinal needle is withdrawn. An epidural catheter is then threaded into the epidural space, the epidural needle is withdrawn, and the catheter is taped to the woman's back.

As the spinal begins to wear off, the anesthesiologist can provide continuous medication through the epidural catheter. As long as the medication used is a narcotic, the woman will retain muscle control and can walk. A "walking epidural" does not provide as deep a level of pain relief, and the woman can perceive the pressure of the contractions. This can be especially beneficial during the second stage of labor. If deeper anesthesia becomes necessary, caine drugs can be added to the epidural.

General Anesthesia

A general anesthetic, which affects every organ, renders the woman unconscious. The risk of complications is higher with this type of anesthesia than any other method. Although rarely given, general anesthesia may be indicated during an emergency cesarean delivery in which there is no time to administer a spinal or epidural. It may also be used if the epidural given for a cesarean delivery is not providing sufficient relief for the surgery. In such a case, an anesthesiologist may need to administer general anesthesia (through an IV, mask, or breathing tube) so the obstetrician is able to complete the procedure. General anesthesia may also be given if a woman's anatomy makes spinal anesthesia unsafe or technically impossible. Very few woman willingly request general anesthesia over a spinal or epidural.

Hints for the Labor Partner

Prior to labor:

✓ Discuss your feelings with your partner about using or not using medication as a labor tool.

✓ Share your desires/birth plan with your partner's caregiver.

✓ Learn all you can about the available medications in case your partner's labor does not progress as expected.

✓ Make sure you understand the risks and benefits of epidurals and the medications used during labor.

MEDICATIONS FOR SPECIAL SITUATIONS

In a labor that is out of the ordinary or involves complications, medication may be required. Preterm labor, hypertension in pregnancy, and post-term pregnancy are examples of these special situations.

Preterm Labor

Women who go into preterm labor may be hospitalized and given a tocolytic medication to relax the uterine muscles and stop the contractions. The most common tocolytic medications are terbutaline sulfate (Brethine) and ritodrine hydrochloride (Yutopar). The side effects of these drugs include rapid heart rate, anxiety, nausea, vomiting, tremors, and insomnia. While on these medications, women are carefully monitored, as they can develop complications such as chest pain, palpitations, high blood pressure, and pulmonary edema. Other medications that may also be used as tocolytics are magnesium sulfate, indomethacin (Indocin), naproxen (Aleve, Anaprox) and nifedipine (Procardia). Depending on the drug, these medications are given orally, subcutaneously (under the skin) with a pump, or intravenously.

If the preterm labor does not stop, the woman may be given steroids such as betamethazone or dexamethazone to prevent or decrease the severity of respiratory distress syndrome (RDS) and the need for a ventilator for the premature infant. Steroids stimulate the production of surfactant, which reduces surface tension in the infant's lungs and allows him to breathe well. However, they must be given twenty-four to forty-eight hours before delivery to be effective. If the preterm labor is a result of an infection, the woman will also be treated with antibiotics.

Tocolytic drugs can also be used to slow contractions if a woman needs an emergency transfer from an out-of-hospital birth center to a hospital. They can also relax the uterus prior to attempting external version.

Hypertension in Pregnancy

Hypertension or high blood pressure in pregnancy places both the woman and baby at risk. The treatment is bed rest and delivery of the baby when mature. If untreated, hypertension can progress to preeclampsia (elevated blood pressure, protein in the urine, and abnormal lab values) and eclampsia (seizures, stroke, and kidney failure).

The most common medication used for preeclampsia is magnesium sulfate, which prevents seizures and also helps lower blood pressure. It is given intravenously prior to labor, during labor, and for twenty-four hours after delivery. The blood pressure, reflexes, respiratory rate, and urine of a woman on this medication are closely monitored. Magnesium sulfate crosses the placenta and is absorbed by the fetus at levels that are close to those of the mother. Side effects to the newborn can include respiratory depression and decreased muscle tone. It may take the newborn days to eliminate the drug from his circulation.

Post-Term Pregnancy

At forty-two weeks, a pregnancy is considered post-term. Since there may be concern about the function of the placenta after this time, many doctors induce labor. Prostaglandin E_2 (dinoprostone) may be applied in or around the cervix before labor is induced to help soften or "ripen" it. This drug may be in the form of a gel (Prepidil) or a vaginal insert with a string attached for easy removal (Cervidil.) A pill containing

---

Hints for the Labor Partner

During labor:

✓ Upon admission, inform the nurse of your partner's desire to avoid medication. Request that no one offers her medication during the labor. (If your partner changes her mind, she can ask for it.)

✓ Before requesting medication or an epidural for your partner, ask a nurse about her progress. If she is close to the pushing stage, this type of medication may not be helpful.

✓ Suggest that your partner first try nondrug pain relievers, such as changing positions, emptying her bladder, receiving a massage, and laboring in a tub or shower.

✓ Ask the nurse if your partner is allowed to get up and walk around. If she is, help her do this.

✓ Tell your partner that she is doing great.

misoprostol (Cytotec) may be taken orally, rectally, or crushed and placed behind the cervix. Misoprostol, a synthetic prostaglandin has not been approved by the FDA for this purpose, but due to its lower cost, it has become more widely used. The FDA has issued an alert that this drug should not be used by women who have had several previous births, a cesarean delivery, or uterine surgery. Risks involve a torn uterus, which can result in severe bleeding, hysterectomy, and death of the mother and baby.[12] After insertion of the medications, the woman and fetus must be monitored for several hours as hyperstimulation of the uterus can occur, resulting in fetal distress.

The use of these agents increases the success rate of labor induction with Pitocin and reduces the need for a cesarean. Occasionally, they initiate labor on their own. (Chapter 11 presents a number of natural methods used to induce labor.)

Inducing labor in the hospital with Pitocin is typically started within two to twenty-four hours after the removal or discontinued use of prostaglandins. If the woman is planning to deliver in an out-of-hospital birth center, she may have a prostaglandin applied the day before in the hospital. The following day, at the birth center, the midwife may rupture the membranes to initiate labor. If these methods do not start labor, she will need to transfer to the hospital for induction with Pitocin.

CONCLUSION

While certain women will require medication and anesthesia during labor and birth for medical reasons, the majority of pain relief is elective. As with any choice, if the benefits outweigh the risks, you may want to accept the medication. But if you accept the medication without informed consent or the knowledge of how your labor is progressing, you may regret your decision. Know your choices and make decisions based on your personal labor experience.

Interventions During Labor and Birth

or Machines that Go Beep

Your caregiver has various procedures at her disposal for obtaining diagnostic information, preventing complications, and even altering the course of labor. The use of a number of interventions is medically necessary in certain circumstances, while the need for others may be questionable, especially during a normal, uncomplicated labor. This chapter presents information on the most common interventions used—for hydrating the laboring woman, for monitoring her well-being and that of her unborn child, and for inducing or augmenting labor. Also discussed are interventions used for complications that may occur during birth. It is important for expectant parents to understand when and why they are used.

As you will see, every intervention carries some degree of risk and, therefore, should not be used unless medically necessary. For this reason, it is important to be prepared. You need to discuss the various interventions with your caregiver prior to labor. Let her know your desires concerning their possible use and find out at what point she feels they are indicated. Clearly understanding her intentions in advance will avoid misunderstandings later, during labor.

There has been an increase in the use of interventions in recent years. Some, such as the electronic fetal monitor, have become standards of care during hospital births, even though their routine use is not evidence-based. In some cases, unforeseen complications may arise that require certain medical or surgical interventions. It is for this reason that, although you may not be planning to use them during labor, it is important to understand when and why they are used.

INTERVENTIONS DURING LABOR

The most commonly used interventions during labor in a hospital setting include the use of intravenous fluids, electronic fetal monitors, and induction or augmentation.

Intravenous Fluids

An *intravenous (IV) fluid* is a solution that is fed into the body through a vein. It may be indicated in a prolonged labor to prevent dehydration. IVs are also used when inducing labor because they provide the most accurate administration of the drug Pitocin, which initiates or strengthens contractions. Prior to an epidural, IV fluids expand the blood volume to reduce the risk of a drop in blood pressure. An IV needle also provides easy access for medication or blood, if needed. For instance, if the

245

woman has a positive group B strep culture, antibiotics are recommended and easily administered through an IV during labor. In certain cases, women with a history of mitral valve prolapse may also be given antibiotics during labor. During a cesarean birth and the immediate postsurgical period, an IV is important for supplying fluids and administering medication or blood. Some doctors, however, routinely use IVs "just in case" a problem arises.

To start an IV, a needle is inserted into the woman's vein—usually in the hand or forearm. (If you are given an IV, ask the nurse to use your nondominant arm.) Next, a thin plastic catheter is threaded through the needle into the vein and the needle is withdrawn. The catheter is securely taped into place. Once the IV is started, a solution of sterile water, normal saline, or Lactated Ringers (a solution of sodium chloride, sodium lactate, potassium chloride, and calcium chloride) with or without dextrose (sugar), is continuously infused into the vein. These solutions will keep the woman hydrated and provide a route for medications if needed.

Antibiotics

If you have a history of positive group B strep cultures, IV antibiotics may be administered during labor.

If you are well hydrated and allowed to drink, and your labor is progressing normally, you probably will not need IV fluids. Many facilities encourage women to drink clear liquids or suck on ice pops during labor. Normal healthy women are well hydrated at term—their bodies store up to two liters of water. They also experience dependent edema, which adds to their store of fluid. This fluid is readily available for use by the laboring woman. One negative of being hooked up to an IV is that it restricts mobility and hampers effective relaxation. If you do have an IV and would like to walk around during labor, ask for the bag of fluid to be hooked up a moveable pole. You could also request a saline lock, in which the catheter is flushed with saline to keep the vein open, and the bag of fluid can be disconnected.

Complications that can result from IV use include infiltration (leakage of fluid into surrounding tissues) and phlebitis (vein inflammation). Some women experience discomfort during the insertion of the needle. A more serious complication, water intoxication, can occur from the use of electrolyte-free IV fluids, such as 5-percent dextrose in water (D_5W). Water intoxication can cause vomiting, convulsions, and pulmonary edema in the woman. Therefore, the use of D_5W should be limited to one liter during labor. Another problem associated with the administration of a dextrose solution is that it can cause an increased level of glucose in the woman's bloodstream. This, in turn, can increase the fetus's sugar level (hyperglycemia), which can rapidly drop and become too low (hypoglycemia) during the newborn period. This is most common when the infusion lasts longer than four hours.[1]

Electronic Fetal Monitor

An *electronic fetal monitor (EFM)* is a device that measures and records the intensity, frequency, and duration of uterine contractions as well as the baby's heart rate. Of special interest to the caregiver is the way the baby's heart rate is affected during and immediately after contractions. A normal fetal heart rate is between 120 and 160 beats per minute. Recurrent deviations from this range may be an indication that the baby is in distress.

The terms used to classify the interpretation of the monitor readout are reassuring, nonreassuring, and ominous. A *reassuring* pattern indicates that the baby is tolerating labor well. A *nonreassuring* pattern may indicate possible distress that may require interventions to speed up the birth. An *ominous* pattern usually means that the baby should be delivered immediately and may require resuscitation.

Monitoring of both the fetal heart rate and uterine contractions can be done either externally or internally. External monitoring is used more frequently, as it is noninvasive and easy to apply. Internal monitoring provides more continuous information and may be used if the external monitor is unable to pick up a continuous reading through the external leads. It is, however, more invasive and the amniotic membranes must be ruptured in order to use it. In both types of monitoring, the leads are connected to a bedside unit that records and prints out the information on graph paper. The information is also relayed to central monitors at the nurses' station.

The baby's heart rate can be monitored externally by securing an ultrasound transducer on the woman's abdomen with an adjustable belt. If it is necessary to monitor the fetal heart rate internally, an electrode is inserted through the vagina and partially dilated cervix, and placed beneath the skin of the baby's head or buttocks. A small number of babies have developed scalp abscesses from the use of this internal electrode.

The most common method for measuring uterine contractions is through a pressure-sensitive transducer that is applied to the woman's abdomen with an adjustable belt. When the uterus hardens, the transducer picks up the muscle contraction and a corresponding wave appears on the graph paper. If a more accurate determination of the contractions is needed, an *intrauterine pressure catheter (IUPC)* may be inserted through the cervix and into the uterus. An IUPC measures the exact amount of pressure exerted by the contractions and may be indicated in a labor involving the use of Pitocin. The IUPC can also be used to infuse saline into the uterus—a procedure called *amniofusion*—to increase the volume of amniotic fluid. A low level of amniotic fluid does not provide buoyancy, and the umbilical cord can become compressed during contractions and result in fetal distress.

An electronic fetal monitor is indicated for pregnancies that are considered high risk. If labor is induced or stimulated with Pitocin, an EFM determines how well the baby is handling the stress of labor and assesses the strength and duration of the contractions. It is also required during epidurals to make sure the baby is stable. A labor that becomes dysfunctional or a fetus that exhibits nonreassuring heart rate patterns also benefits from continuous monitoring.

A number of doctors feel that monitoring all patients, even normal healthy women, is beneficial in determining fetal well-being or detecting distress. Some fear a lawsuit if a problem arises and the monitor was not used. It is also believed that the documentation provided by the monitor will be beneficial in a potential lawsuit. However, monitor readings are open to interpretation. This means that litigants can usually find an "expert" to refute a caregiver's analysis of the readings. Rather than being a benefit, the documentation can become a detriment to hospitals and caregivers.

Experts continue to debate the need for monitoring healthy women whose labors are progressing normally. Electronic fetal monitors were introduced into practice in the 1960s before controlled randomized studies were performed to determine their efficacy and safety. A major controversy concerns the accuracy of the results obtained from these monitors, especially the external types. Many authorities feel that external EFMs show only that the baby is doing well. The information on the printout is open to misinterpretation by the medical staff. Sometimes the monitor picks up the woman's heartbeat, or stomach and intestinal sounds, rather than the baby's heartbeat.[2] Many doctors consider late decelerations of the heart rate (slowdown of the fetal heartbeat at the end of each contraction) as a sign that the baby is in distress. Several studies, how-

A Hint for the Mother-to-Be

Ask if your hospital has telemetry units, which enable you to walk around during labor while being continuously monitored.

ever, have shown that up to 60 percent of fetuses exhibiting late decelerations were not in distress at birth.[3]

Because the monitor readings are interpreted by individuals with a vast difference in experience and knowledge, additional studies have concluded that it is not possible to always predict brain damage based on identifying specific patterns. When the fetal heart tracing is nonreassuring, stimulating the baby's scalp during an internal exam may provide information on the baby's condition. If the heart rate accelerates, it indicates that the baby is not in distress. If the heart rate does not increase or if fetal distress is suspected, the physician may take a sample of the baby's blood to check the pH. This test, called a *fetal scalp sampling,* may be able to determine if the baby is truly in distress and immediate delivery is necessary. This procedure is not available in all hospitals.

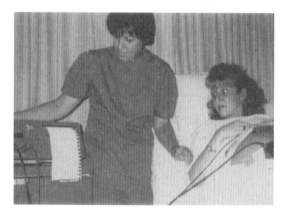

Contractions and the baby's heart rate are being monitored with an external fetal monitor.

Skyrocketing cesarean birth rates have also been associated with increased use of EFMs. Multiple studies have evaluated and compared the use of continuous electronic fetal monitoring with periodic or intermittent monitoring, called *intermittent auscultation.* During these studies, the fetal heart rate was periodically monitored with a fetal stethoscope or a hand-held ultrasound fetal monitor every fifteen minutes during the first stage of labor, and every five minutes (or after every contraction) during the second stage. Both cesarean deliveries and the use of vacuum extraction or forceps (discussed later in this chapter) increased with continuous electronic fetal monitoring. If fetal scalp sampling was not available, the increase in cesarean section was much higher.[4]

Some doctors believe that routine EFMs lower the incidence of maternal and infant illness (including cerebral palsy), and infant death resulting from lack of oxygen during labor or the trauma of birth. However, an analysis of twelve controlled randomized studies performed by Dr. Stephen Thacker and colleagues at the Centers for Disease Control (CDC) established that routine EFM use did not result in a significant decrease in maternal or infant morbidity (illness) or mortality.[5] Additionally, EFM use has not decreased the incidence of cerebral palsy, which has remained the same since the 1950s, and is more likely the result of prenatal influences such as genetics, toxic exposures, and infection.

Another growing concern over routine EFM use is that nurses and doctors are losing the ability to evaluate patients without referring to the "machine." They tend to pay more attention to the monitor readouts than to the woman and her perception of the labor. Many labor partners also become entranced by the beeps of the machine and the continuous readout, and they forget their main purpose—to support and encourage their partners during labor.

In many hospitals, continuous electronic fetal monitoring is standard. In addition to the fear of liability, the lack of adequate staff is another main reason for its use. If a nurse-midwife is your caregiver within a hospital setting, an initial twenty- to thirty-minute readout from an EFM may be required. Intermittent monitorings by the midwife will follow. If you are delivering out of the hospital, total intermittent monitoring with a fetoscope or a hand-held ultrasound fetal monitor is the norm.

Most women who labor with an electronic fetal monitor remain in bed. Laboring in bed typically increases the length of labor and the need for medical intervention.

Because a woman is restricted to certain positions when laboring in bed, her perception of pain is altered, her stress level is increased, and medication is accepted more frequently. And as discussed in the previous chapter, medication can adversely affect her and her unborn baby. A woman who remains in bed because of the monitor cannot receive the benefits of walking during labor or laboring in water. Nor can she experience the personal attention provided by a nurse who actually listens to the baby's heartbeat. Some hospitals offer continuous fetal monitors called *telemetry units,* which allow the woman to be out of bed and able to walk during labor. But this device is expensive and not available in many areas.

Laboring with a Fetal Monitor

As already discussed, a woman's mobility and position during labor can significantly affect the progress of her labor. Therefore, if you choose or are required to be continuously monitored during labor, it is important to avoid lying on your back. This position can cause hypotension and lead to fetal distress—the very problems the monitor was designed to protect against. While in bed, be sure to change your position about every twenty to thirty minutes. The monitor may need to be repositioned to pick up the baby's heartbeat each time you move, but this adjustment is worthwhile because your mobility and comfort are extremely important. You can also request to be monitored while out of bed—you may be able to stand up or walk around next to the bed, or sit in a chair or rocker that is close to the monitor. The longer you can stand and walk during labor, the more efficient your contractions will be. An upright position promotes the descent of the baby and dilation of the cervix. It also helps the uterus to work at maximum efficiency.

If the concept of routine monitoring disturbs you, talk to your doctor about the possibility of limiting your time while on it. She may agree to monitor you intermittently. Even just waiting until active labor is well established before using a monitor will give you more time to move about and be comfortable. If an internal monitor is used, it can be disconnected every few hours so you can stand up and move around.

If you find that the beeping noises coming from the machine are distracting or annoying, ask the nurse to turn down the volume. You could also ask her to reposition the machine so that the readout is not in constant view, which can be distracting to both you and your labor partner.

STAN S31 Fetal Heart Monitor

In 2005, the FDA approved the STAN S31 fetal heart monitor, which, through a fetal scalp electrode, assesses the well-being of the fetus through an electrocardiogram (ECG). The device has a built-in computer that interprets the ECG readout for the caregiver. This reduces human error in determining whether to allow the woman to continue laboring or to intervene and deliver the baby. This technology has been shown to reduce the number of babies born with a lack of oxygen by 50 percent and decrease the number of emergency cesareans.[6]

Fetal Oxygen Saturation Monitor

When fetal heart rate readings are nonreassuring, the use of a sensor to measure the oxygen saturation of the fetus (the amount of oxygen the fetus is receiving) can be helpful. This monitoring device is inserted into the uterus and the sensor is positioned

Hints for the Labor Partner

If your partner is wearing a fetal monitor:

✓ Encourage her to change position (never let her lie flat on her back).

✓ Have her sit in a chair or stand next to the bed.

✓ Pay attention to her, not the monitor.

✓ Ask to turn down the volume if the "beeping" noises are distracting.

on the baby's cheek or temple. Fetal oxygen saturation values are displayed on the same graph paper that records the fetal heart rate and contractions.

The use of this device has been shown to reduce the cesarean rate for nonreassuring fetal heart rates by 50 percent. But the overall cesarean rate did not decrease because of the increased number of cesarean sections performed for dystocia (a difficult labor, possibly resulting from this device).[7] This device should not be used while the woman is laboring in water, or if she has active genital herpes, HIV, hepatitis B and/or hepatitis E antigens.[8] Some facilities have stopped using this device as the sensor can move off of the baby's face and result in an inaccurate reading. A pressure mark from the sensor can also appear on the newborn, although it usually disappears within a few hours.

Induction of Labor

An *induced labor* is one that is started artificially through chemical or physical stimulation. Induction is medically indicated when continuing the pregnancy would adversely affect either the woman or the baby. Indications can include preeclampsia, diabetes, postmaturity (forty-two weeks), Rh sensitization, prolonged rupture of the amniotic membranes with no onset of labor, intrauterine infection, low amniotic fluid volume, severe intrauterine fetal growth retardation (IUGR), and fetal death.

When the amniotic sac breaks prior to the initiation of labor contractions, it is known as a *premature rupture of the membranes (PROM)*. In many cases, the cause of PROM is unknown, but research indicates that it may be the result of an infection, such as group B strep. It is also more common in women carrying multiples, those with high blood pressure, and those who smoke. Whether or not a woman is induced after PROM depends on the week of gestation during which it occurs. When the amniotic sac breaks at term, most labors will naturally start within six to twelve hours. If it doesn't, most caregivers will want to induce labor to prevent possible infection. However, according to a number of studies, women can safely wait for labor to begin even after twenty-four hours of the membranes rupturing, provided that no vaginal exams are performed and they are monitored for infection.

If PROM occurs between twenty-four and thirty-three weeks gestation, the physician will have to weigh the risks of infection and prematurity. Typically, the woman is placed on bed rest and closely monitored for infection. The fetus is evaluated for lung maturity, and the woman is given steroids to promote fetal lung development. Labor can be induced if the fetus is mature enough for birth or the woman shows clinical signs of infection. Amnioinfusion, which provides additional fluid in the uterus, may be performed during labor if the fluid level is low.

Having a large or very large baby, called *macrosomia,* is not a medical reason for inducing labor. According to a 2002 press release from the American College of Obstetrics and Gynecologists, inducing labor for macrosomia almost doubled the cesarean rate without improving the outcome for the baby.[9] Also, ultrasound measurements are not always accurate and the estimated weight of the baby may be off by up to 10 percent.

Elective Induction

An elective induction is one that is scheduled according to the convenience of the hospital, doctor, or pregnant woman. Such planned labors allow hospital staffs to prepare

---

Note for the Labor Partner

Remember to continue your active coaching and support measures—even if the fetal monitor does not indicate that the contractions are very strong. Since the external contraction monitor is pressure sensitive, if the woman does not have a thick layer of fat between her uterus and the transducer, even a small contraction will cause a significant spike on the graph paper. On the other hand, if she has more "cushioning," or the transducer is not positioned at the top of the uterus, a strong contraction may appear as mild. If your partner says that her contractions are becoming more intense, believe her. She knows what she is talking about.

accordingly and enable doctors to arrange births when it best fits their schedule. Women can make plans to be induced when their favorite doctor is on call. It is also easier for them to plan childcare and work schedules if they know the day their babies will be born. Occasionally a woman with a history of fast labors or who lives far from the hospital may have an elective induction to ensure that the baby is born within the hospital. Be aware, however, that scheduled inductions frequently have to be changed. This means that a woman who has been scheduled for an early morning induction may find that it has been pushed back to later in the day, or even the following day. This is likely to cause her stress and fatigue as she waits.

Another growing reason for elective induction is "maternal exhaustion," which simply means the woman is tired of being pregnant. Most expectant mothers are ready and anxious to give birth during the last weeks of pregnancy, but there is no medical reason to be induced because of this. It is important to remember that natural labor begins when both the mother's body and the baby are ready. Researchers believe that when the baby is mature, her body releases a hormone that signals the mother's body to go into labor.

Deciding to be induced without a medical reason is a sign that the woman believes her body is not functioning normally and needs help. It is also important to remember that an induced labor is often more difficult than one that starts naturally. This increases the desire for an early epidural, which further undermines the woman's confidence

---

Scenario of an Induction for "Maternal Exhaustion"

Jennifer was tired of being pregnant. She was thirty-eight weeks with her third child and discovered that her favorite doctor was going to be leaving for a two-week vacation very soon. She decided that she wanted her labor to be induced before he left. It would also make it easier for her to plan for the care of her other children while she was in the hospital.

Jennifer entered the hospital for an induction of labor due to "maternal exhaustion." Shortly after she was admitted, an IV was started and attached to an infusion pump, an automatic blood pressure cuff was strapped to her arm, and a fetal monitor with two external belts was applied. A pulse oximetry device, which checked Jennifer's oxygen level, was attached to her finger.

Pitocin was injected into the IV fluid and caused Jennifer's contractions to begin. In no time, they became very strong, so she requested an epidural. Because the epidural caused her pelvic area to become numb, a catheter was inserted to drain her bladder. Even though she was having frequent, regular contractions, her progress was slow. After six hours, Jennifer developed a fever and antibiotics were initiated. To monitor the actual pressure caused by the Pitocin, an intrauterine pressure catheter was introduced into her uterus through her vagina. A decision was made to increase the Pitocin drip. Since the baby was active, the nurse was not receiving a continuous reading with the monitor's external lead, so an internal scalp electrode was applied to the baby's head. The reading indicated that the baby's heart rate was nonreassuring, so a fetal oxygen saturation device was introduced into the vagina.

Jennifer was given oxygen and the Pitocin was stopped. The baby continued to have a nonreassuring heart pattern, so a cesarean section was performed. Upon delivery, the newborn's breathing was rapid and she had a fever. She was taken to the neonatal intensive care unit where she was observed. Jennifer was not able to hold or breastfeed her baby immediately after the birth. The next day, when Jennifer was able to visit her new daughter, the nurse said to her, "Your baby is small for her gestational age, are you *sure* you were thirty-eight weeks pregnant?"

in her body's ability to give birth naturally. In a number of cases, cervical changes do not occur after induction. When this happens the woman may be sent home only to attempt the induction another day. Or the failed induction may lead to a cesarean section. Women who undergo elective inductions are more than twice as likely to have a cesarean delivery. If this is a woman's first baby, she is almost three times as likely to end up with a cesarean.[10]

Risks of Induction

Since the late 1980s, weekend births have declined with a corresponding increase during the week—the result of a growing of number of inductions. In addition, the number of cesareans due to failed inductions has also increased. Labor should never be induced simply for the sake of convenience because induction increases the risks to both the woman and the fetus. Studies have shown that there is no medical benefit to routinely inducing labor in women at forty to forty-one weeks. Furthermore, this practice "likely increases labor complications and operative delivery without significantly improving neonatal outcomes."[11] Waiting for the pregnancy to reach forty-two weeks will allow babies to be born when they are ready and reduce elective inductions and their risks.

Rather than waiting until after the due date, some physicians are inducing women for convenience at thirty-eight or thirty-nine weeks. If the due date is not exact, there is a possibility of a baby being born preterm. This increases the baby's risk of respiratory distress and other prematurity complications, such as difficulty with breastfeeding. It also means the baby will be separated from her mother and placed in a neonatal intensive care unit for observation and/or treatment.

The use of the labor-inducing medication Pitocin requires additional interventions. To administer this drug, an IV is required. The woman must also have continuous electronic fetal monitoring, which means she is likely to be confined to bed or have to remain close to the bed. Induced contractions tend to start out much stronger than natural contractions, which build up gradually during labor. They also occur more frequently, last longer, and often peak immediately rather than in the middle of the contraction. Induced contractions make labor much more difficult to manage and often result in the desire for pain medication. If your labor is induced, you must stay on top of the contractions from the very beginning or you may lose control. Because of their strength, you may need to use multiple comfort measures in addition to breathing techniques. Your partner is extremely important during this kind of labor. His encouragement and support are essential. He should keep an eye on the monitor to help prepare you for the start of each contraction. If a contraction lasts longer than two minutes, he must immediately alert the nursing staff. Because most induced women find it very hard to stay in control during contractions and avoid panicking, it is important for their labor partners to stay with them. If your partner must leave you to use the bathroom or to get something to eat, it is important that he ask a nurse to stand in for him while he is gone. His assistance in keeping you comfortable and relaxed will help you conserve the energy you need for giving birth.

During natural labor, the oxygen supply to the fetus decreases during each contraction. The long, intense contractions of an induced labor can deprive the fetus of even more oxygen and result in possible fetal distress and a cesarean birth. An over-

*"So what if I **am** post-term? It's nice and cozy in here!"*

dose of Pitocin can result in extremely long, hard *tetanic contractions,* which can cause premature separation of the placenta from the uterus. This can disrupt the oxygen supply to the fetus and lead to an emergency cesarean delivery if a vaginal birth cannot occur immediately. A possible catastrophic risk of tetanic contractions is uterine rupture, which can cause the woman to experience severe blood loss and undergo a possible hysterectomy if the bleeding cannot be controlled. The baby must also be delivered immediately by cesarean.

Other possible maternal side effects of induced labor include lowered blood pressure, rapid heart rate, anxiety, and swelling. The use of Pitocin is also associated with increased jaundice in the newborn.

It is important to remember that when the mother or the baby is at risk, a medical induction is necessary. But an elective induction for the sake of convenience can pose risks that are simply not worth taking.

Medically Induced Labor Methods

After you have passed your due date, there are a number of ways in which doctors or midwives can bring on labor. Some of these methods, which are presented in the following list, are effective in ripening or readying the cervix, while others can help bring on the labor itself. Keep in mind that if the cervix is not ready for labor, induction is less likely to be successful.

■ **Stripping the membranes.** During a vaginal exam, the doctor or midwife can "strip" the amniotic membranes from the uterus to help ripen the cervix or induce labor if the cervix is ready. She does this by inserting her fingers between the partially dilated cervix and the amniotic sac. This will irritate and loosen or strip the sac from the uterine wall, and cause a release of prostaglandins. Some women experience a burning or stinging sensation or even pain during this procedure. Unless labor is imminent, however, this procedure will not initiate true labor, although it may cause contractions for a time.

■ **Dilating the cervix.** Dilation of the cervix can be assisted through mechanical methods, which may also stimulate prostaglandin production. In one common procedure, an *indwelling Foley catheter*, which is normally used to empty the bladder, is inserted into the vagina and through the cervix. The balloon, which normally holds the catheter in the bladder, is then inflated and traction is applied to the internal opening of the cervix to assist in dilation. This device may be left in for more than twenty-four hours as long as the membranes are not ruptured. Once the cervical dilation reaches the size of the balloon, the catheter will fall out.

Another method for dilating the cervix involves the use of inserts called *laminaria tents.* Made from sterile seaweed or a synthetic material, laminaria tents are introduced into the cervical canal, where they gradually begin to swell when they come in contact with moisture. They can swell up to four times their original size. Anywhere from two to five laminaria tents can be inserted at one time. They are removed and replaced after twenty-four hours.

■ **Administering prostaglandins.** Prostaglandins, hormone-like fatty acids that are released naturally by the body, help to ripen the cervix and increase the success of an induced labor. Prostaglandin E_2 (PGE_2), a medicinal form of prostaglandin that is

Hints for the Labor Partner

If your partner is induced:

✓ Expect stronger contractions.

✓ Be an active coach.

✓ Prepare her for the next contraction by watching the fetal monitor and alerting her when it begins.

✓ Do not leave her alone.

available as a gel (Prepidil) or vaginal insert (Cervidil), can be applied either in or on the cervix to encourage ripening. Possible side effects of PGE$_2$ include nausea, vomiting, and diarrhea. It can also cause strong contractions. Women who haveglaucoma, asthma, liver problems, or kidney problems should not use PGE$_2$. Misoprostol, a synthetic form of PGE$_2$ is also available and can be used orally, rectally or vaginally. Although the FDA has not approved misoprostol for this purpose, it has become widely used due to its low cost and lower rate of failed inductions. It can, however, cause frequent, excessive contractions.

The baby's heart rate and uterine activity should be monitored continuously during and after the administration of prostaglandins. Pitocin is usually started within two to twenty-four hours after the discontinuation of prostaglandins if cervical ripening is successful. Prostaglandin administration is not recommended for women who have had uterine surgery, a previous cesarean, or more than three previous births.

A Hint for the Mother-to-Be

Labor should *not* be induced for your convenience or the convenience of your doctor.

■ **Rupturing the amniotic membranes.** *Amniotomy,* the artificial rupture of the membranes (AROM), is another physical method of inducing labor. A tear is made in the amniotic sac with an *amnihook,* a long hook-like instrument that is inserted through the vagina and the partially dilated cervix. The procedure is no more painful than a vaginal exam because the membranes do not contain any nerves, but it does present some risks. If the baby's head is not deep in the pelvis, the cord could slip below the baby's head—called *umbilical cord prolapse*—and cause a loss of oxygen if the weight of the baby's head compresses the cord. The result is fetal distress, which necessitates an emergency cesarean section.

Once her membranes are ruptured, the woman is committed to giving birth, usually within twenty-four hours. If labor does not begin within that time period, both the woman and her baby will face an increased likelihood of infection. For this reason, Pitocin may have to be given. If, however, Pitocin does not produce results within twenty-four hours, a cesarean delivery is usually performed. Studies have shown that starting Pitocin as soon as an amniotomy is performed will result in a shorter labor and less frequent use of forceps or the need for cesarean sections.[12]

■ **Administering Pitocin.** The most common method for inducing labor is the administration of Pitocin, a synthetic form of the hormone oxytocin. Pitocin should always be administered through an intravenous drip that is electronically monitored. Some doctors also use an intrauterine pressure catheter (IUPC) to determine contraction strength. An IUPC is also used to observe for overstimulation, which can result in less oxygen to the baby and, in rare cases, uterine rupture.

Pitocin is an antidiuretic, which means it may cause the woman to retain excess water and increase tissue swelling in her body. It causes some women to experience edema in the areolar tissue surrounding the nipples, making it difficult for the baby to latch on while breastfeeding. The increase in swelling may also affect the baby by causing an artificial increase in birth weight. When the baby loses some of this "water weight" after birth, it may cause concern if the loss is excessive (doctors tend to be concerned when there is a 10-percent loss). This may encourage supplementation among breastfeeding women. In addition, Pitocin given during labor may cause the baby to have *hyperbilirubinemia* (elevated levels of bilirubin), requiring treatment for jaundice.

Alternative Methods to Induce Labor

A pregnancy that is past the due date is the main reason most women want to get labor started. As previously stated, the most common method for inducing labor is the use of Pitocin in an IV drip. But many women want to avoid the more difficult contractions of a Pitocin-induced labor and may seek other ways to encourage the onset of labor. Since Pitocin requires a hospital labor and birth, midwives commonly suggest a variety of alternative methods for women who are having their baby in a birth center or at home. Women scheduled for induction in a hospital (for non-medical reasons), might also attempt to induce labor prior to their scheduled date, provided the pregnancy is at term. It is important to avoid trying any of the following labor-inducing methods prior to thirty-eight weeks gestation.

■ **Castor oil "cocktail."** Drinking one ounce of castor oil mixed in a small glass of orange or grapefruit juice is a popular method for self-inducing labor. Grapefruit juice is preferable because of its tartness, which helps mask the flavor of the castor oil. Before drinking, apply a thick layer of lipstick to your lips. Quickly stir the castor oil in the juice and then drink. Wipe off the lipstick, which is likely to contain residue from the oil. Follow with a fresh glass of plain juice.

Spleen 6 acupressure point.

■ **Sexual stimulation.** One of the more pleasurable methods for stimulating labor—provided the amniotic membranes have not ruptured—is to have sexual intercourse. Semen contains prostaglandins, which can help "ripen" the cervix and bring on contractions. Nipple stimulation (or any stimulation that causes orgasm) releases oxytocin, which can also cause uterine contractions. You or your partner can stimulate your nipples, or you can use a breast pump for fifteen to twenty minutes. (Pumping longer may cause soreness.) If this type of stimulation brings on contractions that last over a minute, or are more frequent than every five minutes, discontinue. Some caregivers prefer that the fetal heart rate be monitored during nipple stimulation to ensure that the baby is tolerating the contractions.

■ **Acupressure.** There are specific acupressure points that, when stimulated, can help encourage contractions. One is the Spleen 6 point, which is located approximately three to four finger widths (the woman's fingers) above the inner ankle bone (see photo at right). This spot will be tender upon pressure. Perform firm, circular pressure with your thumb or fingertip for up to a minute. Intermittently rest and repeat up to six times. Another spot that can encourage contractions is the Hoku acupressure point, located between the thumb and forefinger where the crease makes a "V" (see photo). Apply pressure in the same manner as with the Spleen 6 point. In addition to acupressure, some women visit licensed acupuncture physicians for stimulation of specific points with fine needles.

Hoku acupressure point.

■ **Herbal/homeopathic remedies.** Some midwives and practitioners may recommend herbal or homeopathic methods to induce labor. Herbs such as blue and black cohosh, red raspberry leaf, and evening primrose, as well as homeopathic remedies like caulophyllum and cimcifuga are commonly used to stimulate labor. Consider taking these methods *only* if prescribed by a caregiver who is knowledgeable regarding their use. Be aware that some preparations should not be taken by women with certain medical conditions such as high blood pressure. Follow instructions carefully.

■ **Bowel movement stimulation.** The intestinal cramping brought on by a bowel movement helps to stimulate prostaglandin production, which can encourage contractions. For this reason, taking a small enema can be helpful. You can also eat whatever foods tend to increase movement of your intestines and/or cause loose bowel movements. Some restaurants even claim that certain items on their menu will help encourage labor.

Although these methods may help initiate labor, if your baby is not ready to be born, there is no guarantee that any will work. They may, however, help to ripen the cervix in preparation for labor.

Augmentation of Labor

If your caregiver feels that your labor is not progressing normally, she may decide to augment it, which means "speed it up." The timetables used to determine "normal" labor are based on averages, and very few women are average. This means that before you agree to any kind of intervention to accelerate labor, ask for a little more time and try some non-invasive techniques, such as walking, changing positions, applying acupressure techniques, and stimulating your nipples to release natural oxytocin. If anyone in the room is causing you stress, ask that person to leave. Your labor partner should offer you hugs, caresses, encouraging words, and other loving signs of support.

If, however, natural measures do not seem to be helping speed up your labor, your caregiver may want to perform an amniotomy to rupture the amniotic membranes. Performing an amniotomy to augment labor carries the same risks that it does when used to induce labor. In addition, it removes the protective buffer of fluid between the baby's head and the cervix. As a result, babies who go through labor for an extended period of time with ruptured amniotic membranes experience more head molding and *caput succedaneum* (swelling of the soft tissues of the scalp), and possible *cephalhematoma* (a blood-filled lump or swelling on the scalp). These possible outcomes are not dangerous, although a caput succedaneum can take several days to subside, while a cephalhematoma may take months to reabsorb.

Contractions often increase in intensity and duration after an amniotomy. In addition, the labor may become increasingly uncomfortable and more difficult to control. A drop in the fetal heart rate is also associated with the procedure.

In addition to inducing or augmenting labor, an amniotomy may be performed if the baby appears to be in distress. It may be a necessary procedure if your caregiver needs to insert an internal fetal monitor or a fetal oxygen saturation monitor, or if he has to obtain a fetal blood sample to measure the pH of the infant's blood. She may also want to check for the presence of meconium (fetal bowel movement) in the amniotic fluid. Babies who are in distress may move their bowels, which will turn the fluid green.

If you have an amniotomy to speed up your labor but it is not effective, your caregiver may start a Pitocin IV drip to stimulate your uterus to produce more efficient contractions. Be prepared for stronger and more frequent contractions, the same as in an induced labor. You may need to begin using advanced breathing and relaxation techniques to stay on top of the contractions. The risks associated with the use of Pitocin are the same for augmentation of labor as they are for labor induction.

Active Management of Labor

Some physicians routinely practice *active management of labor* to ensure that it will be completed within twelve hours. The standard for this practice, which originated in Ireland, calls for the woman to be in active labor before it is initiated.

Once active labor is determined, the caregiver performs an amniotomy. If the woman does not progress 1 centimeter per hour, a high dose of Pitocin is started to augment labor. Another important component of this practice is the presence of a personal nurse who provides continuous emotional support for the laboring woman.

Currently, many physicians use this technique, but employ it before active labor begins. Also, few women are fortunate enough to have a nurse provide continuous support throughout labor. If your physician actively manages labor, you might consider hiring a doula for support. On the other hand, you may choose not to have your labor actively managed, but instead allow it to progress at its own pace.

INTERVENTIONS DURING BIRTH

Along with the various induction and augmentation methods already presented in this chapter, there are a number of other techniques and measures that may be used during the second stage of labor. Episiotomies and the use of extraction equipment (forceps and vacuum extractors) are usually unplanned options that are sometimes necessary to aid in giving birth.

Episiotomy

An *episiotomy* is a surgical incision made from the vagina toward the rectum to enlarge the vaginal outlet and assist the birth. The incision is usually midline (straight), but can also be mediolateral (angled to the side). Both types of incisions are shown in Figure 11.3 on page 258. Episiotomies are most often performed when the baby's head begins to stretch the perineum. At that time, the body produces a natural anesthesia, so the woman may not feel the incision. Most caregivers, however, give a local anesthetic prior to making the cut. This type of anesthetic is also necessary for the repair of the episiotomy following birth.

Caregivers perform an episiotomy to expedite birth in cases of fetal distress or during a prolonged second stage of labor if the woman is exhausted and her perineum is taut. Some doctors do them routinely because they feel that a straight incision is easier to repair and heals better than a jagged tear, which may result when the baby's head is born. Recent studies, however refute these sentiments. While women who deliver with intact perineums recover the fastest, those who have episiotomies take just about the same time to heal as women with spontaneous tears.[13] Also, some doctors feel that an episiotomy may prevent tearing, but once a cut is made, the incision is more likely to tear further. In addition, if an episiotomy is not performed and tearing occurs, the tearing may be superficial in nature, whereas an episiotomy cuts into muscle and is more likely to extend into the rectum. Episiotomy risks include infection, bruising, swelling, bleeding, and urinary or fecal incontinence. For these reasons, the American College of Obstetricians and Gynecologists does not recommend episiotomies in uncomplicated deliveries. Since the 1990s, their incidence has decreased dramatically.

Another reason doctors give for performing episiotomies is to prevent the woman from experiencing loss of vaginal tone and control, which could result in prolapsed organs and a decrease in sexual pleasure for both partners. This reasoning, however, is questionable because there is no evidence that episiotomies, which are not performed until the perineum is already stretched, prevent these problems. Practicing Kegel exercises during pregnancy and following birth strengthens the vaginal muscles and eliminates these problems naturally.

Women who have episiotomies are more likely to experience pain during intercourse and wait longer to resume sex after giving birth.[14] Some caregivers overstitch the repair to "tighten up" the vaginal opening. If overstitching, also called the *honeymoon stitch,* is done too tightly, it can result in painful intercourse in the future.

You can decrease your chances of having an episiotomy in several ways. Most important, tell your caregiver that you do not desire to have one. Performing perineal massage (see page 131) beginning around the thirty-fourth week of pregnancy may also help. Many caregivers feel that perineal massage not only stretches the tissues, but also prepares a woman emotionally for some of the physical sensations of birth. While pushing during the second stage, some caregivers perform perineal massage and apply hot compresses to stretch the tissues. Listen to your caregiver's directions and push gently to allow the baby to slowly stretch the birth canal. Also avoid the lithotomy position (lying flat on your back) while pushing. With your legs apart and your feet in stirrups, your perineum will be taut and more likely to tear.

If you have an episiotomy, expect to experience soreness and itching in the area as it heals, which may take several weeks. To alleviate some of the discomfort, sit on pillows or air rings, take warm-water sitz baths, and apply anesthetic pads, creams, and/or sprays to the area.

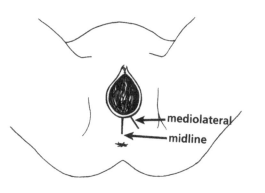

Figure 11.3. The two types of episiotomy incisions are midline and mediolateral.

Rotation and Extraction Methods

Forceps and the vacuum extractor are two obstetrical tools that are used to rotate a baby to a more advantageous position for birth and to help her move down the birth canal. They are used when the baby's head resists rotating from a posterior or transverse position, when a woman's pushing ability is diminished because of epidural anesthesia or fatigue, or when the baby is in fetal distress. Before using either of these instruments, many doctors administer a regional anesthetic and/or perform an episiotomy. The risks involved with these tools are contingent upon the skill and judgment of the person using them.

Forceps

Forceps are large, curved metal tongs. They consist of two blades that are inserted into the vagina and placed on either side of the baby's head. The blades are then locked into place and used to manipulate or extract the baby. If birth is imminent, forceps can be an alternative to cesarean section.

There are four types of forceps procedures—high, mid, low, and outlet. Their use is dependent on where the baby's head is engaged in the pelvis. The *high forceps* procedure, in which the forceps are applied before the baby's head is engaged in the pelvis, is very dangerous and no longer used. It has been replaced by cesarean delivery, which is safer for both the woman and the baby. In a *midforceps* application, the forceps are used when the baby's head is at zero to above +2 station. (Explanation of pelvic stations appears on page 191.) It presents some risk to both the maternal tissue and the baby, and should be performed only by an experienced doctor. A *low forceps* procedure is used when the head is felt at +2 or more station, and it is not rotated more than 45 degrees past the midline. The use of *outlet forceps* is the most common and carries the least risk to the woman and baby. The forceps are applied when the baby's scalp is visible between contractions, and used to aid in the final expulsion.

Maternal complications due to the use of forceps can include increased blood loss, hematoma, extension of an episiotomy, rupture of the uterus, and lacerations of the cervix, vagina, perineum, or bladder. Injury to the pelvic support tissues and organs may also occur, resulting in possible loss of bladder control, fecal incontinence, damage to the anal sphincter, and pelvic organ prolapse.

Forceps can also bruise or lacerate a baby's soft head and facial tissue. Damage to cranial nerves may affect the baby's ability to breastfeed.[15] Other possible complications may include cephalhematoma, facial nerve injuries, skull fractures, and intracranial hemorrhage.

Vacuum Extractor

A *vacuum extractor* is a cap-like device that is attached to the baby's head using suction. The suction cup fits over the top portion of the baby's head and helps ease the infant out through the contours of the birth canal. The doctor is able to adjust the amount of suction. As a safety feature, if too much tension is applied, the suction releases automatically from the baby's head. After twenty minutes, three attempts, or lack of any progress down the birth canal, this procedure should be abandoned.

The use of a vacuum extractor could result in caput succedaneum, a cephalhematoma, or lacerations or abrasions to the baby's scalp. Hemorrhages within the brain or retina are other possible results. A very serious possible complication caused by a vacuum extractor is a *subgaleal hemorrhage* in which there is significant bleeding in a potential space between the bones of the head and the scalp. This can result in major blood loss and even death of the newborn. Babies with a subgaleal hemorrhage are pale and have rapid heart rates. They also have a head circumference that becomes larger, gradually increasing over the first seventy-two hours after birth. In response to this risk, the US Food and Drug Administration published a public health advisory warning doctors to use caution when using the vacuum extractor and to alert the nursing staff to monitor the infant for "signs and symptoms of device-related injuries."[16] Long-term prognosis is generally good for these infants.

For the woman, there are a few advantages of using a vacuum extractor over forceps. It causes fewer traumas to the bladder and vaginal tissues, and has a lowered risk of extending an episiotomy. Unlike forceps, the use of anesthesia is not always necessary with the vacuum extractor. In rare cases, the vacuum extractor can be applied before the cervix is completely dilated to avoid a cesarean section if fetal distress indicates the need for immediate delivery.

Postpartum Hemorrhage

After giving birth, if bleeding is excessive (about two cups), the woman is experiencing a *postpartum hemorrhage*. The most common reason for this is *uterine atony,* which means the uterus is not contracting firmly. To stimulate uterine contractions and stop the blood flow, the caregiver will firmly massage the uterus and, if necessary, administer Pitocin or Methergine, which is often used to stop hemorrhage. Some caregivers routinely administer Pitocin to the woman after she gives birth, while others use this medication only as needed. To help encourage contractions through the release of her own natural oxytocin, the woman can stimulate her nipples either by massaging them or by breastfeeding the baby.

Excessive bleeding can also be caused by internal lacerations in the cervix or vaginal walls, or from an episiotomy or perineal tear. The doctor or midwife will suture the tissues to control and stop the bleeding. Packing the vagina with sterile gauze may also be necessary.

Another cause of postpartum hemorrhage is *retained placental tissue* in which parts of the placenta remain in the uterus after delivery. If this occurs, the uterus will not contract firmly and the vessels at the insertion site will continue to bleed. If Pitocin and massage are not effective in stimulating contractions and expelling the retained placenta, the caregiver may need to manually extract the remaining placenta. If this is not successful, surgery that involves scraping the uterine walls may be necessary. In rare cases, the placenta attaches too deeply and does not detach. This is known as *placenta accreta* and may require a hysterectomy to stop the bleeding.

UNEXPECTED OUTCOMES

This chapter has presented variations in the usual progression of labor and the possible medical interventions that could result. The next chapter discusses cesarean birth. If you are like most expectant parents, you are probably saying, "These situations don't apply to me." But the reality is that every labor and birth is unpredictable, and yours may not be the "ideal" experience you have been hoping for. It is important that while you are designing your birth plan, you consider all the possibilities and try to conclude how you would respond if confronted with an unexpected outcome.

Any variation from your birth plan is considered an unexpected outcome. A labor that goes faster or easier than you had planned is also considered unexpected, although this type of experience elicits positive feelings for most women. On the other hand, when the unplanned outcome is upsetting, you may require help in dealing with your feelings.

An unexpected outcome may be a cesarean delivery when you had planned on having a vaginal birth. It could also be accepting an epidural when you wanted an unmedicated birth. Occasionally, women feel as if they were told one thing by their caregiver before labor, but were then treated differently or without regard to their desires once admitted to the hospital. They may have felt rushed or pushed into accepting procedures they did not want. Women who plan to deliver at a birth center and then require a transfer to a hospital often have to deal with their own feelings when faced with the questions and comments from family and friends. An unexpected outcome could also be baby-related. The newborn may be premature, require treatment in the intensive care nursery, or have a physical problem.

When things do not go as planned, at the very least, you can expect to have feelings of disappointment. Get adequate rest and try not to be Superwoman to compensate. Guilt and anger are also common emotions at this time. These feelings are normal and should not be minimized. It is important for you and your partner to share these thoughts. If they persist, attending a new parents' support group may prove helpful.

Get a copy of your medical record, which may give you additional information on the course of your labor. It may also provide you with the knowledge to avoid repeating this experience with a subsequent pregnancy. For instance, you may want to avoid certain interventions next time, or change caregivers or place of delivery. And you should eventually come to the realization that, while you may have influence, you cannot control all the circumstances during labor.

The most upsetting unexpected outcome is the stillbirth or death of a baby, either before, at, or shortly after birth. Nothing can prepare you for dealing with this type of devastating event. It is very important that you express your feelings of grief and be allowed to mourn the loss of your child.

The following suggestions are from parents who have experienced such a loss. They may help other parents cope with a similar experience.

■ Give your baby a name. It affirms that you are a parent and that there was a life lost for which you are grieving.

■ Hold and touch your baby. If she has been wrapped in a blanket, remove it so you can get a full image of her. Count her fingers and toes. The baby's grandparents or siblings may also want to see and hold her. This will enable all of you to say hello and good-bye, and to acknowledge that you really did have a baby.

■ You may want to get a lock of the baby's hair, and have handprints and footprints made.

■ Have a photo taken of your baby, even if she has a physical abnormality. If you are not sure that you want the picture, have a friend or relative keep the photo until you ask for it.

■ You may want to hold a memorial service for the baby with family and close friends. This will affirm that the child was born into the family; it also allows others to share in your sorrow and grief.

It goes without saying that you will mourn the loss of your child. It is very important that you and your partner share your grief openly with each other. Women tend to grieve more intensely and longer than men. This is understandable because they are the ones who carried the baby and began the bonding process long before the birth.

As you go through the grieving process, expect to experience a number of emotions. Initially, you may be in a state of shock, which is one of nature's coping mechanisms. This is often followed by denial. Feelings of anxiety and/or depression, as well as anger, are very common and can be felt for some time after the death. Feeling guilty and blaming yourself (or others) for causing the baby's death is also normal. Experiencing some jealousy when you see babies and pregnant women is not unusual—some women have difficulty attending baby showers or being around pregnant friends. A future pregnancy may also revive these feelings of sadness and vulnerability. While the people around you may assume that you are happy about being pregnant, you may, in fact, have mixed feelings. It is not unusual for women who have lost a child, either through miscarriage in early pregnancy or a loss in late pregnancy, to experience recurring periods of grief.

Obviously, grieving takes time. For some women, it can take many months or even years to reach a point of acceptance that allows them to move forward with their lives. The more open you can be about your feelings, the quicker you will heal. Let others know that it is okay to talk about the baby. You may also find it helpful to join a support group for bereaved families such as Compassionate Friends or First Candle/SIDS Alliance. (For contact information, see the Resources beginning on page 449.) Professional counseling or talking to a member of the clergy can also be beneficial. Some families choose to preserve the memory of their baby by donating to a favorite charity or having a tree planted in her name. Some excellent books on the subject of bereavement include *Empty Arms* by Sherokee Ilse, *When Pregnancy Isn't Perfect* by Laurie A. Rich, and *Silent Sorrow* by Ingrid Kohn, Perry-Lynn Moffitt, and Isabelle A. Wilkins.

CONCLUSION

If you happen to experience a labor that varies from the norm or requires some type of intervention, it does not mean that you have failed. Giving birth is not a performance, and the only real goal is a healthy baby. If you know that you did the best you could, accept the fact that certain circumstances were out of your control. Be grateful for the technology and the medical advancements that made available the necessary procedures or interventions that assisted you in giving birth to your baby.

Cesarean Birth
or I Wish I Had a Zipper

A cesarean birth is one in which the baby is delivered through incisions in the abdominal wall and uterus, instead of through the vagina. The medical term for this type of birth is *cesarean section,* which is often shortened to *c-section.* Currently, one in three women will give birth by cesarean section—either planned or unplanned. It is important to be aware of the procedures and options for this type of surgical delivery, the factors that increase your chances of having one, as well as the ways to avoid giving birth this way unnecessarily.

Julius Caesar is usually credited as the first baby delivered by cesarean section and for having the procedure named after him. Actually, it is unlikely that he was delivered this way, since during his time, a baby was delivered surgically only if the mother had died—and documents indicate that Caesar's mother was alive for many years following his birth. It is more likely that the term comes from the Latin word *caedere,* which means, "to cut." Hundreds of years before Caesar, the Roman law *lex caesarea* stated that a dying woman who was pregnant should be operated on to save the infant.

The first successful cesarean (meaning that the woman survived) was recorded in 1500. In 1882, Dr. Max Sanger was the first doctor to suture the uterus closed after this procedure instead of removing it, which had been the previous practice. Over the years, advances in anesthesia, antibiotics, surgical techniques, and pain medication have increased the safety of the procedure tremendously.

Since many cesarean births are not planned, it is important to read this chapter carefully to become familiar with the standard surgical procedure (and possible options) in case you need it. Most childbirth preparation classes cover cesarean delivery, but they don't always include ways to decrease your chances of having one. If your cesarean is planned, check with your local hospitals—many offer special classes on this type of delivery. These classes may also provide specialized instruction on exercises and postpartum care, as well as breastfeeding hints geared to the cesarean mother. Although a cesarean section is considered major abdominal surgery, proper preparation can make it a satisfying birth experience for the entire family.

FAMILY-CENTERED CESAREAN BIRTH

A cesarean section is more than an operation. It is the birth of a baby. The way a father and mother feel about their childbirth experience may affect their ability to bond with their newborn. Seeing, touching, and comforting the baby immediately after birth begins the bonding process that is so important for the fostering of maternal and paternal feelings. Therefore, many cesarean couples want to share in the miracle of birth just as they would for a vaginal delivery.

In addition to witnessing the birth, many fathers want to comfort and support their partners during the procedure. Most hospitals permit labor partners to attend cesarean deliveries as long as regional anesthetics are used. However, if general anesthesia is necessary, couples need prior permission from the obstetrician and anesthesiologist. Some doctors feel that the labor partner does not need to be present when general anesthesia is used because the woman is asleep and unaware of any emotional support. They also fear that her unconscious appearance may be upsetting to the labor partner. If you would like your labor partner to be present while you are under general anesthesia, talk to your doctor. If, however, a true emergency exists, this option may not be available. Also, if more than one support person is present during labor, only one may be allowed to attend the cesarean because of space limitations.

A cesarean couple needs to find a pediatrician who is flexible and open to their desires. They should discuss their wishes to touch, hold, and breastfeed their newborn as soon as possible, even in the delivery room or recovery room, provided the baby's condition is good. Of course, if complications arise and the baby needs special care, even the most flexible pediatrician will delay bonding and breastfeeding.

Some facilities will allow the baby to remain in the operating room with his mother and then move with her to the recovery room. Others may have the baby taken to the nursery after a brief introduction to his mother. Later on, he will be reunited with her in the recovery room or postpartum room. As long as the baby is stable, you can request that he be brought to you as soon as possible.

During the birth of a baby, whether vaginally or by cesarean, a couple needs each other's emotional support. Some couples experience a poignant climax at the moment of birth—a feeling that should be shared. During a cesarean delivery, your partner can hold your hand, wipe your forehead, and talk to you. His emotional support can be invaluable in encouraging you to maintain a positive attitude, which can help you relax and recover faster. Many fathers like to take photographs or videos during and after the cesarean delivery. Ask about your hospital's policy on filming in the operating room. Your partner may also be able to take his equipment into the nursery to film the baby's admission procedures. This is a good opportunity to have him record the events that you are unable to view. Couples who are not allowed to share in a cesarean birth may end up sharing feelings of disappointment and even resentment. For these couples, it is even more important to bond with their baby as soon as possible and share their feelings with one another.

One option that should not be affected by the method of delivery is rooming-in. With help from her labor partner, a cesarean mother can enjoy all the benefits of having her baby stay in the same room with her. If she is in a private room, her partner can usually have unlimited visitation and provide the needed assistance, day and night. For the first twenty-four hours, if the partner is unable to remain with the woman, a nurse can take the baby to the nursery when the mother is sleeping and then bring him to the mother to breastfeed.

If there is a possibility that you will be delivering by cesarean, you need to participate actively with your doctor, anesthesiologist, and pediatrician in planning the birth. Your partner should join you for several of your doctor's appointments. Together you should talk with him about the surgery, anesthesia, and postpartum period to make sure he knows your desires. Do not take anything for granted or you may be disappointed. Your requests, of course, must be reasonable because a cesarean section is major surgery and involves risks to both you and your baby. However, having a doctor who strongly believes in the benefits of family-centered maternity care will increase your chances of having the type of birth you desire.

Another good source of help is your local cesarean support group. The members of such a group can give you additional emotional encouragement after your birth. Many cesarean mothers find it helpful to talk to someone else who has had the procedure and who can relate to what she is going through. If you are unable to find a local support group, the International Cesarean Awareness Network (ICAN) can provide resources for local members and online support groups. (For contact information, see the Resources beginning on page 449.)

MEDICAL INDICATIONS FOR CESAREAN BIRTH

Cesarean deliveries are performed for many reasons. Because opinions concerning these reasons vary, you might want to get a second opinion if, during your pregnancy, you are told that you will be needing a c-section.

Many cesareans in the United States are performed because of previous cesarean births. In the 1990s, increasing numbers of women attempted a vaginal birth after a cesarean (VBAC). However, that trend changed when the American College of Obstetricians and Gynecologists recommended that women who desire a VBAC should deliver in the hospital, where an emergency cesarean section could be performed if necessary. Many out-of-hospital birth centers and hospitals that did not have access to twenty-four hour in-house anesthesia and obstetric coverage (and, therefore, unable to perform immediate c-sections) were no longer comfortable doing VBAC deliveries. Today, the practice of VBAC is often discouraged. If a woman desires to have one, she may have to search for a physician and hospital that are willing to provide that option. (See "Vaginal Birth After Cesarean" on page 267.)

During labor, *failure to progress* is the most common indication for performing a cesarean. It means that the labor is not moving ahead normally. In some cases, the baby's head is not rotating correctly through the woman's pelvis and has become wedged. Other cases involve prolonged labor with no change in cervical dilation or station of the baby, an extended period of time since the rupture of the membranes, or weak and ineffective uterine contractions.

Nonreassuring heart-rate tracings on the electronic fetal monitor may indicate that the baby is exhibiting signs of distress, and this may result in a cesarean delivery. In some of these cases, the babies show no evidence of distress once they are delivered. (Distress can be confirmed by testing the pH of the fetal blood, although this is not always done.) Meconium-stained amniotic fluid, which is greenish in color, may also be associated with fetal distress. Fetal intolerance of labor, a condition in which the baby is not actually in distress, may be exhibited by questionable heart-rate patterns as well. If the woman is not close to delivering, the doctor may decide to perform a cesarean rather than wait and see if the fetus is in actual distress. (Most obstetricians prefer to err on the side of caution, as a negative outcome could result in a lawsuit.) If the amount of amniotic fluid is too low, the umbilical cord could become compressed during contractions and cause nonreassuring fetal heart-rate patterns. The volume of amniotic fluid may be increased through *amniofusion*—a procedure through which saline solution is infused into the uterus. This may be a way of allowing labor to continue when a cesarean would otherwise be necessary.

If the baby is in an abnormal presentation within the uterus, a cesarean may be indicated. For the baby who is lying sideways in the uterus in a transverse lie, a vaginal delivery is impossible. A baby in a breech presentation, in which his buttocks or feet present first, may be delivered either vaginally or by cesarean section, depending on several factors. If the doctor is experienced in delivering breech babies, he may more readily agree to a vaginal birth. He will need to make sure that the size of the woman's pelvis is adequate and the baby is not too large. He will also need to determine the type of breech presentation, including the position of the baby's head, and confirm that the labor is progressing normally. Many newer doctors are not trained in the vaginal delivery of breech babies. Others feel that the additional risks involved do not warrant the attempt, so they deliver all breech babies by cesarean. With both transverse lies and breech presentations, the physician may perform an *external version*—an attempt to turn the baby from outside the abdomen into a head-down position. He may do this prior to or even during labor.

In cases of *placental abruption,* the placenta separates from the uterine wall (either partially or completely) before the baby is born. This is considered an emergency situation as it may cause the woman to hemorrhage and baby's oxygen supply to become compromised. In such cases, a cesarean is performed immediately. Placental abruption is a rare condition in normal healthy women.

A *prolapsed cord* occurs when the umbilical cord protrudes into the vagina ahead of the baby, as seen in Figure 12.1 at left. This happens after the amniotic membranes rupture and the baby is either in a breech presentation or his head is not well engaged in the pelvis. As the presenting part compresses the cord, the baby's oxygen supply becomes cut off. While you are still at home, if you feel the umbilical cord in your vagina, or you see it protruding from the vagina, immediately get down on your hands and knees, and position your hips higher than your head to relieve the pressure on the cord. Call 911 and *remain in the knee-chest position* until help arrives. If the cord is protruding from your vagina, cover it with a wet cloth to keep it moist. However, do this only if you can accomplish it without leaving the knee-chest position. When you arrive at the hospital, your doctor will perform an immediate cesarean.

Placenta previa is a condition in which the placenta partially or completely covers the cervix. A cesarean is performed because excessive bleeding can occur as the cervix dilates. This condition is usually identified prior to labor through an ultrasound.

When preeclampsia—a condition resulting from hypertension—is present, the woman may have a stroke, experience kidney failure, or progress to *eclampsia,* which is characterized by seizures. The treatment for this condition is delivery. Preeclampsia affects the welfare of the fetus as well as that of the woman, thereby necessitating delivery, either by induction or cesarean.

If the woman is diabetic, early delivery may be necessary for the baby's sake. Her placental blood flow may be poor, the baby may be excessively large, or he may respond poorly to the stress of labor. If induction is unsuccessful, a cesarean will be needed.

When an Rh-negative woman has been sensitized by Rh-positive blood, her baby may develop *erythroblastosis fetalis.* During the pregnancy, antibodies may pass through the placenta and attack the baby's Rh-positive blood cells, leading to anemia and other problems that necessitate an early induced labor. If unsuccessful, a cesarean will be performed. With the advent of Rh-immune globulin (RhoGAM), erythroblastosis fetalis is now rare, but may still occur.

A woman who has an active herpes simplex virus (HSV) infection on her vulva and/or vagina at the time of birth needs a cesarean section to prevent the baby from becoming infected. HSV can be transmitted to the baby if he comes in contact with an active lesion or even if the membranes have ruptured. Antiviral medications can be given to both the mother and baby, but the mortality rate for infected infants is high. Even after treatment, 25 percent of babies infected with the virus during birth will not survive. If untreated, 65 percent will not survive.[1]

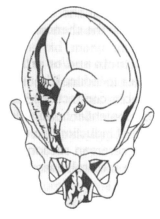

Figure 12.1. Prolapsed cord.

Knee-chest position.

Vaginal Birth After Cesarean

During the 1980s and 1990s, women who had a cesarean section were encouraged to have a *vaginal birth after cesarean* or *VBAC* (pronounced *VEE back*) with subsequent pregnancies. Studies over those two decades showed that 70 percent of women had successful VBACs. But the climate changed when the American College of Obstetricians and Gynecologists (ACOG) recommended that VBACs take place only in hospitals or birth centers where an emergency cesarean could be performed if necessary. This meant that the facility had to have an available obstetrician throughout active labor, as well as anesthesia and a surgical team available twenty-four hours a day. As a result, many smaller hospitals and birth centers were no longer comfortable in practicing VBACs.

Since 2004, many hospitals and doctors have instituted a no-VBAC policy. This has made it increasingly difficult for women who desire a vaginal birth to find a caregiver who is willing to allow them to labor. As a result, the cesarean rate has skyrocketed while the number of VBACs has fallen dramatically.

The reasons cited for this change in hospital policy include legal liability and concern that the previous scar on the uterus from the c-section will rupture. This possibility of rupture, however, is very slight if the woman has had only one cesarean, and her uterine incision was transverse and made in the lower segment. The risk of a woman needing an emergency cesarean section during a VBAC for uterine rupture is thirty times lower than a woman needing an emergency cesarean section for any other unpredictable childbirth emergency, such as acute fetal distress, prolapsed umbilical cord, or excessive bleeding in labor.[2] What *does* increase the chance of uterine rupture are closely spaced pregnancies and induction with a prostaglandin.

Waiting for spontaneous labor after forty weeks gestation also decreases the success of a VBAC, but it does not cause an increase in uterine rupture. If a woman has had a vaginal birth prior to her cesarean, she is also a candidate for VBAC after two cesarean sections, as well as if she is carrying a very large baby.[3]

Many women and healthcare professionals are greatly disturbed by this trend as forced cesareans increase the risk to both mother and baby. This is true for current and all subsequent cesareans. It also limits a woman's choices in her method of giving birth and the number of children she desires. (See "Risks of Cesarean Birth" on page 270.)

In some communities, women are able to locate doctors who are willing to let them have a VBAC, but in many areas, there is no choice. Because of this, some women have resorted to drastic measures to avoid forced cesareans. There have been reported cases of women in labor who have refused to sign a surgical consent form for the cesarean section. Some women have chosen to have unattended home births.

In 2005, the American Academy of Family Physicians issued a report that states, "Women with one previous cesarean delivery with a low transverse incision are candidates for and should be offered a trial of labor."[4] According to *A Guide to Effective Care in Pregnancy and Childbirth,* any obstetrical department that is prepared to deal with emergencies such as placenta previa, placental abruption, prolapsed umbilical cord, or acute fetal distress can safely care for women choosing a VBAC after a low-segment uterine incision.[5]

Women planning a VBAC require strong emotional and physical support, since they may have to deal with negative comments from family and friends, as well as professionals. Cesarean births have become commonplace and women are expected to be happy about their experience, no matter how the baby is delivered. But many women experience feelings of failure and depression after a cesarean. Their feelings of inadequacy are even greater when they believe the surgery was unnecessary. After having a VBAC, many women report that they felt "complete," even if they had accepted that the previous cesarean was justified.

If you would like more information about VBAC, *What Every Pregnant Woman Needs to Know About Cesarean Section*—a free booklet by the Childbirth Connection—is a helpful source. Contact information for this association, as well as the International Cesarean Awareness Network, which also provides helpful information and current research, is found in the Resources beginning on page 449.

Women carrying twins may attempt a vaginal delivery if the first baby is head down. Occasionally, the second baby is delivered by cesarean if he does not move into a favorable position or shows signs of trouble. Many physicians recommend performing a cesarean delivery for all cases of multiples. Triplets (or greater multiples) are an indication for a cesarean.

Some doctors schedule a cesarean if they feel that the baby's size is excessive. They are concerned that the shoulders might become stuck, which can be a serious complication. Since the methods of determining a baby's size are inaccurate, many doctors observe the woman's progress during labor and while pushing to determine whether a cesarean is necessary.

ELECTIVE CESAREANS

Elective cesareans, also called "patient-choice" cesareans, are those surgeries that are performed without a medical indication. Over the past few years, an increasing number of women are requesting cesarean deliveries rather than going into labor. While some are choosing this option for their second or later child, many are requesting it for their first. Fear of labor is one of their most common reasons. Most express a fear of the pain and an inability to cope with contractions. Others are afraid of the complications that might occur during labor or birth. A number of women who previously experienced a difficult labor and/or birth want a surgical birth rather than repeat the experience.

While a fear of labor pain is common among pregnant women, there are many tools available to reduce it. Taking childbirth classes and practicing relaxation, breathing, and other pain-reducing techniques can break the fear-tension-pain cycle. Education along with coping skills empowers a woman to trust in her body's ability to give birth the way nature intended. If a woman experiences uncontrollable pain in labor, she has the option of receiving an epidural, which can provide almost complete pain relief. Many women, however, are surprised at their inner strength and ability to deal with the work of labor. Being prepared also gives them the confidence to cope with any unexpected events and makes them aware that certain choices can positively or negatively affect the process of labor and birth. Extreme fear of childbirth should be explored with a counselor who is experienced in this matter.

Another reason some women choose to have a cesarean is their concern that delivering a baby vaginally will injure the pelvic floor and lead to urinary or fecal incontinence (the leaking of urine, gas, or feces). Recent studies do not support this belief. Incontinence is more closely related to family history,[6] smoking, and excess weight.[7] While a number of women may have bladder or bowel incontinence for a period of time after a vaginal birth, it is usually short term. It is also closely related to birth practices, such as episiotomy, giving birth while lying on the back, the use of forceps or a vacuum extractor, forceful bearing-down efforts, fundal pressure by a nurse or doctor, or pressure against the vaginal opening during the baby's birth.[8]

Some women are concerned about vaginal stretching and a possible decrease in sexual pleasure for both partners. Others are also worried that after watching the baby stretch the vaginal outlet during birth, their partners will feel a decrease in sexual desire for them. All women can strengthen and maintain pelvic muscle tone by performing Kegels daily. The body has a remarkable ability to bounce back after childbirth.

A number of women choose to have their babies by cesarean simply for the sake of convenience. As they have become more common, cesarean births are viewed as safe and "just another way to have a baby." Scheduled cesareans take the guesswork out of when the baby will come and who will deliver the child. The American College of Obstetricians and Gynecologists does not agree, and has released a statement that cesarean section "should not be selected over a natural process without immediate and compelling medical need."[9]

Benefits of Vaginal Birth

For the full-term healthy baby, the stress of labor and the journey down the birth canal help prepare him for survival outside the womb. During normal labor, contractions decrease the amount of oxygen that is delivered to the baby. This causes his adrenal glands to secrete stress hormones called *catecholamines*—primarily adrenaline (epinephrine) and noradrenalin (norepinephrine). Catecholamines protect the baby during these regular periods of decreased oxygen by helping him conserve his energy and oxygen, and by preserving blood flow to the brain and heart.[10] They also "increase blood sugar and mobilize free fatty acids and carbohydrates for energy and heat production."[11] This is very important in the immediate newborn period as the baby begins maintaining his blood glucose levels and self-regulating his body temperature.

During the birth process, the baby is squeezed during his descent down the birth canal. This compresses his chest and the amniotic fluid is expelled from his lungs. High levels of catecholamines aid in the reabsorption of fluid in the baby's lungs. They also encourage the release of *surfactant*, a substance that assists oxygen exchange within the lungs.[12]

Babies who are born by planned or elective cesarean do not have the benefit of this catecholamine surge. But babies who are born by cesarean after several hours of labor do have a higher level of hormones and benefit from their effects. They are also less likely to experience respiratory distress syndrome after birth. A planned cesarean birth would be more beneficial to the baby if the woman went into labor spontaneously, rather than through a scheduled surgery.

During the first couple of hours after a vaginal birth, catecholamines stimulate the newborn's central nervous system, putting him in a quiet alert state, ready to interact with his parents. Labor pain also stimulates the release of endorphins, the body's natural pain relievers. This may provide the baby with analgesic effects during birth. Endorphins are also present in colostrum and mother's milk. The levels are considerably lower in women who have a cesarean section.[13]

Another benefit of being born vaginally is that the baby is colonized with the mother's bacteria. When a baby is in utero, he is sterile. Immediately after entering the world, he is introduced to bacteria that are present in the environment. Ideally, he is first exposed through his mother—he comes in contact with the vaginal and rectal bacteria during birth, and then to the skin flora as he is placed against his mother's bare chest. A baby born by cesarean does not receive this benefit, as he is handled by a number of people before being touched by his mother. In addition, early and exclusive breastfeeding introduces the ideal type of bacteria into the intestinal tract, along with a high level of immunity factors. Skin-to-skin contact also triggers the mother to develop antibodies against any bacteria to which her infant is exposed. These antibodies are then transferred to the baby through breastfeeding. Babies born by cesarean need early skin-to-skin contact to establish this important connection and initiate breastfeeding.

CONTRIBUTORS TO THE HIGH CESAREAN RATE

The cesarean birth rate in the United States skyrocketed from 4.5 percent in 1965 to its highest current level of about one in three. Some caregivers deliver 50 percent of their patients by c-section. There are a number of contributing factors to this high rate.

As mentioned earlier in this chapter, over the past several years, doctors have been less willing or are refusing to allow women to attempt a vaginal birth after cesarean. As these rates have dramatically declined, the practice of "once a cesarean, always a cesarean" is now being imposed again. Elective cesarean sections or patient-request cesareans are becoming more common as women's awareness of this option is growing. These surgeries are performed with no medical indication and are considered by many consumers as a safe alternative to a vaginal birth.

Many other factors contribute to the high cesarean rate. Some doctors fear the threat of a malpractice suit if a cesarean is not done and a "less than perfect" baby results. At least 79 percent of obstetricians have been sued at least once. About 80 percent of those lawsuits involve a claim that a cesarean was not done or was not done soon enough.[14] Doctors are also concerned that if a woman demands an elective cesarean and the doctor refuses to perform the surgery—even though it is unnecessary—he increases his liability.

The training that obstetricians receive is also changing. Because of the risks involved in the use of forceps, doctors now receive less training in using this tool to manage difficult deliveries. High-forceps deliveries have been completely replaced by cesarean sections, and some doctors now also substitute surgical intervention for the difficult midforceps delivery. The majority of breech babies are delivered by cesarean section to reduce the risks to the baby. While some caregivers will attempt to rotate a breech baby into a head-down position, which would allow the woman to labor and give birth vaginally, some physicians simply schedule surgery instead.

Obstetrical training primarily involves handling complications. As a result, many doctors treat all laboring women as potentially high-risk and rely on medical interventions such as electronic fetal monitors, routine inductions, IVs, and epidurals. Few women are encouraged to be upright and walk while in labor or to eat and drink during this time.

The increase in women over thirty years of age giving birth is another factor for the high cesarean rate. These women are at an increased risk for complications, and physicians are often more likely to quickly perform cesareans if they perceive that an adverse outcome may result. Women who are obese are also more likely to develop diabetes or hypertension, which puts them at greater risk for needing a cesarean delivery. Also, multiple births have increased dramatically since the 1980s. These infants are more likely to be delivered by cesarean, especially if one of the babies is in an abnormal presentation. Some physicians automatically schedule a cesarean if the woman is carrying multiples. Additionally, c-section is often used for very low birth weight babies.

Some professionals feel that at least a small percentage of the rise in cesareans is due to the convenience and increased income that the procedure offers doctors. The surgery results in higher fees, longer hospital stays, and guaranteed insurance coverage.

RISKS OF CESAREAN BIRTH

A cesarean section may be necessary to save the life of the woman or baby. But an unnecessary cesarean should be avoided, as there are risks involved. Cesarean section is major abdominal surgery. It carries with it the risk of infection, hemorrhage, pneumonia, blood clots, and anesthesia-related complications. Surgical injury to the bladder, ureters, or bowel; emergency hysterectomy; and maternal death are other risks. In fact, the Centers for Disease Control has reported that the current maternal mortality rate is at it highest level in decades, and a contributing factor is the rise in cesarean sections.[15] According to a study that appeared in the *Journal of the American Medical Association* comparing women who have vaginal deliveries to those who have cesareans, women with c-sections are nearly twice as likely to be back in the hospital within sixty days.[16] Cesareans also have increased financial costs, cause additional pain, and involve a longer recovery period. Women who have cesareans also report more dissatisfaction with their birth experience. They have less early contact with their infant and have to wait longer before they are able to hold their newborn.[17] They also experience more breastfeeding difficulties.

Long-term risks of cesarean birth include chronic pain, adhesion formation, small bowel obstruction, and difficulty in becoming pregnant in the future.[18] Women can also experience problems in subsequent pregnancies. Once there is a scar within the uterus, the woman is at greater risk for an ectopic pregnancy, placenta previa, or placenta accreta—an abnormally firm attachment of the placenta to the uterine wall. Each additional pregnancy increases the risk for accreta. If the placenta is embedded too firmly, hysterectomy is the treatment. Women with previous cesareans are also more like to have a placental abruption or ruptured uterus.

If a woman desires a large family, having a cesarean birth may limit the number of children she can have. Because the risk for complications increases with each cesarean, many doctors strongly caution women to restrict the number of children they have who are born this way.

Cesarean babies are also at a higher risk than those who are delivered vaginally. During surgery, the baby might sustain accidental cuts, which, although not necessarily serious, can be upsetting to the new parent. Breathing difficulties are also more common in c-section babies because the fluid within their lungs is not forced out as with a vaginal birth. They can develop a rapid-breathing condition called *transient tachypnea of the newborn (TTN),* which requires observation and treatment in the neonatal intensive care unit. (The additional financial costs for such treatments can be overwhelming.) Babies born by cesarean are also less likely to breastfeed or they may have breastfeeding difficulties.[19] They also have four times the risk of stillbirth or neonatal death than babies born vaginally.[20] And there is evidence that those who are born by cesarean are 30 percent more likely to be admitted to the hospital for asthma during their childhood.[21] Babies delivered through scheduled cesareans are more likely to suffer from premature birth, as due dates can be inaccurate.

Once the woman's uterus has a scar, the health of subsequent babies may be impacted. The scar tissue may affect the amount of oxygen and nutrients that the placenta and developing fetus receive. Each additional cesarean increases the risk, and these babies are more likely to be born preterm, have a low birth weight, malformations, or injury to the central nervous system.[22]

AVOIDING AN UNNECESSARY CESAREAN

The chances of having a cesarean delivery can be affected by certain hospital practices during labor and even by the choice of caregiver. Selecting a midwife or doctor who

Hints for the Mother-to-Be

To lower your chances of a cesarean:

✓ Select a caregiver with a low cesarean rate.

✓ Hire a doula.

✓ Have a supportive labor partner.

✓ Avoid Pitocin and elective induction.

✓ Walk during labor.

✓ Avoid an epidural and medication.

✓ Request that monitoring be done intermittently.

favors family-centered childbirth and has a low cesarean rate (under 15 percent) will decrease your chance of having a cesarean. Women who have a certified nurse-midwife as their caregiver have the lowest rate of cesarean deliveries. This is because these practitioners treat mainly normal healthy women and are less likely to use interventions without a medical indication during labor. They encourage women to walk during labor, and they offer one-on-one personalized care. Midwives are less likely to suggest routine inductions or elective cesarean births. Having continuous support from a labor partner can also lessen the chances of a cesarean. The supportive presence of a doula can reduce the chances even further.

Inducing labor through the use of Pitocin or by artificially rupturing the membranes can change the force of the labor contractions, precipitate fetal distress, and create potential hazards for the woman and baby. Failure of induction is a common reason for an emergency cesarean section; therefore, labor should be induced only if a medical reason exists.

In a normal labor, early intervention (such as amniotomy, Pitocin, pain medication, epidural anesthesia) may lead to complications that indicate a cesarean delivery. The "rule" that every baby should be delivered within twenty-four hours after rupture of the membranes (or within a specific time after labor begins) to avoid infection, also increases the chance of a cesarean section. Some doctors, however, do not follow this rule and instead, choose to closely monitor the laboring woman for signs of infection by keeping track of her temperature and white blood cell count.

A woman's position during labor is another factor that can affect her need for a cesarean. Lying flat on the back can cause supine hypotension and fetal distress, while walking during labor can assist the normal progression. Walking has been shown to improve the quality of contractions, shorten labor, and improve the baby's condition during labor and delivery.

An electronic fetal monitor is indicated during labor for high-risk women, and for those who are given Pitocin or an epidural. But when it is used routinely for a woman having a normal healthy pregnancy, it can increase her chance of having a cesarean delivery.[23] This can occur for a number of reasons. Insufficiently trained personnel may misinterpret the monitor's readings and overreact to tracings that may just *appear* to indicate fetal distress. The monitor also limits mobility during labor as some nurses insist that a monitored woman lie on her back to ensure a good tracing. And as just mentioned, lying flat on the back can lead to supine hypotension and fetal distress.

An epidural can also increase the likelihood of a cesarean delivery. It can complicate a potentially normal labor and delivery by lowering the woman's blood pressure, thereby decreasing the baby's oxygen supply, which can result in fetal distress. It may also relax the pelvic muscles and, thus, affect the rotation and descent of the baby. Epidural anesthesia can inhibit the force of contractions and prolong the second stage of labor, affecting the urge to push and the effectiveness of the pushing. If this causes the labor to go on for too long, a cesarean is likely to be performed.

The use of analgesics and sedatives can also prompt the need for a cesarean section. These medications can slow labor, inhibit the force of contractions, and depress the baby's heart rate.

PLANNED AND UNPLANNED CESAREANS

There are two types of cesarean births—planned and unplanned. Most first-time cesarean births are unplanned. Many of the same routines are followed for both types of cesareans, although they might be done in a different order and often more hurried for unplanned cesareans. When dealing with an emergency cesarean, stress is usually heightened since the woman has not had adequate time to prepare emotionally. And if she is separated from her labor partner during delivery, the trauma of the experience is intensified.

A planned cesarean birth is usually scheduled just prior to the anticipated due date. Early confirmation of pregnancy and accurate documentation of fetal growth are essential for determining the date precisely. Because the due date is only an estimate, prematurity is a risk. Preterm babies are more likely to develop *respiratory distress syndrome (RDS)* and are generally less capable of handling life outside the uterus than full-term babies. They are, therefore, more likely to be kept in the hospital for an extended period of time, separated from their mothers and fathers. This increases the anxiety of new parents regarding the birth experience and inhibits their bonding with the baby.

If you will be having a planned cesarean, request permission to go into labor spontaneously. Labor is the best indicator that a baby is adequately mature and ready to be born. RDS is less frequent in babies who were delivered after labor had commenced than in those who experienced no labor. As mentioned earlier, labor contractions stimulate the baby's body and trigger a surge of stress hormones that prepare his lungs for breathing, and reduce his chance of respiratory difficulties. Since contractions also draw up and shorten the cervix, many doctors feel that an incision made in this area is the strongest one possible and offers less chance of rupture if a vaginal birth is attempted in the future. When labor begins, call your doctor at once. *Do not labor at home.*

A doctor can perform several tests to help determine fetal maturity and, therefore, lessen the risk of delivering prematurely. He might choose to do a sonogram to measure the biparietal (ear to ear) diameter of the baby's head, which can estimate gestational age. This test is most accurate when performed early in the pregnancy.

Some doctors also perform amniocentesis to assess the maturity of the baby's lungs. This test evaluates the amniotic fluid for the proportions of lecithin and sphingomyelin, substances that are produced by the lungs. The proportion of lecithin to sphingomyelin is called the *L/S ratio.* This ratio changes toward the end of pregnancy, with a sudden increase in lecithin occurring after thirty-four weeks. A ratio of two to one or greater indicates lung maturity.

In certain high-risk conditions, such as diabetes and preeclampsia, it may be necessary to deliver the baby prior to labor. In these cases, specific lab studies and a biophysical profile may be done to determine the optimum time for delivery.

PREOPERATIVE PROCEDURES

If you are having a planned cesarean, you will be admitted to the hospital several hours before the scheduled surgery. Although every doctor and every hospital follow a different set of procedures, there are certain practices that are standard almost everywhere.

You will be instructed to eat nothing solid for eight hours before surgery. This is to prevent possible aspiration of your stomach contents if general anesthesia is needed. Your doctor may allow you to drink clear liquids up to three hours prior to the surgery. You will need to have blood drawn for several tests and for typing and cross

Hints for the Labor Partner

If your partner is having a cesarean:

✓ Stay with her during the surgery.

✓ Hold her hand and reassure her during the surgery.

✓ Take videos and photos of the newborn.

✓ Go with the baby to the nursery and film the events (weighing, measuring).

matching. Most doctors also require a urinalysis. Some may request a chest x-ray and respiratory function tests if you are a smoker or are congested. You can have all of these tests done on an outpatient basis.

A hospital representative will ask you to sign a consent form for the anesthesia and surgery. She will also ask if you have a living will. Read all documents carefully before signing them. Once you are admitted to the hospital room, a nurse may shave or trim the pubic hair that is close to the surgical site, and start an IV in your arm in preparation for the surgery. An anesthesiologist will visit you to discuss preoperative medication and surgical anesthesia. Tell him about any allergies or sensitivities you may have to medications, and discuss your medication preferences with him. If you are having an epidural for the procedure, the catheter may be inserted at this time, prior to your transfer to the operating room.

Whether your cesarean is planned or unplanned, you may be offered a sedative or tranquilizer before the surgery. Prepared women often feel that they do not need anything, choosing instead to rely on relaxation techniques. A sedative or tranquilizer can make both the woman and baby sleepy at the time of birth.

The two types of anesthesia that are used for a cesarean birth are regional and general. Most women and doctors prefer regional because it allows the mother and father to actively participate in the birth and does not depress the baby. Unless an extreme emergency exists, there is usually adequate time for the administration of regional anesthesia.

Regional anesthesia includes spinals and epidurals, which produce similar effects, although spinals provide deeper anesthesia. When the anesthesia is administered, you will feel warm, then tingly, and finally numb. With an epidural, you may still experience some physical sensations, such as tugging and pulling, as the baby is born. Some women feel that this allows them to experience the baby's birth more completely. Because an epidural is usually administered through a catheter, it can be continuously dosed to give you comfort during the bonding period, and then continue to provide pain relief during the first twenty-four hours after surgery.

Signing consent forms before surgery.

A spinal is administered in one injection. Although rare, a general anesthetic is sometimes required for the repair work if the surgery took longer than expected and the effects of the spinal have begun to wear off. It may also be required if the epidural was not effective.

When the health of the woman or baby demands immediate delivery, general anesthesia is used. Because this puts the woman in an unconscious state, her labor partner is usually not permitted to participate in the birth. Some doctors, however, allow the husband to be present. This enables him to bond with the baby. It also allows him to tell his partner the story of the birth.

If you need general anesthesia, you will first be put to sleep with medication that is injected into your IV. Next, a medication will be given to relax your muscles, and a tube will be inserted into your trachea (windpipe). A mixture of oxygen and a gas will be administered through a tube to help you maintain breathing and keep you unconscious throughout the surgery.

SKIN AND UTERINE INCISIONS

A cesarean delivery requires two incisions—one that is made in the skin and another that is made in the uterus. Both can be done either vertically or horizontally. Most commonly, they are made horizontally. If you have had previous abdominal surgery, the doctor will remove the old scar and use that area for the skin incision. Therefore, if the original scar was vertical, the skin incision may not match the uterine incision. The incision in the skin is usually chosen for cosmetic reasons, while the one in the uterus is chosen for medical reasons.

The *low transverse skin incision,* often called a *bikini cut,* is made crosswise along the pubic hairline, as seen in Figure 12.2. It is preferred for cosmetic reasons because the scar is barely noticeable. However, this takes longer to perform than a vertical incision and gives the doctor limited space in which to work. Therefore, it might not be used in an extreme emergency. On the plus side, it causes less discomfort than a vertical incision and the wound heals more quickly. A *vertical skin incision,* shown in Figure 12.3, is faster to make and gives the doctor more room in which to work. It allows for a quicker delivery in an emergency situation.

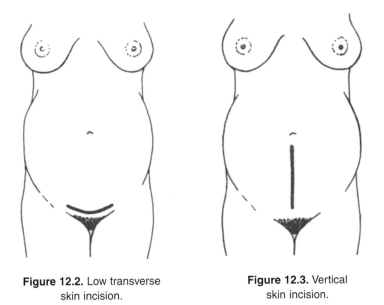

Figure 12.2. Low transverse skin incision.

Figure 12.3. Vertical skin incision.

The most common uterine incision is the *low transverse cervical incision,* which is made horizontally in the cervical area as seen in Figure 12.4 on page 276. Because it is not in the part of the uterus that contracts, it forms the strongest scar with the least danger of rupture. A woman planning a VBAC must have this type of incision in order for her physician to permit a trial of labor.

As illustrated in Figure 12.5, a *classical uterine incision* is made vertically in the fundal area, and gives the doctor ample working room. This type of incision is rarely used and only performed when the baby must be delivered immediately. A classical incision forms the weakest scar; therefore, a vaginal birth after a cesarean is not attempted with this incision.

Figure 12.4. Low transverse cervical incision.

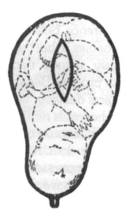

Figure 12.5. Classical uterine incision.

Occasionally a doctor will make a vertical incision lower in the uterus, where the wall is thinner, if the baby is in a difficult position. This low vertical incision carries a smaller risk of uterine rupture than the classical uterine incision, but a greater risk than the low transverse cervical incision. Most physicians will discourage a VBAC with a low vertical incision since it is hard to determine if the incision is confined to the lower segment of the uterus. In rare cases, if a low transverse incision is made and an emergency develops during the surgery, the doctor may extend the incision in the shape of an inverted T or a J to deliver the baby quickly. Women who have this incision are not candidates for VBAC.

SURGICAL PROCEDURE

Depending on the hospital, your delivery will take place either in an operating room that is located in the labor and delivery area or in a surgical operating room. The location might be a factor in your partner's participation. Some hospitals have a policy of not allowing any relatives in an operating room that is separate from the labor and delivery area.

Whether your cesarean is planned or unplanned, you may feel apprehensive as you are being wheeled in for surgery. You can minimize this anxiety with advanced preparation and the use of relaxation techniques. If your partner plans to be present for the birth, he will change into scrub clothes (a mask, scrub suit, cap, and shoe covers) while you are being taken to the delivery room. Unless you have made prior arrangements with your doctor, your partner will not rejoin you until the surgical team is ready to begin the operation.

Once you have been placed on the table, the arm that has the IV may be strapped to a board. A blood pressure cuff will be put on your other arm, and electrocardiogram leads will be attached to your chest. If you would like to hold your partner's hand during surgery and touch your baby once he is born, you will need to request that one arm be left free.

Next, the anesthesiologist will administer the chosen regional anesthesia. He may also offer you oxygen, which you can breathe through a mask until the baby is born. A nurse will insert a urinary catheter to drain your bladder. She will probably do this after the regional anesthetic has taken effect to minimize the discomfort. Because of its location, the bladder must be kept flat and out of the way to avoid being damaged during the surgery. Your abdomen and thighs will be scrubbed with an antiseptic solution, a screen will be placed across your shoulders, and sterile drapes will be adjusted to cover your lower body. Because of the screen, you and your partner will not see anything you do not wish to see. If you would like to see the baby emerge, talk to your doctor about having a mirror in the room or having the screen lowered at the moment of birth. When everything is set up and the doctor is ready to begin the surgery, your partner will be brought into the room and seated next to your head. If general anesthesia is used, it will not be administered until this time to minimize the amount that the baby receives.

The type of skin and uterine incisions that your doctor uses will be influenced by his preferences, the baby's position, your desires, and the speed at which the baby must be delivered. During the surgery, if your doctor needs to cauterize small blood vessels to stop them from bleeding, you may notice a burnt odor. After making the necessary incisions, he will suction the amniotic fluid, which you may hear. Within a few minutes, you may feel a tugging or pulling sensation as your baby is born. If your doctor uses *fundal pressure*—downward pressure on the top of your abdomen—to assist the delivery, you may feel a great deal of pressure. The doctor will then lift the baby out, using his hands, forceps, or a vacuum extractor. If you feel discomfort from this, try slow breathing. Within moments, you will hear your baby's first cry. The umbilical cord will be clamped and cut, and the baby will be handed to the nursery nurse (or possibly a pediatrician), who will show you your new son or daughter. The baby will then be examined by a nurse who will also perform routine identification procedures. (See "Welcome to the World" on page 283.) These exams can usually be done within your view.

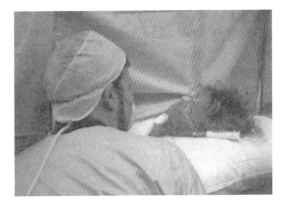

Your doctor will also deliver your placenta through the incision and will give you Pitocin through the IV to help your uterus contract. He will examine your uterus, ovaries, and fallopian tubes, and then repair the uterus, abdominal muscles, subcutaneous tissues, and skin. There are a variety of methods for closing up the skin incision: clamps, staples, sutures, and even glue. This repair work normally takes about thirty minutes. If you feel nauseated or experience any other uncomfortable sensations, tell the anesthesiologist.

Her labor partner's emotional support is invaluable to this mother-to-be as she awaits the cesarean birth of her baby.

While the repair work is being completed, you can ask to touch and hold your baby. If your arms are strapped, your partner may be allowed to hold the baby next to your cheek. Many facilities will allow mothers to have close contact and hold the newborn soon after birth. Your baby may be able to remain with you while in your partner's arms. More commonly, since the operating room will be cold, your baby may be taken to the nursery while you are being repaired, and your partner can accompany him. When you are moved to the recovery room, your partner and newborn can be reunited with you. If your partner was not present for the delivery, the baby can be brought out to him immediately after the birth. Seeing the baby will help to relieve any anxiety he may have about your condition and that of the baby.

RECOVERY ROOM

Once the repair work is completed, you will be taken to the recovery room, where you will stay until the staff feels that you are stable, usually about one to two hours. During this time, a nurse will check your blood pressure, temperature, pulse, respiration, and vaginal and incisional bleeding. If your uterus becomes soft, she may massage it to prevent bleeding. If you feel any discomfort, use your breathing and relaxation techniques. You can also request pain medication. If you had an epidural, the pain medication can continue to be administered via the epidural catheter. This will enable you to bond with your baby and initiate breastfeeding with minimal discomfort.

To help prevent pneumonia, the nurse may ask you to breathe deeply and cough. Splint your incision by holding a pillow firmly against your abdomen and "huff" if coughing seems difficult. (For huffing instructions, see "Day One" on page 280.)

Mom and Dad welcoming their newborn in the operating room.

If you had a regional anesthetic, you will notice the feeling returning first to your toes and feet, and then progressively up toward your abdomen. Medication given continuously through the epidural catheter, if you have one, will give you good pain relief while you regain movement in your extremities. In some hospitals, prior to leaving the operating room, a single injection of a long-acting morphine is given through the epidural catheter, and then the catheter is removed. This provides good pain relief for the next twelve to eighteen hours. General itching and nausea are possible side effects of this medication. If you had general anesthesia, you may be groggy or nauseated upon awakening and feel the need for pain medication.

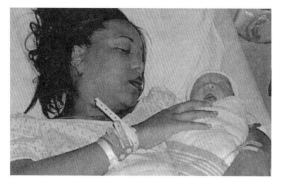
Bonding in the recovery room.

Many hospitals will allow your partner to stay with you in the maternity recovery room. Your baby's pediatrician may permit you some bonding time, provided the baby's condition is good. Bonding, including skin-to-skin touching, is just as important for cesarean parents as it is for couples that experience a vaginal birth.

THE CESAREAN BABY

No two babies are alike, cesarean babies included. One noticeable difference between vaginally delivered and planned cesarean babies is that the head of a cesarean infant is more rounded. This is because it was not molded by the birth process. If you were in labor for many hours prior to the cesarean, some molding may be noticeable. Generally, a cesarean baby needs to be more closely observed because of the surgical delivery. Since he did not pass through the birth canal, which compresses the amniotic fluid from his lungs, he may have more mucus or amniotic fluid in his lungs. This condition will be lessened if the mother experienced some labor. Also, if the mother was given medication or general anesthesia, the baby may be drowsy.

If your baby's condition is good, ask to have him brought to you in the recovery room so you can have early contact with him. If, however, he was in distress at birth, he may be placed in the intensive care nursery immediately. When you feel able, you can visit him there. If your partner is with you, he can push you there in a wheelchair.

If the baby is unable to nurse, you should begin pumping your breasts as soon as possible to provide him with your colostrum, which is high in nutrients and antibodies. Even if he must remain in the warming unit or an isolette, your baby still needs you to touch him and talk to him.

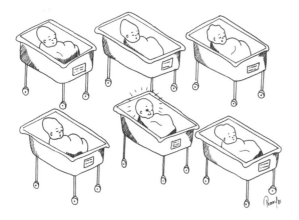
"Can't you tell I'm the cesarean baby?!"

POSTPARTUM PERIOD

The average stay in the hospital after a cesarean birth is three to four days. The IV and catheter will remain in place for approximately twenty-four hours following the surgery. Through the IV, you will receive medication and adequate fluids until your intestines begin to function again. The catheter will give your bladder time to recover from the surgery and keep it empty until you are able to walk to the bathroom yourself. If you are given narcotics through the epidural catheter, you may have a device attached to your finger known as a *pulse oximeter.*

This device measures the amount of oxygen in your blood to ensure adequate levels, since narcotics can decrease your respirations. You may feel nauseated or experience itching as a side effect of the narcotics. Your nurse can give you medication to relieve these discomforts.

At first, your diet will consist of liquids, before gradually increasing to a regular diet. Adequate intake of fluids is important to ensure proper kidney function and prevent dehydration and fever. You will be encouraged to get up and walk around twelve to twenty-four hours after your surgery. Walking promotes good circulation, which reduces the chance of blood clots. It also helps relieve gas. Your first attempt at walking will be the most difficult, but each successive attempt will be easier. Some doctors order support stockings or an abdominal binder for added comfort.

You may feel discomfort in one or both of your shoulders as a result of a collection of blood and air under your diaphragm. The pain is felt in the shoulders because of nerves that connect with the diaphragm. If you had general anesthesia, your throat may be sore because of the tube that was inserted down your throat. Also, even though you have given birth by cesarean, you will still have a vaginal flow. For this, you can use beltless pads.

You will have abdominal pain for several days following the surgery. If you had an epidural, you may have been given a single dose of a narcotic that is injected into the catheter prior to its removal in the recovery room, or you may receive a continuous infusion of a narcotic via the epidural catheter. If you had general anesthesia, narcotic pain medication can be provided through intramuscular injections every three to four hours. It can also be administered through a patient-controlled analgesic (PCA) device, which allows you to intermittently release a small dose of the medication through the IV.

Once the epidural or IV is out and you are taking fluids orally, you will be given pain medication in pill form. You will likely need this medication to be able to interact comfortably with your baby. You can also use relaxation techniques to maximize the effect of the medication. These medications will not interfere with breastfeeding.

As your intestines begin to function again, you may experience sharp gas pains. Chewing on gum will help activate the release of hormones that stimulate your intestines. Avoid apple juice and carbonated beverages, which can increase gas. Hot tea and lemon water are better, more soothing choices. Walking and using a heating pad while in bed will help the gas to pass. Some doctors order medication to aid digestion.

As your incision heals, it will probably itch, possibly for several months. Wear cotton panties rather than nylon during this time. Your doctor will remove the clamps or staples from your incision either before you leave the hospital or within a week after being discharged. He will place sterile tape over the incision to keep the edges together. This tape will peel away and fall off during the next week. You and your partner may want to look at the incision together before going home. Any change in its appearance, such as redness, swelling, separation, a foul odor, or discharge should be reported to your doctor.

Rooming-in is especially important for the cesarean couple to help them develop feelings of attachment to their baby. You will need assistance, however, since you will have difficulty moving around for several days. Do not hesitate to ask for help from the nursing staff. If you have a private room, your partner will probably be able stay with you around the clock. Rooming-in will also help you get breastfeeding off to a good start. For comfort during breastfeeding, make sure you have plenty of

Hints for the Labor Partner

If your partner had a cesarean:

✓ Take the baby to see her in the recovery room, if possible.

✓ Help her position the baby at her breast.

✓ Stay with her overnight in the hospital to help with the baby.

✓ Reassure her that she did well.

✓ If the surgery was unplanned, remind her that some events cannot be controlled.

✓ Give her gum to chew.

✓ Help her find relief from gas pains by encouraging her to walk and giving her warm liquids to drink.

✓ Make sure she has help at home.

When breastfeeding after a cesarean, consider using the football hold to reduce the pressure on your incision.

pillows to take the weight of the baby off the abdomen. Any breastfeeding position presented in Chapter 15 can be used, but many women find the football hold the most comfortable.

Once you return home, you will need household help for the first few weeks. Housework should not be one of your priorities at this time. Setting reasonable goals and expectations for yourself and your baby will make life much easier for all concerned. Take time to relax and nap when the baby does. Your recovery will be more rapid if you concentrate on your health and the baby's welfare, rather than on entertaining visitors or cleaning the house. Continue taking your prenatal vitamins and maintain a high level of protein in your postpartum diet. A healing wound requires lots of protein, just as a growing fetus does during pregnancy. Nutrition plays an important part in how strongly your incision heals.

The correct time to resume sexual relations is different for every couple. Your decision should be based on whether the placental site has healed, which is signaled by cessation of vaginal discharge and the amount of abdominal discomfort you are experiencing. Your doctor's advice and your own desire for sex are also important factors. Most physicians will encourage you to wait until you return for your postpartum checkup at six weeks.

While you are not dealing with an episiotomy, you are coping with an abdominal incision, which is even larger and more painful. During sex, you may find that some of the positions you used during the last months of pregnancy are most comfortable. (See "Postpartum Sex" on page 423.) Many women also experience a changed body image—because of their incision, they worry that they are no longer attractive to their husbands and may need lots of reassurance that they are still appealing.

Your emotional recovery from your cesarean birth can take from two to six months, and your feelings may vary from relief that it is over to painful depression. You may find that you need to be reassured that having a cesarean birth does not mean you are inadequate or a failure. It may have been your only option for giving birth safely. Getting in touch with a local cesarean support group can be very helpful at this time. (For contact information, see the Resources beginning on page 449.)

EXERCISE AFTER A CESAREAN

Because having a cesarean involves major surgery, you will be sore afterwards and require more time to fully recover than if you had delivered vaginally. Postpartum exercises will need to be delayed for a couple of weeks, and always check with your doctor before beginning them. You can, however, start some simple exercises immediately. They will help your body get back to normal more quickly. (For complete descriptions of the following recommended exercises, see "Postpartum Exercises," beginning on page 417.)

Day One

Placing your baby on pillows when breastfeeding helps alleviate pressure on your incision.

Since you may spend the first twelve to twenty-four hours in bed, you can begin doing Ankle Rotating, and Foot Flexing/Stretching as soon as possible after surgery. These two exercises stimulate circulation and lower the risk of blood clots and dizziness. You can begin them in the recovery room when sensation returns after regional anesthesia or as soon as you are alert after general anesthesia.

You can also begin deep breathing to expand your lungs. While in the recovery room or as soon as you awake, take ten slow, deep chest breaths. Repeat once an hour to loosen any phlegm and mucus that may have collected in your lungs during the surgery. This deep breathing is important to prevent pneumonia. Along with it, you can "huff" to bring up phlegm. To do this, hold your incision with both hands, take in a deep breath, then breathe out with short, sharp "ha" sounds. Huffing is not as uncomfortable as coughing and is very effective if you take in enough air first. Don't worry about your stitches breaking. Stitches are done in multiple layers and are very strong.

Log Rolling.

To relieve gas and help the incision heal, practice abdominal tightening. While sitting, lying down, or standing, slowly tighten your abdominal muscles as you exhale and hold them tight for one or two seconds. Gradually increase the holding time to five seconds or more. Doing this exercise may be difficult at first, but the increased circulation will help the incision heal, and the muscle contractions will actually draw the ends of the incision closer together. The first few days you do this exercise; support the incision with your hands for added comfort.

Proper body mechanics can help ease the strain on your abdomen as you roll over and sit up in bed. To turn to your left side, bend your right knee and bring it over your straight left knee. As you turn your body, reach for the left side of the bed with your right arm. This maneuver is called Log Rolling. If you want to turn to your right, reverse the procedure. If you want to sit up, you can easily raise yourself using your arm and shoulder muscles, then swing your legs over the side of the bed without putting undue strain on your abdomen.

Day Two and Beyond

When you are in bed on the second day, continue doing your Ankle Rotating and Foot Flexing/Stretching exercises. Start taking short walks, which you can gradually increase as tolerated. You should also continue huffing until your lungs are clear.

Deep breathing along with the Pelvic Tilt and Kegel exercises will help stimulate intestinal activity and reduce the discomfort caused by gas. To do the Pelvic Tilt, lie on your back or side with your knees bent, and gently rock your pelvis backwards and forwards using your abdominal and buttocks muscles. Also begin doing Super Kegels, contracting the muscles of your pelvic floor for twenty seconds. Do one Super Kegel ten times a day.

Knee Reaching.

To begin strengthening your abdominal muscles, practice Knee Reaching. Sit semi-reclined at a 45-degree angle with the bed raised or your back and head supported by pillows. Breathe in deeply, then exhale, tucking in your chin and reaching for (but not touching) your knees with both hands. Breathe in again, lowering your head to the pillow, and relax. Repeat several times. Start slowly and gradually increase to ten repetitions. If necessary, support your incision as you raise your head.

Before leaving the hospital, check for separation of the recti muscles. (See "Day Three" on page 419). This separation must be restored to normal before doing any further abdominal strengthening exercises. After your doctor gives his permission, progress at your own pace with postpartum exercising, Avoid lifting, straining, and unduly exerting yourself. Be sure to get plenty of rest to speed your recovery.

CONCLUSION

Having a baby by cesarean can be a rewarding, family-centered experience. And in those rare cases in which an emergency situation exists, it can be the only avenue to a healthy baby. However, because a cesarean involves major surgery, with risks to both you and your baby, you should make every effort to avoid having one, if possible.

Your best bet for reducing your chances of a cesarean is your careful choice of a caregiver and birth setting. Another important factor is making sure you have continuous support from a caring labor partner. The presence of a doula further reduces your chances. Allowing your body to labor naturally without interventions is another important element. It is particularly crucial to avoid interventions such as Pitocin or an epidural in early labor. Walking during labor and utilizing upright laboring positions also help to encourage a vaginal birth.

Another very important factor is your trust in your body's ability to give birth. Our society has come to accept a high cesarean rate as normal, implying that one out of three women's bodies do not function properly. We need to reverse this trend by realizing and demonstrating that birth is a natural, normal event. Use your visualizations to "see" yourself giving birth, knowing that your body is designed to give birth vaginally. Use your relaxation techniques to get in touch with your body and realize that, in most cases, babies will be born healthy on their own, without any help or interventions. Having complete confidence that your body will know how to carry out this age-old process can be the key to ensuring a vaginal birth.

The Newborn
or Welcome to Our World

After spending many months preparing for the arrival of your newborn, she has finally made her entrance. As you welcome her into your arms, you may be surprised at her appearance, her alertness, and the overwhelming emotions that you begin to feel the moment she is born. The information presented in this chapter will let you know what to expect immediately following your baby's birth. Also discussed are the initial procedures and testing your newborn will undergo at the hospital or birth facility. And because many new parents are often surprised and sometimes concerned over various unexpected aspects of their new baby's appearance, this chapter offers a head-to-toe description of the common physical characteristics you can expect to see when you look at your newborn.

WELCOME TO THE WORLD

Within the first minutes after your baby is born, she will be given an Apgar score. This is an evaluation of her physical condition at one minute after birth and again at five minutes. (For more information on the Apgar score, see page 206). The nurse will continue to observe the baby's physical condition throughout the first hours. She will give her a thorough examination, as well as monitor her vital signs, including temperature, heart rate, and respirations. This monitoring can be done while the baby is lying skin to skin against your abdomen or chest, and covered with a blanket to stay warm. If the room is cold, ask the nurse to increase the temperature. Unless the baby is having difficulty breathing, routine suctioning of the mouth and nose is no longer recommended.

At this time, the baby will also be weighed. The length of her body will be measured, as will the circumference of her chest and head. The nurse will record a print of your index finger and your baby's footprints on the proper documents. If you brought your baby book with you, ask the nurse to record the baby's footprints in it, as well. The nurse will also give both you and your newborn identification bracelets, which will be checked throughout your hospital stay. These bracelets are intended to prevent nursery mix-ups. In some facilities, the father also receives an identification bracelet, which allows him to retrieve the baby from the nursery.

While the mother is being moved from the birthing room, some hospitals have the baby taken to the nursery for observation. Dad may accompany his newborn there. Other facilities transport the mother and baby together to the postpartum unit without any separation.

Measuring the head is part of the admission procedure following birth.

A baby's footprints are recorded as part of the identification procedure following birth.

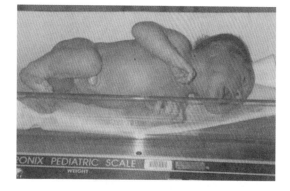

This baby weighs in during the admission procedure after birth.

APPEARANCE AND PHYSIOLOGICAL CHANGES OF THE NEWBORN

The first questions that most parents ask after confirming or learning the sex of their baby are, "How much does she weigh?" and "How long is she?" Full-term babies weigh an average of seven to eight pounds and are from nineteen to twenty inches in length. Their head circumference is approximately thirteen inches, while the average chest circumference measures twelve to thirteen inches. A newborn may lose up to 8 percent of her birth weight within the first few days. This is due to the excretion of extra tissue fluid and the meconium that has built up in her intestines. This weight loss is normal and usually regained within two weeks. A weight loss of 10 percent or more requires an evaluation to ensure that the baby is feeding well.

An unseen change that occurs at the moment of your baby's birth involves her circulatory system. While she was in your uterus, blood bypassed her lungs and she received oxygen via the umbilical cord. The blood was diverted from the lungs through the *ductus arteriosus,* a blood vessel located between the pulmonary artery and the aorta; it was also diverted between a small hole in the right and left upper chambers of the heart called the *foramen ovale.* When your baby began to breathe, the ductus arteriosus and the foramen ovale closed and the blood went to the lungs for oxygenation. Also, after the umbilical cord was cut, certain internal blood vessels that carried blood to and from the cord were no longer needed. These vessels would eventually become ligaments.

Most people do not know what newly born babies look like and expect them to resemble the babies seen on magazine covers. You may be surprised or even concerned over your baby's initial appearance. Immediately after birth, she may appear bluish or gray. Once she starts to cry or begins to breathe, her body will become pink. Her hands and feet, however, may remain slightly bluish for a few hours or even days (it will be more noticeable when she is chilled). This bluish discoloration, called *acrocyanosis,* is normal. Her body may also be streaked with blood.

What follows next is a head-to-toe examination of the newborn. It offers a general discussion of the physical characteristics you can expect to find when looking at your baby.

Head

A newborn baby's face may appear swollen. This is generally due to pressure from a vaginal birth and will subside in a day or two. Her nose may be flattened and her ears may be pressed to her head. Initially, the newborn's head may be misshapen and elongated due to *molding,* which takes place during a vaginal birth. (See Figure 13.1 on page 285.) Molding is caused by the overlapping of the skull bones, which helps ease the passage of the baby's head through the birth canal. The head may take a couple of days to become rounder. It may also exhibit swelling, called *caput succedaneum,* which could last for several days but is not serious. In addition to possible molding, your baby's head may appear to be too large for her body. Typically, a baby's head is about one quarter of its body size. The newborn's neck muscles will be too weak to hold the wobbly head, which you should support at all times.

There will be two areas on the baby's head—one on the top and one on the back—where the skull bones have not yet joined. These *fontanels* or *soft spots* helped facilitate the head molding that was necessary during pushing. They also allow for further growth of the skull after birth. The posterior fontanel, found on the back of the head, is triangular in shape and will close when the baby is around six weeks of age. The diamond-shaped anterior fontanel, located on top of the head, will close by about eighteen months. Both spots are covered by a tough protective membrane called the *dura,* so you do not have to be overly concerned about touching these areas.

If a vacuum extractor or forceps were used during delivery, or if the baby's head was pressed against the pelvic bones during labor or birth, a *cephalhematoma* may have formed. This collection of blood, caused by pressure, appears as a bump under the scalp and may gradually increase in size during the first few days. Cephalhematomas are not life threatening, but they may take months to reabsorb and disappear.

Some babies are born with a full head of hair, while others are bald. If your baby is born with hair, she will probably lose some or all of it within the first few months.

Eyes

At birth, the eye color of Caucasian babies is usually blue, while brown is the eye color of most non-Caucasian babies. Your baby's permanent eye color will probably be determined by six months of age, although it can change for up to a year.

Most babies will blink at bright lights and may not nurse well or look at you if a light is shined directly in their face. Because their eye muscles are not well developed, newborns may appear cross-eyed when looking around. By six months, their eyes should be focusing together. If, after six months, your baby's eyes appear crossed, ask your pediatrician to refer you to an ophthalmologist, who specializes in eye disorders.

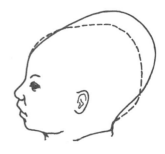

Figure 13.1.
The solid line indicates what a newborn's head may look like if it was molded during the birth process. The dotted line indicates the normal shape of an infant's head, which most newborns attain within a few days.

A Word About Hospital Security

Although rare, infant abduction from hospitals is an unfortunate reality. Since the 1990s, many hospitals have taken serious steps to tighten security, particularly in maternity wards and pediatric units.

In addition to increased security guards, video surveillance, and restricted visitation, a growing number of facilities are using electronic tagging systems. With this type of system, a tag is placed around a baby's ankle that responds to sensor panels located at the exits. If the baby is taken through or even near an exit, an alarm goes off, alerting the hospital's security

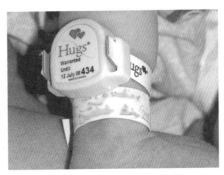

In many hospitals, electronic security tags are placed on the baby's ankle.

team. Photo identification badges for hospital personnel, indicating that they work in the mother/baby unit are also fairly standard. Many of these units are locked and no one is able to enter without proper identification. While in the hospital, do not give your baby to anyone who is unfamiliar or who does not have proper identification.

For peace of mind, be sure to learn about the security procedures of your facility. It is important to know that you and your baby are in a protected environment.

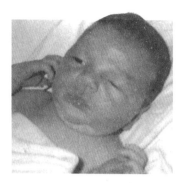

This newborn's eyes are puffy from birth.

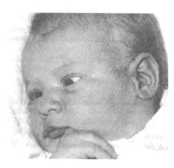

Don't worry if your baby's eyes are crossed at birth. The eye muscles are still developing. By around six months of age, the eyes should focus properly.

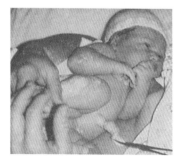

Many babies are born with a protective creamy white coating called vernix caseosa.

Tearless crying is common in newborns because the tear-producing *lacrimal glands* are not completely functional. It could be many months before your baby begins to cry real tears. You might also notice some eye puffiness, which could be from excess fluid or pressure during the birth process, or from the administration of eye medication after birth. This will subside in a day or two. A discharge from the eyes may indicate that the tear ducts are blocked. Notify the pediatrician, who may prescribe an antibiotic ointment or show you how to perform a massage technique that is designed to open the ducts. If you notice blood in the whites of your baby's eyes, don't panic. These small hemorrhages are usually caused by the pressure of childbirth and are not uncommon. They may, however, take several weeks to disappear.

Skin

When babies are in utero, they are covered with fine downy hair called *lanugo*. By the time they are born, most of this hair is gone. Some babies, however, particularly those who are preterm, may be born with some lanugo. This is often most noticeable on the ears, the sides of the face, and the back, and usually disappears within a few weeks. The skin of some babies may have traces of the creamy white *vernix caseosa* that covered their bodies in utero. This natural "cold cream" protected your baby's skin while she floated in the amniotic fluid. In newborns it is typically found in the creases of the skin, the armpits, and inside the labia of females. The closer to term your baby is born, the less vernix she will have. Some mothers prefer to massage the vernix into their newborn's skin to serve as a natural skin conditioner, rather than washing it off. Do not try to remove the vernix from inside the labia, as it will be absorbed naturally.

Some babies, particularly those born post-term, have dry, scaly skin that is most noticeable on their hands and feet, often with some peeling that occurs one to two weeks after birth. If your baby has dry skin, avoid treating it with commercial lotions or mineral-based baby oil, which can rob the skin of vitamins. Instead, use a small amount of natural, edible oil like almond, sunflower, or safflower. You may also notice little whiteheads called *milia* on your baby's chin, nose, and/or cheeks. These are immature oil glands and will go away without any treatment when the glands begin to function. Do not attempt to remove them.

Dark- or olive-skinned babies—most commonly of African-American, Asian, Native American, or southern European descent—may be born with a purplish-brown discoloration on their lower back, buttocks, or the back of their thighs. These discolorations, called *Mongolian spots,* have the appearance of old bruises and will fade within the first years of life. As they may be mistaken for bruises, it is important that childcare providers are aware of their presence. Some babies have clusters of small capillaries that appear on the nape of the neck, on the eyelids, or on the bridge of the nose. Often called *stork bites* or *angel kisses,* these minute blood vessels become more obvious when the baby cries. They usually fade by nine months of age.

Your newborn's skin will be very sensitive. If she becomes chilled, her skin may appear blotchy and/or the capillaries located below the surface may be apparent. Her hands and feet may turn slightly bluish. If she is overdressed or wearing irritating clothing, a rash may develop. During the first days after birth, some babies develop a harmless rash known as *erythema toxicum.* Resembling heat rash—red splotches with small yellowish white bumps in the center—erythema toxicum has no known cause and will disappear without treatment.

Breathing and Heart Rate

Expect your baby's breathing to be fast, between twenty and sixty breaths per minute. It will also be irregular, shallow, and abdominal in nature. The hiccups you may have felt during pregnancy may continue until the baby's diaphragm matures. (These hiccups tend to bother the parents more than the baby.) Your baby's heart rate will also be rapid, between 100 and 160 beats per minute. When she cries, it may accelerate to between 180 to 200 beats per minute.

Breasts and Genitals

Due to the high level of maternal hormones that cross the placenta while babies are still in utero, some newborns (both male and female) may be born with firm enlarged breasts. The swelling usually goes down within two weeks, but during that time, the breasts may secrete milk, sometimes called *witch's milk*. The genitals of both sexes may also be enlarged or swollen. A newborn girl's clitoris and labia can be large enough for her to be mistaken for a boy at quick glance. She may also have a milky vaginal discharge or a small amount of vaginal bleeding called *false menstruation*. The scrotum of a newborn boy may be swollen and unusually dark in color. His testes may move in and out of the scrotum. They may retract as high as the crease at the top of the thigh. This is normal as long as they are located in the scrotum most of the time.

Abdomen

Typically, a newborn's abdomen is round and protruding. This is due to poor abdominal muscle tone and relatively long intestines that are confined to a small area. You can expect the umbilical cord stump to dry up and fall off in one to two weeks. Make sure the cord clamp is removed prior to discharge from the hospital. It is not necessary to swab the stump with alcohol. Simply wash the area with soap and water during bath time and dry it well. Folding down the front of the diaper below the stump will help to dry it.

Arms and Legs

Babies are born with flat feet, and arms and legs that are proportionately short for their bodies. A newborn will keep her arms bent and close to her chest with hands that are usually clenched in fists. Typically, she will hold her legs, which may appear bowed, in a position that is similar to the one she had assumed in utero. A newborn's nails, which are soft and pliable, may be very long at birth and need cutting. After a few weeks, you can trim them with baby scissors or clippers, but prior to that, it is best to simply file them with an emery board or nail file. This will prevent accidental cutting of the skin. Many parents find it easiest to trim the baby's nails while she is sleeping. Do not cover her hands with mittens to prevent her from scratching herself. Babies need to be able to suck on their fingers or touch their mouth just as they did before they were born.

The Senses

Just how keen is a newborn baby's sense of sight, hearing, taste, touch, and smell? For years, mothers were told that their babies could not see until they were several weeks old. Research, however, has proven that even though their vision is not perfect, babies *are* able to see. It is also believed that their best vision is at a distance of eight to ten

Not to Worry . . .

The following are common, normal newborn variations that may surprise you:

✓ Hiccups are common until the baby's diaphragm matures.

✓ Newborns sneeze to get rid of mucus.

✓ Both male and female babies can be born with swollen breasts and genitals from the mother's hormones.

✓ A newborn's nails may be so long that she was able to scratch herself in utero.

✓ Babies can be born with blisters or bruises on their hands and wrists from sucking on them in utero.

Keep in mind that this list is not inclusive. Your newborn may display a behavior or a physical trait that is not noted here, but that nevertheless is normal and common. Talk to your pediatrician if you have any concerns.

Sucking reflex.

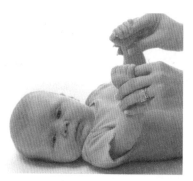

Grasp reflex.

inches—the approximate distance between a breastfeeding baby and her mother's face.

Even before birth, a fetus exhibits sensitivity to sound. Hearing becomes more acute within several days following birth as the amniotic fluid evaporates within the ear canal. Many babies recognize and react positively to the familiar sound of their parents' voices, which they had listened to before they were born. And be aware that it is not necessary to keep the house quiet around your new baby. When you were carrying her, the decibel level in the uterus was as loud as a vacuum cleaner. She may be happier, more comfortable in a noisy environment than in a completely quiet room.

A newborn's sense of taste and smell are also well developed. Newborns have a preference for sweet, which is exactly how colostrum tastes. Immediately after birth, the smell and taste of the amniotic fluid on the baby's hands help her navigate toward a similar-smelling substance that is secreted by the areola. Research has shown that by the age of six days, a baby can recognize the smell of her own mother.[1] Some babies react negatively to the smell of smoke or perfume. For this reason, be cautious about applying strong-scented lotions to your body, especially if you are breastfeeding.

The sense of touch is very important for the newborn. Fetuses are cuddled and massaged by the uterus, and continue to crave these feelings after they are born. Having skin-to-skin contact with your infant, along with massaging or stroking her helps satisfy this vital need. When holding their babies, most mothers instinctively and lovingly stroke them. Touch and interaction is critical for normal development—babies who are rarely held or spoken to do not thrive.

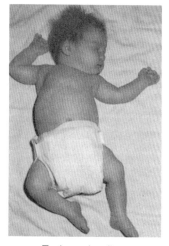

Tonic neck reflex.

Reflexes

A number of reflexes will be present in your newborn at birth. Some will be vital to her survival. Many she will have "practiced" while in utero. All are signs of gestational maturity.

Your baby's *sucking reflex* will be very strong soon after birth. Any stimulation of her lips will elicit a sucking motion. It is not unusual to see a newborn sucking on her thumb, fingers, or fist. This is just a continuation of what she did before she was born. You may even see bruises on her hands or arms from sucking in utero. Because the fetus swallows amniotic fluid, the *swallowing reflex* is present at birth. A baby is also born with a *rooting reflex,* which is most evident when her cheek or lips are stroked. This reflex causes her to turn their head in the direction of the touch and open her mouth. The sucking, swallowing, and rooting reflexes all assist in breastfeeding.

Several protective reflexes are also apparent at birth. These include the *gag reflex,* which prevents choking, and the *cough* and *sneezing reflexes,* which help get rid of mucus. A newborn also instinctively attempts to protect herself. If her face becomes covered with a blanket, she will flail her arms and move her head to remove it. If a limb is exposed to cold, she will draw it close to her body to warm it. If she experiences pain—is pinched or stuck with a pin, for instance—she will quickly withdraw.

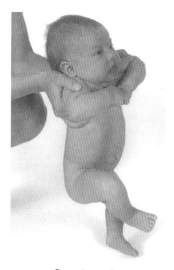

Stepping reflex.

Recreating the environment in the womb can stimulate the *calming reflex,* which quiets fussy or crying babies.

If you place your fingers in your baby's palms, she will grasp them tightly due to the *grasp reflex.* This grasp may even be strong enough to allow you to raise her body up. However, *do not* try this because she may let go and fall. When holding the baby under her arms in a standing position, she will move her legs as if walking. This is the *stepping reflex.* When lying on her back, an infant may assume what looks like a fencing position—her head will be turned to the side, the arm on that side will be extended, and the leg on that side will be flexed. This is called the *tonic neck reflex.* If the baby is startled, she will thrust out her arms as if to embrace you in a movement called the *Moro reflex.*

Two reflexes involve the soles of the infant's feet. The *plantar toe reflex* causes the toes to curl if you press your finger at their base. If you stroke the sole from the heel to the toes, you will notice that the foot hyperextends and the toes fan outward. This is the *Babinski toe reflex.* All of these reflexes usually disappear between two and four months of age.

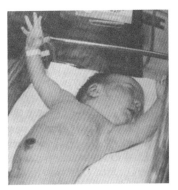

Moro reflex.

COMMON NEWBORN CONCERNS

Jaundice—a condition that affects a large number of newborns—is one of the most common areas of concern among new parents. Whether or not to circumcise a male infant is another major concern. The following section will address some of the frequently asked questions on these subjects.

Jaundice

Normal physiologic jaundice is a condition that affects 50 percent of all newborns. While in utero, the fetus has a large number of red blood cells, which carry oxygen. After birth, the extra red blood cells are no longer needed and begin to deteriorate. Bilirubin, a product of this breakdown, is normally detoxified by the liver and excreted by the bowel. However, because a baby's liver is immature, it may be unable to handle the bilirubin, and the excess may cause jaundice. Generally a non-threatening condition, jaundice is characterized by a yellowish tint to the baby's skin and whites of the eyes. It usually appears on the second or third day of life and disappears within two to three weeks. Jaundice that becomes apparent in the first twenty-four hours is usually due to a maternal-fetal blood type incompatibility, which is discussed later in this section.

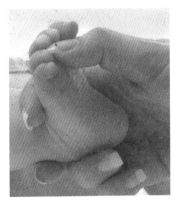

Plantar toe reflex.

Treatment for physiologic jaundice is usually not necessary, as it is a normal condition found in newborns. But even this type of jaundice can reach elevated levels of bilirubin called *hyperbilirubinemia,* a condition that requires intervention. It is important to be aware of the risk factors that can increase bilirubin levels and what you can do to avoid them.

Delayed or poor feeding and excessive weight loss in a full-term newborn can cause dehydration. This can increase bilirubin levels, heighten the risk of jaundice, and require treatment. Other risk factors can include a high red blood cell count, delayed passing of the first stool (after twenty-four hours), the use of Pitocin during labor, and a preterm birth (thirty-five or thirty-six weeks gestation). If the baby has a mother with diabetes or an older sibling who required treatment for jaundice when born, or if she is of Asian, Native American, or African American descent, she has an increased chance of developing jaundice as well.

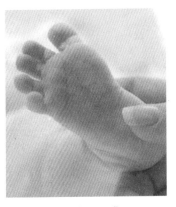

Babinski toe reflex.

The American Academy of Pediatrics (AAP) recommends breastfeeding mothers to nurse their babies at least eight to twelve times in the first days to prevent jaundice caused by dehydration. Routine supplementation of breastfed babies who are not dehydrated with water or glucose water is not recommended by the AAP, as it does not prevent hyperbilirubinemia or decrease the risk of jaundice.[2] If the baby is not breast-feeding well, ask for assistance from a nurse or a lactation consultant. Sleepy babies must be awakened so they can feed at least eight times a day. If supplementation is suggested, nurse more frequently. If your baby is nursing poorly, pump your breastmilk and give it to her between feedings. If supplementation is required due to excessive weight loss or dehydration and you are unable to pump sufficient quantities of breastmilk, formula may be recommended until your milk volume increases.

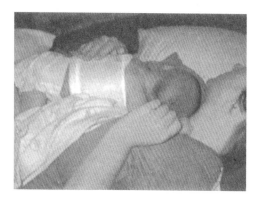

A fiberoptic bili-blanket can help treat jaundice without glaring bili-lights or separation of mother and baby.

Babies who begin nursing soon after birth or who room-in with their mothers and enjoy frequent breastfeeding every two to three hours are less likely to develop jaundice. Early breastfeeding also stimulates the intestines to pass the meconium, which contains a high level of bilirubin. Ridding the body of meconium helps decrease reabsorption of the bilirubin through the intestinal wall. Breastmilk also contains protein-rich colostrum. The protein binds with the bilirubin and is then excreted from the baby's body through bowel movements.

Recently, physicians have taken a more aggressive approach to the treatment of jaundice. This is to prevent *kernicterus*—a type of brain damage caused by extremely high levels of bilirubin that can result in cerebral palsy and hearing loss. *Phototherapy,* which uses light waves to break down the bilirubin through the skin, is a common form of treatment. In 2004, the AAP established criteria that determine when a baby requires phototherapy. The guidelines are based on bilirubin levels according to the infant's age in hours. These levels are measured through the skin with a transcutaneous monitor or determined through a blood test.

To receive phototherapy treatment, the undressed infant is placed under special "bili-lights." These lights emit blue to white waves that are absorbed into the baby's skin and blood, and break down the bilirubin. While under the lights, soft patches are placed over the baby's eyes to protect them from damage. Because phototherapy can cause dehydration, as well as force the separation of the mother and baby, it should be avoided if the bilirubin level is not significantly elevated. Many hospitals have portable bili-lights that can be set up within the mother's hospital room so mother and baby can stay together. Once the baby is home, phototherapy, in the form of either bili-lights or a fiberoptic bili-blanket that is wrapped around the baby, is another possible option. It is a way to prevent mother and child from separation, as they are when the baby remains in the hospital for treatment. In such cases, a home health nurse will set up the equipment in the home, perform the necessary blood tests, and provide reports to the pediatrician. Exposure to filtered sunlight can also help decrease normal jaundice, although this practice is not recommended. Keeping the baby next to a window while she is undressed may cause her to become cold. And taking her outside to expose her to direct sunlight may result in sunburn.

Prolonged jaundice may need further testing to determine the cause. While some mothers' milk contains a factor that tends to prolong jaundice, true breastmilk jaundice is rare. It begins to appear and continues to rise after the third day of life and may peak between the seventh and, in untreated cases, the fifteenth day.[3] Prolonged jaundice can also be caused by other factors, including infection, liver disease, impaired thyroid function, galactosemia, and glucose-6-phosphatase deficiency (G6PD). If the infant is not responding to treatment, she should be evaluated for these conditions.

Blood-Type Incompatibility and Jaundice

The most common type of maternal-fetal blood incompatibility that can cause jaundice is an ABO incompatibility. When a mother is blood type O and the father is either A, B, or AB, the baby may have the father's blood type. The mother's O blood type means she has no A or B factors in her blood. She might, however, have anti-A or anti-B factors. This means that if, for example, the baby is blood type A and the mother has anti-A in her blood, the anti-A will destroy even more red blood cells than are usually broken down. The result is an elevated bilirubin level. This usually begins to occur within the first twenty-four hours after birth.

A more serious type of incompatibility is due to the Rh factor—the other part of your blood type. This type of sensitization, however, is rare since the use of RhoGAM. (For information on RhoGAM, see page 77.)

The pediatrician can have the cord blood tested to determine the baby's blood type. A Coombs test will determine whether or not antibodies are present that are breaking down the red blood cells. Hyperbilirubinemia that results from an ABO or Rh incompatibility will require treatment with phototherapy and, if severe, a possible blood transfusion.

Circumcision

Circumcision is a surgical procedure in which the foreskin is removed from the head of the penis. In the United States, this procedure, which is generally performed by an obstetrician or pediatrician, is traditionally done prior to discharge from the hospital or in the doctor's office within the baby's first week of life. Circumcisions are most commonly performed for religious, cultural, and health reasons.

At one time, experts believed that removal of the foreskin promoted health and cleanliness, and prevented masturbation. Studies, however, have shown that circumcision is not necessary for good health or hygiene, and that it has no effect on the desire to masturbate. One argument still used for routine circumcision is that it prevents cancer of the vagina or cervix in the female sex partners of these men, but little evidence exists to support this. The United States remains the only country that practices non-religious circumcision almost routinely.

Unless you are sure that your baby is a girl, you should decide before your due date if you wish to have your son circumcised. The American Academy of Pediatrics issued a policy statement in 1999 that was reaffirmed in 2005; it declared that, "Existing scientific evidence demonstrates potential medical benefits of newborn male circumcision; however, these data are not sufficient to recommend routine neonatal circumcision. If a decision for circumcision is made, procedural analgesia should be provided."[4]

One potential medical benefit of circumcision is fewer urinary tract infections. While this may be true, performing surgery to decrease urinary tract infections is an extreme measure. Females have a higher incidence of urinary tract infections than males after six months of age—and they are treated with antibiotics, not surgery. Circumcised men also have a lower risk of developing cancer of the penis, although this form of cancer is very rare in both circumcised and uncircumcised men. Cancer of the penis is also associated with poor hygiene and certain sexually transmitted diseases. Circumcision can prevent foreskin infections and *phimosis*—the inability to pull back the foreskin. There is some evidence that circumcised men have a slightly lower risk of sexually transmitted diseases, including HIV; but safe sexual practices and proper hygiene are more effective in their prevention.

Many parents have the surgery performed for religious reasons or to make it easier for the child to clean himself. Others want their son to look like his father or his peers. Circumcision without a medical reason is considered cosmetic surgery and an elective procedure. For this reason, some insurance companies do not pay for routine circumcision.

A growing number of parents are choosing not to have their sons circumcised. Many view the surgery as unnecessary. Furthermore, it can cause complications, which occur in 1 out of every 476 circumcisions.[5] The procedure can result in bleeding, infection, the cutting of too much or not enough foreskin, and improper healing.[6]

Another reason to leave the foreskin intact is that it protects the tip of the penis. Removal can allow the tip to become irritated; it can also cause the urethra to constrict, which may require surgery to open. Foreskin removal can cause a loss of sensitivity to the head of the penis, resulting in a possible decrease in sexual pleasure as an adult. Proper hygiene and practicing safe sex will decrease the chance of an uncircumcised male from developing infections, cancer of the penis, and sexually transmitted diseases.[7] Many parents have decided that if their son desires circumcision in the future, he will be able to give his own informed consent for it as an adult.

Circumcision is also a painful procedure in that it causes temporary changes in the infant's heart rate, blood pressure, oxygen saturation, and cortisol levels.[8] The effects of this pain can be lasting. Studies have indicated that circumcised infants exhibit a stronger pain response to subsequent routine immunizations than do uncircumcised infants.[9] If you choose to have your son circumcised, ask the doctor if he uses an anesthetic for the procedure. Infants who receive local anesthesia cry less and have lower stress hormone levels in their bloodstreams.

There are a number of methods for anesthetizing the area. With a *dorsal penile nerve block (DPNB),* the nerves at the base of the penis are injected with lidocaine. The application of a topical anesthetic cream called *lidocaine-prilocaine (EMLA)* is sometimes used instead of or prior to the DPNB. Applied to the penis sixty to eighty minutes before circumcision, this cream decreases the pain of the surgery, has no adverse effects, and its application is pain-free.[10] EMLA cream is also approved for use on children over one month of age as a topical anesthetic prior to injections, blood work, IV starts, and minor surgery.

The *subcutaneous ring block,* in which a local anesthetic is injected under the skin of the penis—either below the head, in the midpoint of the shaft, or at the base of the shaft—is another simple and effective method of providing pain relief during circumcisions. This method was found to be more effective for pain relief than either EMLA cream or DPNB.[11, 12]

Another method of providing pain relief in combination with a nerve block is to have the infant suck on a 24-percent sucrose solution at least two minutes prior to the start of the injection. This super-saturated sugar solution attaches to the opium receptors in the brain and can provide pain relief for minor procedures. EMLA cream together with the sucrose solution can decrease the pain associated with a lidocaine injection, but it is not a good substitute—a local anesthetic provides the best pain relief for the surgery. If, however, the doctor does not use a nerve block, either of these methods is better than no anesthesia at all.

If you decide to have your son circumcised, try to delay the procedure for at least twenty-four hours. This will give him some time to adjust to his new life outside the uterus. Keep in mind that the procedure should be performed only on healthy, stable infants. If your baby was born preterm or is not breastfeeding well, delay the procedure.

There are also a number of medical conditions for which circumcision is not recommended. Babies born with *hypospadia,* a malformation in which the opening for the urethra is on the side or base of the penis, should not be circumcised. An intact foreskin is sometimes needed for surgical correction of this malformation. Circumcision is also not recommended for infants with a high fever, ambiguous genitalia, or a family history of hemophilia.

Do not request a particular method of circumcision. Each physician performs the method he was trained in or the one with which he is most comfortable. Of the procedures used today, one type does not give better results than another. It is more important to choose a doctor who performs this surgery frequently and is competent in the technique.

After the surgery, request that your baby is returned to you immediately so you can soothe him and try to breastfeed. Do not be surprised if he goes into a deep sleep and refuses to feed for four to five hours. Make an effort to rouse him after several hours. He should also urinate within eight hours after the procedure. Since circumcision can be performed in different ways, with each method requiring different post-surgical attention, make sure you receive instructions on proper home care. In general, placing the baby on his side (when awake) or back may make him more comfortable. When washing him, be sure to gently pull back the small remaining foreskin to prevent scar tissue from growing between the foreskin and the head. Keep an eye out for bleeding, abnormal swelling, persistent redness, and signs of infection, such as a foul smell or fluid-filled sores. Notify your pediatrician if you notice any of these signs or if you have any other concerns.

An uncircumcised penis requires no extra cleaning. Just wash, rinse, and dry it along with the rest of the baby's bottom. Do not pull the foreskin back over the head of the penis. In a newborn, the foreskin is almost always attached to the head, and forcing it back may cause damage. In most cases, by three years of age, the foreskin can be completely retracted in up to 90 percent of uncircumcised boys. In others, it can take longer before separation occurs, even into puberty. Forcibly retracting the foreskin before it detaches naturally from the head can cause pain, bleeding, adhesions, and inflammation of the foreskin and head of the penis. It can also cause *paraphimosis*—the inability of the foreskin to return to its original position. Once the foreskin is fully retractable, pull it back gently to wash the penis and then replace it gently. Your son can learn to do this himself when he bathes.

The decision of whether or not to circumcise a baby is a personal one and should be made by the parents in consultation with their pediatrician. After examining both the benefits and risks, an increasing number of parents today are deciding against routine circumcision. The number of uncircumcised males—who were once looked at as "different"—is increasing. They are not so different anymore.

A Hint for the New Mother

Request an anesthetic when a circumcision is performed.

NEWBORN TESTING AND PROCEDURES

Your infant will undergo a number of tests and procedures before she is discharged from the hospital or birth facility. Some are required, while others will depend on your child's specific needs or situation.

Eye Prophylaxis

All states have a law requiring that an antibiotic ointment (erythromycin or tetracycline) or silver nitrate drops be placed in a baby's eyes within an hour after birth. The purpose of this medicine is to prevent the baby from developing an eye infection caused by bacteria that may be present in the birth canal—particularly bacteria associated with gonorrhea, which can cause blindness. You can ask the nurse to delay administering this medicine for an hour, as it will blur the vision of the baby, who may be alert and looking at you during this time. The antibiotic ointment is less irritating to the eyes than silver nitrate drops and is used more commonly. Occasionally, women who are in a monogamous relationship and have been screened for sexually transmitted diseases during pregnancy may choose to sign a waiver refusing this procedure.

Vitamin K Injection

Vitamin K, an important factor in blood clotting, is manufactured in the intestines once certain normal bacteria are present. Newborns, however, are deficient in vitamin K as their normal bacteria are inadequate. Because of this, within the first hour of life, your baby will receive an injection of vitamin K to prevent a bleeding disorder called *hemorrhagic disease of the newborn.* The injection is given in the baby's thigh while in the birthing room or upon admission to the newborn nursery. In some areas of the country, vitamin K may be available in oral form. If the baby receives oral vitamin K, additional doses will be given at one or two weeks and again at four weeks. Do not refuse vitamin K if you have a son and are choosing to have him circumcised, since bleeding is one of the risks of the procedure.

Test for Hypoglycemia

If your baby displays signs of low blood sugar (jittery, crying abnormally, lethargic, poor sucking reflex), or if she is small or large for her gestational age, she may be tested for hypoglycemia within the first hour after birth. Other factors such as a low Apgar score, suspected infection, a high or low temperature, prematurity, or a mother who was diabetic during pregnancy, may also require monitoring of her blood sugar.

Blood is drawn from the baby's heel for this test. For accurate results, the heel should be warmed before the blood is drawn. This test may be repeated multiple times for infants who have low blood sugar or who are at risk for developing it. The newborn's initial bath is usually delayed until this testing is completed, as any stress can lower blood sugar levels.

To help prevent low blood sugar, keep your naked baby against your skin and breastfeed her as soon after the delivery as possible, especially before sending her to the nursery (if required). If the test results indicate the blood sugar is below normal and the baby is not displaying any symptoms, breastfeed her, and have her blood tested again before possibly offering her a bottle of formula. Severely low blood sugar may require admittance to the intensive care nursery, where she will receive sugar intravenously in the form of dextrose.

Drawing Blood

The heel stick procedure is the most common way to draw blood for testing from newborns. After warming the baby's heel and then pricking it, a drop of blood is collected on a glucose monitor strip (to check for low blood sugar) and/or multiple drops are placed on special paper for metabolic testing. If more blood is needed, it can be collected in a narrow tube or vial and then sent to the lab. Afterward, a gauze pad or cotton ball is placed over the puncture site and pressure is applied. The site is then covered with a bandage.

Test for Jaundice

Newborns are first examined visually for signs of jaundice. The nurse may apply finger pressure to the baby's nose, chest, and abdomen while observing for a yellow discoloration when releasing the pressure. If jaundice is suspected, a test will be done to determine the level of bilirubin in the blood. A hand-held *transcutaneous bilirubin level (TcB)* monitor is used to determine this level through the skin. (Some facilities have begun to routinely screen all babies for elevated bilirubin levels with the TcB monitor every twelve hours.) If the level is above normal, blood will be taken from the baby's heel and further checked for bilirubin.

RhoGAM Studies

If the mother is Rh negative, blood from the baby's umbilical cord will be collected and sent to the lab to determine the baby's blood type and Rh classification. If the baby is Rh positive, the mother will receive an injection of RhoGAM within seventy-two hours of giving birth. (For more information on the Rh factor and RhoGAM, see page 77.)

Cord Blood Studies

If the mother is blood type O, cord blood will be collected and sent to the lab to determine the baby's blood type and to see whether or not antibodies are present. If the baby is a blood type other than O and antibodies are present, she is at risk for developing jaundice as a result of an ABO incompatibility. (For more information, see "Blood-Type Incompatibility and Jaundice" on page 291.)

Hepatitis B Vaccine (HepB)

If the mother tested positive for hepatitis B, her infant should receive both immune globulin and the first dose of the hepatitis B vaccine within twelve hours of birth. If the mother's hepatitis B status is unknown, her infant should receive the first dose of the vaccine within twelve hours of birth. Infants born to women who have a negative hepatitis B status may receive the first dose of the vaccine either in the hospital, or by age two months.

Septic Workup

If the newborn has an elevated temperature or other signs of infection, a septic workup will be done. This may include a complete blood count (CBC), blood cultures, and possibly a spinal tap. If the baby is showing signs of infection, antibiotics will be initiated until the culture results, which can take forty-eight hours, are known.

Testing for Car Seat Travel

Before leaving the hospital, certain babies require a test to ensure that they can safely travel in a newborn safety seat. This includes babies who are born before thirty-seven weeks gestational age and those who weigh less than 2,500 grams (5 pounds 9 ounces) at discharge. It also applies to babies whose oxygen levels are below 88 percent, those with medical conditions that place them at risk for apnea (a condition in which they stop breathing for over twenty seconds), and those with bradycardia (a condition in which the heart rate is under eighty beats per minute).

For this test, the baby is strapped into the car seat at a 45-degree angle while attached to a monitor. A nurse will observe the baby's breathing, heart rate, and oxygen saturation level for one hour in the safety seat and then an additional thirty minutes in a crib. If the newborn fails the test, she may be retested after twenty-four hours. An infant who is unable to use a standard car safety seat may need to be transported in a special car bed.

NEWBORN SCREENINGS

The American Academy of Pediatrics and the March of Dimes recommends that all babies are screened for hearing, and that they undergo metabolic screening (through blood tests) to test for a minimum of twenty-nine disorders. While some states screen for as few as four medical conditions, many states have expanded their testing to include over thirty. To see which tests are required by your state, or where you can have additional testing done (if your state does not have expanded testing), contact the March of Dimes or the National Newborn Screening and Genetics Resource Center. (For contact information, see the Resources beginning on page 449.)

Hearing Screening

Before the baby is discharged from the hospital, she may undergo a hearing test to determine if she has significant hearing loss. If the baby does not pass this test initially, it may be due to fluid in the ear, and the test can be repeated the next day or prior to discharge. If hearing loss is identified, it is important to initiate interventions, such as hearing devices or implants, before the child is six months old. This is so the child, who will start learning speech and language before she can talk, will have a better chance of developing proper speech and language skills.

Two screening methods are used—otoacoustic emissions (OAE) and auditory brainstem response (ABR). For both tests, the baby must be asleep or in a quiet state for the results to register. For the *otoacoustic emissions* test, an earplug is inserted into the baby's ear, where it emits soft sounds that stimulate vibrations in the inner ear. These vibrations produce inaudible emissions (sounds) that echo back to the middle ear where they can be measured. A lack of emissions may indicate hearing loss. The *auditory brainstem response* is a more sophisticated type of hearing screening and is often done if the newborn does not pass the otoacoustic emissions test. For this test, small headphones that emit soft clicking sounds are placed over the baby's ears. Sensors or electrodes are placed on different parts of the head and measure the baby's brain wave responses to the clicking sounds. If your facility does not provide hearing screening, you can have it done through an audiologist.

Naming Your Baby

The ritual of choosing a name for your baby is an important one. Not only is it an activity that involves both you and your partner, it also helps you prepare for the reality of parenthood. Some parents who learn of their baby's gender may decide on a name months before the birth. (This may even aid in the bonding process as they begin referring to their child by name before actually meeting her.) Other couples, while possibly narrowing their list to three or four choices, prefer to wait until the baby is born before settling on a name. They want to choose whichever name seems to "fit" their particular baby.

Many couples find the task of choosing a name easy because they have decided to honor a parent, grandparent, or other relative by using that person's name for their child. Others search for something unique or for a name that has special meaning for them. And with the rich, culturally diverse population in the United States, a growing number of children are given names in accordance with their ethnic backgrounds.

Popular names seem to run in cycles. Every decade sees the emergence of certain names, often because of well-known national figures or entertainers who are popular at that time. According to recent social security card applications, Jacob, Michael, Joshua, Ethan, Matthew, Daniel, Christopher, Andrew, Anthony, and William are the top ten names for boys. Also popular are Joseph, Aidan, Nicholas, Tyler, and Jack. The top ten name choices for girls are Emily, Emma, Madison, Isabella, Ava, Abigail, Olivia, Hannah, Sophia, and Samantha. Other popular choices include Kaitlyn, Makayla, Ashley, and Elizabeth.

If you are debating between a traditional name and an unusual one, be aware that the number-one reason given by parents for staying with a traditional name is that most people will find it acceptable. When considering an unusual name, ask yourself if it will be appropriate as your child grows older and becomes an adult. Also keep in mind any stereotypes that may be associated with certain names. Unfortunately, some people expect a certain type of behavior or appearance from a person based simply on his or her name.

Other questions to consider as you evaluate name options include the following:

- ❑ How does the full name flow?
- ❑ Do the initials form a word that could be embarrassing to your child?
- ❑ What are the possible nicknames for the name?
- ❑ Is the name appropriate for the child's gender?
- ❑ Will an unusual spelling of the name be a nuisance?

Avoid using the diminutive or nickname for your child's legal name. Billy Joe instead of William Joseph, for example, may not be considered appropriate when your child becomes an adult.

If you need help deciding on a name, check your local library or bookstore—numerous books have been written on the subject. An Internet search can also be helpful. In the final analysis, it is most important that you decide on a name that you think will please both you *and* your child for a lifetime.

Metabolic Screening

After blood is taken from the infant's heel, it is sent to the state lab where it will be screened for certain medical conditions. In addition to the standard testing for hypothyroidism, phenylketonuria (PKU), and galactosemia, each state screens for a variety of specific metabolic, hormonal, functional, and genetic diseases.

Congenital hypothyroidism is the most common disorder among newborns. Caused by a deficiency of the thyroid hormone, this condition can lead to mental inadequacy and growth retardation. Early treatment with oral thyroid hormone replacement allows normal development.

A newborn with PKU is missing an enzyme that is necessary to metabolize the amino acid phenylalanine. If left untreated, phenylalanine builds up in the blood and tissues, and can cause brain damage and mental deficiency. Treatment consists of a lifelong restriction of foods that contain this amino acid. Limited breastfeeding is permitted and combined with a phenylalanine-free formula. Frequent blood tests are necessary to monitor the baby's phenylalanine levels.

Babies born with galactosemia are missing the enzyme that breaks down galactose (a sugar in milk) into glucose. Galactosemia can cause death, blindness, and mental deficiency. Infants with this condition are unable to breastfeed and must be placed on a galactose-free formula.

Other diseases and disorders that are included in a full screen include cystic fibrosis, sickle cell disease, Tay-Sachs, and thalassemia, which are discussed in Chapter 4. Congenital adrenal hyperplasia (CAH) is another. CAH is a genetic disorder of the adrenal glands in which the body does not produce enough of the hormones cortisol and aldosterone, but produces too much of the male sex hormone androgen. This causes an early appearance of male characteristics in males, and genitals that appear to be male in female infants. Treatment consists of daily administration of cortisol. If the baby's sex is ambiguous, chromosome studies can determine the gender.

In order for the test results of certain medical conditions to be accurate, metabolic screening is not done until twenty-four hours after the first feeding. If the baby is discharged from the hospital or birth center before that time, the screening must be performed or repeated as an outpatient or at the pediatrician's office. Most hospitals will do the test automatically upon discharge. You can, however, sign a waiver refusing this screening, but only with the understanding that you will have it done later.

If the test results, which are sent to the pediatrician's office, indicate a problem, the parents will be notified within two weeks. Just keep in mind that this does not mean that the child has the condition, only that more precise testing is needed to make the diagnosis.

DISCHARGE FROM THE HOSPITAL/BIRTH CENTER

Babies born in out-of-hospital birth centers generally go home within four to six hours. Although insurance must cover forty-eight hours for hospital deliveries, many parents desire to go home sooner. In 2004, the American Academy of Pediatrics released a policy statement outlining the minimum criteria for discharging healthy full-term newborns.[13] These criteria include:

- An uncomplicated pregnancy and vaginal delivery of a single infant born between thirty-eight and forty-two weeks gestation.
- A baby with healthy weight and good vital signs.
- A baby with normal feeding, urination, and stool patterns.
- A baby without abnormalities, bleeding, or significant jaundice.
- Completion of infant hearing screening and other testing.
- Administration of an initial hepatitis B vaccine based on the infant's risk status.

Discharge should be delayed if there are barriers to adequate medical follow-up for the infant within forty-eight hours.

Prior to discharge, the mother should receive adequate care instructions for her newborn. It is also important to determine that she has help at home to care for herself and the infant. If risk factors—such as substance abuse by the mother, or a family history of domestic violence, child abuse, or neglect—are present, the discharge should be delayed until a solution to the problem is available.

Before leaving the hospital, you will have to fill out and sign the completed birth certificate, which will be sent to the state. Make sure you proofread the typed copy to make sure there are no errors. If you and the baby's father are not legally married, he will need proof of identity to be named on the birth certificate. You can order a copy of the birth certificate through the state's Office of Vital Statistics. By checking the appropriate box found on the birth certificate form, you can request a social security number for your baby, which will be sent to you within six to eight weeks.

When the baby is three to five days old, she should have a follow-up visit with the pediatrician to check for jaundice and possible weight loss. She should be checked again at two weeks to make sure she has regained her birth weight and is feeding well.

CONCLUSION

While you are in the hospital or birth center, and starting to become familiar with this new little person in your life, be sure to utilize the expertise of the nursing staff and the lactation consultants, if available. Your time in the facility is short, so be sure to ask as many questions as you can regarding the care of your newborn. Once you are home, accept help from friends and family, but make sure to get your rest. The next chapter is all about adjusting to your new life. It addresses the most common concerns of new parents.

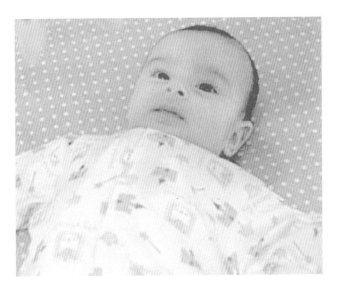

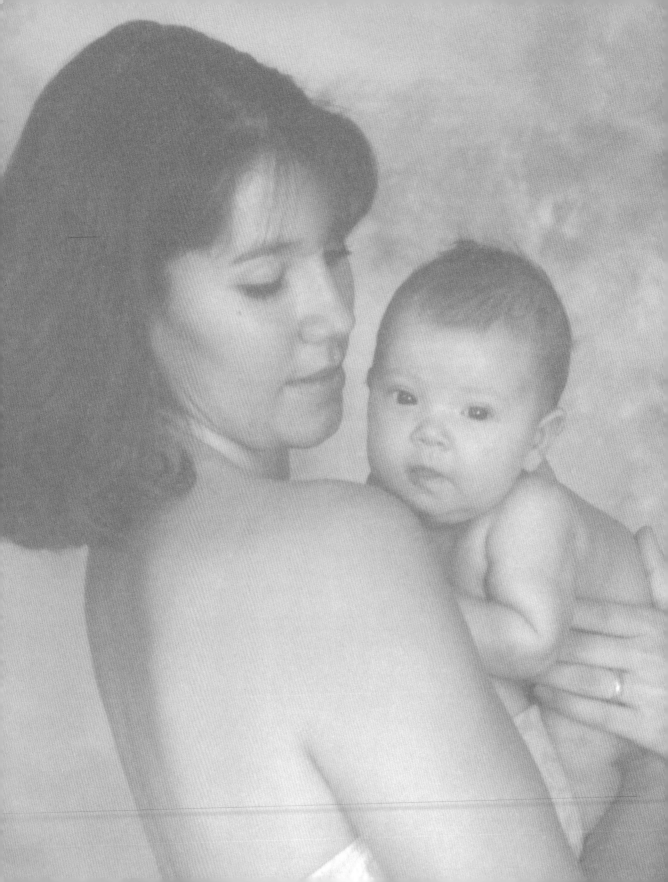

Baby Care and Concerns

or There'll Be Some Changes Made

*C*hange is a keyword when it comes to babies. Not only do newborns change the lives of their parents and siblings, they themselves change physically, almost on a daily basis during the first few months. Having a new baby in the house, especially for first-time parents, can bring about lots of questions and concerns . . . "Am I doing this right?" . . . "Is this normal?" . . . "Why is he still crying?" . . . "Should I call the doctor?" This chapter begins by addressing some of the most common areas of concern for new parents. It encompasses such subjects as immunizations, baby proofing your house, car safety tips, and the lifestyle changes you can expect to make now that there is a baby in your life. Advice on purchasing toys, clothing, and baby equipment are also included, as are emergency procedures for choking and other life-threatening situations. Yes, this chapter is all about the changes (including diaper changes) that you can expect in your life. Embrace the challenge!

COMMON AREAS OF CONCERN

Parents, especially first-time parents, are likely to feel unsure of themselves when it comes to the care of their new infant. This is certainly understandable as they often find themselves in unchartered territory. What follows are some common areas of concern expressed by new parents.

Cord Care

One of the biggest concerns of new parents is how to care for the umbilical cord stump. If the cord was clamped at birth, the clamp is usually removed after twenty-four hours. (Make sure it is removed prior to discharge from the hospital.) If the cord was tied off, the tie will remain there until the stump dries up and falls off, which usually happens in a week or two. Some pediatricians, who believe bathing the newborn may cause the stump to become infected, tell parents to give their babies only sponge baths until the cord falls off. Others allow tub baths right from birth, citing studies that show bathing causes no increase in infection. Whether you give your baby tub baths or sponge baths, try to keep his cord dry between baths. To prevent the diaper (which will eventually become wet) from covering the cord, fold down the front to a level below the baby's navel or use the newborn disposable diapers that are designed with a cutout.

At one time, wiping the cord with alcohol with each diaper change was recommended. This practice is no longer necessary. In a study that compared a group of infants whose cords were cleaned with alcohol with another group whose cords were allowed to dry naturally with no treatment, the umbilical cords in the group without alcohol fell off a day earlier. Neither group showed signs of infection.[1] If you notice that the cord has redness or emits a foul odor or discharge, notify your pediatrician. You might notice some blood when the cord finally does fall off. This is normal.

Bathing

Never . . .
leave an infant alone in a bath. Not even for a second!

While you are in the hospital, try to observe the nurse giving your baby his initial bath, or request that she supervise you as you bathe him. Once you are home, bathing your baby is one task that you *do not* have to do every day. After all, your new baby does not go out and play in the dirt! The only area of his body that you *do* need to wash daily is the diaper area. Make sure that you thoroughly clean his bottom with soap and water after each bowel movement to prevent diaper rash. If he just urinated, plain water is sufficient. Take care to dry the entire area, especially the creases. If, during a feeding, milk drips into the creases of his neck, you will want to make sure to clean and dry that area as well.

When bathing your child during those early weeks, you can immerse him in water or give him a sponge bath. For a sponge bath, lay him on a towel. As you wash and dry each body part, keep the rest of his body covered. Studies have shown that babies cry less and are less likely to become chilled when they are given immersion baths in a tub. Some parents are afraid that this type of bath will delay the cord from falling off, but this is not true. If, however, your son is circumcised, wait a couple days before immersing him. You should however, rinse his penis with water during diaper changes to prevent urine from irritating the surgical site. To do this, squeeze the water from a very wet washcloth over the area.

There are several ways to give your baby an immersion bath. You can take him into the tub with you to combine the task with fun. Dads especially seem to love this "chore." It is safest if you have someone else with you so that when the bath is finished, you can hand the baby to that person before standing up. If you're alone, wrap the baby in a towel and carefully place him on the floor while you get out of the tub. You can also use one of the many commercial tubs that have a special hammock in which to place the baby so that both of your hands are free. If you wish, you can even use a large sink, but wrap a cloth around the faucet to protect the baby from possible injury. By cradling the baby in the crook of your arm and holding his arm with your hand, you will have a free hand with which to wash him. Before the bath, make sure you have all your supplies handy. And *never leave an infant alone in a bath, not even for a second.*

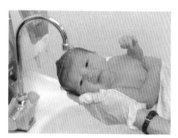

During this newborn's first bath, the nurse uses the football hold while shampooing his hair.

Whether you give your baby a sponge bath or a tub bath, the directions are the same. Use only water to wash his face. Use a separate area of the clean washcloth to wipe each eye from the inside to the outer corner. Wash his body with mild baby soap and then rinse well. In the early weeks, when your baby is more susceptible to getting chilled, remove him from the tub after bathing his body before washing his head. Wrap him in a towel and hold him a football hold position. While supporting his neck, shampoo his head, then rinse and dry well. When bath time is over, make sure to dry around the base of the umbilical cord stump.

Skin Care

Your baby's skin is sensitive and special care should be used to prevent rashes or other reactions. It is not necessary to use lotions, powders, or oils. Use soaps and shampoos that are formulated especially for babies. As a general rule, wash all the baby's clothes and bedding with a mild baby detergent before using them for the first time. This will help prevent rashes caused by allergic reactions to strong laundry detergent or to the chemicals found in new clothes or bedding. Also avoid using dryer sheets. Unlike fabric softeners, which are diluted in the rinse water, dryer sheets are not rinsed out. They are usually heavily perfumed with chemicals that transfer to the clothing in the dryer.

During the first weeks of life, your newborn may develop a harmless rash called *erythema toxicum.* This rash, which is common in newborns, appears as tiny red bumps with yellowish white dots in the center that appear and disappear. It has no known cause, requires no treatment, and will disappear on its own.

Diaper rash is also common among babies. This skin irritation is often caused by prolonged exposure to urine or stool, although the laundry products used on cloth diapers and the chemicals contained in disposable diapers can be culprits as well. Other substances that can cause or add to the problem include the ingredients found in some baby wipes, lotions, powders, and oils. Some babies break out in a diaper rash while they are teething. Breastfed babies are less likely to develop diaper rash.

You can help prevent diaper rash by changing your baby frequently and washing his bottom with warm water. After bowel movements, wash the area with soap and water and dry it well, especially in the folds of his skin. If the area is irritated, apply petroleum jelly or medicated ointment if you desire. If you use cloth diapers, avoid plastic pants, which hold in the moisture. Exposing the irritated area to air is helpful, as is rinsing cloth diapers twice to remove all traces of soap. If you use disposable diapers and diaper rash is a problem, consider changing brands.

When changing diapers, as a general rule, avoid applying powder to the genitals. It can cake in the creases and irritate sensitive tissues, especially in girls. If you use talcum powder or cornstarch on the rest of the baby's body, first sprinkle it in your hand and then apply it sparingly. If you shake it directly onto the baby, he may breathe it into his lungs. Baby oil or lotion that has a mineral oil base robs the skin of vitamins and should not be used on infants. During the first couple of weeks, if the skin on your baby's wrists or ankles is dry and peeling, apply a small amount of an unscented edible nut or vegetable oil, such as almond, sunflower, or safflower.

Prickly heat is another type of rash that is common in babies. It usually occurs if the weather is warm or the baby is overdressed—and most new parents tend to overdress their infants. Keep in mind that a baby should be dressed just like an adult or an older child. If it is 90 degrees outside, you certainly won't need a sweater and neither will your baby.

Cradle cap is a skin condition that appears as flakes, scales, or crusts on the baby's scalp or behind his ears. Wash the area daily and brush it vigorously with a baby brush. Prior to shampooing, you may want to apply oil to the area to help loosen the flakes. Using oil and *not* washing it out would allow the flakes to build up on the scalp. If necessary, ask your pediatrician to prescribe a special soap for this condition.

Urination

Until the volume of mother's milk increases, which usually occurs a few days after the birth, breastfeeding babies will not receive a large amount of milk. The amount of urination, therefore, is small during the first few days. Since formula-fed infants consume a greater volume of milk, they tend to have more wet diapers.

Hints for the New Mother

✓ Avoid using powder on the baby. It can cake in the creases of his skin, and he can breathe it into his lungs.

✓ Do not use mineral oil-based lotions, which can rob the skin of vitamins.

During the first week, the minimum number of wet diapers for both formula-fed and breastfed babies should correspond to their day of life. For example, during the first twenty-four hours, the baby should have a minimum of one wet diaper. He should have at least two wet diapers on day two, three diapers on day three, and four on day four. Once the mother's milk is in, the number of wet diapers will increase. By the end of the fifth to sixth day, the baby should have at least six very wet diapers, and continue with that amount from that point on. During the first few days, the urine may have a red-orange tint, called *brick dust urine,* as the result of urate crystals. This is normal. If, however, brick dust urine is observed after the first few days, it is a sign of dehydration and the pediatrician should be notified immediately.

Bowel Movements

Your baby's first bowel movements, called *meconium,* will be black, tarry, and sticky. Meconium consists of matter that the fetus ingested while in utero, including cells from his skin and intestinal tract, lanugo, mucus, amniotic fluid, bile, and water. During the first four to five days, the stools will gradually change from tarry black to greenish brown to greenish yellow. After the transitional period, they will become "milk stools." Breastfed babies have bowel movements that are yellow and loose with no offensive odor. They may appear to have "seeds," although they will be soft. If the baby is receiving formula, his stools will be soft and yellow with an unpleasant odor.

The number of bowel movements can vary from at least three to eight per day (a small amount with each diaper change). Infrequent bowel movements during the first few weeks may indicate that the baby is not receiving enough milk. After two months, bowel movements may occur as infrequently as once every several days; breastfed babies may have only one a week.

Constipation occurs when the stools are hard, dry, and difficult to pass. This is not related to the frequency of bowel movements. Infants who are totally breastfed and do not receive any supplements of formula or solids rarely become constipated. If you feed your baby formula and he experiences severe constipation, you may need to change his formula.

If your baby has diarrhea, he will need medical attention to prevent dehydration. Diarrhea is characterized by frequent stools that are watery, green in color, and/or foul smelling. They may also contain mucus. Be prepared to tell your pediatrician the number, color, and consistency of the stools. Remember, the stools of a totally breastfed baby are normally loose. They aren't considered diarrhea unless other signs are present.

Spitting Up

Spitting up is a common concern among new parents, especially during the early weeks. The sphincter muscle at the top of the baby's stomach may be immature. When you burp the baby after feeding him, some milk may escape along with air. Be prepared by keeping an extra diaper handy to clean up the milk. Overfeeding and taking in too much air are common causes for spitting up. If you bottle-feed, hold your baby at a 45-degree angle while he feeds and burp him often to prevent air buildup. If you nurse your baby and your let-down (release of milk) is forceful, he may choke and gulp air. Gently remove him from your breast until the flow of milk slows. Also, don't allow your baby to cry for too long before feeding him, as this may cause him to take in large amounts of air. After each feeding, make sure to burp him and elevate his head to aid digestion. As your baby matures, his sphincter muscle will become stronger and the spitting up will subside.

Hints for the New Father

When the baby gets fussy:

✓ Take him for a walk while your partner takes a break.

✓ Take a bath with him.

✓ Lay him skin to skin on your chest.

✓ Talk or sing to him.

✓ Turn on the vacuum cleaner. "White noise" often lulls fussy babies.

✓ Check for a soiled or wet diaper.

✓ Check to see if he is overdressed or underdressed.

✓ Learn and apply the 5 S's (see page 307).

Crying

Crying is your baby's only way of expressing his needs. It is meant to alert you, so that you can respond to him and meet those needs. Being attentive to your baby's cries does not mean you are spoiling him—and don't let anyone tell you that you are. Remember, your baby was snuggled, rocked, fed, and listened to your heartbeat twenty-four hours a day for nine months. Allowing him to "cry it out" is unnecessary and has risks. Prolonged crying in the newborn can increase his blood pressure and result in less oxygen circulating in the blood. It can also impede blood flow to the heart and affect the closure of the ductus arteriosus—the opening that diverts the blood from the lungs during pregnancy and closes shortly after birth. Extended crying in the newborn increases pressure in the head, which can result in bleeding within the brain.[2]

Trying to cope with a crying newborn can be a very frustrating experience for new parents. Hearing your baby cry can make you physically uncomfortable—your own heart rate and blood pressure may rise and you may begin to sweat. Many babies have "fussy periods," which usually occur at the same time each day, commonly in the late afternoon when you are trying to make dinner. In fact, so many babies become fussy at this time that in earlier days, mothers aptly named it "Grandma's hour"—the time when Grandma could help by rocking and cuddling her grandchild.

It is very difficult to always know why your baby is crying. What follows are the most common reasons for a fussy baby. Helpful suggestions are also provided that may be effective in calming him down.

■ **Is he hungry?** If your baby is crying and has not eaten for two hours or more, he may be hungry. If he is breastfed, he may be trying to build up your milk supply with more frequent feedings. Even if he recently nursed, he may want to breastfeed some more just for comfort or a little extra milk. Babies have a strong need to suck. After three weeks of age, you can also try giving your baby a pacifier if he enjoys it and needs more sucking.

■ **Is he uncomfortable?** If your baby is crying but not hungry, check him for a soiled or wet diaper, or an irritating condition such as diaper rash or a diaper that is too tight. Is he underdressed or overdressed? Is his clothing too tight or too rough? Is the room too hot or too cold? Any of these conditions can make a baby fussy.

■ **Does he need to burp?** A fussy baby may have a air bubble and need to burp or expel gas. Hold him upright and pat his back, which may bring up a burp. You can also place him over your knees with a warm towel under his tummy. (To easily warm a towel, place it in the dryer.) If he looks like he is trying to move his bowels, place him on his back and gently move his legs as if he is riding a bicycle. This may help him expel the gas.

■ **Is he lonely?** For nine months, your baby was safe and snug within your warm body, listening to your heartbeat and other sounds. Once he was born, he suddenly found himself lying alone in a crib that was not nearly as comfortable as his mother's body. Your crying baby may just need to be cuddled and held close. A front-pack baby carrier, a wrap, or a sling may be of tremendous help. They will enable your baby to be held close to you, which will make him happy while allowing your hands to be free.

Do Not . . .

let anyone convince you that crying is good for the baby's lungs. A baby's lungs do not need "exercise."

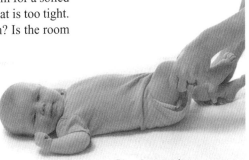

Bicycle exercise for expelling gas.

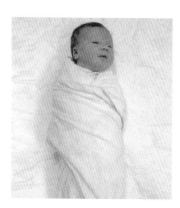

A swaddled baby.

■ **Is he bored?** Some babies need more interaction than others. Change the environment by taking your baby outside or into another room. Take him on a tour of the house to see what interests him. Try to distract him with a mobile or show him bright objects. Talk or sing to him, or read him a book. The book does not have to be for a child. Choose any book or magazine article that interests you and read it aloud. The sound of your voice may be all your baby needs to stop fussing.

■ **Has he been overstimulated?** Too much handling by visitors or long periods of wakefulness can exhaust your baby. Try using motion of any kind—a stroller, car ride, baby swing, walking—to help calm him down. If you are feeling tense, have someone else hold him. You can also try removing all of your baby's clothes except for his diaper, and then lay him on your breast or your partner's bare chest and lightly massage him. Taking the baby into a warm bath with you is another option. This accomplishes three things—it quiets the baby, enables him to be bathed, and allows you to take a bath yourself. Try to have someone available to take the baby out of the tub. If you are alone, carefully wrap him in a towel and place him on the floor while you get out of the tub. Wrapping him snugly in a blanket, called *swaddling,* may also soothe him.

■ **Is he understimulated?** While babies are in utero, they experience constant rocking while listening to the strong sounds within the uterus. Surprisingly, the sound of a vacuum cleaner may be just the trick to quiet your little one. The constant hum or "white noise" mimics the whooshing sound of the placenta and can lull and relax some fussy babies. There are also tapes available that mimic the mother's heartbeat or other sounds that babies hear inside the womb.

Colic

Colic is a condition that is characterized by inconsolable crying for over three hours a day, three or more times a week, and for at least three weeks. It usually does not start until the child is two weeks old (or two weeks after the due date in a preterm baby) and is commonly over after three months of age. Babies usually experience colic symptoms at the same time each day. Typically, they appear to have abdominal cramps or spasms. A baby with colic may draw up his knees as he cries in pain, sometimes while passing gas. This response may be an overreaction to the *gastro-colic reflex,* the signal for the intestines to expel its contents during or after a meal. Medical experts, however, disagree on the cause of colic.

Cow-based protein is believed to be the most common food item that causes colic. If your baby is drinking a cow-based formula, switching him to a soy-based product may improve the condition. Be aware, however, that many babies are also sensitive to soy proteins. For this reason, colic is rare among breastfed babies, although a very small percentage may be sensitive to something the mother has eaten, including dairy or other foods. If you notice that your breastfed baby has a colicky reaction after a feeding, think of any "suspect" food you may have eaten. Before automatically eliminating that food from your diet, try it again about two weeks later. If the baby has the same reaction, eliminate that food from your diet. Hopefully, this will improve the baby's condition.

Severe acid reflux (heartburn) is cited as another cause of colic. Although this may be true in a small percentage of babies, most babies with severe reflux do not have pain.[3] Some doctors place the blame for colic on nervous mothers, whose babies, they believe, can sense their anxiety. Others feel the condition occurs because the baby is challenging or has a difficult temperament. Certain doctors believe that colic is not a gastrointestinal condition at all, but rather a response to overstimulation through too much noise, bright lights, and activity. They suggest that providing the baby with a

Crying Babies and the Missing Fourth Trimester

Dr. Harvey Karp, noted pediatrician and author of *The Happiest Baby on the Block,* does not agree with the common belief that gas, acid reflux, maternal anxiety, or babies with difficult temperaments are real reasons for the severe, persistent crying that some babies experience during their first few months of life. Based on extensive research, Dr. Karp believes that the true cause of colic is what he calls the "missing fourth trimester." Compared to other mammals, human infants are born early. (This is so their large heads can pass through the mother's pelvis

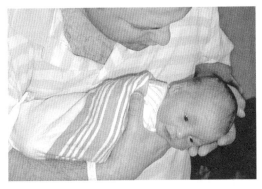

This new dad uses the Five S's
to soothe his fussy baby.

during birth.) He feels that some newborn babies need another three-month gestation period to be better equipped for adjusting to life outside the womb.

Dr. Karp has developed a valuable method that helps recreate the in utero environment. Based on five components that he calls the Five S's, his method, when done properly, can stimulate the baby's *calming reflex* and effectively soothe crying and colicky babies. What follows is a brief description of the Five S's. Some babies need all five, while others require just a few.

THE FIVE S's

Swaddling. Wrapping the baby securely in a soft blanket with his arms at his sides helps mimic the snugness of the uterus. It also prevents him from flailing his arms and helps him focus his attention on the other S's.

Side/Stomach Position. This position, which is done while holding the baby, imitates his position in the uterus. It can also assist in digestion, prevent the startle reflex, and trigger the calming reflex.

Shushing Sounds. These sounds mimic the whooshing sound of the blood as it continuously flows through the placenta. A vacuum cleaner or hair dryer, radio static, and a loud verbal "shhhhhh" can all provide this type of white noise. White noise CDs are also available.

Swinging. Rocking the baby, placing him in a baby swing, or gently jiggling his head can help mimic the comfortable, calming, swinging motions that he experienced whenever his mother moved around or walked up and down stairs.

Sucking. Whether on the breast, a pacifier, or a finger, sucking can trigger the calming reflex and help soothe most babies.

This approach can be amazingly helpful in calming even the fussiest babies, but it is important that the techniques are done exactly right or they may not work. To learn more about Dr. Karp's method, you can read his book or view his DVD, also called *The Happiest Baby on the Block.* (The DVD is recommended as the best way to learn the Five S's technique.) Classes that teach Dr. Karp's techniques are also available in some areas. Visit *www.thehappiestbaby.com* for more information.

quiet, dimly lit environment, especially during feeding, may help. Noted pediatrician Dr. Harvey Karp, who has done extensive research on colic, believes just the opposite. For him, a more plausible explanation for this condition is understimulation. He believes the baby is missing the noisy, rhythmic, and entrancing stimulation he enjoyed while in the uterus.[4] Based on his extensive research, Dr. Karp has developed a method for reducing, if not eliminating, colic symptoms in babies. More information on his method—called the Five S's—is presented in "Crying Babies and the Missing Fourth Trimester" above.

The way in which you hold a colicky baby may be effective in calming him down. He may prefer to be held facing away from you, with your forearm across his belly. The *colic hold* may also provide relief. To do this, hold your baby by straddling his legs over your arm and supporting his head with your hand, as seen in the photo at left. Use your forearm to apply pressure against his upper abdomen and chest.

Crying spells, especially when caused by colic, can make a parent frustrated and even angry. If you have tried everything to calm your crying baby, but nothing is working and you feel as if you are at the breaking point, place him in his crib, remove yourself from the room, and close the door. Turn on the vacuum cleaner, put on earphones, take a shower, or go to another area of the house. Give yourself time to calm down so you can better take care of your infant. After five or ten minutes, go back and try to soothe your baby. Never take your anger out on him. Shaken baby syndrome and child abuse can result when a parent feels unable to handle the situation.

If you are dealing with a colicky infant, do not feel guilty or responsible. Colic is not a result of poor parenting. Talking about it, accepting offers of help, or even laughing about it with your partner may help you get past this difficult time. Remember that the baby is not mad at you or constantly crying on purpose. Fortunately, colic usually disappears by the third or fourth month.

Colic hold.

Sleeping

Newborns sleep from fourteen to eighteen hours per day. The periods of sleeping and wakefulness vary from baby to baby, depending upon individual sleep cycles and eating patterns. Some babies seem to be awake all the time. Most newborns wake up when they are hungry and fall asleep again when they are satisfied. This rhythm usually continues throughout the day and night, except for that possible late-afternoon fussy period. If your baby has his days and nights mixed up, do not try to change them immediately. If you are breastfeeding, nurse him when he is awake and sleep when he sleeps until breastfeeding is well established. Then you can start to encourage him to sleep longer at night. During nighttime feeds, keep the light in the room dim; change and feed the baby without providing additional stimulation that will fully rouse him. Swaddling him and having white noise in the background may help him sleep longer.

By three or four months of age, the baby may have longer periods of wakefulness, as well as longer sleep cycles. In other words, while a newborn may be awake for only an hour and then sleep for two or three hours, by four months of age, he may be awake for several hours at a time and sleep from six to eight hours during the night. As a baby grows, his need for sleep lessens. At nine months, most babies need only a morning and afternoon nap; by twelve to fifteen months, they usually take just one. Remember, however, that each baby is an individual and will establish his own routine.

Studies indicate that twins who sleep together as infants grow faster and are healthier.

Some babies have trouble falling asleep. They are not lulled to sleep by sucking and may fuss or cry for a few minutes. If your baby has this problem, try rocking him or singing him a lullaby. You can also try Dr. Karp's Five S's. You will find that a comfortable rocking chair is a necessity. After three months, most babies begin to learn how to self soothe and they will fall asleep on their own. Placing your baby in bed while he is slightly awake, or slightly rousing your sleeping baby may help encourage this self-soothing practice.

James J. McKenna, PhD, director of the Mother-Baby Sleep Laboratory at the University of Notre Dame, states that infants and older babies fall asleep more easily with a background of family noise, rather than in silence.[5] This is because the baby is likely to feel more secure hearing a parent nearby.

Co-Sleeping and Bed Sharing

Most babi
anywhere
and still o
infant bec
bed, prov
ing. It als
onto the

Co-sle
mother a
tact. Co-
other's s
This can
crib or b
sharing,
another

In 19
sion issu
if there
Americ
ed, "Th
sharing
hazard
that m
with t
father

Bu
procla
bed fc
arate
in clo
room
naps
(alth
age

Children who refuse a pacifier should ...
into taking one.

The Academy of Breastfeeding Medicine (ABM) has expressed concerns over these new recommendations having a negative impact on breastfeeding. Studies have shown that exclusively breastfed infants have a lowered risk of SIDS during the first four months of life.[7] Breastfed infants wake and feed frequently throughout the night and experience less deep sleep,

same way that pacifiers are believed to help pre-[vent] SIDS. They do not need pacifiers as they receive [ade]quate nighttime stimulation through nursing. The [risks] of pacifiers include "an increased chance of ear [infe]ctions, later dental problems, and reduced breast-[fee]ding."[8]

Dr. James J. McKenna, while a consultant to the [AA]P on the new policy, also disagrees with the conclu-[sio]ns and believes that safe co-sleeping needs to be [pu]blicized. He defines co-sleeping as "sleeping in close [pro]ximity to the infant, which can include but does not [ne]cessarily imply being in the same bed." According to [sa]fe co-sleeping practices, the mother and/or her part-[n]er should not be under the influence of alcohol, seda-[ti]ves, drugs, or narcotics. Smokers or extremely obese [p]arents should not share a bed with an infant. Babies [u]nder a year of age should not share a bed with other [c]hildren. The sleep surface should not be a sofa or [w]aterbed, contain soft bedding, or be adjacent to a [s]pace that could trap an infant.[9] Women should avoid [w]earing nightgowns with long ties, and those with [l]ong hair should tie it up to avoid entanglement with the baby.[10] No matter where your child sleeps, follow the recommendations for preventing sudden infant death syndrome that are discussed on page 310.

Some people feel that allowing your older baby to sleep in bed with you can help make him feel secure. Many adults do not like sleeping alone and understand why a baby feels comforted and sleeps better when in his parents' bed. According to Dr. McKenna, studies are showing that co-sleeping can contribute to "strong independence, social competence, feeling of high self esteem, good comportment (behavior) by children in school, ability to handle stress, and strong gender or sex identities."[11] There is no evidence that co-sleeping has harmful long-term effects on the child's emotional development.

You should do whatever is comfortable for you and your baby. When your child is older, he may prefer sleeping in his own bed and may just return to your bed when he is sick or frightened. A dark, shadowy room can be quite scary to a young child with an active imagination.

Sudden Infant Death Syndrome

"Back" to Sleep

Placing your baby on his back to sleep reduces the risk of SIDS. Other recommendations for lowered risk include breastfeeding and the avoidance of smoking in the house. Also, don't allow the baby to become overheated while he sleeps by dressing him in too many layers of clothing or covering him with loose blankets.

Sudden infant death syndrome (SIDS) refers to an unexplained death of an apparently healthy baby under one year of age. It is sometimes called *crib death* because it typically occurs when babies are in their crib. About 91 percent of SIDS cases occur in infants between one and six months of age, with most happening between two to four months. Most incidents occur during the winter months and many of the affected families have reported an upper respiratory infection prior to the death. SIDS occurs more often in males than females.

While the cause of SIDS is unknown, according to one theory, SIDS babies have an abnormality in the portion of the brain that controls breathing and waking during sleep. Babies may experience a decrease in oxygen and excessive carbon dioxide levels if they have a cold that obstructs their breathing, or if they rebreathe exhaled air that is trapped in bedding or blankets if they are sleeping on their stomachs. The brains of normal babies will respond to this decrease in oxygen by causing them to wake up and cry. According to this theory, babies who lack this protective mechanism do not respond to the lack of oxygen and stop breathing.

Factors that increase a child's risk of SIDS include sleeping in a prone position (on the stomach), sleeping on a soft surface, being overheated, having a mother who smoked during pregnancy, and exposure to secondhand smoke in the household. A child who is male, born preterm or of low birth weight, or who is of African American, Native American, or Native Alaskan descent is also at increased risk, as are the firstborn children of women who are under the age of twenty.[12, 13]

While SIDS may be frightening, there are a number of things you can do to decrease the risk:

■ Always place your baby on his back for sleeping, even for naps. Since the AAP has advocated placing babies on their "back to sleep," there has been an over 40 percent decrease in the incidence of SIDS.[14]

■ Make sure the sleep surface is firm. Soft mattresses, waterbeds, sofas, sheepskins, and comforters are not safe for a baby to sleep on.

■ Avoid pillows and loose bed covers.

■ Make sure your baby cannot get trapped between the mattress and the headboard or footboard, a wall, or other furniture.

■ Do not use bumper pads in the crib. If you do, use mesh ones.

■ Remove stuffed toys from your baby's sleep area.

■ Swaddle your baby with a light blanket or infant wrap, or dress him in a sleeper. If you do use a blanket or another covering, place the baby with his feet at the bottom of the crib. Place the blanket no higher than his chest, and tuck it securely in the bottom of the crib mattress. Make sure the blanket does not cover his head.

■ Do not smoke during pregnancy or allow smoking around your baby.

■ Do not overdress your baby for sleep, which can cause him to overheat. His room should be the same temperature that is comfortable for you.

■ Breastfeed your baby. It will strengthen his immune system, making him less likely to pick up an infection, which may increase his susceptibility to SIDS.

Make sure anyone who cares for your baby, including childcare providers, grandparents, and babysitters, knows to place him on his back to sleep. Avoid products that are designed to keep your baby in one position while sleeping. They have not been tested for safety and are not recommended. Take your baby for regular checkups and have him vaccinated. There is no evidence that links immunizations to SIDS, nor is there proof that home monitors decrease its risk.[15]

You may be concerned that your baby will choke if he spits up while sleeping on his back. There has been no evidence to support this. It is safer for a baby to sleep on his back than on his side. Babies who sleep on their sides can roll onto their stomachs. Certain health conditions may require a baby to sleep on his stomach, but your doctor will inform you if he feels this is necessary.

For more information on SIDS and SIDS prevention, contact the National Institute of Child Health and Human Development or the First Candle/SIDS Alliance. For contact information, see the Resources beginning on page 449.

The Need for Human Interaction

You may be wondering if you are spoiling your new baby by giving him too much attention. Current authorities firmly believe that it is impossible to spoil an infant. Babies need lots of love, warmth, tenderness, affection, and holding, which are very important for their security and development. If you compare a human baby to the offspring of other mammals, you will find that the humans are more immature when born and remain so for a much longer period of time. Most other mammals, for example, are able to walk shortly after birth. According to noted anthropologist Ashley Montagu, a human baby's gestational period is only partially completed by the time he is born; the remainder is completed outside the womb. This is necessary because of the rapid brain development that occurs in human infants. If a human baby was not born until he was completely developed, he would not be able to fit through his mother's pelvis. Therefore, the same way that he is carried within his mother's body for nine months, he needs to be carried and held until he is able to move around on his own, which is at least another nine months, according to Montagu.[16]

Your young baby is completely ego-centered. He wants his needs met immediately, and if they are not, he lets you know. Keep in mind that he really does not plan to fuss or cry at inopportune times, such as when you are just starting to make dinner, or talking on the phone, or sitting down with a good book. Your baby is only expressing his needs—with no hidden intentions.

An infant's needs include both physical desires such as food and warmth, and emotional cravings like comfort and love. Babies who receive only physical care exhibit slower emotional and physical development than babies who are given plenty of attention and love. If your baby stops crying when you pick him up, it is because he is happy to see you and needs to be held. Your baby will be tiny for such a short time— enjoy him and give him plenty of love. As he matures, he will cry less frequently and become less demanding because he will know that comfort is coming.

Tummy Time

All infants require "tummy time" when they are awake and someone is watching them. This allows them to exercise their chest, neck and leg muscles. It also prevents them from developing a flat head.

Baby enjoying "tummy time."

Lots of Lovin'

Infants cannot be spoiled. They *need* to be held in order to thrive.

WHEN TO CALL THE DOCTOR

A mother's intuition is often correct when it comes to her child. Never hesitate to call your pediatrician if "something is not right." Your pediatrician may be able to calm your fears or suggest an appropriate treatment. The following common conditions may (or may not) be reasons for calling the pediatrician.

Fever

A fever is a symptom of an illness, not a disease itself, and may or may not be a reason to call the doctor. It can be caused by an infection, a virus, an immunization, or teething. (Doctors refute that teething can cause a fever, but mothers see it happen time and again.) Suspect a fever if your baby feels hot, has dry skin and a flushed face, and seems listless. A low temperature may also be a sign of infection.

Immediately report to your pediatrician any temperature that is lower than 97°F or higher than 100.2°F in an infant under three months old, or higher than 103°F in a child of any age. You should also notify the doctor if a fever lasts longer than twenty-four hours and is of unknown origin. If the fever is above 101°F and the child is uncomfortable, give him a non-aspirin fever reducer according to your doctor's orders and a fifteen-minute lukewarm bath. Never give your child aspirin to reduce a fever because it has been linked to Reye's syndrome, which can be fatal. Dress your child lightly; *do not* bundle him up because heavy clothes and wrappers retain heat. If your child has a mild fever, he does not need any medication because a moderately high temperature stimulates the body's protective immune defenses.

Dangerous Thermometers

Do not use oral glass thermometers that contain mercury. They should be disposed of at a toxic waste disposal site.

Taking Your Baby's Temperature

There are several methods for taking your baby's temperature. For an axillary temperature, place a digital thermometer under the baby's armpit until it beeps. Make sure the armpit is dry. Special axillary thermometers that have a flatter tip are also available. Tympanic thermometers, which read the temperature in the child's ear, are not recommended for children under six months of age. When using a tympanic thermometer on a child who is older than six months, if you feel the reading is inaccurate, recheck the temperature under the arm with a digital or axillary thermometer.

Temporal artery thermometers read the temperature of the blood flow through an artery on the forehead and are very accurate when used according to instructions. Simply place the probe flat on the forehead and slide it across to the hairline while keeping it in contact with the skin. A beeping sound and blinking light lets you know it is taking a measurement; a digital temperature is displayed when completed.

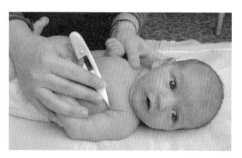

Taking the axillary temperature.

Do not take a child's temperature orally until he is older and able to hold a thermometer in his mouth. And when doing so, do not use an oral thermometer that is made of glass and contains mercury. In the event of breakage, the mercury, which is toxic, can be hazardous to the child's health as well as the environment. If you have this type of thermometer, it should be disposed of at a toxic waste disposal site.

It is no longer recommended to take your baby's temperature rectally. Rectal tissues are very sensitive and damage can result if the thermometer is inserted incorrectly. Two other types of thermometers that should not be used because of the difficulty in recording accurate readings are the forehead strip and the pacifier thermometer. Moisture can affect the result of the forehead strip, and the infant must continuously suck on the pacifier thermometer for five minutes to get an accurate result.

When reporting your baby's temperature to your pediatrician, it is important to tell him how you took the reading.

Vomiting/Spitting Up

At times, a baby will consume more milk than his stomach can hold and will spit it up. As long as your baby is happy and growing well, this is more of a laundry problem than anything else. If, however, he repeatedly or frequently vomits following a feeding, alert your pediatrician. Also let him know if the baby appears to be in pain after a feeding—with or without significant vomiting—as this can be a sign of reflux. If the baby wheezes or exhibits respiratory difficulty during feedings, he may be aspirating the milk into his lungs and may need an evaluation.

Diarrhea

If your baby has diarrhea (loose, watery, greenish, foul-smelling bowel movements) or bowel movements that contain mucus or blood, call the pediatrician. Vomiting and/or diarrhea are reasons for concern because they can cause dehydration, which can occur very rapidly in a tiny baby. The signs of dehydration include loss of tears or saliva (dry mouth), sunken eyes, a decrease or absence of urine, the presence of dark amber-color urine, a depressed soft spot on top of the head, and/or lethargy. Dehydration is considered a medical emergency and needs to be treated immediately.

Coughing/Congestion

Coughing and a stuffy or runny nose are signs of a cold. Running a cool-mist vaporizer near the baby's crib will help ease his breathing. If your baby's nose is congested, your pediatrician may recommend saline nose drops. Simply dissolve $1/4$ teaspoon of salt in eight ounces of water. Place the baby across your lap on his back. Holding him firmly, place two drops of the saline solution in each of his nostrils with an eye dropper. Wait a moment, then suction the mucus from his nostrils with a bulb syringe. (Remember to compress the bulb before inserting the tip into his nose.) Give your baby these nose drops before meals and at bedtime to help him nurse and sleep better. If he also has a fever and/or is irritable, or if he is pulling on his ears, he may have an ear infection. Severe hoarseness, difficulty in breathing, or a "barking cough" also need to be reported.

In 2007, the FDA voted to ban the use of over-the-counter cold products for children under age six. These products are not effective and can have serious side effects. To quiet the cough of a child *over one year of age*, a teaspoon of honey before bedtime is recommended. This soothes an irritated throat and will help him sleep better.

Change in Temperament

Alert your pediatrician if your baby displays a change in temperament or habits. If, for example, he cries excessively, is unusually irritable, is extremely drowsy, has trouble sleeping, is restless, or has a severe loss of appetite, a call to the doctor is in order.

Eye Inflammation or Discharge

If your baby's eye is inflamed, swollen, or has a watery or pus-like discharge, it may be the sign of an infection or a blocked tear duct. Contact your pediatrician as medication may be indicated. He may also instruct you to massage the area if the tear duct is blocked.

When to Call the Pediatrician

Call your doctor if your newborn displays any of the following symptoms:

✓ A temperature over 100.2°F or under 97°F. (Call immediately if the child is under three months of age.)

✓ Projectile vomiting.

✓ Severe diarrhea.

✓ Poor appetite or refusal to feed.

✓ Unusual behavior.

✓ Extreme lethargy (difficulty being roused, floppy limbs).

✓ Inconsolable crying.

✓ Shrill cry or constant moans.

✓ Bulging soft spot.

✓ Depressed soft spot.

✓ Few wet diapers or bowel movements.

Catching and treating a problem early may prevent a more serious condition and possible complications.

Cold Products

Do not give over-the-counter cold products to children under the age of six. They are not effective and can have serious side effects.

Hints for the New Father

✓ Attend a baby-care class.

✓ Talk and sing to your baby.

✓ Give your newborn a bath, or help your partner bathe him.

✓ Take your baby into the bath with you.

✓ Rock your baby.

✓ Change your baby's diaper.

✓ Put the baby to sleep on his back to reduce the risk of SIDS.

✓ Take pictures and videos of your baby.

✓ Attend an infant CPR class with your mate.

✓ Massage your baby.

✓ Play games with your baby.

✓ Carry your baby in a front-pack carrier or sling.

✓ Baby-proof your house.

✓ Use a safety seat every time the baby is in the car.

✓ Never place the safety seat or any child in the front seat of your car if you have dual air bags.

✓ Invest in a comfortable rocking chair for the fussy times.

Rash

Many rashes, such as prickly heat, diaper rash, and cradle cap, are common among infants. When properly cared for, they are also harmless. If your baby displays any bodily rash that is not cured by the methods presented in the Skin Care discussion on page 302, have the doctor take a look at him. The rash may indicate a condition that requires medicinal treatment.

Hearing Loss

Most facilities perform a hearing screening of the newborn as part of routine hospital care. But if you have concerns that your baby is not responding to environmental noises, or you question your child's ability to hear, have his hearing checked. The chart on page 315 provides basic hearing guidelines for a child from birth through twenty-four months.

Twitching/Convulsions

If your child has a convulsion or displays any signs of twitching or rigidity, contact the pediatrician at once. Frequently, young children will have a seizure that is related to a high fever. Call for medical assistance immediately.

Head/Body Injuries

If your child suffers a head injury, observe him for extreme sleepiness with difficulty waking, a change in mental alertness, vomiting, discharge from the ears or nose, unequal pupil sizes, bulging soft spot, or skull deformity. Elevate his head and alert the doctor immediately. When a limb is injured, check for and report any redness, swelling, extreme tenderness, inability to use the limb, or signs of distortion. An open wound may require suturing. For cosmetic reasons, some parents prefer a plastic surgeon to repair cuts, especially those on the face.

Skin Infection

If your child has a skin infection that looks like a pimple or boil; is red, swollen, and painful; and/or contains pus or other fluid; be sure to have the pediatrician take a look at it, as it may require an antibiotic or other treatment. The bacteria *Staphylococcus aureus* (more commonly known as *staph*) normally lives on the skin. A dangerous form of these bacteria, called *methicillin-resistant Staphylococcus aureus (MRSA),* is becoming more prevalent in schools and day care centers. What makes MRSA so dangerous is that it is resistant to antibiotics and can result in serious, sometimes fatal, complications. Be sure to have any suspicious-looking skin infections examined by the doctor.

Sunburn

Severe sunburn in a child under a year old is considered a medical emergency that needs evaluation and treatment by the pediatrician. Prevent sunburn by limiting your child's exposure to direct sunlight. Sunscreens are not recommended for children under six months of age. After that time, choose a broad-spectrum sunscreen that filters both ultraviolet B (UVB) and ultraviolet A (UVA) rays. It should have a sun protection factor (SPF) of at least 15 and be applied at least thirty minutes prior to exposure. Also check the label for a product that is hypoallergenic and PABA-free.

BASIC HEARING GUIDELINES FROM BIRTH THROUGH TWENTY-FOUR MONTHS

Age	Signs of Hearing
Birth to 3 months	Moves or jumps at loud sounds.
	"Coos" or makes vowel sounds like "ooh" and "ahh."
	Blinks or startles at loud sounds.
	Stops crying or smiles when spoken to.
3 to 6 months	Turns his head toward sounds, especially your voice.
	Babbles, says "dada," or uses other consonants, such as "b" or "m."
	Responds to toys that make noise.
	Squeals, laughs.
6 to 9 months	Turns toward new sounds, even if they are not loud.
	Stops activity when his name is called.
	Says "mama" or imitates sounds.
	Understands "no" or "bye-bye."
9 to 12 months	Uses hand movements—waving bye-bye, pointing—to communicate.
	"Jabbers" using different speech sounds and different tones of voice.
	Repeats simple words or sounds that you make.
	Responds to music or sings.
12 to 18 months	Points to familiar objects when you name them.
	Uses three to twenty words.
	Points to one to three body parts.
18 to 24 months	Understands about three hundred words.
	Puts two words together.
	Follows simple directions.
	Points to five or more body parts.

Ingestion of Poison or Nonfood Item

If your child swallows a poisonous substance or nonfood item, immediately call your pediatrician or local Poison Control center for instructions. At one time, syrup of ipecac was prescribed to induce vomiting for such cases; however, the American Academy of Pediatrics no longer recommends this. If you do not know your local Poison Control number, call the American Association of Poison Control Centers at 1-800-222-1222 or visit their website at *www.aapcc.org/findyour.htm.*

Poison Control

Keep the following toll-free Poison Control number on hand:

1-800-222-1222

IMMUNIZATIONS

Immunizations are an important part of your baby's healthcare because they protect him from potentially harmful, often life-threatening diseases. After receiving an immunization, some babies have mild side effects that may include pain and redness at the injection site, fever, and irritability. After receiving the measles vaccine, a baby may break out in a rash six to twelve days later. To reduce the fever or pain, give your child a non-aspirin medication, such as acetaminophen or ibuprofen, as ordered by your pediatrician. If your child develops a high fever or seizures, seek help immediately. In rare cases, a child may develop a severe allergic reaction within minutes or hours of receiving a vaccination. Symptoms may include difficulty in breathing, wheezing, hives, dizziness, fainting, and erratic heartbeat.[17] For such reactions, immediate medical care is necessary.

Table 14.1 below presents the recommended immunization schedule for children and adolescents. Prepared by the Centers for Disease Control (CDC), this schedule indicates the recommended ages for routine administration of currently licensed vaccines for children through age six. What follows on page 317 is a brief discussion of the vaccines and the diseases that they prevent.

TABLE 14.1. RECOMMENDED IMMUNIZATION SCHEDULE

For Persons Ages 0-6 Years • United States • 2008
Department of Health and Human Services, Centers for Disease Control and Prevention

VACCINE ▼ AGE ▶	Birth	1 month	2 months	4 months	6 months	12 months	15 months	18 months	19–23 months	2–3 years	4–6 years
Hepatitis B	HepB	HepB	HepB			HepB					
Rotavirus			Rota	Rota	Rota						
Diphtheria, Tetanus, Pertussis			DTaP	DTaP	DTaP		DTap				DTap
Haemophilus influenzae type b			Hib	Hib	Hib	Hib					
Pneumococcal			PCV	PCV	PCV	PCV				PPV	
Inactivated Poliovirus			IPV	IPV		IPV					IPV
Influenza						Influenza (Yearly)					
Measles, Mumps, Rubella						MMR					MMR
Varicella						Varicella					Varicella
Hepatitis A						HepA (2 doses)				HepA Series	
Meningococcal										MCV4	

▪ Range of recommended ages   ▪ Certain high-risk groups

This schedule indicates the recommended ages for routine administration of currently licensed childhood vaccines, as of December 1, 2007, for children ages 0 through 6 years. Additional information is available at www.cdc.gov/vaccines/recs/schedules. Any dose not administered at the recommended age should be administered at any subsequent visit, when indicated and feasible. Additional vaccines may be licensed and recommended during the year. Licensed combination vaccines may be used whenever any components of the combination are indicated and other components of the vaccine are not contraindicated and if approved by the Food and Drug Administration for that dose of the series.

Hepatitis B

Hepatitis B (HepB) can lead to chronic liver disease or cancer. The first dose of this vaccine may be administered in the hospital or by two months of age if the mother's hepatitis B test is negative. A total of three doses (or four if the first dose was given in the hospital and the remainder are in a combination vaccine) are given. If the mother tested positive for HepB, the newborn should receive Hepatitis B Immune Globulin within twelve hours after birth and in addition to his first HepB vaccination.

Rotavirus

Rotavirus gastroenteritis is a highly contagious disease that leads to severe diarrhea. This virus can survive for a long time on toys or other objects and is resistant to many soaps and disinfectants. The first vaccination should be administered between six and twelve weeks of age (no later), and completed no later than thirty-two weeks.

Diphtheria, Tetanus, Pertussis (DTaP)

Diphtheria is an upper respiratory tract illness caused by bacteria that lives in the mouth, throat, and nose of an infected person. It is highly contagious and easily passed to others through coughing or sneezing. It may cause difficulty in swallowing and, in serious cases, suffocation. Heart failure, paralysis, and even death can occur.

Also known as *lockjaw, tetanus* is a serious but preventable disease that affects the muscles and nerves. Typically, it is caused by a skin wound (usually a cut or deep puncture) that becomes contaminated with *Clostridium tetani* bacteria. The toxins caused by the bacteria affect the nerves and cause muscle spasms. Without treatment, tetanus can be fatal.

Pertussis, also called *whooping cough*, is a highly communicable respiratory illness characterized by prolonged coughing and choking. Unvaccinated infants are at highest risk for complications, which can include pneumonia, seizures, brain damage, and death.

Haemophilus Influenzae Type b

The *Haemophilus Influenzae Type b (Hib)* bacteria are a major cause of childhood meningitis (inflammation of the covering of the brain and spinal cord) as well as bacterial pneumonia in children. (It does not cause the flu, even though "influenzae" is part of its name.) The bacteria colonize in the nose or upper throat and are spread through sneezing or coughing. Illness does not occur unless the bacteria travel to the lungs or enter the bloodstream.

Pneumococcal Disease

Pneumococcal disease is an infection caused by the *Streptococcus pneumoniae* bacteria, which cause pneumonia, bacteremia (infection of the blood), and meningitis. It is recommended that four doses of the pneumococcal conjugate vaccine (PCV) are given to children under age two. In addition, the polysaccharide vaccine (PPV) should be administered to certain high-risk groups over two years old.

Polio

Caused by a virus, *polio* results in fever, muscle paralysis (including those that aid breathing), and possible death. In the past, a live oral polio vaccine was administered in the United States. Currently, three separate injections of inactivated polio are given. Although the live vaccine provided better protection, for certain people—those with compromised immune systems—it also carried a slight risk of contracting the disease. There has not been a case of polio from a wild (non-vaccine related) virus since 1979.

Influenza

Influenza or the *flu* is characterized by high fever, muscles aches, sore throat, and nasal congestion. Complications of the flu can be more severe in young children than adults, and can include pneumonia, bronchitis, and sinus and ear infections. Therefore, healthy children ages six months through their fifth birthday should receive the flu vaccine each year. Their caregivers should receive the vaccine as well. The CDC recommends that children who are six months to nine years of age and getting a flu shot for the first time should receive two doses of the vaccine. The first dose "primes" the immune system, while the second dose provides immunity. This vaccine can be given in two methods. The flu "shot" contains inactivated virus and is injected with a syringe, while the nasal-spray vaccine is made with live, weakened flu viruses that will not cause the flu. The spray is approved for healthy individuals age two to forty-nine years. It should not be taken by women who are pregnant.

Measles, Mumps, Rubella

Measles is a highly contagious, viral respiratory infection. Characterized by a total-body skin rash and flu-like symptoms, including a fever, hacking cough, and runny nose, measles is easily spread through coughing or sneezing. Serious complications of the illness include pneumonia, brain damage, and even death.

Caused by a virus, *mumps* usually spreads through saliva and can infect many parts of the body—usually the parotid salivary glands. Mumps causes these glands, which produce saliva for the mouth and are found toward the back of each cheek, to swell and become painful. Other symptoms of the illness may include high fever, stiff neck, headache, nausea and vomiting, drowsiness, and convulsions. Although not common, mumps can lead to inflammation and swelling of the brain and other organs. If contracted by males during adolescence, it can cause swelling of the testicles.

Commonly known as the *German measles, rubella* is an infection caused by the rubella virus. It is usually transmitted through droplets from the nose or throat. Symptoms in children usually include low-grade fever, swollen lymph nodes that are tender, and a rash that appears on the body. Rubella is most serious to the developing fetus of a pregnant woman. If she is exposed to rubella, her baby may be born with serious birth defects. See Chapter 4 for more information on rubella and pregnancy.

Varicella

Varicella, more commonly known as *chicken pox*, is a common, usually mild but contagious childhood disease that, once contracted, provides lifelong immunity. Caused by the varicella-zoster virus, chicken pox is characterized by mild fever, an itchy rash, and red spots or blisters that appear all over the body. Serious complications are extremely rare in young children. Those over age thirteen who contract chicken pox have a higher risk of complications, which may include encephalitis, pneumonitis, kidney problems, and bacterial infections of the skin. The varicella vaccine may require one or more boosters, and compliance to a booster schedule becomes more difficult as children mature. It is recommended that adults and children over age thirteen who have not had the disease receive two doses of the vaccine. The vaccine is not recommended for anyone with a suppressed immune system.

Hepatitis A

Hepatitis A is a disease that attacks the liver and causes jaundice. Symptoms can include nausea, stomach pain, fatigue, and general weakness. They can also be vague and go undetected. Hepatitis A occurs primarily in areas with poor sanitation—the bacteria are often found in the water and the feces of animals and humans. It can also be contracted by eating uncooked or inadequately cooked foods, or foods prepared by infected food handlers. In 2006, the CDC recommended that all children receive two doses of the vaccine starting at twelve months of age.

Meningitis

Meningococcal disease or *meningitis* is an infection of the membranes surrounding the brain and the spinal cord. It is usually caused by bacteria or a virus and can be life threatening if not treated promptly. The meningococcal vaccine prevents bacterial meningitis—the more serious form of the disease. Meningitis can be easily spread among people living in close quarters, which puts college and boarding school students at a high risk. The vaccine is recommended for children over two years of age who are in high-risk groups and for other children around eleven or twelve years old, prior to entering high school.

Pediarix

In 2003, the FDA approved *Pediarix*, a one-shot vaccine that protects infants against five different diseases—hepatitis B, diphtheria, tetanus, pertussis, and polio. It is recommended to be given as a three-dose primary series to infants at about two, four, and six months of age. Pediarix should not be given to infants before six weeks; it is not indicated for babies born to mothers who are infected with hepatitis B or whose hepatitis B status is unknown. This five-in-one vaccine means six fewer shots for babies during their first year of life.

VACCINE MYTHS AND CONTROVERSIES

Many of today's parents have never seen a case of polio, measles, or mumps—and they may question the validity of the immunizations for these and other illnesses. Before the widespread use of these vaccines, each year nearly 10,000 children were paralyzed from polio; over 4 million contracted the measles and 3,000 died from it; whooping cough caused the deaths of thousands of infants; diphtheria was a common cause of death in school-aged children; and 15,000 children developed meningitis from Hib, leaving many with permanent brain damage. Rubella was the cause of mental retardation and birth defects in as many as 20,000 newborns of mothers who contracted the disease during pregnancy.[18] While each vaccine has possible side effects, the complications caused by the diseases themselves are higher in number and more severe.

According to one theory, the decrease in diseases has more to do with improved sanitation and antibiotics than immunizations. While these factors have certainly added to the decrease in illness, the most dramatic declines followed the introduction of the vaccines. Before the measles vaccine was introduced, almost everyone got the measles. Since then, there has been a 99-percent reduction.[19] Also, the incidence of chicken pox did not decrease until the vaccine was introduced.

Caution: Tylenol Overdosing

When giving acetaminophen (Tylenol) to your infant or young child, be sure to give the proper dose. Overdosing can result in irreversible liver damage or even death. Because Infants' Tylenol can be up to three-and-a-half times more concentrated than Children's Tylenol, *always* check with your pediatrician for the proper dosage and let him know which concentration you are using. Then double-check the dosage instructions on the bottle. *Never* give more than the recommended amount. Even small overdoses can present the risk of serious health problems.

In the 1970s and 1980s, the media portrayed the dangers of the pertussis vaccine during interviews with parents whose children suffered rare but serious side effects from the immunization. In response to the public outcry regarding the vaccine's adverse effects, three developed countries—Great Britain, Sweden, and Japan—cut back on its use. Within several years, the cases of pertussis soared to thousands per year in these countries. Russia has also seen an epidemic of diphtheria since the decrease in immunization.

One common concern among parents is the possible link between autism and thimerosal, a mercury-containing preservative used in some vaccines. The Institute of Medicine (IOM) reviewed multiple studies on thimerosal that involved hundreds of thousands of children in a number of countries. No association between exposure to thimerosal in vaccines and autism was found.[20] Regardless, since 2003, none of the current vaccines (with the exception of the flu vaccine) contains thimerosal. And the amount of mercury from thimerosal that a child would receive from the flu vaccine is below the maximum level of exposure set by the FDA and the EPA.

Many parents are also concerned about serious side effects, long-term problems, or even death following the administration of a vaccine. Most side effects include mild fever and soreness at the injection site. According to the CDC, "serious adverse events occur rarely (on the order of one per thousands to one per millions of doses) and so few deaths can plausibly be attributed to vaccines that it is hard to assess the risk statistically."[21] In addition, the IOM reports that there is no association between the DTP vaccine and SIDS,[22] which was another fear of some parents.

Autism

Autism is a neurological, developmental disorder characterized by problems with social interaction, language and other communication, and learning; repetitive behavior; the desire for routine; and, in certain cases, remarkable mental abilities. Currently, as many as 1 in 150 children have been diagnosed with this disorder, which is more common in males. While the cause of autism is unknown, recent studies point to a combination of genetics and possible environmental triggers.

In 2007, the American Academy of Pediatrics recommended that all children be screened for Autism Spectrum Disorder (ASD) twice before age two—once at eighteen months and once at twenty-four months—as part of well-baby checkups. According to First Signs, an organization that is dedicated to the early identification and intervention of children with developmental delays and disorders, the following signs are considered possible red flags for autism and should be reported to your pediatrician.

❑ No big smiles or other warm, joyful expressions by six months or thereafter.

❑ No back-and-forth sharing of sounds, smiles, or other facial expressions by nine months or thereafter.

❑ No babbling by twelve months.

❑ No back-and-forth gestures, such as pointing, showing, reaching, or waving by twelve months.

❑ No words by sixteen months.

❑ No two-word meaningful phrases (without imitating or repeating) by twenty-four months.

❑ Any loss of speech (or babbling) or social skills at any age.

For more information, contact First Signs and/or Autism Speaks—both organizations are dedicated to increasing awareness of this disorder. For contact information, see the Resources beginning on page 449.

The potency of vaccines can be affected if they are not stored at the right temperature. Although this does not make them dangerous, it could cause them to be ineffective. This means the child may not receive the proper immunity and may need to be revaccinated. Ask your pediatrician if daily temperatures of the office refrigerator are recorded to safegaurd vaccine potency.

It is important to weigh the benefits of the vaccination against its slight risk. A child is far more likely to be seriously affected by one of these diseases than by the vaccine that prevents it. There is also no evidence that giving combination vaccinations increases the risk of side effects.

Large-scale immunization programs are also important for protecting those individuals who cannot be vaccinated because they are allergic to the components in the vaccine. They also help protect the small number of people who do not respond to the vaccines. Some parents who choose not to immunize their children rely on the fact that everyone else in the community will be vaccinated, so their children will be less likely to come in contact with the diseases.

Some parents want to wait until the infant is older before starting the immunizations. However, the schedule is set up to protect children when they are most vulnerable to the complications from the diseases.

HANDLING EMERGENCIES

Some situations should be considered emergencies and treated immediately. If your child is choking or stops breathing, it is important to know how to handle such life-threatening conditions. Familiarize yourself with the following procedures so you will know exactly what to do if the need ever arises.

CPR

When practicing CPR, *never* do so on a living person.

All parents should take a course in infant cardiopulmonary resuscitation (CPR) to get firsthand practice of this procedure (on a manikin) under the guidance of a certified instructor. Babysitters, grandparents, and other caregivers should also be trained, as accidents can occur at any time. For more information or to find a class in your area, contact the American Heart Association or the American Red Cross. (For contact information, see the Resources beginning on page 449.)

First Aid for Choking

If an infant or small child is choking because of a blocked airway, you will have to dislodge the obstruction. The signs of a blocked airway include blue lips, hoarse or crowing breathing, and the inability to speak or cough. (If the child is able to speak or cough, allow him to expel the object on his own. Unnecessary intervention may cause further problems.) Call for help if you can. However, if you are alone, do not take the time to use the phone. You are the lifesaver at this time.

If you can see the object in the throat or mouth, try to remove it—and try to remain calm while doing so. Although your natural reaction may be to sweep your finger blindly in the baby's mouth to dislodge the obstruction, it could make the blockage worse. According to the recommendations of the American Heart Association, if you cannot easily dislodge the object, use back slaps and chest compressions for a child under one year old. For a child over one year, use abdominal thrusts, also known as the *Heimlich maneuver. Never perform abdominal thrusts on an infant under one year of age, as they can cause injury to the abdominal organs.*

Back slaps for
a conscious infant.

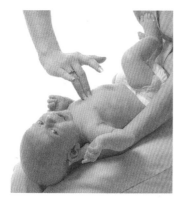

Chest compressions
for a conscious infant.

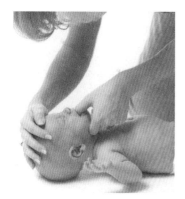

Obstruction check for an
unconscious infant.

For a Choking Baby Under One Year Old

Treat a choking baby who is conscious and under one year of age with back slaps and chest compressions.

1. On your lap, place the baby facedown over the length of your arm. Position his head so it is lower than his chest, and support it with your hand.

2. Using the heel of your free hand, give the baby five sharp slaps between his shoulder blades.

3. Turn the baby onto his back, continuing to support him on your arm with his head lower than his chest. Give him five chest compressions. To do this, use two fingers of your free hand to quickly and firmly compress the breastbone just below the nipple line.

4. Repeat these steps until the object is expelled.

   If the baby loses consciousness at any time, discontinue the previous steps and initiate CPR by doing the following:

5. Place him on his back and kneel next to him.

6. Open his mouth and look for the obstruction. If you see it, remove it.

7. If the obstruction is not visible or is inaccessible, open the baby's airway. To do this, tilt his head back, lift up his chin gently with one finger, and push his forehead down with your other hand.

8. Cover his nose and mouth with your mouth and give two effective (1-second) *rescue breaths*, using just enough force to make his chest rise as in normal breathing. Reposition his head and repeat the rescue breaths if the first ones were unsuccessful.

9. If the airway is still blocked, give thirty chest compressions (as in Step 3).

10. Check the mouth for the object and remove it if possible.

11. If the airway is still blocked, give another two rescue breaths, followed by another thirty chest compressions, followed by a check for the object. Continue this cycle for no longer than two minutes (five cycles).

12. If the airway is still blocked and you are alone, call 911. Then go back to giving rescue breaths and chest compressions until the material is expelled; or the baby begins coughing or breathing on his own; or another person can take over for you; or emergency help arrives.

For a Choking Child Over One Year Old

Treat a choking child who is conscious and over one year of age the same as you would an adult—with abdominal thrusts (Heimlich maneuver).

1. Stand or kneel behind your child and wrap your arms around his waist.

2. Make a fist with one hand and clasp your other hand over the fist. Position the thumb side of your fist against the child's abdomen, above the navel and just below the rib cage.

3. Make a quick upward thrust with your fist into the child's abdomen to force air up through his windpipe.

4. Repeat these steps until the obstruction is expelled.

If the child loses consciousness at any time, discontinue the previous steps and initiate CPR by doing the following:

5. Place him on his back and kneel next to him.

6. Open his mouth and look for the obstruction. If you see it, remove it.

7. If the obstruction is not visible or is inaccessible, open the child's airway. Tilt his head back by lifting up his chin gently with the fingers of one hand, and pushing his forehead down with your other hand.

8. Pinch his nostrils closed, cover his mouth with yours, and give two effective (1-second) rescue breaths, using just enough force to make his chest rise as in normal breathing. Reposition his head and repeat the rescue breaths if the first ones were unsuccessful.

9. If the airway is still blocked, give thirty chest compressions (not abdominal thrusts). Place the heel of one or both hands (one on top of the other) between the child's breastbone at about the nipple line. Compress the sternum hard and fast (about one-third to one-half the depth of the chest), allowing the chest to recoil after each compression.

10. Check the mouth for the object and remove it if possible.

11. If the airway is still blocked, give another two rescue breaths, followed by another thirty chest compressions, followed by a check for the object. Continue this cycle for no longer than two minutes (five cycles).

12. If the airway is still blocked and you are alone, call 911. Then go back to giving rescue breaths and chest compressions until the material is expelled; or the child begins coughing or breathing on his own; or another person can take over for you; or emergency help arrives.

Abdominal thrusts for a conscious child over one year old.

Ways to Prevent Choking

The best way to save your child from choking is to take precautions beforehand. Although most people realize that small objects such as buttons, toy parts, marbles, balloons, and coins can be dangerous to babies and young children, many parents are not aware that some foods also pose hazards. The following foods are the most frequent causes of choking in children under the age of five:

- ❑ Hot dogs and sausage.
- ❑ Round candy.
- ❑ Peanuts and other nuts.
- ❑ Whole grapes.
- ❑ Hard cookies and biscuits.

- ❑ Meat chunks and sticks.
- ❑ Raw carrot slices and sticks.
- ❑ Peanut butter and peanut butter sandwiches.
- ❑ Apple pieces.
- ❑ Popcorn.

Never leave a baby alone while he is eating or drinking, and always make sure that a small child is adequately supervised at mealtime. Babies can also choke when drinking from a bottle that is propped up while they are lying down. Children can choke when they run or play with food in their mouth, or when they talk or laugh while eating. A child should not eat while in a moving vehicle. In the event that he begins choking, it may be difficult to pull over and tend to him.

Cardiopulmonary Resuscitation (CPR)

If a child's breathing and/or heart have stopped, circulation also stops and his body will start becoming deprived of oxygen. Without oxygen, brain cells begin to die within four to six minutes. By performing *cardiopulmonary resuscitation (CPR)*—which involves breathing into the lungs and applying chest compressions to pump the heart—you can maintain blood flow and oxygen to the brain and other organs until the child recovers or emergency medical personnel can take over.

CPR may be necessary during a variety of emergency situations, such as a near drowning, suffocation, choking, electrocution, poisoning, smoke inhalation, and suspected sudden infant death syndrome. If your child loses consciousness and is not breathing, performing CPR can save his life. Although knowing the following steps is valuable, it is best to obtain training under the guidance of a qualified instructor. The American Red Cross and many local hospitals offer emergency first-aid courses.

If your child is in need of CPR and another person is with you, have him call for emergency help while you immediately initiate CPR. If you are alone, perform CPR for at least two minutes before calling 911 yourself. Then immediately return to performing CPR until the child begins breathing, someone takes over for you, or medical help arrives.

When performing CPR on a baby under one year old, first gently tap or shake his shoulder to gauge his responsiveness. Then remember your ABCs—Airway, Breathing, Compressions:

Clear the Airway:

1. Place the baby on his back and kneel next to him.

2. Tilt his head back by gently lifting up his chin with one of your fingers while pushing his forehead down with your other hand. His head should be positioned as if he were trying to sniff something.
   Warning: Do not exaggerate the tilt, as this may close the airway completely.

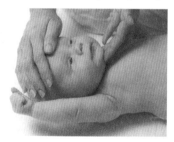

Gauge the baby's responsiveness.   Tilt his head back *slightly.*

Provide Rescue Breaths:

3. Place your ear over the baby's mouth, your face pointing toward his chest, to look, listen, and feel for breathing (take no longer than 10 seconds to do this.)

4. If signs of breathing are absent, cover the baby's nose and mouth with your mouth and give two effective (1-second) rescue breaths, using just enough force to make his chest rise as in normal breathing. (For a child over one year old, pinch his nostrils shut and cover his mouth with yours before giving rescue breaths.)

Warning: Do not blow hard as this can injure the baby's lungs. However, blowing too softly will not give him enough oxygen.

Look, listen, and feel for breathing.

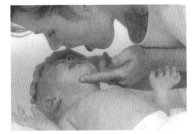

Provide rescue breaths.

Start Chest Compressions:

5. Imagine a horizontal line between the baby's nipples. Place two fingers just below the line, and use the tips of those fingers to compress the breastbone. Make sure that they are not on the tip of the breastbone. (For a child over one year old, instead of using fingers for chest compressions, use the heel of one or both hands—one on top of the other.)

6. Compress the area hard and fast, one-third to one-half the depth of the chest at a rate of 100 times a minute. Allow the chest to recoil after each compression. Use your other hand to maintain the baby's head position.

7. Perform cycles of thirty compressions and two rescue breaths. After two minutes (five cycles), if the child has not started breathing and you are alone, call 911. Then continue compressing the chest and giving breaths until the child begins breathing or medical help arrives. *If another person is available, he can call 911 immediately and take over for you after two minutes.*

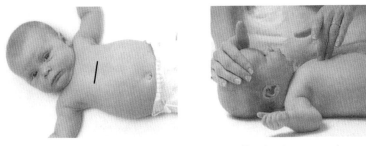

Imagine a line between
the nipples.

Do chest compressions
and rescue breathing.

Using an Automated External Defibrillator

An *automated external defibrillator (AED)* is an electronic device that is designed to deliver an electric shock to victims of sudden cardiac arrest. When used promptly, an AED can restore a normal heartbeat in a large percentage of cases. Once available primarily in hospitals, these devices are now found in many public places. The AED has voice capability and will talk you through the directions for proper use.

For a sudden witnessed collapse of a child who stops breathing and is over one year of age, use an AED (if available) and as soon as possible. (It is not recommended for children under a year old.) For an unwitnessed collapse, use the AED after two minutes of CPR. If pediatric pads are not available, use the adult pads.

BABY PROOFING YOUR HOME

Before your baby begins to creep or crawl, you must baby proof your house—that is, make it safe for curious little fingers. It is easy to put this job off, but if you do, you may find that while your baby is rapidly learning to move around, he is getting into *everything.* The best time to make your home safe for your baby is during your last trimester of pregnancy.

To baby proof your house or apartment, get down on your hands and knees and take a crawling tour through every room to get a baby's eye view. Remove anything that looks even remotely enticing or dangerous. As you move these items out of the way, try to replace them with interesting, safe objects your baby can play with. A stimulating environment contributes to a child's creative development.

There are a number of ways in which you can make your home—both inside and outside—a safe place for your baby. Here are some helpful suggestions:

The House in General

■ Install smoke detectors and carbon monoxide detectors. Check the batteries monthly and change them annually.

■ Place fire extinguishers in areas of fire risk. Plan two escape routes and hold periodic fire drills.

■ Elevate your gas hot water heater to eighteen inches above the floor. This will reduce the risk of a flash fire in case of a flammable liquid spill. Store all flammable liquids in closed containers.

■ Turn the water heater thermostat down to 120°F to protect against scalding, or use anti-scald devices for faucets and showerheads.

■ Check all baby furniture for the Juvenile Products Manufacturers Association (JPMA) Safety Certification Seal to make sure that it meets the basic safety standards. Check for this seal before purchasing anything. For more information on baby furniture safety guidelines, contact the Consumer Product Safety Commission. (For contact information, see the Resources beginning on page 449.)

■ Babies can fall through windows. Move furniture away from the windows and/or install window guards. Leave one window accessible in each room for escape in case of fire.

■ Attach safety netting on balcony railings.

■ Secure furniture to walls with angle braces or anchors. Children can climb up furniture that then topples onto them.

■ Move furniture in front of as many electrical outlets as possible to protect against electric shock.

■ Insert plastic covers in all unused electrical outlets and put large boxlike covers over those that are in use.

■ Cover all unused telephone outlets with duct tape.

■ Hide all electrical and telephone cords, as babies like to chew on them.

■ Store your iron out of sight to prevent the baby from tugging on its cord and pulling it down onto his head. Never leave a hot iron unattended.

■ Mini blinds and window treatments with cords made before 2001 should be replaced or repaired to avoid potential strangulation. The Window Covering Safety Council offers free retrofit kits for this. (For contact information, see the Resources beginning on page 449.)

■ Keep all window pull cords and inner lift cords out of a child's reach. Make sure that tasseled pull cords are short, that continuous-loop cords are permanently anchored to the floor or wall, and that cord stops are properly installed and adjusted to limit movement of inner lift cords.

■ If your home was built before 1970 or you have second-hand painted furniture, strip and repaint any surface on which your baby might chew. The original paint may contain lead. For information about lead, contact the National

Lead Information Center of the Environmental Protection Agency. (For contact information, see the Resources beginning on page 449.)

■ Move ashtrays, pipes, cigarettes, matches, and lighters out of reach. Tobacco can be fatal when eaten by a small child.

■ Unload and lock up all firearms. Never keep a gun in a bedroom drawer or purse, and never let a small child see you using one.

■ If you have any toxic houseplants, hang them out of reach, move them outside, or put them into loving "foster care."

■ Set aside a special utensil set for measuring and applying fertilizer to your houseplants. Do not use household utensils for poisons.

■ Put a safety doorknob cover or a very high lock on every door leading either outdoors or to an unsafe room, such as a sewing room, bathroom, or garage.

The Kitchen

■ Install a gate across the doorway to keep the baby out of the kitchen when you are not there.

■ Install safety latches on all cupboard doors that you do not want little hands to open.

■ Put all vitamins, medicines, wastebaskets, plastic bags, glassware, knives, and other potentially dangerous items in locked cupboards.

■ Move all wine and liquor to a locked cabinet. Do not leave leftover drinks sitting out where a toddler can find and drink them. Alcohol can be toxic.

■ Make sure all household cleaners, detergents, and similar products are out of reach.

■ Tie plastic bags in knots and throw them away after use.

■ Remove all tablecloths from tables that a toddler can pull.

■ When the dishwasher is not in use, keep the door latched.

The Bathroom

■ Lock the medicine cabinet or move all toxic and dangerous medical supplies out of reach.

■ Move perfumes, cosmetics, and other grooming products out of reach.

■ Store all razors out of reach.

■ Move the wastebasket out of reach.

■ Keep all exercise equipment closed up in a room away from the baby. Do not allow the baby to be near when you exercise.

■ Mark all sliding glass doors with decals and do not allow any heavy toys near them.

■ Install a baby gate at the top and bottom of every staircase to prevent climbing and falling. Make sure the gate is securely anchored. Avoid accordion-style gates, which can trap an arm or leg. Gates that have vertical slats or a mesh design are recommended. Those that are held in place with an expanding pressure bar should not be used at the top of stairs.

■ Apply corner and edge bumpers to furniture and fireplace hearths to prevent injuries from falls against sharp edges.

■ Apply door stops and door holders on doors and door hinges to help prevent small fingers and hands from being pinched or crushed.

■ Keep appliances away from the edges of countertops. Unplug and wrap the cords.

■ Put some safe kitchen items, such as plastic bowls and wooden spoons, in a low cabinet away from the stove for the baby to play with. This will help divert his attention from items that are not as safe and keep him occupied while you are cooking.

■ If your stove has knobs on a front panel, either remove the knobs or install knob covers when you are not using the stove.

■ When filling the dishwasher, position sharp utensils with the pointed ends down. Do not add detergent until you are ready to run the machine.

■ Highchairs should have a waist strap and a strap that runs between the legs. Make sure to always use them. Don't use the tray as a restraining device instead of the straps.

■ Pad the bathtub faucet to prevent bumps.

■ Put adhesive nonskid decals on the bottom of the bathtub to prevent slipping.

■ Install a lock on the toilet lid and always keep the lid down and the bathroom door closed. Toddlers can drown in a toilet.

The Nursery

■ Replace the crib if its slats are more than $2\frac{3}{8}$ inches apart (or if a can of soda fits between the slats). Also replace it if the rail, when raised, is less than 26 inches above the mattress support when the support is in the lowest position or, when lowered, is less than 9 inches above the mattress support when the support is in its highest position. Cribs manufactured after 1974 meet all these requirements.

■ Corner posts should not extend more than $\frac{1}{16}$ inch above the top of the end panel to prevent the child's clothing from getting caught.

■ Do not use an antique crib, which may not meet the necessary safety requirements.

■ If the mattress does not fit snugly in the crib, replace it. Remove any plastic wrapping materials. Never use plastic bags as mattress covers. Mattress support hangers should have closed hooks or be secured by bolts.

■ Position the crib mattress support at the highest position for your newborn. Lower the mattress support as the baby grows. Once the baby reaches 35 inches in height or can crawl out of the crib, put him in a regular bed.

■ Be sure the locking latch that holds up the side of the crib is sturdy and cannot be released by a child. Always leave the side up when your baby is in the crib.

■ It is best not to use bumper pads, but if used, choose mesh ones, which allow more airflow through the crib.

When your baby can pull himself up to a standing position, remove the bumper.

■ Do not leave stuffed animals, pillows, or loose blankets in the crib when the baby is sleeping. Crib sheets should fit snugly.

■ Move the crib away from heaters, air vents, and window treatment cords. For warmth, poistion the crib against an inside wall.

■ Do not hang glass mirrors or picture frames on the wall above the crib.

■ Choose a changing table that is sturdy and has a 2-inch guardrail on all sides and a safety strap.

■ Store diaper pins, cotton balls, baby oil, and talcum powder out of the baby's reach. Also, keep these items away from other young children, as they may try to use them on the baby.

■ To prevent strangulation, never tie a pacifier around your child's neck. Remove bibs and necklaces whenever you put your baby in a crib or playpen.

■ Make sure that crib gyms are installed securely so they cannot be pulled down into the crib.

■ Mobiles should be out of the child's reach.

■ Remove crib gyms and mobiles from the crib when your baby is five months old or begins to push up on his hands and knees.

The Playroom

■ Move all toys that have small parts or sharp points to a shelf that the baby cannot reach but that your older children can.

■ Discard all stuffed toys and dolls that have eyes, noses, or other features that might come off. Embroidered features are the safest; sewn or glued parts can be pulled off.

■ Do not use lightweight hammocks without spreader bars to store toys. They can cause strangulation.

■ Do not add soft bedding (quilts, pillows) to the playpen if the baby sleeps there.

■ Use a toy chest with a support that will hold the hinged lid open in any position, or buy one with doors or a detached lid.

The Garage or Workroom

■ Move all pesticides, paints, and petroleum products to a high shelf or locked cabinet. Do not store them in containers such as soft drink bottles or food jars—this could cause them to be mistaken for something else.

■ Move dangerous tools out of reach.

■ Put small items like nails and screws, in closed containers.

■ If you have an old automatic garage door opener, replace it with a model that has an electric eye or that is programmed to stop and reverse if the door touches an object before reaching the ground. Test the door by using a roll of paper towels to simulate a small child. The door should reverse within two seconds.

The Yard

■ Remove any poisonous plants. Daffodils and other plants of the narcissus family, oleander, caladium, elephant's ear, English ivy, castor bean plants, common lantana, rosemary pea, pokeweed, foxglove, Carolina yellow jasmine, jatropha, gloriosa lily, dieffenbachia, hyacinth, holly, mistletoe, Jerusalem cherry, azalea, angel's trumpet, poinsettia, philodendron, and rhododendron are among the toxic plant varieties. Your local poison control center can identify other toxic plants for you.

■ If you use pesticides or herbicides on your plants or lawn, follow the instructions carefully. Do not allow a child to walk or play on a treated lawn for at least forty-eight hours.

■ If you have a pool, block it off with a tall, sturdy fence that has a self-locking gate. Many states require this by law. Hot tubs and spas should be covered when not in use. Also, make sure you have the proper lifesaving equipment on hand.

■ Even if your child is a good swimmer, keep an eye on him when he is in or near a pool or hot tub. Drains and intake valves can draw in water at great pressure, which can entangle long hair and trap a child under water. If the drain cover is broken or dislodged, a child could be sucked underwater by the pressure of the drain.

■ Use caution when placing your infant in a swimming program that involves dunking or repeated submergence. Swallowing large amounts of water can dilute a baby's blood and cause a life-threatening condition known as water intoxication. Infants can also develop severe diarrhea from bacteria in the water that comes from the diapers of other babies. Additionally, even if your child has been through a swimming or water survival program, do not expect him to remember how to swim or "float" from year to year. The techniques he has learned need to be reinforced frequently.

■ Discard or store out of reach any large buckets or containers in which rain or sprinkler water can collect. A child can drown in a five-gallon bucket.

■ Remove any clothes with hoods or strings when your child plays on playground equipment. These items can get caught on the top of a slide or entangled in a swing chain.

■ Do not allow your infant or toddler to suck or chew on the bars of playground equipment, which may contain lead as well as harmful bacteria.

Whenever you take your child to someone else's house, it is important to check for these same hazards.

Lead Poisoning

Lead is a highly toxic metal, especially to children. Common symptoms of lead poisoning include headaches, stomachaches, hearing problems, learning disabilities, behavioral problems, anemia, seizures, and lowered IQ. Although lead is no longer used in gasoline or paint, it is still found in toxic levels in many common everyday items, such as dishes, coffee mugs, and jewelry. Children's products, including toys, toy jewelry, lunch boxes, and vinyl backpacks have also been found to contain harmful levels. The year 2007 saw a massive recall of imported children's toys that contained lead paint. Although attempts were made to remove them from store shelves, many of these toys were still available, especially through online sites.

A blood test can determine if your child has high lead levels. The Environmental Protection Agency recommends that all children be tested at ages one and two. Home test kits are available but may not be reliable. For more information, contact the EPA's National Lead Information Center. For contact information, including its toll-free hotline, see the Resources beginning on page 449.

BABY-SAFE HABITS

In addition to baby proofing your house, you should baby proof yourself and other family members. Take a look at your habits. Do you do anything automatically that could spell trouble for your baby? What about your spouse, other children, parents, friends, or anyone else who is in your home on a regular basis? Replacing a dangerous habit with a safe practice could avoid a possible life-threatening tragedy.

The following are just a few of the habits that you can correct (or never establish in the first place) to make your child's life safer:

■ Do not allow smoking in the house. Children exposed to secondhand smoke in their homes have more colds and upper respiratory infections, and miss more school than those in nonsmoking households. They are also at a greater risk for SIDS.

■ Do not drink or pass hot beverages while your child is nearby or on your lap.

■ Do not leave your baby in a drop-side playpen with the side lowered. He can roll into the space between the pad and the loose mesh side, and possibly suffocate. The best kind of playpen has a firm lower edge in which an infant cannot be entrapped.

■ Never leave your baby or small child alone in the tub.

■ Never leave your baby alone on the changing table or on any other high surface.

■ Do not leave your infant unattended in a bassinet if you have other small children. They could try to pick up the baby or rock the cradle.

■ Avoid the use of walkers. They can result in serious injuries.

■ Never drape clothes or blankets over the side of the crib because they can fall or be pulled over the baby's head.

■ Do not use a cord or string to tie rattles or pacifiers to your baby's clothing or around his neck.

■ Purchase pacifiers that cannot come apart. Solid, one-piece molded plastic varieties are the safest. Check them periodically for deterioration. Never use the top and nipple from a baby bottle as a pacifier.

■ Never give balloons to a baby or small child. An uninflated balloon or pieces from a popped balloon, if swallowed, could get stuck in his throat and cause him to choke.

■ Never leave a baby who is sitting in a Bumbo seat or Bébé pod unattended, as he can get out of it himself. For this reason, do not use this seat on a table or other elevated surface. (For more information on Bumbo seats and Bébé pods, see page 333.)

■ When you are cooking, turn the handles of your pots and pans toward the back of the stove.

■ Do not take medication or vitamins in front of your child.

■ After your pet has eaten, remove the food dishes from the floor.

■ When you have visitors or overnight guests, make sure that their purses and suitcases are locked or out of the reach of curious hands.

■ When shopping in the grocery store, it is safer to carry your child in a front-pack carrier than it is to place the car seat in a shopping cart. Carts can tip over or children can fall out and become injured.

In addition to baby proofing your house (and yourself), teach your child the concept of danger as soon as possible. Show him what is dangerous and what is not. For example, teach him early on what "hot" means.

Keep a list of emergency telephone numbers near or taped to the phone. Be sure to include your local poison control center, rescue unit, fire department, police department, and pediatrician. When the time is right, teach your child how to dial 911 and when to call it.

AUTOMOBILE SAFETY

Automobile accidents are the leading cause of death in young children. When it comes to infants and children riding in cars, a safety seat is a must. In the event of a crash, swerve, or sudden stop, if your baby is not securely placed in a safety seat, he could be thrown into the dashboard, windshield, or another passenger. He could also be thrown out of the car. Although your arms are usually the best place for your baby, they aren't when riding in a car. Tests have shown that volunteers holding seventeen-pound baby-size dummies were not able to hold onto the "babies" in impacts of both fifteen and thirty miles per hour, even though they were prepared for the crashes. Even a tiny ten-pound infant can be thrown forward with a force of 300 pounds in a thirty-mile-per-hour impact. This is equivalent to a fall from a three-story building. Putting your baby in the seat belt with you is not safe either because the force of your body would crush him.

Begin using a car safety seat the day you bring your baby home from the hospital. Many hospitals, in fact, do not allow parents to take the baby home until they show a hospital representative that they have one. Continue using a safety seat for your child until he outgrows it, which is usually when he is four years old or weighs over forty pounds. You will know your child has outgrown the seat when he reaches its upper weight limit, or when his ears are level with the top of the seat and his shoulders are higher than the slots for the top straps.

When children outgrow their safety seats, they should start sitting in a booster seat and use the car's lap/shoulder belts. (Remember, lap/shoulder belts are designed for adult bodies, so a booster seat is necessary.) They should continue using the seat until the lap/shoulder belts fit properly without it. Generally, this is when they are at least four feet nine inches tall, weigh eighty pounds, and are between eight and twelve years of age. Every state has a child restraint law. Check with your local Department of Motor Vehicles to learn the restrictions in your state.

Do not purchase a used safety seat from a consignment store or through the Internet unless you can verify its history. If the seat was involved in a moderate or severe car crash, it is not considered safe to use. It may, however, still be used if the car was involved in a minor crash. A crash is considered minor if the car was able to be driven from the accident, the door closest to the safety seat was not damaged, no one was injured, the air bags did not go off, and the safety seat did not sustain any visible damage. If your safety seat is secondhand or several years old, contact the National Highway Traffic Safety Administration to see if the model was recalled. (For contact information, see the Resources beginning on page 449.)

For infants, as well as babies under twenty pounds and less than one year of age, the safety seat should be placed in the car in a semi-reclined position, facing backwards and anchored snugly with a lap belt. This installation should be done according to the instructions of both the safety seat manufacturer and the automobile manual. Some newer model cars have a seat anchoring system called LATCH (Lower Anchors and Tethers for Children). This system uses a set of hooks and straps—called tethers—on the safety seat that are attached to bars and hooks embedded in the vehicle seats. It does not use the vehicle's lap-shoulder seat belts, which should be hooked so they are not hanging free and able to injure the child during a sudden stop.

When your baby is over one year of age *and* at least twenty pounds, he can be safely moved to a securely anchored forward-facing safety seat. If your car has dual air bags, do not place the safety seat or any child under the age of thirteen in the front passenger seat. An air bag can discharge with enough force to cause serious, even fatal injuries in children.

Bathtub Safety

Do not assume that your child is safe in an infant bathtub seat. A number of children have drowned when left alone in one. According to the US Consumer Product Safety Commission, the seats are safe when used properly. However, if children are left alone in the seats, they can "tip them over, slide into the water through the leg openings, and climb out of the seats into the water, posing the risk of drowning."

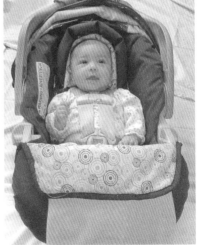

Infant safety seat.

Poison Control

Syrup of ipecac is no longer recommended by the American Academy of Pediatrics to induce vomiting following the ingestion of poison. The FDA may even remove its status as an over-the-counter product. If you are concerned that your child has ingested a poisonous substance, call your pediatrician or the Poison Control Hotline at 1-800-222-1222. If your child is severely ill, call 911.

Newborns with specific risk factors may need to be transported in a special car bed rather than the standard infant seat. They include preterm and low birth weight infants, infants who have experienced apnea, and infants with certain genetic disorders such as Down syndrome. If your infant falls into any of these categories, check with your pediatrician about the need for a special car bed.

Remember that no safety seat will protect your child from injury unless he is secured in it properly. Take the time to strap him in, even for short trips. Most accidents happen within twenty-five miles of home. Studies have shown that up to 90 percent of child restraints are used improperly. Read your car owner's manual and the safety seat instructions. Check to make sure the seat is properly fastened each time. When you tug on the seat, it should not move more than one inch. Do not wrap your child in blankets before securing the straps. The straps should fit snugly against his body. Only use a head support that comes with the seat. It is recommended that a certified Child Passenger Safety (CPS) Technician check the safety seat itself for correct installation. (For CPS contact information, see the Resources beginning on page 449.)

Never leave your child (or pet) in an unattended car for any amount of time. By doing so, you run the risk of your child wandering off or being abducted. The interior of the car can also heat up rapidly, even with the windows down. There have been numerous cases of children who have died in cars due to overheating.

AIR TRAVEL

Traveling by air with young children can be stressful. It is a good idea to leave yourself plenty of time before your flight so that you will not feel rushed. When you arrive at a security checkpoint, remove your child from the car seat or stroller. Medications, breastmilk, formula, baby food, and juice are allowed on the plane in reasonable quantities that exceed the standard three-ounce limit. They are also not required to be in a zip-top plastic bag.

It is best to wait until your child is at least two weeks old before planning a trip by plane. Some pediatricians will encourage you to avoid air travel even longer as the passengers on board and the recirculated cabin air can expose your child to germs. Request a bulkhead seat for extra leg room or choose one close to the wings—the white noise provided by the sound of the engines can help keep your baby calm.

Fluctuations in air pressure during takeoff and landing can cause the baby to experience ear pain. Feeding him or offering a pacifier during these times can equalize the ear pressure and reduce or avoid this problem. Children with a cold or an ear infection should not fly, as this could result in a ruptured eardrum.

While some airlines allow children under the age of two to sit in a parent's lap, the American Academy of Pediatrics recommends that your child sit in a safety seat that is secured in the seat next to you. Most child safety seats will state that they are certified for use in motor vehicles and aircraft. A booster seat may not be used on an airplane. When booking your tickets, be sure to ask the airline about reduced fares for children under two.

Baby Walkers are Dangerous

According to the American Academy of Pediatricians, baby walkers are responsible for a number of serious, often life-threatening injuries. While scooting around in their walkers, children have fallen down stairs and into swimming pools. Because they are also elevated when sitting in walkers, babies are able to touch or grab potentially dangerous items that should be out of their reach.

BABY CLOTHING AND EQUIPMENT

When you begin shopping for baby equipment, you may notice that the advertising is designed to appeal to your most tender and protective feelings. Some ads even attempt to arouse your guilt and anxiety if you do not to buy the products. You may be tempted to buy everything you see, especially if this is your first child. Resist buying too much too soon.

The needs of a newborn are very simple. In the early weeks, a new baby requires only a car safety seat, a few nightgowns or sleepers, diapers, and a place to sleep. You can add other items gradually. Babies quickly outgrow newborn-size garments. By four to six weeks, your baby may be wearing three- to six-month sizes. If friends ask what you could use for the baby, encourage them to buy twelve-month or larger size clothing. Otherwise, before you know it, you will have a dresser full of "little" clothes that do not fit and nothing for your baby to wear.

Be sure that all the garments you buy or receive are soft to the touch and easy to put on. Babies dislike having their heads covered for more than a second. Also, choose clothing that has room for growth in the form of extra wide hems, extra long or adjustable straps, and so on.

Front-pack carriers, wraps, and slings offer babies good transportation plus a warm place to sleep during the first months of life. As your baby reaches two to three months of age, you may prefer a stroller for shopping trips and other long excursions.

The American Academy of Pediatrics strongly discourages the use of baby walkers, which cause more injuries each year than any other nursery product. They allow infants to be more mobile and more vertical than they normally would be at that age. As a result, unsupervised infants can fall down stairs or reach potentially harmful items on the stove or tabletops that should be out of their reach. (There have, for instance, been numerous cases of burns and the ingestion of toxic substances among babies in walkers.) Fingers and toes have also gotten pinched when caught between this piece of equipment and furniture. In addition to the possible physical injuries that can occur, baby walkers can actually impede a baby's progress in learning to walk. Several companies now make bouncers or "saucers" to be used in place of walkers. These products enable the child to be upright without allowing him to be mobile. They also provide activities to entertain him.

You will not need a highchair until your baby is about six months old. Before then, his back and neck will not be strong enough to allow him to sit upright. One item that allows very young children to sit upright is the soft foam baby seat known as a Bumbo seat or Bébé pod. This type of chair should not be used until the child is able to sit up and fully support his head. Never leave a baby who is sitting in one of these seats unattended, as he can get out of it himself. For the same reason, do not use a Bumbo or Bébé pod on a table or other elevated surface.

A sling-style carrier.

A wrap-style carrier.

Baby in a Bébé pod.

Among the items that most parents feel are necessary for meeting an infant's basic needs include the following:

For Sleeping

- A sturdy crib with a firm mattress that can be used for at least two years.

- A bassinet to provide the small, confined space that most newborns prefer during the first weeks of life. This, however, is an expensive purchase considering the short time it is used.

- An infant bed that attaches to your bed to make bed sharing safer.

- One to two warm blankets.

- One to two mattress pads that fit snugly to protect the baby against wetness and to absorb perspiration.

- Two sets of crib sheets. Fitted sheets stay on a mattress better than flat sheets, and knitted cotton is the softest material.

- Four to five receiving/swaddle blankets for wrapping the baby in when he is sleeping or when you take him outdoors on a cool day. An adjustable infant wrap makes swaddling easier.

For Diapering

- Diapers. Most newborns go through about ten diapers a day. The choice of whether to use cloth or disposable varieties is a personal one. (See "Diapers—Cloth or Disposable?" on page 336.)

- Diaper liners. When placed inside cloth diapers, liners help keep moisture away from the baby's skin and make cleanup after bowel movements easier. They will, however, add to your weekly expenses.

- A diaper pail. Choose one that can hold two to three days' worth of diapers.

Clothing

- Three to six cotton nightgowns that close at the bottom to make diaper changing easier.

- Two to three one-piece stretch sleepers in the six-month size. These are great for day and night wear as your baby grows and becomes more active.

- Three to six waterproof pants if using cloth diapers. Use plastic-coated fabric pants that snap on the sides to allow air circulation and to lessen the risk of skin irritation.

- Seasonal items—short-sleeve snap-front shirts, a sweater and cap, or a snowsuit.

For Bathing

- A baby bathtub. The kitchen sink, lined with a towel, works just as well.

- Mild bar or liquid baby soap for cleaning tender skin.

- Three to four soft washcloths for bathing and for wiping little bottoms.

- Two to three baby bath towels. Regular towels also work.

For Traveling

- A car safety seat. (See "Buy and Install a Car Safety Seat" on page 184 and "Automobile Safety" on page 330 for details.)

- A front-pack baby carrier, wrap, or sling.

- A stroller.

Optional Items

- A baby swing to provide movement and diversion for your baby when your hands are busy. Make sure that it is well balanced to prevent tipping.

- A backpack carrier for shopping trips and excursions when your baby is older.

- A playpen to protect your baby from the activities of older children. Never use a playpen to "cage" your baby. If you have baby proofed your house, you won't need one.

- A baby monitor so you can hear or see your baby from another room.

If you spread out your purchases over an extended period of time, you will not be overwhelmed by their cost. You could also ask friends and relatives who no longer need certain items if they would loan them to you or sell them at a fraction of their original cost. Garage sales and consignment shops are other good sources of "nice as new" furniture, clothing, and toys. Babies do not wear out things the way older children do. Do not purchase a used safety seat if you do not know its "crash" history. Also, if you purchase a used crib or other baby furniture, make sure to check for the safety features mentioned throughout this chapter.

PLAYING WITH YOUR BABY

Positive interaction is a crucial factor in the proper mental and emotional development of a baby. Visual, vocal, and tactile stimulation are all valuable aids to learning. Talk to your baby

"I'm sorry, dear. You'll have to take the bus!"

while you change his diaper. Read to him from the time of birth. Even though he cannot understand what you are saying, the sounds of the words will become familiar to him, and it will not be long before he *is* comprehending them.

Set aside some time each day to simply play with your baby. During this time, he should be wide awake, happy, and well fed. Sing to your baby or recite nursery rhymes to help him gain an awareness of language. To keep him entertained, involve him in clapping and other hand movements through such classic interactive rhymes as "Pat-a-Cake," "This Little Piggy Went to Market," and "Itsy Bitsy Spider."

Bath time provides a good opportunity for playful interaction. It is an ideal time to help your baby learn the names of his various body parts by saying them as you wash them. Using the tune from the children's song "Here We Go 'Round the Mulberry Bush," sing verses like: "This is the way we wash your face." As your baby gets older, he will enjoy splashing and playing with bathtub toys.

Selecting Toys

Always choose toys for your child according to his age and abilities. Toys that are too advanced will not only frustrate him, they may also hurt him. For a child under one year old, toys should be large, simple, brightly colored or black and white, and lightweight. In addition, they should not have any small parts that the baby can remove. Household items such as plastic cups and bowls, wooden spoons, and pots and pans are fascinating to little ones. Other good choices include squeak toys with noisemakers that are molded within; sturdy, nonflammable rattles, washable dolls, and stuffed animals with embroidered features; and teethers and other smooth items that can be chewed. If you purchase toys from garage sales or consignment stores, be sure to check them for recalls and lead paint.

"I wonder how long before they learn to talk!"

Send in Those Cards and . . .

Send in the warranty cards you receive with new purchases. If an item is recalled, you will be notified directly.

What follows are some additional toys you might consider purchasing for a baby who is:

Under Two Months Old

■ A mobile that looks interesting from underneath (the baby's point of view). Remove the mobile from the crib when the baby is able to pull it down.

■ Pictures or decals to decorate the walls of his room.

Two to Four Months Old

■ A stainless steel mirror that you can hold about six inches from the baby's eyes.

■ A cradle gym.

Four to Six Months Old

■ Rattles, squeak toys, and teethers.

■ Cloth books with colorful pictures.

■ Stuffed animals.

Six to Eight Months Old

■ Balls.

■ A box filled with simple objects that the baby can take out and put back.

■ Stacking and nesting toys.

Eight to Twelve Months Old

■ An activity box for the bathtub.

■ Bath toys that float or fill up with water that can be poured out.

■ A box filled with interesting objects that are too large to be swallowed.

Diapers—Cloth or Disposable?

Although the choice of using cloth diapers or disposables is a personal one, it is important to consider the following. Disposable diapers are convenient, but they are also expensive and harmful to the environment. The initial cost of cloth diapers may seem high, but the money saved by not buying disposables more than offsets the cost of the fuel, hot water, and soap needed to wash them.

Cloth diapers come in two types—flat and prefolded. Flat diapers are less expensive and dry more quickly, but prefolded types are more absorbent and save time. Preshaped cloth diapers with Velcro tabs are convenient and make diaper pins unnecessary.

If you use cloth diapers, you will need three to four dozen. Be aware that diaper service is as expensive as the cost of disposables. It is also of questionable benefit ecologically if your particular service rinses its diapers five to six times. In many areas, diaper service is not available. If you plan to use cloth diapers, do not start using them until your baby's bowel movements have changed from meconium to milk stools. Meconium does not wash out and will cause permanent stains.

Most newborns go through about ten diapers a day. If using disposables, you will need to buy about seventy a week. Even if you use cloth diapers, you may want to use disposables during trips to the mall or other outings. Disposable diapers are available in a range of sizes and absorbencies. When using the super-absorbent types, be sure to change your baby just as often as you do with the less absorbent varieties. Leaving any size diaper on too long can cause diaper rash.

Remember that a young baby does not need expensive or elaborate toys—and don't be swayed by advertising claims that encourage you to buy them. Although toys can be useful in helping a baby learn about his world, no toy is as fascinating to a child as his mother's face and voice. The time that you spend playing with your baby is more beneficial than any toy could ever be.

INFANT MASSAGE

Infant massage is another pleasurable way that you can interact with your baby. Not only does massage fulfill his need for your gentle touch, it also produces many healthful benefits. Massage can help calm a crying or fussy baby. It can help relieve gas, reduce colic, improve circulation, stimulate the immune system, enhance neurological development, and tone the muscles. Massage can also promote parent-infant bonding and allow parents to synchronize their body rhythms with those of their baby.

You do not have to be an expert to perform massage on your infant, and it does not have to be complicated. Massage is a natural extension of the loving touch you give him every day. Many mothers naturally stroke their baby's arms and legs while he nurses. Or they rub the baby gently all over with lotion following a bath. Incorporating a massage into your daily routine of caring for your baby should be easy.

When performing massage, it is best to choose a quiet, relaxed location where you can be free from distractions and where the baby is comfortable. The room should be warm, so you can remove his clothing, including the diaper if you wish—just be sure to place a waterproof pad beneath him. (For a very young infant, cover his body with a blanket and expose only the area you are working on.) The addition of soft music helps to create a calming, pleasurable atmosphere. Soft or dimmed lighting is preferable to bright lights. The use of an unscented, edible light vegetable or nut oil, such as almond, sunflower, or safflower, will reduce the friction between your hands and your baby's skin. Place a few drops of the oil on your hands and rub your palms together to warm the oil before applying it to the baby.

Make sure your nails are short and you are not wearing jewelry that could scratch the baby. The quality of your touch should be gentle, yet firm. Downward strokes are soothing and calming, while upward strokes are stimulating. Your baby's smiles, coos, and wiggling will let you know that it feels good to him. Any crying, grimacing, or stiffening signals that you are hurting him or that he is not enjoying it. Your hands should remain soft and relaxed as they move in a smooth, flowing manner over his body. Keep your movements slow and rhythmic. Avoid abrupt, jerky moves or lifting your hands from his body. Because your baby will not lie perfectly still, you have to work with, not against, his movements. Never force an arm or leg to straighten out if it is bent tightly.

Wait until the baby is about one month old before performing massage routines. Do not massage him if he is sick or has received an injection within forty-eight hours. Wait at least ninety minutes after a feeding. It is not necessary to do a full body massage each time; you can massage only a specific area if you prefer.

A good time for a full body massage is right before a bath. Your baby will already be undressed and in a warm environment. Any excess oil will wash off in the bath. A massage, followed by a warm bath, should ease him into naptime.

What follows next is a sample massage routine. You will soon learn which strokes are the most enjoyable for you and your baby.

Black and White

Black and white designs on toys and walls stimulate the growth and development of the baby's brain. They provide the optimal contrast for the infant's visual development. According to Jeff Mann, PhD, clinical psychologist and neurological psychology specialist, "Looking at black and white designs helps the baby's brain to grow and even helps to increase his powers of concentration and memory. And, it has a soothing and comforting effect on the infant."

Chest and Abdomen

1. Place your baby on his back with his feet toward you.
2. Place your fingers in the center of his chest and gently stroke outward to the sides, following the ribs.
3. Using a clockwise motion (to relieve gas and improve the digestion), make circles around his belly with your fingers.
4. Gently stroke the sides of his torso.
5. Gently stroke down the front of his torso.

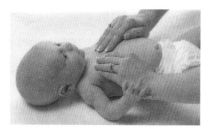

Place your fingers in the center of the chest and gently stroke outward to the sides, following the ribs.

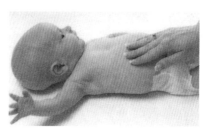

Use a clockwise motion to make circles around his belly with your fingers.

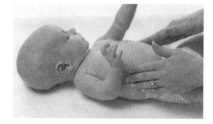

Gently stroke the sides of the torso.

Arms and Hands

1. With the baby on his back, gently stretch his arms out to the sides to form a cross. Use your thumbs to massage the palms and open his hands.
2. Support one hand and wrist with your hand, and gently stroke up the arm from the wrist to the shoulder.
3. Lightly knead the arm from the wrist to the shoulder.
4. Repeat steps 2 and 3 with the other arm.

Gently stretch the arms out to the sides to form a cross.

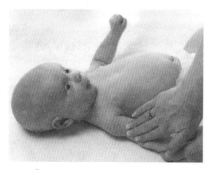

Gently stroke up the arm from the wrist to the shoulder.

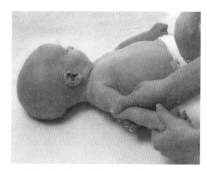

Gently knead the arm from the wrist to the shoulder.

Legs and Feet

1. With the baby on his back, support one leg with both your hands. Gently knead the leg, beginning with the fleshy part of the thigh and working down to the ankle.

2. Supporting the leg with one hand under the knee, stroke the leg from the ankle up the thigh and back down again.

3. Move your supporting hand down to the ankle. Gently smooth the palm of your other hand over the top of the foot to the toes.

4. Repeat steps 1 through 3 with the other leg.

5. Move your thumbs in a circular motion on the bottom of both feet.

Gently knead the leg, beginning with the fleshy part of the thigh and working down to the ankle.

Supporting the leg with one hand under the knee, stroke the leg from the ankle up the thigh and back down again.

Gently smooth the palm of your other hand over the top of the foot to the toes.

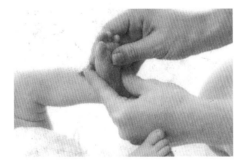

Move your thumb in a circular motion on the bottom of the foot.

Back and Buttocks

1. Lay the baby on his stomach with his feet toward you, making sure that he can breathe easily. Use long stroking motions to distribute some oil on his back.

2. Place the fingertips of both hands near the spine and slowly move them outward to the sides, following the ribs. Start at the shoulders and move all the way down the back to the buttocks.

3. Cup your hands around his sides and use your thumbs to perform the same massage as in Step 2.

4. Gently knead the buttocks using a circular motion.

5. Using long stroking motions, massage the baby from his shoulders to his toes, including the arms.

6. As the massage ends, open your fingers and use a progressively lighter touch with each downward stroke.

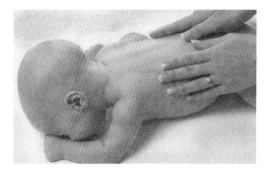

Use the fingertips of both hands near the spine and slowly move them outward to the sides, following the ribs.

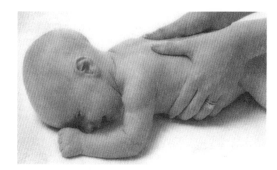

Cup your hands around his sides and use your thumbs to perform light massage from his shoulders to his buttocks.

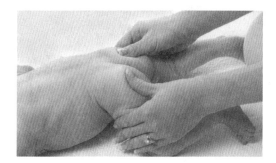

Gently knead the buttocks using a circular motion.

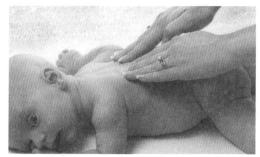

Repeat the long stroking motions, massaging from the shoulders to the toes and including the arms.

For more detailed massage techniques, the book *Infant Massage: A Handbook for Loving Parents* by Vimala Schneider McClure is recommended. You can also contact Infant Massage USA. This group offers training programs for parents and can inform you about training in your area. (For contact information, see the Resources beginning on page 449.)

THE CHILDCARE DECISION

Sooner or later, you will have to leave your baby in someone else's care. It may be for just a few hours so that you can run to the mall, attend a doctor's appointment, or go out to dinner with friends, or it may entail more long-term childcare on a regular basis.

Undoubtedly, you will feel most comfortable if the person who watches your baby is a trusted relative or a friend who is already familiar with him and his routines. Sometimes, however, this is not possible, and you will be forced to look beyond the realm of friends and relatives.

If you will need childcare on a regular basis, you must first decide on the type of care you want. Do you prefer individual care in your own home, in the caregiver's home, or in a childcare center? Each has its own advantages and disadvantages. For example, if having individual care or not exposing your baby to other children is your top priority, try to find a care provider who can come to your home. However, if leaving your baby with someone who is certified or has a license is most important, a licensed daycare center or a licensed family childcare home would be your best choice. Financial considerations may also influence your decision.

It is always a good idea to speak with other parents who use childcare services. They can offer advice and possible references. Most important, you need to meet with any potential childcare providers and observe their interaction with your baby. Discover their approaches to baby care, and make your views clear. Anyone you select should be willing to comply with your wishes, especially when it comes to desires such as holding your baby while he is being fed or not letting him cry alone in his crib. If you have any doubts about a certain person or facility, or you just "don't feel right" about it, do not leave your child there. Sometimes your gut feelings can be the best indicators when making this important decision.

When you do leave your baby under someone else's charge, be sure to provide explicit instructions for his care. And whether the caregiver will be in your home or at another location, be sure there is plenty of breastmilk or formula, a familiar toy or blanket for the baby, and extra diapers and clothing. It is also very important to provide important emergency phone numbers, including the number where you can be reached immediately.

CONCLUSION

Having a newborn is an exciting experience. Your new child will fill your life with discovery, amazement, and joy. Take the opportunity to marvel at each milestone and new adventure. Never again will this little person be changing and learning at such a rapid rate. Enjoy each moment, and invest the energy necessary to make sure that you are providing the best environment for his maximum emotional, mental, and physical development. Every daily interaction and each happy experience you share will help to establish a lifelong family bond.

Breastfeeding

or More Than a Meal

Breastfeeding, also called *nursing,* is the gold standard for infant nutrition. It creates a symbiotic relationship between mother and baby, who both derive physical and emotional benefits from it. Nursing is a natural continuation of the birth process because it completes the maternity cycle and is essential for an infant's optimum growth and development. Just as you nourished your baby prior to birth with nutrients from your body, you continue to supply her with the food that is best suited to her needs—your breastmilk.

In addition to providing nutrients, breastfeeding also helps you foster a special relationship, a close physical and emotional bond with your baby. This relationship is unique in that your baby is totally dependent on you for nourishment. This giving of yourself is an expression of your love and can result in many enjoyable and rewarding hours for both of you. Some of your fondest memories will be of the times spent nursing your baby.

Your success at breastfeeding will depend greatly on your desire to nurse, as well as on the encouragement you receive from those around you. Because of the importance of your partner's support, the decision to breastfeed should be a mutual one. His knowledge and understanding can provide you with a source of strength on those "trying" days when you might be tempted to give up. In addition, support from your caregiver, relatives, and friends is most helpful. Knowing a mother who successfully breastfed a child or who is a member of La Leche League or a nursing mothers' support group can be extremely beneficial when you have questions. The professional support of an international board certified lactation consultant (IBCLC) can offer a higher level of expertise to answer your questions and to assist you with any problems. (These sources of breastfeeding assistance are discussed later in this chapter.)

Several other important factors can help you have a successful breastfeeding experience. Understanding how breastmilk is produced and supplied to the baby, along with how to properly position her at the breast will help prevent most of the problems associated with nursing. Having realistic expectations about the demands of the early weeks of breastfeeding, eating nutritious food, and getting adequate rest will also increase your odds of success. If possible, plan for extra help around the house, especially if you have other children.

Breastmilk is recognized by the American Academy of Pediatrics (AAP) as nutritionally superior to breastmilk substitutes (formula). In 1997 and again in 2005, the

AAP updated its policy on breastfeeding. It recommends that women nurse exclusively until the baby is six months old—when solid foods are usually introduced—and continue past the first birthday, or for as long as is mutually desired. This length for optimum nursing was in response to the increased knowledge about its health, nutritional, immunologic, developmental, psychological, social, economic, and environmental benefits.

The Federal Government also recognizes the importance of breastfeeding for the health of babies and mothers. In 2000, the office of the US Surgeon General released the *HHS Blueprint for Action on Breastfeeding.* This work outlines the nation's health agenda for the decade. By the year 2010, its goals are to increase the proportion of mothers who breastfeed their babies in the early postpartum period to 75 percent and to 50 percent at six months. To carry out these recommendations, the National Women's Health Information Center (part of the Department of Health and Human Services) initiated a media campaign with the slogan "Babies were Born to be Breastfed." Visit *www.4woman.gov* for more information.

This chapter presents everything you want (or need) to know about breastfeeding. It begins with a discussion of its many advantages, not just for the baby, but also for the mother, father, and even the environment. What follows next is a discussion of contraindications to breastfeeding and widespread myths regarding women and breastfeeding. Information on milk production and nursing techniques is presented, as well as answers to common questions on nursing in general. Rounding out the chapter are guidelines for special situations, such as working mothers and breastfeeding multiples.

BENEFITS FOR BABY

As researchers examine breastmilk and its unique qualities, it must be noted that breastfeeding is the standard by which other feeding preparations must be evaluated. No breastmilk substitute will ever equal or come close to duplicating human milk.

First, and most important, breastmilk is the ideal food for a human infant. Each species of mammal produces milk that is especially suited to the needs of its young. Human milk is biochemically geared for brain development, while animal milk promotes muscular development. Most breastmilk substitutes are made from cow's milk (which is meant for baby cows) or from soy plants. Formula companies often claim that their products are "most like mother's milk," but no formula can equal or even come close to breastmilk. Enzymes, living cells, hormones, and other components of breastmilk cannot be replicated and added to formula.

Nutritional Value

Although cow's milk has a higher protein content than breastmilk, the protein in human milk is superior in quality and geared to the specific needs of the human infant. While a baby completely utilizes the protein in breastmilk, she excretes about half the protein contained in cow's milk.

The fat content in breastmilk and formula is similar, but breastmilk fat is more readily absorbed. To imitate mother's milk, formula companies replace the butterfat in cow's milk with mono- and polyunsaturated vegetable oils. This substitution, however, removes cholesterol, which is necessary for several vital functions. Cholesterol aids in the absorption of nutrients and the development of the protective covering of the nerves. Some researchers believe that these high levels of cholesterol in infancy may protect breastfed babies from developing high levels later in life, offering long-term benefits for cardiovascular health.[1] Two fatty acids, docosahexaenoic acid (DHA) and arachidonic acid (ARA) have been added to formula. Preterm babies seem to benefit from this—because they are born early, they receive much less DHA and ARA in utero. Studies on full-term babies are mixed. According to the FDA, there are currently no studies that address whether or not long-term benefits of adding these fatty acids to formula exist for the full-term infant.[2]

Although low, the iron content in human milk is much more readily absorbed than the iron that is added to formula or given as a supplement. Formula-fed infants are at greater risk for iron deficiency anemia because only 10 percent of the iron in modified cow's milk is absorbed, as compared to almost total absorption of the iron contained in mother's milk.[3] Cow's milk can also cause minute bleeding in the intestines, which can further increase the risk of anemia. Full-term breastfed infants should not be supplemented with iron because it interferes with lactoferrin, a special protein that binds the iron in the infant's intestinal tract and, in turn, prevents harmful bacteria from multiplying.

Human milk contains very small amounts of fat-soluble and water-soluble vitamin D, the "sunshine" vitamin that helps metabolize calcium and prevents rickets. This is not, however, a serious problem—a few minutes of sunshine a day on the baby's cheeks should ensure plenty of vitamin D. For those rare cases in which the family lives in an area that does not receive much sunlight or if the baby is not exposed to the sun, it may be advisable for either the nursing mother or the child to take vitamin D supplements. The AAP recommends routine supplementation. If, however, the mother is healthy and the breastfed baby receives some exposure to the sun, many physicians feel it may be unnecessary to supplement the baby with vitamin D.[4]

Breastmilk is raw and fresh. It is unprocessed and fed to a baby when at its nutritional peak. Formula is processed and must be stored and then reheated, which destroys important nutrients.

Breastmilk contains everything that the baby needs. Thriving breastfed infants require no supplementation—they should not receive any water, juice, cereal, or any other food until six months of age. Although fluoride supplementation was once recommended for infants under six months old, it is no longer suggested. Between six months and three years, fluoride supplementation is recommended, but only if the water supply does not contain an adequate amount.[5]

Colostrum—The First Milk

Colostrum is the first milk produced by the breasts and, therefore, the first liquid the baby receives. It is thick, sticky, and clear to yellowish in color. It is also small in quantity but high in quality with more protein and less sugar and fat than mature breastmilk. During the first couple days, the baby receives only about a teaspoon to a tablespoon of colostrum at each feeding—the perfect amount for her tiny tummy.

The high level of antibodies present in colostrum protects the newborn, and any immunity that the mother has acquired over her lifetime is passed through it to her infant as well. Another benefit of this first milk is that it helps rid the newborn's body of mucus, and its laxative effect helps cleanse the intestinal tract of meconium. Meconium, the dark stool present in the bowel at birth, contains high levels of bilirubin. If it is not excreted soon after birth, the bilirubin will be reabsorbed into the baby's bloodstream and contribute to a higher risk of jaundice.

Breastmilk . . .

✓ Is the perfect food for human infants.

✓ Produces healthier babies.

✓ Is economical.

✓ Is always available and at the correct temperature.

✓ Promotes brain development and higher IQs.

✓ Protects against allergies.

✓ Offers emotional and physical benefits to the mother.

✓ Is easy to digest.

✓ Promotes good facial development.

✓ Produces bowel movements that are not offensive smelling.

Colostrum is high in epidermal growth factor, which promotes thickening of the intestinal lining, making it less permeable to harmful foreign invaders. It also provides beneficial bacteria for the newborn's digestive tract, which is sterile at birth.

Immunologic Protection

Some of the amazing properties of breastmilk that cannot be duplicated or added to formula are perfectly devised to keep babies healthy and protect them from disease. Because infants are born with immature immune systems, they are not equipped to fight off infection-causing bacteria and viruses. Breastmilk, however, provides the missing protective factors to combat foreign organisms and strengthen the baby's immune system. It is the *only* way your baby can receive this crucial protection.

The major antibody found in breastmilk—secretory immunoglobulin A—is produced in the mother's milk glands. It protects the baby against foreign invaders that may cause vomiting, diarrhea, and respiratory infections. This antibody does not work by killing organisms, but by binding with them and preventing them from attaching to the lining of the baby's intestines or respiratory tract, where they can multiply. As mentioned earlier, any immunity that the mother has acquired will be passed to her infant through breastmilk. And if the mother comes in contact with a new virus or bacteria, she will begin producing antibodies within hours of exposure. This is why breastfed babies rarely get sick or have colds, even if everyone around them is ill.

Further protection comes from the white blood cells contained in breastmilk called *leukocytes.* These cells attack foreign bacteria and destroy harmful disease-causing organisms. Leukocytes, which are at their highest quantity level right after birth, continue to be produced in sufficient quantities for up to five months. Since they cannot survive heat, stored breastmilk should never be heated to high temperatures or microwaved prior to use. White blood cells produce interferon, which protects against viruses. Mother's milk also contains an antibacterial substance called *lysozyme,* which destroys bacterial cell walls by dissolving them. Although this enzyme can be manufactured, it is destroyed by the sterilization process, so it cannot be added to formula.

In addition to the high levels of antibodies that are passed to the infant, other factors are present in breastmilk that protect the baby from diseases. Proteins that help stimulate the baby's immune system and also prevent bacteria from utilizing iron and B_{12} (which are necessary for bacteria to multiply) are present, as are sugars called *oligosaccharides,* which attract harmful bacteria and prevent them from attaching to the gastrointestinal tract. Rather than entering the bloodstream and causing the baby to get sick, these bacteria are then excreted in the baby's bowel movement and eliminated from the body. The *bifidus factor* in breastmilk promotes the growth of beneficial bacteria in the baby's intestines and provides an acidic environment that is not conducive to the growth of harmful bacteria. The intestines of a formula-fed infant are alkaline, an environment in which many harmful bacteria thrive.

Breastfed infants have higher protective antibody responses to vaccinations than formula-fed infants. This protection is so great that some doctors have referred to breastmilk as "nature's vaccine."[6]

It is well documented that babies who are exclusively breastfed remain healthy. They have markedly lower incidents of ear infections, upper and lower respiratory tract infections, and gastrointestinal diseases. Formula-fed infants have a higher risk of developing pneumonia, influenza, botulism, urinary tract infections, bacterial infections, and bacterial meningitis. They are also ten times more likely to require hospitalization for bacterial infection.[7] A 1991 New Zealand study linked formula feeding, the prone sleeping position, and maternal smoking to an increased risk of SIDS.[8]

Breastfeeding can also reduce the risk of infant death in the first year of life. A recent study looked at 1,204 children between twenty-eight days old and one year who died from causes other than congenital anomalies or cancer and compared them to 7,740 children who were alive at one year. The breastfed children had a 20 percent lower risk of dying than children who were fed formula. The scientists concluded that breastfeeding could prevent up to 720 deaths in the United States each year.[9]

Fewer Allergies

Breastmilk also helps protect babies against allergies, eczema, and asthma. The intestines of a newborn are permeable and allow large molecules to pass through to the bloodstream. Allergies are the result of reactions to foreign molecules found in formula or foods. Colostrum and breastmilk contain *epidermal growth factor*, which coats and thickens the lining of the intestines and prevents the passage of large proteins into the bloodstream. Since breastmilk is not a foreign protein, an infant will not become allergic to it.

Cow's milk is one of the most common causes of allergy in babies. Many parents switch their infants from one formula to another, hoping to find one—usually a soybean-based formula—that is agreeable. Many babies who are allergic to cow proteins are also allergic to soy. On rare occasions, a baby is so allergic that he cannot tolerate any type of formula. In such a case, breastmilk is crucial to the infant's survival. If the mother has not been nursing, she must find another source of human milk until she can relactate and build up her own milk supply. Relactation is possible even for women who have never nursed or who have not lactated for several months. The baby's sucking stimulates milk production. Even adoptive mothers can nurse successfully.

Occasionally, if a breastfeeding mother drinks cow's milk, her infant may exhibit a reaction to its proteins. Removing cow's milk and any other dairy products from the diet will usually eliminate the baby's fussiness. The longer an allergy-prone infant is exclusively breastfed, the better her chances are of reducing or eliminating the effects of allergies.

Breastfeeding is the best way to prevent severe allergies. If you have a family history of allergies, it is especially important that you exclusively breastfeed your baby for at least six months and delay introducing her to solid foods. As your baby gets older, her susceptibility to allergic reactions will diminish.

Advantages for Preterm Babies

Breastmilk is particularly important for the preterm infant. It is tolerated better than formula by the baby's sensitive digestive system and can be a critical factor in her survival. Many neonatologists encourage mothers who deliver preterm to provide breastmilk—which they often refer to as medicine—for their babies while in the neonatal intensive care unit (NICU).

Because they are born early, preterm babies have temporary deficiencies of certain enzymes and frequently suffer malabsorption problems. Breastmilk is perfectly suited to their special needs. The proteins and fats in human milk are easily digested

A Variety of Flavors

Unlike a formula-fed infant, a breastfed baby experiences a variety of tastes and flavors based upon the mother's diet. This may be advantageous when introducing solid foods to the baby, who might be more willing to try them more readily.

Breastfeeding and Pain Relief

Colostrum and mother's milk contain high levels of pain-relieving endorphins, which were produced in response to labor contractions. Studies have indicated that when babies breastfeed during painful or uncomfortable procedures, such as heel-stick blood tests, there is a significant reduction in crying, grimacing, and other indications of discomfort.

and absorbed without stress on the immature kidneys. Breastmilk also contains *lipase,* an enzyme that breaks down fat, an important source of energy for the preterm infant. Babies born early are also at higher risk for infections—a risk that can be lowered by receiving mother's milk. Necrotizing enterocolitis, a severe and sometimes fatal bowel condition of preterm infants, is rarely found in those who are fed breastmilk.

Research has found that the milk from the mothers of preterm babies is different from that of mothers who deliver their babies at term. To meet the demands of the preterm baby, preterm breastmilk is actually higher in protein, fatty acids, iron, chloride, and sodium. These additional nutrients improve motor skills and facilitate brain development, leading to better vision and higher IQs.

If your preterm baby is too weak to suck, it is extremely important that you pump your breasts to give her the colostrum and mature milk that your body is producing. For best results, use a hospital-grade electric breast pump to build and maintain your milk supply. This will take extra effort on your part, but it is well worth the benefits to your baby. Many hospitals rent electric pumps specifically for this purpose.

While the baby is receiving milk via a feeding tube, it is recommended that she also be allowed to nurse at the breast to improve weight gain and encourage stomach emptying. Many facilities also promote "kangaroo care" by placing the baby skin to skin on the mother or the father for extended periods of time. Typically, preterm babies who experience kangaroo care go home sooner, breastfeed longer, cry less at six months of age, have fewer serious illnesses, and have fewer hospital readmissions.[10]

Studies have shown that, contrary to popular medical belief, nursing from the breast is less stressful and easier for the preterm infant than sucking from a bottle.[11] Once the baby is able to suck, request that she be breastfed. A lactation consultant or the NICU staff will be able to assist you.

The use of breastmilk for preterm babies is so critical that some NICUs purchase banked donor human milk for preterm infants whose mothers are unable to provide a sufficient supply. This donor milk is pasteurized and preferable to formula.

Better Digestion

Typically, the digestive system of a breastfed newborn is better than that of an infant who is fed formula. As stated earlier, breastmilk fosters the growth of beneficial intestinal bacteria, which prevents harmful bacteria from growing. This results in fewer bowel upsets and less diarrhea. A baby's system also utilizes breastmilk more completely than formula. Babies who are fed breastmilk exclusively rarely become constipated, whereas formula-fed babies occasionally experience painful constipation.

When a baby breastfeeds, the hormone *cholecystokinin (CCK)* is released in both the mother and the infant. CCK aids digestion and provides the baby with a satisfying feeling of fullness. In response to this hormone, many mothers and infants become sleepy during feedings.

Healthy Teeth and Oral Development

When nursing from a breast, babies suck differently than they do when sucking on a rubber nipple. Nursing promotes superior facial muscle and jaw development, and encourages the formation of a well-rounded dental arch, which may result in fewer snoring and sleep apnea problems in later life.[12] Sucking on a bottle nipple or a pacifier is considered a major cause of malocclusions and other dental problems.

Breastfeeding has also been associated with generally healthier teeth. The antibacterial and enzymatic qualities of breastmilk inhibit decay-causing bacteria. In one study conducted at Oregon State University, children who were breastfed for three months or longer (and who lived in the same communities) had 45 to 59 percent fewer cavities than their formula-fed counterparts.[13] Of course, whether a child has been breastfed or formula-fed, once she begins eating foods, especially those that contain sugar, the importance of good dental hygiene cannot be stressed enough.

Long-Term Advantages

The benefits of breastmilk remain with the infant throughout her lifetime. Babies who have a family history of allergies and are exclusively breastfed for at least three months receive a significant benefit against the development of food allergies and atopic dermatitis. Lymphomas, leukemia, and Hodgkin disease are observed more often in children who were not breastfed.[14]

Studies have also shown that breastfed babies score higher on mental development tests. *The Journal of Pediatrics* published the results of a New Zealand study that tracked 1,000 children from birth through age eighteen. The young adults who were breastfed as infants, especially for a prolonged period, scored significantly higher on standardized achievement tests, including the SATs, many years later.[15] Breastmilk contains long-chain fatty acids, which are necessary for proper brain growth. While these fatty acids are now added to formula, any long-term benefits to babies born at term are questionable. Multiple studies have shown learning deficiencies in children who were not breastfed.[16]

Exclusive breastfeeding for at least two months protects against childhood obesity.[17] This is extremely important as being overweight as a child can lead to a lifelong battle with obesity and its associated health problems. Multiple studies have also linked formula feeding with the development of insulin-dependent diabetes (type 1) and noninsulin-dependent diabetes (type 2) in children and adults.[18]

Serious chronic intestinal difficulties, including ulcerative colitis and Crohn's disease, are associated with formula feeding,[19] as is an increased risk of celiac disease. Celiac disease is triggered by a toxic reaction to gluten, a protein found in wheat. Breastfed children were found to be 52 percent less likely to develop intolerance to wheat if they were breastfeeding when it was introduced into their diet.[20]

Breastfed infants also tend to be healthier adults. Professor Alan Lucas, director of the Medical Research Council's Childhood Nutrition Research Centre in London, and his team followed a group of children for over twenty years. Cholesterol levels were found to be 14 percent lower in adults who were breastfed as babies than in their formula-fed counterparts. The formula-fed children were also found to experience a rapid growth period early in life. Dr. Lucas believes that the slower weight gain that is typically seen in breastfed babies programs the body to produce less cholesterol in later life.[21]

Safer Than Formula . . .

Over the years, infant formulas have been recalled for many different reasons—insufficient chloride, excessive vitamin D, high levels of iodine, and the presence of metal particles in powdered varieties. In one case, cans of soy formula were recalled because they contained vanilla Sustacal, an adult nutrition supplement.

Breastmilk and Skin Benefits

Diaper rash, eczema, and other skin rashes are rarely seen in breastfed babies. A baby's skin is always soft, but this softness tends to be enhanced in nursing babies. Some doctors claim that they can tell the difference between formula-fed babies and breastfed babies by the feel of their skin.

Bacterial contamination is another danger associated with formula. Powdered formula is not sterile, and once opened, it is subject to further contamination. In 2004, a survey of manufacturing plants reported that up to 35 percent of powdered formula samples contained *Enterobacter sakazakii,* a dangerous bacteria that causes bacteremia, necrotizing enterocolitis, and meningitis.[22] Infants at highest risk of death from bacterial contamination are those who are under twenty days of life, are preterm, have a low birth weight, or have a compromised immune system. Soy formula has also been recalled because of salmonella contamination.

Improper storage of prepared formula can also result in bacterial contamination. When prepared powdered formula is stored in the refrigerator, the bacteria level doubles every ten hours; when left at room temperature, the count doubles in thirty minutes.[23] As soon as the baby drinks from a bottle of formula, her saliva begins to break down the milk and bacteria begin to grow. For this reason, any leftover formula should be discarded within one hour.

Method of preparation can also influence formula safety. In one case, a product label was found to have incorrect Spanish instructions. If the formula had been consumed as directed for several days, it could have resulted in "seizures, irregular heartbeat, or death."[24] If too much or not enough water is mixed with powdered or concentrated formula, the baby will not receive the proper nutrients. And if the water used is not sterile, excessive bacteria can result immediately.

In some areas, the water contains lead. Even when this water is boiled before it is mixed with formula, the infant is at increased risk for lead intoxication. Additionally, using water from a supply that is contaminated with bacteria could have serious consequences—and this problem does not occur only in underdeveloped countries. On occasion, dangerous bacteria levels have been found in the water supplies of a number of American cities. With every discovery, the residents were told not to drink the water until the source of the problem was pinpointed and eliminated. The real danger in such situations is to the babies who are given formula made with contaminated water *before* the problem is discovered. No water supply can ever be guaranteed as safe as mother's milk!

In Emergency Situations

Breastfeeding may actually be crucial to your baby's survival. In recent years, devastating hurricanes, earthquakes, tornadoes, and other major disasters have occurred in this country. In many cases, electrical power was lost and not restored for long periods, and water supplies became contaminated—sometimes for several weeks. Babies who were not breastfed were at serious risk during that time. In some areas, supplies of formula in emergency shelters were found to be outdated and in limited supply. In situations such as these, nursing mothers can relax, knowing that their babies have a continuous supply of safe, uncontaminated food.

BENEFITS FOR MOTHERS

Along with the obvious advantages for your baby, breastfeeding has advantages for you, the nursing mother. Because there is nothing to buy, measure, pour, heat, or sterilize, breastfeeding is less expensive than formula and readily available. You can ease your baby's hunger immediately—without first having to warm a bottle. Health benefits have also been demonstrated for the mother who breastfeeds her children, especially for extended periods.

After the birth of your baby, breastfeeding will release the hormone oxytocin, which causes your uterus to contract. This results in less blood loss and a faster return of the uterus to its prepregnant size. And because you have to sit or lie down to nurse, breastfeeding forces you to get the postpartum rest you need.

The production of milk burns calories, making it easier to lose the weight gained during pregnancy without dieting. The extra fat will be utilized during the months of lactation. Breastfeeding mothers who nurse frequently lose more weight than those who nurse infrequently. Women who breastfeed for an extended period of time also lose more weight than those who breastfeed for a short period. Crash dieting should be avoided while breastfeeding. Rapid weight reduction can cause the environmental toxins that are stored in the body fat to be released into the milk.

Studies have shown that a breastfeeding woman's risk of getting breast cancer is proportionately reduced by the length of time she nurses. This means that the longer you nurse, the better protection you have.[25] Multiple studies have also demonstrated a decrease in ovarian cancer in women who have breastfed.[26] Women who have breast-fed also have improved bone remineralization, which puts them at a decreased risk for osteoporosis and hip fractures in the post-menopausal years.

If you wear the right top, you will be able to discreetly nurse your baby anywhere.

Traveling is easier with a breastfed baby because you do not have to pack any supplies or warm any bottles. Outings are more relaxed because you do not have to rush home for feedings or worry if the formula is becoming spoiled without refrigeration. You will be able to discreetly nurse your baby almost anywhere if you wear the right clothing. Choose tops that can be lifted from the bottom or those that are geared specifically for nursing mothers. Practice breastfeeding in front of a mirror to become comfortable nursing in public.

Nursing delays the return of menstrual periods because of the release of *prolactin*—the hormone that encourages the milk supply and suppresses ovulation. Breastfeeding, therefore, is a method of contraception, known as the Lactational Amenorrhea Method (LAM). This method is 99 percent effective in preventing pregnancy for the first six months if the woman breastfeeds exclusively and her periods have not resumed.[27] Be aware that once the baby begins breastfeeding less frequently, starts taking other foods, or sleeps longer periods, your hormone level will drop and you can ovulate and get pregnant without ever having a period. If you are spacing your children, it is wise to use another method of contraception along with breastfeeding.

The amount of breastfeeding that is necessary to suppress ovulation varies from woman to woman. A number of birth control choices that are compatible with nursing are available. Once your milk supply is well established, the use of progestin-only birth control methods is considered compatible with breastfeeding and should not impact your milk supply. Avoid starting hormonal products until your six-week visit. See Table 17.1 on page 428 for more information on birth control options.

Along with the physical benefits of breastfeeding, there are emotional advantages as well. Most important is the intimate contact you will have with your baby, along with feelings of satisfaction and a sense of fulfillment. In addition, the hormones released while nursing have a soothing, tranquilizing effect that instills feelings of calmness and relaxation each time the baby nurses. They encourage maternal feelings. As an added bonus, the release of stress hormones are suppressed in lactating women, which means that breastfeeding may help you to cope during stressful situations.

Many women have experienced a sense of fulfillment knowing that their bodies produced the breastmilk that sustained their babies. Providing the best for your infant can give you a sense of empowerment that you can carry into the rest of your life.

BENEFITS FOR FATHERS

You will discover that advantages also exist for you, the father of a breastfed baby. For starters, those middle-of-the-night feedings are not likely to disrupt your sleep. Your wife will probably awaken as soon as the baby does, often before she even cries. (The two of them will seem to be on the same wavelength.) Of course, you can help out, especially during the early weeks, by getting up, changing the baby, and bringing her to her mother to nurse. While you are all together in bed, the closeness and body warmth may also encourage the baby to fall back asleep more quickly. While the baby is in bed with you, it is important to follow certain safety guidelines. See "Co-Sleeping and Bed Sharing" on page 309.

Another benefit that you will certainly notice is that exclusively breastfed babies smell good. Even when they spit up, they don't have that sour milk smell that formula-fed babies often have. Their bowel movements do not have an offensive odor, so you will find that changing diapers is not as bad as you may have expected.

You will also appreciate the economic advantages of breastfeeding. Bottles, nipples, "formula water," and breastmilk substitutes cost money; breastmilk does not. (Over a thousand dollars can be spent on formula alone during the first year!) And since breastfed babies tend to be healthier than formula-fed babies, you are likely to have fewer medical bills and less need to purchase medicine.

Some new fathers have reported feeling left out or unimportant because they are unable to feed the baby. If you experience these feelings, keep in mind that feeding is just one aspect of your baby's care. There are many other ways to express your love and get involved. You can bathe her, hold and cuddle her, rock her, and sing to her. You can change her diapers and take her for walks in her stroller. And you can have the satisfaction of knowing that, when it comes to nourishment, she is getting the "real thing." Remember, dads can show love in many, many ways.

BENEFITS FOR THE COMMUNITY AND ENVIRONMENT

According to a study by the US Department of Agriculture, "a minimum of $3.6 billion would be saved annually on childhood healthcare costs if breastfeeding were increased from current levels (64 percent in-hospital and 29 percent at six months) to those recommended by the US Surgeon General (75 percent in-hospital and 50 percent at six months).[28] The savings would actually be higher, as this study looked at only three childhood illnesses, otitis media (ear infection), gastroenteritis (vomiting and diarrhea), and necrotizing enterocolitis.

Breastfeeding also decreases costs for public health programs such as the special supplemental nutrition program for Women, Infants, and Children (WIC) that provides infant formula to low-income families. Over half of all infant formula sold in the United States is obtained through WIC. Consumers who are not subsided by WIC also share the increased costs of purchasing formula for this program's participants. In areas of the country where WIC participation is high, the cost to the general public in grocery stores is higher than average.[29]

County landfills have to accept the burden of increased waste from formula containers and disposable bottles. There is also an increase in energy demands in the manufacturing, transporting, and preparation of artificial breastmilk and products.

As stated earlier, compared to formula-fed babies, breastfed babies tend to have fewer illnesses. This means that children who are formula-fed get sick more often. In turn, their employed parents have to stay home and care for them when they get sick. This absenteeism results in reduced productivity in the workplace and a possible smaller income for the family.

AN INFORMED DECISION

It is not uncommon for doctors and nurses to avoid telling new parents about the risks associated with formula. This is generally because they do not want to make the mother feel "guilty" about her decision not to breastfeed. Bottle-feeding has become the norm in this country and viewed as the way most babies receive nourishment. Many women choose bottle-feeding because they believe that formula is close to mother's milk, just as the advertisements state. Maybe if formula was renamed to reflect what it really is "factory-made artificial human milk substitute with chemical additives,"[30] as suggested by noted pediatrician Dr. William Marshall, Jr., women would think twice before offering it to their babies.

Years ago, women smokers continued to smoke during pregnancy, babies sat in their parent's laps when riding in cars, and nobody wore bicycle helmets. We now know that these practices can have serious consequences. Today, most doctors, nurses, and the general public will speak up, citing the risks of these actions. At one time—much like smoking during pregnancy—health risks associated with formula-feeding were also unknown; but an increasing number of studies conducted over the years has highlighted these risks, while uncovering breastfeeding's many benefits.

A woman should be encouraged to choose breastfeeding over formula-feeding for her child, but ultimately the choice will be hers. This choice, like all healthcare decisions, should be based on facts. It should be educated and informed. And the way a mother feeds her child is a health issue, not a lifestyle choice.

CONTRAINDICATIONS TO BREASTFEEDING

According to Dr. Robert M. Lawrence, Clinical Associate Professor of Pediatric Immunology and Infectious Diseases at the University of Florida, "The benefits of breastfeeding are so compelling that very few situations definitively contraindicate it."

Women who have had a double mastectomy in which all of the breast tissue has been removed will not be able to breastfeed. Those with untreated active tuberculosis or T-cell lymphotropic virus type I (HTLV-I) or type II (HTLV-II) should also refrain from nursing. An infant should not nurse from a breast that has an active herpes lesion, although it is acceptable to nurse from the other breast if it is lesion-free.

In the United States, women who are HIV positive are advised not to breastfeed. Rare cases have been reported of infants acquiring the virus through their mothers' breastmilk. HIV-positive women who strongly desire to feed their infants breastmilk may consider pumping their milk and having it pasteurized to kill the HIV. They should not nurse directly from the breast. Purchasing banked donor milk is another option, although it is expensive.

Women who use cocaine or any other illegal recreational drug should not breastfeed because these substances readily pass into the breastmilk and can cause serious reactions in the baby. Cocaine remains in breastmilk for up to thirty-six hours and can result in death if ingested by the infant.

Nighttime Feedings

Nighttime feedings are easiest if the baby is kept in your room in a co-sleeper or crib that is close to your bed.

No Contest

If babies had a choice, they would always choose their mother's milk over artificial breastmilk substitutes.

Babies diagnosed with galactosemia are missing an enzyme that is needed to metabolize lactose. Since breastmilk is high in lactose, breastfeeding is not suitable for these babies. Doing so would cause mental deficiency. Babies with galactosemia must be placed on a special formula such as Nutramigen. All states check for this disorder as part of the infant screening test.

A number of substances, including radioactive isotopes, antimetabolites, and chemotherapy drugs, require temporary cessation of nursing. A woman who must stop breastfeeding temporarily should maintain her milk supply by continuing to pump, although the milk expressed during this period must be discarded. When the specified amount of time to avoid nursing has elapsed, she can safely begin breastfeeding her baby again.

UNFOUNDED CONTRAINDICATIONS TO BREASTFEEDING

There are a number of myths and misconceptions regarding conditions or situations that may not be compatible with breastfeeding. Because of these false beliefs, women have been incorrectly advised to stop breastfeeding or they never attempt to start.

Breast Surgery

Breast reduction surgery, breast augmentation, or any breast surgery may—or may not—impact a woman's milk supply. The effects will vary based upon the type and degree of the surgical procedure. Any incision that is made close to the areola may cut the nerves or the ducts that deliver milk to the nipple. This means that breast reduction surgery involving the removal and reattachment of the nipple may significantly impact the ability to breastfeed. This also holds true for breast augmentation in which implants have been inserted through an incision around the areola. A woman who has had any type of breast surgery must closely monitor the amount of milk her baby receives to ensure sufficient intake.

A woman who has pierced nipples or who had them pierced in the past but no longer keeps them filled may have scar tissue. While most women with piercings can breastfeed successfully, in some cases, this scar tissue may lead to plugged ducts or a loss of sensation around the nipple, and this can affect the milk-ejection reflex. If scar tissue blocks the ducts, it may impact supply. If your nipples are pierced, be sure to remove any jewelry during breastfeeding. If you are concerned that the hole will close, reinsert the jewelry or insert a temporary plastic retainer between feedings.

Even women who are unable to produce a full milk supply should still breastfeed. Any amount of breastmilk is beneficial, as is the emotional bond it creates between mother and child.

Adoptive Mothers

The belief that adoptive mothers cannot breastfeed is simply not true. With proper stimulation, most women can successfully establish a milk supply. The amount of milk produced will vary. Women who have given birth previously may be more successful as their breasts have already experienced the changes during pregnancy. Also, with each subsequent baby, the ability to produce a larger volume of milk increases. Some physicians prescribe medications to stimulate the growth of an adoptive mother's milk glands. Many women will choose to stimulate their breasts through pumping, which is often initiated prior to the baby's arrival. Others may wait until the baby is born and begin breastfeeding—with supplementation as needed. A knowledgeable physician or lactation consultant is important in guiding adoptive mothers through this lactation process. Even if a woman is unable to produce all of the milk that the baby needs, any breastmilk and the act of nursing alone is always beneficial.

Diabetes

Women with certain pre-existing, chronic health conditions may assume that they cannot nurse, but in many cases, they can. Before deciding not to breastfeed, they should speak with a lactation consultant about their specific concerns.

Women who are diabetic or have a family history of diabetes are actually encouraged to breastfeed. Exclusive breastfeeding reduces the baby's chances of becoming diabetic. Children who are at high risk for developing diabetes are more likely to develop the disease when exposed to cow's milk-based formula, especially within the first three months of life.[31] During the last couple weeks of pregnancy, some diabetic women express their colostrum and freeze it. That way, this nutrient-rich early milk will be available in case the baby's blood sugar is low and requires a supplement in addition to breastfeeding. If a mother is unable to express enough colostrum and a supplement is needed, the hypoallergenic formula Nutramigen is recommended over standard cow's milk-based formula.

Bypass Surgery and Crash Diets

Nursing women who are overweight and trying to lose weight should do so under close supervision of a healthcare professional. Rapid weight loss is not recommended as the environmental toxins that are stored in the body's fat cells will be released and enter the breastmilk. Any weight loss should be gradual, and again, under the watchful eye of a healthcare professional. A woman who has had gastric bypass surgery needs to supplement her diet with vitamins, including monthly injections of vitamin B_{12} as her body and her breastmilk may be deficient in these nutrients. The infant should also be observed for signs of vitamin B_{12} deficiency, which can include developmental delays, low muscle tone, failure to thrive, and hyper reflexes. The infant may require supplements of vitamin B_{12}, folate, and iron.[32]

Colds, Flu, and Other Illnesses

A nursing mother who has a fever from a cold, flu, or a similar illness should continue breastfeeding. The baby will receive the antibodies that her mother is producing to fight the illness and is not likely to get sick. If the baby does become ill, it will be with very mild case of the illness. Women who need to be hospitalized at this time can use an electric pump to maintain their milk supply or arrange to have their baby brought to them for feedings.

Breastfeeding is not contraindicated in mothers who have hepatitis B or hepatitis C. If the woman is a carrier (not recently acquired) of cytomegalovirus (CMV), she can breastfeed her full-term infant. For preterm babies, precautions may be suggested. Freezing and pasteurization can decrease the viral load of CMV in the milk.[33]

If your baby has jaundice, continue breastfeeding her—and frequently. Breastmilk provides the protein that binds with the bilirubin so it can be excreted from the body in bowel movements. In severe cases, the baby may need supplementation if the mother does not have an adequate volume of milk.

Medications

Many medications can be safely used while nursing, but it is important to check with your caregiver or lactation consultant before taking any medication or drug, even an over-the-counter variety. Certain drugs may transfer into breastmilk and have a negative effect on your baby. Stimulant laxatives, for example, can upset your baby's digestive system. Cold medications that dry nasal secretions should also be avoided as they may decrease your milk supply. Healthcare professionals, particularly lactation consultants can provide you with the most up-to-date information regarding medications and breastfeeding. If you are prescribed a drug that is contraindicated with nursing, an alternative may be suggested.

Alcoholic Beverages

A nursing mother can consume an occasional alcohol beverage and still breastfeed. Just be aware that any alcohol consumed will be readily transmitted to the baby in much the same concentration as it is in the mother's blood. It takes the liver approximately two hours to break down the alcohol, so if you wait that length of time before breastfeeding, the amount of alcohol the baby receives will be minimal. You do not need to "pump and dump" the milk. If you consume more than one drink, you will need to double (or triple) the waiting time. It is also important to know that heavy alcohol consumption inhibits the flow of milk.

Smoking

Smoking is not a reason to avoid breastfeeding. It is, however, certainly advisable to stop or drastically cut down the number of cigarettes you smoke per day, as nicotine is transferred to the baby in the breastmilk. Do not smoke immediately before or while breastfeeding. Women who smoke produce less milk, and the milk they produce has a lower fat content. If you smoke over a pack of cigarettes a day, your baby may experience nausea, vomiting, abdominal cramps, and diarrhea after nursing because of the nicotine in the milk. There will also be a reduced level of vitamin C in the milk as your own stores will be diminished.[34]

Even if you don't smoke, it is a good policy to avoid secondhand smoke. In addition to being dangerous for your baby—it puts them at a high risk for respiratory infections, pneumonia, bronchitis, and SIDS during their first year—it can affect your breastmilk as well. Not surprisingly, nicotine has been found in the milk of nonsmokers who are around people who smoke. If anyone in your home smokes, insist that he or she do so outside and not in the presence of you or the baby.

Pregnancy

Many women who become pregnant while breastfeeding can continue to nurse their other children with no serious consequences. There is no evidence that a woman who is experiencing a normal pregnancy needs to wean. It is, however, important that she is well nourished and takes vitamins. For some pregnant women, breastfeeding is not recommended. As discussed earlier in this book, uterine contractions occur while nursing. For women with a history of miscarriages, abnormal bleeding, or previous preterm births, these contractions may be a risk, and weaning may be recommended.

If you become pregnant while breastfeeding, expect nipple tenderness and breast discomfort. As a matter of fact, these signs may be the first indication that you are pregnant. And if you are like most women, you will also notice a dramatic decline in your milk supply. Because of this milk reduction, if you are nursing a baby who is less than a year, you may need to supplement her feedings. If the child is over a year, she may begin weaning herself at this point. If she continues to breastfeed, it may be mostly for comfort. If she is old enough to talk, you may hear her complain that the milk is "all gone" or that it tastes different.

Some children may continue to nurse through the pregnancy and even after the new baby is born. Others who had weaned during the pregnancy may suddenly decide to start nursing again. When breastfeeding a newborn and an older sibling—called *tandem nursing*—be sure to feed the infant first to ensure that she receives the colostrum and enough milk.

MILK PRODUCTION

Many women express concern about their ability to make enough milk for their baby. It is important to remember that just as your body nourished your baby during the pregnancy, your breasts are designed to feed her. Understanding how milk is produced and knowing which factors can impact milk supply are important as well.

Anatomy of the Breast and the Production of Milk

During pregnancy, hormones cause the breasts to enlarge in size and the glandular tissue and ducts to increase. Colostrum production begins during the second trimester. After birth, when the placenta is delivered, the resulting drop in estrogen and progesterone (primarily) signals the body to increase milk production.

As seen in Figure 15.1 on page 358, within the breasts there are areas of glandular tissue made up of small ducts and clusters of tiny sacs called *alveoli*. Milk is produced and stored in the alveoli and then travels through the ducts until it reaches the nipple. Each nipple contains an average of four to ten tiny openings through which the milk flows. (This is far fewer than the fifteen to twenty openings that were previously believed to exist.) Stimulation of the nipple by sucking or even touching causes it to become more erect, making it easier for the infant to latch onto.

During pregnancy, raised bumps on the areola called *Montgomery glands* become prominent. These glands secrete a fluid that lubricates and prevents bacterial growth on the nipple and areola.

Sucking or touching the nipple causes the release of oxytocin into the bloodstream. This causes the alveoli to contract, which pushes the milk into the ducts toward the nipple so it is available for the baby. This process, known as the *milk-ejection reflex (MER)* or *let-down reflex,* occurs shortly after the baby begins each nursing. Most women will have more than one let-down during a feeding. Once the volume of milk increases, there will be a sort of tingling in the breasts during a let-down, along with a surge of milk that can be strong enough to spray out as far as twelve inches. At times, the force of this spray will cause the baby to release the breast. For many women, hearing the baby cry or even just thinking about her can cause a let-down. The milk-ejection reflex can be inhibited by emotional upset, fatigue, or tension. Mothers having difficulty can condition this reflex by developing a nursing routine and using relaxation techniques.

When you breastfeed, don't be surprised if you become sleepy and thirsty, which are side effects of the oxytocin. Also expect to feel uterine contractions, which can range from very mild cramping (usually after a first baby) to strong, uncomfortable spasms (more common after subsequent births). This discomfort usually subsides within a few days. If necessary, take pain medication as suggested by your doctor.

During the first few days of breastfeeding, your infant will be receiving colostrum, about a teaspoon to a tablespoon per feeding. Around the third to fifth day, but sometimes as early as the second day, the volume of milk will increase and you will probably notice that your breasts are heavier, fuller, and firmer. This is not caused by milk alone, but also by extra lymph fluid and blood, which aids in the production of milk. This fullness is normal and generally subsides within several days as long as the baby nurses frequently. It may, however, return if the interval between feedings is too long. If this breast swelling is uncomfortable, applying an ice pack to the area for twenty-minute periods can provide relief. For additional pain relief suggestions, see "Treating Engorged Breasts" on page 395.

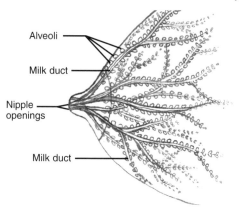

Figure 15.1. Cross-section of a lactating breast.

During the first two weeks, breastmilk transitions from colostrum to a mixture of colostrum and mature milk, and then to mature milk. Mature milk is a thin white or bluish-white liquid that contains the exact combination of water, fat, protein, sugar, minerals, and vitamins that your baby needs for proper nourishment and development, while also providing her with immunities and other protective factors.

Supply and Demand

Your milk supply is determined by the amount of milk your baby requires. The more she nurses, the more milk you will produce. This is why mothers are able to nurse twins and even triplets! During the first days after birth, frequent breastfeeding or stimulation through hand expression or a breast pump sets up the "milk factories" within the breasts.

The first two weeks are the most critical for establishing a good milk supply. To ensure an adequate supply, let the baby nurse whenever she is hungry. Also, delay introducing a pacifier or an occasional bottle for at least three weeks, or until your baby is skilled at nursing and your milk supply is well established. Otherwise, you might disturb nature's perfect demand-supply relationship by decreasing the baby's nursing time at the breast. This will diminish your milk supply. Encourage your baby to nurse at least every two to three hours (eight to twelve times a day). If she wants to nurse sooner than two hours, do not make her wait.

Through recent studies conducted at the University of Australia on the synthesis of milk, it was discovered that the storage capacity of breasts differs from woman to woman and even from a woman's left and right breasts. And this capacity is not related to breast size. The studies showed that the storage capacity ranged from 80 milliliters (almost 3 ounces) to 600 milliliters (2 $\frac{1}{2}$ cups).[35] While women with vastly different storage capacities can equally nourish their babies, those with smaller capacities will need to nurse more frequently. Removing the milk from the breast signals the body to make more. Therefore, increasing breastfeeding will increase the amount of milk that is available to the infant. Conversely, decreasing breastfeeding or lengthening the time between feeds, will decrease the amount of milk that is produced. When milk remains in the breast over four to five hours, a component in the milk called *feedback inhibitor of lactation* signals the breast to reduce milk supply.

The majority of mothers can develop an adequate milk supply for nursing. There are, however, certain medical conditions that can affect a woman's ability to produce sufficient milk. For a complete discussion of these conditions, see "Inadequate Milk Supply" on page 378. Women who have had any type of breast surgery, those who take medication, or those with chronic health problems may want to speak to a certified lactation consultant.

You will find that allowing your baby to set her own pattern will benefit both of you—the baby will be more content and you will avoid both breast engorgement and an inadequate milk supply. Because breastmilk is more easily digested than formula, breastfed babies need to eat more often, sometimes every two hours. As your baby grows, her body will require more milk. During growth spurts, she will want to spend more time at the breast, which will increase your milk supply. Do not misinterpret these increased feedings as a signal that you are not producing enough milk or that it has "dried up." Your initial breast fullness will probably subside within six weeks. If you allow your baby to nurse on demand during growth spurts, after one or two days of these more frequent feedings, your milk supply will increase and she will return to her normal feeding pattern. The most common times for these growth periods are between ten and fourteen days, between four and six weeks, at three months, and at around six months.

Some babies will want to nurse repeatedly in the late evening, then typically they will fall asleep for a longer period of time. This is known as *cluster feeding*, which is normal and can occur at any time of the day.

The milk that is present at the start of the feed, called the *foremilk*, is usually lower in fat. As the feeding progresses, the fat content increases. The high-fat milk at the end of the feed is known as *hindmilk;* it contains more calories and can be especially important for babies who need to gain weight. This is one reason that mothers are instructed not to watch the clock and stop feeding the baby after a specified number of minutes. It has also been discovered that if the interval between feedings is short, the milk that is present at the start of the feed will have a higher fat content. Therefore, the fat content of milk is related to the fullness of the breast. Feeding your baby more frequently when the breast is less full will result in milk that is higher in fat.

LATCH AND POSITIONING

Proper positioning of your baby during breastfeeding is very important. If she does not latch correctly, she may not consume milk efficiently. Improper latching can also cause you to develop sore nipples.

When latching on, the baby's mouth should be opened wide with the tongue down and extended over the bottom gum. When you look at your baby's mouth on your breast, her lips should be apart and well flared. It is best if the latch is asymmetrical, with the bottom gum further from the nipple than the top gum. The placement of the bottom gum is most important as it does most of the work along with the tongue. The baby's chin should be deep into the breast, not flexed onto her own chest, and you may see some slight breast movement as she sucks. The movement of her jaw can be seen near her ear and you may be able to see or hear her swallow.

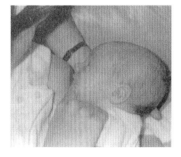

To remove the baby from your breast, place your finger in the corner of her mouth to break the suction.

When the baby first latches, it may be uncomfortable, but the discomfort should quickly dissipate. You should feel a pulling sensation, not a bite. The baby should nurse in bursts of sucking, swallowing, and pausing. The sucking should not be painful, but if it is, remove the baby from your breast and relatch her correctly. To remove her, gently insert your finger into the corner of her mouth to release the suction. Do not allow the baby to slowly draw the nipple into her mouth—she will simply chew on the tip, which will cause soreness.

If the baby has latched on correctly, when she releases the breast, the nipple will appear as it did before the feeding or possibly longer. If the nipple is tilted, mis-shapened, or has a compression stripe across the top, the baby was latched incorrectly. When you look at your baby's mouth, it should appear as if she has taken a large mouthful of breast. If her lips are close together, she should be unlatched and repositioned.

To help the baby latch correctly, support and compress your breast using the *sandwich hold*. To do this, think about how you would eat a large sandwich or burger. First you would hold the burger in front of your face and compress it slightly with your fingers parallel to your lips. Next, you would tilt your head back a little, place your lower jaw on the bottom bun and open your mouth wide as you move your head in to take a bite. To get a bigger mouthful, you would compress the sandwich more. This is the same basic concept for helping the baby latch correctly and deeply on the breast. Compress your breast like a sandwich in the same direction as her lips. This gives you the most control over the shape of your breast and the position of the baby's mouth on it.

Figure 15.2. Position of fingers in the sandwich hold when the baby is lying across your chest.

Breast compression is a valuable technique for stimulating a sleepy baby or increasing the flow of milk for babies with a weak suck. Even when the baby has achieved a good latch, continue holding the breast. If she stops sucking for an extended period of time or you want to bring more milk to her, compress the breast or massage it. Some women use their thumb to stroke the breast during compression to move the milk downward. You can also stroke the baby beneath her chin to encourage her to start sucking again. Repeat this as needed throughout the feed. Do not stroke or compress the breast too firmly, as this can cause soreness; press just enough to bring milk to the baby.

If the baby is biting, her suck will be painful and cause nipple damage. This usually occurs if she keeps her tongue behind the gum or if she is not latched well. If you notice her cheeks dimpling when she sucks, but you do not feel any pressure, she is sucking her tongue. If you tilt her head away from your breast and the nipple easily falls out of her mouth, she was not latched at all. This sometimes fools even nurses, as the baby appears to be sucking.

During the first few days, it may be difficult to hear the baby swallow. While she is sucking, listen for a puff of air from her nose. You may also hear a very soft "ka" sound, or see the baby's throat move. Watch her lower jaw, which should show movement all the way up to her ear when she swallows; also your breast tissue should move. Once your milk volume increases, it will be easier to hear the swallows.

Nursing Positions

There are several comfortable positions for nursing. The cross-cradle, cradle, football hold, and side-lying positions are the most popular. Before you start, make sure you have a few pillows or a nursing pillow to maintain the breastfeeding position. All nursing positions can be used after a cesarean if sufficient pillows are used for support. No matter which position you choose, the baby's head and chest should be in good alignment. This means that her head, chest, and legs are all facing in the same direction. Her head should not be turned to the side, nor tilted toward her shoulder. Picture the tilt of your head as you drink from a glass; your baby should be positioned in a similar manner.

Cross-Cradle Position

The *cross-cradle position* allows the most control over the shape of the breast and the position of the baby's mouth on the breast. It is also the easiest position for the mother to see how the baby is latching. While sitting in a chair or propped up in bed, use a nursing pillow or two standard pillows to support your baby's head and body. Remove any blankets and place her on her side across your chest, tummy to tummy, with her body wrapped around yours and her lower arm across her tummy. Support her upper back and neck with your left hand. Using the sandwich hold for compression, cup your hand beneath your breast with your fingers shaped like a "U." (Use your right hand when nursing from your right breast and left hand when nursing from your left.) Make sure your fingers do not cover the areola—they should be placed directly outside of where your baby's lips will be positioned.

Avoid . . .

touching the back of the baby's head or cheek while she is breastfeeding. This will cause her to turn away from the breast towards the touch.

Tickle the baby's top lip with your nipple. When she turns toward the stimulation—caused by the rooting reflex—and opens her mouth, her bottom gum will automatically be correctly positioned well below the nipple. As she roots, she will move toward the breast with her mouth opened wide. Her tongue will be down and extended over the bottom gum. Compress your breast as you rock her head slightly forward to the nipple. The nipple should be centered or slightly asymmetrical in her mouth, with her bottom jaw positioned well below the nipple and on the areola. Her chin should be pressing into the breast, with her lips flaring outward. Make sure she has a large mouthful of breast.

Have your partner adjust the pillows so that they are providing most of the support for the baby. This position is even comfortable for women who have had a cesarean, provided the pillows are properly positioned to support the baby's weight. Avoid firmly grasping the back of the baby's neck and head. Most of your control should be on her upper back with support for the neck. Do not let your fingers touch the back of her head or her cheeks, as this will cause her to pull away from the breast and move her face toward the touch.

To nurse from the right breast in the cross-cradle position, place the baby across your chest with your left hand supporting her upper back and neck.

Cup your right breast with your fingers in a "U" shape.

Compress your breast and tickle her top lip with your nipple.

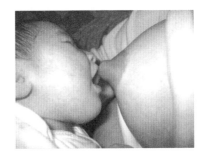

Wait until she opens her mouth wide, her tongue down, and . . .

place her lower lip below the nipple, and rock her head into your breast.

Her chin should press into the breast, and her lips should flare outward.

Maintaining this position throughout the feeding makes it easy to periodically compress the breast and stimulate the baby to continue sucking. If your partner wants to encourage the baby to suck, he can stroke her under the chin. If this position is not comfortable for the entire feed, after the baby is maintaining the latch and nursing well, you can release your right hand from under your breast and hold your baby in the more traditional cradle position.

Cradle Position

Cradle position.

To nurse your baby in the traditional *cradle position,* rest her head in the bend of your arm or your forearm with her lips directly in line with the nipple. Place a pillow under your arm and help raise the baby's mouth to the level of your breast. You can tuck her lower arm under your arm or around your side. With the baby facing you, tummy to tummy, cup your hand around your breast with your fingers in the same direction as her lips. Make sure your fingers do not cover the areola—they should be placed directly outside of where your baby's lips will be positioned. Tickle her top lip with your nipple. When she opens her mouth wide with her tongue down and extended over the bottom gum, pull her toward you. The nipple should be centered or slightly asymmetrical in her mouth, with her jaw positioned well below the nipple and on the areola. Her chin should be pressing into the breast, with her lips flaring outward.

If you are concerned that the baby cannot breathe, draw her legs in closer or slightly lift the breast with your hand. Avoid pressing down on the breast as this may cause her jaw to slide down closer to the tip of the nipple. Also, make sure that your baby faces you and does not need to turn her head to the side to feed.

Football Hold

Football hold.

To nurse using the *football hold,* also called the *clutch position,* place your baby's body next to your side and support her upper back and neck with your hand. Use pillows as necessary to support the baby's weight and bring her up to the level of your breast. If you have large breasts, make sure your breast is not resting on the baby's chest. You may also want to place a folded diaper or hand towel under the breast for support.

As you look at your baby, use your free hand to compress the breast and shape it to your baby's mouth. Tickle her top lip with your nipple. When she opens her mouth wide with her tongue down and extended over the bottom gum, pull her toward you. The nipple should be centered or slightly asymmetrical in her mouth, with her jaw positioned well below the nipple and on the areola. Her chin should be pressing into the breast, with her lips flaring outward. She should be looking up at your face.

Side-Lying Position

Side-lying position.

Some mothers prefer the *side-lying position* when nursing, especially for nighttime feedings. This position is also helpful if your baby is very fussy at the breast. As you lie on your side, position your baby on her side facing you with her top lip even with your nipple. Support the breast as in the other holds (above) and make sure the baby latches deeply.

COMMON BREASTFEEDING QUESTIONS

Most mothers have questions concerning breastfeeding. Unfortunately, they are often given conflicting advice on the subject from family, friends, and even members of the medical profession. What follows are answers to their most common questions.

How often should I feed my baby?

Your baby should breastfeed at least eight to twelve times every day. If she is sleepy and not feeding a minimum of eight times, wake her up after three hours to nurse. If she is averaging enough feeds every twenty-four hours, allow her to set her own pattern. As she wakes up, she will stretch and squirm—and during the early days, any sign that the baby is waking up should be a sign to feed. Look for cues that your baby is ready to nurse, such as moving her hands to her mouth or making sucking motions. Do not wait for her to begin crying, which is a late sign of hunger. If you wait until she cries or screams, you will have to settle her down before nursing.

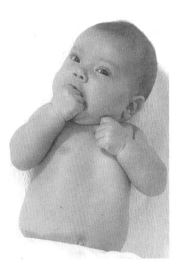

Sucking on the fist means this baby is hungry and ready to breastfeed.

How do I burp my baby?

To burp your baby, place her against your shoulder and gently pat her back. You can also sit her on your knee and support her chest and chin with your hand while rubbing her back with the other hand.

How often should I burp my baby during feedings?

Allow your baby to finish nursing from one breast. If she starts falling asleep or pulls away from the breast, burp her and then offer the other breast. Do not be concerned if she does not burp. Typically, breastfed babies do not take in much air and may not need to burp. Once the volume of milk increases, if the baby gulps down the milk, she may burp more easily.

How long should each feeding last?

Encourage your baby to feed at least ten to twenty minutes on the first breast, but avoid strict adherence to time. If she is still nursing vigorously at twenty minutes, do not disturb her. Each baby has a different suck wants. Some babies will complete a feed in fifteen minutes while others may need forty-five. Treat your baby as an individual and allow her to nurse as much as she wants. As your baby matures, she may become very efficient at emptying the breast and the length of time it takes to feed will decrease. During the first couple weeks of nursing, offering both breasts will increase milk stimulation and help prevent engorgement.

Will longer feeding times cause nipple soreness?

The length of a feeding time is not the cause of nipple soreness—improper positioning of the baby's mouth on the breast is the most common reason.

Is it okay to begin nursing from the same breast at each feeding?

Because your baby's initial sucking will be strongest at each feeding, it is best to alternate the first breast you offer her. This ensures that an adequate milk supply is built up in both breasts. To remind yourself which breast to offer first at the next feeding, attach a safety pin to your bra on that side. Many women have discovered, though, that one breast produces more milk than the other. If your baby nurses from the side that produces less, she may want the second breast, but if she consumes plenty of milk from the side with the larger storage capacity, she may not take the second.

Burping the baby.

How will I know if my baby is getting enough milk?

This is the one of the most frequently asked questions regarding breastfeeding, and of special concern during the baby's first few weeks of life. The answer to this question is usually determined by the number of times the baby feeds in a day, as well as the number of wet and soiled diapers she produces.

It is important to remember that during the first few days, your baby will be receiving small amounts of colostrum. Your milk supply will gradually increase, as will the number of wet and soiled diapers. Also be aware that it is normal for the baby to lose some weight during the first few days as she excretes the meconium that was present in her intestines at birth.

Until you are confident that breastfeeding is going well, keep a record of feedings and wet and soiled diapers. Use the Breastfeeding Record on page 365 to monitor your baby's progress. Day 1 starts at the time of birth, Day 2 starts twenty-four hours later. (If you delivered at 10AM, Day 2 starts at 10AM the following day.) Mark off each time you feed your baby and each time she has a wet or soiled diaper. Make sure you look closely for urine whenever there is a bowel movement. If the meconium is mixed with urine, the edges of the meconium will have a green tinge. In females, the urine is usually located towards the back of the diaper, while the urine in a male's diaper is typically found toward the front or between the legs.

By the end of the first week, the newborn's urine should be pale yellow and easily detected. Bowel movements should have turned from black/green meconium to loose green, and then loose yellow. If your baby is not meeting the minimum number of wet and soiled diapers, contact a lactation consultant for guidance.

By the end of the first week, if your baby is receiving only breastmilk and has six or more very wet diapers a day, along with at least three bowel movements, you can be sure that you are producing enough milk. During the early weeks, your baby may have five or more bowel movements a day, sometimes as often as after every nursing. After two months, she may have a bowel movement as infrequently as once every five days. She may even switch from one routine to the other. You will soon know what is "normal" for your baby and will be able to recognize any variations. The stools of a totally breastfed baby are yellow in color, and mushy or loose. These loose stools do not indicate diarrhea unless they are also green in color, contain mucus, or have a strong unpleasant odor.

How much weight should my baby gain?

After the initial weight loss following birth (less than 10 percent), your baby should regain her birth weight by two weeks of age, double it by six months, and triple it by the time she is a year old. From birth to four months, babies should gain at least four to seven ounces per week. Between four to six months, they will slow down and gain about three to five ounces per week. From six months to a year, they may gain only about three ounces a week. Babies are individuals and gain weight at different rates. Some of the older growth charts that are used to track infant growth were based on infants who were fed formula. Newer growth charts reflect the normal breastfed infant. If your baby is not gaining appropriate weight, seek the advice of a lactation consultant.

BREASTFEEDING RECORD

Day 1 (first 24 hours) Date and Time of Birth _____

Feedings (minimum 7–8)	1 2 3 4 5 6 7 8 9 10
Wet diapers (minimum 1–2)	1 2 3 4
Meconium bowel movements (minimum 1–2)	1 2 3 4

Day 2 starts _____

Feedings (minimum 8–12)	1 2 3 4 5 6 7 8 9 10 11 12
Wet diapers (minimum 2–3)	1 2 3 4
Meconium bowel movements (minimum 2–3)	1 2 3 4

Day 3 starts _____

Feedings (minimum 8–12)	1 2 3 4 5 6 7 8 9 10 11 12
Wet diapers (minimum 3–4)	1 2 3 4 5
Green bowel movements (minimum 3)	1 2 3 4 5

Day 4 starts _____

Feedings (minimum 8–12)	1 2 3 4 5 6 7 8 9 10 11 12
Wet diapers (minimum 4–6)	1 2 3 4 5 6
Loose yellow bowel movements (minimum 3)	1 2 3 4 5 6

Day 5 starts _____

Feedings (minimum 8–12)	1 2 3 4 5 6 7 8 9 10 11 12
Wet diapers (minimum 6)	1 2 3 4 5 6
Loose yellow bowel movements (minimum 3)	1 2 3 4 5 6

Day 6 starts _____

Feedings (minimum 8–12)	1 2 3 4 5 6 7 8 9 10 11 12
Wet diapers (minimum 6)	1 2 3 4 5 6
Loose yellow bowel movements (minimum 3)	1 2 3 4 5 6

Day 7 starts _____

Feedings (minimum 8–12)	1 2 3 4 5 6 7 8 9 10 11 12
Wet diapers (minimum 6)	1 2 3 4 5 6
Loose yellow bowel movements (minimum 3)	1 2 3 4 5 6

If your baby gains weight more rapidly than the average, this does not indicate a problem. Remember that the average weight is the median of all weights. Even if your baby appears "fat," if her only food is breastmilk, you won't have to worry. She is receiving the perfect food, containing no empty calories. This chubbiness will not remain with her throughout life—she won't need a reducing diet. Continue nursing her, and she will slim down as soon as she becomes active and begins moving around.

Is it true that a nursing baby gets the most milk in the first ten minutes, and after that she is just using me as a pacifier?

Each baby is unique in her ability to transfer milk from the mother. Some babies will finish nursing quickly and be satisfied, while others need longer feeds to obtain the same amount of milk. Throughout the feeds, mothers can have repeated let-downs to bring more milk to the baby. Also, the fat content increases throughout the feed, so a baby may need to nurse longer to obtain the high-fat hindmilk.

Remember, a pacifier is a substitute for the breast. Some babies just need extra cuddling when nursing, and what better way to do so than by giving her your breast.

Do I have to go on a special diet while breastfeeding?

It is important and you will feel better if you maintain a nutritious diet while nursing. You do not have to follow any special or complex diets, although you may be hungrier and thirstier than before. Eat when you are hungry and drink sufficient liquids to quench your thirst. Do not feel that you have to drink excessive liquids. Drinking too much may actually decrease your milk supply. And you do not have to drink milk to make milk. If you do not like milk, drink water and fruit juices that are fortified with calcium, and eat high-calcium foods such as cheese and yogurt. It is also important to eat foods that contain omega-3 fatty acids, such as wild salmon, albacore tuna (limit to once or twice a week), trout, walnuts, and tofu, or take a supplement. Use canola, soybean, or flaxseed oil for cooking. You no longer have to adhere to the dietary restrictions that you followed during pregnancy to prevent listeriosis, so you can enjoy sushi, soft cheeses, and cold cuts.

It is not necessary to cut out spicy or gassy foods while breastfeeding. Your baby has already begun tasting these different flavors through the amniotic fluid. If she is particularly fussy after a feeding and you suspect it may be caused by a particular food you have just eaten, avoid that food for at least two weeks, then try it again and see if she has the same response.

Even mothers who are poorly nourished will make quality milk for their babies, although their own health may suffer. Eating junk food will not cause poor-quality breastmilk. Most women can also consume caffeine in moderation without it affecting their milk. If, however, you notice that your baby isn't sleeping well or seems to be irritable, you may want to avoid caffeine.

The breastmilk of vegetarian women is nutritionally adequate. It is similar in composition to the milk of women who consume a standard diet. Breastfed infants whose mothers do not regularly consume dairy products, foods fortified with vitamin B_{12}, or B_{12} supplements, will need to take this vitamin in supplement form. Infants born to vegan mothers whose diets lack good sources of vitamin B_{12} are at high risk of deficiency.[36] Guidelines for supplementation of iron and vitamin D are the same as for infants of mothers who consume a standard diet.

Do I need a nursing bra?

While you do not have to wear a bra during nursing, many women appreciate the support of a good nursing bra. Choose one that is made of cotton and fits properly. Try to avoid underwires as they can apply pressure to the breast tissue and cause plugged ducts. If, however, you choose to wear an underwire bra, make sure it fits correctly and does not press against the breast itself. During the early weeks, you may find it most comfortable wearing one twenty-four hours a day—even to sleep in. (See "How to Select a Nursing Bra" below.)

If you have a problem with leaking, place nursing pads inside your bra. Do not use plastic pads or liners, which tend to keep the nipples wet. After each feeding, leave the flaps down for a few minutes to allow your nipples to dry thoroughly.

Will breastfeeding cause my breasts to sag?

Breastfeeding does not cause the breasts to sag. Pregnancy causes the increase in size and the change in shape that most women observe in their breasts. Some women even find that their breasts are smaller after nursing.

Can I exercise while breastfeeding?

Although it is safe to exercise during breastfeeding, very strenuous exercise can cause a buildup of lactic acid, which may cause the milk to have a sour taste. If the baby refuses to nurse after you have exercised, first wash the breast to remove any perspiration. You can then manually express some of the milk and discard it before trying to feed the baby again, or you can delay the feeding for an hour or so. You can also feed the baby previously expressed breastmilk. Immunity factors found in breastmilk are also diminished after strenuous exercise, but return to normal levels within an hour. Moderate exercise should have no effect on the taste of breastmilk. For optimal comfort while exercising, a good supportive sports bra is recommended.

Are there benefits to nursing longer than one year?

As long as a child breastfeeds, she will continue to receive optimum nutrition and immune factors. Nursing is also an excellent way to meet your child's emotional needs when she is hurt or upset. If your child becomes sick, breastfeeding will supply need-

---

How to Select a Nursing Bra

To ensure buying a nursing bra with the proper fit, it is best to shop for one during your last month of pregnancy. There are a number of factors to consider when making your selection.

Comfort, of course, is key. The bra should not be tight around the rib cage, and the cups should be loose enough on top to allow for the use of breast pads or fullness as your milk comes in. Avoid underwires as they can constrict the milk flow and possibly result in plugged ducts. If you prefer an underwire bra, make sure the wires rest on your rib cage, not on the breast tissue. As far as fabric, cotton is the softest and most absorbent. Avoid lace and any fabric that may scratch or irritate your baby's skin as he breastfeeds. Look for a cup style that is easy to latch and unlatch with one hand, since you will be holding your infant with the other.

When you find a bra you like, purchase just one initially. Wear it for a day or so to make sure it is comfortable. If it is, purchase at least two more, so you always have a spare.

ed calories and help bolster her immune system. The World Health Organization recommends that children breastfeed for two years. Extended breastfeeding for three to five years is standard practice throughout most of the world.

How should I deal with unwanted or conflicting advice?

If you are receiving conflicting advice about breastfeeding, seek the advice of a lactation consultant or La Leche League leader. They are experts on the subject and will provide you with the most up-to-date information. Turn a deaf ear to any criticism concerning breastfeeding or the way in which you care for your baby. Your baby's happiness and comfort are of the utmost importance—what is *not* important is the opinion of your neighbor or your mother-in-law. Remember, this is your child to raise and nourish in the manner you feel is most appropriate. Keep your priorities straight. You are the one who has to decide what works best for you and your baby.

GETTING OFF TO A GOOD START

Women have been breastfeeding successfully for centuries. You can use the experiences of others to help your own breastfeeding go smoothly. This section offers some suggestions—during pregnancy, in the birth facility, and at home—to optimize your experience.

During Pregnancy

Choosing a pediatrician is one of the most important decisions you will make as a parent, so make it carefully. Meet with prospective choices well before your due date to discuss your feelings and their ideas about childcare, including breastfeeding. When meeting with a potential pediatrician, find out the percentage of her newborns that are breastfed, how she treats jaundice, and when she recommends supplementation. The early months with your baby will be much easier if you and your pediatrician agree on the use of supplements, the introduction of solid foods, and weaning.

The use of prenatal nipple preparation to prevent sore nipples has varied over the years. During pregnancy, your hormones naturally prepare the nipples for breastfeeding. At one time, "toughening" the nipples with a towel was recommended, but this practice is no longer considered beneficial. Nor is the need to massage your breasts or apply a lubricant or cream to your nipples. Avoid nipple stimulation if you have a history of preterm labor. Bathe normally, but do not use soap or alcohol-based products on the nipples as this tends to dry them out by removing the natural lubrication secreted by the Montgomery glands.

Educate yourself on the subject of breastfeeding through books and classes. Read about breastfeeding from authors who are experts, and be sure to check their credentials. Be wary of books that insist you follow strict rules. Take childbirth preparation classes and become aware of techniques to avoid medications and interventions during labor. Having an unmedicated labor and vaginal birth gives your baby the best chance to start breastfeeding right after delivery. Many hospitals, birth centers, and health departments offer breastfeeding classes to prepare for nursing. Attend the class with your partner and ask questions.

During your classes or hospital tour, inquire about the breastfeeding support within the facility. Since the 1990s, hospitals and birth centers that offer an optimal level of care for breastfeeding and have implemented the Baby-Friendly Hospital Initiative

(BFHI) have received a designation of "Baby Friendly." The staff is required to have breastfeeding training and encourage practices that do not interfere with nursing. To find a Baby Friendly hospital or birth center, or for more information on this subject, visit the Baby Friendly USA website at *www.babyfriendlyusa.org.*

Even if your hospital does not have the Baby Friendly designation, you can request the options that are beneficial. Do not accept a gift bag that comes from a formula company. These hospital "freebies" include formula samples that tempt mothers to offer a bottle of formula if breastfeeding becomes difficult or if she questions her milk supply.

If you have personal concerns, contact a lactation specialist, who is specially trained to detect breastfeeding problems and help new mothers find solutions to these difficulties. If you establish this support system of breastfeeding experts *before* you deliver, it will be much easier to get help if problems or questions come up later.

Begin attending La Leche League meetings early in your pregnancy. This is an organization of women who have successfully breastfed their children and enjoy helping others do the same. You will get excellent advice on both breastfeeding and mothering. The advice on "getting started" will be invaluable once your baby arrives. After giving birth, continue attending La Leche League meetings or a mother's support group with your infant. (For more information, see "Breastfeeding Assistance" beginning on page 385.)

In the Hospital or Birth Center

As seen in the inset on page 370, a number of interventions and medications used during labor and delivery, such as elective induction, epidurals, and separation of the newborn from the mother, can have a negative effect on breastfeeding. Whenever possible, avoid them.

Nurse your baby as soon as you can after the birth, ideally within the first hour. The earlier you begin breastfeeding, the easier it will be for both of you. Her sucking reflex will be the strongest in the first hours after birth. At this time, the amount of oxytocin in your blood is very high, which means your baby will receive a good amount of colostrum if she nurses then. Babies are in a quiet alert state for up to two hours after birth, after which they will fall into a deep sleep that can last several hours. The longer you delay breastfeeding, the more difficult it may become. If the light in the birthing room is very bright, shield your baby's eyes or ask that it be dimmed so that she can look at you comfortably.

"What do you mean I can't nurse after a cesarean? I have all the right equipment!"

Request that your baby remains with you until the first breastfeeding. Encourage the staff to delay any bathing or admission procedures so that you can bond and start nursing. If your baby was removed from your abdomen and taken to the warmer, when the nurse hands her back to you, open the blankets, lift up your top and place her naked body against yours. Then cover up with blankets to maintain her temperature.

The special closeness that breastfeeding provides will be particularly important if your baby was born after a cesarean section. Since you will not have experienced the physical sensations of a vaginal birth, nursing will afford you the intimate contact and comfort that are essential for both you and your baby. Your breasts will fill up with milk just as if you had delivered vaginally. Plan to nurse as soon after delivery as

Labor and Delivery Procedures That Can Affect Breastfeeding

When labor begins and the birth process is underway, be aware that certain interventions that occur during this time can have a negative impact on breastfeeding.

❑ Elective Induction and Elective Cesarean

It is not unusual for babies who are born after an elective induction or cesarean to be preterm due to an incorrect due date calculation. Many preterm babies have to be admitted to an intensive care unit for various conditions, and they may have a weak sucking reflex, which has a direct impact on feeding.

❑ Pain Medication During Labor

Stabol and Nubain are two popular narcotics used during labor. If given to the woman less than an hour before the baby is born, little of the medication will reach the baby's system. If, however, either drug is given over an hour before the woman gives birth, a large amount will reach the baby. Babies with this medication in their system will take longer to establish effective breastfeeding compared to infants of unmedicated mothers or mothers who took the drug within an hour of giving birth.[37]

❑ Epidural Anesthesia

Epidurals have a "negative impact on breastfeeding during the first twenty-four hours of life."[38] One study noted that babies born to mothers who had epidural anesthesia were less alert and had disorganized motor behavior that continued up to the first month. They were also more likely to receive a bottle while in the hospital.[39]

❑ Pitocin and IV Fluids

A large amount of intravenous fluid during labor can cause fluid retention in the woman's areolas and breast tissue. This can make it difficult for the baby to latch onto the breast when nursing. Pitocin, which is given to induce labor contractions, also causes fluid retention and is associated with an increased risk of jaundice in the baby. Jaundice, which is characterized by high bilirubin levels, can make babies sleepy. As a result, they do not feed well, and supplementation is often recommended.

❑ Forceps and Vacuum Extractor Assisted Births

Extreme head molding caused by a difficult vaginal birth or a vaginal birth that is assisted with forceps or a vacuum extractor may result in trauma to the cranial bones, facial muscles, and facial nerves. These muscles and nerves are important to the function of jaw movement and sucking. The infant has six cranial nerves and sixty muscles that act in conjunction with the twenty-two skull bones to coordinate sucking, swallowing, and breathing during feeding.[40] A baby with a misshapen head may prefer to breastfeed only in certain positions and become irritated or experience pain if pressure is applied to certain areas of the head.

❑ Suctioning the Mouth and Nose

Aggressive suctioning of the newborn's mouth may irritate or bruise the throat. If the baby was intubated (to remove meconium from the throat, for instance) this can cause even more pain and trauma. Babies who have had this type of experience are at greater risk for oral aversion. They may gag easily or thrust their tongue forward to prevent anything from entering their mouths.

❑ Cesarean Section

During a cesarean section, babies are often lifted out of the uterus using traction at the base of the skull. This can affect the alignment of the bones and involve the nerves that run through that area. Some physicians use forceps or a vacuum extractor during this surgery to assist in the delivery of the baby's head. Any damage to the facial nerves, muscles, or bones can affect sucking and swallowing during feeding. Because they do not have the benefit of coming through the birth canal, cesarean-born newborns are also suctioned more vigorously, which can bruise the mouth and cause oral aversion. Babies born by cesarean section are frequently separated from their mothers at birth, often for several hours. This separation can delay the initiation of breastfeeding. After a cesarean delivery, mothers often return their babies to the nursery at night for the staff to feed because they are exhausted and under the influence of pain medication.

❑ Separation from the Mother

According to the American Academy of Pediatrics, babies should be placed skin to skin with the mother immediately after the birth and remain there until the first breastfeeding.[41] The initial assessment of the newborn can be done while the baby is with the mother, as her body temperature will keep the baby warm. The weighing, measuring, eye prophylaxis, and vitamin K injection can be delayed. Keeping the mother and newborn together without separation is common in birth centers and midwifery births, but not routine in many hospitals and rarely done after a cesarean birth. Removal of the baby shortly after the birth to a warmer is a more common occurrence in many hospital birthing rooms.

❑ Supplemental Bottles

Many caregivers see no problem in giving the baby an occasional bottle of formula until a mother's "milk comes in" while in the hospital. Unless there is a medical reason to do so, this should be avoided. The early introduction of bottles and pacifiers may interfere with the baby's ability to suck correctly at the breast. It decreases the amount of time the baby nurses and may impact milk supply. It is impossible to determine which babies will switch back and forth from bottle to breast and which ones will refuse the breast after "just one bottle." Overfilling the baby's tummy with a larger volume of fluid than she gets at the breast may cause her to expect that "Thanksgiving meal" feeling. When she is at the breast, she may not appear satisfied and become frustrated. Another reason to avoid a supplemental bottle is that even one exposure to formula will alter the bacteria in her intestines. It may take up to three weeks for it to return to the normal flora of a breastfed baby.

❑ Circumcision

After circumcision, it is common for an infant to withdraw and refuse to feed for up to four or five hours. If a newborn was not breastfeeding well prior to the surgery, it will cause more concern among parents and increase the chance of supplemental bottles being introduced.

possible. If you have a spinal or epidural anesthesia, you can nurse your baby right in the recovery room. If you have general anesthesia, however, you will have to wait until you are alert before getting started.

Because of your abdominal incision, you will have to experiment to find nursing positions that are comfortable and easy—many cesarean mothers prefer side-lying. If you nurse while sitting, bend your knees somewhat and support your feet to lessen the strain on your abdomen. Place a couple pillows on your lap to ease the pressure on your abdomen while supporting the baby in the cradle or cross-cradle position. The football hold is another position that relieves pressure on the abdomen.

Whether you gave birth vaginally or by cesarean, you can take pain medication as needed and still breastfeed—your obstetrician will prescribe a compatible medication. Do not become discouraged if you and your baby seem to get off to a slow start. Remember that this is just the beginning of many months of a happy, rewarding nursing relationship.

Women who give birth in an out-of-hospital birthing center go home within four to six hours. They need to initiate and feel competent regarding breastfeeding before being discharged. Nursing will get off to its best start, whether in the hospital or at home, by keeping your baby with you day and night. You can nurse her when she is hungry and become familiar with her awake and sleep pattern. If you *do* send the baby to the nursery for any reason, place a note on the crib that states, "No bottles or pacifiers, please." Nursing on demand uses a baby's natural cues to signify that she is ready to nurse and stimulates the milk to come in. Do not limit the number or length of feeds.

If you are a cesarean mother who prefers the cradle position, place a pillow or two on your lap to support the baby and bring her to your breast.

Breastfeeding is Successful When . . .

✓ The baby is nursing at least eight to twelve times a day.

✓ You can see or hear her swallow.

✓ The breast softens after feeding.

✓ The baby has at least six wet diapers and three or more bowel movements every twenty-four hours by day six.

✓ The baby regains her birth weight by two weeks of age.

✓ The baby continues to gain four to seven ounces per week.

Naturally Clean

There is no need to wash your nipples before each breastfeeding—they secrete a substance that keeps them clean naturally. Bathe normally, but avoid using soap directly on your nipples as it may remove the natural protection. Also avoid using oils, lotions, and any product that contains alcohol. The use of modified lanolin can soothe sore nipples, although it won't prevent them.

If you give birth in the hospital, limit the number of visitors and restrict the amount of time that they stay. Many women are hesitant about telling their guests to leave so that they can feed the baby. Often, feeding cues are missed because the baby is being passed around and held by the visitors. You also need to take naps during the day, and if you have a room full of company, you will be unable to get the proper rest. Remember, your visitors will be going home and sleeping all night. You, on the other hand, will be awakened throughout the night to care for your newborn.

During the baby's first twenty-four hours, many new parents discover that they have to make an extra effort to encourage her to remain awake for feedings. Watch for her alert times and encourage her to nurse every two hours when she is awake or shows signs of readiness. In the first days, if she sleeps over three hours at a time, you may want to wake her so that she will have a minimum of eight feeds.

Between the second and third day, these sleepy babies usually become more alert. They may want to be held constantly and nurse very frequently. And it may not be so much hunger they are craving, but rather the environment that they had in utero when they heard their mothers' heartbeat and were constantly held, rocked, and fed. Occasionally, a mother will give a bottle at these times because her "milk is not in and the baby appears to be hungry," but this is counterproductive.

Keep your baby with you, breastfeed often, and do not quickly remove her from your chest after feeding. If she has stopped nursing, gently remove the nipple from her mouth and let her sleep on your chest. Wait until she is in a deep sleep before moving her to the bassinette. You can also pass the baby to your partner, who can spend some quality time rocking, singing, and comforting her. This need to be close to mom with frequent, sometimes very long feedings is a common frustration for many parents during the baby's second twenty-four hours, but it will pass. Also, once the baby does fall into a deep sleep, which usually happens after a long breastfeeding session, you also need to sleep. Think back to when she was in utero. When was she most active? There is a good chance that she will continue that same pattern after birth.

During the first three weeks, avoid giving your baby even one supplemental feeding with a bottle. This can seriously undermine your breastfeeding efforts (See "Just One Bottle" on page 374.) Pacifiers can also have a negative effect on the way a baby nurses. Don't offer one to your baby until your milk supply is well established.

Do not be discouraged if you and your baby have trouble getting started with breastfeeding. She will be learning how to coordinate sucking and swallowing, which will create the stimulus for increasing your milk supply. If your hospital has a lactation consultant on staff, ask her to observe a feeding so you can be sure you are using the proper technique before leaving for home. Remember, breastfeeding is new for both of you. Have patience. Before long, you will both be pros.

At Home

Give yourself about six weeks to establish a good nursing relationship. These first weeks may seem hectic and difficult, but any newborn, breastfed or not, is demanding. Just imagine having to wash bottles and prepare formula besides! After about six weeks, your life will calm down a bit as you and your baby adjust to each other.

During your first week or two at home, your main priorities are to recuperate from birth, rest, and breastfeed your baby. Be careful to avoid exhaustion by taking naps whenever the baby sleeps. Make sure you have someone with you who will take care of the household duties.

Some babies have greater sucking needs than others. You can easily soothe your baby by putting her to your breast. Even if her need for the breast is not as much for hunger as it is to be held close and to be comforted, it is still important. You will be meeting her needs, not spoiling her (as some people may tell you). It is crucial to your baby's security that you meet her needs as soon as possible. According to Dr. Herbert Ratner, a breastfeeding advocate and advisor for La Leche League, "The quickest way to make your child independent is to take care of his needs when he is dependent."[42]

As mentioned earlier, unless there is a medical indication, do not introduce a bottle or pacifier before your baby is three weeks old. Once she is well established on the breast, and you have a good milk supply, you can offer an occasional bottle if desired. Also, if your baby has a high suck need, an occasional pacifier may not be a problem if your baby is nursing well and gaining weight.

Do not give your baby water. She will get plenty from your breastmilk, which is 87.5 percent water. The AAP does not recommend water for infants because it can cause oral water intoxication—a dangerous condition in which the sodium in the blood becomes diluted through the ingestion of too much water. When this happens, the body cannot function properly. An altered mental state, abnormally low body temperature, bloating, and even seizures could result. Babies less than one month old are especially susceptible. While an infant *may* require more fluid in hot weather, encouraging her to nurse more frequently will ensure an adequate intake.

Around the third to fifth day, and sometimes as early as the second day, you will feel your breasts become fuller and hear more swallows at the breast as the volume of milk increases. Even though your breasts will be somewhat larger and fuller at first, your milk supply will even out after a few weeks and your breasts will return to a more normal size. Do not confuse this with "losing your milk." You will still have plenty. The decrease in size is due to a reduction of the excess tissue fluid that helped with the initial production of milk.

Any breast or nipple soreness should be gone within two weeks. If you continue to have painful nipples or notice that their shape becomes tilted or compressed when the baby releases the breast, seek the advice of a lactation consultant to observe the feeding and determine the problem. Your nipples should never get to the point of bleeding or cracking.

Do not put your baby on a feeding schedule or try to change her sleep patterns. In the early weeks, use her alert times for feeding and her sleep cycles for getting some much-needed rest yourself. If you try to change these cycles too quickly or too drastically, she won't feed well when you wake her from a deep sleep, nor will she go back to sleep when she is wide awake. Gradually, over the next weeks, a pattern will develop and you may be able to encourage her to sleep better at night.

When to Seek Help

Call a lactation consultant for guidance if any of the following situations occur:

✓ Baby is nursing less than eight times a day or does not appear satisfied after feedings.

✓ Infrequent or no swallows are heard.

✓ Breast remains hard after a feeding.

✓ Baby is not meeting minimums for wet and soiled diapers.

✓ Meconium is still being passed after day five.

✓ Baby has not regained her birth weight by two weeks of age, or is not gaining weight appropriately after that time.

✓ The baby has latching problems.

✓ Your nipples are sore.

✓ Mastitis symptoms appear.

The Breast Crawl

During the first hours after birth, it has been observed that when an unmedicated baby is placed on her mother's bare abdomen, she has the ability to crawl to the breast and attach to it unaided. The baby is guided by the scent of the amniotic fluid on her hands to a similar scent secreted by the nipple. Using her legs and aided by the stepping reflex, she can propel herself toward the breast. (The darker color of the areola may help provide a more visual target.) She is then able to lift up her head and position herself on the breast, where she can begin to nurse unassisted. This is why it is important to leave newborns on top of their mothers after birth.

Cues for Feeding the Baby

The following signs are indications that your baby is ready to nurse:

✓ Sucking on hands or fingers.

✓ Being in a quiet alert state.

✓ Making sucking motions with the mouth.

✓ Exhibiting the rooting reflex.

✓ Fussiness.

If you have an older child, nursing is the perfect time for reading a story together, talking, or just being close.

A number of books and programs offer guidelines for getting babies to sleep through the night by the time they are two months old. Be very cautious about following such advice, which often involves setting rigid sleeping and feeding schedules that are unrealistic for all babies. While some babies will naturally fall into their own pattern, forcing a baby into a rigid schedule can cause problems. As a result, some babies who need to feed more frequently or for longer periods may not gain the proper amount of weight. It can also cause unnecessary stress on the parent, who is encouraged to put the baby down and not pick her up again until the next feeding. Human touch is essential to human infants. Dr. Harvey Karp, author of *Happiest Baby on the Block,* encourages parents to treat their newborns for the first three months as if they are still fetuses. The result will be happy babies whose needs are being met in a loving manner.

Ideally, during the early weeks, you will have help from your partner, mother, mother-in-law, or perhaps a paid helper, so that you can devote your time to your new baby. If you do not have help, you will have to manage your time wisely. When your baby goes to sleep in the afternoon, you, too, should use that time for napping, rather than running around cleaning house. Your milk supply and your disposition will benefit. You will find that a comfortable chair, preferably a rocker, is mandatory. At times, you may want to breastfeed lying down. You can lie on your side with your baby next to you and close your eyes while she feeds.

Breastfeeding is convenient, since it leaves one hand free to do other things. You can keep a book, magazine, or paper and pen by your chair and catch up on your reading or correspondence. How about those thank-you notes for all the baby and shower gifts you received? It is the perfect opportunity for making grocery lists, things-to-do lists, or holiday lists (it's never too early to start). If you have other children, nursing is a perfect time for reading to them, talking with them, or just being close. Do not, however, feel that you always have to accomplish something while nursing. You might prefer to enjoy this quiet time with your baby by cuddling her, talking to her, or singing her a lullaby.

Attend La Leche League meetings, join a mother's support group, or seek the counsel of a lactation consultant when necessary. Encouragement and support from other nursing mothers or professionals can be a lifesaver for you, particularly if problems arise.

Just One Bottle

Unless there is a medical reason for doing so, do not give your baby formula during the first three weeks of life. Giving her "just one bottle"[43] can seriously affect your breastfeeding efforts. Most obviously, it gives the baby an opportunity to prefer the bottle nipple over the breast, and may cause her to refuse to nurse. In addition, even one bottle of formula can do the following:

❑ Change the normal healthy bacteria flora and pH in the baby's intestine to a less desirable environment that can take two to four weeks to return to normal.

❑ Increase the risk of developing allergies and insulin-dependent diabetes in susceptible children.

❑ Increase the possibility of engorgement in the mother.

❑ Affect the ability to produce a good milk supply.

Furthermore, supplementing with formula can have a negative mental effect on a mother. It can undermine the confidence in her ability to nourish her baby. After the first three weeks, once breastfeeding has been well established, you can give your baby an occasional bottle of breastmilk if desired.

BREASTFEEDING PROBLEMS

Certain problems connected with breastfeeding, such as sore nipples, engorged breasts, and inadequate milk supply, occur in some women. For the most part, these problems can be easily remedied, especially if you are properly prepared to deal with them. Don't hesitate to use the services of a lactation consultant. She is an expert in assessing these conditions, providing solutions, and monitoring progress.

Nipple Soreness

Sore nipples are usually the result of improper positioning of the baby on your breast. It is crucial that she takes the entire nipple into her mouth, along with a good portion of the areola—at least one inch—so that she does not "chew" on the end of your nipple. Figure 15.3 shows the proper positioning of the baby's mouth on the breast. When the baby has finished feeding, the nipple should appear the same as before she nursed, only longer in length. If you notice that the nipple has changed shape—tilted, compressed, creased—when the baby releases the breast, it means she was latched incorrectly. In most cases, sore, cracked, or bleeding nipples can be remedied by simply adjusting the way the baby is positioned and latches onto the breast. When you begin breastfeeding, a little tenderness is normal. Sore, cracked nipples are not.

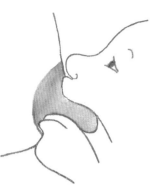

Figure 15.3. The proper positioning of the baby's mouth on the breast.

After feeding, express some of your milk and apply it to the nipples. Modified lanolin may also be used sparingly for comfort. Cool gel pads can also be soothing. Do not use lanolin if you are using gel pads, as it may affect the gel pad. Do not use preparations that contain other ingredients even if they are advertised as breast creams. Vitamin E is no longer recommended as babies can absorb toxic levels if the mother applies it to the nipples.

Some practitioners recommend cleansing the nipples with mild soap and water and applying an antibiotic ointment to kill bacteria if the nipples are cracked. Warm water compresses may also be comforting. Avoid drying agents on your breasts because they wash away the natural protection. Expose your breasts to air and sunshine, or use a blow dryer on the warm setting to help the nipples heal.

Frequent nursing can help reduce sore nipples. It often prevents the breasts from becoming too firm, which can make it difficult for the baby to latch well. If your breasts are engorged and the milk is not flowing, apply ice packs to reduce the tissue swelling so the milk will flow. If necessary, perform reverse pressure softening (see page 376), or express some of the milk before your baby nurses to soften the breast. Even if your nipples become sore or cracked, continue nursing. Any blood swallowed by your baby will not hurt her.

Do not allow wet nursing pads to remain on your nipples for long periods, and never use plastic liners as they retain moisture. If a pad is stuck, loosen it with warm water before removing. Remember that nipple soreness is a temporary condition. With good care and perseverance, you can help your nipples heal in a very short time.

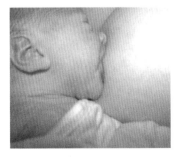

To avoid nipple soreness, make sure the baby's mouth is positioned correctly.

Snuggle your baby up close to your breast to avoid unnecessary tugging, and use a variety of nursing positions that allow her jaw to apply pressure to different areas of the areola. Use plenty of pillows to support your arm and maintain the proper position of the baby, who should remain at breast level for the entire feeding.

Nipple pain that becomes worse or lasts beyond the first week may be caused by thrush, a harmless yeast infection that the baby may have acquired as she traveled down the birth canal. This is then transmitted to the mother's nipples during nursing.

Women are more susceptible to a yeast overgrowth if they were given antibiotics during labor or as the result of a cesarean. Thrush may appear as white patches on the nipples and in the baby's mouth, or as a diaper rash. It is most important that both mother and baby are treated to eliminate this cause of nipple soreness.

If you experience throbbing or stabbing pains in the breast along with sore nipples that are white after nursing and then turn blue or red before returning to a normal color, it may be caused by *vasospasms*—constriction of the veins in the breast. Nipple vasospasms are linked to Raynaud's syndrome, a condition usually brought on by exposure to the cold that generally affects the fingers and toes. Applying warm compresses may alleviate the discomfort, although some women may require medication.

Ankyloglossia is another possible cause of sore nipples. Babies with this condition, also known as tongue-tie, are unable to extend their tongues over their bottom gums. Because of this, they cannot latch onto the breast effectively, which causes them to bite the nipple while nursing. More on this condition is presented on page 382.

Breast Fullness and Engorgement

Most new mothers experience a normal increase in the size and fullness of their breasts around the third to the fifth day after birth. This occurs as the mature milk "comes in." It is also the result of extra blood and fluid in the area that assist in the production of milk. This condition is temporary and can be prevented by frequent nursing. The milk supply and excess swelling will readjust within a short time.

If the breasts become overfilled and hard, if pain or fever accompanies the increase, or if the milk is unable to flow due to this extreme swelling, the condition is known as *engorgement*. Engorgement is usually due to infrequent or insufficient feedings and is common among women who have chosen not to breastfeed. This condition varies considerably among individuals, but occurs most often in first-time mothers.

To prevent the normal fullness from progressing to engorgement, nurse the baby frequently and encourage her to feed from both breasts. The use of ice packs or cold cabbage leaves can also reduce swelling and provide comfort. (For more information, see page 395.) If she has difficulty grasping the nipple because it is too hard, she may become frustrated and cry. Using the reverse-pressure softening technique (see below) will make the areola soft and pliable.

Many women report a swelling under the arm that becomes noticeable when the milk comes in and then gradually subsides. This is breast tissue that goes undetected until the hormones of pregnancy cause it to enlarge.

Swollen Areolar Tissue and Reverse Pressure Softening

Some women have areolas that are quite firm to the touch during the first week after giving birth. This may be due to IV fluid and/or Pitocin used in labor, extreme breast fullness as the mature milk is coming in, or pressure from milk buildup due to missed feedings. Your areola must be pliable in order to extend the nipple deep enough inside the baby's mouth. If your baby is unable to latch as a result of this extreme swelling, before each feeding, apply steady inward pressure to the central areola. This will temporarily shift the edema and soften the areolar tissue. RN and lactation consultant Jean Cotterman describes this technique as *reverse pressure softening (RPS)*.[44] When performing RPS:

1. Place your fingers and thumb around the sides of the nipple.

2. Gently but firmly press inward toward your chest.

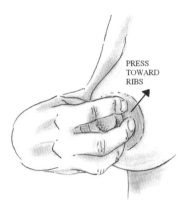

Figure 15.4.
Flower-hold method.

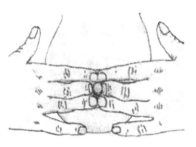

Figure 15.5.
Two-handed method.

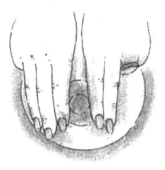

Figure 15.6.
Two-step method.

3. Hold the pressure for at least one to three minutes. If the swelling is quite severe, lie on your back, and hold the pressure for ten to fifteen minutes or more.

If you have short fingernails, you can use the one-handed *flower-hold method,* as shown in Figure 15.4 above. You can also use the *two-handed method* in which the middle three fingers of both hands are placed around the nipple and pressure is applied with curved fingertips, as seen in Figure 15.5. If your fingernails are long, the *two-step method* illustrated in Figure 15.6 is recommended. Keeping your fingers straight, place your index and middle fingers on either side of the nipple pointing downward, then press inward toward the chest for one to three minutes. Next, place the fingers above and below the nipple, pointing sideways, and apply pressure for another one to three minutes.

Milk Leakage

Milk leaking or spraying usually occurs when the milk starts to flow during a let-down. It often happens close to feeding time, but can also occur when you just think about your baby or hear her cry. Leakage is usually preceded by a tingling in the nipples. If you feel this tingling, you may be able to prevent leakage by pushing the heel of your hand against the nipple. When out in public, to appear less conspicuous, you can apply pressure by crossing your arms across your chest. Wear nursing pads to protect your clothing.

Large Breasts

Women with large breasts will need to support them throughout the feed. Resting the nursing breast on a pillow or rolling a small baby blanket and placing it under the breast will provide good support. When using the football position to nurse, the weight of the breast must not be allowed to rest on the baby's chest. It is safer to position the baby on her side with her body against the breast.

"Oops! Looks like it's time to nurse."

Popular breastfeeding position
for large-breasted women.

Inadequate Milk Supply

Babies whose mothers have an inadequate milk supply will display signs such as excessive weight loss after birth, low weight gain, few wet diapers, dark concentrated urine, meconium bowel movements after the fourth day, and a general state of unhappiness. (Use the Breastfeeding Record on page 365 to keep track of the number of feeds, as well as the amount of wet and soiled diapers your baby has every day.) If your baby develops these symptoms, call your pediatrician immediately. Although most mild cases can be remedied at home, if the baby is severely dehydrated, hospitalization may be required.

Inadequate milk supply can result from a rigid feeding schedule, infrequent or poor feedings due to a sleepy baby, the use of supplements, or severe stress. The early introduction of supplements can result in a vicious cycle—the more supplements you give, the less milk you will produce, the more supplements you need to give, and the further your milk supply diminishes.

Spend twenty-four hours in bed with your baby and breastfeed frequently, every two hours during the day and every three hours or more at night if the baby is interested. Make sure to offer the baby both breasts at each feeding and nurse long enough for her to receive the high-calorie hindmilk. Compress your breast during the feed to bring her additional milk.

You may consider using a breast pump to further stimulate milk production. If supplements are required, this milk can then be offered with a supplemental nurser at the breast, a flexible cup, a bottle, or through finger feeding. Chapter 16 offers details for these and other feeding methods.

A decreased milk supply can also be attributed to previous breast surgery or medical history. A woman may be unable to produce sufficient milk if her thyroid is underactive, if she is severely anemic, or if she has untreated diabetes. In rare cases, due to improper development, a woman's breasts may not contain the necessary glandular tissue for nursing. In this situation, there is usually no change in the breasts during pregnancy or with continued nursing. In addition, if a piece of the placenta was retained after the birth, the woman's body may think she is still pregnant and won't produce enough hormones for lactation. Excessive or long-term bleeding should be reported to your caregiver.

If you are taking certain medications and experiencing an inadequate milk supply, you may want to check with a lactation consultant. These medications include prescription drugs and over-the-counter preparations for allergies, asthma, depression, hypertension, migraines, insomnia, autoimmune diseases, and heart problems. Any medication for allergies or a cold that dry up secretions may also decrease milk supply. Other factors that may have the same effect include smoking, alcohol consumption, caffeine consumption, combined (estrogen and progestin) oral contraceptives, and high doses of vitamins. Some women have reported a decrease in milk after consuming the herb sage (frequently used in turkey stuffing) and peppermint.

In some cases, medications or herbal supplements can help increase milk production. Some of the more common prescribed medications include Reglan, which should not be used by women with a history of depression, and Domperidone, which is commonly used in Canada but not widely available in the United States. It is important to understand that along with this type of medication, you must also increase the number of feedings/pumpings every twenty-four hours. Medication alone will not improve milk supply long term. Some women have found that the herbs fenugreek and blessed thistle help increase breastmilk. Because fenugreek can decrease blood sugar, it must be avoided by women who are diabetic or hypoglycemic. Other herbs that have also been used to increase milk supply include fennel, garlic, goat's rue, milk thistle, alfalfa, anise, caraway, coriander, cilantro, dandelion, dill, hops, and raspberry leaf.

You may think that your baby is not getting enough milk if she wants to nurse every two hours. This desire to nurse frequently is normal in a baby during the early weeks and during growth spurts. It is not a cause for alarm as long as she is not showing any of the symptoms mentioned above.

Oversupply of Milk

Most women have a large initial supply of milk that gradually becomes more regulated within the first few weeks. Once breastfeeding is underway, some women will produce more milk than the baby needs and may complain about having "too much milk." Oversupply can be caused by frequent pumping in addition to breastfeeding. This is a common practice among working women who are trying to stockpile milk before returning to work. If you have an oversupply and nurse your baby from both breasts, she will receive a lot of foremilk, rather than the rich hindmilk that comes at the end of a feeding. To reduce milk production and even it out within a few days, breastfeed the baby from only one breast at a feeding. If the other breast is uncomfortable, express only a small amount of milk for comfort, apply an ice pack, or use one of the other recommended comfort measures given in "Treating Engorged Breasts" on page 395.

Plugged Ducts

If you notice soreness and a lump in an area of your breast, you may have a plugged duct, which can occur if milk is not removed. Incomplete emptying of the duct by the baby, missed feedings, wearing a tight bra (especially one with underwires), carrying a heavy purse or diaper bag that puts pressure on the breast, or even the position in which you sleep can cause a plugged duct.

You can clear a plugged duct within twenty-four hours by resting, drinking plenty of fluids, and nursing the baby frequently on the affected breast. To help stimulate the milk flow, massage the breast by applying gentle pressure with your thumb from the chest wall toward the nipple. You can also promote the flow by applying warm compresses to the breast. While your baby is nursing, be sure to offer her the affected breast first, when her sucking is the strongest. Also alter her position to help her drain all the ducts. Aim her chin towards the affected area. *Do not stop nursing.* Untreated plugged ducts can lead to mastitis.

Mastitis

Mastitis refers to an inflammation or infection of the breast that is typically characterized by tenderness, redness, fever, and/or flu-like symptoms. It is often caused by ineffective treatment of plugged ducts or cracked nipples, stress, or fatigue. If you believe you have mastitis, contact your doctor or midwife, and continue to nurse your baby frequently. *Do not stop nursing.* In addition to causing a physical and emotional shock to both you and the baby, stopping would cause the ducts to overfill and make the problem worse.

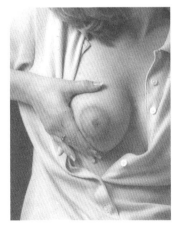

To stimulate milk flow, massage the breast by pressing gently from the chest wall towards the nipple.

Drink plenty of fluids and get lots of rest. Remove your bra and lie in bed with your baby to allow unlimited breastfeeding. Apply heat in the form of a hot water bottle or heating pad to the inflamed area. Your caregiver may also prescribe antibiotics that are safe to take while nursing.

Mastitis also causes an increase in the sodium and chloride levels in breastmilk, resulting in milk that may taste salty. If the baby refuses to nurse, express the milk from the affected breast and nurse from the other.

In rare cases, mastitis can progress to a pus-filled abscess. Along with antibiotics, the abscess may need to be drained. This minor surgery is normally done in the doctor's office and heals quickly. If the incision is close to the nipple, the baby may not be able to breastfeed from that side. Until the cut has healed, a good-quality pump should be used to express the milk from that breast. Once the healing is complete, nursing can resume on both sides.

Flat or Inverted Nipples

To determine if your nipples are inverted, place your thumb and index finger around the base of the nipple and press together. If the nipple shrinks inward, the nipple is inverted. Flat or inverted nipples, which frequently improve as the pregnancy progresses, do not interfere with breastfeeding. When nursing, a baby applies pressure to the areola, not the nipple. Also, the sucking motion will naturally draw out the nipple. Use the sandwich hold to shape the breast and make it easier for the baby to grasp. Avoid giving the baby bottles or pacifiers because she may find them easier than the breast, which she may then refuse. A nipple shield can also be an effective tool if the baby is unable to grasp the nipple.

BABY-RELATED BREASTFEEDING DIFFICULTIES

Your baby's unique personality and condition at birth may have an effect on your nursing relationship. If your baby is fussy or sleepy, or if she nurses too vigorously (or not vigorously enough), you may find it difficult to breastfeed. Don't give up! Remember that every baby is an individual and no baby "goes by the book." Meet your baby's individual needs and, hopefully, any difficulty she presents will quickly be overcome. If, however, the problem continues, don't hesitate to contact a lactation consultant, who will be able to help you find an effective solution.

A Sleepy Baby

If you were medicated shortly before giving birth, given an epidural for an extended period of time, or received general anesthesia for a cesarean, your newborn may be sleepy and somewhat sluggish about nursing. Undress her and place her against your naked chest, then cover yourselves with a blanket. Just the scent of your breasts may cause her to become interested. During those first few days, to help stimulate your baby from her sleepy state, try changing her diaper, moving her around, or gently rubbing her back. Uncover her and expose her to the air. Alternate sitting her up and laying her down, while supporting her head and back. Pat her feet, talk to her, and play with her. Express colostrum onto her lips and feed her as often as possible to prevent weight loss. Offer her your breast every two to three hours and compress it for increased flow. If your baby is sleepy as a result of jaundice, you may need to wake her more frequently or offer supplementation with your pumped breastmilk.

Many newborns have short periods in which they are quietly alert, followed by periods of deep sleep during the first days. Make the most of your baby's awake times, especially if she is a "sleepy" baby. Nurse her as soon as she wakes up. Don't allow visitors to pick her up and play with her first—by the time you get the baby back to feed her, she may have fallen back into a deep sleep. Also, watch for cues that she wants to nurse, such as sucking motions or bringing her hand up to her mouth. Try nursing her immediately when you see those signals.

A Baby Who Refuses the Breast

During the first few days after birth, some babies will use their tongue to thrust the nipple from their mouth. If your baby does this, encourage her extend her tongue by expressing some colostrum onto her lips.

Don't give her milk from a bottle, as this may cause her to further refuse the breast—she may prefer the quick reward from the bottle rather than the small amount of colostrum that comes only after vigorous sucking. Frustrated and impatient, she may turn away from the breast, shake her head, and even scream. To help keep her interested at the breast until your milk increases in volume and flows faster, have your partner drip some milk (preferably breastmilk) in the corner of her mouth as she sucks. Once she begins breastfeeding effectively, try not to offer her bottles.

Check your hand position. Are you touching her cheeks or the back of her head and stimulating reflexes that cause her to move toward your touch?

Infants are nose breathers, so if your baby has a stuffy nose, she may latch onto the breast, but then pull away in order to inhale. To help her breathe, place saline drops in her nose before a feeding and then suction out the mucus with a bulb syringe.

A woman's milk-ejection reflex may be delayed if she is under a lot of stress, or if she smokes or drinks excessive amounts of alcohol or caffeine. This could frustrate the baby, who may not like having to wait for her meal and who may reject the breast while she's waiting. If you are experiencing this problem due to anxiety or stress, try to create a relaxing environment before you nurse—put on some soft music, dim the lights, and settle into a comfortable chair or rocker. You can also stimulate your milk flow by applying warm compresses to your breasts or by massaging them. Closing your eyes and visualizing the milk flowing to your baby may also be helpful.

A Fussy Baby

Although breastfeeding can actually calm a fussy baby, if your baby is frantic or crying hysterically, try to calm her down first before offering the breast. (A number of recommended techniques for soothing a crying baby are provided on page 305.) If your baby is fussy and appears to be hungry all the time, she may not be getting enough milk. Have her weight checked, listen for swallows as she feeds, and make sure she is producing a sufficient number of wet and soiled diapers each day.

If your baby becomes very fussy *after* eating, you may need to look at what you are eating. Occasionally, your diet may include foods that upset your baby. If you suspect her post-nursing fussiness may be caused by something you ate, write down everything you ate that day. If you see a pattern, the fussiness may be caused by the suspect food. Are you eating a lot of dairy products? Some babies are sensitive to them. Does your diet contain large amounts of caffeine? If you consume it in the evening, your baby may be wide awake when it is time for her to go to sleep.

Do you exercise vigorously? The buildup of lactic acid after strenuous exercise can cause your milk to taste sour. Are you menstruating? Some babies become fussy or reject the breast at the beginning of the mother's period. Also, if you use hair spray, deodorant, or any other perfumes or sprays, keep them away from your breasts. They may mask your normal scent and cause your baby to become fussy or reject the breast. And sometimes, babies become fussy for no apparent reason at all.

A Vigorous Nurser

If your baby nurses vigorously, she may gulp too much milk along with air, which can cause a buildup of gas in her stomach. This can result in discomfort and the likely possibility of spitting up. If she takes in too much milk in response to a strong let-down, hand-express some milk before offering her your breast. To reduce the force of the milk that sprays into the back of the baby's throat, breastfeed while in a leaning-back position. Gravity will reduce the force naturally. If she is a spirited nurser by nature, remove her from your breast several times during a feeding and burp her. This will interrupt and calm down her enthusiastic sucking. Also avoid making your baby wait too long before feeding her. If she is overly hungry, she may begin sucking too vigorously, or perhaps bite down hard on your breast and cause soreness.

An Ineffective Nurser

Occasionally, a baby may appear to be feeding well, but she will swallow infrequently and produce an insufficient number of wet or soiled diapers. She may not be transferring enough milk at the breast. This may be due to a preterm birth or birth defect, a poor latch, muscle weakness, tongue-tie, or a medicated delivery. If your baby is a weak nurser, feed her more frequently and for longer periods—for as long as she wants. Help her get started at each nursing by hand-expressing some milk into her mouth. You may need to pump your breasts to maintain an adequate supply. And she may need supplementation until she is able to breastfeed effectively.

Visit a lactation consultant to assess the problem, which may be as simple as correcting a shallow latch. If your baby has weak oral muscles, the consultant may suggest that you bring her to an oral therapist for evaluation and treatment. Whatever the cause, it is important to catch this problem quickly and find the correct solution.

Ankyloglossia (Tongue-Tie)

Ankyloglossia or *tongue-tie* is a condition (usually hereditary) in which the baby is unable to extend her tongue over her gum, touch it to the roof of her mouth, or move it from side to side. It is caused by a piece of tissue called the *lingual frenulum* that is attached to the underside of the tongue. If this tissue is too taut or located too close to the tip of the tongue, ankyloglossia is the result. When babies with this condition try to stick out their tongue, it may have a heart-shaped appearance.

Treatment involves a simple snipping of the frenulum, and can be done in the hospital or the pediatrician's office. It is important to have the procedure as soon as possible to prevent the baby from developing poor sucking habits (and possible speech problems later on). The procedure causes minimal bleeding, and nursing the baby afterward provides analgesia and comfort. Most women notice an immediate improvement in the baby's suck. If ankyloglossia is left untreated, feeding difficulties are likely to occur, leading to poor weight gain. The mother may also suffer from sore nipples.

BREASTFEEDING AND WORKING MOTHERS

If you plan to return to work after your baby is born, you can still enjoy a happy and successful nursing experience. Your baby will benefit from whatever time you spend breastfeeding her, as she continues to receive nourishment from your breastmilk.

If possible, arrange to visit and nurse your baby on your lunch hour, or have her brought to you. If this is not possible, leave breastmilk for the sitter to give your baby while you are at work. Many women prefer their infants to continue having only breastmilk and arrange to pump their breasts once or twice each day while they are at work. While at home, they continue nursing their babies on request.

Many women keep a supply of milk in the freezer to have on hand in case they miss an occasional pumping at work. If you want to maintain such as supply, begin pumping several weeks prior to your back-to-work date. There may not be an abundance of milk at first, but repeated pumping will increase your supply. Once you begin breastfeeding, while your child is nursing at one breast, you can pump the opposite breast and freeze the milk. (You can also pump the opposite breast or both breasts after the baby has finished feeding.) Most women have extra milk in the morning after resting well at night. When their babies start sleeping through the night, some women will pump during the night. Others prefer to get a full night's sleep and do extra pumping during the day.

While at work, don't be surprised if you pump less milk by the end of each week. (Pumps are not as effective in stimulating milk production as babies.) Breastfeeding your baby exclusively on your days off will help maintain your supply.

A bathroom is not an appropriate place to pump breastmilk while at work. Try to find a private area where you can pump undisturbed. If you have your own office, you may be able to arrange the furniture in a way that offers privacy at this time. Many companies designate "lactation lounges" or "pump stations" for nursing mothers. Some even provide hospital-grade pumps.

If there isn't a designated or specific place to pump while at work, look around for an unused office or an area that can be used for this purpose. Ideally, the room should have a sink, comfortable chairs, and possibly a refrigerator for storing the expressed milk. You can also keep your milk in a cooler. Encourage your employer to provide this type of area and inform him how he will benefit from it. Explain how children who drink breastmilk are healthier. This means a woman who breastfeeds will miss fewer days of work to stay home and care for her sick child. Some companies have on-site daycare to accommodate their female employees who have small children. This arrangement allows women to visit their children or breastfeed during the workday.

If you have the type of job that does not lend itself to regular pumping, you may have to reduce stimulation of your breasts during work hours, while continuing to breastfeed at home in the evenings and through the night. About a week before returning to work, replace the first breastfeeding that would occur during work hours with a bottle. You may need to express a small amount of milk at this time for comfort. After a couple of days, your breasts will reduce its milk production at that time. Then replace the last breastfeeding that would occur during the workday with a bottle. Continue to eliminate feedings that would normally occur during the workday, so that by the time you are ready to return to work, you are no longer breastfeeding during work hours. You will also have to continue this schedule during the weekends.

If possible, plan for your first day back at work to be at the end of the week, so you will have the weekend to be back with your baby. Also, try a reduced work schedule at first to ease into the separation. If at all possible, delay returning to work outside the home until your baby is a year old. The first year is very important in a child's development and a very precious time for mothers. The time you spend with your baby will be more beneficial to your family than the income you will receive from working, especially after you deduct taxes, babysitting fees, the possible cost of formula, extra clothes needed for work, travel expenses, and other work-related costs.

If you must work, choose your babysitter carefully. A trusted relative or friend is your best choice. Otherwise, be sure to thoroughly check references before leaving your child with a stranger. Ideally, you will find someone who will care for your baby as you would. A person who watches only one or two children is more likely to provide a homelike atmosphere and offer plenty of cuddling and interaction with your child. In addition, exposure to fewer children will reduce your baby's chances of catching colds or other illnesses. "The Childcare Decision" on page 340, offers further considerations on this subject.

BREASTFEEDING IN SPECIAL OR UNUSUAL SITUATIONS

Many mothers have successfully breastfed in special or unusual situations. If you have twins, triplets, or a preterm baby, you can receive valuable support and helpful advice from a lactation consultant or La Leche League member. These sources also provide information on how to nurse if you need to be hospitalized for an illness such as tuberculosis, hepatitis, epilepsy, or cancer. Help is also available if your baby has Down syndrome, a cleft palate, a mental or physical handicap, or if she must be hospitalized.

Nursing Multiples

Women who give birth to more than one child can produce enough milk to sustain them as long as they are nursing well and the babies stimulate an adequate supply. Breastfeed within an hour of birth and continue to offer the breast at least eight times every twenty-four hours for each baby. At first, it is easier to breastfeed one baby at a time, unless you have assistance to latch the second baby. After breastfeeding is well established, you will become adept at breastfeeding two babies at once. Specially designed pillows for nursing twins are also available.

If you are separated from your babies after birth, make sure you start pumping with a hospital-grade pump as soon as possible after delivery, ideally within six hours. Pump ten to twelve times a day to encourage milk production.

Breastfeeding twins using a specially designed "twin" nursing pillow.

Once an adequate milk supply has been established, supply and demand will ensure that you have enough milk. After giving birth, your only jobs during the first few weeks will be to rest, eat, and feed the babies. As the babies mature, you will find yourself with more time for other activities. Keep a record to ensure that each baby is feeding well. It is difficult enough to recall the number of feeds and diaper changes with only one baby, let alone multiples. Use the Breastfeeding Record on page 365 to help you keep track.

The Near-Term Infant

A near-term infant is one who is born between thirty-four and thirty-seven weeks, but is not admitted to the neonatal intensive care for observation. More near-term infants are being cared for in their mothers' rooms and going home within forty-eight hours. Babies who are born early may have a suck that is weak and may not transfer milk effectively. They may lack the coordination to suck, swallow, and breathe, which is necessary for successful feeding. It is critical that you monitor the feedings and diaper changes of a near-term infant to ensure that she is nursing well. Use the Breastfeeding Record on page 365 to help you keep track. These babies are also more likely to have limited fat stores and may have difficulty regulating their temperature. They are often readmitted to the hospital for inadequate feeding or jaundice. Close follow-up by a lactation consultant or your pediatrician is important.

BREASTFEEDING ASSISTANCE

There are many options available to women who need assistance with breastfeeding. La Leche League members, peer counselors, and the services of lactation consultants are recommended.

La Leche League International

La Leche League International (LLL) is an organization of women who have successfully breastfed their children and who enjoy helping others do the same. The organization had its beginnings at a family picnic in Franklin Park, Illinois, in 1956. Two nursing mothers attending the picnic recognized the need for new mothers to receive factual advice on breastfeeding.

Today, La Leche League includes over 3,000 groups in fifty countries. It offers information in twenty-three languages, including English Braille. Each chapter meets monthly and covers a series of topics concerning nursing. If you are considering breastfeeding, it is best to begin attending LLL meetings at least four months before your due date to complete the series. There is no charge to attend the meetings, although you may be encouraged to join the organization. After your baby is born, you can take her with you to the meetings. Contact La Leche League to find a chapter near you. See the Resources beginning on page 449 for contact information.

Once you join La Leche League, keep the telephone number of your leader handy and feel free to call her at any time if a problem arises. Her knowledge and experience can help ease you through any rough spots. The advice of these breastfeeding counselors, who volunteer their time and knowledge to assist breastfeeding mothers, is free. Some LLL leaders are also lactation consultants. If you utilize their services outside of meetings, there may be a fee.

Lactation Consultants

International board certified lactation consultants (IBCLCs) are paid professionals who have completed a prescribed course of study and passed an examination. They are qualified to do breastfeeding assessments on mothers and babies, and to assist with all types of breastfeeding problems. They provide hospital, at-home, and office consultations; conduct prenatal and working mothers' classes; and offer breastfeeding supplies. The first lactation consultants were La Leche League volunteers who devised a system to certify breastfeeding counselors who met certain standards. The first test was administered in 1985. Since then, this specialized field has gained wide acceptance in the medical community.

Many hospitals employ lactation consultants to assist new mothers with breast-feeding. Consultations are usually included during the hospital stay. If you continue to have breastfeeding problems while at home, ask your pediatrician, local hospital, or childbirth instructor to recommend a lactation consultant, or contact the International Lactation Consultant Association (ILCA). For contact information, see the Resources beginning on page 449.

Many state health departments have lactation consultants on staff. In addition to providing information to breastfeeding mothers, they train them to become peer counselors. A volunteer breastfeeding peer counselor has accumulated her knowledge through personal experience, reading, and classes. She does not charge a fee. Counselors can provide phone consultations as well as instruction within group settings. They may be part of an organization such as La Leche League.

Donor Milk Banks

Donor human milk banks are located throughout the United States and Canada. They provide breastmilk for high-risk infants whose mothers are unable to provide their own milk. Common reasons for using donor milk include preterm births, allergies, intolerance to formula, immunologic deficiencies, inborn errors of metabolism, infections, and nutrition after surgery.[45] A prescription is necessary to obtain donor milk.

Women who donate their milk have been carefully screened for communicable diseases. They must also be nonsmokers and free of any medication (including mega-vitamins). The milk is pasteurized to kill any bacteria or viruses.

The Human Milk Banking Association of North America (HMBANA) sets the guidelines for donor milk banks. For contact information, see the Resources beginning on page 449.

THE RIGHT TO BREASTFEED IN PUBLIC

At some point, most women who breastfeed will need to feed their baby when out in public. While some women may take a bottle of expressed breastmilk—to avoid embarrassment or the need to find a secluded area—this requires preplanning. To be prepared for those times when you must nurse in public, it is a good idea to practice nursing discreetly at home in front of a mirror. Choose clothing that is either specifically designed for nursing or that can easily be pulled up at the waist. Some women strategically position blankets to provide privacy. A sling or wrap can also be worn and adjusted to make it easy to feed the baby in public.

Most states have enacted breastfeeding legislation to ensure that women have a right to breastfeed their children in public. Whether or not your state has a law, you still have that right. You cannot be cited for indecent exposure or nudity even if your breast is exposed during feeding. The purpose of the law is not to legalize breastfeeding in public, but to clarify that it is not a criminal offense.

Also, stores, restaurants, and other public establishments are not permitted to force a woman to breastfeed in specified areas as this is considered

You can breastfeed anywhere.

segregation. In 1999, a federal law was enacted to provide a woman with the right to breastfeed her child anywhere on federal property that she has the right to be with her child.

THE MARKETING OF FORMULA

From the time a woman finds out she is pregnant and visits her obstetrician, she is inundated with information from formula companies. If she signs up for a "baby club" at her doctor's office or a local maternity store, she is placed on a formula company mailing list. Right before her due date, samples of formula will start to appear at her door. Approximately two weeks after her due date, more samples of formula will arrive. In most hospitals, the new mother is discharged with her baby and a diaper bag that is specially designed for breastfeeding mothers. Prepared by the manufacturers of formula, this bag contains breastfeeding advice and a supply of formula.

Why do the makers of breastmilk substitutes spend so much money on breastfeeding mothers? They know that if a mother is having difficulty with breastfeeding or questions her milk supply, she is likely to offer her baby a bottle of formula if it is readily available. They are counting on this early introduction of formula, which will impact the mother's milk supply and, thus, create the need to buy more formula. Every mother who switches to formula feeding provides significant revenue to the company, and over 95 percent will purchase the brand that was given to them in the hospital.[46] In some instances, the information included in the breastfeeding pamphlets is inaccurate, or it makes breastfeeding seem harder than it actually is. In an effort to prevent mothers from feeling guilty about using formula, it is described as being "close" to mother's milk.

The World Health Assembly does not ban the sale of formula, but it developed an International Code of Marketing of Breastmilk Substitutes that is designed to protect and promote breastfeeding. The Code states that formula companies should not advertise infant formula or other products such as cereal, teas, juice, and bottles for babies under six months of age. They should not provide free samples to mothers or promote their products in healthcare facilities, or through free or low-cost supplies. The Code also forbids formula companies from giving gifts, including money, food, or trips, to health workers.

In the United States, the Code is violated repeatedly. The media continues to bombard consumers with print ads and television commercials that promote formula. Company sales reps regularly visit hospital units and provide free formula. They also offer educational seminars for nursing staffs that tout the benefits of their formula over the competition's. In an effort to accommodate each supplier, many hospitals rotate the brand of formula they use (three months for brand X, then three months for brand Y). Many nurses, while knowing that breastfeeding is the optimal nutrition for babies, do not feel that offering bottles in the hospital is a problem—but you know that it can be. Refuse the "free" bag. It could cost you your breastfeeding experience.

WEANING

Many expectant mothers plan to nurse for a set amount of time—three months, six months, or one year. However, once they begin nursing, women often find it so rewarding that they are not anxious for it to end. They know, too, that breastfeeding is more than just a method of physical nourishment. It is an emotional bond. An abrupt severing of that bond could be traumatic for both the mother and her baby.

Most nursing mothers find that weaning is easiest when done gradually. Authorities, too, are realizing that this separation from the breast for nourishment should be determined by each child's individual needs. Just as babies begin sitting up, rolling over, walking, and talking at different ages, their needs to continue nursing vary. Therefore, weaning ideally should be a baby-led process. You will know when your baby is ready through the signs she displays. (Often, this behavior is so subtle and gradual that you may hardly recognize it.) As she becomes more interested in other activities and in the world around her, and as she becomes better at feeding herself from the table and drinking from a cup, her need to nurse will diminish. Of course, when she is hurt or ill, she may want to resort to her "baby" ways—and you will be glad that you can comfort her through nursing. In fact, nursing can be a real "life-saver." If your toddler becomes sick and does not want to eat or drink, but she does want to nurse, your milk can prevent her from becoming dehydrated. Gradually, however, you will find that she will be interested in nursing less frequently. The best way to assist in this weaning process is to stop offering her the breast, but continue giving it to her if she needs it.

Remember that you will be helping your child to become an independent human being at her own rate. Through your months of involvement in the nursing relationship, you will become sensitive to her exact needs. If you feel that prolonged nursing is best for you and your baby, do not allow public opinion to affect your decision. Our society supports babies remaining attached to the bottle until age two or three. It should be the same for breastfeeding—after all, isn't it much better to be attached to a person than to a thing? The American Academy of Pediatrics supports breastfeeding for as long as it is mutually desired. The nutritional and psychological benefits from nursing will continue; through it, you will be helping to create a happy, healthy, well-adjusted human being.

CONCLUSION

Feeding your baby is a natural continuation of the way in which you protected and nourished her before she was born. Your breastmilk is the food that nature intended for her. Its nutritional and immunologic properties can never be duplicated. Receiving these benefits is your baby's birthright.

Breastmilk is the "gold standard" by which all formulas are compared. Why give your baby artificial baby milk when you can provide her with the "real thing"? Formula manufacturers would have you believe that their product is almost as good as yours. But these companies are not in the mother's milk business—they are in the business of making money. Your milk is far superior to all the substitutes, and it is free!

By breastfeeding, you can relax and find comfort in the knowledge that you are providing your baby with the best possible start in life. Educate yourself about breastfeeding before giving birth. Attend La Leche League meetings, talk with mothers who have nursed successfully, and utilize the assistance of a lactation consultant. You and your baby will share many happy hours together through this rewarding experience.

Alternative Feeding Methods
or Pumps, Bottles, and Other Supplies

Breastfeeding your baby is the optimum way to nourish him. When mothers who breastfeed return to work, when breastfeeding difficulties arise, or when a mother chooses not to breastfeed at all, other methods of feeding become necessary. This chapter discusses the various ways to feed your child—bottles and other methods—when the physical act of breastfeeding is either not possible or not desired. It includes guidelines for expressing breastmilk with a good quality breast pump or through hand expression. For women who choose not to breastfeed, information on bottle-feeding breastmilk substitutes (infant formula) is covered. Also included are helpful guidelines for introducing solid foods.

HAND EXPRESSING BREASTMILK

One of the ways in which nursing mothers can express the milk from their breasts is with their hands. Many women become proficient at hand expressing and find they do not need to use a breast pump—the other method of expressing breastmilk. Even if you use a pump, it is important to learn how to hand express for those times when a pump is not available.

Some women find that hand expressing works very well, while others find it more difficult and are able to express only a drop or two. It is often easiest to collect breastmilk while the baby is nursing from the other breast. This is because your milk letsdown on both sides during a feeding. While nursing on one breast, you can place a collection bag over the nipple of the other breast and gently express the milk into it.

To help stimulate the flow of milk prior to expressing, cover the breasts with a warm moist towel for five minutes and then massage them for three to four minutes. Use your fingers to lightly stroke down the breasts as you lean forward. To express the milk, gently press into the breast at the outer edge of the areola (or about $1\frac{1}{2}$ inches behind the nipple) with your thumb and forefinger. Keeping your fingers in place, gently press as you roll your thumb and finger. (Do not squeeze or pull on the nipple as this is ineffective in removing milk and can cause pain.) Continue pressing and rolling until the milk stops flowing.

PUMPING BREASTMILK

Many women prefer the convenience of a breast pump to express milk for their babies. These pumps can be manual or electric, but they are not all equal. Look for brands that specialize in breast pumps, as they will offer the highest quality and provide the best results. Many hospitals and lactation consultants have pumps available for purchase or rent. A lactation consultant can discuss your situation and help you decide which pump will best fit your needs.

Most electric pumps sold in stores are considered for single use—that is, they should be used by only one person. This is to avoid cross contamination of transmittable diseases such as HIV or hepatitis B. Electric pump motors cannot be sterilized, and simply purchasing new tubing will not prevent cross contamination. Do not buy a used pump at a garage sale or consignment shop, or borrow one from a friend. You won't know the health history of the previous user.

If you plan to provide an occasional bottle for times when you will miss a feeding, a *manual pump* is probably sufficient. Although a variety of these devices are available, those that can be easily used with one hand are recommended. They enable you to pump one breast while the baby nurses at the other. Because manual pumps do not require electricity, they are convenient when pumping away from home. Models that allow you to vary the degree of pressure for comfort and effective pumping are other characteristics to look for; those with handles that use a trigger motion are most efficient.

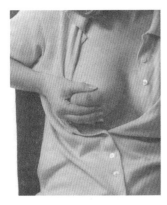

Hand expressing milk.

Women who pump often—to increase their supply or to provide milk to caregivers after returning to work, for example—usually prefer the convenience of an *electric pump*. Electric pumps come in single models (for expressing milk from one breast at a time) and double models (for pumping both breasts at once). Obviously, double pumps are more time efficient than single models. A small motorized single pump may not be as effective as a double variety, and if used daily, the motor may not last very long. Look for a model that is easy to set up and use. Some units have a section for cooler packs, so you can store the pumped milk within the case.

A *hospital-grade electric pump* is built to be used numerous times each day and for many years. It is also intended for use by many women and has features to prevent cross contamination. Some of the newest pumps are preset to simulate the pattern of a baby nursing at the breast. These advances are the result of years of research into the best methods of pumping milk. If your baby is born preterm or needs hospitalization for a period, a hospital-grade pump is a necessity. A lactation consultant will help you initiate pumping while you are in the hospital. After you have been discharged, you can rent a pump to continue stimulating your breasts and providing your milk for the baby. Some women who return to work also prefer to rent hospital-grade pumps. If you plan to pump long term, keep in mind that once your milk supply is well established, you could purchase a high-quality pump for the same amount of money that it would cost to rent a hospital-grade pump for four to five months.

Flange size is another important consideration when using a breast pump. The *flange* is the horn-like part of the device that is applied to the breast. During pumping, the nipple needs to move in and out of this opening freely. Most pumps come with flanges that have a standard size opening. If you notice rubbing, pain, or nipple damage while using a pump, you may need to purchase a larger flange. Most women notice that the amount of milk they express will increase with the proper size flange.

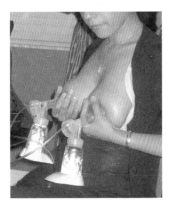

sUsing an electric double pump.

When purchasing a pump, do not let the cost be the most important factor, especially if you are planning to use it every day. The motor of a lower-priced electric pump may not be durable enough to last for extended pumping sessions. Before making a purchase, investigate the different types of pumps and try to speak with a lactation professional for advice.

Pumping Guidelines

No matter which type of pump you choose, the following directions will serve as a helpful guide. Pumping in a quiet, relaxed setting usually helps to get the milk flowing. To help stimulate the flow of milk, place a warm moist towel on your breasts for five minutes prior to expressing, then massage your breasts for three to four minutes. If your pump allows you to increase or decrease the number of cycles per minute (each pull and release of the nipple is considered a cycle), you can adjust it for maximum milk flow. More rapid cycling at the start of pumping also stimulates the milk flow. This mimics the rapid way in which a baby sucks at the start of a feed. Begin pumping on the lowest suction setting to avoid discomfort. Gradually increase to your maximum comfort level, but do not exceed it. Pumping should not be painful.

If you use a single pump, pump for ten minutes on each breast, followed by an additional three to five minutes on each breast for a total of twenty-five to thirty minutes. If you use a double pump, the total time should be approximately fifteen minutes, or until the flow of milk ceases.

While you are in the hospital (or birth facility) after giving birth, if your baby is unable to breastfeed, pumping should be initiated as soon as possible. To stimulate your milk to come in and to maintain your supply, pump every two to three hours during the day and every three hours at night (or at least eight to twelve times a day). Store the milk according to the guidelines in the following section. If, however, you are pumping for a baby in the neonatal intensive care unit, the staff will give you specific instructions for pumping and transporting the milk. The milk storage guidelines are also different from those for normal healthy babies.

You can also "power pump" to stimulate milk production after giving birth or to increase supply once breastfeeding has begun. Power pumping is done once a day in place of one of your standard pumping sessions. Simply double pump your breasts for ten minutes, rest for ten minutes, double pump another ten minutes, rest for ten minutes, then double pump for a final ten minutes.

STORING BREASTMILK

Breastmilk stores very well. When refrigerated or frozen, it can last a relatively long time. Always make sure that your hands and the container you use for collecting the milk are clean. Specially designed breastmilk storage bags, which are durable, self-sealing, and presterilized, are recommended. Sterile plastic bottle liners are another storage option, although they are less durable and require the use of twist ties or clips for closing. To help prevent liners from tearing, double them before filling.

Plastic is preferable over glass for milk that is to be stored in the refrigerator. This is because the leukocytes (white blood cells) that are contained in breastmilk—and that help protect the body from infections—adhere to glass and will be destroyed. If the milk is to be frozen, glass and plastic are equally acceptable because freezing will destroy the leucocytes no matter which type of container is used.

Amazingly, breastmilk has properties that protect it from bacterial contamination. It can, therefore, be left out at room temperature for up to ten hours.[1] It can also remain in an insulated cooler bag for twenty-four hours. When refrigerated immediately, breastmilk can keep up to eight days. When frozen, it can stay up to four months in a standard freezer with a temperature of 0°F. (Be sure to place it in the back, away from

Pumping While Away From the Baby

Many working mothers regularly spend their breaks and lunch hours with a breast pump. The following tips should help your milk flow get started:

✓ Find a quiet, private area with a comfortable chair to express your milk.

✓ Listen to soft, relaxing music.

✓ Look at a picture of your baby.

✓ Place a baby blanket with the scent of baby powder or lotion over your shoulder or on your lap.

✓ Before pumping, place a warm cloth on your breasts.

✓ Massage your breasts before pumping.

✓ Relax your shoulders and visualize your baby.

✓ Visualize the milk flowing.

✓ Drink a beverage while you are expressing.

Also be sure to wear clothing that makes it easy to pump. Daily pumping will soon be a natural part of your routine.

the door.) If your freezer is not 0°F or lower, breastmilk that is stored there should be used within two weeks. In a deep freezer with a temperature of -4°F, breastmilk can last up to twelve months.[2] Use the following chart for quick reference to these storage guidelines.

GUIDELINES FOR STORING BREASTMILK				
	At Room Temp (68° F)	In the Refrigerator	In a Standard Freezer (0°F)	In a Deep Freezer (–4°F)
Freshly Expressed	10 hours	8 days	3 to 6 months	6 to 12 months
Previously Frozen and Thawed	Do not leave at room temp	24 hours	Do not refreeze	Do not refreeze

It is most convenient to store milk in two- to four-ounce portions. Small quantities thaw and warm quickly. If the baby does not finish the bottle, save it in the refrigerator and give it to him at the next feeding. Also, because babies utilize breastmilk so completely, less is needed at a feeding than if the baby were taking formula.

If you are not able to pump full portions, chill smaller amounts separately in the refrigerator and then combine them for freezing. When adding chilled milk to already frozen milk, add only half of the amount that is already frozen. For example, if you have 1 ounce of frozen breastmilk, you can chill another $1/2$ ounce and add it. Now the container has $1^1/_2$ ounces. Once it is frozen, you can add another $3/_4$ ounce of chilled breastmilk.

To defrost the frozen milk, simply run it under cold water until it gets mushy. Then use warmer water to take the chill out. Do not thaw frozen breastmilk in a microwave. Microwaving not only produces hot spots that can burn the baby, it also destroys the antibodies found in the milk. Once the milk is thawed, it cannot be refrozen, but it can be safely returned to the refrigerator for up to twenty-four hours.

Unlike cow's milk, breastmilk is not homogenized so it may separate. Don't be concerned by this. Simply shake the milk gently to mix it before a feeding. It is also normal for human milk to be bluish, yellowish, or even brownish in color. When frozen, it may turn yellow; but this does not mean it is spoiled unless it smells sour.

BOTTLE-FEEDING

Hint for the New Mother

Refrigerate fresh breastmilk in plastic rather than glass to maintain its protective properties.

If you have chosen to bottle-feed your baby, whether breastmilk or infant formula, remember that the act of feeding does more than just provide nourishment. While feeding, your baby will also be receiving love, warmth, intimate human contact, and a feeling of security. Close physical contact, especially skin to skin, as well as cuddling are extremely important in the psychological and physical development of a baby. For this reason, never have your baby drink from a propped up bottle or let him sit in an infant seat while you feed him. Feeding this way does not provide the necessary elements of human contact. Even when your baby can hold his own bottle, he should not be left alone. You can still hold him and cuddle him as he holds his bottle and drinks.

Make each feeding time special by cradling your baby close to you in the bend of your arm—the *nursing position*. And don't rush the feeding. Talking and singing to him will make feeding time a sociable and pleasant experience for both of you.

Equipment

When bottle-feeding exclusively, you will need about eight bottles and nipples. Because some babies may develop an allergy to latex, silicone nipples are preferred. Nipples also come in many shapes and varieties. Be sure that your baby will accept a certain kind of nipple before stocking up on it. Also make sure that the hole in the nipple is the correct size. When you hold the bottle upside down and shake it, the milk should drip easily, one drop at a time. If your baby takes a long time (over thirty minutes) to finish a bottle, or if he becomes fussy or tired before finishing, the hole may be too small. If he takes in a lot of air or finishes the bottle very quickly, the hole is probably too large. For breastfed babies who take an occasional bottle, a slow-flow, wide-based nipple is recommended. This makes for greater ease in transitioning back and forth from the bottle to the breast.

Baby bottles, which are made of glass or plastic, also come in a variety of shapes and colors. Avoid odd-shaped bottles, though, as they are more difficult to clean—milk tends to cling to the crevices. Polycarbonate plastic bottles contain bisphenol A (BPA), which makes them clear and unbreakable. There is some concern that BPA, which mimics estrogen, can leach from the bottles over time or from the use of heat. If you are worried about BPA, use glass or non-polycarbonate opaque plastic bottles, or use disposable liners.

Air intake while feeding is another consideration when choosing bottles. When fed in a semi-upright position, babies are less likely to swallow air from angle-necked bottles as compared to standard straight-sided ones. Disposable liners also permit less air into baby's stomach because they collapse as the milk drains. They are also convenient because you can simply throw them away, which also makes them more expensive. A natural-flow bottle with a straw-like venting system for decreased air intake is also available. It is, however, somewhat difficult to clean.

Before their first use, bottles and nipples should be sterilized in boiling water for five minutes. (Washing them in a dishwasher is also sufficient.) After each subsequent use, they should be run through the dishwasher or washed in hot soapy water and rinsed well. Make sure the nipple holes are open.

Feeding Guidelines

Because overheating destroys important vitamins, both breastmilk and formula should be given at room temperature. Never heat the milk in a microwave. While the bottle may feel cool, the milk will continue to heat. Microwaving can also produce hot spots, which can burn the baby. Overheating might even cause the bottle to explode.

Feed your baby every two to four hours or whenever he seems hungry. In the first couple of days after birth, do not give him more than an ounce at a feeding (breastfed babies who are being supplemented should be given only a half-ounce). Doing so will overfill his tummy and likely cause him to vomit. Once he is accustomed to taking an ounce, but wants more, increase the amount gradually. If he falls asleep during a feeding, or refuses to take any more, he has probably had enough.

When you feed your baby, cradle him in your arms in a semi-upright position. Hold the bottle at a 45-degree angle so that the milk always fills the nipple. Otherwise, the baby will take in a lot of air. Burp your baby halfway through and at the end of each feeding. If he was crying hard before being fed or if he gulped his milk, he may need extra burping. Place a diaper over your shoulder to prevent "spit-up" stains on your clothes.

When holding your baby during feedings, alternate sides. Bottle-fed babies who are always held on the same side develop different strengths in their eyes. The eye that is closest to your breast will not receive adequate stimulation and can become weak from non-use.

When your baby is old enough to hold his own bottle, do not be tempted to put him to bed with it. Formula and juice contain sugar that can remain on his teeth while he sleeps. This can lead to severe tooth decay—a condition called *bottle mouth syndrome.* Furthermore, leaving a baby unattended with a bottle as he sleeps could cause him to choke. Better yet, hold and rock your baby as he enjoys his night feeding, and then put him to bed without a bottle. This not only prevents tooth problems, but also gives him that extra love and cuddling that every child needs.

Bottle-Feeding Alternatives

To correct a short-term feeding problem in breastfed babies, lactation consultants may recommend alternative methods of feeding—finger-feeding, cup-feeding, spoon-feeding, supplemental nursing—in place of using a bottle. These methods are beneficial to breastfeeding because they help prevent a young baby from getting used to a bottle nipple and preferring it over the breast.

■ **Finger-Feeding.** A finger can help stimulate a baby to suck properly. The finger-feeding method is often used when a baby thrusts his tongue forward and pushes the breast from his mouth. It can also be used if the mother is away and the baby refuses a bottle. To finger-feed, place your finger in the baby's mouth with the pad side up to stimulate him to suck. Once the baby is sucking (and *only* when he is sucking), drip the milk into his mouth with a syringe or eyedropper. A periodontal syringe is preferred as it holds more milk and has a curved tip for easy insertion into the corner of the baby's mouth.

■ **Cup-Feeding.** Even very young babies can be fed using a small soft flexible cup or shot glass. When cup feeding, the baby should be in a sitting position. Place the rim of the cup on his lower lip and tilt it until a small amount of milk just touches his lips. The baby will bring his tongue out to lap up or sip the milk.

■ **Spoon-Feeding.** This technique is similar to cup-feeding. Place the baby in a sitting position. Fill or express breastmilk into a teaspoon and place the edge of the spoon against his lower lip. When the milk just touches his lips, he will bring his tongue out to lap it up. Spoon-feeding breastmilk is particularly useful during the first days, when the small amounts of colostrum may be lost in a larger container.

■ **Supplemental Nursing.** A supplemental nurser is a bottle with a thin tube that is introduced into the baby's mouth while he is breastfeeding. This type of bottle can be used to supplement a baby who is nursing well but needs additional calories. It can also be beneficial for increasing the mother's milk supply—the baby stimulates the breast while being supplemented with milk from the tube. This device was originally created for adoptive mothers who wanted to breastfeed. After a period of days or weeks, the baby's sucking triggers a hormonal mechanism that causes the adoptive mother to begin producing milk. This is also a good device for mothers with insufficient milk supply. They can use it to breastfeed long-term while providing adequate nutrition. A supplemental nurser can also be used with finger-feeding by taping the tube on the finger.

Bottle Mouth Syndrome

When your baby is old enough to hold his own bottle, do not be tempted to put him to bed with it. Formula and juice contain sugar that can remain on his teeth while he sleeps and lead to bottle mouth syndrome, which is evidenced by severe tooth decay.

These feeding alternatives are usually utilized for a short time, only until the feeding problem is corrected. If, however, the problem persists, the baby may need to be fed from a bottle to receive a sufficient amount of milk.

FORMULA—BREASTMILK SUBSTITUTE

Even if you choose not to breastfeed, you may consider pumping your breasts and feeding your baby breastmilk from a bottle. Otherwise you will need to give your baby infant formula—a breastmilk substitute. Before deciding to feed your baby formula over breastmilk, it's important to understand the differences between the two. In the last chapter, the benefits of breastmilk are clearly detailed, and the differences between mother's milk and breastmilk substitutes are presented in "Safer Than Formula" on page 349. Also, be aware that whether or not you choose to breastfeed, your body will produce milk for your baby. If you have chosen not to breastfeed or you wean abruptly, your breasts will become engorged with milk. Treating this painful condition is discussed in "Treating Engorged Breasts" below.

Formula, which is basically artificial human milk, is made from cow's milk or soybeans, and modified to include important ingredients that resemble those in human

---

Treating Engorged Breasts

If you have decided not to breastfeed or if you need to wean abruptly, your breasts will become engorged with milk. This mild to extremely painful condition is usually characterized by breasts that swell, throb, and become hard. It usually takes one or more weeks to resolve. The following suggestions will assist you in coping with this condition:

❏ **Apply cold packs.** Applying ice packs or bags of frozen vegetables to your breasts for twenty minutes at a time can bring temporary relief. Just be sure to wrap the cold packs in cloth before placing them against your skin. The bags of vegetables can be reused multiple times and then discarded when no longer needed. You can also pour water into baby diapers and freeze them before applying to your breasts. If your breasts leak, the diapers will absorb the milk.

❏ **Apply cool cabbage leaves.** Wash the leaves from a head of green cabbage and place them in the refrigerator to keep cold. Place a cold leaf against each breast and keep them in place with a bra. When the leaves wilt (and begin to emit an odor), discard them and apply fresh ones. Wear them continuously for best results.

❏ **Express some of the milk.** Hand express or pump out just enough milk to offer some comfort. Do not discard this milk, as you may still feed it to your baby. It contains antibodies and other important health-promoting properties. (This does not apply to the milk of women who are taking a medication that is contraindicated to breastfeeding.)

❏ **Do not apply heat.** Applying heat to the area will stimulate more blood flow and make the swelling worse.

❏ **Do not bind your breasts.** Tightly binding the breasts causes unnecessary discomfort. Wear a sports bra for support.

❏ **Avoid breast stimulation.** Direct stimulation, whether by the touch of a hand or the spray of a shower, may encourage milk production.

If you develop a fever, call your doctor. This could be a sign of mastitis and may require antibiotics. When the swelling has gone down and your breasts have softened, you can decrease the treatments. If the swelling recurs, resume the suggested actions above. If you have initiated breastfeeding and must stop, to help prevent severe engorgement, try to wean slowly, dropping one feeding every few days.

milk. Mother's milk has hundreds of ingredients that cannot be duplicated; the FDA has set a minimum standard of twenty-nine nutrients in formula. The type of formula you use will probably depend upon your pediatrician's preference, with cow's-milk based formulas recommended first. Keep in mind that savvy advertisers have done an excellent job in convincing mothers and healthcare providers that their formula is "close" to mother's milk.

Some babies cannot tolerate certain formulas, which may cause them to become constipated or suffer digestive upsets. Some are allergic to cow's milk-based formula and may break out in a rash or suffer from diarrhea, chronic cold symptoms, colic, or asthma. If your baby shows these signs, your pediatrician may switch him to a soybean-based formula. Occasionally, a baby is so allergic to any type of formula that he can tolerate only breastmilk. If this occurs, you can relactate by breastfeeding or pumping. Banked human milk is also available for highly allergic infants, but it is expensive. Do not use rice "milk" or rice drinks as a substitute for breastmilk or infant formula. They do not contain sufficient protein for an infant's nutritional needs.

About Rice Milk

Do not use rice "milk" or rice drinks as a substitute for breastmilk or infant formula. They do not contain sufficient protein for an infant's nutritional needs.

Formula Types

Formula comes in several forms. The single-serving ready-to-feed bottles are the easiest to use, but also the most expensive. Canned liquid formula also comes premixed and ready-to-use, as well as in concentrated form, which needs to be diluted with water. Once the can is opened, it must refrigerated and used within forty-eight hours. Powdered formula does not need refrigeration until it is mixed with water; but once mixed, it must be used within twenty-four hours. Ideally, powdered formula should be prepared close to the time of feeding.

When preparing the liquid concentrate or powdered formula, make sure to follow the directions exactly. Adding extra water to stretch the formula or not adding enough water is dangerous to your baby's health and development.

It is important to know that powdered formula is not sterile. It may contain bacteria that can make the baby sick. Once it is prepared, the bacteria will begin to multiply—at room temperature, it can double every thirty minutes; in the refrigerator, it

---

Removing Formula Stains

Infant formula can certainly stain clothing—both yours and your baby's! To "save" clothes from formula stains, do the following:

1. Soak the stained garment in cold water, a solution of baking soda and water, or white vinegar and water as soon as possible. Soaking makes pretreating more effective, plus it helps remove some of the formula itself.

2. Pretreat the stains with a paste made of baking soda and water, or use a commercial prewash stain remover. Applying some liquid detergent to the stain

and working it in can also be effective. Taking the time to work on the stains prior to washing will help remove them.

3. Set your washing machine to the prewash cycle, and launder the clothes as usual.

Note: If the stain is due to the iron in the infant formula, use a pretreating product that is specifically designed for removing iron from clothing. This type of stain remover is readily available in grocery, discount, and hardware stores. Do not add bleach to the washing machine as this will "set" iron stains.

can double every ten hours. For this reason, it is recommended that you either mix the formula right before each feeding or that you do not give your baby powdered formula during the first two months of life, when he is most susceptible to infection.

Formula Safeguards

Do not place an unfinished bottle of formula in the refrigerator for later use. The baby's saliva will already be mixed with it and bacteria will start to multiply. Also, do not save formula for re-use if it has been out of the refrigerator for several hours. If you plan to go out, it's best to take "ready-to-feed" bottles so you do not have to worry about spoilage. But if you will be using powdered formula, measure the powder and water in separate containers to mix right before feeding. If using prepared formula, place it in a cooler to prevent spoilage. Contaminated or spoiled milk can cause vomiting and diarrhea, which can lead to dehydration, a very serious problem in infants.

Canned liquid formula should be stored at temperatures below 72°F and above freezing. If it was stored in a hot warehouse during the summer, it may have curdled. Always check the expiration date, especially if you bought the container when it was on sale. Never use canned formula that smells "funny" or has separated into layers with an oily yellow substance on top that cannot be dispersed by shaking. Do not use a can that has been dented—the liner could be damaged and the contents spoiled. Powdered formula should not be stored in the refrigerator as the humidity could cause it to clump.

Since formula has the potential for being recalled, you may want to record the lot numbers. This way, if a recall is announced, you will know if your formula is affected. If you have a complaint about a formula or if you are concerned that your baby has become ill from it, report the problem to MedWatch, the FDA Safety Information and Adverse Event Reporting Program. For contact information, see the Resources beginning on page 449. Make sure you have the can available to read the lot number and expiration date.

Formula Preparation Guidelines

This section presents helpful guidelines for preparing the various types of formula—powdered, concentrate, and even the ready-to-use variety. It is important to first be aware of the following general recommendations and precautions:

- Before preparing infant formula, wash your hands with soap and warm water.

- Use sterile (boiled) water to prepare formula for babies under three months old, or as your pediatrician advises. (See "When Sterilizing Water" on page 400.)

- Do not leave prepared formula at room temperature for more than two hours. When going out and taking it with you, keep it in a cooler.

- Refrigerate prepared formula immediately until needed.

- Check expiration dates.

- Record lot numbers in case of formula recalls.

Sticking to these formula "basics" will allow you to feel confident in preparing any type of infant formula. What follows are detailed preparation instructions.

Bottle-Feeding Tips

For a healthy and rewarding bottle-feeding experience:

✓ During feedings, alternate the side on which you hold the baby, so that both of his eyes will be equally stimulated. Bottle-fed babies who are always held on the same side develop different strengths in their eyes.

✓ Remember to check the expiration date on every can of formula.

✓ When preparing formula, follow the directions carefully.

✓ Always hold your baby while he is feeding.

✓ Do not heat bottles in the microwave.

✓ If the baby does not drink the entire bottle of breastmilk, it can be returned to the refrigerator and finished at the next feeding.

✓ If the baby does not drink the entire bottle of formula, discard it after an hour. Bacteria from the baby's saliva will be mixed with it and start to multiply.

Ready-to-Use Formula

This type of formula comes premixed. Do not add water.

1. Wash the top of the can with soap and water.

2. Wash the can opener.

3. Shake the can well and then open.

4. Pour the desired amount of formula into a clean bottle. Use within two hours.

5. Refrigerate the remaining formula immediately. Use within forty-eight hours.

6. Throw away any formula that is left in the bottle within one hour after feeding.

Concentrated Liquid Formula

Concentrate must be diluted with equal parts water.

1. Wash the top of the can with soap and water.

2. Wash the can opener.

3. Shake the can well and then open.

4. Pour the can of concentrate into a clean container.

5. Add an equal amount of sterile water to the concentrate and stir or shake well.

6. Pour the desired amount into a clean bottle. Use within two hours.

7. Refrigerate the remaining formula immediately. Use within forty-eight hours.

8. Throw away any formula that is left in the bottle within one hour after feeding.

Powdered Formula

To ensure freshness, use powdered formula within four weeks after opening the can. Once the can is opened, cover it tightly with the plastic lid and store in a cool, dry place. Do not mix large quantities at one time.

1. Pour the desired amount of sterile water into a clean bottle. Use the line markings on the bottle to measure the ounces.

2. Using the scoop that comes with the can, add 1 level loosely packed scoop of the powdered formula for every two ounces of sterilized water. (Do not pack the powder into the scoop as this will make the formula too concentrated.)

3. Attach the nipple and lid to the bottle and shake well.

4. Feed the baby immediately (especially if younger than a few months old) or refrigerate the formula and use within twenty-four hours.

5. Throw away any formula that is left in the bottle within one hour after feeding.

INTRODUCING SOLID FOODS

Breastmilk or a breastmilk substitute is a complete food for your baby until around six months of age. At that time, the iron supply he was born with may begin to diminish. It is also when many babies start teething—an indication that they are ready to begin chewing. This is usually a good time to introduce them to solid foods. Let your baby be your guide. Some babies will be eager to eat and will reach for food. Others may not be ready and will refuse it. Proceed very slowly. If your baby does not seem to be interested in food, do not force him to eat. Continue to offer it occasionally, and when he is ready, he will take it. Do not concern yourself with how much he eats. He will just be learning to eat and will still need some time before he is ready for three "square meals" a day.

Breastmilk or formula should remain your baby's primary source of nutrition throughout the first year. The American Academy of Pediatrics recommends that babies receive only breastmilk for the first six months of life and then continue to receive it as the primary source of nutrition throughout the second half of the first year while starting to eat solid foods. Mothers are encouraged to continue breastfeeding for as long as is mutually desired. If you do not breastfeed for the entire first year, you should substitute with formula.

Experts in infant nutrition and the American Academy of Pediatrics believe that introducing solids before six months offers no advantages. The enzymes that are necessary to completely digest cereal and other foods are usually not present in full quantity until a baby is three to six months old. Also, before three to four months, a baby does not have the ability to move food from the front of his mouth to the back. His tongue will thrust most of the food out. Furthermore, because a baby's gastrointestinal tract is not yet mature, the early introduction of solids can cause improper absorption and food allergies. It might also lead to obesity in later life—many mothers encourage their babies to finish the jar or to clean the plate to prevent wasting food.

Some parents believe that giving a baby cereal during the early months will make him sleep through the night. This is not true. Sleeping all night is a function of neurological maturity and independent of feeding. Babies usually begin to sleep through the night at two to three months of age.

Guidelines and Cautions

When you do begin giving solid foods to your baby, introduce one food at a time. Rice cereal mixed with breastmilk or formula is a common suggestion. Mashed banana is another good first food, as are mashed white or sweet potatoes. Allow one week between the introduction of any new food. If your baby has an adverse reaction, such as a rash or stomach upset, you will know which food is responsible.

Certain foods are highly allergenic and should be delayed to prevent reactions. Approximately 20 percent of children are allergic to cow's milk. For this reason, do not give your baby dairy products (milk, cheese, yogurt, cottage cheese) or soy products (soymilk, tofu) until he is one year old. Avoid introducing orange juice, citrus fruits, strawberries, peanut butter, and eggs, which are also highly allergic foods.

Some foods are dangerous for babies for other reasons. Once you begin giving your child cow's milk, it should be whole milk until he is two or three years old. The high protein and salt content of skim milk and other reduced-fat varieties put too much stress on a young child's kidneys. In addition, skim milk does not contain enough calories to meet a toddler's growth and energy needs. It is also deficient in iron, vitamin C, and the essential fatty acids. Honey is another food that should not be given to babies under a year old because of the risk of infant botulism, which can be fatal.

Because of the possibility of choking, a number of foods should not be offered to a child until he is at least three years old. These foods include nuts, grapes, popcorn,

Honey Warning

Honey may contain botulism spores. Do *not* dip a pacifier in honey to entice your infant to accept it.

When Sterilizing Water . . .

Sterilized water is necessary for preparing concentrated and powdered infant formula. When sterilizing water, keep the following points in mind:

❑ Always start with cold water. Hot water from the faucet can leach lead from pipes.

❑ Let tap water run for two minutes before using. This will flush out any impurities that may have collected in the standing water within the pipes.

❑ Bring the water to a boil and continue to boil for one minute. Let cool to lukewarm (100°F) to use with liquid concentrate. When used with powdered formula, which is not sterile and may contain harmful bacteria, the water should be hotter (158°F). Once the formula is mixed, run it under cold water and bring to room temperature for feeding.

❑ Do not boil water in a microwave. Microwaving can heat liquids above their boiling point.

❑ Do not boil the water too long or more than once as this can actually increase the concentration of impurities.

❑ Avoid boiling water in a kettle unless you know the kettle is not lead-based.

❑ Unless marked, bottled water and nursery water are not sterile. It should be boiled before mixing with formula.

❑ To prevent fluorosis—a cosmetic condition that causes white streaks on adult teeth from over-exposure to fluoride during their development—mix formula with water that is fluoride free or low in fluoride. Purified, demineralized, deionized, distilled, or reverse-osmosis filtered water is recommended.

❑ Before using well water, it should be tested for the presence of nitrates. If nitrates are present, do not use the water for making formula.[3]

spoonfuls of peanut butter, and carrot and celery sticks. When children are older, foods such as meat, raw vegetables, hard fruit, nuts, and cookies can pose a choking hazard if they are not chewed well. Even gummy bears, fruit rolls, and marshmallows can stick in a child's throat. Children should always be supervised at mealtime. They should not be permitted to eat while playing, walking, or riding in a vehicle. For instructions on what to do if your child is choking, see page 321.

Making Your Own Baby Food

You can avoid using expensive, overprocessed commercial baby foods by taking the nutritious (and unsalted) foods from your table, and mashing or blending them for your baby. You can even freeze portions of these mashed foods in ice cube trays. Once the food is frozen, remove the cubes from the tray and pack them in plastic bags. Label the contents and store in the freezer. To use, simply take out the needed amount and defrost at room temperature.

Caution
Do not give unpasteurized apple juice or cider to infants or young children. These products may contain harmful bacteria.

Even commercial baby cereals are unnecessary if you regularly serve your family cooked cereals that are low in salt and sugar, such as oatmeal and Cream of Wheat. Prepare the cereal for your baby with water instead of milk, and serve it without any added sweetener. You can also add some breastmilk to the cereal.

To avoid the expense and trouble of puréeing foods for your baby, wait until he is truly ready for finger foods. By eight to ten months of age, he will be able to handle many of the foods from your table and enjoy the independence of feeding himself. Offer him small pieces of softened vegetable, such as baked white or sweet potato, or tiny pieces of chicken, fish, or beef. Foods that you can easily mash between your fingers are good choices. Finger-sized pieces of dried or toasted whole wheat bread are convenient and easy for babies to chew. Packaged cereals that are low in salt and sugar, such as Cheerios, also make good finger foods. Spoon feeding won't be necessary and mealtimes will be more pleasurable.

Commercial Baby Food

Commercial baby food manufacturers have been tremendously successful at marketing their products by convincing parents that puréed food is a necessary step before table food. They have even invented different levels of prepared foods from "smooth" to "chunky" to prolong the length of time that parents think they "need" to purchase them. Advertising experts have influenced our culture so strongly that many mothers feel negligent if they do not use these products. Baby food manufacturers even promote the purchase of small jars of special "baby" fruit juices when the same juices are available much more economically in larger bottles.

What other mammal purées food for its young? Most breastfeed their infants until they are able to feed themselves adult-type food. By breastfeeding or formula-feeding your baby and delaying the introduction of solids until he is ready, you can avoid giving your child commercial or even homemade puréed foods. To know when your child is ready, watch for him to grab for your glass or reach for your food.

If you do decide to purchase prepared baby foods, look for varieties that have no added salt, sugar, starches, or other fillers. Many brands now offer products that contain only the puréed food and no additives. These foods provide more nutrition, so be sure to read the labels carefully.

Older siblings often want to help. This big brother is helping feed his sister.

Do not feed your baby right from the jar, since his saliva contains enzymes and bacteria that will start to break down the food and prevent you from saving any leftover portion for later use. In addition, be aware of products containing chicken—high levels of fluoride have been found in some commercial varieties. Fluoride is stored in bone and may be released during the deboning process. Too much fluoride can result in fluorosis, which causes white spots on the permanent teeth.[4] If you use commercial baby food, offer chicken products sparingly. Better yet, grind your own chicken or wait until your child can handle eating small pieces himself.

Children's Snacks

With so many quality foods available, it should be easy to avoid giving your child packaged cookies and soft drinks as snacks. When mothers simply do not purchase junk foods, their children readily accept and come to prefer the more nutritious choices. Offer your child cheese, fresh fruits and vegetables, raisins and other dried fruit, and whole wheat crackers. If your child is over three, you can include nuts, seeds, and popcorn to the list.

Turn your favorite cookie recipes into health cookies by substituting whole wheat flour for a portion of the white flour and adding wheat germ, brewer's yeast, and powdered milk. If your child is over one year old, you can also substitute honey for the refined sugar. The cookies should turn out fine as long as your total dry ingredients equal the total dry ingredients in the original recipe. If the batter is too thick, just add an extra egg. Many cookie recipes call for raisins, nuts, peanut butter, or oatmeal, which make them doubly nutritious.

Soft drinks are devoid of any food element except sugar. They are full of acids, preservatives, emulsifiers, stabilizers, artificial flavorings, and dyes. Although researchers have tested these additives individually for safety, little is known about their combined effect on the human body. What we do know is soft drinks cause tooth decay and take away the appetite for more nutritious foods. They also act as stimulants by causing the blood sugar to soar temporarily and create a short-lived burst of energy. When your child is thirsty, offer him milk, water, or unsweetened fruit juice.

Presweetened packaged gelatin desserts also have a high sugar content—about 85 percent. For a healthier version, use unflavored gelatin and prepare it with fresh fruit juice.

CONCLUSION

Whether you decide to feed your baby breastmilk or infant formula, what is most important is that you enjoy this quality time together. Use feeding time to strengthen the connection with your little one—to hug, cuddle, and interact with him. Take pleasure in these special moments—they are truly priceless.

The New Parent

or Happy Daze

17

During your first days as a new parent, you can expect a wide range of feelings and emotions—from relief and excitement that your baby is finally here, to fear and apprehension over the tremendous responsibility you have undertaken. Most of all, there will be feelings of love for this unique little person you helped to create. In spite of this heartfelt love, you may experience unexplained feelings of sadness and a sense of being overwhelmed. At times, all you may feel is total exhaustion! All of these feelings are normal reactions to new parenthood.

This chapter discusses the physical and emotional changes that are experienced by most new parents and offers suggestions for making this adjustment period a little easier. It also includes advice for helping your other children cope with their new sibling, as well as guidelines for handling pets and the newborn. Rounding out this chapter is a section on suggested postpartum exercises to help you regain your prepregnant strength and figure.

PHYSICAL AND EMOTIONAL CHANGES

During the first six weeks after giving birth, you can expect a number of changes, both physical and emotional. Your uterus will gradually become smaller and return to its prepregnant size and position in a process called *involution*. You may notice periodic contractions during this time. If you nurse your baby, you will feel your uterus contract each time you put your baby to your breast during the first few days. Because of these contractions, involution of the uterus occurs faster in breastfeeding mothers. If this is your second or subsequent child, you may find that these "after pains" cause discomfort. A mild pain reliever such as ibuprofen or acetaminophen may provide relief.

You will have a vaginal discharge called *lochia* for up to three weeks as the lining of your uterus returns to normal. For ease in cleansing, use your "peri-bottle" to spray the area after urinating or having a bowel movement. Initially, the discharge will be bright red. It will then become light pink, gradually turn brownish, and then finally become clear. Once the discharge has decreased in amount and is pink or brown in color, if it becomes bright red again, you have probably overexerted yourself. Slow down, stay in bed for a couple of days, and try to get plenty of rest. If the bleeding is excessive, call your caregiver. It could be a sign of postpartum hemorrhage.

During the postpartum period, do not use tampons, douches, or have intercourse

403

Driving

You should be able to start driving again within a week after a vaginal birth. Most physicians encourage women who have had a cesarean to wait two weeks before getting behind the wheel. Do not drive your car if you are taking a prescription pain reliever, as it is a narcotic.

until the discharge has stopped and you are well healed. Also avoid heavy lifting and overactivity. For the first two weeks, do not pick up anything heavier than the baby. You may resume activities as desired, but if the bleeding increases, you have overdone it. Start with short walks and gradually increase their length as your stamina increases. Make sure you are napping when the baby sleeps. It is the only way to get sufficient rest during the early days. And make sure someone is helping with the household chores until you feel able to resume those responsibilities. Women who have had a cesarean birth need additional time to recover.

You will start eliminating the extra fluid that you retained during pregnancy through frequent urination and perspiration. Some women notice an increase in swelling within the first days after birth. This is likely caused by a large amount of IV fluid during labor and/or the use of Pitocin, which has an antidiuretic effect.

Continue the comfort measures that you used in the hospital for your stitches or hemorrhoids. For added pain relief, place cool witch hazel compresses (refrigerate homemade or commercial brands) directly onto a sanitary pad before applying it to the perineum. If you did not receive a portable sitz bath in the hospital, you can sit in a clean tub of warm water or use a hand-held showerhead to run water over the perineal area. Do this a few times a day. You will also find that squeezing your buttocks together before sitting down or standing up helps reduce the strain on perineal stitches. Some women prefer sitting slightly to the side.

Many women are concerned about their first post-delivery bowel movement, especially if they have stitches or hemorrhoids. Your bowel movements should resume within two to three days. Eat a diet with sufficient green leafy vegetables, fresh fruit, and whole grain products. Also drink plenty of fluids. Prunes or prune juice may also help. If necessary, your caregiver may recommend a stool softener. Hemorrhoids will gradually shrink over time.

Around the third to fifth day after giving birth, your breasts will increase in size—possibly becoming several sizes larger than they were at the end of your pregnancy. This is because your body sends additional blood and fluid to the breasts to aid in the production of milk. If you do not breastfeed, your breasts will still undergo these changes. Although medication was once given to suppress milk production, this is no longer done. During this time, which lasts about a week, you may want to wear a comfortable sports bra and apply ice packs to reduce the swelling of engorged breasts. For additional "relief" suggestions, see "Treating Engorged Breasts" on page 395. Women who breastfeed will notice that by six weeks, their breasts have returned to the size they were at the end of pregnancy. This does not mean the milk has dried up; there is still plenty for the baby.

Weight loss will be gradual and may take a few months. Remember that it took you nine months to put the weight on, so you cannot expect to lose it all overnight. Nursing will help since the body uses 500 to 800 calories each day in the production of milk. Continue to eat well and take your prenatal vitamins. Do not go on a strict reducing diet if you are breastfeeding. When you first come home, expect your abdomen to be flabby—you may still look four or five months pregnant. If you start a postpartum exercise program (such as the one beginning on page 417) while still in the hospital, you will have a head start on reconditioning the muscles that were stretched during pregnancy.

The Baby Blues

You may experience emotional highs as well as lows during the first weeks after birth. Because new moms are faced with so many sudden changes, it is not surprising that as many as 80 percent experience some degree of the *baby blues.* Signs and symptoms, which vary, typically include episodes of crying, moodiness, sleeping difficulty, irritability, anxiety, lack of sexual desire, and ambivalence about the decision to have a baby. In most cases these symptoms last just a few days or weeks. Most women expect to be consistently happy and loving toward their new babies, so they may be surprised and guilty to experience these negative feelings.

During the first few weeks after giving birth, physically, your body will undergo abrupt shifts in hormonal levels, a 30-percent decrease in blood volume, possible painful uterine contractions, and/or a sore bottom. If you had a cesarean birth, you will also be recovering from major surgery. Pregnancy grows on you month by month, but motherhood is thrust upon you very suddenly. One moment your baby is still a part of you, and the next she is a separate, unique human being. To further compound the shock, the spotlight shifts from you to the baby. You are no longer the center of attention, pampered and coddled by family, friends, and even strangers. After giving birth, this loss of the spotlight may make you feel isolated and unimportant.

Your partner may also be affected by these changes. No longer will he be the primary focus of your attention. He may feel resentment and jealousy toward the baby, especially if he is not allowed to be an active partner in the newcomer's care and nurturing. In addition, the sudden awareness of the enormous responsibility that he has just assumed may overwhelm and even frighten him for a time.

More than any other factor, exhaustion is the primary reason women experience the blues. Therefore, you should consider it a priority to get as much rest as possible during your first two weeks at home. Since it will be several weeks before you can fit into your prepregnant clothes again, stay in your nightgown and be comfortable. You will also appear to be recovering and will be treated as such. If you get dressed as soon as you arrive home, you will appear fully recovered and will find yourself pushed into hostess and housekeeper roles before you are ready. This will result in fatigue and irritability, and your recovery will be slower. If possible, nap whenever your baby does. In fact, the two of you should spend the first days at home in bed together. Do not feel guilty about this. Your body needs the extra rest at this time.

If you take care of yourself and follow the suggestions in this chapter, you can minimize and possibly avoid the down feelings that women have come to expect following childbirth. If, however, you become severely depressed and lose interest in taking care of yourself and the baby, you need to seek professional help. (See "Postpartum Depression" on page 407)

ADJUSTING TO PARENTHOOD

Imagine this scene: You are home with your new baby. You have just bathed, fed, and cuddled her, and she is now sleeping peacefully in a clean and tidy house. You are relaxing with your feet up and reading a good book, exchanging occasional fond glances with your loving, content mate. This is a wonderful picture, but is it realistic? And if you actually *do* have moments like this, how long do they last?

No matter what romanticized ideas you may have regarding parenthood, there will be times (and many of them) when your reality will not match these ideals. You can-

When to Call Your Caregiver

The following symptoms may indicate serious problems during the postpartum period. If you experience any of these "warning signs," do not hesitate to call your doctor. Immediate treatment may prevent these conditions from becoming serious.

✓ Temperature over 100°F and chills.

✓ Heavy bleeding. Bleeding should gradually decrease, not increase.

✓ Passing a large clot or many clots.

✓ Unpleasant odor from the vaginal discharge.

✓ Increased pain or swelling in the vaginal or perineal area.

✓ Abdominal pain or tenderness (other than the normal uterine cramping).

✓ Increased pain, redness, drainage, or separation of the cesarean incision.

✓ Chest pain.

✓ Hot, sore breasts with a lump or area of redness.

✓ Cracked and/or bleeding nipples.

✓ A lump or pain in the calves or severe swelling in the legs.

✓ Pain in the mid to lower back.

✓ Difficulty, frequency, or urgency with urination.

✓ Burning sensation while urinating.

✓ Severe depression, sadness, or withdrawal.

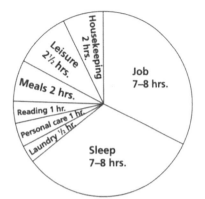

Figure 17.1. A sample "Before Baby" time management chart.

Figure 17.2. A sample "After Baby" time management chart.

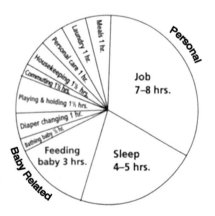

Figure 17.3. A sample "Working Mother" time management chart.

not program yourself to have boundless energy and be relaxed, confident, consistently loving, and still meet the needs of your baby (and partner). You cannot be a perfect parent—it doesn't exist. Parents are human beings! The perfect-parent image you may try to project to the people around you—parents, relatives, friends—is simply unrealistic. And if you take time to discuss this topic openly with them, you will find that they, too, have had frenzied and anxious moments as new parents.

Manage Your Time

In many ways, the adjustments you will make after having a baby are similar to the ones you made following marriage (or other committed relationships). New roles will be defined; new household tasks will be assigned. While you are still pregnant, sit down with your partner and, together, perform the following exercise. It will help you realistically prepare for the days that lie ahead.

On separate sheets of paper (one for you and one for your spouse), draw two large circles on each sheet. Each circle is to represent a twenty-four hour period. Label the first circle "Before Baby" and the second circle "After Baby." Now, starting with the "Before Baby" circle, divide it (like a pie chart) according to the various activities that currently make up your day. Typical divisions include working, preparing and eating meals, housekeeping, paying bills, banking, shopping, making love, gardening, relaxing, enjoying a hobby, sleeping, bathing, and so on. Size each section in this pie chart to reflect the percentage of time you spend on the activity during a twenty-four hour day. For example, if you work eight hours a day, the "work section" should be one-third of the chart. For a sample "Before Baby" time management chart, see Figure 17.1 at left.

Now move to the "After Baby" chart, and note the activities you expect to (or hope to) continue once the baby is born. Also include the new baby-related activities that you expect will be part of your day. As seen in Figure 17.2 they will probably include such activities as feeding, bathing, diaper changing, and doing the laundry. The size of these sections should reflect the amount of time you expect to devote to these activities each day.

When you have both finished your pie charts, compare them. Is one partner indicating more changes than the other? Are the "After Baby" charts realistic? Do the childcare activities and time estimates that each of you have indicated match each other's expectations? How will the "After Baby" chart change if the mother returns to outside employment? Figure 17.3 offers a sample "Working Mother" time management chart.

After performing this exercise, it should be clear that the time you currently devote to your daily routine will change considerably once you add the role of parent to your life. Discuss any differences in your expectations with your partner now. This way, after the baby is born, you will not argue over who should do what and when. Save your charts. You will have fun looking at them again after your baby is born.

Expect Confusing Emotions

When you and your partner become new parents, you will share many positive feelings—personal gratification, challenge, and achievement; a deepened love; and a renewed appreciation of each other. You will enjoy discovering new dimensions in each other as parents and may even become closer with your own parents.

Any negative feelings that accompany new parenthood may come as a surprise to you, as will the feelings of guilt that often follow. When you have done simply everything to soothe a fussy baby and she is still crying, when you have gotten up for the third time during the night to feed her, or when the anticipated two-hour nap lasts for only thirty minutes, you may find yourself getting upset or even hostile toward this baby who is so "ungrateful" for all that you have done for her. You are not alone! Par-

"Pregnancy is easy, you have time to gradually get used to it. But being a mom is instantaneous, there is no transition."

Amy

Postpartum Depression

While up to 80 percent of women experience a mild case of baby blues after giving birth, 10 to 15 percent suffer a more debilitating condition known as *postpartum depression*. Some women also feel depressed during pregnancy or within a year after the birth.

A woman who suffers from this type of depression typically develops prolonged feelings of sadness and anxiety. She experiences frequent episodes of crying, a loss of appetite, insomnia, extreme and constant fatigue, lack of concentration, severe mood swings, a sense of failure, lack of concern (or excessive concern) for herself or her baby, and a sense of being overwhelmed. She may have thoughts that the baby might be better off without her. Some women entertain thoughts of suicide or of causing harm to the infant. These unwanted thoughts may intensify existing feelings of guilt and worthlessness. Postpartum depression affects a woman's well-being and prevents her from functioning normally. It is a serious condition that needs to be treated by a doctor.

Postpartum psychosis—a rare, very severe manifestation of this condition occurs in less than 1 percent of women, and usually begins in the first six weeks postpartum. Women with this condition may experience delusions, hallucinations, sleep disturbances, paranoia, confusion, and thoughts of harming themselves or their babies. Rapid mood swings that range from deep depression to feelings of euphoria are also common. Women at the highest risk for developing postpartum psychosis are those who have bipolar disorder or other psychiatric conditions.

The most widely accepted theory relates postpartum depression to the drastic hormonal changes that accompany birth. In addition, the constant demands of a newborn can leave a new mother completely fatigued and overwhelmed. A woman who has high expectations and tries to accomplish too much may also set herself up for depression. The inability to be the "perfect parent" may affect her self-esteem and increase her feelings of inadequacy. If the birth did not go according to her plans, it may add to her feelings of failure. Heredity or previous history of depression may also play a role. A history of mental illness or a difficult postpartum adjustment either by the woman or by another family member may increase her risk.

Breastfeeding releases hormones that help new mothers feel calm and relaxed. It has also been shown to prevent the release of stress hormones in new mothers. Women who abruptly stop breastfeeding may experience a drop in hormone levels, which can increase feelings of depression.

Identifying postpartum depression is the first step. Adequate rest, good nutrition, compassion and understanding from family members, and assistance with daily activities are a must. Counseling and support groups may also be beneficial. Occasionally, drug therapy with antidepressants is effective. If, however, the woman takes antidepressants during pregnancy, her baby may experience withdrawal symptoms. If antidepressants are necessary, only the minimum dose should be taken.[1]

Coping with "Baby Blues"

The following suggestions may help reduce the incidence of the blues or help you cope with them.

✓ Sleep when the baby sleeps.

✓ Limit guests to short visits.

✓ Take warm relaxing baths.

✓ Have a massage.

✓ Use relaxation/meditation techniques.

✓ If breastfeeding, have your partner assist in nighttime feedings by bringing the baby to you.

✓ Eat small frequent snacks or meals if you don't have an appetite. Drink when thirsty.

✓ Take a multivitamin or continue your prenatal vitamins.

✓ Avoid alcohol.

✓ Get regular exercise or take walks.

✓ Join a mother's support group.

✓ Pamper yourself with a haircut, facial, or manicure.

✓ Avoid rigid schedules.

✓ Ask for help with household chores.

✓ Don't aim for "perfection."

ents are human and have feelings of anger and guilt from time to time, whether they admit it or not. The feelings, however, are not the problem. Rather, the concern is over how you handle them and cope with the situation at hand. Often just talking with other new mothers who are experiencing the same feelings and difficulties will help you put the situation in perspective and arrive at a creative solution.

Sometimes, the baby is not the reason that these emotions surface in a parent. Cabin fever, lowered self-confidence, lack of intellectual stimulation, or loss of freedom is often the cause. If you feel upset in any way after your baby is born, try to pinpoint the reason you feel as you do. You will then be able to work toward a solution. Be sure to share your feelings with your partner. Problems seem less important when they are shared and solved together.

Ask for Help and Limit Guests

It can be very helpful if your partner is able to take off a week or two as you settle into your new roles as parents. You may appreciate this opportunity to be together as you help each other learn new responsibilities. You might also consider hiring a postpartum doula to provide care for you—even it is just for a few hours a day. Many doulas can also offer advice regarding breastfeeding and baby care.

Try to get household assistance for your first couple weeks at home to help ease you through the adjustment period. A relative with whom you feel truly comfortable is a joy. She can help with basic housecleaning, preparing meals, washing dishes, doing laundry, and/or caring for your other children. This will allow you to better care for yourself and your baby.

Just make sure that your helper understands her role. These first weeks are essential for you to bond with your baby and become confident in caring for her. Your helper can offer her expertise as she watches you care for your new infant; but don't let her turn into the "baby nurse." Letting her take over the baby's care will impede your proficiency in baby-related skills. You are also likely to find yourself exhausted from performing hostess duties. Once your helper goes home, you may not feel adequately prepared to care for your new baby.

If you are breastfeeding, in order to be successful, it is extremely important to be surrounded by a supportive atmosphere. Family members who offer to feed the baby so that you can rest may sabotage your breastfeeding efforts. If your household helper has not breastfed, have her read Chapter 15 before the baby's arrival so that she will become familiar with the ways in which she can help you.

During those first few weeks, if you are concerned that your visitors will bring more stress than assistance, ask them to come over for just short visits. You may find it most beneficial if these well-intentioned friends and relatives simply provide nutritious meals and help with some light housekeeping chores. Once you feel better physically and are more comfortable with baby care, you may be ready to handle visitors. Many couples find that it is better for out-of-town visitors to wait a few weeks before making the trip.

Set Job Priorities

As a couple, organize your priorities and agree to do only those jobs and tasks that you both feel are important and necessary. The new baby, who will need almost constant physical care, will be most demanding on your time during the first few weeks. In addition, your body will undergo tremendous physical changes that will affect your energy level. Many people find that to-do lists are helpful. You could include things that you *must* do, things that you *can* do if time permits, and things that *can wait* until the baby is older. You could also make a list of substitutes that could save you work, like using paper plates or having take-out rather than cooking every night.

Along with this listing of jobs and their importance, also note who will perform them. You may find that temporarily paying for some of these tasks is well worth the money. For instance, you may consider hiring a housecleaning service or lawn care company, or you may pay a responsible teenager to help out with your other children, prepare easy meals, or do the laundry.

If you are breastfeeding, your baby may want to nurse nearly every two or three hours around the clock during the first weeks. Gradually, you will find more and more time elapsing between feedings as she grows older. You will be able to catch up on your housework later. Noted childbirth educator and author Donna Ewy suggests that the best gift you can give your baby is *you* for the first six weeks of her life.

Identify Personal Priorities

It is important to become aware of the activities in your current lifestyle that are important to you and your partner both individually and as a couple. Although it is not likely that you will be able to continue all of these activities after the baby arrives, try to find ways to maintain at least some of them. The following simple exercise will help you clarify your priorities.

Sit down with your partner and, on separate sheets of paper, complete the following phrases: "Three things that I like to do alone are. . ." and "Three things that I like to do with my partner are . . ." Then answer the question, "How will the baby change these activities?"

When you have both finished writing your answers, trade lists. You may find items missing from your partner's list that you thought were important, as well as things on his list that you did not realize were important to him. Decide together which activities are most important and which you can give up temporarily. Also discuss how to maintain those that are priorities.

For example, if you enjoy going to the movies but do not want to leave the baby, rent a DVD or select a movie from a cable network. You can also go to an early feature at the movies (nursing babies do very well in theaters). Rather than going out to dinner with friends, entertain them in your home. And you don't have to fuss. Order take-out food from your favorite restaurant and set the table with flowers, candles, and your best china.

So that you and your partner can each get some "alone time," take turns watching the baby for a few hours. Also look for blocks of time to spend alone as a couple that may be different from those you currently share. Take advantage of the baby's naptimes for conversation and shared activity, rather than using them to rush to the grocery store or do yard work.

You can accomplish many things while you nurse your baby—make a grocery list, read a book, listen to music, eat a snack, or lie down and rest. Learn to utilize nursing time in whatever ways you find most satisfying. And do not feel guilty if you just want to relax and enjoy these quiet moments.

Take Time to Adjust

Avoid exceedingly high expectations for yourself, your spouse, and your baby during those first months. As a couple, you and your partner will be adjusting to tremendous changes in the forms of an altered family structure, new demands on time, and changes in your relationship. The early months will be the most demanding—on your time both alone and as a couple. Communication will be essential. Be assured that as your baby grows and you mature as parents, your lifestyle can and will adjust to what you want it to be.

Use Your Resources

Parenthood is one of life's most thrilling adventures—one in which both you and your partner will bring many positive attributes to your new roles. Spend time talking about the special qualities that each of you will be bringing to parenthood. Take turns discussing your individual strengths. You will probably find that your positive attributes complement each other's and will make you well-rounded parents. Qualities like a good sense of humor, self-confidence, flexibility, organizational ability, compassion, and an affectionate nature will go a long way to get you over the rough spots during the early weeks and through all the years of parenthood. Build on these strengths to become the kind of parents you want to be.

Analyzing what you liked and disliked about the parenting you received as a child can also be helpful. Try to remember the things your parents did that you would like to copy. Also try to recall the weaknesses in your parents' methods. In this way, you can avoid becoming trapped in the same negative patterns that you disliked as a child.

You may also want to talk about your concerns and perceived weaknesses. Many young couples feel unprepared for the immense job of parenting. Don't forget that there are many resources, including books, parenting magazines, and the advice of your pediatrician, that can help you gain confidence in this area. Share your feelings and compare notes with other parents, and spend time with them and their babies. A new parents' group or class may be available in your area and provide wonderful opportunities for sharing concerns and helpful hints, and for acting as a support group. If not, you can start one. Place a notice in your church bulletin or community newsletter. Hang a flyer in the grocery store or the neighborhood park. Set a day and time, and encourage new mothers to meet at the designated location and to bring a bag lunch, their baby, their concerns, and their advice. You may be surprised at the response you receive. New mothers, especially, benefit from time out with their babies in an atmosphere of acceptance and common experience.

A new mothers' group is ideal for sharing concerns and helpful hints, and for getting much-needed support.

Make the Most of Those Special Times

As a couple, make the most of all the precious, close, happy times you share with each other and your baby. Feelings are very catching, and the baby who is surrounded by loving feelings in the early years is likely to give them back later. Most of all, *remember to maintain a sense of humor!*

HELPING YOUR OTHER CHILDREN ADJUST

If you have other children, it is important to prepare them for the new arrival. You will also want to plan ways to help them become accustomed to the new baby in the house. Their adjustment, in fact, will probably be greater than yours, since you did most of your adjusting with your first child.

During Your Pregnancy

The time to start preparing your other children for the new baby depends on their age. Toddlers have no concept of time, so talking about a new baby before your seventh or eighth month will only make the wait more difficult. Preschoolers, like toddlers, have limited time conception—the wait can seem endless if you start talking about the baby too soon. You can tell a preschooler of three or four years when she begins showing an interest in your growing abdomen. She may also ask questions if she hears you discussing the topic. Older children can be told immediately, and they can be involved in the preparations for the baby from the beginning.

Have your child come with you to your checkups where she will be able to hear the baby's heartbeat and see other pregnant women. If you have a sonogram, she can

Attachment Parenting

Named by renowned pediatrician Dr. William Sears, *attachment parenting* is a style of child rearing that encourages the parent to be responsive to the baby's emotional needs. It is in direct contrast to the philosophy that encourages strict scheduling of the baby's feeds, playtime and sleep time, and in letting babies cry themselves to sleep.

Attachment parenting incorporates seven tools known as the "7 Baby B's." They are **B**irth bonding, **B**reastfeeding, **B**abywearing, **B**edding close to baby, **B**elief in the language value of your baby's cry, **B**eware of baby trainers, and **B**alance. These tools are designed to help the parent interact with the infant. In turn, the infant comes to trust that the parent will meet her needs.

Proponents of this parenting style believe that it develops secure and loving children. According to Dr. Sears, "A child must go through a stage of healthy dependence in order to later become securely independent."[2] For more information on attachment parenting and a detailed explanation of the 7 Baby B's, visit Dr. Sears' website at *www.askdrsears.com*.

observe the baby within the uterus. This is a good opportunity to answer any questions she is likely to have. If your child is going to attend the birth, she will need further preparation. Many facilities offer classes that are specifically designed to help prepare siblings. This may be either a short class that provides basic information and a tour of the facility, or a longer class (or classes) that offers more detailed instruction. (See "Children at the Birth" on page 214.)

Most children love to look at their baby pictures and hear the story of their own birth. By sharing these memories with your other children, you can assure them that you felt the same excitement and anticipation for them that you feel for the new baby. You can also use these stories to paint a realistic picture of what the new baby will be like. Many young children expect a ready-made playmate and are greatly disappointed when they find a baby who does little more than eat, sleep, wet, and cry. If you have friends who have young babies, take your preschooler to visit so that she can get an idea of what babies are really like.

If you have a toddler who still sleeps in the crib that you plan to use for the baby, move her to her "grown-up bed" at least two months before your due date. Dismantle the crib and put it out of sight until the baby is born. This way, your toddler will not feel that the baby has stolen her bed. And do not take away stuffed animals and baby toys from your older child and give them to the baby. Let her do this when (and if) she is ready. There is a good chance that she is going to feel that the baby has taken over as it is. Do not add to her distress by asking her to give up some of her possessions.

During Your Hospital Stay

When you go to the hospital or birth center, be sure to have someone your child knows well and likes stay with her while you are away. It is best if the person can stay at your home. If this is not possible and your child must be cared for at the sitter's home, have your child stay overnight with her a few times before your due date. This way, she will become used to staying at the person's home and will not become frightened when you leave for the hospital.

Two big-brothers-to-be learn about pregnancy and birth in a sibling preparation class.

While in the hospital, call home at set times each day to talk to your child. And do not be upset if she refuses to come to the telephone. She may be "busy" playing, or she might be feeling angry that you left her. To make her feel special, consider hiding several small toys or treats around the house before you leave. Each time you call, give her directions to one of these hidden treasures. She will enjoy it immensely.

Take advantage of sibling visiting hours at your birth facility. This can help ease your child's anxiety over your absence and give her the opportunity to meet her new brother or sister. Together, celebrate the baby's birth day with a cake and a "0" candle. You might even consider a special gift from the newborn to her older sibling.

At Home

When you arrive home, let your husband carry the baby into the house so that your arms are free to hold and cuddle your other child. You may be amazed at how *big* she suddenly appears to you. If you like, bring her some gifts and spend some time with her as soon as you get home. Wait until she asks to see the baby, then satisfy her curiosity by letting her touch, hold, talk to, and talk about this new family member.

Dealing with Negative Behavior

When it comes to older siblings, don't expect them to readily accept the new family addition without possibly expressing feelings of jealousy, anger, or resentment. And don't be surprised if they also display signs of regression. Although such behaviors can be upsetting to you (and your child), understand that they are not uncommon and there are ways to deal with them.

Jealousy toward a new baby brother or sister is a fact of life and cannot be completely prevented. It is usually stronger in children under age five because they are more dependent on their parents and have few outside interests. Older children adapt more easily because less of their time and interest is centered in the home. You can

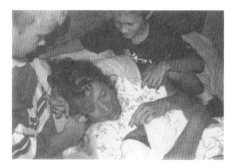

ease feelings of jealousy in your preschooler by spending time alone with her each day. Make the baby's morning naptime your preschooler's special play time, during which she can be the sole focus of your attention. Children also feel special when enjoying "dates" with Dad—a trip to the park or lunch at a restaurant can be a special treat for a child of any age.

Another way to decrease a preschooler's feelings of jealousy is by giving her (or him) a new doll to play with so that she has a "baby" of her own. While you are taking care of your new baby, she can take care of hers. Like you, she can change, feed, and bathe her "baby." You can also let her help you take care of her new sibling, even in little ways—she can assist you during bath time and diaper changes, pack diapers in the diaper bag when leaving the house, and sing lullabies to her new baby brother or sister. This will make her feel like an important member of the family.

If your child shows signs of anger—through words, misbehavior, harmful physical actions—toward you or the baby, encourage her to talk about them. Tell her that you understand these feelings and, in fact, even feel them yourself sometimes. If your child has expressed anger by physically harming the baby, take immediate action. Reassure her that you love her, but be very firm in telling her that you will not allow her to hurt the baby. To safely vent her anger, you might consider giving her a punching bag or a pegboard and hammer, for example.

Toddlers become very frustrated when they want something and have difficulty communicating. Temper tantrums are often the result. *The Happiest Toddler on the Block* by Dr. Harvey Karp offers effective suggestions for dealing with tantrums. He presents a new way to look at your toddler (as a caveman) and teaches you how to communicate in "Toddler-ese" to stop the tirades.

You can also expect some regressive behavior on the part of your toddler or pre-schooler. Wet or soiled pants, sudden interest in a pacifier, and requests for the breast or a bottle are common among young siblings. If you look at the situation from her point of view, it makes sense. She reasons that if the baby gets so much attention by doing these things, she will, too. Let your child try to nurse or drink from a bottle if she wishes. Most children do not remember how to nurse if it has been awhile. After a few attempts, she will realize that it is not much fun and will head off to do some-thing else. Although rare, a toddler who was recently weaned may return to breastfeed-ing for a time. If you are uncomfortable with allowing your child to nurse, express some milk into a cup for her to taste. This may satisfy her curiosity. If she is not already potty trained by the time the baby is born, wait at least four to six months (or until you are sure that she is ready) before attempting to train her.

Reinforce the side of your child that wants to grow up. Give her a chance to be proud of her maturity and make comments that foster her self-esteem: "You do that so well." "You are such a help to Mommy." "Our new baby is so lucky to have such a helpful older sister." Remind her that there are disadvantages to being a baby—babies cannot play ball, go to birthday parties, or eat ice cream. Have lots of patience and be prepared for the adjustment to take some time.

Once children enter school, they are likely to be more interested in outside activ-ities and not as affected by the new addition. Don't be surprised though, if they feel some resentment toward you and the new baby. This feeling usually occurs if you and/or your husband are unable to be as involved with your older child's activities as you were before having the baby. Adolescents and older children who understand the mechanics of reproduction may also be embarrassed that their parents are having a baby. This feeling usually lasts just a short time. Encourage older children to interact with the new baby by reading out loud to her, even if it is just a homework assignment. They can also stimulate the baby's senses by singing and playing games with her like "peekaboo."

Another common cause of concern, especially among older children, involves blended families. When a parent remarries and has a baby with a different mate, some children worry that their parent will love this new baby more than them. It is very important that blended families work very hard to ensure that children from previous relationships continue to feel secure.

Cautions

Very young siblings need close supervision. They are still babies and not responsible for their actions, which can be harmful to the baby. For example, if they want to give the baby a toy, they may hurl it into the crib. Out of curiosity, they may poke the baby's eyes, bend her fingers, or "smack" at her. You will need an extra set of hands to cope with a toddler and a newborn. During those early weeks, consider asking for help with your toddler. Even an older neighborhood child, although too young to be left alone with younger children, can help entertain your toddler while under your supervision.

"The baby lives in the belly room."

Hannah, 3 years old when talking to the midwife

Sample List for Helpers

If friends or relatives offer to help you during those first few weeks after the baby is born, be prepared with some suggestions. Hang your list on the refrigerator or message board and allow them to choose a task (or two) that suits them. What follows are some suggestions:

✓ Watch your other children for a few hours.

✓ Take over the carpool for a couple of weeks.

✓ Prepare some food.

✓ Make a snack.

✓ Run the vacuum cleaner.

✓ Wash the dishes.

✓ Clean the bathroom.

✓ Clean the kitchen.

✓ Do a load of laundry.

✓ Wash the dog.

✓ Run an errand (drugstore, dry cleaner, deli, hardware store).

✓ Pick up items from the grocery store.

Keep "Surprises" on Hand

Keep little wrapped gifts on hand. Give one to an older sibling when visitors bring presents for the new baby. These gifts are also nice for rewarding good behavior.

Keep a close eye on preschoolers as well. Three- and four-year olds can be wonderful "helpers," but sometimes they attempt tasks that could endanger the baby. They may, for instance, try to pick her up and carry her, or attempt to take her out of the crib. They may also try to share their food or try to change the baby's diaper. Be sure to keep baby supplies out of their reach so that powders and creams are not available. Putting the infant in a playpen is often helpful just to protect her from a sibling's "help." It is also a good idea to place a baby monitor near the infant and keep the receiver on and near you. That way, you can be aware of any unwanted "assistance."

PETS AND THE NEW BABY

Just as siblings need to be prepared for the new baby's arrival, so do pets. For many couples, their pet is their "first baby." They may have concerns about how the pet will adapt to the new baby, and even fear that it may harm her. Although most pets adapt very well and grow to accept and love the new addition, some show signs of aggression. It is very important to remember that close supervision of all pets is required.

A big brother lovingly welcomes his new sister into the family.

If you have a dog, keep in mind that he is a pack animal, and he sees the people in the home as the members of his pack. His view of his place in the pack and of this "new" pack member will affect his response to the baby. If he believes this new addition threatens his position, he may not adapt as well. Your dog's personality will help you determine how he might react to the baby. Is he good with other children? How does he react when a baby cries? Is he tolerant of being handled, or does he snap if certain areas of his body are touched or grabbed? Does he become aggressive if his food bowl is touched or if you try to take something from his mouth? Is he easily excited or nippy? Is he protective of his territory, or does he welcome strangers into his home? If your dog shows aggressive behavior, it is important to invest in specialized training to alter this behavior. He should learn how to follow the commands *sit, stay, down, no,* and *come.*

Begin to prepare your dog for the baby during the last weeks of pregnancy. A dog uses his senses of smell and sound to learn about his environment. Allow him to investigate the nursery and sniff the new scents. Cradle a blanket that has been sprinkled with powder, lotion, or even diaper cream. Speak to him in a pleasant, soothing tone of voice, pet him, and offer him a treat so he has a positive association with these smells. Never play tug of war with a baby blanket or baby toy. Reinforce calm interest and discourage jumping or aggressive behavior. Play a tape of a baby crying to see how he reacts. If you have friends or family members with babies or young children, ask them to visit, especially if your dog has not been around many children.

"I walked in to find my newborn covered in Vaseline from head to toe and my toddler exclaiming, 'Look Mom, I'm changing the baby!'"

Becky

If your pet has not had a physical recently or is not on monthly heartworm/parasite medication, it may be a good idea to take him to the vet for a complete physical, including an examination for parasites. Make sure he is up to date on all vaccinations. This would also provide an opportunity to discuss the subject of the new baby with a veterinarian who knows your pet.

While you are still in the hospital, have your partner wrap the baby in a blanket, and then take the blanket home so the dog can become familiar with the baby's smell. When you arrive home, have your partner carry the baby into the house and place her directly in the crib. You can then greet your pet, who will be excited to see you after your absence. A little later, you can gradually introduce him to the baby. Let him first look at the baby in the crib, and then in your arms. Allow him to be curious and observe you while feeding, changing, and holding the baby. Do not act overly frightened or react angrily if your dog approaches or licks the baby. This would reinforce that the baby is something negative. If he becomes upset when the baby cries, reassure and stroke him just as you would if he were frightened by thunder or other loud noises.

If your dog is territorial, it may be best to bring him outside (a neutral location) for his first view of the baby. Then you can enter the house together. If he becomes overly excited with lots of company, don't have extra people present for the first meeting.

Sharing a pacifier moment.

Occasionally, a dog will react to this new addition by having accidents, chewing furniture, refusing to eat, or displaying other signs that he is feeling abandoned. Make sure his routine is not altered drastically and that he is given the attention he is used to having. Continue taking him for his daily walk. Take time to play with him and offer him lots of pats and kind words. Do not hit your dog for bad deeds—rather than accentuate negative behavior, reward the positive. A dog that becomes aggressive is instinctively protecting his territory from an invader. This can have very serious consequences. If the behavior is not altered, you may have to find another home for him.

To avoid a possible tragedy, do not leave your dog alone with the baby until you are absolutely sure you can trust him. When your baby starts to crawl, you need to be equally alert, as a dog can be seen as an attractive plaything. Even the best animal may not take kindly to being grabbed or pinched. Teach your child to stroke and pet the dog; never allow hair pulling or ear tugging.

Cats are more independent than dogs and need to be handled a little differently. In general, follow the same suggestions for introducing a dog to a new baby. Knowing your cat's personality and how he responds to people and new situations is your best guide to how he will act with the baby. An older cat that is used to lots of attention may act jealous or misbehave. Extra attention, especially when the baby is awake, should solve the problem.

Contrary to popular myth, cats cannot suck the air out of a baby's mouth. A cat may, however, cuddle up with or sleep on top of an infant and accidentally smother her. Because they can easily jump onto dressers and into cribs, cats should not be allowed in the baby's room unless you are there. Securely fasten netting over the crib to discourage jumping. Before your baby is born, placing crumpled-up pieces of aluminum foil in the empty crib will discourage your cat from jumping in. Doing this during your pregnancy will break your cat of the habit before the baby is born. Do not leave aluminum foil in the crib with a baby.

Clip your cat's nails to prevent accidental scratches. If you have a mature male cat, he may spray to mark his territory. To avoid this, you might consider having him neutered prior to the baby's arrival. Neutering may also diminish aggressive behavior.

Lizards, snakes, turtles, and other reptiles can carry and shed salmonella bacteria. They may not show any signs of illness and they can transmit the disease without direct contact. Any surface that the reptile comes in contact with can harbor the bacteria. Children under a year old or individuals with compromised immune systems are at the greatest risk for developing sepsis and meningitis from these bacteria.[3] It is best

A Hint for the New Mother

Do not get a new puppy when your baby is first born thinking that you will have plenty of time to train him.

if these pets are kept in a remote area of the house. Good hand washing and disinfecting any surfaces that the reptiles touch is another important precaution.

Most pets learn to love the new addition to the family and become close companions. Avoid problems by preparing your pet. Identify possible problems and remedy them before they become worse. Some couples plan to get a puppy during their first weeks at home with a new baby, thinking that they will have lots of time to spend training it. But most parents are already overwhelmed by the lack of sleep and the responsibility of the new baby. It would be best to delay getting a puppy until the baby is older and sleeping better. Then you will be able to give a new puppy the attention she deserves.

FOR THE NEW FATHER: CHANGES IN YOUR LIFE

While mom adjusts to the major physical and emotional changes that the birth of a baby brings, you will also experience a major alteration in your life. You may find that this new addition requires your partner's undivided attention. Visitors will also focus on the new baby and mother. At times, you may feel neglected and left out, and experience feelings of jealousy toward the infant. To avoid these feelings, become an active participant in her care. Change diapers, give baths, and take her for walks. Do not hesitate to perform these tasks because you fear you may not do them exactly as your mate does. The important thing is that you are bonding with your baby and developing a lasting relationship. You may even be more skilled than your partner at performing certain baby-related jobs. Except for breastfeeding, you can do anything mom can do.

If possible, take off time from work during those first weeks. It will encourage you to bond as a family (as well as sharpen your baby-care skills). If a close friend or family member has also offered to spend time helping out—and she is the type of person who, although well-meaning, tends to "take over"—she may interfere with the interaction between you and your newborn. In such a case, it might be best to have her delay her visit until you go back to work. In addition to letting you to enjoy the first few weeks with your new baby, it allows your partner to have help for a longer period.

Be aware that a new addition to the family can cause fathers, just like mothers, to feel "blue." These feelings can be mild and short-lived or develop into depression. Although initially new fathers typically experience feelings of elation, some may suddenly find themselves overwhelmed by the new responsibilities of parenthood. They may feel trapped and alone, both emotionally and physically. Obsessing over issues like finances and the health of the mother and new baby is typical. Because they have a new person depending on them, they may suddenly begin worrying about their own health and safety. For some men, these new stresses can be overwhelming, especially when they are also dealing with lack of sleep and adjustment to the new family structure. Signs of depression can include mood swings, loss of appetite, anxiety, irritability, and impatience. A lack of interest in or sudden obsession with hobbies or activities is also common. If you find yourself overwhelmed with your new responsibilities and experiencing signs of depression, realize that these feelings are fairly common and should pass. Talk to other men and discover how they coped. If, however, feelings of depression linger or you begin developing thoughts of aggression, it is time to seek professional help.

You may find that your sexual feelings have changed since the birth of the baby. Some men find it difficult to view a woman who has become "a mother" as sexy (at least

Bonding with Daddy.

right away). This *Madonna complex* may cause you to believe that sexual feelings are inappropriate. Other men express ambivalence toward sex after viewing the birth of their baby. It may take some time before they can view the vagina as sexual, rather than the opening through which the new baby came into the world. Your mate's body will also have changed and may still retain some of the effects of pregnancy, including added weight and breasts that secrete milk. Many men find the larger breasts attractive, but some are uncomfortable, knowing that touching or kissing them may cause them to leak milk. They may feel that the breasts are only for nourishing babies. If the woman had an episiotomy or other perineal lacerations, there may also be concern over initiating intercourse.

"This breastfeeding pillow makes a great TV table!"

Your partner may also be reluctant to resume intimacy if she is exhausted, concerned about pain, or worried that the baby will wake up. Take it slowly, and start with a little romance. Take her out on a date. Bring her some fresh flowers. Offer her a full body massage. Gradually, she will become more receptive to your touch and eventually be ready for sexual intercourse. If you are concerned that she may be experiencing vaginal or perineal pain, first gently touch the area and ask for feedback. Massage vitamin E oil into the scar tissue. During sex, use a good water-soluble lubricant and provide adequate foreplay. When the woman assumes the superior position, she can control the depth of penetration. This is especially important for women who have had cesareans, as being in the superior position will avoid any discomfort to the incision. While resuming sex may not be automatic and exactly as before, patience and understanding can make this aspect of your relationship just as fulfilling.

You may be pleasantly surprised by the enormity of your love for the new baby. In order to spend more time with her, you may even find yourself reducing your own outside interests. The huge responsibility of having a baby will offer you an opportunity to bond and to develop a lasting relationship with your child. While parenting is not easy, it offers tremendous satisfaction and benefits to those who invest time and energy in their children.

POSTPARTUM EXERCISES

You should begin exercising as soon as possible after childbirth, even within twenty-four hours. In fact, if your perineum is not numb from anesthesia, you can begin doing Kegels within the first two hours. You can also perform ankle and foot exercises while lying in bed.

The muscle work involved in the immediate postpartum exercises is not strenuous or harmful. These exercises will help restore tone to your pelvic floor and abdominal muscles, as well as encourage good circulation in your legs. Your caregiver may give you a list of exercises to begin after delivery. If she does not, show her the following exercises and get her approval. See if she recommends any modifications that may be necessary in your particular case. Start gradually, and add exercises and repetitions as your strength and comfort permit. Do not overdo!

Unless otherwise noted, perform each exercise twice a day, beginning with two to three repetitions and gradually working up to the number of repetitions listed. Consistency is much more important than the length of the session.

For a cesarean delivery, a suggested exercise program is found beginning on page 280. Before starting any exercise program, be sure to get your caregiver's approval.

DAY ONE

Perform the following exercises while still in the birthing room or as soon afterward as possible.

Super Kegel

Benefits: Tones the pelvic floor muscles. Improves circulation. Promotes healing of the perineum.

Directions: While lying down, sitting, or standing, contract the muscles of the pelvic floor and hold for 20 seconds. Continue to breathe normally.

Frequency: Perform 1 Super Kegel every two hours, for a total of 10 a day. If possible, perform the first one in the birthing room. Also perform one after every urination.

Abdominal Tightening

Benefits: Decreases abdominal flabbiness and helps restore muscle tone to the abdominal wall.

Directions: While sitting or standing, pull in the abdominal muscles and hold tightly for 5 seconds. Continue to breathe normally. Gradually increase the holding time to 10 seconds.

Frequency: As often as possible.

Ankle Rotating

Benefits: Aids blood circulation and prevents blood clots.

Directions: While in bed, lie down or sit with your legs stretched out in front of you. Rotate your right foot at the ankle three times in one direction, then three times in the other direction. Repeat with the left foot.

Frequency: 5 to 10 repetitions with each ankle.

Foot Flexing/Stretching

Benefits: Aids blood circulation and prevents blood clots.

Directions: While in bed, lie down or sit with your legs stretched out in front of you. Flex your right foot, slowly pointing your toes toward your body and hold for a count of five. You will feel stretching in the calf muscle. Relax the foot, then slowly point the toes away from you. Repeat with the other foot.

Frequency: 5 to 10 repetitions with each foot.

DAY TWO

Continue the Super Kegels and Abdominal Tightening from the first day and add the following two exercises:

Pelvic Tilt

Benefit: Tones the abdominal muscles.

Directions: Lie on your back with your knees bent and feet flat on the floor. Arch your back and press your buttocks against the floor. Then release your buttocks and press the small of your back against the floor, contracting your abdominal muscles. Continue to breathe normally. (This can also be done in bed.)

Frequency: 5 to 10 repetitions.

Prone Resting Position

Benefit: Helps the uterus return to its normal position.

Directions: Lie on your stomach with a folded blanket or pillow under your abdomen and upper thighs, and another one under your ankles. Turn your face to one side, eyes opened or closed, and rest for as long as you wish.

Prone Resting position.

Frequency: As often as possible.

DAY THREE

On the third day, check for separation of the recti muscles before you do any further abdominal exercising. This band of muscles runs vertically through the center of the abdomen. It is divided into two halves, which are joined by connective tissue. Many pregnant women experience separation of these muscles, especially if they did not use good body mechanics while lifting during pregnancy.

To check for separation, lie on your back with your legs bent and feet flat on the floor. Press the fingers of one hand in a horizontal line into the area below your navel, then slowly raise your head and shoulders about 8 inches off the floor. You should feel the bands of muscles on both sides of your abdomen pull toward the center and move your fingers out of the way. If three or more fingers slide into a gap between the muscle bands, the recti muscles are separated.

Checking for separation of the recti muscles.

Performing the Head Lifting exercise (below) will correct the problem. The gap should close to the normal half-inch width within seven to ten days. Do not continue the exercise program until the gap is closed. Also, do not rotate or bend your trunk from side to side or twist your hips, which could cause the muscles to pull further apart.

If, after checking for separation, you discover that your recti muscles are fine, continue doing the Super Kegels, Abdominal Tightening, Pelvic Tilt, and Prone Resting position for the next four days.

Head Lifting

Benefit: Restores the recti muscles to their proper position.

Directions: Lie on your back with your knees bent and feet flat on the floor. Cross your arms over your abdomen and take a deep breath. Slowly exhale and raise your head off the floor, pulling your abdominal muscles together with your hands. Inhale and slowly lower your head.

Frequency: 10 repetitions per set. Perform 5 sets per day.

Head Lifting to correct separated recti muscles.

WEEK TWO

Continue the Super Kegels from the first week. Replace the remaining first-week exercises with the following, more advanced versions. Aim for at least two exercise sessions per day or as directed.

Modified Sit-Up.

Modified Sit-Up (variation).

Modified Sit-Up

Benefit: Tones the abdominal muscles.

Directions: Lie on your back with your knees bent and feet flat on the floor. Inhale, then exhale while raising your head and shoulders off the floor and reaching both of your hands toward your knees. Inhale while lying back down.

Variation: As you exhale and raise your head and shoulders off the floor, reach both of your hands to the outside of your right knee. Inhale while lying back down. Exhale again, while raising your head and shoulders and reaching both of your hands to the outside of your left knee. Inhale while lying back down.

Frequency: 5 to 10 repetitions.

Caution: If the recti muscles are still separated, support them as you do this advanced head lifting exercise. Do not do the variation until the recti muscles are restored.

Postpartum Pelvic Rock

Benefit: Tones the abdominal muscles.

Directions: Kneel on the floor on your hands and knees. Align your head with your spine, tuck in your bottom, pull up your abdominal muscles, and press up your spine at the lower back. Hold this position for a few seconds, then return to the starting position. Repeat the exercise with a constant rhythm and a rocking motion.

Frequency: 5 to 10 repetitions per set. Perform 3 sets per day.

Knee-Chest Position

Knee-Chest position.

Benefit: Encourages the uterus to return to its proper position.

Directions: Get down on your knees, spacing them about 12 to 18 inches apart. Bend forward at the hips, lower your chest to the floor, and place the side of your face on top of your folded hands. Your elbows should be pointing out to the sides. (If desired, position a pillow under your face and chest.) Contract and relax your abdominal muscles.

Frequency: As many times as you wish, followed by at least 5 minutes of rest.

WEEK THREE

Continue the Super Kegels, Postpartum Pelvic Rock, and Knee-Chest position from the first two weeks and add the following five exercises. In addition, to strengthen your cardiovascular system and tone your body, begin taking brisk walks every day.

Side Kicks

Benefit: Helps restore the waistline.

Directions: Lie on the floor on your right side with your arms over your head and your head resting on your right arm. Keeping your right leg slightly bent, raise your left arm and leg toward the ceiling and touch your left hand to your knee. Return your arm and leg to the starting position, stretching the arm over your head and elongating your waist and rib cage. Repeat 5 to 10 times. Relax. Turn onto your left side and repeat with the other arm and leg.

Frequency: 5 to 10 repetitions on each side.

Side Kicks.

Modified Sit-Up II

Benefit: Tones the abdominal muscles.

Directions: Lie on your back with your knees bent, feet flat on the floor, and hands clasped behind your head. Inhale, then exhale while raising your head and shoulders off the floor and reaching your elbows toward your knees. Do not touch the knees. Inhale while lying back down.

Frequency: 5 to 10 repetitions..

Modified Sit-Up II.

Modified Sit-Up III

Benefit: Tones the abdominal muscles.

Directions: Lie on your back with your knees bent, feet flat on the floor, and hands clasped behind your head. Inhale, then exhale while raising your head and shoulders off the floor and reaching both elbows to the outside of your right knee. Do not touch the knee. Inhale while lying back down, then exhale while raising your head and shoulders and reaching both elbows to the outside of your left knee. Inhale while lying back down.

Frequency: 5 to 10 repetitions.

Modified Sit-Up III.

Single Leg Raises

Benefits: Tones the leg and abdominal muscles. Improves the blood circulation.

Directions: Lie on your back with your knees bent, feet flat on the floor, and hands clasped behind your head. Draw your right knee toward your chest, then inhale, point your toes, and continue raising the leg toward the ceiling until the knee is straight. Exhale, flex the foot, and slowly lower the straightened leg to the floor. Return the leg to the starting position and repeat with the left leg.

Frequency: 5 to 10 repetitions with each leg.

Single Leg Raises:

Draw your knee . . .   raise your leg with   then flex your foot and
                           the toes pointed . . .   slowly lower your leg.

Single Leg Slide

Benefits: Tones the leg and abdominal muscles. Improves the blood circulation.

Single Leg Slide.

Directions: Lie on your back with your knees bent, feet flat on the floor, and hands clasped behind your head. Inhaling through your nose, draw your right knee toward your chest, flexing your foot. Then exhaling through your mouth, slowly return the foot to the floor and slide the leg downward, pressing the small of your back to the floor and contracting your abdominal muscles. Return the leg to the starting position and repeat with the left leg.

Frequency: 5 to 10 repetitions with each leg.

WEEKS FOUR THROUGH SIX

Continue doing the Super Kegels, Side Kicks, Single Leg Raises, and Single Leg Slides from the first three weeks and add the following two exercises. In addition, increase the time you spend walking.

Hip Rolls

Benefit: Helps restore the waistline.

Directions: Lie on your back with your arms stretched out sideways like a "T." Draw your knees toward your chest, then roll your hips to the right, lowering your knees and legs to the floor on your right side; keep your back and arms flat on the floor. Return your hips and knees to the center position, then roll your hips to the left, and lower your knees and legs to the floor on your left. Return to the center position.

Frequency: 5 to 10 repetitions on each side.

Modified Sit-Up IV

Benefit: Strengthens the abdominal muscles.

Directions: Lie on your back with your knees bent, feet flat on the floor, and arms folded across your chest. Inhale, then exhale while raising your head and shoulders to a 30-degree angle. Inhale while lying back down.

Frequency: 5 to 10 repetitions.

Hip Roll.

Modified Sit-Up IV.

AFTER THE SIX-WEEK CHECKUP

After the six-week checkup, continue practicing all the exercises from weeks four through six—Side Kicks, Single Leg Raises, Single Leg Slides, Hip Rolls, and Modified Sit-Up IV—for at least the next two months. In addition, continue walking briskly around your neighborhood and add an aerobic exercise, such as jogging, swimming, or bicycle riding. Continue doing your Super Kegels (for the rest of your life).

POSTPARTUM SEX

The time following the birth of your baby will be exciting, complicated, and busy. Your body will go through rapid changes, adjusting from the pregnant to the nonpregnant state. As new parents, you and your partner will have an altered relationship—being pregnant and in love is quite different from being parents and in love. After being free and spontaneous as lovers, you will now also be parents with new roles, new responsibilities, and a whole new life.

The love relationship between you and your husband will continue to grow in many ways, and part of that relationship will be the enjoyment of sex. You may be confused by what you are told or even by your own feelings as individuals and as a couple. A number of factors, including fatigue, pain, and whether or not you are breastfeeding, will influence your decision about when to resume sexual intercourse.

Medical Indications

Some caregivers advise their patients to delay having sex until after the six-week postpartum checkup. Others suggest waiting just until the vaginal discharge has stopped. Waiting ensures that both the stitches and the placental site within the uterus have healed. With a cesarean birth, the abdominal scar must also heal completely, otherwise bacteria could be introduced and cause an infection. Having intercourse within the first weeks after birth while the placental site is healing can also be dangerous. It can cause a potentially fatal air embolism to enter the bloodstream.

Fatigue

The first few weeks and months with a new baby will be the busiest. Your time will not really be your own. The days will be exhausting and you may not get a decent night's sleep for a long while. Although your partner's routine will be somewhat changed, your lifestyle will change much more dramatically. It will be difficult to be a good parent around the clock—but sexy, too? Resuming sexual activity just may not seem possible (or a priority) for a while!

Hormones

Your body's hormones are actively involved in all the changes connected with birth and breastfeeding. It may take them some time to get back into balance. These hormonal changes may affect your feelings and sexual responsiveness. You may want very much to make love, or you may feel turned off by sex for a time. If you are turned off, do not berate yourself— the desire will return. The following four-step method, which appeared in the *International Journal of Childbirth Education,* can be used to help reawaken your sexual desire:

Step 1. Nonsexual touch
Daily hugging and cuddling, showering together, and nonsexual massage can help both partners rediscover the pleasure of touch and increase their sexual anticipation.

Step 2. Sexual touch
Using massage on each other in a sexual way while continuing to avoid all genital contact will further increase desire and enhance awareness of each other's sexuality.

Step 3. Genital stimulation
Gentle massage of the vagina, using sterile water-soluble lubricating jelly, will help to determine the woman's sensitivity and whether she is ready for intercourse. She can reciprocate by massaging her partner's genital area manually or orally.

Step 4. Sexual intercourse
Using repeated *partial* penetration and withdrawal will ease the stretching of the vagina by the penis.

These steps will be helpful in gradually introducing sexual activity. They should be practiced with a relaxed attitude.

Pain

Some new mothers find intercourse painful or uncomfortable, especially if they resume it too soon after giving birth. Some new dads are hesitant because of this concern. Patience and gentleness are important. It is also important that your perineum and vagina are healed. If your perineal stitches have made your vaginal opening smaller than it was before, or if you have vaginal adhesions, before attempting intercourse, try gentle dilation, first using the fingers and then vaginal dilators from your caregiver. If your vaginal area is still tender, you may find that the most comfortable position for intercourse is lying side by side, which takes the pressure off the episiotomy site. A warm bath before lovemaking may also help.

Decreased vaginal lubrication due to hormonal changes might also make intercourse painful. This situation may last longer for the breastfeeding mother. Applying a water-soluble jelly to the penis and vagina helps remedy this problem. Do not use a non-water-soluble lubricant, such as petroleum jelly, because it keeps air out and allows bacteria to grow.

Breastfeeding

Some breastfeeding mothers enjoy sex immensely; others do not, at least for a while. Fathers have feelings about breastfeeding also. Some find it very attractive, while others find that it inhibits their sexual feelings somewhat.

Breasts are an important part of human sexuality—first, as the means of nourishment for babies, and second, as a source of sexual stimulation and pleasure. If you and your partner have thought of breasts solely as objects of sexual pleasure, you will both need some time to get used to the idea that they are filled with milk. Some nursing mothers do not enjoy breast stimulation. Along with their partners, many of these women explore new areas of the body for sexual foreplay. At the same time, be assured that the baby will not contract an infection if your partner kisses your breasts or stimulates them orally.

One thing that may catch you unaware is the leaking of milk during love play or orgasm. This happens because sexual stimulation releases oxytocin, which triggers the milk-ejection reflex. This release of milk is normal and natural. It may help to make love after nursing, when the breasts are relatively empty (and the baby is more likely to be asleep). You could also try wearing a nursing bra and pads to prevent leaking at a stimulating moment. Using towels to keep the bedding dry is another recommendation.

If you do not breastfeed your baby, you may still have an uncomfortable amount of milk within your breasts for a few weeks after delivery. Since sexual activity involving the breasts encourages milk production, you should avoid the breasts during sexual foreplay to discourage this.

Lack of Spontaneity

The baby, no matter how adorable she is, may almost seem to function as a "chaperone," which can be very inhibiting at times. The spontaneity in your love life may take a dive: "Is the baby going to wake up?" "Do we have enough time between feedings?" Sexy feelings hardly get a chance to develop if you are always listening for a cry.

Your new responsibilities may fatigue both of you, especially during the early weeks of adjustment. But the tension and fatigue may build even further if you do not take some time for yourselves. Change, feed, and cuddle the baby, then put her to bed, shut the door, and take time to talk to each other, relax, caress, and make love.

Fear of Becoming Pregnant

No matter how thrilled both of you will be with the new baby, the thought of having another one right away can be alarming. The fear of becoming pregnant can be a major factor in having (or not having) postpartum sex. As a couple, address family planning before the postpartum checkup, and then discuss it with your caregiver.

Hints for the New Father

✓ Encourage your partner to begin doing Super Kegels after giving birth.

✓ Take your partner on a date.

✓ As a couple, discuss your birth control options.

✓ Express your affection for your mate. Make her feel special with a thoughtful gift, some flowers, or by preparing a nice dinner. Tell her, "I love you."

✓ Give your partner a massage.

✓ Allow yourself time to adjust to your new role as a parent.

✓ Enjoy being a dad.

Spacing children at least eighteen months apart but no longer than five years decreases the risk of preterm birth and low birth weight. This time between pregnancies allows the body to recover nutritionally from the previous pregnancy and breastfeeding. The risks related to spacing children longer than five years may be related to maternal factors that decrease fertility and could also lead to poor fetal development.[4]

Exclusive and frequent breastfeeding inhibits ovulation and the onset of your period, and is effective at preventing pregnancy for the first six months. Keep in mind that this is true only if the woman is breastfeeding *exclusively* (no bottles or pacifiers) and the baby is nursing throughout the night. This is called the Lactational Amenorrhea Method (LAM) of family planning. Breastfeeding mothers may experience many period-free months. Women who do not breastfeed will resume their menstrual cycles at six week postpartum.

Most methods of birth control can be used during breastfeeding. Menstrual periods must resume with regularity before practicing the *rhythm method*—a means of contraception in which intercourse is avoided on high-fertility days. A condom and spermicidal foam or jelly may be the best means of birth control for the first few weeks. The condom will decrease the possibility of introducing infection, and the foam or jelly will lubricate the vagina. Not recommended is a contraceptive sponge, which is not an effective method of birth control within the first year of giving birth. Also be aware that due to changes in the vagina and uterus following childbirth, your old diaphragm or cervical cap may not fit correctly. It may also be dried out and contain tiny holes. You can be refitted at your six-week checkup. Do not use a cervical cap prior to ten weeks following childbirth.

While still in the hospital, some women are given an injection of Depo-Provera (the synthetic progesterone *progestin*) as a means of contraception. This is not recommended for women who are planning to breastfeed because a drop in this hormone (when the placenta is delivered) is the body's signal for milk production. An injection at this time may inhibit milk supply. Nursing mothers should delay the initiation of any progestin-only birth control pills or injections until their milk supply is well established—about six weeks after giving birth.

Contraceptives that contain both estrogen and progestin are not compatible with breastfeeding either, since estrogen also reduces milk production and alters the composition of the milk. This type of contraception is found in combined birth control pills, the transdermal patch, and the vaginal ring. To ensure adequate milk supply and success with breastfeeding, wait six months before using any type of contraception that contains both of these hormones.

In 1996, the FDA endorsed two methods that could be used for emergency contraception in cases of unprotected sex and cases in which the primary method failed (condom breakage, for example). The Plan B or "morning after pill" is a high-dose birth control pill that is taken in two doses. The first dose must be taken within 120 hours after unprotected intercourse; the second is taken 12 hours later. This is a one-time method with 75- to 89-percent effectiveness when the first dose is taken within 72 hours of intercourse. After using emergency contraception, it is important that the woman also begins using a reliable form of birth control.

Planning Your Next Pregnancy?

Thinking about getting pregnant? Whether you have been pregnant before or are planning a first pregnancy, there are a number of factors that will increase your chances of conception and help ensure a healthy pregnancy.

If you and your partner are planning to conceive, it is essential to start your pregnancy while in the best possible condition. A preconception or early pregnancy class, which provides basic information regarding diet, exercise, and medication, as well as other helpful recommendations, is a good place to start. Your caregiver will also be able to offer helpful guidelines.

If you have a history of multiple miscarriages, preterm births, or children with birth defects, it is important for your caregiver to rule out any treatable causes, such as infection or folic acid deficiency. He may also recommend genetic counseling if you are at high risk for passing on such conditions as Tay-Sachs disease, sickle cell disease, thalassemia, or cystic fibrosis, which are all detailed in Chapter 4. A genetic counselor may also consider other problems, such as Down syndrome, that tend to increase as a woman ages. Knowledge of such information can allay the concerns of low-risk couples, as well as prepare high-risk couples for additional prenatal screening.

If you are planning to become pregnant, consider the following recommendations. At least three months prior to possible conception:

❑ Have a complete physical to rule out pre-existing medical conditions. If you have a chronic illness that requires medication, your caregiver will recommend the safest type to use during your pregnancy.

❑ Get checked for immunity to rubella and, if necessary, get immunized. Do not get pregnant for at least three months following the vaccination.

❑ If you did not have chicken pox as a child, get immunized. Do not get pregnant for at least three months following the vaccination.

❑ Stop taking birth control pills. Use another form of contraception that does not contain hormones.

❑ Start taking a folic acid supplement and prenatal vitamins.

❑ Stop or reduce the consumption of products containing caffeine. Some studies have indicated a link between high caffeine consumption and delayed conception.

❑ Stop smoking, drinking alcoholic beverages, and/or taking recreational drugs, which can reduce fertility in both men and women.

❑ If you are overweight, try to lose the extra pounds and begin your pregnancy at an ideal weight.

❑ If you own or have previously handled cats or litter boxes, have a blood test to verify that you have immunity to toxoplasmosis.

Plan B is available over the counter (OTC) for women who are eighteen years of age and older. Those under eighteen need a prescription. Women can also use certain birth control pills as emergency contraception methods. For information on dosages and specific brands, contact the Association of Reproductive Health Professionals or Planned Parenthood. These organizations also provide general information on contraception, as well as local caregivers who will prescribe emergency contraceptives. (For contact information, see the Resources beginning on page 449.)

Another effective method of emergency contraception is the copper-T intrauterine device (IUD), which must be inserted within five days after unprotected intercourse. Following insertion, this IUD can be left in place up to twelve years. Studies have shown no long-term or serious side effects for any of the emergency contraception methods just discussed. For summaries of these and other birth control methods currently available in the United States, see Table 17.1 on page 428.

TABLE 17.1. METHODS OF CONTRACEPTION USED IN THE UNITED STATES

Method	What Is It?	How Does It Work?	How Effective Is It?
Behavioral *Does not protect against HIV or other STDs.*			
LAM (Lactational Amenorrhea Method)	Exclusive breastfeeding (no bottles, pacifiers), including nursing during the night.	Prevents the ovaries from releasing an egg.	99% for the first six months after giving birth.
Fertility Awareness (natural family planning; rhythm method)	The avoidance of intercourse each month on the days when one is most likely to become pregnant.	The release of the egg is calculated through such methods as maintaining a chart of body temperature, checking vaginal secretions, and keeping a calendar of menstrual periods. Sex is avoided at times of fertility.	75%–99% or less, depending on the method and consistency of use, and on the avoidance of sex during those days. Effectiveness is greatest when all calculation methods (in box at left) are combined.
Barrier (over the counter)			
Condom (male)	A sheath, made of either latex or polyurethane, designed to fit snugly over the erect penis. May be prelubricated. May have a reservoir tip to hold the sperm.	Prevents sperm from getting inside the vagina during intercourse.	85%–98%. Effectiveness is greatest when used with a spermicide. Check expiration date.
Condom (female)	A lubricated polyurethane sheath with flexible rings on each end.	Prevents sperm from entering the uterus during intercourse.	79%–95%
Sponge	A pillow-shaped disposable sponge that is infused with spermicide. The spermicide is released over twenty-four hours. The sponge has a loop for easy removal.	Blocks the cervix and prevents sperm from passing. The spermicide kills the sperm.	68%–91%. Less effective within the first year after giving birth.
Barrier (prescription) *Does not protect against HIV or other STDs.*			
Diaphragm	A dome shaped cup with a flexible rim. Should always be used with spermicidal jelly or cream.	Fits inside the vagina and forms a barrier between the cervix and the sperm. Spermicide kills the sperm.	84%–94%

How Is It Used?	What Are the Advantages?	What Are the Disadvantages?	Possible Side Effects or Complications
Through exclusive breastfeeding.	Free; no side effects; requires no supplies or medical supervision.	Effective for only six months.	None
By maintaining careful calculation records to help predict ovulation.	Free; safe; no religious objection; teaches women about their menstrual cycles.	Difficult to use if menstrual cycle is irregular. Requires abstinence or use of a barrier birth control method during "unsafe"days. If done for religious reasons, nothing that kills sperm (even condoms) can be used.	None.
Placed on the erect penis prior to contact with the vagina. After ejaculation, the penis should be removed from the vagina immediately.	Effective; safe; available without a prescription; latex provides more protection against HIV and other STDs.	Often found objectionable. Interrupts intercourse; can be messy; can break. Should be used only with a water-based lubricant, such as K-Y jelly; is weakened by petroleum-based products, such as Vaseline and baby oil.	Possible allergic reaction to latex.
Inserted in the vagina before intercourse with one ring in and the other out. Must be removed very carefully.	Available without prescription. Protects somewhat against HIV and other STDs. Can be used with any type of lubricant.	Awkward to insert. May slip during use. Not aesthetically appealing to some couples.	Vaginal irritation. Penile irritation.
Moisten with water and insert deep into the vagina. Must remain for six hours after intercourse.	Available without prescription. Offers continuous protection for 24 hours. Does not affect hormones. Safe with breastfeeding. Convenient (can be carried in purse).	Does not protect against STDs. Should not be used during menstruation.	Vaginal irritation. Risk of toxic shock syndrome if left in over twenty-four hours.
Coated with spermicide and inserted in the vagina before intercourse. Can be inserted up to six hours beforehand. Must stay in at least six hours after intercourse, but no longer than twenty-four hours.	Does not affect hormones. Safe with breastfeeding. Convenient (can be carried in purse).	Must be fitted by healthcare professional. Can be difficult to insert, inconvenient, and messy. Requires reapplication of spermicide for repeated intercourse after six hours. Weight gain or loss of over ten pounds may affect the fit. Should not be used during menstruation.	Vaginal irritation. Frequent bladder infections. Although rare, may cause toxic shock syndrome if allowed to remain in for a prolonged period of time.

Method	What Is It?	How Does It Work?	How Effective Is It?
Lea's Shield	A silicone cup with an air valve and a loop to aid in removal. Should always be used with spermicidal jelly or cream.	Fits snugly over the cervix, and forms a barrier between the uterus and the sperm. Spermicide kills the sperm.	85%
Cervical cap Fem Cap	A soft latex thimble-shaped cap or a silicone cup shaped like a sailor's hat. Should always be used with spermicidal jelly or cream.	Fits snugly over the cervix, forming a barrier between the uterus and the sperm. Spermicide kills the sperm.	84%–91%; 68%–74% after giving birth vaginally.
Spermicide			
Cream Jelly Foam Suppository Film	Cream and jelly available in tubes; foam available in cans or individual applicators. Also available in suppository form or dissolvable film.	Acts as physical barrier between the sperm and the uterus. Contains a chemical that kills sperm.	71%–85%. Effectiveness is greater when used with another method, such as a condom.
Hormonal (progestin only) *Does not protect against HIV or other STDs.*			
Progestin-only pill (mini-pills)	Pills containing the synthetic hormone progestin (similar to the progesterone made in the ovaries).	Thickens the cervical mucus and changes the uterine lining, making it difficult for a fertilized egg to begin growing. Less often, it prevents the egg's release from the ovary.	92%–99% if used consistently; much less if used carelessly.
Depo-Provera Depo-SubQ Provero 104 (30% less hormone)	An intramuscular injection of the synthetic hormone progestin (similar to the progesterone made in the ovaries).	Inhibits ovulation. Less often, it thickens the cervical mucus and changes the uterine lining, making it difficult for a fertilized egg to begin growing.	99%

How Is It Used?	What Are the Advantages?	What Are the Disadvantages?	Possible Side Effects or Complications
Coated with spermicide and inserted in vagina before intercourse. Must be left in place at least eight hours, but no longer than forty-eight hours. Should reapply spermicide with each intercourse.	One size only. Can be inserted hours prior to sex. Does not affect hormones. Safe with breastfeeding. Convenient (can be carried in purse).	Can be difficult to insert. Should not be used during menstruation.	Frequent bladder infections.
Filled with spermicide and inserted in the vagina over the cervix before intercourse. Must remain for at least eight hours after intercourse, but no more than forty-eight hours.	Can be inserted many hours before intercourse. Reapplication of spermicide is not necessary for repeated intercourse, but it is suggested. Does not affect hormones. Safe with breastfeeding. Convenient (can be carried in purse).	Cannot always be fitted properly. May be difficult to insert. Cannot use until ten weeks after giving birth. Should not be used during menstruation	Uterine or cervical infection. Increased risk of toxic shock syndrome. Genital burning, irritation.
Inserted in vagina before intercourse. Can be used up to ten minutes before and remain effective for one hour after insertion. Must be reapplied with repeated intercourse. Must remain undisturbed (no douching) for at least eight hours afterwards.	Effective and safe. Offers good lubrication. Available without prescription.	Must be inserted just before intercourse. Can be inconvenient or messy. Products containing nonoxynol-9 used many times a day may irritate tissue and increase the risk of HIV and other STDs.	Vaginal irritation. Penile irritation.
Taken orally. One pill is taken at the same time every day.	Convenient and extremely effective. Does not interfere with sex. May reduce menstrual cramps. Can be used with breastfeeding.	Requires a prescription. A medical exam is recommended. Cannot be taken by all women. Must be taken at the same time every day and in the right order. Antibiotic (rifampin), anti-fungals, St. John's wort, HIV protease inhibitors, and anti-seizure medications can reduce effectiveness.	Nausea, headache, irregular periods, missed periods, breast tenderness, depression.
Injected every three months by office nurse.	Convenient. Effective for twelve weeks. Results in lighter or no periods. Can be used while breastfeeding.	Must be re-injected every three months. Takes six months or more to regain fertility. If side effects occur, must wait until medication wears off.	Irregular periods, spotting, longer and heavier periods, depression, weight gain, headaches, increased risk of osteoporosis.

Method	What Is It?	How Does It Work?	How Effective Is It?
Implant (Implanon)	A thin, flexible, matchstick size plastic implant that contains progestin.	Inhibits ovulation. Less often, it thickens the cervical mucus and changes the uterine lining, making it difficult for a fertilized egg to begin growing.	99% for three years
Hormonal (combined) *Should not be used by smokers, women over thirty-five, or those with diabetes, high blood pressure, high cholesterol, or blood clotting disorders. Antibiotic (rifampin), anti-fungals, St. John's wort, HIV protease inhibitors, and anti-seizure medications can reduce effectiveness. Does not protect against HIV or other STDs.*			
Combined pill Three-month pill (Seasonale) No periods (Lybrel)	Pills containing synthetic estrogen and progestin, or estrogen and a new progestin called drospirenone.	Prevents the egg's release from the ovary. Also thickens the cervical mucus and changes the uterine lining, making it difficult for a fertilized egg to begin growing.	92%–99% if used consistently; much less if used carelessly.
Transdermal Patch (Ortho Evra)	A patch containing synthetic estrogen and progestin, which are absorbed through skin.	Prevents the egg's release from the ovary. Also thickens the cervical mucus and changes the uterine lining, making it difficult for a fertilized egg to begin growing.	99%
Vaginal Contraceptive Ring (NuvaRing)	A ring placed in the vagina that releases synthetic estrogen and progestin, which are absorbed through the vagina.	Prevents the egg's release from the ovary. Also thickens the cervical mucus and changes the uterine lining, making it difficult for a fertilized egg to begin growing.	98%–99%

How Is It Used?	What Are the Advantages?	What Are the Disadvantages?	Possible Side Effects or Complications
Inserted under skin of upper arm after a local anesthetic.	Convenient. Protection is immediate if inserted during the first five days of period. Otherwise, an additional method contraception method is required for the first seven days. Can be used with breastfeeding. After one year, some women have no periods. Fertility returns quickly after removal.	Less effective if very overweight. Antibiotic (rifampin), St. John's wort, anti-fungals, and certain drugs used to treat mental illness, seizures, or HIV may reduce effectiveness.	Irregular periods, spotting, longer and heavier periods, depression, weight gain, headaches. Infection, scarring at insertion site. Difficulty in removing.
Taken orally. One pill taken every day for three weeks, with one week off. Three-month pill is taken daily for twelve weeks with one week off. Lybrel is taken daily without any breaks and results in the absence of periods. Femcon Fe is a chewable version which also contains iron in the "inactive" pills.	Convenient and extremely effective. Does does not interfere with sex. May reduce menstrual cramps. Will have only four periods a year with the three-month pill or none with Lybrel.	Requires a prescription. A medical exam is recommended. Best if taken at same time every day.	Nausea, weight gain, irregular or missed periods, spotting, darkened facial skin, mood changes. Although rare, may cause heart attack; blood clots in the legs, lungs, or brain.
Patch is applied to the abdomen, buttocks, or upper body once a week for three weeks with one week off.	Convenient and effective. Not necessary to remember to take daily pills.	Less effective in women weighing over 198 pounds. May detach or irritate skin. Because heat can increase absorption rate to potentially dangerous levels, avoid hot tubs, sun exposure, or increased skin temperature for extended periods.[1]	Irregular bleeding, weight gain or loss, breast tenderness, nausea, mood changes. Increased risk of blood clots or high blood pressure. Exposure to 60% more estrogen than typical birth control pills.
Ring is worn for three weeks, then removed for one week. New ring is then inserted.	Convenient and effective. Not necessary to remember to take daily pills.	Increased vaginal discharge.	Vaginal irritation and/or infection. Irregular bleeding, weight gain or loss, breast tenderness, nausea, mood changes. Increased risk of blood clots, high blood pressure.

Method	What Is It?	How Does It Work?	How Effective Is It?
Intrauterine Devices			
Progestasert Mirena ParaGard	A small plastic T-shaped device with a thin string that is inserted into the uterus.	Causes reaction within uterus that impedes fertilization, or stops a fertilized egg from attaching to uterine wall. (Progestasert releases progesterone; Mirena releases the progestin leyonorgestrel, and ParaGard releases copper.)	99%
Sterilization *Does not protect against HIV or other STDs.*			
Tubal ligation (female)	Surgical procedure in which a section of each fallopian tube is cut out and the ends are tied off and cauterized, or sealed by clips, clamps, or rings.	Prevents the sperm from reaching the egg and the egg from reaching the uterus.	95% in the first year, 99% thereafter.
Essure (female)	No-incision procedure in which an insert is placed in the fallopian tube. Growth around the insert closes the tube.	Prevents the sperm from reaching the egg and the egg from reaching the uterus.	95% in the first year, 99% thereafter. Not effective until twelve weeks after the procedure.
Vasectomy (male)	Surgical procedure in which a section of the vas deferens is removed and the ends are tied off, cauterized, or blocked with surgical clips. In the no-incision no-scalpel method, a tiny puncture is made to reach both tubes, which are sealed.	Prevents sperm from being released during ejaculation.	99%–100%
Emergency Contraception			
Plan B (Morning After Pill)	A high-dose birth control pill given in two doses. It is taken after unprotected intercourse.	Alters the lining of the uterus to prevent the implantation of a fertilized egg.	75%–89%
Copper-T IUD (ParaGard)	A small plastic T-shaped device with a thin string that is inserted into the uterus. For emergency contraception, it must be inserted within five days of unprotected intercourse.	Causes a reaction within the uterus that impedes fertilization, or prevents a fertilized egg from becoming attached to the uterine wall.	99%

How Is It Used?	What Are the Advantages?	What Are the Disadvantages?	Possible Side Effects or Complications
Inserted in uterus by caregiver. Progestasert replaced yearly; Mirena effective for 5 years; Para Gard effective up to 12 years. The string must be checked by user after each period to ensure device is still in place.	Effective; allows spontaneity; usually not felt by either partner during intercourse.	Should not be used by women with a history of pelvic inflammatory disease. Can be expelled by the uterus. Does not protect against HIV or other STDs.	Cramps, bleeding, fever, vaginal discharge. Uterine infection/inflammation can cause scarring of reproductive organs or sterility. Possible uterine perforation during insertion. If pregnancy occurs with IUD, can be ectopic or miscarriage can occur.
Performed by a surgeon either postpartum or on an outpatient basis.	Effective; low rate of complications; no loss of sexual desire or ability; no fear of pregnancy.	Involves surgery. Usually not reversible.	Pain for several days after procedure. Wrong structure can be tied off or tube can grow back together. If pregnancy occurs, may be ectopic.
Performed by a surgeon either postpartum or on an outpatient basis	Effective; low rate of complications; no loss of sexual desire or ability; no fear of pregnancy, which can improve sexual relations.	Involves surgery. Usually not reversible.	Pain for several days after procedure. The insert could be expelled or perforate the fallopian tube.
Performed by a urologist in the office.	Effective; low rate of complications; no loss of sexual desire or ability; no fear of pregnancy; less invasive than tubal ligation or essure.	Involves surgery. Usually not reversible.	Pain and possible swelling after procedure. The wrong structure can be tied off or the tube can grow back together. Should have sperm count taken prior to having unprotected intercourse (usually after 3 months).
Taken orally. First dose should be taken within 72 hours after unprotected intercourse, but can also be taken up to 120 hours afterward. Second dose taken 12 hours after the first.	Convenient; no long-term or serious side effects.	Over-the-counter for women over eighteen years of age; younger women require a prescription. If vomiting occurs within two hours after taking a dose, the dose must be retaken.	Nausea, vomiting.
Must be inserted by a caregiver.	High level of effectiveness.	Should not be used by women with a history of pelvic inflammatory disease. Can be expelled by the uterus.	Cramps, bleeding, fever, vaginal discharge. Uterine infection/inflammation can cause scarring of reproductive organs or sterility. Possible uterine perforation during insertion.

DON'T LOSE SIGHT OF EACH OTHER

Warmth and affection are vital for new parents.

Warmth and affection mean a lot to new parents, especially during the early adjustment period. A cuddle and hug may be more desirable than making love, at least for a while. For many couples, the baby arrives before they have had a chance to become content with their sexual life. A satisfying, exciting sex life can take years to develop.

Many a new dad has felt pushed aside at the arrival of the baby, who needs so much attention. Instead of feeling that he has gained a child, he may feel that he has lost a lover. If your partner feels this way, it is important to reassure him that your seemingly endless involvement with the baby does not mean that your love for him has diminished. You will receive a lot of touching and body contact while caring for your baby all day; but your partner, who is likely to be away from home at work, will not have this physical contact. He will need it when he gets home. Encourage him to help with the baby, and be sure to give him an extra hug and kiss now and then.

You yourself may find it quite a change to be home alone with a baby, especially if you have always worked outside the home. You will need to be reassured that your new role as a mother is important, even though you will not be earning money for it. Like your partner, you will also require love and confidence boosting; you will need to hear you that you are still desirable. If he takes no special notice of you until you flop into bed exhausted, your frustration, as well as resentment, may build.

Although you may not yet be ready for intercourse, don't turn away from your partner's signs of affection. It would be sad if you chose to forgo his warmth or loving gestures because you are concerned that it will lead to sex. Try not to put so much emphasis on having sexual intercourse and wondering if "tonight is the night." Loving each other does not have to be intercourse only. Cuddling in each other's arms, touching, kissing, giving or receiving a massage, and simply enjoying each other are very important ways of showing love and feeling close.

As a couple, it is most important to stay in touch with each other's feelings. The concerns that you will have as new parents are not isolated problems; rather they are typical of the challenges you will be facing together throughout your life. If you can both talk about your feelings and physical needs now, you will find that your understanding of each other will enhance your sexual relationship for the rest of your life together. Couples who are honest and patient with each other do not have trouble finding solutions to problems—sexual or otherwise. Talk about your feelings, keep your sense of humor, and look for solutions together. After all, you will be friends and lovers long after your child has grown up and left home.

CONCLUSION

Having a baby is one of life's most exciting adventures. More than any other single act, it will change your life and your lifestyle. The journey begins during pregnancy as you learn new things about your body and your unborn child. The mother-child bond will begin to develop as soon as you are aware of the baby growing within you—and it will continue to blossom with every kick and flutter that you feel. The act of labor and giving birth will help to cement this relationship.

Your commitment to this tiny individual will last throughout her lifetime. Make wise and informed choices right from the start of the pregnancy and continue doing so after your precious child is born. Parenthood is the most important (and most challenging) job that you will ever have. And with the right spirit, attitude, and determination, it can also be the most rewarding.

Glossary

All words that appear in *italic type* are defined within the glossary.

abdomen. The area between the ribs and the *pubic bone.*

abortion. Any termination of pregnancy, either spontaneously (*miscarriage*) or intentionally, before the *fetus* is able to survive outside the *uterus.*

abruptio placentae. See placental abruption.

acquired immune deficiency syndrome (AIDS). A viral disease that attacks the body's natural defenses.

active labor. The second phase of the *first stage of labor.* During this phase, the *cervix* dilates 4 to 8 *centimeters.*

active management of labor. The use of *amniotomy* and *augmentation* to ensure a *labor* that is under twelve hours.

acupressure. The use of fingertip pressure on specific points on the body for the relief of such problems as pain, nausea, and fatigue.

acupuncture. The insertion of fine needles into specific points on the body for the relief of such problems as pain, nausea, and fatigue.

adrenal glands. Two small glands located on the upper part of the kidneys. They are the source of various *hormones,* including the stress hormones epinephrine (adrenaline) and cortisol.

AFP. *See* alpha-fetoprotein.

afterbirth. The *placenta* and surrounding *membranes* that pass from the *uterus* during the *third stage of labor.*

afterpains. Contractions of the *uterus* after giving birth.

AIDS. *See* acquired immune deficiency syndrome.

albumin. A simple protein. When detected through a urine test during pregnancy, albumin may indicate kidney damage or *preeclampsia.*

alpha-fetoprotein (AFP). A protein normally produced by the fetal liver and detected in the woman's blood.

alpha-fetoprotein (AFP) screening. A blood test to screen for open neural tube defects (spina bifida), and chromosomal abnormalities (Down syndrome and Edward syndrome) through the detection of abnormal AFP levels.

alveoli. Cluster of tiny sacs found within the lungs and breasts. In the breasts, they produce milk; in the lungs, they absorb oxygen.

amino acids. The building blocks of protein molecules.

amnihook. Instrument used to perform an *amniotomy.*

amniocentesis. Removal of a small amount of *amniotic fluid,* often to determine fetal age and genetic composition.

amnioinfusion. The technique of infusing saline through an *intrauterine pressure catheter* to provide additional fluid within the *uterus.*

amnion. The innermost *membrane* of the *amniotic sac.*

amniotic fluid. The liquid contained in the *amniotic sac.*

amniotic membranes. Two membrane layers (the *amnion* and the *chorion*) surrounding the *fetus* and the *amniotic fluid.* Also called the *amniotic sac.*

amniotic sac. *See* amniotic membranes.

amniotomy. Artificial rupture of the *amniotic membranes.*

analgesic. A drug that relieves or reduces pain without causing unconsciousness.

anesthetic. An agent that produces loss of sensation with or without loss of consciousness.

angel kisses. *See* stork bites.

anoxia. Deficiency of oxygen.

antibody. A type of protein produced by the immune system to attack harmful *antigens*.

antigen. A foreign substance, such as dust, food, or bacteria, that may be a threat to the health of the body. The presence of antigens stimulates *antibody* production.

antepartum. *See* prenatal.

anus. The rectal opening through which solid waste is eliminated from the body.

Apgar score. An evaluation of the infant's condition at one minute and five minutes after birth.

areola. The pigmented area of the breast surrounding the nipple.

augmentation. The act of speeding up *labor* through various methods, such as the use of *Pitocin* or *amniotomy*.

Babinski toe reflex. A reflex in newborns that causes the toes to fan outward when the sole of the foot is stroked.

baby blues. A temporary period of sadness that may occur after giving birth.

belly button. *See* navel.

beta strep. *See* group B streptococcus.

bilirubin. A product of the breakdown of red blood cells. In newborns, an excess of bilirubin can cause *jaundice*.

biophysical profile. An *ultrasound* test to check for fetal well-being.

birth canal. The passageway through which the baby is born; the *vagina*.

bladder. The reservoir for urine.

blastocyst. A stage in the early development of the *embryo* before *implantation*.

blood pH. Blood alkalinity or acidity.

bloody show. A blood-tinged vaginal discharge that occurs at the beginning of or during *labor*.

bond. The strong attachment that develops between parents and their babies.

Braxton-Hicks contractions. The intermittent and usually painless uterine *contractions* that may occur during pregnancy after the first trimester. Not a sign of true *labor*.

breastfeeding counselor. A volunteer who encourages breastfeeding through telephone consultations and in-group settings.

breech. A fetal *presentation* in which the baby's buttocks or feet are closest to the *cervix*.

caput succedaneum. Swelling of a newborn's scalp caused by pressure during birth.

cardinal movements. The rotations of the baby through the *pelvis*.

catheterization. The insertion of a small pliable tube through the *urethra* to empty the bladder.

centimeter. A unit of measure used to describe progress in the dilation of the *cervix* during *labor*.

cephalhematoma. A collection of blood under a newborn's scalp caused by pressure or trauma during delivery.

cephalic. Pertaining to the head.

certified nurse-midwife (CNM). A registered nurse who has completed an accredited midwifery program and is licensed by the state to manage normal pregnancies and births.

cervix. The narrow necklike end of the *uterus* that leads into the *vagina*. It must thin out and open during *labor* to allow the baby to pass into the *birth canal*.

cesarean birth. *Delivery* of the baby by means of incisions in the abdominal and uterine walls; also called *cesarean section, c-section,* or simply *section*.

cesarean delivery. *See* cesarean birth.

cesarean section. *See* cesarean birth.

chlamydia. A sexually transmitted disease that can be passed to the newborn during a vaginal delivery and cause eye or lung infections.

chorion. The outermost *membrane* of the *amniotic sac*.

chorionic villi. Fingerlike projections covering the developing *embryo* and containing cells with the same genetic composition as the *embryo*.

chorionic villus sampling (CVS). A procedure in which a sample of the *chorionic villi* is removed to determine genetic composition.

cilia. Hairlike projections that propel the *ovum* through the *fallopian tube* toward the *uterus.*

circumcision. Surgical removal of the *foreskin* of the *penis.*

CNM. *See* certified nurse-midwife.

coccyx. The small bone at the end of the spinal column; the tailbone.

colostrum. A sticky yellowish fluid secreted by the breasts in small amounts during late pregnancy and for several days following birth before the mature milk comes in. It is low in fat, and high in carbohydrates, protein, and antibodies.

conception. *Fertilization;* the union of a *sperm* and egg.

congenital. Existing at or before birth; hereditary.

contraceptive. Any method or device used to prevent pregnancy.

contraction. A tightening and shortening of the uterine muscles during *labor* that causes *effacement* and *dilation* of the *cervix,* and encourages the descent of the baby.

contraction stress test. *See* oxytocin challenge test.

cord blood. Blood from the *umbilical cord.*

cord blood banking. The process of collecting and freezing blood from the *umbilical cord* after birth.

cradle cap. A skin condition that appears as flakes, scales, or crusts on the infant's scalp or behind his ears.

crowning. Point during birth when the *presenting part* of the baby (usually the crown of the head) is visible at the vaginal opening and no longer slips back out of sight between *contractions.*

cryobank. A blood bank that freezes and stores blood.

c-section. *See* cesarean birth.

CVS. *See* chorionic villus sampling.

delivery. Birth; the baby's passage from the *uterus* into the external world through the *birth canal* or via *cesarean birth.*

dilation. Gradual opening of the *cervix* through uterine *contractions.* Permits passage of the baby out of the *uterus. Dilation* is complete at 10 *centimeters.*

diuretic. A medication that removes water from the body; commonly called *water pills.*

Doppler. A hand-held device used to listen to the *fetal heart rate.*

doula. A trained *labor* companion.

dry birth. A birth with a decreased amount of *amniotic fluid.* It is a misconception that if the *amniotic membranes* rupture, all the *amniotic fluid* is lost.

due date. The estimated date of birth; also called the *estimated date of confinement (EDC).*

dystocia. An abnormal or prolonged *labor.*

early labor. The first phase of the *first stage of labor,* during which the *cervix* dilates from 0 to 4 *centimeters.*

eclampsia. A serious form of *hypertension* in pregnancy accompanied by convulsions and coma that can occur before, during, or after *delivery.*

EDC. *See* estimated date of confinement.

edema. The presence of excessive fluid in body tissues.

effacement. Thinning and shortening of the *cervix* that occurs before or during *dilation;* expressed in terms of a percentage from 0 to 100.

effleurage. A light fingertip massage of the *abdomen,* buttocks, or thighs that aids relaxation during *labor.*

electronic fetal monitor. *See* fetal monitor.

embolism. An air bubble or blood clot that obstructs a blood vessel.

embryo. Term for a baby during the first eight weeks in the *uterus.*

endorphins. Natural painkillers produced by the body.

enema. A solution that is inserted into the rectum for the purpose of emptying the colon.

engagement. The process in which the baby's *presenting part* becomes secured in the upper opening of the woman's pelvic cavity in preparation for passage through the pelvic bones. It may be felt as *lightening* by the woman.

engorgement. Excessive fullness, usually when referring to the breasts.

epidermal growth factor. A property of breastmilk that promotes cell growth and thickens the intestinal walls to act as a barrier against foreign substances.

epidural anesthesia. The injection of an *anesthetic* into the epidural space, which surrounds the spinal fluid. Causes a complete or partial loss of sensation from the *abdomen* to the toes.

episiotomy. An incision made in the *perineum* to enlarge the vaginal outlet; done prior to *birth*.

erythema toxicum. A harmless newborn skin rash.

estimated date of confinement (EDC). Another term for *due date*.

estriol. An *estrogen-type hormone* made by the *placenta*.

estrogen. A female *hormone* produced in the *ovaries* and *placenta*.

expulsion. The actual movement of the baby through and out of the *birth canal*.

external version. The manual turning of a baby from a *breech* or *transverse lie* to a head-down *presentation*.

fallopian tubes. Two small muscular canals extending from the *uterus* toward the left and right *ovaries*. When an egg is released from an ovary during *ovulation*, it is drawn into one of the tubes and moved toward the *uterus*.

false labor. *See* prelabor.

fertilization. The meeting of a *sperm* and an egg, normally occurring in one of the *fallopian tubes*.

fetal distress. Condition in which the oxygen supply of the *fetus* is threatened; detected by a change in *fetal heart rate* or the presence of *meconium*-stained *amniotic fluid*.

fetal heart rate (FHR). The heartbeat of the *fetus*, normally 120 to 160 beats per minute.

fetal kick count. *See* fetal movement evaluation.

fetal monitor. An electronic machine used to detect and record the *fetal heart rate* in relation to the *contractions* of the *uterus*; also called an *electronic fetal monitor*.

fetal movement evaluation. A method of determining fetal well-being by keeping track of the baby's movements; also called the *fetal kick count*.

fetal scalp sampling. A test during *labor* in which a sample of blood is obtained from the scalp of the *fetus* to determine the *blood pH*.

fetoscope. An instrument used for listening to the *fetal heart rate* and sounds of the *placenta*.

fetus. Term for the baby from the eighth week of pregnancy until birth.

FHR. *See* fetal heart rate.

finger. A unit of measure used to describe the progress of *dilation*. One finger equals 2 *centimeters*.

first stage of labor. The period of *labor* during which the *cervix* dilates to 10 *centimeters*. Includes *early labor, active labor,* and *transition*.

folic acid. An important B vitamin that is believed to help prevent certain birth defects.

fontanels. Two soft areas on the top and back of the baby's head. These spots enable the *molding* that is necessary during a vaginal birth. Also called *soft spots*.

forceps. An obstetrical instrument resembling a pair of tongs that may be used to aid in *delivery*.

foreskin. A fold of skin that covers the head of a *penis*.

fourth stage of labor. The first hours after birth. Also called the *recovery period*.

frenulum. The membrane that connects the tongue to the bottom of the mouth.

fundus. The top or upper portion of the *uterus*.

GBS. *See* group B streptococcus.

general anesthesia. The induction of a state of unconsciousness through the administration of an *anesthetic* drug, which may be inhaled as a gas or delivered *intravenously* as a liquid.

genitals. The external reproductive organs.

gentle birth. *See* Leboyer method.

German measles. *See* rubella.

gestation. The period of development in the *uterus* from conception to birth. For humans, gestation is approximately forty weeks long.

gestational age. The age of the *fetus* as determined from the first day of the last menstrual period.

gestational diabetes. Diabetes that occurs during pregnancy; usually temporary.

glucose tolerance test (GTT). A blood test to screen for diabetes.

gonorrhea. A sexually transmitted disease.

group B strep. *See* group B streptococcus.

group B streptococcus (GBS). A bacterium that causes illness in newborns and pregnant women; also called *beta strep* or *group B strep.*

GTT. *See* glucose tolerance test.

heartburn. A burning sensation in the esophagus caused by the seepage of gastric juices from the stomach.

hemolytic disease of the newborn. A severe illness characterized by massive destruction of red blood cells, usually caused by Rh incompatibility.

hemorrhoids. *Varicose veins* of the *anus;* usually temporary when they first appear during pregnancy.

hepatitis B. A viral infection that is transmitted sexually or through contact with body fluids.

herpes simplex virus II (HSV II). A contagious venereal virus that, if active, can have disastrous effects on the *fetus* during vaginal *delivery.* It is an indication for a *cesarean section.*

high-risk pregnancy. A pregnancy in which the mother and/or baby are believed to be at risk for developing complications.

HIV. *See* human immunodeficiency virus.

hormone. A chemical substance produced by a gland or organ.

HSV II. *See* herpes simplex virus II.

human immunodeficiency virus (HIV). The virus that causes *AIDS.*

hyperglycemia. High blood sugar.

hypertension. High blood pressure.

hypertension in pregnancy. Also known as *pregnancy-induced hypertension,* this metabolic disorder has symptoms that include *hypertension* and *albumin* in the urine. Formerly called *toxemia.*

hyperventilation. Rapid breathing that causes excessive depletion of carbon dioxide in the blood; characterized by dizziness and tingling of the extremities.

hypoglycemia. Low blood sugar.

hypotension. Low blood pressure.

IBCLC. *See* International Board Certified Lactation Consultant.

IgA. *See* secretory immunoglobulin A.

immunity. Resistance to a particular disease.

implantation. The attachment of the fertilized egg to the wall of the *uterus.*

in utero. Within the *uterus.*

incompetent cervix. A *cervix* that begins dilating too early, usually during the second *trimester.*

incontinence. The inability to voluntarily control the flow of urine and waste matter.

induction. The artificial initiation of *labor* through the use of medication or mechanical techniques.

infant screening test. A blood test done on the infant within the first week of life to screen for multiple metabolic diseases. Also includes a hearing test.

International Board Certified Lactation Consultant (IBCLC). A person who has completed a prescribed course of study and is authorized to assist mothers with breastfeeding techniques and concerns.

intradermal. Under the skin.

intrathecal. Into the spine. Used when referring to *spinal anesthesia.*

intrauterine. Within the *uterus.*

intrauterine pressure catheter (IUPC). A catheter that is inserted into the *uterus* for measuring the exact pressure exerted by a *contraction.*

intravenous (IV). In the vein.

intravenous (IV) fluid. A sterile fluid that is fed into the body through a vein for the purpose of nutrition, hydration, or medication.

intubation. The insertion of a breathing tube into the windpipe for the administration of *general anesthesia.*

involution. The process through which the *uterus* returns to its nonpregnant size and position after giving birth; usually takes four to six weeks.

IUPC. *See* intrauterine pressure catheter.

IV. *See* intravenous.

jaundice. Yellow discoloration of the skin and the whites of the eyes due to a high level of *bilirubin.*

Kegel exercises. A set of exercises devised by Dr. Arnold Kegel to strengthen the *pelvic floor* muscles.

labia. The lips or external folds surrounding the *vagina* and *urethra.*

labor. Uterine *contractions* that are productive, causing *effacement* and *dilation* of the *cervix,* and the descent and *expulsion* of the baby.

lactation. The production and secretion of milk by the breasts.

lactation consultant. *See* International Board Certified Lactation Consultant.

lactiferous ducts. Milk ducts.

Lamaze method. A method of childbirth developed by Dr. Fernand Lamaze that involves emotional and physical preparation; also called *psychoprophylaxis.*

lanugo. The fine downy hair on the body of the *fetus* after the fourth month.

Leboyer method. A quiet, peaceful birth experience, designed by Dr. Frederick Leboyer, to reduce birth trauma in infants; also called *gentle birth.*

let-down reflex. The involuntary ejection of milk that occurs during breastfeeding; also called the *milk-ejection reflex.*

leukocytes. White blood cells that attack bacteria.

lightening. The settling of the baby's head downward into the pelvic cavity, one to six weeks before delivery.

linea nigra. A dark vertical line that appears during pregnancy and extends from the navel to the pubic bone.

listeria. A bacterium that can contaminate food and, if ingested, can cause *miscarriages* and stillbirths in pregnant women.

lithotomy. A *delivery position* in which the woman lies on her back, usually with her feet in the stirrups that are located at the bottom of the bed.

local anesthetic. An *anesthetic* designed to numb a specific area; used during childbirth to numb the *perineum* for the repair of the *episiotomy.*

lochia. A discharge of blood, mucus, and tissue that is expelled from the *uterus* after the birth of a baby.

lysozyme. An antibacterial substance found in breastmilk that dissolves bacterial cell walls.

macrosomia. Term used to describe a newborn with an excessive birth weight.

mask of pregnancy. A brownish pigmentation of the forehead, cheeks, and nose that may occur during pregnancy.

mastitis. Inflammation or infection of the breast.

meconium. The dark green or black tarry substance that is present in the baby's large intestine and forms his first stools after birth.

membranes. *See* amniotic membranes.

milia. Immature oil glands that appear as tiny whiteheads on the face of some newborns. They will disappear without any treatment when the glands begin to function.

milk-ejection reflex. *See* let-down reflex.

miscarriage. Premature delivery of a nonviable fetus from the uterus. Also called *spontaneous abortion.*

molding. An elongation of the baby's head as it adjusts to the size and shape of the *birth canal.*

Mongolian spots. A temporary purplish-brown discoloration that is found on the backs of some dark- or olive-skinned babies.

Montgomery glands. Small bumps on the *areola* that enlarge during pregnancy and *lactation.* They secrete a fluid that lubricates and prevents bacterial growth on the nipple and areola.

morbidity. The presence of illness or disease.

morning sickness. The nausea and vomiting some pregnant women experience, mostly during the first *trimester.*

Moro reflex. A reflex that causes a startled infant to open his arms wide and reach forward as if to embrace the person before him.

mortality. Term referring to death.

morula. The cluster of cells resulting from the early division of the fertilized *ovum.*

mucous plug. The heavy collection of mucus that blocks the cervical canal during pregnancy.

multiple pregnancy. A pregnancy in which the woman is carrying more than one baby.

natal. Pertaining to birth or the day of birth.

navel. The site where the *umbilical cord* was attached to the baby in utero; also called the *belly button* or *umbilicus.*

necrotizing enterocolitis. A severe and sometimes fatal bowel condition of *preterm* infants.

neonatal period. The first four weeks of life.

nonstress test. A noninvasive test to help determine fetal well-being.

nuchal fold scan. *See* nuchal translucency screening.

nuchal translucency screening. An ultrasound test to check for chromosomal abnormalities, also called a *nuchal fold scan.*

nursing. Another term for breastfeeding.

obstetrics. Branch of medicine covering the care of women during pregnancy, childbirth, and the *postpartum* period.

occiput. The back area of a baby's head.

OCT. *See* oxytocin challenge test.

ovaries. The two female reproductive glands in which *ova, estrogen,* and *progesterone* are produced.

ovulation. The monthly release of a ripe *ovum* from one of the *ovaries.*

ova. Plural of *ovum.*

ovum. The egg cell produced in one of the *ovaries.*

oxytocin. The *hormone* that stimulates *contractions* of the *uterus* and the *let-down reflex.*

oxytocin challenge test (OCT). A test in which *contractions* are temporarily induced (with *oxytocin*); helps determine how well the baby will undergo the stress of *labor.*

paracervical anesthetic. An *anesthetic* that is injected into the *cervix;* not commonly used.

paraphimosis. The inability to return the *foreskin* of an uncircumcised *penis* to its original position.

patient controlled analgesia (PCA) device. A device that allows the patient to control the *intravenous* administration of narcotics.

PCA device. *See* patient controlled analgesia device.

pelvic floor. The hammock-like ligaments and muscles that support the reproductive organs.

pelvis. The bony structure that joins the spine and legs. In the female, its central opening encases the *uterus, vagina, bladder,* and *rectum.*

penis. The male sex organ.

perineal. Pertaining to the *perineum.*

perineal massage. Massage of the *perineal* tissues.

perineum. The area between the *vagina* and the *anus.*

phenylketonuria (PKU) test. A procedure in which the newborn's blood is screened for a specific *amino acid* deficiency.

phimosis. The inability to pull back the *foreskin* of an uncircumcised *penis.*

phototherapy. The use of ultraviolet light to treat newborn *jaundice.*

physiological. Pertaining to normal body functioning.

pica. An unusual craving or appetite for nonfood items, such as clay or dirt.

PIH. *See* pregnancy-induced hypertension.

Pitocin. An oxytocic *hormone* used to induce or stimulate *contractions* of the *uterus.*

PKU test. *See* phenylketonuria test.

placenta. Temporary organ of pregnancy that exchanges oxygen, nutrients, and waste products between the mother and the *fetus;* part of the *afterbirth.*

placenta previa. A *placenta* that is implanted in the lower *uterine* segment, possibly covering the cervical opening partially or completely.

placental abruption. Premature separation of the *placenta* from the *uterus.*

plantar toe reflex. A reflex in infants that causes the toes to curl when the bottom of the foot is pressed at the base of the toes.

position. The way in which the *presenting part* of the *fetus* is situated in the mother's *pelvis.*

posterior. The fetal *position* in which the back part of the baby's head is against the mother's spine.

postpartum. The time period following birth.

postpartum depression. A prolonged period of melancholy that some women experience after giving birth.

post-term. A pregnancy at forty-two or more weeks *gestation.*

potentiate. To intensify the action of a medication.

precipitate delivery. A sudden and unexpected birth, usually following a very short *labor.*

precipitate labor. A *labor* that is completed within three hours.

preeclampsia. A severe form of *hypertension in pregnancy* that, if left untreated, may lead to *eclampsia.*

pregnancy-induced hypertension (PIH). *See* hypertension in pregnancy.

prelabor. *Uterine contractions* that are strong enough to be interpreted as true *labor,* but that have no dilating effect on the *cervix;* also called *false labor.*

premature. Term referring to an infant weighing less than 2,500 grams (5 pounds 8 ounces) at birth, or to a *delivery* before thirty-seven weeks *gestation;* also called *preterm.*

prenatal. The period of pregnancy from *conception* to birth; also called *antepartum.*

prep. The shaving or trimming of the pubic hair in preparation for the birth.

presentation. The way in which the baby is positioned for birth.

presenting part. The part of the baby that is closest to the *cervix.*

preterm. *See* premature.

progesterone. The *hormone* responsible for building up the *uterine* lining and for maintaining that lining during pregnancy.

prolactin. The *hormone* that stimulates *lactation.*

prostaglandins. A hormone-like substance that is released at the end of pregnancy to *ripen* the *cervix* and cause *contractions.*

psychoprophylaxis. Mind-prevention method of lessening pain awareness. *See also* Lamaze method.

pubic bone. The forward portion of either of the hip bones that forms the pelvic girdle. The pubic bones are connected by the *symphysis pubis* and ligaments, which soften during pregnancy.

pudendal block. The injection of an *anesthetic* into the pudendal nerves, resulting in loss of sensation in the *vagina* and *perineum.*

pulse oximeter. A device placed on the finger to measure the oxygen level in the blood.

quickening. The first movements of the *fetus* felt by the woman, usually between sixteen and eighteen weeks.

recovery period. *See* fourth stage of labor.

rectum. The lower part of the large intestine.

relaxin. The *hormone* that helps relax the pelvic ligaments and other joints during pregnancy.

Rh factor. A blood factor found in the red blood cells and present in 85 percent of the population. It is expressed as "Rh-positive" if present and "Rh-negative" if absent.

Rh-immune globulin. A medication (RhoGAM) given to an Rh-negative woman within seventy-two hours of giving birth to an Rh-positive baby, after having an *abortion,* or after undergoing *amniocentesis.* It is given to prevent her body from producing *antibodies* that could endanger subsequent babies.

RhoGAM. *See* Rh-immune globulin.

ripen. Term that refers to the softening of the *cervix,* which occurs when it is ready for the onset of *labor.*

rooming-in. An arrangement in which a mother and her baby stay in the same hospital room for extended periods, rather than just for feedings.

rooting reflex. The instinctive movement of the baby's head and mouth toward a touch on the cheek or mouth.

round ligaments. The two ligaments that are the main support of the uterus.

rubella. Also called German measles, this viral infection is transmitted through respiratory contact with an infected person. If contracted during pregnancy, the developing baby can be seriously affected.

sacrum. The triangular bone situated below the last spinal vertebra and above the *coccyx.*

saddle block. The injection of an *anesthetic* into the lower spinal canal causing a loss of sensation from the pubic area to the toes; not commonly used.

scopolamine. A medication used for its amnesic effects; also called scope; rarely used.

scrotum. External sac of skin in males that contains the testes.

second stage of labor. The period of *labor* from *complete dilation* through the birth of the baby.

secretory immunoglobulin A (IgA). An *immunity*-inducing substance contained in breastmilk.

section. *See* cesarean birth.

sibling. A brother or sister.

sickle cell anemia. Inherited blood disorder common in African Americans and descendants from the Caribbean, Central and South America, and the Mediterranean.

SIDS. *See* sudden infant death syndrome.

soft spots. *See* fontanels.

sonogram. *See* ultrasound.

sperm. The male reproductive cell produced in the *testes*.

sphincter. A ringlike muscle that closes a natural body opening, such as the *anus* and *urethra*.

spinal anesthesia. The injection of an *anesthetic* into the spinal fluid, causing a loss of sensation.

spontaneous abortion. *See* miscarriage.

station. The location of the baby's *presenting part* in relation to the woman's pelvic bones.

stem cells. Immature blood cells.

stork bites. A reddened area on a newborn's skin caused by capillaries close to the skin; also called *angel kisses*.

stretch marks. *See* striae gravidarium.

striae gravidarum. Pinkish or purplish lines that may appear on the *abdomen* and breasts during pregnancy; also called *stretch marks*.

stripping the membranes. The procedure in which the *amniotic membranes* are pulled away from the *cervix* to induce *labor*.

sudden infant death syndrome (SIDS). The unexplained death of a baby under one year of age.

Super Kegel. A more effective type of *Kegel exercise*.

supine hypotension. Low blood pressure when lying down.

symphysis pubis. The cartilage that connects the *pubic bones* and softens during pregnancy.

Tay-Sachs disease. Progressive neurological genetic disorder most common among people of Eastern European ancestry and Askhenazi Jewish descent.

temporal artery thermometer. Type of thermometer that is moved across the forehead and determines body temperature through blood flow.

TENS unit. *See* transcutaneous electrical nerve stimulation unit.

term. The completed cycle of pregnancy; full term is forty weeks.

testes. The two organs that are located in the *scrotum* and produce *sperm*.

tetanic contraction. *Uterine contraction* that is extremely long and strong; often associated with induced *labor*.

thalassemia. Diverse group of genetic blood diseases resulting in varying degrees of anemia.

third stage of labor. The period of *labor* from the birth of the baby through the *delivery* of the *placenta*.

tocolytic drug. A type of medication used to stop *contractions* of the *uterus*.

tonic neck reflex. A reflex in infants that causes them to assume a fencing position when lying on their backs.

toxemia. *See* hypertension in pregnancy.

toxoplasmosis. A disease that is spread primarily through the waste products of cats; can be harmful during pregnancy.

tranquilizer. A medication that relieves anxiety.

transcutaneous electrical nerve stimulation (TENS) unit. A small battery-operated device used for pain relief.

transition. The last phase of the *first stage of labor*, during which the *cervix* dilates from 8 to 10 *centimeters*.

transverse lie. A fetal *presentation* in which the baby lies sideways in the uterus.

trimester. A period of three months.

tympanic thermometer. A thermometer that records body temperature via the ear.

ultrasound. High frequency sound waves used for diagnostic purposes; also called a *sonogram*.

umbilical cord. Cordlike structure containing two arteries and one vein that connects the baby and the placenta.

umbilicus. *See* navel.

urethra. The tube that carries the urine from the bladder to the outside of the body.

uterine. Referring to the *uterus*.

uterus. The muscular pear-shaped organ of *gestation;* also called the *womb*.

vacuum extractor. A suction device used to assist in the *delivery* of the baby's head.

vagina. The curved, very elastic canal, measuring four to six inches long, between the *uterus* and the *vulva*.

Valsalva maneuver. Long breath-holding and forceful pushing during the *second stage of labor*.

varicose veins. Unnaturally distended veins, commonly found during pregnancy in the legs, *vulva,* and *anus*.

vernix caseosa. White creamy protective coating that covers the baby's skin in utero.

vertex. The crown (or top area) of the head.

viability. The ability to survive outside the *uterus*.

vibroacoustic stimulation test (VST). A *nonstress test* that determines fetal well-being through stimulation with a buzzing sound.

visualization. The formation of a mental image.

VST. *See* vibroacoustic stimulation test.

vulva. The external female reproductive organs, consisting of the clitoris and the *labia*.

walking epidural. An *epidural* in which narcotics are used, but without affecting motor sensations; with this type of epidural, the woman is able to walk during labor.

water intoxication. A serious complication that occurs if large amounts of electrolyte-free *intravenous fluids* are infused or too much water is ingested.

water pills. *See* diuretic.

Wharton's jelly. The gel-like substance surrounding the vessels of the *umbilical cord*.

womb. *See* uterus.

Trimester Checklists

FIRST TRIMESTER

____ Contact your insurance company for coverage; discover any restrictions.

____ Tour local birth centers and hospitals.

____ Choose your caregiver.

____ Attend an early pregnancy class.

____ Visit your dentist for a cleaning.

____ Enroll in a prenatal exercise or yoga class.

____ Take your dog for obedience training or reinforce prior training.

____ Start a memory book about your pregnancy.

____ Take photos of your newly pregnant body for your memory book.

SECOND TRIMESTER

____ Continue exercising.

____ Start to prepare older siblings for the new arrival.

____ Interview and hire a doula for labor and the postpartum period.

____ Take photos of your changing body.

THIRD TRIMESTER

_____ Enroll in childbirth preparation classes.

_____ Take a breastfeeding class.

_____ Take your other children to a sibling preparation class.

_____ Encourage your parents to attend a class for grandparents.

_____ Continue taking photos of your changing body.

_____ Do a belly casting.

_____ Prepare the nursery and set up supplies for the baby.

_____ Start to baby proof your home.

_____ Make a trial run to the hospital and find alternate routes.

_____ Choose a pediatrician.

_____ Preregister at the hospital.

_____ Arrange for cord blood banking.

_____ Perform "fetal kick counts."

_____ Pack your bags—for labor and for your hospital stay.

_____ Install the car safety seat and have it checked by someone who is certified.

_____ Arrange for postpartum help.

_____ Make a list of household chores for family and friends who offer to help.

_____ Decide on a name for your baby.

_____Practice relaxation and breathing exercises daily.

Resources

Childbirth Connection
281 Park Avenue South, 5th Floor
New York, NY 10010
Phone: 212-777-5000
Fax: 212-777-9320
Website: www.childbirthconnection.org

Founded in 1918 as Maternity Center Association, Childbirth Connection is a national organization whose mission is to improve the quality of maternity care through research, education, advocacy, and policy. It promotes safe, effective, and satisfying evidence-based maternity care.

Coalition for Improving Maternity Services (CIMS)
PO Box 2346
Ponte Vedra Beach, FL 32004
Phone: 888-282-CIMS (2467)
        904-285-1613
Fax: 904-285-2120
Website: www.motherfriendly.org

The focus of this volunteer-based coalition of individuals and organizations is the care and well-being of mothers, babies, and families. CIMS developed the Mother-Friendly Childbirth Initiative, an evidence-based model that outlines and promotes the principles and practices of maternity care to improve birth outcomes and substantially reduce costs. This initiative, which has been endorsed by over fifty organizations representing over 90,000 members, provides guidelines for identifying and designating "mother-friendly" birth sites, including hospitals, birth centers, and home-birth services.

DONA International
PO Box 626
Jasper, IN 47547
Phone: 888-788-DONA (3662)
Fax: 812-634-1491
Website: www.dona.org

Formerly Doulas of North America, DONA International is the largest association of doulas in the world. It provides quality training and certification for doulas, while offering information to the public on childbirth and the postpartum experience. DONA also provides a doula referral service.

Infant Massage USA
7481 Huntsman Blvd, Suite 635
Springfield, VA 22153
Phone: 800-497-5996
        703-455-3455
Website: www.infantmassageusa.org

This group, which offers infant massage training programs, is the United States chapter of the International Association of Infant Massage (IAIM). Its mission is "To promote nurturing touch through training, education, and research so that babies, parents, and caregivers are loved, valued, and respected throughout the world community."

March of Dimes
1275 Mamaroneck Avenue
White Plains, NY 10605
Phone: 914-997-4488
Website: www.marchofdimes.com

Established in 1938 by President Franklin D. Roosevelt, the

March of Dimes began as the National Foundation for Infantile Paralysis to fund research in the fight against polio. Since the development of the Salk vaccine, the focus of this organization has been on preventing birth defects and premature birth through cutting-edge research, innovative programs, community service, education, and advocacy.

National Institute of Child Health and Human Development (NICHD)

31 Center Drive
MSC-2425, Room 2A32
Bethesda, MD 20892-2425
Phone: 800-370-2943
     301-496-5133
TTY: 888-320-6942
Fax: 301-496-7101
SIDS Information Line: 800-505-CRIB (2742)
Website: www.nichd.nih.gov/

A division of the National Institutes of Health, the NICHD conducts and supports clinical research involving all stages of human development from preconception to adulthood. Its extensive database provides information on such topics as family planning, fertility and infertility, birth defects, breastfeeding, sudden infant death syndrome, infant health, childhood diseases, genetics, and nutrition.

National Newborn Screening and Genetics Resource Center (NNSGRC)

1912 West Anderson Lane, Suite 210
Austin, TX 78757
Phone: 512-454-6419
Fax: 512-454-6509
Website: http://genes-r-us.uthscsa.edu/

In addition to supplying information in the areas of newborn screening and genetics, this national resource center provides a listing of the newborn tests that are required in each state. If your state does not have expanded testing and you want your newborn to have additional tests done, the NNSGRC offers a list of commercial and nonprofit laboratories to contact.

CHILDBIRTH EDUCATION

American Academy of Husband-Coached Childbirth

Box 5224
Sherman Oaks, CA 91413-5224
Phone: 800-4-A-BIRTH (800-422-4784)

Website: www.bradleybirth.com

Through a series of small comprehensive classes led by certified instructors, this organization offers training on the Bradley Method of natural childbirth. Women learn how to work with their bodies to reduce pain and experience efficient labor. In addition, classes cover the coach's role, exercise during pregnancy, nutrition, possible complications, cesarean birth, postpartum care, breastfeeding, and baby care.

American Association of Birth Centers (AABC)

3123 Gottschall Road
Perkiomenville, PA 18074
Phone: 866-54-BIRTH (866-542-4784)
     215-234-8068
Fax: 215-234-8829
Website: www.birthcenters.org

A comprehensive resource on birth centers, this organization—formerly the National Association of Childbearing Centers—is also an informative source on birth, labor, delivery, and women's healthcare and reproduction issues. It is an association for parents and parents-to-be, as well as healthcare workers and professionals who specialize in prenatal and postnatal care. Provides a list of birth centers throughout the United States.

American College of Nurse-Midwives (ACNM)

8403 Colesville Road, Suite 1550
Silver Spring MD 20910
Phone: 888-MIDWIFE (888-643-9433)
     240-485-1800
Fax: 240-485-1818
Website: www.midwife.org

Established in 1929, the American College of Nurse-Midwives is the oldest women's healthcare organization in the United States. It promotes the health and well-being of women and infants through the development and support of certified midwives and nurse-midwives. Its "Find a Midwife" service helps consumers and healthcare professionals locate midwives in their area.

Hypnobabies

7108 Katella Avenue, Suite 241
Stanton, CA 90680
Phone: 714-898-BABY (2229)
Website: www.hypnobabies.com

"No drugs for baby; no pain for mommy" is the goal of Hypnobabies—a complete childbirth education course that offers

medical hypnosis techniques for creating a peaceful, relaxing pregnancy; a calm, confident Hypno-Daddy; and an easier, fearless, often pain-free birthing. Provides a listing of local instructors, as well as materials for a home-study course.

HypnoBirthing

PO Box 810
Epsom, NH 03234 USA
Phone: 603-798-3286
Website: www.hypnobirthing.com

Based upon the techniques of natural childbirth pioneer Dr. Grantly Dick-Read, HypnoBirthing—The Mongan Method—was developed by certified hypnotherapist Marie Mongan. Through this method, women learn deep relaxation and self-hypnosis, visualization, guided imagery, and breathing techniques to achieve a gentle birth while alert and in control. Offers information about classes and maternal services, as well as books, audiotapes, and other material.

International Cesarean Awareness Network (ICAN)

1304 Kingsdale Avenue
Redondo Beach, CA 90278
Phone: 800-686-ICAN (4226)
Fax: 310-697-3056
Website: www.ican-online.org

Formerly the Cesarean Prevention Movement, the International Cesarean Awareness Network is a nonprofit organization whose mission is to improve maternal-child health by preventing unnecessary cesareans. It accomplishes this goal through education, by providing support for cesarean recovery, and by promoting Vaginal Birth After Cesarean (VBAC).

International Childbirth Education Association (ICEA)

PO Box 20048
Minneapolis, MN 55420
Phone: 952-854-8660
Fax: 952-854-8772
Website: www.icea.org

The International Childbirth Education Association is a federation of groups and individuals who believe in the promotion of family-centered maternity and infant care. It does not encourage a specific method of childbirth preparation, but rather promotes freedom of choice based on the knowledge of alternative methods. The ICEA provides training and certification in childbirth education, postnatal education, perinatal fitness, and doula and labor support.

Lamaze International

2025 M Street, Suite 800
Washington, DC 20036-3309
Phone: 800-368-4404
          202-367-1128
Website: www.lamaze.org

Formerly the American Society for Psychoprophylaxis in Obstetrics, Lamaze International promotes, supports, and protects normal birth—one that occurs naturally, free of unnecessary interventions. Childbirth educators, labor support specialists, lactation consultants, midwives, physicians, and parents are among its members. Provides a list of local Lamaze instructors.

Waterbirth International

PO Box 1400
Wilsonville, OR 97070
Phone: 800-641-BABY (2229)
          503-673-0026
Fax: 503-673-0029
Website: www.waterbirth.org

Part of the larger Global Maternal/Child Health Association, Waterbirth International was founded in 1988 to promote waterbirth as an available childbirth option for all women. It provides education, training, consultations, programs, and practitioner referrals for parents and healthcare professionals alike. Also offers books, videos, and portable pool sales and rentals.

BREASTFEEDING

Human Milk Banking Association of North America (HMBANA)

1500 Sunday Drive, Suite 102
Raleigh, NC 27607
Phone: 919-787-5181
Website: www.hmbana.org

The Human Milk Banking Association of North America is a multidisciplinary group of healthcare providers that promotes, protects, and supports donor milk banking. The only professional membership association for milk banks in the United States, Canada, and Mexico, HMBANA sets the standards and guidelines for donor milk banking. It also offers information to the general public and healthcare providers on the subject, as well as how to contact a milk bank, how to donate milk, and how to order donor milk.

International Lactation Consultants Association (ILCA)

1500 Sunday Drive, Suite 102
Raleigh, NC 27607
Phone: 919-861-5577
Fax: 919-787-4916
Website: www.ilca.org

International Lactation Consultants Association is the professional association for International Board Certified Lactation Consultants—healthcare professionals who specialize in the clinical management of breastfeeding. Its mission is to advance the profession of lactation consulting through leadership, advocacy, professional development, and research. ILCA provides referrals to board certified lactation consultants in the United States and countries throughout the world.

La Leche League International (LLLI)

957 North Plum Grove Road
Schaumburg, IL 60173
Phone: 800-LA-LECHE (800-525-3243)
        847-519-7730
Fax: 847-969-0460
TTY: 847-592-7570
Website: www.lalecheleague.org

The mission of La Leche League International is to help women breastfeed through personal mother-to-mother support, encouragement, information, and education. This organization had its unplanned start in 1956 when a small group of women came together to encourage the practice of breastfeeding at a time when formula-feeding was the norm. Today, LLLI has over 3,000 groups in sixty-seven countries. Contact them to find a local chapter.

CORD BLOOD BANKING

CorCell, Inc.

1717 Arch Street, Suite 1410
Philadelphia, PA 19103
Phone: 888-326-7235
Fax: 215-864-0312
Website: www.corcell.com

CorCell was the first private family cord blood bank licensed for cord blood preservation, and provides services nationwide for private storage. It processes and stores the blood under FDA requirements using the high standards of Good Manufacturing Practice.

Cord Blood Donor Foundation (CBDF)

1200 Bayhill Drive, Suite 301
San Bruno, CA 94066
Phone: 650-635-1452
Fax: 650-635-1428
Website: www.CordBloodDonor.org

The Cord Blood Donor Foundation is dedicated to promoting the research of umbilical blood stem cell usage for the treatment of disease. It accepts cord blood donations for unrelated transplants and further research at no cost to you.

Cord Blood Registry (CBR)

1200 Bayhill Drive, Suite 301
San Bruno, CA 94066
Phone: 800-844-2202
Wesite: www.cordblood.com

The Cord Blood Registry is the world's largest family cord blood stem cell bank.

Cryobanks International

270 Northlake Boulevard, Suite 1000
Altamonte Springs, FL 32701
Phone: 800-869-8608
        407-834-8333
Fax: 407-834-3533
Website: www.cryo-intl.com

Cryobanks offers private storage for families who wish to store their baby's stem cells, as well as a public cord blood donation program for those who prefer to donate.

Cryo-Cell International

700 Boulder Creek Boulevard, Suite 1800
Olsdsmar, FL 34677
Phone: 800-STOR-CELL (800-786-7235)
Fax: 813-855-4745
Website: www.cryo-cell.com

Cryo-Cell is one of the world's largest and most established family cord blood storage banks. Call to speak with a nurse twenty-four hours a day, seven days a week, or visit its website for a live online chat.

National Marrow Donor Program (NMDP)

3001 Broadway Street NE, Suite 100
Minneapolis, MN 55413-1753
Phone: 800-MARROW2 (800-627-7692)
Website: www.marrow.org

Through its Registry, the National Marrow Donor Program provides searching patients with access to more than 10 million donors and cord blood units throughout the world.

ViaCord
245 First Street
Cambridge, MA 02142
Phone: 866-668-4895
Fax: 866-565-2243
Website: www.viacord.com.

In addition to being a cord blood banking facility, ViaCord is a recognized leader in cord blood research.

POISON CONTROL

Poison Control Emergency Hotline
800-222-1222

National Lead Information Center (NLIC)
422 South Clinton Avenue
Rochester, NY 14620
Phone: 800-424-LEAD (5323)
Website: www.epa.gov/lead/pubs/nlic.htm

The NLIC provides the general public and professionals with information about lead hazards and their prevention. It operates under the US Environmental Protection Agency (EPA), with funding from the EPA, the Centers for Disease Control and Prevention, and the Department of Housing and Urban Development. Call to speak with a specialist Monday through Friday, 8 am to 6 pm EST. You can also leave a recorded message in English or Spanish twenty-four hours a day, seven days a week.

EMERGENCY FIRST-AID INSTRUCTION

American Heart Association (AHA)
National Center
7272 Greenville Avenue
Dallas, TX 75231
Phone: 800-AHA-USA-1 (800-242-8721)
Website: www.americanheart.org

The American Heart Association, whose mission is to build healthier lives that are free of cardiovascular disease and stroke, offers training classes for infant cardiopulmonary resuscitation (CPR). It also offers the "Infant CPR Anytime Personal Learning Program"—a kit containing everything needed to learn the basics of infant CPR and relief of choking. Developed in coordination with the American Academy of Pediatrics, the kit allows families, friends, grandparents, siblings, and others who care for infants to learn the core skills of these lifesaving methods in just twenty-two minutes.

American Red Cross
2025 E Street, NW
Washington, DC 20006
Phone: 202-303-4498
Website: www.redcross.org

Founded in 1881, the American Red Cross is the nation's premier emergency response organization. It prepares people to save lives through health and safety education and training. From first aid and cardiopulmonary resuscitation (CPR)—including infant CPR—to swimming and lifeguarding, HIV/AIDS education, and Babysitter's Training, the American Red Cross Preparedness programs have helped people lead safer, healthier lives. Contact them for local chapters.

PRODUCT SAFETY

Auto Safety Hotline
888-DASH-2-DOT (888-327-4236)
Website: www-odi.nhtsa.dot.gov/ivoq/

When purchasing a used car safety seat, call the Auto Safety Hotline to determine if that particular model has been recalled. This hotline is sponsored by the National Highway Traffic Safety Administration.

Consumer Product Safety Commission (CPSC)
4330 East West Highway
Bethesda, MD 20814
Phone: 301-504-7923
Fax: 301-504-0124
Consumer Hotline: 800-638-2772
TTY: 800-638-8270
Website: www.cpsc.gov

The US Consumer Product Safety Commission protects the public from unreasonable risks of serious injury or death from more than 15,000 types of consumer products that pose a fire, electrical, chemical, or mechanical hazard, or that can injure children (toys, cribs, baby furniture). To obtain product safety information or to report any unsafe products, call the Consumer Hotline Monday through Friday, 8:30 am to 5:00 pm EST. You can also leave a recorded message in English or Spanish twenty-four hours a day, seven days a week.

MedWatch

Food and Drug Administration

5600 Fishers Lane

Rockville, MD 20857

Phone: 800-FDA-1088 (800-332-1088)

Website: www.fda.gov/medwatch

MedWatch is the FDA Safety Information and Adverse Event Reporting Program. If you have a complaint about an infant formula or if you are concerned that your baby has become ill from formula, report the problem to MedWatch.

SeatCheck

866-SEAT-CHECK (866-732-8243)

Website: www.seatcheck.org

The SeatCheck Program was created in 2002 by Chrysler, the National Highway Traffic Safety Administration, the National Safety Council, Graco Children's Products, Toys "R" Us, and Babies "R" Us. Its mission is to reduce the number of children who are hurt or killed in killed in car accidents due to improperly installed car safety seats. SeatCheck promotes the proper inspection of car safety seats by qualified Child Passenger Safety (CPS) technicians. Inspections are free and available at over 4,000 locations.

Window Covering Safety Council (WCSC)

355 Lexington Avenue, Suite 1500

New York, NY 10017

Phone: 800-506-4636

          212-297-2109

Fax: 212-370-9047

Website: www.windowcoverings.org

The Window Covering Safety Council (WCSC) is a coalition of major US manufacturers, importers, and retailers of window coverings dedicated to educating consumers about window cord safety. Mini blinds and window treatments with cords made before 2001 should be replaced or repaired to avoid potential strangulation hazards. Free retrofit kits can be ordered through WCSC.

MULTIPLE BIRTHS

National Organization of Mothers of Twins Clubs (NOMOTC)

PO Box 700860

Plymouth, MI 48170-0955

Phone: 877-540-2200

          248-231-4480

Website: www.nomotc.org

This national network of more than 450 local clubs represents over 25,000 individual parents of multiples (twins, triplets, quadruplets, and more). It is dedicated to supporting families of multiple birth children through education, research, and networking.

The Triplet Connection

PO Box 429

Spring City, UT 84662

Phone: 435-851-1105

Fax: 435-462-7466

Website: www.tripletconnection.org

The Triplet Connection is an international "network of caring and sharing for multiple birth families." It offers support and resources to parents (and expectant parents) of triplets and other multiples. It also has the world's largest database of medical information regarding triplets and higher-order multiple births.

AUTISM

Autism Speaks

2 Park Avenue, 11th Floor

New York, NY 10016

Phone: 212-252-8584

Fax: 212-252-8676

Website: www.autismspeaks.org

Founded in 2005, Autism Speaks is dedicated to funding biomedical research into the causes, prevention, treatment, and cure for autism. It is also focused on raising public awareness of autism and bringing hope to all who deal with it.

First Signs, Inc.

PO Box 358

Merimac, MA 01860

Phone: 978-346-4380

Fax: 978-346-4638

Website: www.firstsigns.org

A national nonprofit organization founded in 1998, First Signs is dedicated to educating parents and pediatric professionals about the early warning signs of autism.

BEREAVEMENT

Compassionate Friends

PO Box 3696

Oak Brook, IL 60522-3696

Phone: 877-969-0010
      630-990-0010
Fax: 630-990-0246
Website: www.compassionatefriends.org

A national nonprofit, self-help support organization, Compassionate Friends assists families that have lost a child of any age. It offers friendship, understanding, and hope to bereaved parents, grandparents, and siblings.

First Candle

1314 Bedford Avenue, Suite 210
Baltimore, MD 21208
Phone: 800-221-7437
      410-653-8226
Websites: www.firstcandle.org
         www.sidsalliance.org

First Candle started as the National SIDS Foundation, whose primary focus was supporting families that had lost babies from sudden infant death syndrome. The organization changed its name in 2002, when it broadened its mission to address all areas of infant death, including stillbirth and miscarriage. Bilingual crisis counselors are available twenty-four hours a day, seven days a week.

DOMESTIC VIOLENCE

Domestic Violence Hotline

800-799-SAFE (7233)
TTY: 800-787-3224

National Coalition Against Domestic Violence (NCADV)

1120 Lincoln Street, Suite 1603
Denver, CO 80203
Phone: 303-839-1852
Fax: 303-831-9251

TTY: 303-839-1681

Formally organized in 1978, the NCADV is the only national organization of grassroots shelter and service programs for battered women. Its programs support battered women of all racial, social, religious, and economic groups; ages; and lifestyles.

FAMILY PLANNING

Emergency Contraception Hotline

888-NOT-2-LATE (888-668-2528)

The Association of Reproductive Health Professionals (ARHP)

2401 Pennsylvania Avenue NW, Suite 350
Washington, DC 20037
Phone: 202-466-3825
Fax: 202-466-3826
Website: www.arhp.org

Comprised of highly qualified experts in the field of reproduction, the Association of Reproductive Health Professionals is a "leading source of trusted clinical education and information on reproductive and sexual health."

Planned Parenthood Foundation of America (PPFA)

434 West 33rd Street
New York, NY 10001
Phone: 800-230-PLAN (7526)
      212-541-7800
Fax: 212-245-1845
Website: www.plannedparenthood.org

The nation's leading women's healthcare provider, educator, and advocate, Planned Parenthood has over 860 affiliated health centers throughout the country. It offers high-quality family planning and reproductive healthcare to women, men, and teens.

Notes

Chapter 1. Birth, Your Way

1. "Fact Sheet—CNM-Attended Births Still on the Rise!" American College of Nurse-Midwives website, updated March 1, 2004. www.midwife.org

2. "New Crop of Midwives Shatter Stereotype," *The Florida Times-Union,* 22 October 1996.

3. Judith P. Rooks, *Journal of Nurse-Midwifery* Vol 44, No 4 (July/August 1999), p. 370.

4. "ICEA Position Statement and Review: The Birth Place," *International Journal of Childbirth Education* Vol 17, No 1, ICEA, Inc., Minnesota (2002), p. 38.

5. Ibid: p. 36.

6. Ibid: p. 39.

7. "Home Birth as Safe as Hospital Delivery for Low-Risk Pregnancies," *British Medical Journal* 330 (June 16, 2005): 1416–1419.

Chapter 2. Pregnancy

1. Marshall H. Klaus and Phyllis H. Klaus, *Your Amazing Newborn.* Read, MA: Perseus Books, 1998, p. 47.

2. Ibid: p. 5.

3. Ibid: p. 5.

4. "Ginger Supplement Helps Relieve Pregnancy-Related Nausea and Vomiting," American College of Obstetrics and Gynecology News Release (March 29, 2004). www.acog.org

Chapter 3. Questions and Concerns

1. "Seatbelts Greatly Reduce Harm to Pregnant Drivers and Fetuses During Car Crashes," American College of Obstetrics and Gynecology News Release (July 31, 2003). www.acog.org

2. Kim A. Boggess, Susi Lieff, Amy P. Murtha, Kevin Moss, James Beck, and Steven Offenbacher, "Maternal Periodontal Disease is Associated with an Increased Risk for Preeclampsia," *American College of Obstetrics and Gynecology Green Journal* Vol 101, No 2 (February 2003), p. 227. www.acog.org

3. "Ante Partum Dental Radiography and Infant Low Birth Weight," *Journal of the American Medical Association,* American Dental Association News Release (April 28, 2004). www.ada.org/public/media/releases/0404_release03.asp

4. L.B. Signorello and J.K. McLaughlin, "Maternal caffeine consumption and spontaneous abortion: a review of the epidemiologic evidence," *Epidemiology* 15(2), (2004 March): 229–239.

5. B. Eskenazi, A.L. Stapleton, M. Kharrazi, WY Chee, "The association between maternal decaffeinated and caffeinated coffee consumption and fetal growth and gestation duration." *Epidemiology* 155(5), (1999): 429–436, as reported in March of Dimes Fact Sheet 2004, p. 2.

6. B. Clausson, F. Granath, A. Ekbom, S. Lundgren, A. Nordmark, L.B. Signorello, S. Cnattingius. "Effect of caffeine exposure during pregnancy on birth weight and gestational age," *American Journal of Epidemiology* 155(5), (2002): 429–436.

7. B. Eskenazi, "Caffeine—filtering the facts," *The New England Journal of Medicine* 341(22), (1999): 688–689, as reported in March of Dimes Fact Sheet 2004.

8. Ibid.

9. Gerald G. Briggs, Roger K. Freeman, and Sumner J.Yaffe, *Drugs in Pregnancy and Lactation,* 5th edition. Baltimore: Williams and Wilkins, 1998, p. 72a.

10. John Henkel. "Sugar Substitutes: Americans Opt for Sweetness and Lite," (1999). www.fda.gov/fdac/

11. National Toxicology Program Report on Carcinogens, Subcommittee Meeting Oct. 30–31, 1997. http://ntp-server.niehs.nih.gov

12. Ibid.

13. Michael B. Bracken, et al, "Asthma Symptoms, Severity, and Drug Therapy: A Prospective Study of Effects on 2,205 Pregnancies," *Obstetrics & Gynecology* Vol 102(4), (October 2003): 730–752.

14. "Accutane and Other Retinoids," March of Dimes Fact Sheet 2004, March of Dimes Birth Defects Foundation website, p. 1. www.marchofdimes.com

15. Ibid: p. 3.

16. Ibid: p. 2.

17. Ibid: p. 2.

18. Gerald G. Briggs, Roger K. Freeman, and Sumner J.Yaffe, *Drugs in Pregnancy and Lactation,* 5th edition. Baltimore: Williams and Wilkins, 1998, p. 128/c.

19. Li-Xing Man and Benjamin Chang, "Maternal Cigarette Smoking during Pregnancy Increases the Risk of Having a Child with a Congenital Digital Anomaly," *Plastic & Reconstructive Surgery* 117(1) (January 2006): 301–308.

20. "California Birth Defects Monitoring Program Fact Sheet on Smoking." www.cbdmp.org

21. "Smoking Can Raise SIDS Risk," *The Orlando Sentinel,* 8 March 1995.

22. Xiao-ou Shu, Julie A. Ross, et al, "Parental Alcohol Consumption, Cigarette Smoking, and Risk of Infant Leukemia: a Children's Cancer Group Study," *Journal of the National Cancer Institute* Vol 88, No 1 (January 3, 1996), pp. 24–31.

23. "New Study Finds Babies Born To Mothers Who Drink Alcohol Heavily May Suffer Permanent Nerve Damage," The National Institutes of Child Health and Human Development Press Release (March 8, 2004). www.nichd.nih.gov

24. "US Surgeon General Releases Advisory on Alcohol Use in Pregnancy," US Department of Health and Human Services News Release (February 21, 2005). www.hhs.gov/surgeongeneral/pressreleases/sg02222005.html

25. "Cocaine Follow-up," *Childbirth Instructor Magazine* (Winter 2004), p. 8.

26. "CPSC Warns About Hazards of 'Do it Yourself" Removal of Lead Based Paint: Safety Alert," CPSC Document #5055. www.cpsc.gov/CPSCPUB/PUBS/5055.html

Chapter 4. Prenatal Care and Testing

1. "Limb-Reduction Defects and Chorion Villus Sampling," *The Lancet* (4 May 1991), pp. 1091–1092.

2. "Multiple marker screening (AFP)," (October 15, 2004). www.BabyCenter.com

3. "Prudent Use," American Institute of Ultrasound in Medicine Official Statement (May 2, 1999). www.aium.org/publication/statements

4. Bernard G. Ewigman, et al., "Effect of Prenatal Ultrasound Screening on Perinatal Outcome," *The New England Journal of Medicine* 329 (16 September 1993), p. 821.

5. "New Marker for Preterm Labor," *Childbirth Instructor Magazine* (First Quarter 1996), p. 7.

6. Ronald S. Gibbs, "Herpes simplex virus infection in pregnancy," *Infection Protocols for Obstetrics and Gynecology.* Montvale, NJ: Medical Economics Publishing, 1992, p. 85.

7. Brent Laartz, "Viral Infections and Pregnancy," eMedicine. com, Inc., updated July 19, 2004.

8. Ibid.

9. Stanley A. Gall, "Human papillomavirus infection," *Infection Protocols for Obstetrics and Gynecology.* Montvale, NJ: Medical Economics Publishing, 1992, p. 215.

10. "Infectious Diseases During Pregnancy: Expanding Prevention and Treatments," American College of Obstetrics and Gynecology News Release (December 12, 2001). www.acog.org

11. Larry C. Gilstrap III and George D. Wendel, Jr., "Syphilis in pregnancy," *Infection Protocols for Obstetrics and Gynecology.* Montvale, NJ: Medical Economics Publishing, 1992, p. 53–54.

12. "Baby Poisoned by Food Spurs Couple's Crusade," *New York Post,* 18 August 1977.

13. "Lymphocytic choriomeningitis," CDC Fact Sheet. www.cdc.gov/ncidod/dvrd/spb/mnpages/dispages/Fact_Sheets/Lymphocytic_Choriomeningitis_Fact_Sheet.pdf

14. Stephanie Schrag, D. Phil, Rachel Gorwitz, Kristi Fultz-Butts, and Anne Schuchat, "Prevention of Perinatal Group B Streptococcal Disease, 2002 Revised Guidelines from CDC." www.cdc.gov/groupbstrep

15. Ibid.

16. Ibid.

17. Ibid.

18. "Lyme Disease Treatment and Prognosis," CDC website. www.cdc.gov/ncidod/dvbid/lyme/ld_humandisease_treatment.htm

19. Christine L. Williams and Peter Welch, "Lyme disease in pregnancy," *Infection Protocols for Obstetrics and Gynecology.* Montvale, NJ: Medical Economics Publishing, 1992, pp.57–58.

20. "News," *Birth* 24 (December 1997), p. 266.

21. Robert L. Goldenberg, "Most Efforts to Prevent Preterm Labor Not Effective," American College of Obstetrics and Gynecology News Release (November 1, 2002). www.acog.org

22. Ibid.

23. Ibid.

24. Anna Sanderson, "Coping with Bedrest During Pregnancy," *Childbirth Forum* (Winter 2002). OH:Willow Creative Group.

25. "Violence and Reproductive Health," CDC website. www.cdc.gov/reproductivehealth/violence/index.htm

Chapter 5. Nutrition

1. "Health and Fitness," *The Orlando Sentinel,* 30 April 1996, p. E-4.

2. Murray Enkin, Marc J.N.C. Keirse, James Neilson, Caroline Crowther, Lelia Duley, Ellen Hodnett, and Justus Hofmeyr, *A Guide to Effective Care in Pregnancy and Childbirth,* 3rd edition. New York: Oxford University Press, 2000, pp. 43–45.

3. "Folic Acid," March of Dimes Fact Sheet 2004. www.marchofdimes.com

4. Ibid.

5. Barbara Hayes, "Folic Acid—What a Difference a Pill Makes!" *Childbirth Forum* (Summer/Fall 2003). OH: Willow Creative Group, p. 1.

6. Ann Linden, "Morning Sickness: Causes, Concerns, Treatments." www.babycenter.com/refcap/pregnancy/morningsickness

7. "Vitamin A May Increase Risk of Birth Defects," *The Orlando Sentinel,* 7 October 1995, p. A-1.

8. Murray Enkin, Marc J.N.C. Keirse, James Neilson, Caroline Crowther, Lelia Duley, Ellen Hodnett, and Justus Hofmeyr, *A Guide to Effective Care in Pregnancy and Childbirth,* 3rd edition. New York: Oxford University Press, 2000, p. 45.

9. M.S. Kramer and R. Kakuma, "Energy and protein intake in pregnancy," *Cochrane Reviews.* www.cochrane.org/reviews/en/ab000032.html

10. "Dietary Guidelines for Americans 2005," Executive Summary, p. 2. www.health.gov/dietaryguidelines/dga2005/report/

11. "Dietary Reference Intakes," Food and Nutrition Information Center. www.nal.usda.gov/fnic/

12. "Vegetarian Diets,"American Dietetic Assoc. Abstract (2003). www.eatright.org/Public/GovernmentAffairs/92_17084. cfm

13. Ibid.

14. Joey Shulman, "Eating Salmon Safely," Environmental Working Group (January 18, 2006). www.ewg.org/news/story.php?id=4957

Chapter 6. Prenatal Exercise

1. Robin Bell and Maureen O'Neill, "Exercise and Pregnancy: A Review," *Birth* 21 (June 1994), p. 85.

2. "Pregnancy Outcomes Among Active and Sedentary Women," *Baby Care Forum* (Summer 1996), p. 5.

Chapter 7. Tools for Labor

1. Penny Simkin, Janet Whalley, and Ann Keppler, *Pregnancy, Childbirth and the Newborn.* New York: Meadowbrook Press, 2001, pp.172–173.

2. "The Bradley Method Goals" (2004), The Bradley Method website. www.bradleybirth.com

3. Barbara Harper, "Waterbirth: An Increasingly Attractive Gentle Birth Choice," *International Journal of Childbirth Education* 9 (February–March 1994), p.17.

4. Murray Enkin, Marc J.N.C. Keirse, James Neilson, Caroline Crowther, Lelia Duley, Ellen Hodnett, and Justus Hofmeyr, *A Guide to Effective Care in Pregnancy and Childbirth,* 3rd edition. New York: Oxford University Press, 2000, p. 291.

5. Ibid: p. 292.

Chapter 8. Labor and Birth

1. Marshall Klaus, John Kennell, and Phyllis Klaus, *Bonding: Building the Foundations of Secure Attachment and Independence.* New York: Addison-Wesley Publishing, Co., 1995, p. 38.

2. Catherine C. Roberts and Leslie M. Ludka, "Food for Thought: The Debate Over Eating and Drinking in Labor," *Childbirth Instructor Magazine* (Spring 1994), pp. 25–29.

3. Murray Enkin, Marc J.N.C. Keirse, James Neilson, Caroline Crowther, Lelia Duley, Ellen Hodnett, and Justus Hofmeyr, *A Guide to Effective Care in Pregnancy and Childbirth,* 3rd edition. New York: Oxford University Press, 2000, p. 260.

4. Catherine C. Roberts and Leslie M. Ludka, "Food for Thought: The Debate Over Eating and Drinking in Labor," *Childbirth Instructor Magazine* (Spring 1994), p. 27.

5. Murray Enkin, Marc J.N.C. Keirse, James Neilson, Caroline Crowther, Lelia Duley, Ellen Hodnett, and Justus Hofmeyr, *A Guide to Effective Care in Pregnancy and Childbirth,* 3rd edition. New York: Oxford University Press, 2000, p. 298.

Chapter 9. Labor Variations

1. "Moxibustion for correction of breech presentation: a randomized controlled trial," *Journal of the American Medical Association* 280(18), (November 11, 1998): 1580–1584. www.ncbi.nlm.nih.gov

2. Barbara Hotelling and Ann Tumblin, "Encouraging Your Baby Into the Best Position for Labor and Birth." Resource: Sutton & Scott, *Understanding and Teaching Optimal Foetal Positioning,* New Zealand: Birth Concepts, 1996.

3. Henci Goer, "The Occiput Posterior Baby," *Childbirth Instructor Magazine* (Summer 1994), pp. 36–40.

4. Barbara Harper, "Waterbirth: An Increasingly Attractive Gentle Birth Choice," *International Journal of Childbirth Education* 9 (February–March 1994).

5. Adrienne Lieberman, *Easing Labor Pain.* Boston: The Harvard Common Press, 1992, p. 113.

6. Ibid: p. 49.

Chapter 10. Medications and Anesthesia

1. Diana Korte and Roberta M. Scaer, *A Good Birth, A Safe Birth,* 3rd edition. Boston: Harvard Common Press, 1992, p. 31.

2. Mary Kroeger, *Impact of Birthing Practices on Breastfeeding.* Sudbury, MA: Jones and Bartlett Publishers, Inc., 2004, p. 105.

3. James A. Thorp and Ginger Breedlove, "Epidural Analgesia in Labor: An Evaluation of Risks and Benefits," *Birth* 23 (June 1996), p. 74.

4. "Epidural Analgesia During Labor Increases Risk of Abnormal Fetal Head Position," *Obstetrics & Gynecology* (2005), p. 105. www.medscape.com/viewarticle/504026

5. James A. Thorp and Ginger Breedlove, "Epidural Analgesia in Labor: An Evaluation of Risks and Benefits," *Birth* 23 (June 1996), pp. 69–73.

6. Henci Goer, "Epidural: Myth vs. Reality," *Childbirth Instructor Magazine* (Special Issue 1997), p. 22.

7. Janelle Durham, "Side Effects of Epidurals: A Summary of Recent Research Data," *International Journal of Childbirth Education* Vol 18, No 3 (2003), p. 15.

8. "Intrapartum Fever Common with Epidural; Has Adverse Effect on Infant," Reuters Medical News for the Professional. http://pediatrics.medscape.com/reuters/prof/2000/01

9. Janelle Durham, "Side Effects of Epidurals: A Summary of Recent Research Data," *International Journal of Childbirth Education* Vol 18, No 3 (2003), p. 15.

10. Ibid: p.14.

11. James A. Thorp and Ginger Breedlove, "Epidural Analgesia in Labor: An Evaluation of Risks and Benefits," *Birth* 23 (June 1996), p. 81.

12. "Patient Information Sheet, Misoprostol (marketed as Cytotec)" FDA ALERT (May 2005). www.fda.gov/cder/drug/InfoSheets/patient/misoprostolPIS.htm

Chapter 11. Interventions During Labor and Birth

1. Kathy Charbonneau, "Healthy Lifestyles: Intravenous Infusion: The Chemical Impact," *International Journal of Childbirth Education* 9 (February–March 1994).

2. Margot Edwards and Penny Simkin, *Obstetric Tests and Technology: A Consumer's Guide.* Minneapolis: International Childbirth Education Association, p. 7.

3. Ibid.

4. Murray Enkin, Marc J.N.C. Keirse, James Neilson, Caroline Crowther, Lelia Duley, Ellen Hodnett, and Justus Hofmeyr, *A Guide to Effective Care in Pregnancy and Childbirth,* 3rd edition. New York: Oxford University Press, 2000, p. 271.

5. "News," *Birth* 23 (March 1996), pp. 49–50.

6. Christian Thye-Petersen, "New device prevents oxygen deficiency during birth." www.neoventa.com/US/Articles/Publications_Press/Newspaper_Articles/Newdevicepreventsoxygende.html

7. G.A. Dildy, "A multicenter randomized trial of fetal pulse oximetry," *American Journal of Obstetrics and Gynecology* 182, No 1, part 2 (2000): 12.

8. "OxiFirst Fetal Oxygen Saturation Monitoring System, CDRH Consumer Information website (June 8, 2005). www.fda.gov/cdrh/mda/docs/P990053.html

9. "Cesarean delivery more likely with labor induction of a large baby," American College of Obstetricians and Gynecologists Press Release (November 1, 2002). www.acog.org

10. Paula Moyer, "Inducing Labor: Don't Force Mother Nature's Hand," WebMD Medical News. http://aolsvc.health.webmed.aol.com/content/Article/26/1728_58677.htm

11. J.M. Alexander, D.D. McIntire, and K.J. Leveno, "Forty weeks and beyond: Pregnancy outcomes by week of gestation." *Obstetrics & Gynecology,* 96(2), (2000): 291–294.

12. Murray Enkin, Marc J.N.C. Keirse, James Neilson, Caroline Crowther, Lelia Duley, Ellen Hodnett, and Justus Hofmeyr, *A Guide to Effective Care in Pregnancy and Childbirth,* 3rd edition. New York: Oxford University Press, 2000, p. 386.

13. Jean Marie Campen, "Routine Episiotomy," *Childbirth Instructor Magazine* 1 (Winter 1991), p. 29.

14. K. Hartmann, M. Viswanathan, R. Palmieri, G. Gartlehner, J. Thorp, Jr, and K.N. Lohr. "Outcomes of routine episiotomy: a systematic review." *Journal of the American Medical Association* 293(17) (May 4, 2005): 2141–2148.

15. Mary Kroger, *Impact of Birthing Practices on Breastfeeding.* Sudbury, MA: Jones and Bartlett Publishers, 2004, p. 132.

16. "FDA Public Health Advisory: Need for CAUTION When Using Vacuum Assisted Delivery Devices," US Department of Agriculture (May 21, 1998). www.fda.gov/cdrh/fetal598.html

Chapter 12. Cesarean Birth

1. Brent Laartz, "Viral Infections and Pregnancy," eMedicine.com, Inc., updated July 19, 2004.

2. Murray Enkin, Marc J.N.C. Keirse, James Neilson, Caroline Crowther, Lelia Duley, Ellen Hodnett, and Justus Hofmeyr, *A Guide to Effective Care in Pregnancy and Childbirth,* 3rd edition. New York: Oxford University Press, 2000, p. 358.

3. "ACOG Practice Bulletin Number 54 Vaginal Birth After Previous Cesarean Delivery," *Obstetrics and Gynecology* Vol 104, No 1 (July 2004).

4. "Trial of Labor After Cesarean (TOLAC), Formerly Trial of Labor Versus Elective Repeat Cesarean Section for the Woman

With a Previous Cesarean Section," American Academy of Family Physicians. www.aafp.org/PreBuilt/clinicalrec_tolac.pdf.

5. Murray Enkin, Marc J.N.C. Keirse, James Neilson, Caroline Crowther, Lelia Duley, Ellen Hodnett, and Justus Hofmeyr, *A Guide to Effective Care in Pregnancy and Childbirth,* 3rd edition. New York: Oxford University Press, 2000, p. 358.

6. "Vaginal Birth Not Associated With Incontinence Later in Life," American College of Obstetrics and Gynecology News Release (November 30, 2005). www.acog.org/from_home/publications/press_press_releases/nr 11-30-05-1.cfm

7. Maternity Center Association, *What Every Pregnant Woman Needs to Know About Cesarean Section.* New York: MCA, July 2004, p. 11.

8. Ibid: p. 7.

9. "New ACOG Opinion Addresses Elective Cesarean Controversy," American College of Obstetrics and Gynecology News Release (October 31, 2003). www.acog.org

10. Marcy White, "Birth is Good for Babies," *International Journal of Childbirth Education* Vol 20, No 4 (December 2005), p. 4.

11. Ibid: p. 5.

12. Ibid: p. 5.

13. Linda J. Smith, "Physics, Forces, and Mechanical Effects of Birth on Breastfeeding," *Impact of Birthing Practices on Breastfeeding.* Sudbury, MA: Jones and Bartlett Publishers, 2004, p. 126.

14. Bruce Flamm, "Cesarean Delivery 1970–1995: Where Have We Been and Where Are We Going?" *International Journal of Childbirth Education* 9 (November 1994), p. 7.

15. "Pregnancy & Childbirth /Maternal Mortality Rate in US Highest in Decades, Experts Say," August 27, 2007. www.kaisernetwork.org/daily_reports/rep_index.cfm?DR_ID=4 7116

16. Paula Moyer, "Inducing Labor: Don't Force Mother Nature's Hand," WebMD Medical News. http://aolsvc.health.webmed.aol.com/content/Article/26/1728_58677.htm

17. Peter S. Bernstein, "Complications of Cesarean Deliveries," Medscape, pp 6–7. www.medscape.com/viewprogram/4546_pnt.

18. Ibid: p. 7.

19. Ibid: p. 8.

20. Ibid: p. 7.

21. Ibid: p. 7.

22. Maternity Center Association, *What Every Pregnant Woman Needs to Know About Cesarean Section.* New York: MCA, July 2004, p. 25.

23. Ibid: p.14.

Chapter 13. The Newborn

1. Marshall Klaus, John Kennell, and Phyllis Klaus, *Bonding: Building the Foundations of Secure Attachment and Independence.* New York: Addison-Wesley Publishing Co., 1995, p. 53.

2. "Management of Hyperbilirubinemia in the Newborn Infant 35 or More Weeks of Gestation," Clinical Practice Guideline, the American Academy of Pediatrics, *The Journal of Pediatrics* Vol 114, No 1 (July 2004), p. 298.

3. Ruth A. Lawrence and Robert M. Lawrence, *Breastfeeding: A Guide for the Medical Profession.* St. Louis: Mosby, 1999, p. 486.

4. American Academy of Pediatrics Circumcision Policy Statement. Task Force on Circumcision. *The Journal of Pediatrics* Vol 103, No 3 (March 1999), pp. 686–693. www.medem.com/medlb/article_detaillb.cfm?article_ID=ZZZ6 HG9QE8C&sub_cat=0

5. "A Trade-off Analysis of Routine Newborn Circumcision," American Academy of Pediatrics News Release (January 10, 2000). www.aap.org/advocacy/archives/jannb.htm

6. "Circumcision Information for Parents," American Academy of Pediatrics website. www.aap.org/pubed/ZZZJZMEMH4C.htm ?&sub_cat=1

7. "A Trade-off Analysis of Routine Newborn Circumcision," American Academy of Pediatrics News Release (January 10, 2000). www.aap.org/advocacy/archives/jannb.htm

8. L.M. Talbert, E.N. Kraybill, and H.D. Potter. "Adrenal cortical response to circumcision in the neonate," *Obstetrics & Gynecology* 48 (1976): 208–210.

9. A. Taddio, J. Katz, A.L. Ilersich, and G. Koren, "Effect of neonatal circumcision on pain response during subsequent routine vaccination," *The Lancet* 349 (1997): 599–603.

10. "Lidocaine-Prilocaine for Circumcision Pain," *Childbirth Instructor Magazine* (Third Quarter 1997), p. 6. Cited in *New England Journal of Medicine,* 24 April 1997.

11. J. Lander, B. Brady-Fryer, J.B. Metcalfe, S. Nazarali, and S. Muttitt, "Comparison of ring block, dorsal penile nerve block, and topical anesthesia for neonatal circumcision: a randomized clinical trial," *Journal of the American Medical Association* 278 (1997): 2157–2162.

12. A.L. Masciello, "Anesthesia for neonatal circumcision: local anesthesia is better than dorsal penile nerve block," *Obstetrics & Gynecology* 75 (1990): 834–838.

13. "AAP Releases Early Hospital Discharge Requirements for Healthy Newborns," American Academy of Pediatrics Press Release (May 3, 2004). www.aap.org/advocacy/releases/mayhospital.htm

Chapter 14. Baby Care and Concerns

1. S. Dore et al., "Alcohol versus Natural Drying for Newborn Cord Care," *Journal of Obstetric Gynecologic and Neonatal Nursing* 27 (1998): 621–27.

2. Mary Kroeger, *Impact of Birthing Practices on Breastfeeding.* Sudbury MA: Jones and Bartlett Publishers, 2004, p. 199.

3. Harvey Karp, *Happiest Baby on the Block.* New York: Bantam Dell, 2002, p. 43.

4. Personal communication with Harvey Karp, April 14, 2006.

5. James J. McKenna, "Maximizing the Chances of Safe Infant Sleep in the Solitary and Cosleeping (Specifically, Bed-Sharing) Contexts." www.nd.edu/~jmckenn1/lab/faq.html#safesleep

6. "Changing Concepts of Sudden Infant Death Syndrome: Implications for Infant Sleeping Environment and Sleep Position Task Force on Infant Sleep Position and Sudden Infant Death Syndrome," American Academy of Pediatrics Policy Statement, *The Journal of Pediatrics* Vol 105, No 3 (March 2000), pp. 650–656.

7. "Protocol #6: Guidelines on co-sleeping and breastfeeding," ABM Protocols. www.bfmed.org

8. Nancy E. Wright and James J. McKenna, "Breastfeeding is Associated with a Lower Risk of SIDS According to The Academy of Breastfeeding Medicine," ABM Press Release October 14, 2005. www.bfmed.org/documents/SIDS-Bedsharing.doc

9. Ibid: p. 1.

10. Ibid: p. 2.

11. Ibid: p. 5.

12. National Institute of Child Health and Human Development Fact Sheet: Sudden Infant Death Syndrome. www.nichd.nih.gov/publications/pubs/sidsfact.htm

13. "AAP Revises SIDS Prevention Recommendations," American Academy of Pediatrics Press Release October 10, 2005. www.aap.org/ncepr/sids.htm

14. "Changing Concepts of Sudden Infant Death Syndrome: Implications for Infant Sleeping Environment and Sleep Position Task Force on Infant Sleep Position and Sudden Infant Death Syndrome," American Academy of Pediatrics Policy Statement, The Journal of Pediatrics Vol 105, No 3 (March 2000), pp. 650–656.

15. "AAP Revises SIDS Prevention Recommendations," American Academy of Pediatrics Press Release October 10, 2005. www.aap.org/ncepr/sids.htm

16. Ashley Montagu, *Touching: The Human Significance of the Skin,* 2nd edition. New York: Harper and Row, 1978, pp. 39–41.

17. "Vaccinations," March of Dimes website. www.marchofdimes.com/printableArticles/298_9087.asp

18. "Vaccine Education," The Children's Hospital of Philadelphia web page, October 2, 2005. www.chop.edu/consumer/

19. "Compare the Risks." American Academy of Pediatrics website. www.cispimmunize.org/pro/pro_main.html

20. "Mercury and Vaccines (Thimerosal)," CDC web page, April 1, 2005. www.cdc.gov/nip/vacsafe/concerns/thimerosal/default.htm

21. "Six Common Misconceptions about Vaccination and How to Respond to Them," CDC web page. www.cdc.gov/nip/publications/6mishome.htm#Diseaseshadalready

22. "Compare the Risks." American Academy of Pediatrics website. www.cispimmunize.org/pro/pro_main.html

Chapter 15. Breastfeeding

1. Christopher G. Owen, Peter H. Whincup, Katherine Odoki, Julie A. Gilg, and Derek G. Cook, "Infant Feeding and Blood Cholesterol: A Study in Adolescents and a Systematic Review," *The Journal of Pediatrics* Vol 110, No 3 (September 2002), pp. 597–608.

2. "What is the evidence that addition of DHA and ARA to infant formulas is beneficial," FDA/CFSAN Office of Nutritional Products, Labeling and Dietary Supplements, July 2002. www.cfsan.fda.gov/~dms/qa-inf17.html

3. Ruth A. Lawrence and Robert M. Lawrence. *Breastfeeding, A Guide for the Medical Profession.* St. Louis: Mosby, 1999, p. 218.

4. Ibid: p. 322.

5. "Breastfeeding and the Use of Human Milk," The American Academy of Pediatrics Policy Statement, *The Journal of Pediatrics* Vol 115, No 2 (February 2005), p. 500.

6. La Leche League International, *The Womanly Art of Breastfeeding,* 5th edition. New York: Penguin Books, 1991, p. 349.

7. M.E. Fallot, J. Boyd, III, and F. Oski, "Breastfeeding reduces incidence of hospital admissions for infections in infants," *The Journal of Pediatrics* 65 (1980), pp. 1121–1124.

8. E.A. Mitchell, R. Scragg, A.W. Stewart, et al. "Cot death supplement: results from the first year of the New Zealand cot death study," *New Zealand Medical Journal* 104 (1991), pp. 71–76.

9. "Breastfeeding Decreases Infant Mortality," National Institutes of Health News Press Release (May 2, 2004). www.nih.gov/news/pr/may2004/niehs-02.htm

10. Nancy Mohrbacher and Julie Stock, *The Breastfeeding Answer Book.* Schaumburg, IL: La Leche League International, 1997, p. 247.

11. Ibid: pp. 255–256.

12. Brian Palmer, "The Influence of Breastfeeding on the Devel-

opment of the Oral Cavity: A Commentary," *Journal of Human Lactation,* Vol 14, Issue 2, pp. 93–98.

13. Karen Pryor and Gale Pryor, *Nursing Your Baby.* New York: Pocket Books, 1991, p. 83.

14. "Breastfeeding and the Use of Human Milk," American Academy of Pediatrics Policy Statement, *The Journal of Pediatrics* Vol 115, No 2 (February 2005), p. 497.

15. "Breastmilk: Wide-Ranging Benefits," *The Florida Times-Union,* 13 January 1998, p. C-1.

16. Marsha Walker, "Summary of the Hazards of Infant Formula," International Lactation Consultant Association, 1992, p. 1.

17. Bergmann, et al. "Early determinants of childhood overweight and adiposity in birth cohort study: role of breastfeeding," *International Journal of Obesity* 27 (2003), p. 162–172.

18. "Breastfeeding and the Use of Human Milk," American Academy of Pediatrics Policy Statement, *The Journal of Pediatrics* Vol 115, No 2 (February 2005), pp. 496–497.

19. Marsha Walker, "Summary of the Hazards of Infant Formula," International Lactation Consultant Association, 1992, p. 2.

20. "Breastfeeding may reduce risk of celiac disease," Medline Plus web page, January 20, 2006. www.nlm.nih.gov/medlineplus/news/fullstory_29253.html

21. Sarah Boseley, "Bottle-fed babies 'face higher risk of heart death,'" *The Guardian,* May 14, 2004. www.guardian.co.uk/print/0,3858,4923793-103690,00.html

22. M.C. Kandhai, M.W. Reij, L.G.M. Gorris, et al. "Occurrence of Enterobacter sakazakii in food production environments and households," *The Lancet* 363 (2004), pp. 39–40.

23. James Randerson, "Baby food could trigger meningitis," NewScientist.com (June 3, 2004). www.newscientist.com/article.ns?id=dn5062&print=true

24. Marsha Walker, *Selling Out Mothers and Babies.* Weston MA: National Alliance for Breastfeeding Advocacy, Research, Education and Legal Branch, 2001, p. 95.

25. Polly A. Newcomb, Barry E. Storer, Matthew P. Longnecker, et al., "Lactation and a Reduced Risk of Premenopausal Breast Cancer," *New England Journal of Medicine* Vol 330 (January 13, 1994), pp. 81–87.

26. Ruth A. Lawrence and Robert M. Lawrence. *Breastfeeding, A Guide for the Medical Profession.* St. Louis: Mosby, 1999, p. 220.

27. Miriam H. Labbock, "The Lactational Amenorrhea Method (LAM): Another Choice for Mothers," *Breastfeeding Abstracts,* Vol 13, No1 (August 1993), pp. 3–4.

28. Jon Weimer, "The Economic Benefits of Breastfeeding: A Review and Analysis," US Department of Agriculture Food Assistance and Nutrition Research Report (FANRR), No 13 (March 2001), p. 20. www.ers.usda.gov/Publications/fanrr13/

29. Victor Oliveira and Mark Prell, "Sharing the Economic Burden: Who Pays for WIC's Infant Formula?" Amber Waves website. www.ers.usda.gov/AmberWaves/September04/Features/Infantformula.htm

30. "Why Use the Word "Formula?" letter to the editor, *The Journal of Pediatrics* Vol 99, No 2 (February 1997), p. 309.

31. Marsha Walker, "Breastfeeding and Diabetes," at FLCA conference (April 22, 2006).

32. Ibid.

33. "Breastfeeding and the Use of Human Milk," American Academy of Pediatrics Policy Statement, *The Journal of Pediatrics* Vol 115, No 2 (February 2005), pp. 496–497.

34. Candace Woessner, Judith Lauwers, and Barbara Bernard, Breastfeeding Today: A Mother's Companion. Garden City Park, New York: Avery Publishing Group, 1994, pp. 39–40.

35. "Current Research," The University of Western Australia web page, updated April 14, 2005. www.biochem.biomedchem.uwa.edu.au/Our_People/home_pages/academic_staff/hartmann/peter_hartmann/current_research

36. "Vegetarian Diets," American Dietetic Assoc. Abstract, 2003. www.eatright.org/Public/GovernmentAffairs/92_17084. cfm

37. Mary Kroeger, *Impact of Birthing Practices on Breastfeeding.* Sudbury MA: Jones and Bartlett Publishers, 2004, p. 104.

38. Dennis J Baumgarder, Patricia Muehl, Mary Fisher and Bridget Pribbenow, "Effect of Labor Epidural Anesthesia on Breastfeeding of Healthy Full-term Newborns Delivered Vaginally," *The Journal of the American Board of Family Practice* 16, (2003): 7–13.

39. Mary Kroeger, *Impact of Birthing Practices on Breastfeeding.* Sudbury MA: Jones and Bartlett Publishers, 2004, p. 107.

40. Linda J. Smith, "Physics, Forces, and Mechanical Effects of Birth on Breastfeeding," *Impact of Birthing Practices on Breastfeeding.* Sudbury MA: Jones and Bartlett Publishers, 2004, p. 142.

41. "Breastfeeding and the Use of Human Milk," American Academy of Pediatrics Policy Statement, *The Journal of Pediatrics* Vol 115, No 2 (February 2005): 498.

42. Karen Pryor, *Nursing Your Baby.* New York: Pocket Books, 1991, p. 64.

43. Marsha Walker, "Supplementation of the Breastfed Baby, Just One Bottle Won't Hurt—or Will It?"

44. K. Jean Cotterman, "Reverse Pressure Softening," 2004 handout and personal communication.

45. Human Milk Banking Association of North America website. www.hmbana.org/

46. Marsha Walker, "Selling Out Mothers and Babies: Marketing breast milk substitutes in the USA." Weston MA: NABA REAL, 2001, p. 13.

Chapter 16. Alternative Feeding Methods

1. La Leche League International, *The Womanly Art of Breastfeeding,* 5th edition. New York: Penguin Books, 1991, p. 167.

2. "Proper Handling and Storage of Breastmilk." CDC website. www.cdc.gov/breastfeeding/recommendations/handling_breast milk.htm

3. "New Report Outlines Dangers of Well Water in Infant Nitrate Poisoning," American Academy of Pediatrics News Release (September 6, 2005). www.aap.org/advocacy/releases/sept05 wellwater.htm

4. Judy Heilman, et al, "Fluoride Concentrations of Infant Foods," *Journal of the American Dental Association* 128 (July 1997), p. 857.

Chapter 17. The New Parent

1. "Antidepressant Use During Pregnancy Appears Associated with Withdrawal Symptoms in Newborns," Medem: AMA Medical Library website, February 8, 2006. www.medem.com/medlb/article_detaillb.cfm?article_ID=ZZZBPWFPHJE&sub_cat=0

2. "Attachment Research," askDrSears.com website. www.askdrsears.com/html/10/T131300.asp

3. "Beware Pet Reptiles," *Childbirth Instructor* (March/April 2000), p. 5.

4. "Experts suggest spacing pregnancies," www.usatoday.com website (April 18, 2006). www.usatoday.com/news/health/2006-04-18-birth-spacing_x.htm

5. Robert A. Hatcher, et al., *Contraceptive Technology 1998,* 17th edition. New York: Ardent Media, Inc., 1990, pp. 277–608.

6. Planned Parenthood Federation of America website, updated 2005. www.plannedparenthood.org

7. "FDA will Review Safety of Medicated Patches, Including Ortho Evra," Kaiser Daily Woman's Health Policy, March 7, 2006. www.kaisernetwork.org/daily_reports/print_report.cfm?DR_ID=35820&dr_cat=2

Bibliography

"A Trade-off Analysis of Routine Newborn Circumcision." American Academy of Pediatrics News Release (January 10, 2000). www.aap.org/advocacy/archives/jannb.htm

"AAP Releases Early Hospital Discharge Requirements for Healthy Newborns." American Academy of Pediatrics Press Release (May 3, 2004). www.aap.org/advocacy/releases/mayhospital.htm

"AAP Revises SIDS Prevention Recommendations." American Academy of Pediatrics Press Release (October 10, 2005). www.aap.org/ncepr/sids.htm

"Accutane and Other Retinoids." March of Dimes Fact Sheet 2004. March of Dimes Birth Defects Foundation website. www.marchofdimes.com

"ACOG Practice Bulletin Number 54, Vaginal Birth After Previous Cesarean Delivery." *Obstetrics & Gynecology* Vol 104, No 1 (July 2004).

Alexander, J.M., D.D. McIntire, and K.J. Leveno. "Forty weeks and beyond: Pregnancy outcomes by week of gestation." *Obstetrics & Gynecology* 96(2), (2000).

American Academy of Pediatrics Circumcision Policy Statement. Task Force on Circumcision. *The Journal of Pediatrics* Vol 103, No 3 (March 1999). www.medem.com/medlb/article_detaillb.cfm?article_ID=ZZZ6HG9QE8C&sub_cat=0

American Heart Association. *Basic Life Support, Heartsaver Guide.* Tulsa: CPR Publishers, Inc., 1993.

"Ante Partum Dental Radiography and Infant Low Birth Weight." *Journal of the American Medical Association.* American Dental Association News Release (April 28, 2004). www.ada.org/public/media/releases/0404_release03.asp

"Antidepressant Use During Pregnancy Appears Associated with Withdrawal Symptoms in Newborns." Medem: AMA Medical Library website (February 8, 2006). www.medem.com/medlb/article_detaillb.cfm?article_ID=ZZZBPWFPHJE&sub_cat=0

"Attachment Research." askDrSears.com website. www.askdrsears.com/html/10/T131300.asp

"Baby Poisoned by Food Spurs Couple's Crusade." *New York Post* (18 August 1997).

Baumgarder, Dennis J., Patricia Muehl, Mary Fisher, and Bridget Pribbenow. "Effect of Labor Epidural Anesthesia on Breast-feeding of Healthy Full-term Newborns Delivered Vaginally." *The Journal of the American Board of Family Practice* 16, (2003).

Bell, Robin, and Maureen O'Neill. "Exercise and Pregnancy: A Review." *Birth* 21 (June 1994).

Berezin, Nancy. *The Gentle Birth Book.* New York: Simon & Schuster, 1980.

Bergmann, et al. "Early determinants of childhood overweight and adiposity in birth cohort study: role of breastfeeding." *International Journal of Obesity* 27 (2003).

Bernstein, Peter S. "Complications of Cesarean Deliveries." Medscape. www.medscape.com/viewprogram/4546_pnt

"Beware Pet Reptiles." *Childbirth Instructor* (March/April 2000).

Bing, Elisabeth D., and Libby Colman. *Making Love During Pregnancy.* New York: Farrar, Straus & Giroux, 1989.

Boggess, Kim A., Susi Lieff, Amy P. Murtha, Kevin Moss, James Beck, and Steven Offenbacher. "Maternal Periodontal Disease is Associated with an Increased Risk for Preeclampsia." *American College of Obstetrics & Gynecology Green Journal* Vol 101, No 2 (February 2003). www.acog.org

Boseley, Sarah. "Bottle-fed babies 'face higher risk of heart death.'" *The Guardian* (May 14, 2004). www.guardian.co.uk/print/0,3858,4923793-103690,00.html

Bracken, Michael B., et al. "Asthma Symptoms, Severity, and Drug Therapy: A Prospective Study of Effects on 2205 Pregnancies." *Obstetrics & Gynecology* Vol 102(4), (October 2003).

"The Bradley Method Goals." The Bradley Method website (2004). www.bradleybirth.com

"Breastfeeding and the Use of Human Milk." The American Academy of Pediatrics Policy Statement. *The Journal of Pediatrics* Vol 115, No 2 (February 2005).

"Breastfeeding Decreases Infant Mortality." National Institutes of Health News Press Release (May 2, 2004). www.nih.gov/news/pr/may2004/niehs-02.htm

"Breastfeeding may reduce risk of celiac disease." Medline Plus web page (January 20, 2006). www.nlm.nih.gov/medlineplus/news/fullstory_29253.html

"Breastmilk: Wide-Ranging Benefits." *The Florida Times-Union* (13 January 1998).

Briggs, Gerald G., Roger K. Freeman, and Sumner J.Yaffe. *Drugs in Pregnancy and Lactation,* 5th edition. Baltimore: Williams and Wilkins, 1998.

"California Birth Defects Monitoring Program Fact Sheet on Smoking." www.cbdmp.org

Campen, Jean Marie. "Routine Episiotomy." *Childbirth Instructor Magazine* 1 (Winter 1991).

"Cesarean delivery more likely with labor induction of a large baby." American College of Obstetricians and Gynecologists Press Release (November 1, 2002). www.acog.org

"Changing Concepts of Sudden Infant Death Syndrome: Implications for Infant Sleeping Environment and Sleep Position Task Force on Infant Sleep Position and Sudden Infant Death Syndrome." American Academy of Pediatrics Policy Statement. *The Journal of Pediatrics* Vol 105, No 3 (March 2000).

Charbonneau, Kathy. "Healthy Lifestyles: Intravenous Infusion: The Chemical Impact." *International Journal of Childbirth Education* 9 (February–March 1994).

"Circumcision Information for Parents." American Academy of Pediatrics website. www.aap.org/pubed/ZZZJZMEMH4C.htm?&sub_cat=1

Clausson, B., F. Granath, A. Ekbom, S. Lundgren, A. Nordmark, L.B. Signorello, and S. Cnattingius. "Effect of caffeine exposure during pregnancy on birth weight and gestational age." *American Journal of Epidemiology*155(5), (2002).

"Cocaine Follow-up." *Childbirth Instructor Magazine* (Winter 1994).

"Cocaine Follow-up." *Childbirth Instructor Magazine* (Winter 2004).

"Compare the Risks." American Academy of Pediatrics website. www.cispimmunize.org/pro/pro_main.html

Cotterman, K. Jean. "Reverse Pressure Softening." 2004 handout and personal communication.

"CPSC Warns About Hazards of 'Do it Yourself' Removal of Lead Based Paint: Safety Alert." CPSC Document #5055. www.cpsc.gov/CPSCPUB/PUBS/5055.html

"Current Research." The University of Western Australia web page, updated April 14, 2005. www.biochem.biomedchem.uwa.edu.au/

Our_People/home_pages/academic_staff/hartmann/peter_hartmann/current_research

"Currents in Emergency Cardiovascular Care." American Heart Association. Vol 16, No 4 (Winter 2005–2006). www.americanheart.org/downloadable/heart/1132621842912Winter2005.pdf

Dick-Read, Grantly. *Childbirth Without Fear.* New York: Harper and Row, 1959.

"Dietary Guidelines for Americans 2005." Executive Summary. www.health.gov/dietaryguidelines/dga2005/report/

"Dietary Reference Intakes." Food and Nutrition Information Center. www.nal.usda.gov/fnic/

Dildy, G.A. "A multicenter randomized trial of fetal pulse oximetry." *American Journal of Obstetrics and Gynecology* 182, No 1, part 2 (2000).

Dore, S., et al. "Alcohol versus Natural Drying for Newborn Cord Care." *Journal of Obstetric, Gynecologic, & Neonatal Nursing* 27 (1998).

Durham, Janelle. "Side Effects of Epidurals: A Summary of Recent Research Data." *International Journal of Childbirth Education* Vol 18, No 3 (2003).

Edwards, Margot, and Penny Simkin. *Obstetric Tests and Technology: A Consumer's Guide.* Minneapolis: International Childbirth Education Association.

Enkin, Murray, Marc J.N.C. Keirse, James Neilson, Caroline Crowther, Lelia Duley, Ellen Hodnett, and Justus Hofmeyr. *A Guide to Effective Care in Pregnancy and Childbirth,* 3rd edition. New York: Oxford University Press, 2000.

"Epidural Analgesia During Labor Increases Risk of Abnormal Fetal Head Position." *Journal of Obstetrics & Gynecology* (2005). www.medscape.com/viewarticle/504026

Eskenazi, B. "Caffeine—filtering the facts." *The New England Journal of Medicine* 341(22), (1999), as reported in March of Dimes Fact Sheet (2004).

Eskenazi, B., A.L. Stapleton, M. Kharrazi, and WY Chee. "The association between maternal decaffeinated and caffeinated coffee consumption and fetal growth and gestation duration." *Epidemiology* 155(5), (1999), as reported in March of Dimes Fact Sheet (2004).

Ewigman, Bernard G., et al. "Effect of Prenatal Ultrasound Screening on Perinatal Outcome." *The New England Journal of Medicine* 329 (16 September 1993).

"Experts suggest spacing pregnancies." www.usatoday.com website (April 18, 2006). www.usatoday.com/news/health/2006-04-18-birth-spacing_x.htm

"Fact Sheet—CNM-Attended Births Still on the Rise!" American College of Nurse-Midwives website, updated March 1, 2004. www.midwife.org

Fallot, M.E., J. Boyd, III, and F. Oski. "Breastfeeding reduces incidence of hospital admissions for infections in infants." *The Journal of Pediatrics* 65 (1980).

"FDA Public Health Advisory: Need for CAUTION When Using Vacuum Assisted Delivery Devices." US Department of Agriculture (May 21, 1998). www.fda.gov/cdrh/fetal598.html

"FDA will Review Safety of Medicated Patches, Including Ortho Evra." Kaiser Daily Woman's Health Policy (March 7, 2006). www.kaisernetwork.org/daily_reports/print_report.cfm?DR_ID=35820&dr_cat=2

Flamm, Bruce L. *Birth After Cesarean: The Medical Facts.* New York: Simon & Schuster Trade, 1992.

Flamm, Bruce. "Cesarean Delivery 1970–1995: Where Have We Been and Where Are We Going?" *International Journal of Childbirth Education* 9 (November 1994).

"Folic Acid." March of Dimes Fact Sheet (2004). www.marchofdimes.com

Gall, Stanley A. "Human papillomavirus infection." *Infection Protocols for Obstetrics and Gynecology.* Montvale, NJ: Medical Economics Publishing, 1992.

Gebhardt, Susan E. and Robin G. Thomas. "Nutritive Value of Foods." *Home and Garden Bulletin #72.* Beltsville, MD: US Department of Agriculture, 2002.

Gibbs, Ronald S. "Herpes simplex virus infection in pregnancy." *Infection Protocols for Obstetrics and Gynecology.* Montvale, NJ: Medical Economics Publishing, 1992.

Gilstrap III, Larry C. and George D. Wendel, Jr. "Syphilis in pregnancy." *Infection Protocols for Obstetrics and Gynecology.* Montvale, NJ: Medical Economics Publishing, 1992.

"Ginger Supplement Helps Relieve Pregnancy-Related Nausea and Vomiting." American College of Obstetrics & Gynecology News Release (March 29, 2004). www.acog.org

Goer, Henci. "Epidural: Myth vs. Reality." *Childbirth Instructor Magazine,* Special Issue 1997.

Goer, Henci. "The Occiput Posterior Baby." *Childbirth Instructor Magazine* (Summer 1994).

Goldenberg, Robert L. "Most Efforts to Prevent Preterm Labor Not Effective." American College of Obstetrics and Gynecology News Release (November 1, 2002). www.acog.org

Harper, Barbara. "Waterbirth: An Increasingly Attractive Gentle Birth Choice." *International Journal of Childbirth Education* 9 (February–March 1994).

Hartmann, K., M. Viswanathan, R. Palmieri, G. Gartlehner, J. Thorp, Jr, and K.N. Lohr. "Outcomes of routine episiotomy: a systematic review." *Journal of the American Medical Association* 293(17) (May 4, 2005).

Hatcher, Robert A., et al. Contraceptive Technology 1998, 17th edition. New York: Ardent Media, Inc., 1990.

Hayes, Barbara. "Folic Acid—What a Difference a Pill Makes!" *Childbirth Forum* (Summer/Fall 2003). OH: Willow Creative Group.

"Health and Fitness." *The Orlando Sentinel* (30 April 1996).

Heilman, Judy, et al. "Fluoride Concentrations of Infant Foods." *Journal of the American Dental Association* 128 (July 1997).

Henkel, John. "Sugar Substitutes: Americans Opt for Sweetness and Lite." (1999). www.fda.gov/fdac/

"Home Birth as Safe as Hospital Delivery for Low-Risk Pregnancies." *British Medical Journal* 330 (June 16, 2005).

Hotelling, Barbara, and Ann Tumblin, "Encouraging Your Baby Into the Best Position for Labor and Birth." Resource: Sutton & Scott, *Understanding and Teaching Optimal Foetal Positioning,* New Zealand: Birth Concepts, 1996.

Human Milk Banking Association of North America website. www.hmbana.org/

"ICEA Position Statement and Review: The Birth Place." *International Journal of Childbirth Education* Vol 17, No 1, ICEA, Inc., Minnesota (2002).

"Infant Eye Cues." *Childbirth Instructor Magazine* (First Quarter 1996).

"Infectious Diseases During Pregnancy: Expanding Prevention and Treatments." American College of Obstetrics and Gynecology News Release (December 12, 2001). www.acog.org

"Intrapartum Fever Common with Epidural; Has Adverse Effect on Infant." *Reuters Medical News for the Professional.* http://pediatrics.medscape.com/reuters/prof/2000/01

Ilse, Sherokee. *Empty Arms.* Minneapolis: Wintergreen Press, 1990.

Jordan, Kate, and Carole Osborne-Sheets. *Bodywork for the Childbearing Years,* 10th edition. La Jolla, California: American Massage Therapy Association, 1995.

Kandhai, M.C., M.W. Reij, L.G.M. Gorris, et al. "Occurrence of Enterobacter sakazakii in food production environments and households." *The Lancet* 363 (2004).

Karmel, Marjorie. *Thank You, Dr. Lamaze.* New York: Dolphin Books, 1965.

Karp, Harvey. *Happiest Baby on the Block.* New York: Bantam Dell, 2002.

Karp, Harvey. Personal communication (April 14, 2006).

Klaus, Marshall, and John Kennell. *Maternal-Infant Bonding.* St. Louis: C.V. Mosby Co., 1976.

Klaus, Marshall, John Kennell, and Phyllis Klaus. *Bonding: Building the Foundations of Secure Attachment and Independence.* New York: Addison-Wesley Publishing Co., 1995.

Klaus, Marshall and Phyllis H. Klaus. *Your Amazing Newborn.* Read, MA: Perseus Books, 1998.

Kramer, M.S., and R. Kakuma. "Energy and protein intake in pregnancy." *Cochrane Reviews.* www.cochrane.org/reviews/en/ab000032.html

Korte, Diana, and Roberta M. Scaer. *A Good Birth, A Safe Birth,* 3rd edition. Boston: Harvard Common Press, 1992.

Kroeger, Mary. *Impact of Birthing Practices on Breastfeeding.* Sudbury, MA: Jones and Bartlett Publishers, Inc., 2004.

La Leche League International. *The Womanly Art of Breastfeeding,* 5th edition. New York: Penguin Books, 1991.

Laartz, Brent. "Viral Infections and Pregnancy." eMedicine.com, Inc., (updated July 19, 2004).

Labbock, Miriam H. "The Lactational Amenorrhea Method (LAM): Another Choice for Mothers." *Breastfeeding Abstracts,* Vol 13, No 1 (August 1993).

Lander, J., B. Brady-Fryer, J.B. Metcalfe, S. Nazarali, and S. Muttitt. "Comparison of ring block, dorsal penile nerve block, and topical anesthesia for neonatal circumcision: a randomized clinical trial." *Journal of the American Medical Association* 278 (1997).

Lauwers, Judith, and Candace Woessner. *Counseling the Nursing Mother.* Garden City Park, New York: Avery Publishing Group, 1990.

Lawrence, Ruth A. "Can We Expect Greater Intelligence from Human Milk Feedings?" *Birth* 19 (June 1992).

Lawrence, Ruth A., and Robert M. Lawrence. *Breastfeeding: A Guide for the Medical Profession.* St. Louis: Mosby, 1999.

Leboyer, Frederick. *Birth without Violence.* Rochester, Vermont: Inner Traditions International Ltd., 1995.

"Lidocaine-Prilocaine for Circumcision Pain." *Childbirth Instructor Magazine* (Third Quarter, 1997).

Lieberman, Adrienne. *Easing Labor Pain.* Boston: Harvard Common Press, 1992.

"Limb-Reduction Defects and Chorion Villus Sampling." *The Lancet* (4 May 1991).

Linden, Ann. "Morning Sickness: Causes, Concerns, Treatments." www.babycenter.com/refcap/pregnancy/morningsickness

"Lyme Disease Treatment and Prognosis." CDC website. www.cdc.gov/ncidod/dvbid/lyme/ld_humandisease_treatment.htm

"Lymphocytic choriomeningitis." CDC Fact Sheet. www.cdc.gov/ncidod/dvrd/spb/mnpages/dispages/Fact_Sheets/Lymphocytic_Choriomeningitis_Fact_Sheet.pdf

Man, Li-Xing, and Benjamin Chang. "Maternal Cigarette Smoking during Pregnancy Increases the Risk of Having a Child with a Congenital Digital Anomaly." *Plastic & Reconstructive Surgery* 117(1), (January 2006).

"Management of Hyperbilirubinemia in the Newborn Infant 35 or More Weeks of Gestation." Clinical Practice Guideline, the American Academy of Pediatrics. *The Journal of Pediatrics* Vol 114, No 1 (July 2004).

Masciello, A.L. "Anesthesia for neonatal circumcision: local anesthesia is better than dorsal penile nerve block." *Obstetrics & Gynecology* 75 (1990).

Maternity Center Association. *What Every Pregnant Woman Needs to Know About Cesarean Section.* New York: MCA, July 2004.

McKenna, James J. "Maximizing the Chances of Safe Infant Sleep in the Solitary and Cosleeping (Specifically, Bed-Sharing) Contexts." www.nd.edu/~jmckenn1/lab/faq.html#safesleep

"Mercury and Vaccines (Thimerosal)." CDC web page, April 1, 2005. www.cdc.gov/nip/vacsafe/concerns/thimerosal/default.htm

Mitchell, E.A., R. Scragg, A.W. Stewart, et al. "Cot death supplement: results from the first year of the New Zealand cot death study." *New Zealand Medical Journal* 104 (1991).

Mohrbacher, Nancy and Julie Stock. *The Breastfeeding Answer Book.* Schaumburg, IL: La Leche League International, 1997.

"Moms Who Smoke Increase Babies' Risk of Ear Infections." *Growing Child Research Review* (May 1995).

Montagu, Ashley. *Touching. The Human Significance of the Skin,* 2nd edition. New York: Harper and Row, 1978.

"Moxibustion for correction of breech presentation: a randomized controlled trial," *Journal of the American Medical Association* 280(18), (November 11, 1998). www.ncbi.nlm.nih.gov

Moyer, Paula. "Inducing Labor: Don't Force Mother Nature's Hand." WebMD Medical News. http://aolsvc.health.webmed.aol.com/content/Article/26/1728_58677.htm

"Multiple marker screening (AFP)," October 15, 2004. www.BabyCenter.com

National Institute of Child Health and Human Development Fact Sheet: Sudden Infant Death Syndrome. www.nichd.nih.gov/publications/pubs/sidsfact.htm

National Toxicology Program Report on Carcinogens. Subcommittee Meeting, October 30–31, 1997. http://ntp-server.niehs.nih.gov

"New ACOG Opinion Addresses Elective Cesarean Controversy." American College of Obstetrics and Gynecology News Release (October 31, 2003). www.acog.org

"New Crop of Midwives Shatter Stereotype." *The Florida Times-Union* (22 October 1996).

"New Marker for Preterm Labor." *Childbirth Instructor Magazine* (First Quarter 1996).

"New Report Outlines Dangers of Well Water in Infant Nitrate Poisoning." American Academy of Pediatrics News Release (September 6, 2005). www.aap.org/advocacy/releases/sept05wellwater.htm

"New Study Finds Babies Born To Mothers Who Drink Alcohol Heavily May Suffer Permanent Nerve Damage." The National Institutes of Child Health and Human Development Press Release (March 8, 2004). www.nichd.nih.gov

Newcomb, Polly A., Barry E. Storer, Matthew P. Longnecker, et al. "Lactation and a Reduced Risk of Premenopausal Breast Cancer." *New England Journal of Medicine* Vol 330 (January 13, 1994).

"News." *Birth* 24 (December 1997).

Nilsson, Lennart. *A Child Is Born.* New York: Delacorte, 1990.

Oliveira, Victor, and Mark Prell. "Sharing the Economic Burden:

Who Pays for WIC's Infant Formula?" Amber Waves website. www.ers.usda.gov/AmberWaves/September04/Features/Infantformula.htm

Owen, Christopher G., Peter H. Whincup, Katherine Odoki, Julie A. Gilg, and Derek G. Cook. "Infant Feeding and Blood Cholesterol: A Study in Adolescents and a Systematic Review." *The Journal of Pediatrics* Vol 110, No 3 (September 2002).

"OxiFirst Fetal Oxygen Saturation Monitoring System. CDRH Consumer Information website (June 8, 2005). www.fda.gov/cdrh/mda/docs/P990053.html

Oxorn, Harry. *Oxorn-Foote Human Labor and Birth,* 5th edition. Norwalk, Connecticut: Appleton-Century-Crofts, 1986.

Palmer, Brian. "The Influence of Breastfeeding on the Development of the Oral Cavity: A Commentary." *Journal of Human Lactation* Vol 14, Issue 2.

"Patient Information Sheet, Misoprostol (marketed as Cytotec)." FDA ALERT (May 2005). www.fda.gov/cder/drug/InfoSheets/patient/misoprostolPIS.htm

Palmer, Gabrielle. *The Politics of Breastfeeding.* London: Pandora Press, 1988.

Peterson, Gayle. *Birthing Normally,* 2nd edition. Berkeley, California: Mindbody Press, 1984.

Planned Parenthood Federation of America website, updated 2005. www.plannedparenthood.org

"Proper Handling and Storage of Breastmilk." CDC website. www.cdc.gov/breastfeeding/recommendations/handling_breastmilk.htm

Pryor, Karen. *Nursing Your Baby.* New York: Pocket Books, 1991.

Polomeno, Viola. "Sexual Intercourse After the Birth of a Baby." *International Journal of Childbirth Education* 11(December 1996).

"Pregnancy & Childbirth /Maternal Mortality Rate in US Highest in Decades, Experts Say," August 27, 2007. www.kaisernetwork.org/daily_reports/rep_index.cfm?DR_ID=47116

"Pregnancy Outcomes Among Active and Sedentary Women." *Baby Care Forum* (Summer 1996).

"Protocol #6: Guideline on co-sleeping and breastfeeding," ABM Protocols. www.bfmed.org

"Prudent Use." *American Institute of Ultrasound in Medicine Official Statement* (May 2, 1999). www.aium.org/publication/statements

James Randerson. "Baby food could trigger meningitis." NewScientist.com website (June 3, 2004). www.newscientist.com/article.ns?id=dn5062&print=true

Riordan, Jan, and Kathleen Auerback. *Breastfeeding and Human Lactation.* Boston: Jones and Bartlett Publishers, 1993.

Roberts, Catherine C., and Leslie M. Ludka. "Food for Thought: The Debate Over Eating and Drinking in Labor." *Childbirth Instructor Magazine* (Spring 1994).

Rooks, Judith P. *Journal of Nurse-Midwifery* Vol 44, No 4 (July/August 1999).

Sanderson. "Coping with Bedrest During Pregnancy." *Childbirth Forum* (Winter 2002). OH: Willow Creative Group.

Schrag, Stephanie, D. Phil, Rachel Gorwitz, Kristi Fultz-Butts, and Anne Schuchat., "Prevention of Perinatal Group B Streptococcal Disease, 2002 Revised Guidelines from CDC." www.cdc.gov/groupbstrep

"Seatbelts Greatly Reduce Harm to Pregnant Drivers and Fetuses During Car Crashes." American College of Obstetrics and Gynecology News Release (July 31, 2003). www.acog.org

Shu, Xiao-ou, Julie A. Ross, et al. "Parental Alcohol Consumption, Cigarette Smoking, and Risk of Infant Leukemia: a Children's Cancer Group Study." *Journal of the National Cancer Institute* Vol 88, No 1 (January 3, 1996).

Shulman, Joey. "Eating Salmon Safely." Environmental Working Group (January 18, 2006). www.ewg.org/news/story.php?id=4957

Signorello, L.B., and J.K. McLaughlin. "Maternal caffeine consumption and spontaneous abortion: a review of the epidemiologic evidence." *Epidemiology* 15(2) (2004 March).

Simkin, Penny. *The Birth Partner: Everything You Need to Know to Help a Woman Through Childbirth.* Boston: Harvard Common Press, 1989.

Simkin, Penny, Janet Whalley, and Ann Keppler. *Pregnancy, Childbirth and the Newborn.* New York: Meadowbrook Press, 2001.

"Six Common Misconceptions about Vaccination and How to Respond to Them." CDC web page. www.cdc.gov/nip/publications/6mishome.htm#Diseaseshadalready

Smith, Linda J. "Physics, Forces, and Mechanical Effects of Birth on Breastfeeding." *Impact of Birthing Practices on Breastfeeding.* Sudbury, MA: Jones and Bartlett Publishers, 2004.

"Smoking Can Raise SIDS Risk." *The Orlando Sentinel* (8 March 1995).

"Study: Drinking Multiplies Risks of Infant Leukemia." *The Orlando Sentinel* (3 January 1996).

Taddio, A., J. Katz, A.L. Ilersich, and G. Koren. "Effect of neonatal circumcision on pain response during subsequent routine vaccination." *The Lancet* 349 (1997).

Talbert, L.M., E.N. Kraybill, and H.D. Potter. "Adrenal cortical response to circumcision in the neonate." *Obstetrics & Gynecology* 48 (1976).

Thorp, James A., and Ginger Breedlove "Epidural Analgesia in Labor: An Evaluation of Risks and Benefits." *Birth* 23 (June 1996).

Thye-Petersen, Christian. "New device prevents oxygen deficiency during birth." www.neoventa.com/US/Articles/Publications_Press/Newspaper_Articles/Newdevicepreventsoxygende.html

"Trial of Labor After Cesarean (TOLAC), Formerly Trial of Labor

Versus Elective Repeat Cesarean Section for the Woman With a Previous Cesarean Section." American Academy of Family Physicians. www.aafp.org/PreBuilt/clinicalrec_tolac.pdf.

"US Surgeon General Releases Advisory on Alcohol Use in Pregnancy." US Department of Health and Human Services News Release (February 21, 2005). www.hhs.gov/surgeongeneral/pressreleases/sg02222005.html

"Vaccinations." March of Dimes website. www.marchofdimes.com/printableArticles/298_9087.asp

"Vaccine Education." The Children's Hospital of Philadelphia web page (October 2, 2005). www.chop.edu/consumer/

"Vaginal Birth Not Associated With Incontinence Later in Life." American College of Obstetrics and Gynecology News Release (November 30, 2005). www.acog.org/from_home/publications/press_press_releases/nr11-30-05-1.cfm

"Vegetarian Diets."American Dietetic Association Abstract (2003). www.eatright.org/Public/GovernmentAffairs/92_17084.cfm

Verny, Thomas, with John Kelly. *The Secret Life of the Unborn Child.* New York: Dell Publishing Co., 1981.

"Violence and Reproductive Health." CDC website. www.cdc.gov/ reproductivehealth/violence/index.htm

"Vitamin A May Increase Risk of Birth Defects." *The Orlando Sentinel* (7 October 1995).

Walker, Marsha. "Breastfeeding and Diabetes." FLCA conference (April 22, 2006).

Walker, Marsha. *Selling Out Mothers and Babies.* Weston MA: National Alliance for Breastfeeding Advocacy, Research, Education and Legal Branch, 2001.

Walker, Marsha."Summary of the Hazards of Infant Formula." International Lactation Consultant Association (1992).

Walker, Marsha. "Supplementation of the Breastfed Baby, Just One Bottle Won't Hurt—or Will It?"

Weimer, Jon. "The Economic Benefits of Breastfeeding: A Review and Analysis." US Department of Agriculture Food Assistance and Nutrition Research Report (FANRR), No 13 (March 2001). www.ers.usda.gov/Publications/fanrr13/

"What is the evidence that addition of DHA and ARA to infant formulas is beneficial?" FDA/CFSAN Office of Nutritional Products, Labeling and Dietary Supplements (July 2002). www.cfsan.fda.gov/~dms/qa-inf17.html

White, Marcy. "Birth is Good for Babies." *International Journal of Childbirth Education* Vol 20, No 4 (December 2005).

"Why Use the Word "Formula?" Letter to the editor, *The Journal of Pediatrics* Vol 99, No 2 (February 1997).

Williams, Christine L., and Peter Welch, "Lyme disease in pregnancy." *Infection Protocols for Obstetrics and Gynecology.* Montvale, NJ: Medical Economics Publishing, 1992.

Woessner, Candace, Judith Lauwers, and Barbara Bernard. *Breastfeeding Today: A Mother's Companion.* Garden City Park, New York: Avery Publishing Group, 1994.

Wright, Nancy E., and James J. McKenna. "Breastfeeding is Associated with a Lower Risk of SIDS According to The Academy of Breastfeeding Medicine." ABM Press Release (October 14, 2005). www.bfmed.org/documents/SIDS-Bedsharing.doc

Young, Diony, and Charles Mahan. *Unnecessary Cesareans: Ways to Avoid Them.* Minneapolis: International Childbirth Education Association, 1989.

About the Author

Linda Goldberg, RN, CCE, IBCLC, is a graduate of the Helene Fuld School of Nursing at West Jersey Hospital. She has taught childbirth classes since 1977 and served as Director of Instructor Training and Certification for the Childbirth Education Association (CEA) of Jacksonville, Florida. She also served as Vice President and President of the CEA of Jacksonville, as well as President of its board of directors, before moving to Winter Springs, Florida, in 1984. Linda taught childbirth education for Special Beginnings, an out-of-hospital birth center in Orlando, from 1985 until it closed in 2006. Prior to becoming an international board certified lactation consultant in 2001, Linda worked as a staff RN on the mother/baby unit of Winter Park Memorial Hospital.

In addition to her lactation consulting duties, Linda teaches classes in early pregnancy, breastfeeding, and childbirth. She is also a certified Happiest Baby on the Block instructor. An active member of the Florida Lactation Consultant Association, Linda has held the board position of Recording Secretary and is currently the Treasurer for the state organization. Along with Ginny Brinkley and Janice Kukar, Linda coauthored the bestsellers *Your Child's First Journey* and *Pregnancy to Parenthood.*

Linda and her husband have three children—Jeff, Becky, and Jonathan—who were all born after unmedicated labors and exclusively breastfed. Jeff and Becky were born in a hospital by a supportive physician, while Jonathan was born in an out-of-hospital birth center attended by a certified nurse-midwife.

Index

AAP. *See* American Academy of Pediatrics.

Abdominal Tightening, 418

ABM. *See* Academy of Breastfeeding Medicine.

ABR screening. *See* Auditory brainstem response screening.

Academy of Breastfeeding Medicine (ABM), 309

ACOG. *See* American College of Obstetricians and Gynecologists.

Acquired immune deficiency syndrome (AIDS), 63

Acrocyanosis, 284

Active labor, 196–197

Active management of labor, 257

Acupressure, 41, 135, 138, 160, 161, 162–163, 182, 197, 199, 223, 255, 256, 243

Acupuncture, 160, 167, 219, 255

AED. *See* Automated external defibrillator.

Aerobic exercises, prenatal, 119–121

AFP. *See* Alpha-fetoprotein.

Afterbirth. *See* Placenta.

Afterpains, 207, 235, 238

AIDS. *See* Acquired immune deficiency syndrome.

Air travel with children, 332

Alcohol consumption
  and breastfeeding, 356, 378, 381
  and co-sleeping, 309
  and pregnancy, 25, 42, 43, 74, 84, 92, 102

Allergies, baby
  breastmilk and, 347, 349
  to all formula, 396
  to cow's milk formula, 347, 386, 396
  to solid foods, 399
  to vaccinations, 316, 321

Allergies, maternal
  medication and, 232, 274
  milk, 102, 104
  peanut, 104–105

Alpha-fetoprotein (AFP), 47, 50

Alveoli, 357

American Academy of Family Physicians, 267

American Academy of Husband-Coached Childbirth, 141

American Academy of Pediatrics (AAP), 68, 231, 290, 291, 296, 298, 309, 310, 315, 320, 332, 333, 343, 344, 345, 371, 373, 388, 399

American College of Obstetricians and Gynecologists (ACOG), 27, 75, 115, 250, 257, 265, 267, 269

American Dental Association, 35

American Heart Association, 321

American Red Cross, 321, 324

American Society for Psychoprophy-laxis in Obstetrics. *See* Lamaze International.

Amniocentesis, 48, 49, 51, 53–54, 57, 61, 77, 79, 273

Amniofusion, 247, 265

Amniotic fluid, 24, 84

Amniotic membranes
  artificial rupture of, 243, 254, 256, 257, 272
  development of, 20
  premature rupture of, 250
  purpose of, 21
  spontaneous rupture of, 188, 192, 196, 198
  stripping of, 221, 253

Amniotic sac. *See* Amniotic membranes.

Amniotomy, 243, 254, 256, 257, 272

Analgesics, 230, 232, 233, 241

Anesthesia, 196, 230–241

Angel kisses, 286

Animal-transmitted infections, and pregnancy, 67

Ankle Rotating, 280, 281, 418

Ankyloglossia, 376, 282

Apgar, Virginia, 206

Apgar score, 204, 206, 240, 283, 294, 438

Areola, 27, 254, 288, 354, 357, 361, 362, 375, 376–377

Arm Circles, 124

Arm Circles in Water, 119

Arm Raises, 122

Aromatherapy, 163, 182

Artificial insemination, 19

Artificial rupture of membranes. *See* Amniotomy.

Artificial sweeteners, 39, 102

Association of Reproductive Health Professionals, 427

Asynclitic position, fetal, 220

Attachment parenting, 411

Auditory brainstorm response (ABR)
    screening, 296
Augmentation of labor and birth,
    256–259
Autism, 320
Autism Speaks, 320
Automated external defibrillator
    (AED), 326
Automobile safety, 330–332. *See also*
    Car safety seat.

Babinski toe reflex, 289, 438
Baby, at birth
    admission procedures for, 205, 283
    and discharge from birth facility,
        298–299
    Apgar scoring of, 204, 206, 283,
        294
    circulatory changes of, 284
    examination of, 283
    maintaining temperature of, 204,
        205, 283
    screenings of, 296–298
    testing/procedures of, 294–296
    See also Baby, newborn,
        characteristics of.
Baby, common concerns regarding
    bathing, 302
    bowel movements, 304, 364, 365
    circumcision, 291–293
    colic, 306–308
    cord care, 301–302
    crying, 305–306
    feeding frequency, 363
    jaundice, 50, 289–291, 299, 355,
        380
    skin care, 302–303
    sleeping, 308, 374
    spitting up, 304
    spoiling, 311
    sudden infant death syndrome,
        310–311
    urination, 303–304, 364, 365
    weight gain, 364, 366
    See also Baby proofing;
        Breastfeeding problems.
Baby, items needed for

car safety seat, 184, 331–332,
    334
clothes, 332, 333, 334
diapers, 333, 334, 336
equipment, 333, 334, 335
toys, 335–337
Baby, medical concerns regarding
    body injury, 314
    choking, 321–323
    convulsions, 314
    coughing, 313
    diarrhea, 313
    eye problems, 313
    fever, 312
    head injury, 314
    hearing loss, 314, 315
    immunizations, 316–321
    poison ingestion, 315
    rash, 314
    skin infection, 314
    sunburn, 314–315
    temperament change, 313
    temperature taking, 312–313
    vomiting, 313
    See also Cardiopulmonary
        resuscitation; Preterm baby.
Baby, naming, 297
Baby, newborn, characteristics of
    abdomen, 287
    arms and legs, 287
    breasts, 287
    breathing, 287
    eyes, 285–286
    feet, 287
    genitals, 287
    head, 284–285
    heart rate, 287
    reflexes, 288–289
    senses, 287–288
    skin, 286
    tear ducts, 286
Baby, newborn tests/procedures
    car-seat travel test, 296
    cord blood studies, 295
    eye prophylaxis, 294
    hepatitis B vaccine, 295
    hypoglycemia test, 294

jaundice test, 295
RhoGAM studies, 295
septic workup, 295
vitamin K injection, 294
Baby blues, 405, 408
Baby bottles, 393
Baby food, solid, 398–401
Baby-Friendly Hospital Initiative,
    368–369
Baby proofing, 326–329
Baby-safe habits, 330
Babysitter. *See* Childcare decision.
Back labor, 222–223
Bacterial vaginosis (BV), 69
Bathing baby, 301, 302
Bébé pod, 330, 333
Bed sharing, 309
Bicep Curls, 122
Bicycling in Water, 121
Biophysical profile (BPP), 52, 55, 56,
    70, 273
Bili-blanket, 290
Bili-lights, 290
Bilirubin, 254, 289, 290, 291, 295, 345,
    355, 370
Birth ball, 159, 160, 164–165, 169, 220
Birth center. *See* Birth facility.
Birth circle, 181
Birth control, 351, 426–435
Birth facility
    admission procedures of, 192–194
    and rooming-in, 209, 212
    and sibling visitation, 212
    Baby-Friendly designation of, 369
    delivery procedures of, 170, 204,
        243
    discharge from, 194, 213, 298–299
    during stay at, 213–215, 369,
        371–372
    preregistering at, 178–179
    tour of, 178, 215
    when to leave for, 192
Birth Partner, The (Simkin), 178
Birth plans, 10–12, 14, 15
Birth without interventions, 225, 228
Birth without medical assistance,
    223–225

Birth Without Violence (Leboyer), 226
Birthing Normally (Peterson), 155
Blastocyst, 20
Blood
    and Rh factor, 48, 49, 51, 57, 77,
        291, 295
    fetal, 25, 284
    incompatibility, 57, 77, 291
    type, 48
    umbilical cord, 179, 203, 295
    volume, 84–85, 88–89, 91, 203
Bloody show, 188, 201
Body Tension Awareness relaxation
        method, 146–148
Bonding, 204, 205, 207, 208–209, 212,
        215, 263, 264, 273, 278, 297, 337,
        416
Bottle-feeding, 392–397
Bottle mouth syndrome, 394
Bowel movement, 304, 364, 365
BPP. *See* Biophysical profile.
Bradley, Robert A., 141
Bradley method, 13, 141
Braxton-Hicks contractions, 29, 31, 38,
        74, 175, 186, 210
Breast pumps, 389, 390
Breastfeeding
    adoptive mothers and, 354–355
    alcohol consumption and, 356
    as contraception method, 351
    assistance for, 385–386
    benefits for baby, 344–350
    benefits for community and
        environment, 352–353
    benefits for fathers, 352
    benefits for mothers, 350–351
    breast surgery and, 354
    burping the baby and, 363
    cesarean birth and, 369–370
    common questions about, 363–364,
        366–368
    contractions during, 351, 357, 403
    contraindications to, 353–354
    convenience of, 350, 351
    diabetes and, 355
    dieting and, 355
    during growth spurts, 359

economic advantages of, 352
emotional advantages of, 351
exercise and, 367
false contraindications to, 354–357
formula manufacturers and, 387
frequency of, 363
hepatitis B and, 355
HIV and, 353
in public, 386
interventions that affect, 370–371
jaundice and, 355
let-down reflex and, 357
medications and, 356
multiples, 384
near-term infants, 384–385
oxytocin release and, 351, 357, 369
pregnancy and, 356
preparing for, 368–374
preparing nipples for, 368
proper latching for, 359–363
smoking and, 356
special diet and, 366
succeeding at, 343–344, 368–369,
        371–374
supplemental bottles and, 372
weaning and, 387–388
working mothers and, 383–384
See also Breastfeeding positions;
        Breastfeeding problems;
        Breastmilk production.
Breastfeeding positions, 360–362, 371
Breastfeeding problems
    ankyloglossia, 382
    breast fullness/engorgement, 376
    flat nipples, 380
    fussy baby, 381–382
    inadequate milk supply, 378–379
    ineffective nurser, 382
    inverted nipples, 380
    large breasts, 377
    mastitis, 379–380
    milk leakage, 377
    nipple soreness, 375–376
    oversupply of milk, 379
    plugged ducts, 379
    refusal of breast, 381
    sleepy baby, 380–381

swollen areolar tissue, 376–377
vigorous nurser, 382
Breastfeeding Record, 365
Breastmilk
    allergies and, 347, 349
    benefits for baby, 344–350
    comparison to cow's milk, 347
    comparison to formula, 349–350
    digestion and, 348
    donor, 348, 353, 386
    foremilk, 359, 379
    herbs that increase, 379
    hindmilk, 359, 366, 378, 379
    immunologic benefits of, 346–347
    intestinal disorders and, 349
    long-term advantages of, 349
    nutritional value of, 344–345
    oral development and, 348–349
    preterm babies and, 347–348
    production of, 357–359
    skin benefits and, 349
    storing of, 391–392
    See also Breastmilk, expressing;
        Colostrum.
Breastmilk, expressing
    guidelines for, 391–392
    hand method for, 389
    in the workplace, 383
    pumping methods for, 389–391
Breastmilk substitute. *See* Formula,
    infant.
Breasts
    anatomy of, 357
    during breastfeeding, 357–359, 363,
        367, 370, 373, 375, 376, 377, 378,
        379
    during postpartum, 345, 357, 376,
        404, 425
    during pregnancy, 27, 29, 30, 91,
        357
Breaststroke Swimming in Place, 120
Breathing techniques
    during labor, 157–158
    while pushing, 168–169
Breech presentation, 189, 217–220,
        222, 265
Breech-tilt position, 218, 219

Brick dust urine, 304
Bumbo seat, 330, 333
Burping the baby, 304, 305, 363, 382, 393
BV. *See* Bacterial vaginosis.

Caffeine, 38, 102, 103
CAH. *See* Congenital adrenal hyperplasia.
Calf Stretch, 125
Calming reflex, 289, 307
Caput succedaneum, 256, 259, 284, 438
Car safety. *See* Automobile safety.
Car safety seat, 184, 331–332, 334. *See also* Automobile safety.
Cardinal movements, 190
Cardiopulmonary resuscitation (CPR), 225, 323, 325–325
Caregiver
    choosing of, 5–6
    questions for, 15–16, 48
    when to call during pregnancy, 55, 58, 74–75,79, 85, 115, 188
    when to call postpartum, 378, 403, 405
    See also Midwife; Pediatrician.
Carrier screenings, 49–50
Centers for Disease Control (CDC), 68, 69, 248, 271, 316, 318, 319, 320
Cephalhematoma, 256, 259, 285, 438
Cephalic presentation, 189, 217
Cerclage, 75
Cervix, 17, 18, 192
    changes during pregnancy, 27, 31
    dilation and effacement of, 167, 177, 186, 187, 188, 189, 190–191, 195, 196, 197, 198–199, 200
    incompetent, 75
    induced dilation of, 242–243, 253–256
Cesarean baby, 278
Cesarean birth, 4, 263
    as family event, 263–265
    contributors to, 270
    elective, 268–269
    exercise after, 280–281
    incisions for, 275–276
    indications for, 265–266, 268
    planned and unplanned, 272, 273
    postpartum, 278–280
    preoperative procedures for, 273–274
    recovery room procedures for, 277–278
    risks of, 270–271
    sexual relations following, 280
    surgical procedures for, 276–277
    ways to avoid, 271–272
    See also Vaginal birth after cesarean.
Cesarean delivery. *See* Cesarean birth.
Cesarean section. *See* Cesarean birth.
CF. *See* Cystic fibrosis.
Chicken pox, 59, 318–319
Child Passenger Safety (CPS) technician, 184, 332
Childbirth preparation methods, 138
    Bradley method, 13, 141
    hypnosis methods, 141
    Lamaze method, 13, 139–141
    relaxation techniques, 142–174
    See also Labor tools/techniques; Pushing during labor.
Childbirth without Fear (Dick-Read), 139
Childcare decision, 340–341
Childhood illnesses and pregnancy, 58–64
Children at the birth, 214–215
Choking, 321–323
Chorion, 21
Chorionic villi, 20, 21, 49
Chorionic villus sampling (CVS), 49
Cigarette smoking
    during breastfeeding, 356, 378, 381
    during pregnancy, 25, 42–43, 74, 250
    effect on children, 310, 330, 347
    effect on fertility, 427
Circulation
    of fetus, 24–25
    of newborn, 203, 284
    of woman during pregnancy, 29
Circumcision, 291–293, 371
Classes
    for childbirth preparation, 13
    for early pregnancy, 427
    for new parents, 410
    for siblings, 411
Clothing, baby, 332–333, 334
Cluster feeding, 359
Clutch position. *See* Football hold nursing position.
CMV. *See* Cytomegalovirus.
Colic, 306–308, 337, 396
Colic hold, 308
Colostrum, 29, 208, 225, 269, 278, 288, 290, 345–346, 348, 355, 357, 358, 364, 369, 380, 381
Compassionate Friends, 262
Complete breech presentation, 217–218
Conception. *See* Fertilization.
Congenital adrenal hyperplasia (CAH), 298
Contraception. *See* Birth control.
Contraction stress test. *See* Oxytocin challenge test.
Contractions
    after amniotomy, 256
    afterpains, 207, 235, 238
    as sign of labor, 187, 188
    during breastfeeding, 351, 357, 403
    during labor, 196–197, 198, 199, 200, 201, 202, 206–207, 220, 221, 222, 273
    induced, 245, 252–254, 255–256, 272, 370
    prelabor versus true labor, 187
    tetanic, 253
    timing of, 187
Cord. *See* Umbilical cord.
Cordocentesis, 57
Co-sleeping, 309
Cotterman, Jean, 376
Cough reflex, 288
Counter pressure, 161–162
Couvade syndrome, 30, 32
CPR. *See* Cardiopulmonary resuscitation.
Cradle cap, 303
Cradle nursing position, 360, 362, 371

Crib death. *See* Sudden infant death syndrome.
Crohn's disease, 105
Cross-cradle nursing position, 360–362, 371
Crowning, 201
Crying in newborns, 305–306, 311. *See also* Colic.
Cryobanks, 179
C-section. *See* Cesarean birth.
Cup-feeding, 394
CVS. *See* Chorionic villus sampling.
Cystic fibrosis (CF), 50, 53, 298, 427
Cytomegalovirus (CMV), 60, 355

DES. *See* Diethylstilbestrol.
DES daughters, 80–81
Diabetes, gestational, 70–71
Diabetic mother, early delivery of, 266
Diapers, 183, 333, 334, 336
Dick-Read, Grantly, 138–139, 141
Dietary guidelines during pregnancy, 92, 94–95, 97–102, 104–105
Diethylstilbestrol (DES), 74, 80–81
Digestion during pregnancy, 27, 31
Dilation, cervical, 75, 176, 186, 190, 191, 192, 210, 212, 229, 238, 249, 253, 424
Diphtheria, 317, 319, 320
Diphtheria, Tetanus, Pertussis (DTaP) vaccine, 317, 320
Directed pushing, 168, 169
DONA International, 178
Donor breastmilk, 348, 353, 386
Doppler blood flow study, 57
Doppler monitor, 22, 52, 57
Double-Hip Squeeze, 161–162, 222
Doula, 4, 8, 140, 178, 196, 199, 257, 272, 282, 408
Dropping. *See* Lightening.
Drugs, recreational, 44–45, 353, 427
Drugs in Pregnancy and Lactation, 38
Dry birth, 188
DTaP. *See* Diphtheria, Tetanus, Pertussis vaccine.
Ductus arteriosus, 203, 284, 305

Due date, 20
Dural membrane, 240, 241
Dystocia, 80

E. coli bacteria, 65–66, 100, 101
Early labor, 195–196, 221
Eclampsia, 72, 242, 266
Ectopic pregnancy, 79
Edema, 29, 84–85, 86, 207, 246, 254
Effacement, cervical, 176, 186, 190, 192, 210, 212
Effleurage, 160, 161
Elevator Kegel, 130, 173
Embryo, 21
Emergencies, handling
    for choking, 321–323
    for poison ingestion, 315, 332
    performing CPR, 324–325
    using automated external defibrillator, 325–326
Emergency birth control, 426–427
Emergency birth kit, 184, 224
Empty Arms (Ilse), 262
Endorphins, 113, 132, 162, 165, 166, 193, 198, 229, 269, 348
Engorged breasts, 376, 379, 395, 404
Environmental Protection Agency (EPA), 101, 320, 327, 329
EPA. *See* Environmental Protection Agency
Epidurals, 7, 8, 12, 13, 16, 178, 198, 200, 204, 205, 222, 230, 231, 232, 233, 238–241, 258, 268, 274, 277, 370
Episiotomy, 130, 131, 172, 173, 207, 232, 257–258
Erythema toxicum, 286, 303
Erythroblastosis fetalis, 266
Escherichia coli. *See* E. coli bacteria.
Estrogen, 26, 29, 80, 84, 86, 186, 357, 426
Exercise
    aerobic, 113, 119–121
    guidelines and precautions for, 114–116
Kegels, 129, 130–131

postpartum, 417–423
postpartum cesarean, 280–281
prenatal yoga, 128
proper attire for, 118–119
recommendations for, 115
strength-training, 113, 122–123
stretching/flexibility, 113, 124–126, 128
to relieve leg cramps, 127
to relieve sciatic pain, 127
External version, 218, 219, 242, 266

FDA. *See* US Food and Drug Administration.
Fear-tension-pain cycle, 139, 141, 268
Fertilization, 17–20
    alternative methods of, 19
Fetal alcohol syndrome (FAS), 43, 102
Fetal fibronectin (fFN), 55, 75
Fetal heart rate
    epidural effect on, 240
    nonreassuring, 56, 246, 247, 248, 249, 250, 265
    ominous, 246
    reassuring, 56, 246
Fetal kick count. *See* Fetal movement evaluation.
Fetal monitor, 168, 192, 194, 205, 222, 233, 249, 256
    electronic, 9, 52, 158, 193, 245, 246–249, 265, 270, 272
    hand-held, 9, 22, 52, 57, 194, 228
    STAN S31, 249
    ultrasound, 52
Fetal movement evaluation, 54–55
Fetal movement tracking chart, 54
Fetal oxygen saturation monitor, 249–250, 251, 256
Fetoscope, 9, 228
Fetus
    development of, 20–24
    distress of, 57, 142, 173, 218, 238, 243, 247, 249, 253, 254, 265, 267, 272
    position of, 189, 217, 220
    presentation of, 73, 177, 189, 201, 217–219, 221, 222, 265, 266, 270.
    See also Fetal heart rate.

fFN. *See* Fetal fibronectin.
Finger-feeding, 394
First Candle/SIDS Alliance, 262, 311
First Signs, 320
First trimester combined screening
  test, 49
Five S's, 307, 308
Flu. *See* Influenza.
Folate, 89
Folic acid, 86, 89
Fontanels, 285
Food-borne infections, and pregnancy,
  64–66
Foot Flexing/Stretching, 280, 281, 418
Foot Stretch, 128
Football hold nursing position, 360, 362
Footling breech presentation, 218
Foramen ovale, 284
Forceps delivery, 3, 172, 173, 178, 215,
  230, 231, 232, 238, 248, 254,
  258–259, 270, 277, 285, 370
Foremilk, 359, 379
Formula
  comparison to breastmilk, 349–398
  marketing of, 387, 396
  preparation guidelines for, 397–398
  removal from clothing, 396
  safeguards for, 397
  safety issues of, 349–350
  sterilizing water for, 400
  types of, 396–397
Frank breech presentation, 218
Freestyle Swimming in Place, 119–120

Gag reflex, 288
Galactosemia, 297, 298, 354
Gate Control Theory of Pain, 138, 157,
  162
GBS. *See* Group B streptococcus.
Genital herpes, 49, 62, 132, 250, 266,
  353
Gentle birth, 225–228
German measles, 61, 318, 319
Gestational age, 20
Giardiasis, 66
Gingivitis, 35
Glucose screening, 51

Glucose tolerance test (GTT), 51
Grasp reflex, 288, 289
Group B strep. *See* Group B
  streptococcus.
Group B strep culture, 55, 188, 192,
  193, 194, 246
Group B streptococcus (GBS), 48, 55,
  58, 67–68, 193, 250
GTT. *See* Glucose tolerance test.

Haemophilus influenza type b (Hib),
  317
Hamstring Stretch, 128
Happiest Baby on the Block (Karp), 13,
  307, 374
Harper, Barbara, 227
Hathaway, Jay, 141
Hathaway, Marjie, 141
Head Lifting, 419
Hearing guidelines, 315
Heartburn fighters, 31, 42
Heel stick blood test, 295, 348
HELLP syndrome, 72
Hemolytic disease of the newborn, 77
Hemorrhagic disease of the newborn,
  294
Hepatitis A, 319
Hepatitis B, 58, 63, 295, 316, 317, 319,
  355
Hepatitis C, 63, 355
Herpes. *See* Genital herpes.
Herpes simplex virus (HSV), 62, 266
Hib. *See* Haemophilus influenza type b.
Hindmilk, 359, 366, 378, 379
Hip Rolls, 422–423
HIV. *See* Human immunodeficiency
  virus.
HMBANA. *See* Human Milk Banking
  Association of North America.
Home birth, 10
Honeymoon stitch, 258
Hospital bags, 181, 183. *See also*
  Lamaze bag.
Hospitals, types of, 9–10. *See also*
  Birth facility.
HSV. *See* Herpes simplex virus.

Human immunodeficiency virus (HIV),
  63–64, 353
Human Milk Banking Association of
  North America (HMBANA), 386
Hyperbilirubinemia, 254, 289, 290, 291
Hypertension, 71, 78, 270. *See also*
  Pregnancy-induced hypertension.
Hypertension in pregnancy. *See*
  Pregnancy-induced hypertension.
Hypnobabies, 141
HypnoBirthing, 13, 141
Hypoglycemia, 70, 246, 294
Hypothyroidism, congenital, 297

IBCLC. *See* International board
  certified lactation consultant.
ILCA. *See* International Lactation
  Consultant Association.
Ilse, Sherokee, 262
Immunizations, 311, 316–321
In vitro fertilization, 19
Incisions for cesarean birth,
  275–276
Induction of labor
  alternative methods for, 255–256
  by dilating cervix, 253
  by stripping membranes, 253
  elective, 250–252
  risks of, 252
  through amniotomy, 254
  through Pitocin, 254
*Infant Massage: A Handbook for
  Loving Parents* (McClure), 340
Infant Massage USA, 340
Influenza, viral, 69, 318
Informed consent, 14–16
Institute of Medicine (IOM), 320
International board certified lactation
  consultant. *See* Lactation
  consultant.
International Childbirth Education
  Association, 178
International Code of Marketing of
  Breastmilk Substitutes, 387
*International Journal of Childbirth
  Education*, 424

International Lactation Consultant Association (ILCA), 386
Interventions
    during birth, 257–259
    during labor, 245–250
    See also Induction of labor.
Intracytoplasmic sperm injection, 19
Intradermal water blocks, 166
Intrauterine pressure catheter, 254
IOM. *See* Institute of Medicine.
JAMA. *See Journal of the American Medical Association.*
Jaundice, 50, 289–291, 299, 355, 380
    causes of, 48, 63, 70, 226, 240, 253, 254, 289, 291, 295, 319, 345, 370
    test for, 215, 295
    treatment for, 289, 290
Jogging in Water, 121
Journal of the American Medical Association, 219, 271
Journal of the National Cancer Institute, 43
Journal of Pediatrics, The, 43, 349
Juvenile Products Manufacturers Association, 326

Kangaroo care, 208, 348
Karmel, Marjorie, 139
Karp, Harvey, 307, 308, 374
Kegel, Arnold, 130
Kegel exercises, 129–131, 173, 201, 207, 214, 258, 268, 281, 417, 418, 419, 421, 422, 423, 425
Kennell, John, 208
Kernicterus, 290
Klaus, Marshall, 208
Knee breech presentation, 218
Knee-chest position, 266, 420
Knee Press, 162
Knee Reaching, 281
Kohn, Ingrid, 262

La Leche League (LLL), 343, 368, 369, 373, 374, 384, 385, 386, 388
Labor
    active management of, 257
    augmentation of, 256

breathing techniques for, 157–158
coping with pain of, 137–138
induction of, 250–256
interventions during, 245–256
positions for, 158–160
preparation methods for, 138–141
process of, 189–192
pushing techniques for, 167–174
relaxation methods for, 142–166
signs of, 185–186, 187, 188–189
variations of, 220–223
See also Birth without medical assistance; Cesarean birth; Gentle birth; Labor tools/techniques; Stages of labor.
Labor partner, 141, 144–146, 149, 153, 154, 194–195, 196, 197, 198–199, 202, 203, 210–213
Labor tools/techniques
    acupressure, 162–163
    acupuncture, 167
    aromatherapy, 163
    birth ball, 159, 160, 164–165, 169, 220
    breathing methods, 157–158, 168–169
    counter pressure, 161–162
    intradermal water blocks, 166
    massage, 160–161
    music, 163
    relaxation methods, 142–166
    transcutaneous electric nerve stimulation, 166
    use of heat/cold, 163–164
    use of rituals, 165–166
    visualization, 153–156
Laboring down, 167, 200
Laboring in water, 9, 160, 164, 165, 193, 205, 249, 250
Lactation Amenorrhea Method (LAM), 351
Lactation consultant, 180, 212, 214, 290, 343, 348, 355, 356, 359, 364, 368, 372, 373, 374, 375, 378, 380, 382, 384, 385–386, 388, 390, 394
Lactose intolerance, 102, 104
LAM. *See* Lactation Amenorrhea Method.

Lamaze, Fernand, 139
Lamaze bag, 181, 182
Lamaze International, 140
Lamaze method, 13, 139–141
Lanugo, 22, 23, 286, 304
Lap squat, 170–171
Latching, 359–360
Lateral Sims' position, 172
Lawrence, Robert M., 353
Lead poisoning, 326–327, 329
Leboyer, Frederick, 203, 226
Leboyer delivery, 225, 226–227
Lecithin to sphingomyelin ratio, 273
Leg Kicks in Water, 121
Leg Kicks in Water While Sitting, 121
Let-down reflex, 304, 357, 366, 382
Lightening, 31, 185, 186, 189, 210
Linea nigra, 29
Listeriosis, 65, 100
Lithotomy position. *See* Supine position.
LLL. *See* Le Leche League.
Local infiltration, 232
Lochia, 207, 214, 403
Log Rolling, 281
Low blood sugar. *See* Hypoglycemia.
L/S ratio. *See* Lecithin to sphingomyelin ratio.
Lucas, Alan, 349
Lunge position, 159, 222
Lymphocytic choriomeningitis, 67

Macrosomia, 80, 250
Madonna complex, 416–417
Magnetic resonance imaging (MRI), 57
Mahan, Charles, 6
March of Dimes, 296
Marshall, William, Jr., 353
Mask of pregnancy, 30
Massage
    during labor, 160–161
    during pregnancy, 131–135
    infant, 337–340
Mastitis, 373, 379–380, 395
Maternal exhaustion, 4, 251
Maternal-Infant Bonding (Klaus and Kennell), 208
McClure, Vimala Schneider, 340

McKenna, James J., 308, 309

Measles, 60, 318, 319. *See also* German measles.

Meconium, 22, 208, 256, 265, 284, 290, 304, 336, 345, 364

Medication
  analgesics, 230, 232–241
  anesthesia, 232, 233, 238–240, 241
  benefits of, 230–231
  commonly used during childbirth, 234–238
  narcotics, 230–231, 233
  risks of, 231–232
  use during pregnancy, 41–42

MedWatch, 397

Melanocyte stimulating hormone, 30

Membranes, amniotic. *See* Amniotic membranes.

Meningitis, 319

Meningococcal disease. *See* Meningitis.

Midwife, 8–9, 204. *See also* Caregiver.

Midwifery model of care, 8–9

Milia, 286

Milk banks, donor, 348, 353, 386

Milk-ejection reflex. *See* Let-down reflex.

Miscarriage, 79–80

Modified Valsalva maneuver, 168–169

Moffitt, Perry-Lynn, 262

Molding, head, 256, 284

Mongolian spots, 286

Montagu, Ashley, 311

Montgomery glands, 27, 357, 368

Morning after pill, 426, 427

Morning sickness, 27, 80, 91

Moro reflex, 289

Moxibustion, 219

MRI. *See* Magnetic resonance imaging.

Mucous plug, 186, 188–189, 210

Multiple marker screening, 50–51

Multiple pregnancy, 72–73, 268

Mumps, 61, 318

National Center on Birth Defects and Developmental Disabilities, 89

National Highway Traffic Safety Administration (NHTSA), 184, 331

National Institute of Child Health & Human Development, 52–53

National Institutes of Health (NIH), 52

National Lead Information Center, 327

National Newborn Screening and Genetics Resource Center, 296

National Organization of Mothers of Twins Clubs, 73

Neck Stretch, 128

Necrotizing enterocolitis, 73

Neonatal intensive care unit (NICU), 347, 348

Nesting urge, 186

New England Journal of Medicine, The, 10, 90

NHTSA. *See* National Highway Traffic Safety Administration.

NICU. *See* Neonatal intensive care unit.

NIH. *See* National Institutes of Health.

Nipples
  and expressing milk, 389, 390, 391
  and mastitis, 379–380
  and reverse-pressure softening, 376–377
  care of, 372, 375
  flat, 380
  inverted, 380
  plugged ducts, 379
  position during breastfeeding, 361, 362, 372
  preparing for breastfeeding, 368
  sore, 359, 360, 363, 368, 373, 375, 382
  stimulation of, 38, 76, 221, 225, 255, 256, 260, 357
  vasospasms, 376

Nipples, bottle, 393

Nonreassuring fetal heart rate, 56, 246, 247, 248, 249, 250, 265

Non-stress test, 55

Nuchal translucency screening, 49

Nursing. *See* Breastfeeding.

Nursing bra, 118, 183, 367, 425

Nutrition during pregnancy
  and daily dietary guidelines, 92, 94
  and daily dietary recall, 97
  and foods to avoid, 100–102
  and making good choices, 95, 96

and trimester needs, 91–92
  basics of, 86–90
  bodily focus of, 84–86
  special concerns of, 102, 104–105
  vegetarian diet and, 98–99

OAE screening. *See* Otoacoustic emissions screening.

OB. *See* Obstetrician.

Obesity and pregnancy, 80

Obstetrician (OB), 7–8. *See also* Caregiver.

OCT. *See* Oxytocin challenge test.

Odent, Michael, 227, 228

Ominous fetal heart rate, 246

Otoacoustic emissions screening, 296

Overhead Press, 123

Oxytocin, 7, 38, 57, 208, 221, 225, 232, 234, 235, 254, 255, 256, 260, 351, 357, 369, 425

Oxytocin challenge test (OCT), 44, 56–57

Paracervical block, 232

Paraphimosis, 293

Parenthood, adjustment to, 405–417, 436

Patient-controlled analgesia (PCA), 233, 279

PCA. *See* Patient-controlled analgesia.

Peanut butter, making, 104

Pediarix, 319

Pediatrician
  choosing, 179–180
  when to call, 312–315

Pelvic Rock, 41, 125, 160, 172, 220, 222

Pelvic Tilt, 281, 418–419

Percutaneous umbilical blood sampling (PUBS). *See* Cordocentesis.

Peri-care, 183, 213–214

Perinatologist, 7

Perineal massage, 129, 131–132, 201, 258

Perineum, 131, 169, 170, 171, 173, 174, 201, 213, 214, 227, 232, 241, 257, 258, 404, 417

Pertussis, 317, 319, 320

Peterson, Gayle, 155

Petrikovsky, Boris, 65

Pets, preparing for newborn, 414–416

Phenylketonuria (PKU), 39, 78, 102, 104, 297, 298

Phimosis, 292

Phototherapy, 290, 291

Physician, family practice, 7. *See also* Caregiver.

Physician model of care, 7–8

Pica, 105

PIH. *See* Pregnancy-induced hypertension.

Pitocin, 234, 443
    for oxytocin challenge test, 56
    risks of, 252–253, 256, 272, 289, 370, 377, 404
    to aid contractions following birth, 260–277
    to augment/induce labor, 4, 178, 188, 221, 222, 243, 245, 252–253, 254, 255, 256, 257

Placenta, 20, 21, 22, 24–25, 27, 84–86, 91, 142, 177, 192, 195, 203, 206–207, 224, 225, 243, 253, 260, 267, 277, 357, 378

Placenta accreta, 260, 271

Placenta previa, 38, 51, 56, 74, 114, 266, 267, 271

Placental abruption, 43, 44, 56, 57, 71, 72, 74, 266, 267

Plan B birth control pill, 426, 427

Planned Parenthood, 427

Plantar toe reflex, 289

Pneumococcal disease, 317

Poison Control Center, 315

Polio, 317–318, 319

Position, fetal, 189, 217, 220

Postpartum
    care following cesarean, 278–279
    care following vaginal delivery, 207, 213
    emotional changes during, 405, 407–408
    exercises, 207, 280–281
    guest limitation, 408
    help at home, 280, 408

physical changes during, 403–404, 405

sex, 280, 423–427

Postpartum depression, 407

Postpartum hemorrhage, 259–260

Postpartum Pelvic Rock, 420

Post-term pregnancy, 242–243

Precipitate labor, 220–221

Preeclampsia, 29, 35, 48, 70, 71–72, 80, 85, 242, 266, 273

Pregnancy-induced hypertension (PIH), 71–72, 242

Pregnancy
    alcohol and, 43
    artificial sweeteners and, 39
    caffeine and, 38
    car safety during, 34
    cigarette smoking and, 42–43
    dental care and, 35–36
    domestic violence and, 81
    ectopic, 79
    emotional changes during, 26, 28, 30, 32
    environmental concerns during, 45–46
    exercise during, 113–116, 119–131
    first trimester of, 26–28, 36, 48–50, 80, 91
    food additives and, 40
    foods to avoid during, 100–102
    herbs and, 39–40
    high risk, 70–78
    illness during, 58–70
    length of, 26
    medications and, 41–42
    miscarriage during, 79–80
    obesity and, 80
    over age thirty-five, 78–79
    physical changes during, 26–28, 29–30, 31
    physical exams during, 47–48
    recreational drugs and, 44–45
    second trimester of, 29–30, 36–37, 50–54, 91
    sexual abuse and, 81
    sexual relations and , 36–38
    signs of complications during, 58

teen, 78

third trimester of, 30–32, 37, 54–57, 91–92

traveling and, 34–35

weight gain during, 85–86

working during, 33

See also Massage during pregnancy; Nutrition during pregnancy; Pregnancy, tests during.

Pregnancy, tests during
    amniocentesis, 53–54
    antibody screening, 51
    biophysical profile, 56
    blood type and Rh factor, 48
    carrier screenings, 49–50
    chorionic villus sampling, 49
    cordocentesis, 57
    Doppler blood flow study, 57
    fetal fibronectin test, 55
    fetal movement evaluation, 54–55
    glucose screening, 51
    group B strep culture, 55
    magnetic resonance imaging, 57
    multiple marker screening, 50–51
    non-stress test, 55
    nuchal translucency screening, 49
    oxytocin challenge test, 56–57
    sonogram (ultrasound), 51–53

Pregnancy-induced hypertension (PIH), 57, 71, 75, 89, 242

Prelabor, 187

Premature rupture of membranes (PROM), 250

Presentation, fetal, 73, 177, 189, 201, 217–219, 221, 222, 265, 266, 270

Preterm baby, 73, 220, 271, 273, 286, 293, 310, 322, 345, 347–348, 390

Preterm labor, 73–77, 220
    bed rest and, 75–77
    signs of, 188–189
    medication for, 242
    risk factors for, 35, 42, 44, 56, 57, 64, 68, 69, 72, 74, 80, 83, 100, 142, 252, 370, 426

Progesterone, 18, 26, 27, 357, 426

Prolapsed umbilical cord, 218, 266

Prolonged labor, 221–222

Prolonged prelabor, 221
PROM. *See* Premature rupture of
    membranes.
Prone resting position, 419
Prostaglandins, 253–254
Psychoprophylaxis techniques, 139
Pubococcygeus muscle, 129
Pudendal block, 232
Pulse oximeter, 278–279
Pumping breastmilk. *See*
    Breastmilk, expressing.
Pumps, breast. *See* Breast pumps.
Pushing during labor, 200–205
    breathing patterns for,
        168–169
    positions for, 169–173
    practice sessions for, 173–174
    types of, 167–168

Quickening, 22

Rashes, newborn, 286, 303
Ratner, Herbert, 373
RDS. *See* Respiratory distress
    syndrome.
Reassuring fetal heart rate, 56, 246
Recti muscle separation, 281, 419
Rectus abdominis muscles, 115
Reflexes, newborn, 288–289
Relaxation
    and signs of tension, 144–146
    basics of, 143–144
    benefits of, 142–143
    methods during labor, 142–174
    positions, 143–144
    See also Labor tools/techniques.
Relaxin, 27, 115
Relaxing breath, 157
Reproductive organs, 17–18
Respiratory distress syndrome , 373
Reverse-pressure softening techniques,
    376–377
Rh factor, 48, 77, 214–215
Rh-immune globulin (RhoGAM), 48,
    49, 51, 54, 77, 214–215, 266, 291,
    295
Rh incompatibility, 77

RhoGAM. *See* Rh-immune globulin.
Rib Cage Stretch, 124
Rich, Laurie A., 262
Ring of fire, 201
Rooming-in, 209, 212, 225, 264, 279
Rooting reflex, 288, 361
Rotavirus gastroenteritis, 317
Rowing, 123
Rubella. *See* German measles.
Rubeola. *See* Measles.

Salmonella, 66, 100
Sandwich hold, 360, 361
Sanger, Max, 263
Screenings, newborn, 296, 297–298
Sears, William, 411
Security, hospital, 178, 285
7 Baby B's, 411
Sexual relations, 36–38, 280, 423
Sexually transmitted diseases, and
    pregnancy, 61–64
Shoulder presentation. *See* Transverse
    lie position.
Shoulder Rotations, 124
Siblings
    and negative behavior, 412–414
    and preparing for newborn, 410–414
    and visitation in birth facility, 212
    See also Children at the birth.
Sickle cell disease, 50, 53, 57, 74, 179,
    298, 427
Side Kicks, 421
Side-lying position, 37, 143, 160, 169,
    172, 222, 223, 360
SIDS. *See* Sudden infant death
    syndrome.
Silent Sorrow (Kohn, Moffitt, Wilkens),
    262
Simkin, Penny, 129, 131, 178
Sims' position, 144, 172, 220
Single Leg Raises, 422
Single Leg Slide, 422
Sit-Ups, Modified, 420–423
Sitz bath, 214, 258
Skin, during pregnancy, 27–28
Skin care, baby, 302–303
Sleep cycles, newborn, 308

Sneezing reflex, 288
Soft spots. *See* Fontanels.
Sonogram, 51–53
Sperm, 17, 18, 19
Spitting up, 304
Spontaneous pushing, 167–168
Spoon-feeding, 394
Squatting positions, 170–172, 223
Stages of labor, 177, 192, 195
    first stage, 195–200
    fourth stage, 207–209
    second stage, 200–205
    third stage, 206–207
STAN S31 fetal monitor, 249
Staphylococcus aureus, 314
Station, fetal, 191
STDs. *See* Sexually transmitted
    diseases.
Stepping reflex, 288, 289
Sterilizing water, 400
Stillbirth, 261-262
Stork bites. *See* Angel kisses.
Strength-training exercises, prenatal,
    122–123
Stretch marks, 30
Stretching/flexibility exercises,
    prenatal, 124–128
Striae gravidarum. *See* Stretch marks.
Stripping the membranes, 221, 253
Subgaleal hemorrhage, 259
Sucking reflex, 288, 294, 369, 370
Sudden infant death syndrome (SIDS),
    43, 209, 310–311
Super Kegel, 130, 131, 214, 281, 418,
    419, 421, 422, 423, 425
Supine hypotension, 172, 272
Supine position, 11, 117, 173, 258
Supplemental nursing, 394
Supplements, prenatal, 90. *See also*
    Nutrition during pregnancy.
Surfactant, 242, 269
Swaddling, 306
Swallowing reflex, 288

Tailor Press, 126
Tailor sitting, 117
Tailor Stretch, 126

Tay-Sachs disease, 50, 53, 298, 427
Temperature
    maintaining newborn's, 204, 205, 283
    taking baby's, 312–313
TENS. *See* Transcutaneous nerve stimulation.
Tetanus, 317, 319
Thalassemia, 50, 298, 427
Thank You, Dr. Lamaze (Karmel), 139
Thermometers, 312–313
Thimerosal, 320
Thrush, 69–70, 375–376
Tocolytic medication, 242
Tongue-tie. *See* Ankyloglossia.
Tonic neck reflex, 289
Total Body Relaxation method, 149, 150–151
Total Relaxation method, 149, 152–153
Toxemia. *See* Pregnancy-induced hypertension.
Toxoplasmosis, 67, 100, 101
Toys, selecting baby, 335–337
Transcutaneous bilirubin level (TaB) monitor, 295
Transcutaneous nerve stimulation (TENS), 166
Transient tachypnea of the newborn, 271
Transition, 197–198
Transverse lie position, 189, 217
Trimesters of pregnancy, 20
    first trimester, 26–28, 36, 48–50, 80, 91
    second trimester, 29–30, 36–37, 50–54, 91
    third trimester, 30–32, 37, 54–57, 91–92
Triple Connection, The, 73

Tummy time, 311
Twin-to-twin transfusion syndrome, 72–73
Tylenol overdosing, 319

Ultrasound, 51–53
Umbilical cord
    and fetal development, 25–26
    around baby's neck, 224
    blood, 179, 203, 295
    compression of, 247, 265
    cutting of, 70, 202, 203, 225, 277, 284
    prolapse of, 218, 254, 266, 267
    stump care, 287, 301–302
Underwater birth, 225, 227–228
Urination
    during pregnancy, 27, 31
    of newborn, 303–304, 364–365
Urine atony, 259–260
US Consumer Product Safety Commission (CPSC), 309, 331
US Department of Agriculture (USDA), 97, 352
US Food and Drug Administration (FDA), 38, 39, 45, 52, 53, 62, 64, 89, 101, 102, 243, 249, 259, 254, 313, 316, 319, 320, 332, 345, 426
US Surgeon General, 43, 352
USDA. *See* US Department of Agriculture.
Uterus, 17, 18, 26–27, 29, 31

Vacuum extractor, 173, 215, 230, 232, 238, 248, 257, 258, 259, 268, 277, 285, 370
Vagina, 18, 19, 27, 29, 31

Vaginal birth, 269
Vaginal birth after cesarean (VBAC), 4–5, 265, 276
Valsalva maneuver, 168
Vanishing twin syndrome, 72
Varicella. *See* Chicken pox.
Vasospasms, 376
VBAC. *See* Vaginal birth after cesarean.
Vegetarian diet during pregnancy, 98–99
Vena cava, 117
Vernix caseosa, 23, 286
Vertex presentation, fetal, 189, 217
Visualization, 153–156
Vitamin K injection, 294
Vitamins, prenatal, 90. *See also* Nutrition during pregnancy.
Walkers, dangers of, 332, 333
Walking epidural, 241
Wall Squats, 123
Waterbirth. *See* Underwater birth.
Weaning, 356, 357, 368, 387–388, 395
Weight gain
    during pregnancy, 85–86
    of newborn, 364, 366
Wharton's jelly, 25
What Every Pregnant Woman Needs to Know About Cesarean Section, 267
When Pregnancy Isn't Perfect (Rich), 262
Whooping cough. *See* Pertussis.
Wilkins, Isabelle A., 262
Witch's milk, 287
World Health Assembly, 387
World Health Organization (WHO), 140, 368

Zygote, 20

HEY! WHO'S HAVING THIS BABY ANYWAY?

Breck Hawk, RN

In this important new book, Breck Hawk explains how pregnant women can avoid the sometimes serious repercussions caused by unnecessary labor drugs and medical interventions. *Hey! Who's Having This Baby Anyway?* begins with the Patient Bill of Rights and Responsibilities so that moms-to-be understand how they can remain involved in their own care. The author then presents information on the types of available caregivers, labor medications, natural remedies, complementary methods of pregnancy and labor, home birth, water birth, birth plans, and breastfeeding. Several chapters close with helpful workbook pages for those readers who learn best by doing. A concluding chapter presents a compilation of women's childbearing experiences. Finally, lists of helpful books and websites point the way to further information and guidance.

$19.95 • 386 pages • 7.5 x 9-inch quality paperback • ISBN 978-0-7570-0248-9

HOW SMART IS YOUR BABY?

Glenn Doman, and Janet Doman

The first months after birth are vital to the long-term well-being of a child. Yet parents do not have the information they need to make their baby's life as stimulating as it should be. *How Smart Is Your Baby?* provides parents with all the information required to help their baby achieve full potential. The authors first explain infant growth, and then guide parents in creating a home environment that enhances brain development. A developmental profile allows parents to track their child's progress, determine strengths, and recognize where additional stimulation is needed.

$16.95 • 280 pages • 7.5 x 9-inch quality paperback • ISBN 978-0-7570-0194-9

DOES YOUR BABY HAVE AUTISM?

Osnat Teitelbaum and Philip Teitelbaum, PhD

For many years, the diagnosis of autism has centered on a child's social interaction—from poor eye contact to lack of language skills. Although the autism community agrees that early intervention is key to effective treatment, the telltale signs of this disorder usually don't reveal themselves until the age of two or three. But what if it were possible to detect the potential for autism within the first year of life?

Osnat and Philip Teitelbaum have worked for nearly two decades to establish ways of detecting signs of potential autism or Asperger's syndrome by examining early motor development. This book first provides general information about the history of autism and The Ladder of Motor Development. Each of four chapters then examines one motor milestone—righting, sitting, crawling, or walking—contrasting typical and atypical development so that it's easy to recognize unusual patterns of movement. Finally, parents are guided in finding professional help for a baby whose motor skills may indicate a problem.

$17.95 • 128 pages • 7.5 x 9-inch quality paperback • ISBN 978-0-7570-0240-3

HOW TO TEACH YOUR BABY TO READ
Glenn Doman and Janet Doman

As the founder of The Institutes for the Achievement of Human Potential, Glenn Doman has demonstrated time and again that young children are far more capable of learning than we ever imagined. In *How To Teach Your Baby To Read,* he and daughter Janet show just how easy it is to teach a young child to read. They explain how to begin and expand the reading program, how to make and organize necessary materials, and how to more fully develop your child's reading potential.

By following the simple daily program presented in *How To Teach Your Baby To Read,* you will give your baby a powerful advantage that will last a lifetime.

$13.95 • 288 pages • 6 x 9-inch quality paperback • ISBN 978-0-7570-0185-7

HOW TO TEACH YOUR BABY MATH
Glenn Doman and Janet Doman

Glenn and Janet Doman have not only shown that children from birth to age six learn better and faster than older children do, but have given it practical application. *How To Teach Your Baby Math* demonstrates just how easy it is to teach a young child mathematics through the development of thinking and reasoning skills. It explains how to begin and expand the math program, how to make and organize necessary materials, and how to more fully develop your child's math potential.

By following the simple daily program in a relaxed and loving way, you will enable your child to experience the joy of learning—as have millions of children the world over.

$13.95 • 240 pages • 6 x 9-inch quality paperback • ISBN 978-0-7570-0184-0

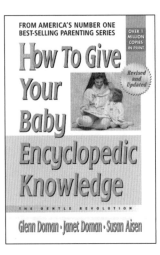

HOW TO GIVE YOUR BABY ENCYCLOPEDIC KNOWLEDGE
Glenn Doman, Janet Doman, and Susan Aisen

How To Give Your Baby Encyclopedic Knowledge shows you how simple it is to teach a young child about the arts, science, and nature. Your child will recognize the insects in the garden, learn about the countries of the world, discover the beauty of a painting by Van Gogh, and more. This book explains how to begin and develop this remarkable program, how to create and organize necessary materials, and how to more fully cultivate your child's learning ability.

Very young children not only can learn, but can learn far better and faster than older children. Let *How To Give Your Baby Encyclopedic Knowledge* be the first step in a lifetime of achievement.

$13.95 • 304 pages • 6 x 9-inch quality paperback • ISBN 978-0-7570-0182-6

HOW TO MULTIPLY YOUR BABY'S INTELLIGENCE

Glenn Doman and Janet Doman

Too often, we waste our children's most important years by refusing to allow them to learn everything they can at a time when it is easiest for them to absorb new information. *How To Multiply Your Baby's Intelligence* provides a comprehensive program that shows you just how easy and pleasurable it is to teach your young child how to read, to understand mathematics, and to literally multiply his or her overall learning potential. It explains how to begin and expand a remarkable proven program, how to make and organize the necessary materials, and how to more fully develop your child's learning ability, preparing him or her for a lifetime of success.

$15.95 • 400 pages • 6 x 9-inch quality paperback • ISBN 978-0-7570-0183-3

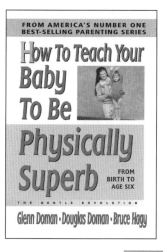

HOW TO TEACH YOUR BABY TO BE PHYSICALLY SUPERB

Glenn Doman, Douglas Doman, and Bruce Hagy

The early development of mobility in newborns is a vital part of their future ability to learn and grow to full potential. In *How to Teach Your Baby To Be Physically Superb,* Glenn Doman—founder of The Institutes for the Achievement of Human Potential—along with Douglas Doman and Bruce Hagy guide you in maximizing your child's physical capabilities. The authors first discuss each stage of mobility, and then explain how you can create an environment that will help your baby more easily reach that stage. Full-color charts, photographs, illustrations, and detailed yet easy-to-follow instructions are included to help you establish and use an effective home program that guides your baby from birth to age six.

$29.95 • 296 pages • 7.5 x 10.5-inch hardback • ISBN 978-0-7570-0192-5

HOW TO TEACH YOUR BABY TO SWIM

Douglas Doman

Teaching an infant or toddler to swim is not only a matter of safety, but also a great way to stimulate the child's physical coordination, concentration, and intelligence. That's right. By teaching your baby the proper swimming techniques, you can actually enhance his or her learning ability. You will also make your child happier, healthier, and more self-confident. Based on the revolutionary learning principles developed at The Institutes for the Achievement of Human Potential, *How To Teach Your Baby To Swim* is a clear and easy-to-follow guide to teaching your child swimming basics.

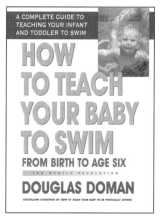

$14.95 • 128 pages • 7.5 x 9-inch quality paperback • ISBN 978-0-7570-0198-7

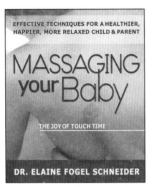

MASSAGING YOUR BABY
The Joy of Touch Time
Dr. Elaine Fogel Schneider

The power of touch is real and has been scientifically shown to have remarkable effects. For infants, it encourages relaxation; improves sleep patterns; reduces discomfort from teething, colic, and gas; strengthens digestive and circulatory systems; and does so much more. For parents, it nurtures bonding, increases communication, promotes parenting skills, and reduces stress levels. Now, massage expert Dr. Elaine Fogel Schneider has written the ultimate guide to using infant massage at home. *Massaging Your Baby* begins by explaining why massage is so beneficial. It then provides an easy-to-follow step-by-step guide to effective massage.

$15.95 • 224 pages • 7.5 x 9-inch quality paperback • ISBN 978-0-7570-0263-2

POTTY TRAINING YOUR BABY
A Practical Guide for Easier Toilet Training

Katie Warren

Contrary to traditional belief, the transition from diaper to potty can be started even before your child's first birthday—and completed by the second! Katie Warren advises taking advantage of the early months, when babies do most of their communicating on an emotional level, as children understand things intuitively much sooner than they understand words. *Potty Training Your Baby* provides information on everything from where to buy a potty to dealing with those inevitable little "accidents." Perhaps most important, the author shows you how to turn this often dreaded and frustrating task into a time of growth and learning for both you and your child.

$9.95 • 104 pages • 6 x 9-inch quality paperback • ISBN 978-0-7570-0180-2

HOW TO MAXIMIZE YOUR CHILD'S LEARNING ABILITY
A Complete Guide to Choosing and Using the Best Computer Games, Activities, Learning Aids, Toys, and Tactics for Your Child
Lauren Bradway, PhD, and Barbara Albers Hill

Over twenty years ago, Dr. Lauren Bradway discovered that all children have specific learning styles. Some learn best through visual stimulation; others, through sound and language; and others, through touch. In this book, Dr. Bradway first shows you how to determine your child's inherent style. She then aids you in carefully selecting the toys, activities, and educational strategies that will help reinforce the talents your child was born with, and encourage those skills that come less easily.

$14.95 • 288 pages • 6 x 9-inch quality paperback • ISBN 978-0-7570-0096-6